# International Handbook on Drug Control

# International Handbook on Drug Control

Edited by

Scott B. MacDonald

and

Bruce Zagaris

GREENWOOD PRESS
Westport, Connecticut • London

**Library of Congress Cataloging-in-Publication Data**

International handbook on drug control / edited by Scott B. MacDonald and Bruce Zagaris.
p. cm.
Includes bibliographical references (p. ) and index.
ISBN 0-313-27375-8 (alk. paper)
1. Narcotics, Control of. 2. Drug traffic. 3. Narcotics, Control of—International cooperation. I. MacDonald, Scott B. II. Zagaris, Bruce.
HV5801.I575 1992
363.4'5—dc20 91-35118

British Library Cataloguing in Publication Data is available.



Library of Congress Catalog Card Number: 91-35118
ISBN: 0-313-27375-8

First published in 1992

Greenwood Press, 88 Post Road West, Westport, CT 06881
An imprint of Greenwood Publishing Group, Inc.

Printed in the United States of America

The paper used in this book complies with the Permanent Paper Standard issued by the National Information Standards Organization (Z39.48-1984).

10 9 8 7 6 5 4 3 2 1

**Copyright Acknowledgment**

The editors and publisher gratefully acknowledge permission to use materials from: Rensselaer W. Lee III. "Soviet Narcotics Trade," *Society* (July/August 1991).

# Contents

# Preface

The international illicit drug trade is an ongoing problem that faces the global community. It influences economic and political development in a number of countries in the developing world and feeds the habits of addicts in the developed world. The nature of the game will probably continue into the next century because so many people experiment with drugs and because so much profit is to be gained in drug sales. In the 1990s, it is likely that more people in developing countries will abuse illicit drugs. One approach to dealing with the problem of drug misuse is education. Along these lines, the editors wish to make a small contribution to the fight against drug abuse by increasing what is known about the global narcotics trade.

The editors wish to thank Mildred Vasan at Greenwood Press for putting up with their trials and tribulations. Sarah Barber also gets special mention for her many contributions to facilitate the completion of the book. Scott MacDonald also wishes to extend his appreciation to his wife Kateri Scott-MacDonald for her enduring patience and to his cat Ringgit for his support in the wee hours.

# I

# Introduction and Problems of International Control

# 1

# Introduction: Controlling the International Drug Problem

SCOTT B. MACDONALD AND BRUCE ZAGARIS

## INTRODUCTION

The international illicit trade in drugs is one of the major problems confronting the world in the 1990s. The global media constantly focuses on the struggle against what has become a modern scourge. Increasingly, countries are trying to cope with problems of rising addict populations and related crime and violence. The power of the drug trade was explicitly manifested in August 1989 when the *narcotraficantes* of the so-called Medellín cartel in Colombia assassinated the leading presidential candidate, Luis Carlos Galan, because of his opposition to their activities. In December 1989 Colombian law enforcement agents killed drug *capo* José Gonzalo Rodríguez Gacha in a shoot-out, and that same month U.S. troops intervened in Panama, removing from power the alleged drug-trading regime of General Manuel Noriega. Moreover, the Ochoas and Pablo Escobar, despite their surrender to Colombian authorities in 1991, both made *Fortune*'s list of leading millionaires in that same year. The assassination of public officials and leading antinarcotics politicians, shoot-outs, bombings, and military interventions all underscore the brutal and ugly nature of the drug trade and the pressing need to bring it under control in the 1990s. The problem of the drug trade confronts not only the supplier countries, but also those countries with the most consumers, especially North America, Western Europe, and, increasingly, Eastern Europe. The problem of illicit drug consumption is also beginning to concern law enforcement and social agencies in Japan and parts of the Middle East.

The drug problem, global in nature, will not conveniently go away; it must be resolved. The globalization of the drug trade requires a global response. Certainly, the advancements in communications have revolutionized the drug trade by enhancing the ability of drug dealers to ship and market their wares, to move money around the world, and to equip themselves with the newest, most sophisticated weapons and advisors. In the late 1980s, the governments in the developed countries in North America, Europe, and Asia and the Pacific began to work more closely with their counterparts in Latin America, the Caribbean, the Middle East, and Southwest Asia, while the United Nations sought to develop an international framework of action against the drug trade. Although certain governments are suspect for their alleged involvement in the drug trade and their links to narco-terrorist groups of both the political left and right, the majority of countries are increasingly preoccupied with the broadening linkages of the drug trade's underground empires. Those broadening linkages of the drug trade's underground empires. Those broadening linkages include the spread of money-laundering activities around the globe to such remote locations as the ministates of the Indian and South Pacific oceans; the penetration of cocaine cartels into Western Europe, Japan, and the Middle East; and a revitalization of drug smuggling in the People's Republic of China. The international seizure of the holdings of the Bank for Credit and Commerce International (BCCI) in the summer of 1991 reflected part of the broad, global scope of drug money and its laundering.

The purpose of this book is to discuss the status of drug-control efforts around the world, covering the key nations and international organizations involved in controlling the drug threat. The drug problem includes the production, exportation, and marketing of illicit drugs as well as worldwide trading and money-laundering networks, gangland-style executions, corruption of public officials, and the creation and maintenance of well-armed private armies capable of conducting full-scale military assaults. The global illicit drug trade, according to *Fortune* magazine, is probably worth $500 billion.[1] The United Nations estimated drug-trafficking proceeds at $300 billion in 1987. In Latin America the drug trade accounts for between $80 and $150 billion, and, as in certain parts of Asia, those who partake in the production and trading of illicit drugs have gained significant political and economic influence.

## OPERATIONALIZING THE TERMS

It is important to operationalize such terms as the international drug trade, the Medellín drug cartel, *narcotraficantes*, cocaine, ice, marijuana, heroin, and money laundering. Each of these terms will be defined for usage throughout the book.

The international drug trade refers to the illicit trafficking of narcotics across national borders. The primary "hot" commodities are cocaine, heroin, hashish (hasheesh), marijuana, and psychotropic drugs. The major dealers in Latin America are called *narcotraficantes*, and the most infamous of such organizations is the Medellín cartel, which operates out of Medellín, Colombia. However, the reader is cautioned that there are other cartels (such as that in Cali, Colombia) and, worldwide, many other groups, such as Burma's Shan United Army. Jon

Wiant, in a study on the drug trade in the Golden Triangle (Burma, Laos, and Thailand), identified four groups as drug dealers: ethnic insurgents, revolutionary movements, warlord organizations, and syndicates and consortia.[2] The point here is that *narcotraficantes*, in the broadest definition, covers all four groups.

Cocaine is a relatively new substance, though the coca plant has been around for several centuries. Although the precise date of the first planting and cultivation of coca is not know, it is thought to have occurred roughly as early as 1800 B.C. in South America's Andes Mountains. The coca plant was used primarily as a mild stimulant to be chewed or drunk in the form of a tea. In these forms, coca dulled hunger and provided some protection against the cold. It was only in the 1860s that European scientists succeeded in extracting the cocaine alkaloid from the coca plant. The drug soon became available in pure form and was in heavy demand in the medical world as a painkiller and anesthetic. Further experimentation in Europe and the United States in the late 1800s gradually created a need for a greater supply of cocaine. Over time, a legal pharmaceutical industry developed in several Latin American countries to meet the demand. By the 1920s, cocaine was being produced in large quantities for the first time. Further research revealed negative side effects, such as addiction, and controls were implemented. Although cocaine, or the coca plant, continued to have a limited role in the medical world, the substance now existed for illegal smuggling and use in Europe and the United States.

Cocaine is part of the same chemical family as nicotine, caffeine, and morphine. It is extracted from the coca plant, which is cultivated chiefly in South America. When the extract is heated with hydrochloric acid, the result is cocaine hydrochloride, a form of salt often mixed with various adulterants. This byproduct is the mainstay of the trade. Since it is water soluble, it is easy to consume in several different ways.

Marijuana and heroin are not limited to the New World, although they do play an important role in the inter-American drug trade. Heroin, in fact, has been and continues to be the most widely traded illicit drug in the world. While the United States was saturated with cocaine in the 1980s, heroin maintained its primary position as the drug of choice for Europe's addicts. Heroin was long thought to be the drug of the inner-city poor in the United States, and marijuana appears to have permeated all levels of society in North America as well as the rest of the world. Marijuana is produced throughout Africa, as in Morocco; in parts of Asia, as in India; and in the Americas, as in Jamaica, Mexico, and Colombia. Marijuana, also known as cannabis, is the second largest cash crop in the United States.

Heroin, a white, odorless, addictive narcotic, is derived from morphine. Its chemical name is diamorphine hydrochloride, and it is obtained from the opium poppy. Gum is tapped from the incised poppy head after the petals have fallen. That gum is prepared and treated so that the morphine base can be chemically extracted from it. From that point, the base is mixed with acetic anhydride and is converted to heroin base (diacetyl morphine) and hence into a soluble salt, diamorphine hydrochloride. Ten kilos of opium convert into approximately 1.1 kilos of heroin, making access to large amounts of poppies essential for commercial operations. As Roger Lewis noted of the other characteristics of the opium plant: "With its high price, high yield per acre, labor-intensive nature and inaccessibility on high, rugged, hard-to-control terrain, opium is a tempting cash crop for impoverished tribal peoples who have successfully integrated the poppy into their domestic economy and culture."[3] In many respects, opium functions in a similar fashion to coca in parts of Asia and in the Middle East.

Though it can be smoked or sniffed, heroin is usually administered intravenously. It is sometimes injected with cocaine as "speedballs." Heroin has been traditionally regarded as the drug of the poor, usually minority, urban dwellers. In the United States it has been associated with the unemployed, minority male who has little education and often commits crimes to support his habit. Due to the ready availability of the drug and to the structure of the relationship of inner-city residents to society, the heroin life-style has become firmly established as an alternative life-style for youngsters. Heroin use, however, is not limited to the poor inhabitants of the inner city. Its use has extended into the more affluent middle class, and not all users become addicts.

Hashish is a purified extract derived from the dried flowers of the hemp plant, smoked or chewed as a mild narcotic. Its major producers, in sequence of importance at the beginning of the 1990s, are Lebanon, Pakistan, Afghanistan, and Morocco. Europe is the major market, although Egypt has emerged as an important consumer.

Psychotropic, or mind-altering, drugs, which are synthetic, are produced in laboratories. This type of drug includes amphetamines and methamphetamines. Both are stimulants to the central nervous system. Methamphetamines are derivatives of amphetamines used in the form of crystalline hydrochloride. The most recent psychotropic drug to become available is "ice," a smokable, crystallized form of methamphetamine.

Ice, which is highly addictive, is made primarily in Asia, particularly in the Philippines where methamphetamine is readily available. It has a high that can last for up to eight hours, quite an improvement over the twenty-minute crack high. Cocaine and ice are alike, however, in that "chronic use can lead to permanent neurological damage, severe weight loss, and life-threatening heart and lung disorders."[4]

Another frequently used term in the drug trade lexicon is money laundering. Money laundering is the process of converting the cash from the drug business (or other illicit activities) into funds available for legitimate investments. Economist Ingo Walters outlines a "typical" money-laundering operation in five stages: (1) Money is transferred (often with wire transfers) to a secret haven overseas; (2) lawyers in the haven create a shell corporation using boilerplate documentation, for which a fee is charged; (3) funds are deposited in the name of the dummy corporation in a cooperative local bank, generally an offshore bank authorized to conduct transactions only with nonresidents; (4) money is transferred to a larger, "clean" international bank; and (5) the corporation borrows money from this bank (secured by the deposits) for legitimate use in the original country. Although many variations exist in practice, Walters' scenario provides an excellent frame of reference for understanding money laundering.

Although efforts are being made to make money laundering illegal around the world, there are a number of countries where it is not officially a crime. For countries with large-scale, offshore financial centers, legislation making money laundering a criminal activity raises difficult questions about banking secrecy and confidentiality. In the United States, money laundering was defined as a criminal activity by the Money Laundering Control Act of 1986. In the early 1990s, several other countries, including the United Kingdom, Australia, Canada, Luxembourg, Switzerland, and France, criminalized money laundering; enacted "know your customer" suspicious transaction record keeping for cash and other transactions; and agreed to assist other countries in the investigation and prosecution of alleged money-laundering offenses.

## AN OVERVIEW OF THE ILLICIT DRUG TRADE IN THE 1980s AND EARLY 1990s

The main forces in the international drug trade are cocaine, heroin, and marijuana. Cocaine is produced primarily in three countries: Bolivia, Colombia, and Peru. Secondary production countries are Brazil, Ecuador, and Venezuela. Heroin has three major source regions: the Golden Triangle countries of Burma, Laois, and Thailand; the Golden Crescent countries of Afghanistan, Iran, and Pakistan; and Mexico and Central America. An emerging production area is Lebanon. Marijuana, the second major cash crop in the United States, is also widely produced throughout Latin America and parts of Africa, the Middle East, and Asia.

The structure of the drug trade in the 1980s was marked by the rise of the Colombian drug cartels in the Americas and by the ongoing relationship between the Golden Triangle and the newly emergent Golden Crescent with Europe. America's habit became cocaine; Europe's remained heroin. The development of drug transport routes throughout the world and the money laundering of drug profits, however, increased the geographical scope of illicit operations in the 1980s. This occurred largely as a result of better communications, which allowed a globalization of the marketplace.

Ten developments occurred in the 1980s and early 1990s that changed the structure of the international drug trade. First and foremost, the United States developed what initially appeared to be an insatiable appetite for cocaine. In response, Colombian drug traffickers quickly moved to eliminate competitors (such as the Cuban mafia in Florida), to develop refining capacity and trade routes, and to neutralize law enforcement and judicial forces in their home country. What evolved was a system of coca cultivation in Colombia, Peru, and Bolivia; a transportation network through Mexico, Central America, the Caribbean, and Brazil; and mass marketing in the United States and Canada. There was also some spillover into Ecuador, Paraguay, Uruguay, and Venezuela. The laundering of narco-profits was facilitated in the Caribbean, Panama, and a number of other Latin American and European countries (such as Switzerland and Luxembourg) as well as in the United States and Canada.

While cocaine emerged as the dynamic of the inter-American drug trade, heroin continued its staple existence for a user community in Western Europe and parts of Asia. This is not to argue that there was no use of cocaine, but that the levels were very low in comparison to those of heroin from the Golden Triangle and, to a lesser extent, to those of Moroccan hashish and cannabis. Europe's concern with heroin brought a European focus on Pakistan and Thailand. In particular, the governments of Britain and Germany sought to bring pressure to bear on these governments to clamp down on production. At the same time, other European countries, such as the Netherlands, Switzerland, and Italy, were willing to experiment with levels of tolerance vis-à-vis what drugs incurred official displeasures as criminal offenses and what society accepted in relation to hard versus soft drugs.

The second major development was the Soviet invasion of Afghanistan in 1979. Although Afghanistan was the home of opium poppy cultivation prior to the invasion, the ensuing war between the Soviet-backed regimes in Kabul and the Afghan rebels, the *mujahidin*, created the proper conditions for an explosion in opium production and trading. These conditions included a breakdown in central authority, the expansion of clandestine trade networks through Iran and Pakistan for both drugs and guns, and the need of the rebels to raise hard currency. Moreover, the Soviet occupying force became a new market for opium and heroin, and the soldiers took the habit back to the Soviet Union when they left. By 1990, the Kabul regime remained unable to take any action to suppress opium cultivation and heroin refining. Afghanistan also had the dubious distinction of being the world's leading producer of opium after Burma. This meant that trafficking increased in neighboring Iran, Pakistan, and India.

The third major development to shape the drug trade was the Islamic revolution that took place in Iran. While the Iranian government did not promote the consumption or production of drugs in its own country, its assistance to radical fundamentalists in the Bekka Valley did little to suppress Lebanon's expanding opium production and heroin processing. At the very least, Iran's involvement in Lebanon's affairs, in which the Syrians actively assisted, contributed to that country's chaos and the inability of any central authority in Beirut to respond to the problem. The turmoil created by the Islamic revolution in Iran also undermined regional enforcement measures. The Iran-Iraq War (1980–1988) and internal politics, such as fighting the Kurdish separatists, were clearly priorities for the government in Teheran over the spread of drug trafficking and rising drug consumption. Sharing borders with Afghanistan, Pakistan, and Turkey, Iran became a major transit point for heroin bound for Europe via Turkey.

The fourth development was a crackdown, in the mid–1980s, on the drug trade in Latin America, which especially affected Mexico and Colombia and led to new offshoots. While regional enforcement agencies sought to suppress entry into Florida, production facilities in Colombia (like Tranquilandía in 1984), and Mexican networks, cocaine production operations were moved to new countries, such as Brazil and Ecuador. New routes were found into North America via Venezuela, Suriname, Paraguay, and Haiti. The crackdown and some softening in U.S. demand began an interest in cocaine export to Europe through the Iberian Peninsula.

The fifth major development was the collapse of the Ne Win regime in Burma in 1988. Long a major producer of opium, the Burmese government had periodically sought to reduce production and heroin refining by large-scale military offenses conducted against the traffickers, who included members of the local Communist party, ethnic Karen rebels, and criminal consortia. With the downfall of the Ne Win regime and the ensuing political turmoil, drug suppression became a minor concern. Consequently, by 1990, Burma was the world's major opium-producing country, transporting heroin through Thailand, India, and China and laundering the profits in banks and non-banks in Thailand, Hong Kong, and Singapore. The expansion of Burma's production and the lack of antinarcotics programs were matched by the probability that Lao military and civilian officials were involved in the drug trade, helping in both opium production and heroin trafficking.

The sixth major development was a combination of the Colombian government's intensified war on the Medellín cartel following the assassination of leading presidential candidate Galan in August 1989 and the U.S. military intervention in Panama in December 1989. The impact of these two events was to close down the use of Panama as a transshipment point for drugs and guns and money laundering. It also led to a subtle restructuring of the inter-American drug trade. That restructuring has meant less coca production in Colombia (a trend already in motion), a greater emphasis on Peru as a producer (the world leader in the late 1980s), and horizontal and vertical integration of the industry in Bolivia. It has also meant the expansion of the narcotics network in Argentina, Chile, Paraguay, and Uruguay. One last development has been the decline of the Medellín cartel and the rise of the Cali cartel as well as other regional Colombian organizations.

The seventh development is the saturation of the U.S. market for cocaine in the early 1990s. While U.S. demand for cocaine is decreasing, narcotics trafficking groups are considering market or product diversification. This means that Latin American drug traders are seeking to expand their market in Europe, Japan, and the Middle East, especially the wealthy Persian Gulf states and Saudi Arabia. This sitution was evident in June 1990 when Belgian authorities captured a 40-kilogram shipment of cocaine on a Colombian ship. The cocaine was bound for Germany, and two Colombians from Medellín were arrested with the seizure. At the same time that the South American criminal consortia are looking to new markets, heroin producers and traders, like the Chinese triads, are reexamining the United States and Canada as possible areas of greater consumption. Added to this are the reports that the Colombian cartels are seeking to plant a Mexican strain of opium poppy for heroin production in the Andes.

The eight major development is the ongoing experimentation with psychotropic or mind-altering drugs, sometimes called synthetic drugs. Psychotropic drugs can be produced just about anywhere, depending on access to chemicals, such as ephedrine. The Philippines, for example, emerged in the late 1980s as a major producer of methamphetamine, most of which went to growing local consumption. Considering the disruption of the Marcos regime and the instability of the Aquino government, the Philippines has emerged as a major production area and transit point for psychotropic drugs. The most recent psychotropic drug to be used is ice, which is produced mainly in Asian laboratories. In the early 1990s, it is likely that such drugs will increasingly be produced in the United States.

The ninth development is the spread of the drug trade around the world. Although many nations do not produce narcotics or have large user populations, their locations on trade routes gives them significance. Nigeria in the 1980s, for example, emerged as a major transshipment point for heroin from Southwest and Southeast Asia earmarked for Europe and North America. Additionally, Nigerian traffickers smuggle South American cocaine to Europe. Another example is Malaysia, which is a transit site and heroin conversion center. Despite the well-advertised and strictly enforced death penalty for trafficking and possession, increased availability of Golden Triangle heroin has shown up in Malaysia.

The tenth and final major trend to shape the illicit international narcotics trade is the movement toward a global governmental response and the emergence of an international regime of antinarcotics enforcement. Governments in both developed and developing countries are signing new information exchange agreements and seeking cooperation in such matters as joint criminal investigations, information sharing, and anti–money laundering efforts. For example, the G–7 countries (the United States, Japan, Germany, France, the United Kingdom, Italy, and Canada) and the European Communities formed a Financial Action Task Force in July 1989 to deal with money laundering. Sweden, the Netherlands, Belgium, Luxembourg, Switzerland, Austria, Spain, and Australia soon joined the task force. The Financial Action Task Force's report provided an analysis of the money-laundering process, the international instruments and national programs already in place to combat money laundering, and action recommendations. In June 1991, the task force obtained from the Organization for Economic Cooperation and Development (OECD) in Paris a secretariat, thereby further institutionalizing its work. The joining of the task force by Singapore and the Gulf Cooperation Council States further broadens its base.

The United Nations is playing an important coordinating role through its various agencies and the 1988 antinarcotics treaty regime. Other regional organizations, such as the Organization of American States (OAS), are seeking to harmonize legal responses and deepen the information pool about financial codes, money-laundering laws, and the structure of production and refining. Moreover, multilateral efforts to clamp down on money laundering, like the June 1990 Aruba Caribbean Conference, are creating an environment in which it is increasingly difficult to enjoy the profits of drug dealing.

Three future shocks should be addressed here: the issue of the European Community's 1992 project, the growing resentment vis-à-vis immigrant populations due to the involvement of members of their ethnic or racial community in the drug trade, and the threat of psychotropic drugs. According to the European Community's 1992 project, by January 1, 1993, all barriers to the free movement of goods, services, people, and capital will come down within the community, which includes twelve members: Belgium, Denmark, France, Germany, Greece, Ireland, Italy, Luxembourg, the Netherlands, Portugal, Spain, and the United Kingdom. Although there will be tremendous commercial advantages to this new development, it will also open new possibilities for both traffickers and money launderers. The final approval in June 1991 of a directive to criminalize and take action against money laundering ensures that the European Community will begin to take steps to combat money laundering.

The second issue concerns the role or at least the identification of immigrant communities in the drug trade. In the United States, the involvement of Colombians and Jamaicans in the narcotics trade, especially some of the more brutal aspects of it, has led to a popular targeting or identification of these nationalities as drug dealers. The same is true in Europe. In the Netherlands, the Surinamese and Moluccan communities are regarded as important outposts for heroin and cocaine trading. In Germany, it is the Turks, Nigerians, Senegalese, and Pakistanis. In France, it is the North Africans and Lebanese. Whatever the group, its existence creates problems in terms of community relations, especially as the borders begin to open up in Europe and as the potential for the spread of trafficking evolves.

The third problem is the spread of psychotropic drugs. If suppression operations continue to make headway against cocaine and if Europe and the Middle East do not develop into major markets, the alternative for the illicit drug industry is to turn to synthetic production of such drugs as ice. Japan and Western Europe could be severely affected by this, considering the existing wealth of those countries and the availability of high-grade chemical ingredients.

By 1992, the global drug trade has undergone several changes. After the 1980s, it became a broader-based phenomenon, cutting across a wide range of ideological regimes and cultures as well as national frontiers. Better communications have enhanced its ability to respond to countermeasures. The bottom line continues to be greed, whether one is trafficking, laundering hot money, or functioning as a hired gun. However, controls have improved, and the 1990s will be a decade of an intensified, high-technology cat-and-mouse game between law enforcement and dealers. At the same time, the real battles to be fought will concern social agendas and contending with the most basic question—why do people take drugs?

## THE SCOPE OF THE BOOK

The scope of this book is global. In the broadest sense, each chapter is broken down into the following sections:

1. *Introduction*: This section outlines the geographical area and the history of the drug trade in the particular region.
2. *The Structure of the Industry/Trade*: This section examines who produces what and why and where the product goes. Consideration is given to the characteristics of organized groups (i.e., age, organizations, links with other groups); the role money laundering plays in the country; and any special mechanisms that exist for money laundering.
3. *The Government's Response*: Any measures that have been taken by the government to suppress the drug trade are delineated, and their success or failure are recounted.
4. *Societal Reaction*: The reaction of the particular society to the emergence of drug-related problems is summarized: Has the response been one of indifference or have nongovernmental organizations, like self-help or support groups, been established to deal with the problem of drug abuse and instilling a greater community-wide awareness?
5. *International Linkages for Control*: This section examines the types of international agreements and other types of cooperation that exist between the particular country and other countries or international organizations to control the drug trade.
6. *Conclusion*: This section summarizes and notes whether there are any lessons to be learned from the particular country's experience with the drug trade.

The scope of the book is meant to cover the main dimensions of the drug trade: production, exportation, marketing, money laundering, enforcement (on the criminal side), and government responses. The last includes legal actions (such as extradition treaties and judicial reform), law enforcement measures, and international cooperation. The overarching issues that will be included in the various chapters (obviously with different emphasis) will be domestic addiction, money laundering, narco-terrorism, and specific programs.

Before proceeding further, it is necessary to discuss the thirty-five targets listed by the United Nations (UN) in combatting the drug trade because it provides a further foundation for this book. One of the major problems confronting researchers of the drug trade is the wide range of information in some areas and the lack of information in others. An additional dilemma is that information is often conflictual and, at times, of dubious validity. In seeking to formulate strategies for its member countries, the United Nations responded to this problem in methodology by creating thirty-five targets for government policymakers. These targets, if properly implemented, can be of significant help in the development of a common information pool. Therefore, each chapter in this book will also seek, as far as possible, to touch upon the guidelines given in the United Nations' *Declaration of the International Conference on Drug Abuse and*

*Illicit Trafficking and Comprehensive Multidisciplinary Outline of Future Activities in Drug Abuse Control* (1988).

The UN study has four major target areas: the prevention and reduction of the illicit demand for narcotic drugs and psychotropic substances, the control of supply, the suppression of illicit trafficking, and the treatment and rehabilitation of users. Regional and national policies have largely tried to emulate this framework. For the purposes of this book, several questions can be asked: What are governments doing to prevent and reduce illicit demand for narcotic drugs, to control supply, to suppress illicit trafficking, and to treat and rehabilitate users? Equally important, what are nongovernmental local organizations doing along the same lines? And what kind of interface do governments have with regional organizations?

The UN study lists seven areas of action under drug prevention and reduction of demand: assessment of the extent of drug misuse and abuse; organization of comprehensive systems for collection and evaluation of data; prevention through education; prevention of drug abuse in the workplace; prevention programs by civic, community, and special interest groups and law enforcement agencies; leisure-time activities in the service of the continuing campaign against drug abuse; and the role of the media.

The second area outlined in the UN study is the control of supply. The eradication of illicitly cultivated opium poppy, coca bush, and cannabis plants is a complex undertaking since the plants are often grown in remote areas, or in areas beyond effective governmental control. Further complications arise because, in some developing countries, these crops provide supplementary or primary sources of livelihood for the rural population. This is clearly the case in parts of Bolivia, Peru, and Burma. Nine requirements are listed under this category: strengthening the international system of control of narcotic drugs and psychotropic substances; rational use of pharmaceuticals containing narcotic drugs or psychotropic substances; strengthening the control of international movements of psychotropic substances; action related to the increase in the number of controlled psychotropic substances; control of the commercial movement of precursors, specific chemicals, and equipment; control of analogues of substances under international control; identification of illicit plant cultivation; elimination of illicit plantings; and redevelopment of areas formerly under illicit drug crop cultivation. Clearly, the issues concerning controls are important, especially, for the purposes of this book, the questions raised over country control of precursor drugs, crop eradication, and redevelopment. This is particularly true in the chapters on Bolivia, Burma, Colombia, Laos, Peru, and Thailand.

The third area in the UN study concerns the suppression of illicit trafficking. The emphasis in suppressing illicit trafficking is reflected in the negotiation of a new United Nations convention, which was signed in December 1988 and which became effective in November, 1990. Much attention has been devoted to increasing cooperation among governments and forfeiture of assets of organized traffickers. Under the heading of suppression of illicit trafficking are twelve guidelines: disrupting major trafficking networks; promoting the use of the technique of controlled delivery; facilitating the extradition of drug dealers; creating mutual judicial and legal assistance pacts; admitting into evidence samples of bulk seizures of drugs; adequacy with a view to improving efficacy of penal provisions; and the forfeiture of the instruments and proceeds of illicit drug trafficking, which involves asset forfeiture laws. Five subareas fall into this last group: the tightening of control of movement through official points of entry; the strengthening of external border controls and of mutual assistance machinery within economic unions of sovereign states, such as the European Community; surveillance of land, water, and air approaches to the frontier; controls over the use of international mail for drug trafficking; and controls over ships on the high seas and aircraft in international airspace.

The fourth area considered is the treatment and rehabilitation of drug users. Because a policy for treatment of drug addiction must include counseling, guidance, sustained motivation, medical assistance, and other factors, the development of a policy for treatment for drug addiction is difficult and complex. One of the major problems confronting countries with consumption problems is that competition from other pressing issues makes it difficult to devote adequate attention to the social, cultural, and environmental factors. In particular, the emphasis, according to the United Nations, should be placed on the multidisciplinary aspects of the strategy of treatment and rehabilitation, which involves the participation of a wide range of experts from several specialties. Account must be made of the establishment and maintenance of parent/family and peer groups designed to support the drug addict throughout the treatment and aftercare process. Such psychosocial structures can improve the potential for recovery and prevention of relapse. As each of the chapters will demonstrate, each national experience varies, especially when one compares the more developed and still developing countries.

Seven subheadings exist under treatment and rehabilitation: the creation of a policy of treatment; the inventory of available modalities and techniques of treatment and rehabilitation; the selection of appropriate treatment programs; the training of personnel working with drug addicts; the reduction of the incidence of diseases and the number of infections transmitted through drug-using habits; the care for drug-addicted offenders within the criminal justice and prison system; and the social reintegration of persons who have undergone programs for treatment and rehabilitation.

The chapters were selected in terms of the country's or region's significance in the international narcotics trade. Along these lines some regions, such as Latin America, the Middle East, and Southwest Asia, are more important than others, such as Sub-Saharan Africa. Consequently, the emphasis is placed on the major consumers and suppliers of illicit narcotics. Since the United States is the world's largest market for illicit drugs and is a major producer of marijuana, it has the dubious distinction of being the subject of the first country-specific chapter. The other specific industrialized countries considered, Canada, the United Kingdom,

Sweden, and the Netherlands, have had particular experience with the drug trade, which single them out for special treatment. A separate chapter exists for the European Community. The Soviet Union has also been given a separate chapter because it provides a relatively new frontier in terms of research and drug problems.

Other chapters concentrate on those countries that are regarded as the primary producers: the Andean states of Bolivia, Colombia, and Peru; Mexico; the Caribbean offshore financial centers; Brazil; the Southern Cone countries of Argentina, Chile, Paraguay, and Uruguay; Turkey and India; the Golden Crescent countries of Afghanistan, Iran, and Pakistan; the Golden Triangle countries of Burma, Laos, and Thailand; and Singapore. A final section discusses the activities of international organizations, such as the United Nations and the Organization of American States.

## CONCLUSION

The drug trade is like the mythical hydra: Every time a head is cut off, another one grows in its place. What is needed is a better understanding of how the beast works. In this, there been considerable progress; however, the next step is often the most difficult: finding the political will to something about the problem. Many governments, as in the cases of Bolivia and Peru, find it difficult to carry through coca crop eradication because of peasant opposition. The United States has similar obstacles to resolving the drug trade: elements of the American public, including President George Bush, are opposed to gun control. The illicit trade in weapons, especially assault rifles which can be bought and sold in the United States, is one of the major props of such organizations as the Medellín cartel and the Mexican drug consortia. This book can provide useful information, but there has to be a will to implement comprehensive and logical policies that address matters in a holistic fashion. The comparative nature of this volume should provide a wider background upon which to view domestic conditions in each country.

## NOTES

The views expressed here are solely those of Scott B. MacDonald, and do not represent in any fashion the Office of the Comptroller of the Currency, of which he is an official.

1. Louis Kraar, "The Drug Trade," *Fortune*, 20 June 1988, 37.
2. For a discussion of these ethnic organized crime groups and their drug-trafficking activities see U.S. Department of Justice, *Drug Trafficking: A Report to the President of the United States* (Washington, D.C.: U.S. Government Printing Office, 3 August 1989). Also see Gerald L. Posner, *Warlords of Crime, Chinese Secret Societies: The New Mafia* (Harmondsworth, England: Penguin Books, 1988) and Claire Sterling, *Octopus: The Long Reach of the International Sicilian Mafia* (New York: W. W. Norton and Company, 1990).

3. Roger Lewis, "Serious Business—the Global Heroin Economy," in *Big Deal: The Politics of the Illicit Drug Business*, ed. Anthony Henman, Roger Lewis, and Tim Maylon (London: Pluto Press, 1985), 10.

4. The White House, *National Drug Control Strategy* (Washington, D.C.: U.S. Government Printing Office, January 1990), 45.

## BIBLIOGRAPHY


Backmann, Christian, and Anne Coppel. "*Le dragon domestique: Deux siècles de relations étranges entre l'Occident et la drogue*." Paris: Editions Albin Michael S.A., 1989.

Bagley, Bruce M. "Colombia and the War on Drugs." *Foreign Affairs* (Fall 1988): 70–92.

de Montvalon, Dominique. "Immigrés l'heure de vérité." *L'Express*, 8 December 1989, 32–33.

Eddy, Paul, with Hugo Sabogal and Sara Walden. *The Cocaine Wars*. New York: W. W. Norton and Company, 1988.

Freemantle, Brian. *The Fix: Inside the World Drug Trade*. New York: Tom Doherty Associates, 1986.

Glynn, Lenny. "Can Bankers Help Win the Drug War?" *Institutional Investor* (February 1990): 77–84.

Lee, Rensselaer W. III. *The White Labyrinth: Cocaine and Political Power*. Rutgers, N.J.: Transaction Press, 1989.

MacDonald, Scott B. *Dancing on a Volcano: The Latin American Drug Trade*. New York: Praeger Publishers, 1988.

———. *Mountain High, White Avalanche: Cocaine and Power in the Andean States and Panama*. New York: Praeger Publishers, 1989.

———. "The Next Wave of the Latin Drug Trade." *The Times of the Americas* (27 June 1990): 7.

———. "Slaying the Drug Hydra." *SAIS Review* 9, 1 (Winter-Spring 1989): 65–85.

———. "Traffic Island Blues." *Money International* (London) (April 1989): 88–89.

Malarek, Victor. *Merchants of Misery: Inside Canada's Illegal Drug Scene*. Toronto: McClelland & Stewart, 1989.

Organization of American States. *Comparative Study of the Legal Regime on Drug Control in Ten South American Member States of the Organization of American States*. Washington, D.C.: Organization of American States, May 1988.

Pacini, Deborah, and Christine Franquemont, ed. *Coca and Cocaine: Effects in People and Policy in Latin America*. Petersborough, N.H.: Transcript Publishing Company, 1986.

Perl, Raphael Francis. "The US Congress, International Drug Policy, and the Anti-Drug Abuse Act of 1988." *Journal of Interamerican Studies and World Affairs* 30, nos. 2, 7, 3 (Summer/Fall 1988: 19–52).

Posner, Gerald L. *Warlords of Crime, Chinese Secret Societies: The New Mafia*. Harmondsworth, England: Penguin, 1988.

Rosenblum, Mort. "Hidden Agendas: The Honduran Connection Makes Hypocrisy out of the Hype about Bush's War on Drugs." *Vanity Fair*, March 1990, 102–20.

Secretaria de relaciónes Exteriores, *El problema del narcotrafico visión internacional*. Mexico City: Government of Mexico, 1989.

Sterling, Claire. *Octopus: The Long Reach of the International Sicilian Mafia*. New York: W. W. Norton and Company, 1990.

Trebach, Arnold S. *The Great Drug War: And Radical Proposals that Could Make America Safe Again*. New York: Macmillan, 1987.

United Nations Division of Narcotic Drugs. *Declaration of the International Conference on Drug Abuse and Illicit Trafficking and Comprehensive Multidisciplinary Outline of Future Activities in Drug Abuse Control*. New York: United Nations, 1988.

U.S. Department of State, Bureau of International Narcotics Matters. *International Narcotics Control Strategy Report*. Washington, D.C.: U.S. Department of State, March 1991.

Walters, Ingo. *Secret Money: The World of International Financial Secrecy*. Lexington, Mass.: Lexington Books, 1985.

Wiant, Jon. ''Narcotics in the Golden Triangle.'' *The Washington Quarterly* 8, 4 (Fall 1985): 130–37.

Zagaris, Bruce. ''Dollar Diplomacy: International Enforcement of Money Movement and Related Matters—A United States Perspective.'' *The George Washington Journal of International Law and Economics* 22, 3 (1989): 465–552.

Zagaris, Bruce, and Markus Bornheim. ''When the Walls Come Tumbling Down.'' *Security Management*, May 1990, 69–74.

Zagaris, Bruce, and Ange-François Fantauzzi. ''Breaking the Connection.'' *Security Management*, June 1990, 46–53.

Ziegler, Jean. *La Suisse lavé plus blanc*. Paris: Editions du Seuil, 1990.

# 2

# Money Laundering: An International Control Problem

BRUCE ZAGARIS

## INTRODUCTION

Since drug traffickers need to convert the large and unmanageable amounts of currency they receive into more manageable and less conspicuous forms of money, they must spend large amounts of time and resources designing and implementing plans to launder money. The process of money laundering necessarily requires involving additional persons who become part of the criminal element when they knowingly participate. These new persons and others who become unwittingly involved become potential informers and cooperating witnesses for law enforcement. The phrase money laundering embraces all procedures to change the identity of illegally obtained money so that it appears to have come from a legitimate source. The use of cash provides anonymity to many types of criminal activity and is the normal medium of exchange in the world of drug trafficking. As a result, three features result: drug traffickers must conceal the true ownership and origin of the money; they need to control the money; and they need to change the form of the money. Although this chapter discusses asset forfeiture law insofar as it is part of the money-laundering initiatives, it does not focus on the details of asset forfeiture policy and law, which are examined in Chapter 3.

Three stages of money laundering can be identified during which numerous transactions may be made by launderers:

1. *Placement*—the physical disposal of cash proceeds derived from illegal activity.
2. *Layering*—the separation of the illicit proceeds from their source by designing complex lawyers of financial transactions designed to disguise the audit trail and to provide anonymity.

3. *Integration*—the provision of apparent legitimacy to criminally derived wealth. If the layering process has succeeded, integration mechanisms place the laundered proceeds back into the economy so that they reenter the financial system appearing to be normal business funds.

Since 1985, many countries and the world community have been devising policies, laws, and strategies to detect money laundering and to both stop the laundering and deprive the perpetrators of their assets.

The need to combat money laundering gains ascendence in the efforts to combat narco-terrorism, which is the term used to describe the role played by drug trafficking in international politics. In recent years the power of narco-terrorists—their ability to manipulate sovereignty and the comparative slowness with which governments adopt to change—has enabled narco-terrorists to gain significant power both nationally and internationally. Organized crime and narco-terrorism increasingly have extended into the international financial system. Their association with economic and white-collar crime has become increasingly more evident. Money laundering and other financial operations carried out by narco-terrorists in developing countries are a source of grave financial problem to those countries. Narcotics trafficking brings a new entrepreneur class, the financial power of which is often used in a manner contrary to national and international interests. Organized narcotics traffickers have a devastating effect in all countries and have spilled over national borders in a most insidious manner.

Another facet of organized drug trafficking is the ubiquity of and profits from drug trafficking that enable persons to use illicit drugs as a type of currency that can be traded for money or for other commodities such as arms or jewels. In recent times technological innovations and huge profits have enabled individuals to obtain what used to be the sole province of governments: The airplane; the radio; satellite communications; electronic fund transfers; and the easy availability of automatic weapons, rockets, grenades, and other military hardware have facilitated the participation of individuals and groups in the engagement of transnational criminal activities.

In the context of the growing power of organized crime, the very survival on national governments and the international order depend on the ability to deprive organized narcotics traffickers of their wherewithal to do business. The pernicious threat of organized traffickers and dynamic alliances with other organized crime groups has garnered the attention of both national governments and intergovernmental actors.

This chapter will highlight anti–money-laundering policies and laws, their impact on both criminal and economic policy, and the prospects for future operation. After reviewing the laws of selected major industrialized countries, the chapter will discuss the policies of intergovernmental organizations.

## NATIONAL LAWS

### The United States

In some ways the United States has been a leading national government in formulating policies and laws to stop money laundering. Part of the leadership comes from the U.S. laws and policy to combat organized crime, particularly through the use of the racketeering laws, and part comes through the U.S. experience with currency transaction reporting laws which have been in force since the 1970s. Since the United States is the largest consuming country of drugs and the largest source of funds, the political support for tough action against money launderers and profiteers has been strong.

In 1986, as part of the Anti-Drug Abuse Act of 1986, the United States enacted a Money Laundering Control Act (MLCA), which subjects individuals to criminal liability for knowing participation in any laundering of money. It authorizes the seizure and forfeiture of cash, or property related to such cash, where the owner causes a financial institution to fail to file a required Bank Secrecy Act (BSA) report. Financial institutions have been required since 1970 to file reports of cash transactions of $10,000 or more. The MLCA also substantially increased both the civil and criminal fines and increased the maximum term of imprisonment for violating the BSA from five to ten years. The MLCA applies to negligent as well as to willful violations of the reporting and record-keeping requirements. The act provided enlarged powers and responsibilities for banking regulators to enforce and try to stop money laundering. The act also provides exceptions for financial privacy, so that financial institutions which observe suspicious transactions can voluntarily report such developments to law enforcement authorities without notifying their customers.

In 1988, the Money Laundering Prosecution Improvements Act of 1988, as part of the Anti-Drug Abuse Act of 1988, was passed. It reduced threshold reporting requirements (e.g., $3,000 or more) in geographical areas of the United States in which substantial money laundering is deemed to exist. An additional exception to the Right to Financial Privacy Act permits a financial institution or supervisory agency to provide the financial records of any major borrower, officer, director, employee, or controlling shareholder of such institution whenever there is reason to believe that the records are relevant to show possible criminal activity by such individuals against the institution or supervisory agency. Higher fines are imposed for persons violating the MLCA.

The 1988 act requires the secretary of the treasury to negotiate with finance ministers of foreign countries to establish an international currency control agency (ICCA). The ICCA will serve as a centralized source of information and data base for international drug enforcement agencies, collect and analyze currency transaction reports filed by the ICCA's member countries, and encourage the enactment of uniform cash-transaction and money-laundering statutes by member countries.

The 1988 act also includes several last-minute provisions, added at the behest of Senator John F. Kerry (D–Mass), which require that the U.S. government undertake international negotiations designed to expand access to information on transactions involving large amounts of U.S. currency, wherever such transactions occur worldwide (since these transactions support the narcotics trade). The act also requires that the Department of Treasury negotiate with the appropriate financial supervisory agencies and other officials of foreign countries, foreign banks, and other financial institutions that do business in U.S. currency. The Treasury must assign the highest priority to countries whose financial institutions may be engaging in currency transactions involving the proceeds of international narcotics trafficking, particularly with U.S. currency from drug sales in the United States.

Under the Kerry provisions, the Treasury must report noncompliance by foreign governments to Congress and must identify countries whose financial institutions are engaging in currency transactions involving the proceeds of international narcotics trafficking, where those countries have not agreed to institute mechanisms for exchanging international currency transaction records in connection with narcotics investigations and proceedings.

The Kerry Amendment requires that the president impose penalties and sanctions on recalcitrant governments when the Treasury advises the president or formally reports that a foreign country:

1. Has jurisdiction over financial institutions that are substantially engaging in currency transactions that affect the United States involving the proceeds of international narcotics trafficking
2. Such country has not reached agreement on a mechanism for exchanging adequate records on international currency transactions in connection with narcotics investigations and proceedings.
3. Such country is not negotiating in good faith to reach such agreement.

The penalties and sanctions that the president must impose include the temporary or permanent restriction of such foreign individuals, institutions, or other entities from participating in any U.S. dollar clearing or wire transfer system and from maintaining an account with any bank or other financial institution chartered under the laws of the United States or any individual state. However, the president may certify to Congress that the national interest dictates delay or waiver of these penalties. In addition, financial institutions in such countries that maintain adequate records will be exempt from such penalties and sanctions.

In effect, these well-intentioned, but misguided, provisions attempt to impose U.S. currency transaction and related laws on foreign governments. However, after three years of attempting to cajole and browbeat countries in Latin America and the Caribbean to finalize such agreements, the United States has succeeded in concluding only one of these agreements: an agreement with Venezuela, which was signed on November 5, 1990.

In regulatory matters, the U.S. Treasury Department on October 12, 1990, promulgated controversial proposed regulations on enhanced record-keeping requirements relating to wire transfers (i.e., all aspects of funds transfers by banks of transmittals of funds by other financial institutions subject to the Bank Secrecy Act). The proposed regulation will apply to non-bank institutions as well as to depository institutions. The proposed regulation is aimed at assisting the Justice Department in tracking money-laundering activity.

Under the proposed regulations, financial institutions must obtain and retain specific information concerning the identity of the persons engaging in funds transfers except funds transfers between domestic banks for their own accounts. Because of the drug and other illegal-source money sent through wire transfers domestically and internationally in all amounts, Treasury's proposed regulations require the originator's bank to retain information for each funds transfer. The beneficiary's bank must also obtain and retain similar information.

The proposed regulations would require a special identification verification and record-keeping procedures for a bank that acts as an originator's bank for a funds transfer for a customer who does not have a deposit account at the institution. There will be a new category for international book transfers not involving wire transfers, such as transfers of credit in the books of a foreign and a domestic institution, to the categories of information that the Treasury may request. These regulations will apply to non-bank transmitters of funds, such as institutions operating as telegraph companies or check cashers or fronting as other businesses, typically as travel agencies. As the scope of money laundering becomes broader, so do the methods employed by money launderers to accomplish their goals.

The United States has legislation that makes extensive use of civil in rem and criminal forfeiture proceedings. Since 1988, the United States also forfeits substitute assets when it can show that forfeitable assets are no longer available and that the perpetrator is responsible for their unavailability. For instance, in the Banco de Occidente case in 1988, Banco de Occidente had no offices, directors, or presence in the United States. It would never have expected that it would be subject to U.S. jurisdiction. Suddenly, its Colombian and Panamanian subsidiaries woke up and found that the government, through ex parte motions, had frozen $20 million. The governments of Germany, Switzerland, and Canada also froze accounts of the bank in their countries. Hence, in three days, the U.S. government had frozen $80 million of the Banco de Occidente. Since the bank had only between $130 and $150 million worth of assets, the Banco de Occidente became insolvent. Although the Banco de Occidente was a very respected organization, the U.S. corporate criminal law prevailed. Banco de Occidente had to argue the illegality of the freeze order in four countries. The U.S. government argued that the "substitute assets" doctrine enabled it to freeze the assets. The defense attorneys argued that this is a novel concept without validity in those countries. German courts ruled in favor of the Banco de Occidente. The U.S. government agreed to accept a plea of guilty of drug conspiracy and a fine of

$5 million over five years in exchange for the release of the rest of the funds so that Banco de Occidente could continue to do business. The United States used the substitute assets provisions successfully in 1989 against the Bank for Credit and Commercial International (BCCI). Months after BCCI was charged, many of its assets were also frozen, making its operation difficult and ultimately resulting in a plea bargain.

## Canada

The right to financial privacy in Canada comes from customary law and bank practice, and violations subject violators to compensation. Bank account information is available for criminal and civil proceedings.

The enactment of Bill C–61 in 1988 permits the attorney general, for the purpose of an investigation of a designated drug offense, to apply to a court for an order for bank and other financial information. The same legislation permits the Canadian government to use income tax information for investigating narcotics and money-laundering offenses.

According to Beare and Schneider, a money launderer is defined as one who

> uses, transfers the possession of, sends or delivers to any person or place, transports, transmits, alters, disposes or otherwise deals with, in any manner and by any means, any property or any proceeds of any property with intent to conceal or convert that property to those proceeds or knowing that all or a part of that property or of those proceeds were obtained or derived directly or indirectly as a result of: a) the commission in Canada of an enterprise crime offense or a designated drug offense; or b) an act or omission anywhere that, if it had occurred in Canada, would have constituted an ''enterprise crime offense'' or a ''designated drug offense.''

Enterprise crime offenses embrace twenty-three offenses, including bribery, fraud, murder, theft, robbery, possessing and using counterfeit money, and laundering of the proceeds of a crime.

Canada provides for forfeiture of assets involved in narcotics transactions and laundering of proceeds. Additionally, the court can in certain cases impose a fine on the offender in lieu of forfeiture. In particular, the court can impose a fine if it has the power to order forfeiture, but the property or interest therein cannot be made subject to such an order if, for instance, it is located outside Canada or has been transferred to a third party.

Canada has a strong national law providing for rendering mutual legal assistance in criminal matters. Canada currently has such treaties with the United States, the United Kingdom, Australia, and France.

## France

French law recognizes financial privacy by the Banking Regulations Act of January 24, 1984, which imposes on bankers an obligation to respect a so-called professional secret, the violation of which may constitute a criminal offense with possible imprisonment from one to six months and a fine of from Fr 50 to Fr 300,000. Additionally, banks and financial institutions have a duty of confidentiality, the violation of which may result in civil liability. This bank secrecy, however, gives way in certain criminal investigations, for example, tax and customs and French securities agencies.

On July 12, 1990, France enacted a new money-laundering law, which was inspired by the G–7 Summit of Industrialized countries in July 1989. The French money-laundering act applies to banks, financial institutions, and other professionals (i.e., pawnshops, money changers, and insurance, stocks, and commodities brokerage firms). In addition, it embraces other professionals engaged in financial activities or those who ''carry out, counsel, or control'' capital flows. Hence, notaries, realtors, auctioneers, accountants, auditors, and traders in precious metals are included. It is not known yet whether it includes attorneys and how it impacts on the attorney-client privilege.

Financial and other covered institutions must disclose the amount and nature of all transactions in circumstances where the institution ''has reasons to believe that the operations are derived from narcotics trafficking.'' The information must be reported to the Office in Charge of Money-Laundering Tracking (TRACFIN) within the Ministry of Treasury. Contrary to the U.S. legislation, the French legislation has not provided specific thresholds, directions, or guidelines to define the concept of ''operations derived from narcotics trafficking.'' Hence, institutional officials must rely on their own standards of evaluation. Other professionals with a duty of disclosure must disclose only those transactions that they know are the product of drug trafficking as opposed to transactions that are suspicious.

The law requires banks to obtain, prior to opening any account, the name of the originator of the transaction as well as the name of any person on whose behalf the transaction is originated, if different from the originator. This provision will principally affect legal entities performing industrial or commercial activities in foreign countries. This requirement also affects occasional customers (i.e., customers who do not have a deposit account at the bank) for certain types of transactions which a governmental decree will define.

Banks must retain information of any ''complex or unusual transaction, whenever this transaction seems not to be part of an economic or lawful background.''

The information collected must be maintained five years from the day on which the bank closes the customer's account or rends its relationship with him or her. Records must be retained for five years from the day of the transaction for nondeposit account holders. Casinos must retain identification of players exchanging or cashing chips and counters.

Financial institutions that do not comply with the mandatory disclosure requirement may face disciplinary action by the market authorities; however, the bank's refusal to cooperate does not constitute a criminal defense, probably because of the subjectivity of the requirement to cooperate.

Financial institutions that have disclosed and forwarded in good faith information on suspicious transactions may not be sued for bank secrecy violations by the customer. Banks are granted total immunity even though money laundering cannot be proved afterward, and the customer is acquitted.

Upon request of the customs authorities, a judge may authorize the seizure of someone's assets. The seizure may be declared only against a person who faces drug trafficking or money-laundering charges. It provides that such a seizure can occur only to secure the payment of fines.

Any international outgoing or incoming transfer of currency or stocks for any amount higher than Fr 50,000 has to be declared to the Customs Service. The failure to comply with this requirement may be punished by the confiscation of the corpus delicti, or an equivalent amount, and a fine of at least a quarter of the amount of the attempted transfer.

The French office implementing TRACFIN may exchange, prior to any judicial prosecution, information with its foreign counterparts. The international cooperation is nevertheless subjected to three restrictions:

1. The exchange of information may not violate any domestic law or international convention concerning the right of privacy.
2. The foreign counterpart must respect the rule of reciprocity in exchanging its own information and must follow regulations dealing with the protection of secrecy equal in value to the French professional secret.
3. The French agency will refuse the communication of any document as soon as a criminal prosecution is started or in the event this communication jeopardizes the French sovereignty, security, or public order.

## Germany

The right to financial privacy in Germany, which has evolved as part of the common law, is recognized in statutes dealing with privileges and personal data protection. The public prosecutor can gain access to bank information in connection with criminal inquiries. In certain cases, criminal sanctions apply to violations of a bank or financial secret.

As of the end of 1990, Germany had enacted neither currency-transaction report laws nor laws criminalizing money laundering. However, a bill to criminalize drug-related money laundering and seize assets and earnings from suspected narcotics transactions is pending and is expected to become law in 1992. As of May 1, 1992, it had not been enacted and is controversial because of its potentially adverse impact on the means by which individuals can anonymously invest in German banks.

Already the German Code of Penal Law authorizes forfeiture of profits and other illicit financial gains, earned through a punishable offense, regardless of the kind of crime.

To ensure judicial assistance to foreign authorities, Germany grants judicial assistance on the basis of international agreements, as well as through its comprehensive national legislation.

## Japan

Bank secrecy in Japan exists through banking contract and banking practice. The violation of bank secrecy gives rise to claims compensation. However, regulatory authorities in specifically defined cases (unrelated to money laundering) can obtain access to bank information.

Although currency reporting is not required for domestic transactions, international transfers in excess of five million yen (approximately U.S. $37,000) must be reported to the Ministry of Finance through the Bank of Japan.

Issued in the summer of 1990, bank supervisory circular notices, effective on October 1, 1990, require the identification of the customers of financial institutions. In particular, identification must be established when a new account is opened. When a person opens an account, when a large cash transaction of foreign exchange involves more than five million yen, or when any transaction involves more than thirty million yen, financial institutions must obtain identification by way of reliable public documents. Financial institutions must report the identification to regulatory agencies semiannually. Financial institutions must keep identification and transaction records for five years. Wherever possible, the circular requires financial institutions to cooperate with courts, investigative organizations, and regulatory agencies. Financial institutions must also begin training programs. Most institutions utilize manuals, videos, and in person instructions to all their staff. Such instruction is periodically updated. Anti–money-laundering enforcement training itself has become an industry.

Money laundering is not defined in Japan as a crime. Article 19 of Japan's penal code provides for the forfeiture of property deriving from infringement of law, and, when the property is no longer recoverable, its equivalent valued in money may be forfeited.

On April 18, 1991, Japan completed a draft of two bills to implement the Vienna Drug Convention. One of the bills criminalizes money laundering and calls for the establishment of a system to control money gained illegally by putting it into bank accounts under fictitious names or sending it abroad by requiring financial institutions to report suspicious accounts, including questionable new accounts and money transfers. Money launderers will be subject to a maximum five-year prison term or a fine of up to three million yen. The other proposed bill authorizes the confiscation of bank deposits and other invisible assets from drug-trafficking profits. Prior to passage, authorities could confiscate only cash, securities, and other visible assets. These bills were passed in late 1991.

## United Kingdom

The principles of bank secrecy in the United Kingdom became well-established with the case of *Tournier v. National Provincial and Union Bank of England* (1924). This decision established that the banker will not disclose any information concerning a customer's account, unless ordered to do so by a court, or where a statute so provides, or where the circumstances give rise to a public duty of disclosure.

New laws, such as the Drug Trafficking Offenses Act (DTOA) of 1986, provide that the police and customs officials can have access to information about a suspect's financial affairs at an early stage of a drug-trafficking investigation after order from a court. Banks are required to keep a close check on the accounts of clients who make large deposits and to pass on to the police any information concerning suspicious accounts. Banks are protected from legal action by clients whose accounts are disclosed to the police.

There is no currency-transaction reporting legislation in the United Kingdom; however, the notification of movements of large amounts of currency was required under the suspended Foreign Exchange Regulation.

The United Kingdom has enacted legislation to address the problem associated with money laundering in three key areas: drugs; terrorism; and other crimes.

The DTOA, which took effect in January 1987, contains provisions for the investigation of suspected drug-derived assets prior to arrest, the freezing of assets on arrest or on the issue of a summons, and the making of confiscation orders following conviction. Section 24 of the DTOA, which makes it an offense to assist a drug trafficker to retain the benefits of his proceeds, is aimed at those who launder drug money; the offense is punishable by a maximum of fourteen years in prison, or a fine, or both. The offense is committed by anyone who, knowing or suspecting that another person is a drug trafficker, holds or controls the proceeds of drug trafficking, puts funds at his or her disposal, or gives him or her any help in investing those proceeds. However, it is a defense to prove that it was not known or suspected that drug trafficking was involved or to have disclosed that knowledge or suspicion to the authorities. The act provides financial institutions with protection from suit by customers for breaches of confidentiality and permits police and customs agents to give consent to continue to operate an account after suspicious activity.

The Criminal Justice (International Co-operation) Act of 1990 makes it a criminal act for a person, who knows or has reasonable grounds to suspect that property is derived wholly or in part from the proceeds of drug trafficking, to conceal, disguise, convert, transfer, or remove that property from the jurisdiction of the courts for the purpose of assisting any person to avoid prosecution for a drug-trafficking offense or the making or enforcement of a confiscation order.

Under the Prevention of Terrorism (Temporary Provisions) Act (POTA) of 1989, an offense is committed by anyone who facilitates retention or control of terrorist funds. It is a defense to prove that it was not known, or there was no reasonable cause to suspect that the arrangements related to terrorist funds, or to have disclosed such knowledge or suspicion to the authorities. It is an offense not to disclose information which is known or believed to be of material assistance in preventing an act of terrorism or to be in relation to someone who has committed a terrorist offense.

Both the DTOA and the POTA allow the law enforcement agencies to apply for production orders from a circuit judge which may be served on a financial institution. In appropriate circumstances, a search warrant may be granted by a judge. When orders are granted or are being sought under the DTOA or POTA, any person who knows of the investigation who then makes a disclosure that is likely to prejudice the investigation commits a criminal offense punishable by up to five years imprisonment, or a fine, or both.

The Criminal Justice Act of 1988 does not contain a money-laundering offense. However, although no obligation exists to disclose information to the authorities about crimes that are not suspected to be related to drugs or terrorism, Section 98 affords protection from suit where disclosure is made of a suspicion that property derives from, or is in connection with, an indictable offense.

On December 10, 1990, the United Kingdom took another step to combat money laundering by issuing a set of guidelines to assist and compel banks in detecting and stopping money laundering, such as reporting suspicious transactions. The twenty-page set of guidelines was prepared by the banking industry with the participation of the National Drug Intelligence Unit (NDIU), Customs and Excise, the police, and the Bank of England. The guidelines concentrate on the banks' statutory duty to alert the enforcement agencies to suspected criminal activity. The consequence of not abiding by the statutes and guidelines is potential criminal liability; the benefits of compliance are exoneration from potential criminal and civil liability from breaching confidentiality.

The guidelines require banks to identify all their customers personally, if possible through a face-to-face meeting. The guidelines advise banks to meet new customers personally and to avoid opening accounts by post. The guidelines define reliable forms of identification. The passport is preferred; other reliable forms of identification include an armed forces identity card, an employer identity card, and a full driving license. Documents considered to be less reliable, owing to their susceptibility to forgery, include birth certificates, credit cards, student union cards, and provisional driving licenses. Banks must keep records for up to six years to facilitate investigations.

One of the key and most controversial segments of the guidelines concerns reporting suspicious transactions. The guidelines state that the staff of the organizations that are subject to the guidelines must be encouraged to cooperate fully with the law enforcement agencies and to provide prompt advice of suspicious transactions.

An important aspect of the guidelines concerns their breadth. They apply both to banks and home loans and savings institutions. They will soon be extended to cover the insurance and investment areas as well. They will also cover auctioneers, car dealers, money changers, and other businesses where criminals can convert large amounts of cash into valuable goods.

An important decision made by the United Kingdom is their emphasis on suspicion-based reporting rather than on blanket cash reporting. The United States and Australia rely on cash reporting. Approximately 20 percent of the reports now received by the NDIU lead to new cases or contribute to existing ones.

Some critics are beginning to wonder whether the United Kingdom has enacted too much restrictive legislation: since 1986 the United Kingdom has enacted four statutory initiatives and three nonstatutory initiatives to combat money laundering. The issue is whether these initiatives might jeopardize London's role as one of the world's largest financial centers.

## Australia

The right to bank secrecy in Australia is derived through bank practice and a contractual duty to limit the disclosure of information. The violation may give rise to a claim of compensation; however, in civil and criminal proceedings, banks must disclose financial information.

On July 1, 1988, the Australian government enacted the Cash Transactions Report (CTR). Its purpose is to facilitate the administration of tax and other federal and state laws, especially where criminal activity is involved. It serves to detect and monitor underground cash flows and to deter money laundering by establishing reporting requirements and verification of identity requirements for a person seeking to make transactions and to obtain accounts. The Australian government enacted the law after studying the U.S. Currency Transactions Reporting Act. Conceptually, many similarities exist. The threshold for reporting is $A10,000 with certain exemptions to some transactions involving financial institutions. Suspicious transactions must also be reported whenever there exists reasonable grounds to suspect evasion of tax, offenses against the law, or proceeds from a crime. Institutionally, a Cash Transaction Reports Agency (CTRA) has been established with the responsibility to collect, retain, compile, analyze, and disseminate information relating to cash transaction reports, suspect transactions, and aspects of accounts with cash dealers. The law requires verification by the cash dealers of the identity of persons seeking to open accounts or seeking to become signatories to existing accounts.

The CTRA implements the act. It receives CTRs and performs oversight on transactions for which exemptions from reporting requirements are claimed. In appropriate cases, it will refer CTRs or suspicious transaction reports for further investigation. It also verifies identities and collects, retains, compiles, and analyzes information relating to the above and disseminates it to relevant taxation and law enforcement authorities.

In 1987, Australia enacted the Proceeds of Crime Act which provides new, important tools for forfeiture and confiscation. The law contains new provisions criminalizing money laundering. A money launderer is defined as a person who is engaged directly or indirectly in a transaction that involves money, or other property, that is the proceed of crime and who knows, or ought reasonably to know, that the money or other property is involved in some form of unlawful activity. Violations are punishable by a fine not to exceed $A200,000 ($A600,000 for a corporation), or imprisonment not to exceed twenty years, or both. In 1989, Australia amended its law to permit enforcement agencies to obtain tax return information when it relates to criminal investigations or to the hiding of the proceeds of crime. The Proceeds of Crime Act provides for confiscation, forfeiture, search, and restraining orders.

In 1987, Australia enacted the Mutual Assistance in Criminal Matters Act to handle requests by foreign countries in cases involving search and seizure.

## INTERNATIONAL LAW

Laws to combat international money laundering are part of the developing international criminal cooperation regime, that is, a set of rules among governments and international organizations that require cooperating in the investigation, prosecution, adjudication, and execution of judgments of criminal matters. Within the regime of international criminal cooperation has arisen a subregime of cooperation on regulating international money movement. Similar in some ways to the international criminal cooperation regime, the new subregime on regulating international money movement owes its origin to the fight against illicit international narcotics trafficking, especially as it is conducted by organized crime. However, the subregime of regulating international money movement is gathering a momentum of its own, and it is expanding beyond merely narcotics trafficking.

### Influences

The development of the rising subregime of regulation of international money movement has resulted from the convergence of the work of governments and international organizations, especially intergovernmental organizations (IGOs). Most important, some of the work has culminated in international conventions that impose binding obligations on signatory countries and intergovernmental organizations, such as the European Community, which is a signatory to the Vienna Drug Convention. Binding obligations are referred to as "hard law." Some of the work of IGOs has resulted in resolutions and reports with recommendatory actions. These actions are not binding on countries or persons and therefore are referred to as "soft law." However, even the soft laws, although not immediately binding, have been precursors to hard law.

## Worldwide Organizations

### *The United Nations*

The United Nations, in particular the United Nations Fund for Drug Abuse Control (UNFDAC), the UN Drug Commission, and the UN Crime Prevention Committee, has played an important role in galvanizing the world in the suppression of illicit trafficking. (The role of the United Nations is discussed in more detail in Chapter 26.) On December 19, 1988, the United Nations Convention against Illicit Traffic in Narcotic Drugs and Psychotropic Substances (hereafter referred to as the Vienna Drug Convention) was signed by more than one hundred countries. On November 1, 1990, the convention took effect. The convention is a law enforcement treaty which contains articles on the subjects of extradition, asset forfeiture, mutual legal assistance, cooperation between law enforcement agencies, control of precursor and essential chemicals, and crop eradication. Most important it establishes in a comprehensive manner the offenses of drug trafficking. The convention also establishes the offenses of money laundering and the aiding and abetting of money laundering. (The asset forfeiture provisions of the UN Drug Convention are discussed in Chapter 3.) The UN Drug Convention requires rendering mutual legal assistance for any of the crimes within the convention, including money laundering, and states that a requested country cannot refuse to render mutual legal assistance on the basis of bank secrecy.

In preparing and negotiating the UN Drug Convention, while they achieved common definitions and concepts, the negotiators developed close bonds and a determination to extend and deepen the asset forfeiture obligations on other bodies, such as the Council of Europe (see also Chapter 14).

Another UN organization that has assisted in molding asset forfeiture law is the United Nations Committee on Crime Prevention and Control. At its Eighth Crime Congress, held on September 7, 1990, the congress, which is organized by the UN Committee on Crime Prevention Control, adopted a series of model treaties on international criminal cooperation that will provide significant assistance to strengthening cooperation in asset forfeiture. One of the treaties adopted was a model treaty on mutual assistance in criminal matters. It contains an optional protocol that would require requested states to ascertain whether any proceeds of alleged crimes are located within their jurisdiction by attempting to trace assets, investigate financial dealings, and obtain other evidence that might assist in securing the recovery of the proceeds of crime. The resulting information would be transmitted to the requesting state. The requested state would, to the extent allowed by its law, give effect to or allow enforcement of a final order forfeiting or confiscating the proceeds. Recommendations will be made to the UN General Assembly to adopt the model treaties.

### *Interpol*

Interpol has been in the forefront of assisting states to cooperate with each other in the investigation of money laundering. It has been instrumental in providing technical assistance and training on combatting money laundering, especially in the Caribbean and Latin America. Interpol's Caribbean and Latin American working groups have successfully initiated model legislation on money laundering that has included provisional measures, which are discussed in Chapter 3. The adoption of a series of resolutions on combatting international money laundering and forfeiting crime proceeds illustrates Interpol's continuing leadership in forging a consensus among its members to cooperate against money laundering.

Interpol has recognized the utility of closer cooperation with international organizations. For example, at a recent meeting, other UN representatives agreed to include the Interpol model as an addendum to the forthcoming UN Convention on Narcotic Drugs, to serve as an example of the national legislation needed to aid law enforcement in the conduct of international financial investigations and the forfeiture of criminal assets. In September 1985, after the model was presented to the Customs Cooperation Council (CCC) meeting in Brussels, Belgium, the CCC endorsed the model and stated its intention to distribute it to the commissioners of customs in its member countries. Additionally, after the model legislation on money laundering and forfeiture of assets was adopted by Interpol during its general assembly in August 1985, Interpol embarked on an extraordinary lobbying campaign to try for enactment of the model legislation outside the Interpol community. For instance, the secretary general of Interpol has written to the ministers of justice and the attorney generals of non-Interpol countries to apprise them of the model legislation. In February 1986, Ray Kendall presented the model legislation to the UNFDAC. As Interpol begins to broaden the scope of its membership to include members of the Communist bloc, such as the Soviet Union which recently rejoined Interpol, its coverage of countries and the budget for the enforcement of money movement will increase.

*The G–7 Group and the Financial Action Task Force*

One of the new enforcement initiatives has resulted from the meetings of the leaders of the seven leading industrialized democracies: the United States, Japan, Germany, France, the United Kingdom, Italy, and Canada. In the June 20, 1988, meeting in Toronto, the G–7 countries pledged to establish a ministerial-level task force on international narcotics trade as part of a broader effort to stop the production, trafficking, and financing of illegal drugs. From the beginning, one of its priorities has been to reduce money-laundering operations, used by drug kingpins to move billions of dollars through the international banking system. The declaration called for additional international cooperation to curb money laundering.

On July 16, 1989, the final communiqué of the G–7 summit conference was issued. It pledged to enhance international criminal cooperation on four key topics: drugs, money laundering, terrorism, and the environment. Most important, the communiqué announced the establishment of an institutional mechanism to deal with money laundering—a financial action task force formed from summit participants and other interested countries. The G–7 countries have been joined by the governments of Australia, Austria, Belgium, Spain, Luxembourg, the Netherlands, Sweden, and Switzerland. The task force is politically significant because it is a step toward the institutionalization of international cooperation without which the international community cannot translate the lofty statements of intent into actual measures of cooperation.

On April 23, 1990, the Financial Action Task Force released a report issuing recommendations on combatting money laundering. The report is a combined effort of three working groups: money laundering statistics and methods, chaired by the United Kingdom; legal questions, chaired by the United States; and administrative and financial cooperation, chaired by Italy. The recommendations have important implications for the conduct of international business by financial institutions and other persons. The report will also impact significantly on the investigation and prosecution of persons accused of money laundering, since member countries have agreed to accelerate cooperation efforts in that regard.

The report allocates the measures to combat money laundering into the following areas: improvements of national legal systems, enhancement of the role of the financial system, and the strengthening of international cooperation. According to the report, the Financial Action Task Force members unanimously agreed that financial institutions' secrecy laws should be conceived so as not to inhibit implementation of the recommendations of the report.

The report states that each country should take measures to criminalize drug money laundering as required by the 1988 UN Drug Convention. In particular, the report directs member governments to consider extending the offense of drug money laundering to any other crimes for which a link to narcotics exists. The United Kingdom adapted this approach in the Drug Trafficking Offenses Act, which other Commonwealth governments, such as Hong Kong, have emulated. Alternatively, the report recommends extending the offense of money laundering to all offenses that generate a significant amount of proceeds or to certain serious offenses. The U.S. and Australian laws take the latter approach (e.g. criminalizing the laundering of the proceeds of serious offenses).

The recommendations also encourage improving the role of the financial system, encompassing not only banks, but also non-bank financial institutions. The report suggests creating rules requiring these institutions to identify customers and to keep certain financial records. In fact, to comply with the Basle Statement of Principles, financial institutions suspecting that funds were derived from a criminal activity should be allowed or required to report promptly their suspicions to competent authorities.

The report considers the utility of a currency transactions reporting system such as those implemented by the United States and Australia. It states that, despite the uncertainty of its efficiency, countries should consider establishing such a system.

The report recommends that international competent authorities, perhaps Interpol and the Customs Cooperation Council, should have responsibility for gathering and disseminating information to competent authorities about the latest developments in money laundering and money-laundering techniques and that central banks and bank regulators should do the same on their network.

An important accord reached agrees that each government should furnish spontaneously, or upon request, international information relating to suspicious transactions and on the persons and corporations involved in those transactions. Strict safeguards should be established to ensure that this exchange of information is consistent with national and international provisions on privacy and data protection.

On cooperation between legal authorities, the report is quite vague. Countries are encouraged to enter into a network of bilateral and multilateral agreements and arrangements using generally shared legal concepts to provide practical measures to effect the widest possible range of mutual assistance. According to the report, countries should implement compulsory measures for mutual assistance in criminal matters including giving the governments authority to take expeditious action in response to requests by foreign countries to identify, freeze, seize, and confiscate proceeds or other property of corresponding value to such proceeds, based on money laundering or the crimes underlying the laundering activity. The report encourages creating procedures to avoid conflicts in prosecuting defendants in more than one country and to coordinate seizure and confiscation proceedings which may include the sharing of confiscated assets. Governments are also urged to establish procedures to extradite individuals charged with a money-laundering or related offense.

In June 1991, the task force agreed to accept an offer from the Organization for Economic Cooperation and Development (OECD) to have its secretariat in the OECD's Paris headquarters. It also broadened the group to include Singapore and the governments of the Gulf Cooperation Council.

*The Organization of Economic Cooperation and Development*

The OECD has played an important role in developing guidelines to minimize the overlapping of jurisdiction and enforcement laws that inhibit international investment and business transactions. Most of the recommendations are of a general nature, although some are directed at specific problem areas in terms of potential for conflicting requirements. However, these guidelines are not binding, and most legislatures and courts do not pay heed to the guidelines. The agreement in June 1991 to have the OECD headquarters in Paris serve as the Financial Action Task Force's secretariat ensures enhanced cooperation between the two organizations.

*The Basle Committee on Banking Regulations and Supervisory Practices*

In December 1986, the Basle Committee on Banking Regulations and Supervisory Practices, which consists of the central bank governors of the major industrialized countries, requested U.S. representatives from the Federal Reserve, the Federal Deposit Insurance Corporation, and the Comptroller of the Currency to draft a general statement of principles that international bank supervisory authorities could encourage banks to follow.

In December 1988, a Statement of Principles was adopted by the committee. The statement encourages banks to know their customers, to spot suspicious transactions, and to cooperate fully with law enforcement authorities. In particular, it states that, when banks have good reason to suppose that money held on deposit derives from criminal activity or that the transactions made are themselves criminal in purpose, appropriate legal measures should be taken. For example, banks should deny assistance, sever relations with the customer, and close or freeze accounts in connection with suspicious activity. It also provides specific means to ensure implementation of the measures.

The Basle committee's work resulted in the establishment of a number of regional supervisory authorities. Some of these would have occurred without the committee's involvement; in two cases, they predated the committee, but more recently, groups in the Caribbean, Latin America, Asia, the Middle East, and Africa have been established. In the future, the network of international cooperation among bank supervisors is expected to widen further into related forms of financial intermediation, such as the writing of insurance, as well as the enforcement of securities and commodities practices. In addition, the Basle committee is working closely with international organizations to become more effective in its implementation, especially after the closure of the operations of the Bank of Credit and Commerce International (BCCI) in nine countries in July, 1991.

## Regional Organizations

### *The Council of Europe*

The Draft Convention on Laundering, Search, Seizure and Confiscation of the Proceeds from Crime (hereafter called the convention) was prepared by the Select Committee of Experts on July 25, 1990, was approved by the Council of Ministers on September 10, 1990, and was signed by twelve countries on the very first day it was opened for signature on November 8, 1990. It contains some far-reaching provisions that have the potential to revolutionize international cooperation and the overall development of the regime of regulating international money movement. In particular, although the convention is based on the December 1988 UN Drug Convention, it allows signatory countries to criminalize laundering for nondrug matters. Significantly, the participants in the drafting and potential signatories include countries outside the Council of Europe. In addition to the experts from sixteen Council of Europe countries, the group of experts included experts from Australia, Canada, and the United States as well as Interpol, the United Nations, the International Association of Penal Law, the International Penal and Penitentiary Foundation, and the International Society of Social Defense. The convention also contains important substantive developments, such as allowing the criminalization of negligent money laundering and explaining that hiring defense counsel is not meant to constitute a laundering offense.

The convention has four chapters: the first explains the use of terms; the second sets forth measures to be taken at a national level; the third defines the obligations and parameters of international cooperation; and the fourth contains final provisions.

The momentum for the preparation of the convention first occurred at the Fifteenth Conference of the European Ministers of Justice in Oslo, Norway, on June 17–19, 1986, when the penal aspects of drug abuse and drug trafficking were discussed. In particular, the participants discussed the need to combat drug abuse by smashing the drugs market, which was often linked with organized crime and even terrorism, for example, by freezing and confiscating the proceeds from drug trafficking. As a result of the meeting, Resolution no. 1 was adopted, in which the ministers recommended that the European Committee on Crime Problems (CDPC) should examine "the formulation in the light *inter alia* of the work of the United Nations, of international norms and standards to guarantee effective international cooperation between judicial (and where necessary police) authorities as regarding the detection, freezing and forfeiture of the proceeds of illicit drug trafficking." The CDPC, at its Thirty-sixth Plenary Session in September 1987, proposed and the Committee of Ministers authorized the creation of a Select Committee of Experts on international cooperation in regard to search, seizure, and confiscation of proceeds from crime (PC-R-SC). At the extraordinary conference of the Pompidou Group in London in May 1989, the ministers urged the Council of Europe to expedite the work of the committee, and thereafter its work was expedited.

*The European Community*

On June 10, 1991, the Council (European Community) adopted by unanimity, in the meeting of the ECOFIN Council of Ministers for the European Community, a directive to enforce anti–money-laundering policy. The directive has been winding its way through the European Community.[1] In March 1990, the proposed directive was submitted to the Council of Ministers. After review by the Economic and Social Committee and the European Parliament, the commission submitted an amended proposal in November 1990. The council reached agreement on a common position in February 1991. The directive provides that European Community countries have until January 1, 1993, to adopt the directive into national law. Sir Leon Brittan stated that the commission, the council, and the parliament have worked efficiently and rapidly together.

The directive prohibits money laundering of funds derived from drug trafficking and other criminal offenses, unlike the 1988 UN Drug Convention and the Financial Action Task Force recommendations, which include only drug-related money laundering. Under the directive, money laundering is defined as intentional conversion or transfer of property while knowing that the property is derived from criminal activity ''for the purpose of concealing or disguising the illicit origin of the property or of assisting any person who is involved in the commission of such to evade the legal consequences of his action.'' The directive also states that knowledge or intent may be ''inferred from objective factual circumstances.''

The directive specifies enhanced ''know your customer?'' requirements. For instance, it requires banks and other credit and financial institutions to obtain identification from customers when they open accounts or when they undertake a transaction of 15,000 European currency units (ECUs) (about U.S. $18,000) or more. The threshold for which financial institutions must demand proof of identity of occasional customers for whom money is placed is 15,000 ECUs ($20,400). Germany had sought a higher threshold of 25,000 ECUs and France a lower threshold of 10,000 ECUs. Member states will be able to impose stricter rules, although, obviously, the adverse economic impact of such rules may limit such action. The directive includes certain exceptions for pension plans.

Following the recommendations of the G–7 Financial Action Task Force, the directive provides for enhanced record keeping. In particular, financial institutions must keep copies of the customer identification records for at least five years after their relationship with the customer has terminated.

Under the directive, attention is given to suspicious transactions. Active cooperation between financial institutions and competent authorities will be ensured by a system of reporting suspicious transactions. Financial and covered institutions must review with special attention any transaction that appears by its nature to be related to money laundering. Banks must pay special attention to transactions with third countries that do not apply comparable standards against money laundering to those established by the European Community or to other equivalent standards established by international organizations and endorsed by the European Community.

The directive also gives assistance in relieving employees or directors of a bank who in good faith report information concerning a suspected money laundering to authorities. They will not be responsible for breaching restrictions on disclosure of information.

The directive requires financial institutions and covered institutions to develop special training programs to enable employees of financial institutions to detect money laundering and to inform them about how to respond to suspected cases.

The directive covers certain branches of credit institutions which have their headquarters outside the European Community.

The directive expressly states that the European Community, while adopting the strictest standards in the world, will continue to participate in the work of the Financial Action Task Force on Money Laundering and help ensure that equivalent standards are applied in other areas of the world. The European Community has an incentive to have equivalent standards apply worldwide; otherwise, they will lose business.

Most significantly, the directive provides in practical terms that banks must be vigilant about transactions with jurisdictions whose anti–money-laundering enforcement laws are not on a par with those of the European Community. In effect, this will reward offshore jurisdictions whose laws meet the standards of the G–7 Summit Financial Action Task Force. The coverage of branches with their headquarters outside the European Community also provide an extraterritorial reach to the directive and ensure their applicability.

The immunization of employees or directors of a bank who disclose information from responsibility for breaching restrictions on disclosure of information contrasts with the U.S. government's position, which is to refuse to provide immunity or even informal relief to such persons.

The European Community Commission will explore associating the new democracies in Eastern Europe with the agreement so that similar measures criminalizing the laundering of proceeds from trafficking will apply in those countries as well.

*The Caribbean Financial Action Task Force*

On June 8–10, 1990, a Caribbean drug money-laundering conference was held in Oranjestad, Aruba. That the leading governments in the region sent delegates and committed themselves, at least at this level, to take action against drug money laundering is noteworthy. The governments in attendance included Aruba, the Bahamas, Barbados, Bermuda, the British Virgin Islands, Canada, the Cayman Islands, Colombia, Costa Rica, the Dominican Republic, France, Honduras, Jamaica, Mexico, the Netherlands, the Netherlands Antilles, Panama, St. Vincent and the Grenadines, Trinidad and Tobago, the United Kingdom, the United States, and Venezuela. The governments agreed to consider the forty recommendations of the Financial Action Task Force of the G–7 countries plus twenty-one additional recommendations.

One of the recommendations stemming from the conference provides that a study be undertaken to determine the extent of the drug and related money-laundering problems in the region. According to the conference report, the drug service industry in the area utilizes banks and sea/air transport companies. Another recommendation states that adequate resources must be dedicated to fighting money laundering and other drug-related financial crimes. Additional specialization is required by competent authorities in countries lacking substantial experience in combatting money laundering and other drug-related financial crimes. Another recommendation, consistent with Recommendation 5 of the Financial Action Task Force, is to determine how to criminalize money laundering and in particular what crimes ought to constitute predicate offenses. More than likely, the Caribbean will agree to criminalize the lowest common denominator—making the predicate crime drug-related crimes and following Britain's laws (Drug Trafficking Offenders Act of 1986) and basic legal concepts. If so, the Caribbean would criminalize conspiracy or association to engage in and aid and abet drug trafficking, money laundering, and other serious drug-related offenses and subject such activities to stringent criminal sanctions. The real issue is how broadly governments will include the predicate offenses for money laundering. More than likely, initially the standard of knowing will be selected as a sufficient standard, and governments will refrain from enacting an ought-to-have-known standard. A narrow standard is especially important for a jurisdiction with an important international financial sector.

*The Inter-American Drug Abuse Commission*

The Inter-American Drug Abuse Commission (CICAD), an autonomous, regional organization within the OAS, has established mechanisms to combat money laundering that may have a long-term impact on money movement enforcement activities. Upon its formation, CICAD established an action program to work against the production and use of illicit substances. Additionally, in November 1990, CICAD convened a group of experts to prepare model asset forfeiture laws for adoption by its members.

The mission of the expert group is to set forth the need for legislation that defines as a crime all activities related to the laundering of property and proceeds related to illicit drug trafficking and enables the identification, tracing, seizing, and forfeiting of such property and proceeds. The group is to recommend to the member states that they encourage financial institutions to cooperate with the competent authorities to, inter alia, facilitate the identification, tracing, seizure, and forfeiture of illegal proceeds from laundering. The recommendations are to enable authorities to identify, trace, seize and forfeit property and proceeds related to illicit drug trafficking. The group met in the spring of 1991 and in September 1991, and produced model regulations in 1992.

*The Caribbean Common Market and Community*

On August 2, 1990, during the Eleventh Meeting of the Conference of Heads of Government of the Caribbean Common Market and Community (CARICOM), which took place in Kingston, Jamaica, the heads of government discussed the importance of developing mechanisms to protect the regional and international banking and financial systems from subversion by international drug traffickers. In this connection, they issued a communiqué containing several items of importance to international enforcement. In it they committed their governments to supporting strategies that are being developed in this area. They also took note of the active participation of many CARICOM states in the drug money-laundering conference held in Aruba in June 1990.

## Bilateral Mechanisms

Almost all national governments have bilateral mechanisms that enable them and the other signatory country to forfeit assets. The primary mechanisms are mutual legal assistance treaties, bilateral narcotics conventions, and extradition agreements. For instance, recent Mutual Legal Assistance Treaties in Criminal

Matters (MLATs) have an article that provides for immobilizing, securing, and forfeiting assets. The article provides that a requesting party may notify the other when it has reason to believe that proceeds, and fruits or instrumentalities of crime, are located in the territory of the other party. The parties are required to assist each other, to the extent permitted by their respective laws, in procedures relating to the immobilizing, securing, and forfeiting of the proceeds, fruits, and instrumentalities of crime, restitution, and collection of fines.

### Unilateral Mechanisms

Some countries by law permit the rendering of assistance to another country on the identification, tracing, seizing, freezing, and forfeiture of funds. Some laws allow rendering assistance only for drug-related crimes; other laws go farther. The procedural requirements vary. In most cases the unilateral mechanisms are new or have undergone much revision and are influenced by developments of universal (e.g., the 1988 UN Drug Convention) or regional (e.g., the Council of Europe Laundering Convention) organizations. As countries gain experience in administering the new or revised asset forfeiture laws, proposals undoubtedly will be made for the implementation and improvement of the conventions of universal and regional organizations.

## CONCLUSION

The convergence of many treaties, such as the Vienna Drug Convention; meetings; declarations; and resolutions, such as the G–7 Summit Declarations and Interpol resolutions has brought about the rise of a subregime on regulating international money movement. In the coming months and years, additional details will regulate how financial institutions and professionals must identify customers, keep records for years, and in some cases transmit identification information and information of suspicious transactions to government authorities.

The countries whose enforcement regime is more vigorous than other countries will see a downturn in foreign investment since both legitimate and illegitimate investors desire anonymity, ease of transmission of funds, and as little bureaucracy and expense as possible.

As the subregime of regulating international money movement becomes increasingly sophisticated, drug money launderers will become more sophisticated and will create additional layers and find new ways of devising initial legitimate transactions. They will also discover new jurisdictions to enter, and they will diversify their investments and the types of jurisdictions used.

At present, the international community has scored important successes in such cases as those involving the Banco de Occidente and the BCCI and, more important, in causing organized narcotics groups to spend significant resources and time to devise new ways to launder money and forcing them to reach out and embrace new persons into the labyrinthian network. As countries began to share assets forfeited and to put into place some of the new cooperative mechanisms (i.e., the 1988 Vienna Drug Convention and the Council of Europe Laundering Convention), international enforcement against money laundering will become even more successful. Meanwhile, organized criminals will continue to exploit the loopholes in the laws and policies of some jurisdictions and employ certain technology to move assets. The older organized narcotics traffickers, whose assets have become washed many years ago with money from legitimate ventures, will become difficult if not impossible to catch, especially if they avoid new narcotics activity. However, if efficient enforcement of anti–money-laundering laws facilitates only retiring old traffickers, as opposed to stopping the newer ones, it will have achieved some success.

## NOTE

1. Time to pass controversial directives can take even more time. Hence, Sir Leon Brittan, vice president of the European Commission responsible for financial services and competition policy, characterized ''its rapid adoption'' as showing ''the priority we give to effective action against money laundering.'' Indeed, the community did meet the schedule set forth by the European Councils of Dublin and Rome for the adoption of the proposal, which was originally presented by the commission in March 1990. (Stated at a press conference, March 1990)

## BIBLIOGRAPHY

American Bankers Association and American Bar Association Section of Criminal Justice. *Money Laundering Enforcement Update: Legislative, Regulatory, Enforcement Developments and Policy Implications* (2 volumes). Washington, D.C.: ABA/ABA, 24–25 Sept. 1990.

Beare R. and B. Schneider. *Tracing of Illicit Funds: Money Laundering in Canada*. Department of the Solicitor General, Canada, 1990.

British Bankers' Association, the Building Societies Association, and the Law Enforcement Agencies in Britain. ''Money Laundering, Guidance Notes for Banks and Building Societies.'' London: December 1990.

Police Foundation. ''Confiscation and Forfeiture Law: English and American Comparisons.'' London: 1989.

President's Commission on Organized Crime. *The Cash Connection: Organized Crime, Financial Institutions and Money Laundering*. Washington, D.C.: U.S. Government Printing Office, October 1984.

Segal, Laurent. ''The New French Money Laundering Act.'' *International Enforcement Law Reporter* 6 (November 1990).

U.S. Congress. Senate. *Crime and Secrecy: The Use of Offshore Banks and Companies*. Hearings before the Permanent Subcommittee on Investigations of the Committee on Governmental Affairs. U.S. Senate, Hrg. 98–151, 15, 16 March, and 24 May 1983.

Zagaris, Bruce. ''Dollar Diplomacy: International Enforcement of Money Movement and Related Matters—A United States Perspective.'' *The George Washington Journal of International Law and Economics* 22 (1989): 465–552.

Zagaris, Bruce, and Richard Bornheim. ''Draft Chapter on Foreign and International Money Laundering Laws.'' Paper presented at the American Bankers Association (ABA) and American Bar Association (ABA) Section on Criminal Justice: Money Laundering Enforcement: Legal and Practical Developments, New York: ABA/ ABA, 26–27 October 1989.

''International Cooperation against Money Laundering in the European Integration Context.'' *1992 The External Impact of European Unification*. Washington D.C.: ABA/ABA, 3 November 1989 13–16.

# 3

# The Emerging Regime of Asset Forfeiture

ELIZABETH KINGMA

## INTRODUCTION

The international and foreign laws for asset forfeiture are just developing as the result of a concerted effort by governments and international organizations to combat illicit drug trafficking and other forms of criminal activity. Asset forfeiture policy and laws constitute an integral part of international money movement regulation, or anti–money-laundering legislation, in that they provide for the tracing, freezing, and seizing of ill-gotten gains, even after those proceeds have been transferred or converted into other forms. The underlying premise is to prevent the criminal from profiting from his crime.

These laws have been gaining momentum in their insurgence. At least twenty-six countries have enacted some version of asset forfeiture laws. The asset forfeiture policies presented by international and regional organizations as well as individual countries are similar, but they vary on some key provisions. This chapter will examine and compare the key aspects of the new treaties, conventions, and laws.

## INFLUENCES

As was mentioned in Chapter 2, the United Nations has had a profound effect upon the emergence of international money laundering and asset forfeiture treaties, agreements, and laws. The United Nations Convention against Illicit Traffic in Narcotic Drugs and Psychotropic Substances (referred to as the UN Drug Convention) mandates the enactment of asset forfeiture laws by its signatory countries. Another UN organization, the United Nations Crime Prevention and Control Committee adopted a series of model treaties on international criminal cooperation that will significantly strengthen cooperation in asset forfeiture.

Interpol has also been in the forefront of assisting states to cooperate with each other in the investigation of money laundering, and it has adopted model legislation which provides for asset forfeiture.

One of the new enforcement initiatives has resulted from the meetings of the leaders of the seven leading industrialized democracies—the United States, Japan, Germany, France, the United Kingdom, Italy, and Canada—known as the G–7. The G–7 instituted a Financial Action Task Force formed from summit participants and other interested countries to address a need for money-laundering legislation and cooperation. Joining the G–7's task force were the governments of Australia, Austria, Belgium, Spain, Luxembourg, the Netherlands, Sweden, and Switzerland. The task force's work culminated in a report recommending methods to combat money laundering.

Another leader in this field is the Basle Committee on Banking Regulations and Supervisory Practices, which consists of the central bank governors of the major industrialized countries. The Basle committee adopted a Statement of Principles which, among other things, suggests that banks freeze accounts when they suspect the accounts are connected to criminal activity. The Council of Europe has also contributed to this field. It opened for signature in September 1990 the Draft Convention on Laundering, Search, Seizure and Confiscation of the Proceeds from Crime (hereafter called the convention), the terms of which will be explored more fully in the following sections. Moreover, the Inter American Drug Abuse Commission (CICAD), an autonomous, regional organization within the Organization of American States (OAS), has convened a group of experts to prepare model asset forfeiture laws for adoption by its members.

## THE SUBSTANCE

Key aspects of forfeiture law in different conventions, agreements, and statutes vary slightly. These issues include establishing cooperative mechanisms for assisting foreign countries in seizing, freezing, and confiscating assets as well as for providing investigative assistance; recognizing rights to refuse cooperation; naming the offenses that will be subject to imposition of asset forfeiture; allowing temporary measures to freeze and seize assets prior to conviction; designating the property subject to forfeiture; defining the extent to which the rights of third parties may be infringed upon and measures for protecting their rights; and providing the ultimate disposal of distribution of the confiscated assets. Also, different agreements and statutes have envisioned and addressed new problem areas. A survey of the different provisions that have been developed to address these aspects of asset forfeiture follows.

## INTERNATIONAL COOPERATION: INTERNATIONAL ORGANIZATIONS' MANDATES

International organizations have encouraged, and in some cases required, countries to enact legislation that provides a mechanism for rendering assistance to other countries' requests that they freeze or seize assets that are evidence, proceeds, or means of a crime that is under investigation or conviction in the requesting state.

One of the purposes of the European Laundering Convention is to supplement the European Convention on Mutual Assistance in Criminal Matters, especially Article 3(1)'s letters rogatory section which provides a mechanism by which countries may obtain evidence to be used in criminal proceedings and which is located in a foreign country. The convention also complements the European Convention on the International Validity of Criminal Judgments, which provides for the possibility of enforcing a foreign "sanction," including measures to confiscate objects. The European Laundering Convention will enable signatory countries to enforce confiscation orders from another requesting state prior to judgment. The European Laundering Convention provides a comprehensive set of rules, covering all the stages of the procedure from the first investigations to the imposition and enforcement of confiscation sentences. It permits flexible but effective mechanisms of international cooperation.

The European Laundering Convention states that bank secrecy cannot constitute an obstacle to domestic criminal investigations or provisional measures. Additionally, it provides for special investigative powers and techniques. Signatory countries are required to at least consider the introduction of the following new techniques to cooperate on an international level:

1. Granting monitoring orders or judicial orders to a financial institution to transmit information about transactions conducted through a particular account, usually for a specific period of time.
2. Observing covertly the movement of persons.
3. Intercepting telecommunications, including telephone conversations, telex, and telefax communications.
4. Ordering access to computer systems.
5. Granting production orders to produce specific records, documents, or other property. Failure to comply with such an order would result in an order for search and seizure.

The G–7 Financial Action Task Force also encourages cooperative investigations among foreign countries. Mutual assistance in criminal matters procedures should be implemented to compel countries to cooperate with each other in searching, seizing, and freezing evidence, including bank records, for use in money-laundering investigations and prosecutions and in related actions in foreign jurisdictions. Similarly, the Caribbean Financial Action Task Force recommended that, at the request of a foreign state, countries should have legislation granting the authority to seize, freeze, and confiscate property located in their jurisdiction regardless of whether the owner of the property or the person who committed the offense is or ever has been within the jurisdiction.

The UN Drug Convention is more stringent. It does not suggest but, rather, requires its signatory countries to adopt measures that will enable them to confiscate narcotic drugs and psychotropic substances, as well as the instrumentalities used in or intended for use in and the proceeds derived from drug offenses. The convention also obligates the signatory countries to endeavor to conclude bilateral and multilateral treaties and agreements to improve the effectiveness of international cooperation in this regard. Moreover, the signatory countries must designate an authority to execute foreign requests for mutual legal assistance or to transmit them to the competent authorities for execution. The request for mutual legal assistance must contain certain information, including the subject matter and nature of the investigation or proceeding; a summary of the relevant facts; a description of the assistance sought; where possible, the identity, location, and nationality of any person concerned; and the purpose for which the evidence, information, or action is sought. Because of this provision and the momentum generated by the preparation and signing of the UN Drug Convention, many countries have entered into bilateral conventions, and several other regional organizations have concluded and are considering adopting similar conventions.

## Foreign Laws

Mutual legal assistance treaties, bilateral narcotics conventions, and extradition agreements are among the most common examples of the bilateral agreements entered into as a result of the UN Drug Convention. Some countries, by means of national statutes, have also provided mechanisms for assisting other countries to identify, trace, seize, freeze, and forfeit assets. Some of these foreign statutes limit assistance to drug-related crimes; other laws apply to a broad spectrum of criminal offenses.

A mutual legal assistance agreement between Mexico and the United States specifically provides that, to the extent permitted by their respective laws, the requested country will assist in immobilizing, securing, and forfeiting the proceeds, fruits, and instrumentalities of crime and will aid in the collection of fines. The mutual legal assistance treaty between Mexico and the United States has been ratified by both countries. This complements a bilateral narcotics cooperation agreement between the two countries, which has a broad scope and could be used for authorizing cooperative measures in asset forfeiture.

In April 1990, the United Kingdom (U.K.) and the United States entered into the U.K.'s first formal confiscation agreement, the Drug Traffickers Offenses Act (U.S.) Order 1989. The United Kingdom has also signed similar agreements which await introduction with at least fourteen other countries. Moreover, in its introductory remarks, the U.K.'s Criminal Justice (International Cooperation) Act of 1990 states but its purpose is to enable the United Kingdom to aid the international effort against drug trafficking by providing a means to enforce foreign seizure, detention, and forfeiture orders.

The United States does not have a statute that generally authorizes and establishes a procedure for international cooperation regarding asset forfeiture. Instead, it relies on agreements, letters rogatory, and international comity as a basis for cooperating with foreign seizure and forfeiture requests. However, three sections of the U.S. Code recognize that, in regard to certain crimes, forfeited assets may be transferred to a foreign country and thereby recognize the ability to cooperate on an international level. These statutes require, among other things, that any transmittal be predicated on a preexisting agreement with the country requesting the transfer.

The Canadian authorities may execute foreign court-imposed fines or asset forfeiture orders and return the assets to the requesting country on the basis of a mutual legal assistance treaty with the country. Canada has such treaties with the United States, the United Kingdom, Australia, Mexico, and the Bahamas. Most important, Canada, unlike the United States, has passed legislation that generally establishes procedures and authorization for international cooperation in seizing and forfeiting assets. The Mutual Legal Assistance in Criminal Matters Act allows Canadian authorities to respect requests for legal assistance from countries with which it does not have a mutual legal assistance treaty.

Australia passed its Mutual Assistance in Criminal Matters Act of 1987, which specifically provides for and designates the procedure for complying with foreign search and seizure requests. It requires that a foreign forfeiture order be predicated on a "serious offense." Additionally, the attorney general must be satisfied that a person has been convicted of the offense and that the conviction is final and not subject to final appeal. Once registered, the foreign order may be enforced as if it were a local order. However, the attorney general may cancel the registration and thus the order should he determine that the order has ceased to have effect in the foreign country.

The U.K.'s Drug Trafficking Offenses Act of 1986 provides that, if another country entered into a formal agreement with the United Kingdom, the courts in England and Wales would enforce that country's confiscation orders within the United Kingdom. The High Court could freeze the assets of a drug trafficker while the requesting country proceeds with the case. Once a conviction is obtained by that country, the High Court can enforce the requesting country's confiscation order. Likewise, the Criminal Justice Act of 1988, which covers assets derived from other indictable crimes, also permits enforcement of restraint and confiscation orders issued by foreign countries, provided a formal agreement was entered into by foreign countries. Finally, the Criminal Justice Act of 1990 provides that foreign orders for forfeiture may be enforced in the United Kingdom provided that the order has been approved by a resolution of each House of Parliament and has become an Order in Council. The order must be predicated on an offense corresponding to or similar to an offense under the Misuse of Drugs Act of 1971, a drug-trafficking offense as proscribed by section 38(1) of the Drug Trafficking Offenses Act of 1986, an offense under section 1 of the Criminal Justice (Scotland) Act of 1987, or an offense to which Part IV of the Criminal Act of 1988 applies.

The developed countries are not alone in creating asset forfeiture laws and in responding to foreign requests: the Bahamas, Barbados, and Panama have also passed such legislation. The new Bahamian asset forfeiture law provides broad power to respond to foreign requests to conduct searches. However, a Bahamian court cannot register an external confiscation order unless the court is satisfied that the confiscation order is final, the defendant had adequate notice to defend himself, and the order has not been satisfied already. Similarly, Barbados law provides that the attorney general may apply the Proceeds of Crime Act, the national asset forfeiture law, in response to a foreign request. Many of the same concerns outlined in the Bahamas law—that the order is final, that the defendant has time for a defense, and that enforcing the order in Barbados would not be contrary to the interests of justice—are evident. Panamanian law provides for cooperation with foreign drug investigations for the same drug-related crimes for which national forfeiture applies.

## RIGHT TO REFUSE AND POSTPONE COOPERATION: INTERNATIONAL ORGANIZATIONS

In order to ensure flexibility in international cooperation, the European Laundering Convention provides for the possibility of refusal and postponement of the cooperation. Additionally, the convention provides that the parties will, before refusing or postponing cooperation, consult each other and consider whether the request may be granted partially or be subject to conditions.

### Foreign Laws

The United Kingdom's Drug Trafficking Offenses Act of 1986 and the Criminal Justice Act of 1988 allow for refusal to execute foreign forfeiture or restraining orders if the defendant may still appeal his conviction or did not receive notice of the proceedings against him and so could not defend his interests, or if enforcement of the foreign orders would be contrary to the interests of justice.

The Canadian Mutual Legal Assistance in Criminal Matters Act, the implementation legislation for mutual legal assistance treaties negotiated with foreign countries, provides that the treaties, in order to be covered by the act, must allow Canada the right to refuse to comply with a request on the grounds of security, sovereignty, or public interest. Additionally, the offense being investigated by the foreign country must also constitute an offense in Canada.

Australia has enacted a comprehensive list of situations under which cooperation must be denied and another set of conditions under which assistance may be denied. The Australian Mutual Assistance in Criminal Matters Act requires refusal of a foreign country's request for assistance when the offense being investigated or prosecuted relates to punishment for political views, prejudice on account of a person's race, sex, religion, nationality, or political opinions; the offense would not constitute an offense under the ordinary criminal law of Australia; and granting the request would impose upon the sovereignty, security, or national interests of Australia. A request may be refused if the defendant has been acquitted or pardoned or if he or she has already served the punishment for the offense and the requesting country is not a country to which the Mutual Assistance in Criminal Matters Act applies. A request may be refused also if the attorney general concludes that the act being investigated would not constitute an offense under Australian law; the act was committed outside of the requesting foreign country and, had a similar act with regard to Australia occurred outside of its territory, it would have been an offense under Australian law; or the statute of limitations would prevent its prosecution. Two additional situations for refusal could apply if providing assistance could prejudice an ongoing Australian investigation or the safety of any person and if assisting would create an "excessive burden" on Australia's resources.

## PREDICATE OFFENSES: INTERNATIONAL ORGANIZATIONS

One of the key provisions that varies among the conventions, reports, and foreign laws is what crimes will be subjected to asset forfeiture. Laws for money laundering and asset forfeiture originated from an effort to curb illegal narcotics trafficking. However, some treaties and foreign laws have expanded the realm of asset forfeiture to include other serious crimes such as kidnapping, murder, and rape.

The UN Drug Convention is narrow in scope, limiting forfeiture and provisional measures to drug crimes. The G–7 Financial Action Task Force Report similarly maintains that the scope of criminalization of money laundering and asset forfeiture should include drug money laundering. However, it allows for expansion by stating that each country should consider extending the offense of money laundering to any other crimes linked to narcotics, and even to laundering profits from serious offenses or from all offenses that generate a significant amount of proceeds.

The Council of Europe's European Laundering Convention expands the scope to include offenses defined by the UN Drug Convention encompassing drug trafficking as well as terrorist offenses, organized crime, violent crimes, offenses involving the sexual exploitation of children and young persons, extortion, kidnapping, environmental offenses, economic fraud, insider trading, and other serious offenses. The drafters thought that, in principle, the scope of predicate crimes should be made as wide as possible. However, they believed that this broad approach required flexibility for states to restrict cooperation under the convention to certain offenses or categories of offenses. Accordingly, signatory states were allowed to enter reservations to some of the crimes, thus allowing them to exempt themselves from applying asset forfeiture to any of the crimes listed.

## Foreign Laws

Foreign laws reflect these divergent theories. Although it was recently enacted, the scope of forfeiture in the Bahamas is limited to drug-trafficking offenses, which include receiving gifts from drug trafficking and dealing with drug-trafficking proceeds and related property, whether directly or indirectly. Similarly, the Proceeds of Crime Act, enacted in Barbados on June 21, 1990, provides a narrow scope, allowing for the forfeiture of property used in connection with the commission of scheduled offenses, including possession of controlled drugs for the purpose of supplying to another person, trafficking in controlled substances, assisting another to retain the benefit of drug trafficking, money laundering related to one of the three preceding drug offenses, and possession of property from one of the three preceding drug offenses.

The United States applies asset forfeiture to a more diverse range of offenses. Civil forfeiture may be applied not only to drug crimes, but also to illegal gambling, motor vehicle theft, sexual exploitation of children, copyright infringement, illegal exploitation of war material, illegal surveillance, illegal transportation of goods manufactured by prisoners, and money laundering. Criminal forfeiture extends to many of the same crimes and also to the illegal transmission of defense information, racketeering (Racketeer-Influenced Corrupt Organizations, or RICO) offenses, and the distribution of illicit obscene materials.

The United Kingdom has enacted several statutes that provide for asset forfeiture. One of these, the Drug Trafficking Offenses Act of 1986, provides for the confiscation of any benefits received as a result of drug trafficking. A later statute, the Criminal Justice Act of 1988, allows for the confiscation of proceeds from other crimes. The Prevention of Terrorism (Temporary Provisions) Act of 1989 provides for the forfeiture of any money or property to be used in connection with terrorist offenses that is within the defendant's control at the time of the offense.

Italy's asset forfeiture legislation is found in the so-called anti-Mafia law, Law no. 646 of September 13, 1982. Originally intended to combat Mafia associations, the anti-Mafia law has been broadly applied by the courts to narcotics traffickers and other criminals, permitting forfeiture for a broad variety of crimes. Italy recently passed additional legislation outlawing money laundering and restricting money transfers. That legislation also provides for the seizure of funds in drug trafficking and organized crime contexts.

Other countries have been active in defining the new legal regime. Recent Canadian legislation authorizes asset seizure and forfeiture for two types of criminal offenses: ''enterprise crime offenses'' and ''designated drug offenses.'' The enterprise crime offense encompasses many infractions, such as bribery, fraud, gambling, and money laundering. A designated drug offense is defined as a breach of specific sections of the Food and Drugs Act and the Narcotics Control Act, both of which prohibit trafficking certain drugs and laundering of the proceeds of that trafficking. Australia's Proceeds of Crime Act of 1987 broadly provides for assistance to foreign countries in tracing and forfeiting property that represents the proceeds and the means of "a serious foreign offense." Singapore's law, also broad, provides that monetary instruments that are the means or proceeds of a crime may be seized as long as the crime was an offense under the Penal Code of the Republic. Similarly, in Switzerland the foreign offenses must also breach the Swiss penal code. Moreover, the Swiss must have jurisdiction over the criminals.

### Confiscation

Confiscation is the heart of asset forfeiture policy. Generally, the laws allow that a defendant's assets may be seized or frozen during investigation and trial. Upon conviction, those assets may be forfeited to the state. On an international level, when one country is investigating a crime or has charged or convicted a defendant, it may request that the assets and property related to the crime be seized, frozen, or forfeited by the country in which those items are located. Often, the procedure taken by a country in response to a request by a foreign country to confiscate assets will be the same procedure used to confiscate assets on a domestic level.

### Provisional Measures

Under U.S. law, assets may be seized prior to conviction if a police officer can obtain a warrant by showing probable cause to believe that a crime has been committed, that certain items will prove to be evidence of that crime, and that those items are located in the place specified by the warrant. It is often helpful if the officer can demonstrate that the accused did not have an alternative legal source of income by which he could have obtained the objects to be confiscated. A warrant is necessary to search an area except when certain exigent circumstance exist, for example, searches incident to arrest, a search consented to by a proper party, automobile searches, plain view seizures, searches of those crossing national borders, investigative stops predicated on reasonable suspicion, and searches of certain abandoned property.

Once the warrant is obtained or the exigent circumstances arise, the officer must have probable cause to believe that the items located will be subject to forfeiture in order to seize them. The officer must report the seizure promptly, and an inquiry must be commenced shortly to determine whether forfeiture is warranted. If there is unnecessary delay in these procedures, the forfeiture may be unattainable.

Canadian legislation allows using provisional seizure in an investigatory manner. New Canadian legislation provides for a special warrant authorizing a peace officer to search a building for other property and to seize any property which the peace officer has reasonable grounds to believe would be subject to forfeiture. The judge may grant the order if satisfied that there are reasonable grounds to believe that there are items subject to forfeiture on the property to be searched. Similarly, the attorney general may obtain a restraining order that would prohibit any person from disposing of or dealing with the property specified in the order.

Additionally, the Canadian minister of justice may authorize the competent government official to apply for a search warrant in compliance with a foreign state's request for seizure of objects sought in connection with a foreign offense. The official must apply to the judge of the relevant province for a search warrant. The judge may grant the warrant if satisfied that there are reasonable grounds to believe that an offense was committed, the foreign state requesting the search and seizure has jurisdiction over the offense, and evidence of the offense will be located in the place specified in the warrant. The officer who executes the warrant may seize things not mentioned in the warrant if he or she has reasonable grounds to believe that the item will provide evidence of or is the means or proceeds of a criminal offense.

Australia's procedure for searching, seizing, and freezing assets is similar to Canada's. Police officers may apply to a magistrate for a search warrant for property tainted by an offense. In executing the warrant, the police officer may seize any property reasonably believed to be property related to the offense, even if not of the kind specified in the warrant; or property related to another offense; or anything relevant to or providing evidence to a criminal proceeding. However, the Australian law differs from the Canadian in that it provides that the officer must also have reasonable grounds to believe that it is necessary to seize that property in order to prevent its concealment, loss, or destruction, or to prevent its continued used in committing the offense. Similarly, a restraining order to freeze the dealings with property may be granted when a person has been convicted, charged, or is about to be charged with an indictable offense. If the person who owns the seized or frozen property cannot meet certain debts or support himself or herself without the property, the court may allow him or her reasonable living expenses out of the property.

Australia's Mutual Assistance in Criminal Matters Act also extends its provisional measures to foreign countries. It allows that, when a foreign proceeding or investigation in regard to a "serious offense" is ongoing in Australia and there are reasonable grounds to believe that related property is present in Australia, upon request from the foreign country, a search warrant may be issued to search for and seize or freeze any property found that the police officer conducting the search believes is relevant to the foreign proceedings. If during the search the officer finds something relevant but not of the type of thing specified by the warrant, the officer may seize the item so long as he or she believes it is tainted by crime and will likely be concealed, lost, or destroyed if left. The court may allow that the property be used for reasonable living expenses by the person and his or her dependents in defending a criminal charge, or in paying off a specified debt. However, the court will not allow the property to be used in that manner if the defendant can meet the expense out of property free from the restraining order.

The United Kingdom's Drug Trafficking Offenses Act of 1986 and the Criminal Justice Act of 1988 are more limited than the legislation of Australia. They do not allow for seizing or freezing property during the investigatory stages prior to indictment. They require that legal proceedings must have commenced against a person and that a confiscation order must have been made or that reasonable grounds must exist for finding that such an order be made. The law is broad, however, in that it encompasses acting upon any property held by the defendant including that which was acquired after the crime and any property that the defendant has transferred to another person as a gift. Also subject to restraint are interests in land and securities held for the benefit of the defendant, as well as the interest that accrues to them. As with other countries' statutes, this law allows the court to exclude the amounts necessary to satisfy any of the defendant's debts and obligations that are due and have priority at that time.

The United Kingdom has also extended its provisional measures to foreign countries under the Criminal Justice (International Cooperation) Act of 1990. A customs officer or constable may seize and detain any cash that is being imported into or exported from the United Kingdom under that act if the officer has reasonable grounds for suspecting that the cash is the direct or indirect proceeds of or is intended for use in drug trafficking and if the cash exceeds a specified sum.

## PERMANENT MEASURES–FORFEITURE

Countries generally provide that forfeiture may be realized upon a final determination of guilt in committing one of the predicate offenses. For instance, in the United Kingdom, property may be forfeited upon conviction of one of the predicate offenses; whether they will forfeit property pursuant to a foreign request varies with the different agreements and statutes.

In Canada property may be forfeited if, upon conviction of an enterprise crime or designated drug offense, the court finds that the property is proceeds of a predicate criminal offense or that the offense was committed in relation to that property. Moreover, if the court fails to find that the crime was committed in relation to the property, but does not find that the property is related to another crime, it may forfeit the property.

U.S. legislation provides for forfeiture under criminal proceedings and also forfeiture under civil proceedings. Both are dependent upon a final determination that seizure is warranted, but otherwise they differ significantly. Jurisdiction for civil forfeiture rests on the property's location; it is an in rem procedure, and the property must be seized in order to obtain jurisdiction. Civil forfeiture also carries a lower burden of proof to obtain a forfeiture order. Once the government shows probable cause to believe that the property is subject to forfeiture, the burden shifts to the defendant to demonstrate that the property should not be forfeited. Criminal forfeiture's jurisdiction is in personam; the defendant must be within the court's jurisdictional reach. The burden of proof to obtain a forfeiture order in a criminal proceeding is also more rigorous, and so more difficult to obtain. Accordingly, a criminal conviction is not necessary for forfeiting assets in the United States. Civil forfeiture orders do not rest on a conviction, only a showing that the preponderance of the evidence indicates that the property is related to the predicate crime.

## PROPERTY SUBJECT TO FORFEITURE

Another important area addressed by different asset forfeiture conventions, agreements, and laws is what property or assets may be forfeited. Traditionally only property that is tainted by the crime or property that is directly related to the crime (e.g., the crime's instrumentalities or profits) may be forfeited. Some international organizations have broadened the scope to allow for any assets held by the defendant to be forfeited up to the value or amount of the profits from the crime. This is commonly known as value confiscation. Some allow for substitute confiscation which will forfeit property that has been bought or traded for the direct proceeds and thus is a substitute for the direct proceeds. Another important issue to be addressed is whether the tainted property, once transferred, may be taken from third parties to whom the property was transferred.

### Tainted Property

The Caribbean Financial Action Task Force recommends a narrow scope—that confiscation measures should apply to crime proceeds and to chemicals, equipment, and materials used or destined for the illicit manufacture, preparation, distribution, and use of narcotic drug and psychotropic substances.

The type of object or property subject to forfeiture in the United States varies with the type of crime committed. In relation to drug crimes, the authorities may seize controlled substances and drug-related equipment, materials, containers, means of conveyance and transportation, financial records, money, negotiable instruments, securities and things of value, and proceeds traceable to illegal drug exchange or used or intended to be used in breach of drug laws. Also real property and any interest in such property that has a connection with illegal use may be forfeited.

The U.S. criminal forfeiture laws provide that, in regard to drug crimes, real and personal property used or intended to be used in committing the crime may be forfeited as well as any contractual or property interest in the criminal enterprise and any proceeds of the crime. Moreover, a rebuttable presumption arises that property acquired during the period of the violation is the proceeds of that violation if the prosecution shows that no legitimate source of the property existed. Some other crimes, such as the sexual exploitation of children and money laundering, allow civil forfeiture of the proceeds as well as the objects and instrumentalities related to the crime. Many others are restricted to simply forfeiting the object or means of the crime, for example, motor theft, gambling, wiretapping, and copyright infringements and violations do not allow forfeiture of the illegal proceeds. Whereas criminal forfeiture provisions provide for the forfeiture of proceeds in the context to many crimes, including RICO, obscene material, sexual exploitation of children, and illicit transmission of defense information violations. Again, criminal copyright infringements do not warrant forfeiture of proceeds.

Canadian law allows for the seizure and forfeiture of proceeds that are defined as "any property, benefit or advantage, within or outside Canada, obtained or derived directly or indirectly as a result" of one of the prescribed crimes, as well as the means and instrumentalities of the crime.

The expansive Italian law provides that, upon conviction of the crime, not only may the instruments, proceeds, product, or profit of crime be forfeited, but additionally any commercial licenses or entitlement to work as the contractor or subcontractor for public works or supplies. Furthermore, during preliminary proceedings, all assets which the defendant cannot prove were legally acquired or which exceed his apparent purchasing power may be seized.

Australia allows all of the defendant's property including after-acquired property to be seized and forfeited. In considering the request for a forfeiture order, the court may consider the hardship that might be caused to anyone by a forfeiture, the use intended or usually intended for like property, and the gravity of the offense. In fulfilling a forfeiture request, Australia will seize real personal property of every description, situated in Australia or elsewhere, tangible or intangible, and any interest in such property.

Mexico will forfeit the instruments of crime as well as things that are the object or product of certain crimes if their use is prohibited and the crime was intentional. Furthermore, the law requires the forfeitures of instruments and objects used by a person in permitting the use of an airport, air landing and takeoff strips, or any other installation for air traffic that is engaged in illicit activities.

Swiss law provides that forfeiture of monetary instruments may be ordered if they were used as the means or the proceeds of a criminal offense. Additionally, the monetary instruments may be seized only to the extent that they redress an illicit situation or profit. As a result, forfeiture will most commonly be ordered when the offender did not return the funds to his victim.

Monetary instruments that represent the means or proceeds of a crime may be seized in Japan either upon a warrant issued by a judge or at the scene of arrest of a flagrant offender. However, certain articles relating to an official secret and held by a public officer or certain government officials may not be seized. Likewise, articles relating to professional secrets (such as secrets between a doctor and patient) may not be seized from the professional person.

### Value and Substitute Confiscation

Some organizations and countries have also provided that, when the original proceeds or means of the crime have been transferred or converted, the assets into which the original proceeds were transformed may be forfeited. For example, if a drug trafficker uses the money he made from a drug deal to buy an airplane, the airplane would be subject to forfeiture. This concept, known as substitute confiscation, is provided for by many international organizations and foreign laws.

Value confiscation is an alternative means for preventing the criminal from reaping the benefit of his or her acts. It resembles substitute confiscation in that other assets are substituted for the proceeds of property originally obtained. It differs in approach, however. Instead of identifying the exact property that was traded for the originally tainted property, the courts assess the value of the original proceeds and levy a fine in that amount against the convicted criminal. The state may exert this penalty against any of the criminal's assets. The UN Drug Convention and the G–7 Financial Action Task Force Report provide for both substitute and value confiscation.

The relation back theory is the basis for the United States' substitute confiscation rule for drug-related offenses in civil forfeiture proceedings. According to the theory, the property or assets subject to forfeiture are legally forfeited at the moment when the illegal act occurs. Any transfer subsequent to the crime is therefore moot because title had already vested in the U.S. government. As a result, all interest, dividends, income, or property derived from the original drug-trafficking proceeds is subject to forfeiture. In other words, if the property that was sold by the defendant legally belonged to the U.S. government, then any assets or property the defendant received as consideration for the forfeitable property also belongs to the U.S. government.

The criminal asset forfeiture provisions under U.S. law state that, if the forfeitable property is unavailable because it has been secreted or removed from the jurisdiction, transferred to a third party, substantially diminished in value, or irretrievably commingled with other property, other property belonging to the defendant is forfeitable instead.

Canadian laws provide for value confiscation when the property cannot be located, has been transferred to a third party, is located outside of Canada, has diminished in value, or has been irretrievably commingled with other property. An additional important aspect of the Canadian law allows that, should the convicted party default in payment of the fine, the court may impose a prison term in lieu of the fine. On an international level, the Canadian Mutual Legal Assistance in Criminal Matters Act provides that the minister of justice may enforce the fine or penalty ordered by a foreign court in a criminal proceeding.

Australian law also provides for value confiscation. It notes that the amount of the penalty shall be reduced by the value of any tainted property that was seized. In assessing the value of proceeds derived from the offense, the court may assess any property that is subject to the effective control of the defendant, including shareholdings in debentures or directorships of any company that has an interest in the property; any trust related to the property; and family, domestic, and business relationships having an interest in the property.

### Notification and Protection of Third Parties' Rights

Another problem in determining what property to include in a confiscation order is what, if any, property may be included which has been transferred to a third party. The laws seek to prevent the criminal from hiding his proceeds by "giving" them to third parties from whom he can retrieve them later. At odds with this goal is the necessity to protect innocent third parties' rights to property to which they have a legal right.

In terms of international organizations, the UN Drug Convention states that the confiscation provisions will not be construed as prejudicing the rights of bona fide third parties. The European Laundering Convention protects the rights of interested parties or persons who claim that their rights with respect to frozen or confiscated property have been unjustifiably affected. For instance, if it is likely or beyond a reasonable doubt that a party is innocent or bona fide, the claims against the property must be honored. Notably, as long as no final confiscation order has been made, the accused also may qualify as interested part. The European convention requires that countries must enact legal provisions to guarantee "effective" legal remedies for interested third parties. The implication is that such parties, if known, must be timely informed by the authorities of the proceedings to provide them an opportunity to challenge the measures taken. When the third party had no earlier opportunity to challenge it; that challenge must be heard even if a confiscation order has already become enforceable. These remedies should permit the right to a hearing in court, the right to be assisted by a lawyer, the right to present witnesses and other evidence, and the right to review the court decision.

On a country basis, in the United States, the rights of innocent third parties override the government's claim to property as established under the relation back theory in civil forfeiture proceedings, and such third parties will prevail in criminal forfeiture proceedings, too. Therefore, when an innocent third party in a civil forfeiture matter proves his or her right to the tainted property, the government must return that property to him or her. Likewise, in a criminal proceeding, a bona fide purchaser for value who had no reasonable cause to believe that the property would be subject to forfeiture and who had a vested interest in the property superior to the defendant's interest at the time of the crime, will receive the property back from the government.

The United Kingdom's Criminal Justice (International Cooperation) Act of 1990 also requires the court to give notice to third parties with an interest in the property when property is seized and detained under the statute. It further mandates that, prior to releasing property that is under a confiscation order, the court must provide a "reasonable opportunity" to hear the representations of anyone holding an interest in the property. The Drug Trafficking Offenses Act of 1986 simply directs the court that is granting restraint or charging orders to do so, as is possible, in a manner to allow innocent third parties to retain or recover the value of any property held by them.

Canadian law provides a detailed procedure for protecting the rights of third parties. Before issuing a seizure or restraining warrant, the judge may require notice and a hearing for any person who appears to have a valid interest in the property. However, the judge shall not order notice to such a person if doing so might result in the disappearance or reduction in value of the property in question. Canadian law also provides that, once property has been seized, any person with an interest in the property may apply to a judge for permission to examine the property or to obtain a revocation or variance of the seizure order. If the applicant is lawfully entitled to possession of the property and appears to be innocent of any complicity in the offense, the judge may return the property to the applicant. However, if the applicant is charged with an offense, or if the applicant had acquired right to the property under circumstances that gave rise to a reasonable inference that the other party was transferring it in order to avoid forfeiture, the judge may revoke the warrant only if he determines that the warrant or restraining order should not have been issued initially. However, in both cases, the judge may only return the property if it will no longer be necessary to any investigation or as evidence. The court may set aside any transfer or conveyance of seized property made by the defendant to a third party that occurred subsequent to the seizure that was not for valuable consideration to a person who acted in good faith and without notice. Once a forfeiture order has been made against the property, the court may return property only to the lawful owner who appears to be innocent of any complicity in the offense.

Australian law provides that a person with a bona fide interest in property that is subject to forfeiture or has been forfeited may apply to the court for an order directing the Commonwealth to either return the property or to pay an amount equal the third party's interest in the property.

In a move that is likely to provoke much litigation, Egypt in the early 1990s passed a drug-trafficking law which provides for the confiscation of assets and property belonging not only to convicted drug traffickers but also to their families. The implications of the legislation have yet to be fully realized, but these are expected to unfold as the law is implemented.

## USE OF FUNDS AND THE DISCRETION TO SHARE CONFISCATED PROCEEDS

Once the assets are confiscated and forfeited, the issue of what to do with them arises. Some laws provide the the country holding the assets will keep them. Others allow the proceeds to be shared with other countries and even with international organizations.

### International Organizations

Under the UN Drug Convention, a requested state, when acting on the request of another party, may enter into agreements to contribute confiscated property, or the funds derived from the sale of such property, to intergovernmental organizations that specialize in combatting illicit traffic in and abuse of narcotic drugs and psychotropic substances. The requested states may also consider concluding agreements to share with other parties, on a regular or case-by-case basis, such proceeds or property, or funds derived from the sale of such proceeds or property.

The G–7 Financial Action Task Force similarly provides that countries should have arrangements for coordinating seizure and confiscation proceedings which may include the sharing of confiscated assets. The Caribbean Financial Action Task Force Recommendation suggests that confiscation measures be transferred directly for use by competent authorities or be sold and the proceeds put into an antinarcotics and anti–money-laundering law enforcement fund.

## Foreign Laws

U.S. statutes allow seized property or proceeds from certain crimes to be transferred to other countries by the attorney general or the secretary of the treasury if the country participated in locating and procuring the property, the secretary of state approves the transfer, and an international agreement that provides for such a transfer exists between the United States and the other country.

Others countries' laws provide for diverse manners of disposing of the forfeited assets. Australian property vests absolutely in the Commonwealth, and the attorney general may direct how to dispose of property confiscated pursuant to a foreign forfeiture order. Canadian victims of crime have priority and will receive the property that is subject to forfeiture in compensation and restitution for the injury suffered. If no victim is identified, the property will be forfeited and rendered to the government. If, however, upon a hearing subsequent to the seizure, the judge finds that the seizure warrant was properly executed and issued, the items seized will be transmitted to a requesting foreign country. Should the judge find to the contrary, he or she must return the seized property either to the person from whom it was seized or to the lawful owner of the property.

Neither Egypt nor Greece allows seized monetary instruments to be returned to a foreign country for breach of its laws. Nor may seized assets in Thailand be returned. Rather, assets seized in Thailand may be used to establish a Narcotics Prevention and Suppression Fund. In Cyprus, the law allows seized monetary instruments to be returned to a foreign country, except in those cases where public interests prohibit it. Bahamian law allows that the seized funds may be transmitted to a foreign country if the rightful owner is proven to be a non-national. Hong Kong law provides that monetary instruments may be returned to a foreign country, but only if that country has already commenced criminal proceedings. The monetary instruments are required exhibits, and an application is made to the High Court in Hong Kong for the instruments. In Germany seized monetary instruments may be reported to and returned to the country whose laws have been infringed upon if doing so is consistent with national mutual legal assistance treaties. Switzerland broadly provides that monetary instruments may be seized even if the offender was not convicted abroad and that the seized instruments may be transmitted to a foreign government in order to redress the victim.

## CONCLUSION

Although the international subregimes of regulation of international money movement and asset forfeiture are new, already there are common definitions, common aims and concepts, and some common procedures. Indeed, most governments employ asset forfeiture as a key tool to deprive narcotics traffickers of the benefits of their crimes and the instruments of the narcotics trade. Perhaps, more important, such economic incentives as the ability to keep the forfeited assets and possibly to receive from another country part of the booty will motivate countries to enforce their own domestic law and to cooperate with other countries in seizing and freezing assets. For instance, when the United States government received $5 million in fines from the Banco de Occidente, S.A., Panama, it shared $1 million each with the countries that assisted. If governments share the proceeds of forfeited assets with other cooperating countries, the many governments that are reluctant to cooperate will have an independent incentive to cooperate. The tension between the traditional role of national sovereignty and the need to move expeditiously against high-level narcotics traffickers as well as other criminals will preoccupy legislators, administrators, courts, academicians, and economists for the foreseeable future.

## BIBLIOGRAPHY

Schneider, Stephan. ''Proceeds of Crime and Money Laundering Enforcement in Canada.'' Paper presented at the American Bankers Association and American Bar Association Section on Criminal Justice: Money Laundering Enforcement Update, Legislative, Regulatory, Enforcement Developments and Policy Implications, Washington, D.C., 24–25 September 1990.

U.S. Department of State, Bureau of International Narcotics Matters. *International Narcotics Control Strategy Report March 1991*. Washington, D.C.: U.S. Government Printing Office, March 1991.

Wren, Tim. ''The Enforcement of Confiscation Law in Great Britain.'' Paper presented at the American Bankers Association and American Bar Association Section on Criminal Justice: Money Laundering Enforcement Update, Legislative, Regulatory, Enforcement Developments and Policy Implications, Washington, D.C., 24–25 September 1990.

Zagaris, Bruce, and Elizabeth Kingma. ''Asset Forfeiture: International and Foreign

Laws.'' Paper presented at the American Bar Association National Institute on Asset Forfeiture, Washington, D.C., 4–5 December 1990.

———. ''Asset Forfeiture International and Foreign Law: An Emerging Regime.'' *Emory J. of International Law* (Fall 1991) (forthcoming).

# II

# Country and Regional Studies: The Americas

# 4

# The United States

RAPHAEL FRANCIS PERL

## INTRODUCTION

The United States is the world's largest consumer of illicit drugs. Best source estimates, U.S. Department of State Bureau of International Narcotics Matters (*International Narcotics*) suggest that consumers spend about $28 billion annually on cocaine, $68 billion on cannabis, and $10–12 billion on heroin. At least four-fifths of all illicit drugs, including all the cocaine and heroin consumed in the United States, are of foreign origin. U.S. users are estimated to consume roughly 3.5 percent of the world's available supply of opium, from 10 to 20 percent of the world's available marijuana (some of which is produced in the United States), and between 9 and 13 percent of the world's available cocaine. Not only is the United States the major consumer of illicit drugs, its financial systems—banks and non-banks—are used to launder narcotics profits. This situation has lead the U.S. government to adopt a comprehensive, antidrug program that entails both domestic and international dimensions. The domestic dimension is reflected by concerns over large numbers of addicts, drug-related crime, and the drug trade's overall impact on U.S. society. Estimates for regular cocaine users, for example, range between 8 and 22 million Americans. The international dimension is mirrored in its efforts to coordinate antinarcotics policy closely with other consumer and producer countries.

The United States has a population of 246 million and covers an area of approximately 9,363,123 square kilometers. In 1988 dollars, it has the world's fourth highest per capita income at $19,840, which places it behind only Switzerland, Japan, and Norway. Life expectancy at birth is 76 years. The country's gross domestic product of $4.85 trillion is the world's largest, giving the United States one of the most affluent societies on the face of the planet. While the United States is a dynamic force in the global economy, its relative affluency as well as its geographical location close to major drug-producing areas in the Western Hemisphere and a lengthy Pacific seaboard have combined to make its drug-consumption problem a major societal concern.

Efforts to reduce substantially the flow of illicit drugs into the United States failed in the 1980s, and the problem continues in the 1990s; the United States is still a major drug-consuming, drug-producing, and drug-transshipping nation as well as a major, international, drug money-laundering center. Polls conducted in the first half of 1988 reflected that Americans consider drug control the leading domestic issue and that nearly half of all Americans regard drug trafficking as the United States' number one international problem. However, the U.S. approach to resolving the issue has been greatly complicated by certain inherent contradictions that regularly appear between the country's antidrug policy and other policy objectives and concerns.

## THE STRUCTURE OF THE INDUSTRY

The United States is the world's biggest market for illicit drugs; 25 million Americans spend more than $100 billion yearly on cannabis, cocaine, and heroin. Such drugs are to varying degrees injurious to the health, judgment, productivity, and general well-being of their users. The addictive nature of many of these drugs, their high price, and their illegality play a role in more than half the street crime committed in the United States. The U.S. illicit drug market generates enormous profits which enable the growth of diversified international criminal organizations to extend their reach into local neighborhoods, legitimate businesses, and even national governments. Such profits provide drug-trafficking organizations with the resources to evade and compete effectively with law enforcement agencies and, in some instances, to challenge the authority of national governments. All of this, of course, has a bearing on the structure of the illicit drug industry in the United States.

Measured in dollar value, at least four-fifths of all illicit drugs consumed in the United States are of foreign origin, including virtually all the cocaine and heroin. Between 25 and 35 percent of the marijuana consumed in the country is produced domestically, and virtually all of the hallucinogens and illegally marketed psychotherapeutic drugs and "designer" drugs are of domestic origin. It is very roughly estimated that, in 1985, cocaine, heroin, and cannabis worth $1.6 billion at foreign source warehouses was worth $10 billion at U.S. points of entry and fetched $51 billion "at retail" on the streets.

Little is known about the distribution of revenues from illicit drug sales, but foreign supply cartels exercise considerable control over wholesale distribution in the United States, and illicit proceeds are often laundered and invested through foreign banks and financial institutions. The major foreign source countries for the United States include Bolivia, Colombia, and Peru for cocaine; Afghanistan, Burma, Pakistan, and Mexico for heroin; and Mexico for cannabis. The Andean countries and Mexico receive, in particular, considerable U.S. attention due to their proximity and the export of cocaine, currently the focal drug of U.S. policymakers.

The cocaine trade that ends up on the streets in the United States commences in the Andean countries of Bolivia, Colombia, and Peru and, to a lesser extent, Brazil and Ecuador. In these nations coca is cultivated and refined into cocaine, which is then exported to the United States through either the Caribbean or Mexico and Central America. Once in the United States, cocaine resurfaces in a number of major metropolitan centers, from which it is distributed. Various criminal organizations, such as the Jamaican Posses and Los Angeles gangs, are prominent in distribution. The cocaine trade also entails the selling of crack, an even more addictive form of coca by-product.

The heroin trade begins in Mexico and Guatemala in the Western Hemisphere; in Afghanistan, Pakistan, and Iran in Southwest Asia; and in Burma, Laos, and Thailand in Southeast Asia. In Asia, opium cultivation is followed by refining which produces heroin. Two major routes exist: from Southwest Asia, heroin flows through Iran, Syria, Lebanon, and Turkey to Europe and North America; and from Southeast Asia, through either the People's Republic of China through Hong Kong and then to the West Coast of the United States or through Malaysia and Singapore to the United States. Production and refining are controlled by various criminal organizations, such as the Chinese Triads. For Mexico and Guatemala, the process is far simpler—cultivation and refining take place close to the United States, and distance is not a problem.

The cannabis trade is largely of domestic production, although some South American marijuana, mainly Mexican and Colombian, has a share of the market. American cannabis production has been found to be widespread, especially in the country's southwest. Production sites have even been discovered in national and state parks. Increasingly, marijuana plantations have been discovered indoors: The plant is grown in large, underground hothouses powered by diesel generators.

An area of growing concern is designer drugs, such as ice. Tougher interdiction policies and the relatively easy access to the necessary ingredients have stimulated the creation of synthetic drugs, giving "Made in the USA" a new and sad dimension. Some percent of this market is foreign. Asian producers, such as the Philippines, are key source countries.

The international illicit drug trade is big business, and large profits are laundered in a number of offshore financial centers as well as in the United States. One estimate, advanced by the U.S. Department of State in 1991, put the amount of illegal money earned by the drug trade as much as $300 billion, of which a part is laundered (or disguised) each year through the U.S. banking system (International Narcotics Control Strategy Report, March 1991). Although estimates vary about the total volume of money laundered, it is a critical link in the international drug trade and is central to giving drug dealers their ill-begotten financial rewards. It should be added that money-laundering operations are not limited to banks; car dealerships, jewelry stores, and real estate agencies have been involved, too.

Criminal organizations involved in the illicit drug trade are diverse. The range includes the Sicilian Mafia and Chinese Triads in heroin and Colombia's Medellín and Cali cartels in cocaine. In the five U.S. government–tagged Designated High Intensity Drug Trafficking Areas—Houston, Los Angeles, New York City, Miami, and the southwestern border cities of San Diego, El Paso, and Phoenix—various criminal organizations are at work. New York City functions as one of the major entry and distribution points for Southeast and Southwest Asian heroin and cocaine and marijuana from South America. Both the Chinese Triads and Colombian cartels (Cali more so than Medellín) are involved. New York City is also a major distribution point for the supply of significant amounts of heroin, cocaine, and crack to many Northeastern and mid-Atlantic states and Washington, D.C. The notorious Jamaican Posses have often functioned as dealers and gunmen, especially in the Washington, D.C., area, where they have been implicated in numerous brutal, execution-like slayings.

Los Angeles is a major port of entry and a transshipment point for South American cocaine, Asian and Mexican heroin, and marijuana. It is also the chief source of the PCP that is distributed throughout the United States. Most of the area's local drug trading is in the hands of gangs. It is estimated that the 750 gangs in Los Angeles County have between 50,000 and 70,000 members. The largest and best-organized of these gangs are the Crips and the Bloods, which account for a total of 15,000 members.

Miami functions as a major entry point for South American cocaine and marijuana. In the past, the city and environs were used to launder money from drug profits. Houston, a major transportation hub in the United States south, is also a center for Mexican heroin and Colombian cocaine. The transshipment of cocaine has been accomplished through cooperation between Mexican criminal elements and the Cali and Medellín cartels. The southwestern border area encompasses the three major cities of San Diego, El Paso, and Phoenix and stretches from the Gulf of Mexico to the Pacific Ocean. Mexican heroin and transshipped Colombian cocaine have, in particular, hit these cities hard.

## THE GOVERNMENT'S RESPONSE

On September 5, 1989, in a nationally televised speech, President George Bush outlined a wide-ranging, antidrug strategy. This program was refined and submitted to the Congress on January 25, 1990 and is today the foundation for both domestic and international antidrug policies. It has two major components: (1) reduction of demand and (2) reduction of supply. Reduction of demand is sought through education to prevent dependence, through treatment to cure addiction, and through measures to increase prices and risk of apprehension at the consumer level. Reduction of supply (which accounted for more than 71 percent of the Federal antidrug control budget for fiscal year 1990) is sought by programs aimed at destabilizing the operations of illicit drug cartels at all levels and by seizing their products and assets. As most illicit drugs are imported, a major interdiction campaign is being conducted on the borders of the United States, at ports of entry, on the high seas, and on major foreign transshipment routes and production sites. An international program of source country eradication is also being pursued.

An important foundation for the Bush administration's drug control policy was the Anti-Drug Abuse Act of 1988, which was introduced on August 11, 1988, by House Majority Leader Thomas Foley as H.R. 5210. The bill had ten titles, and each title was referred to a different committee, with the section on international narcotics control going to the Foreign Affairs Committee, which had established a special task force on narcotics control in the 98th Congress. Other House committees to which parts of the bill were referred were the committees on Banking, Finance, and Urban Affairs; Education and Labor; Government Operations; Interior and Insular Affairs; Judiciary; Merchant Marine and Fisheries; Public Works and Transportation; Ways and Means; and Energy and Commerce.

Debate over the 1988 drug bill's provisions centered not on its international narcotics control and foreign policy provisions, but rather on volatile domestic issues and—to a lesser extent—on the overall question of funding. Major domestic issues included three main questions: (1) whether to add the death penalty for those who commit murder during a drug felony, (2) whether to change the exclusionary rule to make it easier to convict drug offenders, and (3) whether to require a waiting period prior to the purchase of a handgun. On October 21, as one of the last acts of the 100th Congress, both houses approved the Anti-Drug Abuse Act of 1988, as it had been amended, by a vote of 346 to 11 in the House and by voice vote in the Senate. The measure was signed into law on November 13, 1988 (Public Law 100–690).

In the Anti-Drug Abuse Act, Congress acted to secure a clear definition of national and international drug-control objectives, but without itself clearly defining them. The 1988 act required the director of the Office of National Drug Control Policy to establish policies, objectives, and priorities. Additionally, it provided the president 180 days after confirmation of his "drug czar" to promulgate a national drug-control strategy, including long-term goals and short-term measurable objectives.

The act authorized additional federal antidrug expenditures for fiscal year 1989 of $2.7 billion, bringing total U.S. fiscal year drug-control authority under the act to $5.5 billion. Of the total funds appropriated under the act for fiscal year 1989, 56 percent went for supply reduction and 44 percent for demand reduction.

At roughly the same time, Congress promulgated other significant legislation that merits mention. The Foreign Operations, Export Financing and Related Programs Appropriations Act of 1989 was approved on October 1, 1988. This legislation appropriated and established conditions for funds for international narcotics programs under the Foreign Assistance Act of 1961 and amended that act. It had intensification of interdiction and eradication of illegal narcotics as major themes and called for increased emphasis on international cooperation in narcotics enforcement.

The role of the military in narcotics interdiction was addressed separately in the National Defense Authorization Act of 1989, which was approved September 29, 1988. This act established the Department of Defense as the lead agency for detecting and monitoring the aerial and maritime transit of illicit drugs into the United States.

Although the other laws are important, the Anti-Drug Abuse Act of 1988 is the centerpiece for all U.S. drug-control efforts. Considering the emphasis placed on reducing supply, the international component is important, especially as it included Title IV, which amended the Foreign Assistance Act of 1961. This revised country certification process by requiring the secretary of state to establish numerical standards and guidelines for determining which countries are major illicit drug-transit nations and to notify Congress each October 1 of the final list of countries to be determined to be major drug-producing or drug-transit countries. Additionally, Congress was given thirty days (subsequently amended to forty-five) of continuous session to decertify countries certified by the president as exempt from trade and aviation sanctions. Title IV furthermore required the president, when making certifications under the act, to consider whether the government has (1) taken the necessary steps to eliminate (to the maximum extent possible) narcotics-related bribery and public corruption; (2) facilitated narcotics production or distribution; (3) had any of its senior officials involved in the drug trade; (4) investigated aggressively cases in which U.S. drug enforcement agents have suffered violence with the complicity of foreign law enforcement officers and sought to bring such perpetrators to trial; (5) responded with reasonable cooperation to U.S. requests to assist Drug Enforcement Agency activities, including requests for aerial hot pursuit; (6) made necessary changes in legal codes to combat effectively narcotics traffickers (i.e., new conspiracy laws and asset seizure laws); (7) expeditiously processed U.S. extradition requests relating to narcotics trafficking; and (8) refused to give safe haven to known traffickers in addition to processing expeditiously narcotics-related extradition requests to other countries.

In addition, Title IV of the act contained a series of country-specific certification provisions designed to increase congressional control and influence over narcotics policy and supply-reduction programs in key producing and transshipment countries in Latin America and Asia. Many of these country-specific provisions further reduced the flexibility of the president to release aid to these countries.

Another key area that fell under the 1988 act was money laundering. Although money laundering was made illegal by the Anti-Drug Abuse Act of 1986 and although the Justice and Treasury departments, through their various agencies, were responsible for conducting financial investigations, the 1988 act clearly sought to expand the scope and intensity of money-laundering enforcement. Congress increased the number of transactions covered by record-keeping and reporting requirements and eliminated loopholes in certain Bank Secrecy Act (BSA) requirements. The BSA, enacted in 1970, requires private individuals, banks, and other financial institutions to report large-scale transactions to the federal government. The 1986 act provided Currency Transaction Reports (CTRs), which require that all currency transactions of $10,000 and over be reported to the federal government (the Office of the Comptroller of the Currency for all nationally chartered banks) by law. The Money Laundering Prosecution Improvements Act of 1988, part of the 1988 act, added three new elements: a reduced threshold reporting requirement that allowed geographical targeting, an erosion of financial privacy, and enhanced penalties for violators.

Another important dimension of the 1988 act was Section 4702, which mandated that the U.S. government, through the Treasury Department, negotiate with key drug-producing or drug-transit states information-sharing agreements concerning financial data. The aim of such Kerry Amendment agreements, named after the senator who proposed the provision, is to allow U.S. and other national enforcement forces to go after the profits of drug trafficking thereby reducing the ability of drug dealers to launder narco-profits.

With the mandate of the Anti-Drug Abuse Act of 1988, the Bush administration selected William Bennett as its drug czar and went to work to formulate the country's antidrug strategy. Bennett was later replaced by Robert Martinez. What the Bush administration added to existing U.S. antidrug efforts in September 1989 was largely in the international realm, reflecting an ongoing emphasis on supply reduction. New to the U.S. strategy were four provisions: (1) the provision, for the first time, of support for limited economic assistance to major cocaine-producing countries; (2) a greater concentration on disrupting the activities of the trafficking organizations (i.e., on seizing processing labs, chemicals, and assets) and less on disrupting the activities of farmers (i.e., crop eradication); (3) the encouragement of increased levels of Andean country military involvement in counternarcotics operations; and (4) the provision for enhanced U.S. military support to host country counternarcotics forces. Also, coordination of U.S. international drug efforts, among federal agencies, with producer and transit nations, and emerging international initiatives of other consumer nations, receives policy emphasis under the strategy.

The U.S. president's strategy introduced the concept of focusing on high-value traffickers, operations, and drug shipments. High value did not necessarily refer to the dollar value of shipments, or to the prominence of certain traffickers, but rather to their overall importance to drug-trafficking operations and the disruptive effect their removal from the trafficking chain might have on the supply of drugs destined for the United States.

The U.S. president's new direction also called for improved collection, analysis, and dissemination of drug-related intelligence and for enhanced command, control, and communications for the antidrug operations of federal, state, and local law enforcement authorities and Department of Defense antidrug operations. The Bush administration also proposed increases in funding for Department of Defense operations, mainly to interdict drug smuggling across the southern borders of the United States.

An "Andean initiative," estimated to cost $2.2 billion between 1990 and 1995, was a major component of the president's strategy. The initiative sought to provide enhanced law enforcement and military and economic assistance to Bolivia, Colombia, and Peru (totaling $423 million for fiscal year 1991) in an effort (1) to assist these nations to strengthen political and economic conditions and institutional capabilities for effective action against the trafficking organizations; (2) to increase the effectiveness of military and law enforcement activities of these countries against the cocaine trade by supporting their efforts to isolate major coca-growing regions, to destroy labs, and to block delivery of precursor chemicals; and (3) to inflict significant damage to the drug-trafficking organizations operating in these countries by directing U.S. assistance to support Andean measures designed to seize key traffickers and their assets.

Multilateral initiatives are also a part of the president's strategy, which seeks to enlist European Community support for measures to reduce source and transit-country drug production and distribution. It also proposes the creation of a joint intelligence collection center in the Caribbean Basin. Enhanced foreign cooperation in disrupting drug money laundering and precursor chemical flows is another component of the president's international drug strategy.

One highly publicized multilateral initiative was President Bush's attendance at an Andean drug summit in Cartagena, Colombia, on February 15, 1990, where he met with the presidents of Bolivia, Colombia, and Peru. In the communiqué issued, the parties agreed to cooperate and exchange information in a variety of areas, including precursor chemical flows and money-laundering activities and generally to attack the drug trade on all fronts: production, distribution, finance, and use.

## DOMESTIC POLICY

There is considerable debate about the effectiveness of the U.S. government's drug-control policy. In particular, a number of analysts are critical that the emphasis on supply reduction, carried out through the international component of the national drug strategy, has neglected the even more important demand problem at home. Additionally, efforts on the domestic front are regarded by cities as too top-heavy with enforcement efforts to the detriment of preventive education and treatment and rehabilitation. Proponents of federal supply reduction policies, however, stress that federal policy by its very nature must be supply-reduction oriented, as the lion's share of demand-reduction measures (i.e., education, rehabilitation, and treatment) tend to be within the purview of activities performed at the state and local levels. This debate, over the allocation of federal resources between supply versus demand-reduction approaches, also has a social component as it appears, according to survey research in the late 1980s and early 1990s, that better educated and more affluent Americans are reducing their use of illicit drugs, while lesser educated Americans, often residents of the country's troubled inner cities, are still users. This trend, in part, supported by data on the high mortality rate of young black males, points to potentially serious new problems in urban development, health care, and the adequacy of the nation's health care system, which cannot be ignored.

The domestic part of the U.S. government's response to the drug problem places an emphasis on making illicit drugs undesirable and difficult to obtain through a mixture of supply and demand policies. Key areas on the domestic front have encompassed using the criminal justice systems; drug treatment programs; prevention activities in the national school system, businesses, and communities; and an improvement in local and national intelligence and research resources. This has meant that state and local law enforcement operations, regarded as the first line of defense against drugs, were to receive grants from the Bureau of Justice Assistance, amounting to $492 million in fiscal year 1991, to help them secure their neighborhoods from the illicit drug trade and related violence. That sum represented a 228 percent increase from 1988.

The lead antidrug agency in the United States is the Drug Enforcement Administration (DEA), which is part of the Department of Justice. Created in 1973, it has handled a wide range of responsibilities that emphasize the enforcement of the country's drug laws and regulations to the growing, manufacturing, and distribution of controlled substances. Although there is some amount of bureaucratic rivalry, the DEA's efforts are complemented by the Federal Bureau of Investigation (FBI). Other parts of the Justice Department, as well as the Treasury Department, are also active in the U.S. domestic war on drugs.

The Treasury Department—through the Bureau of Alcohol, Tobacco and Firearms (ATF), Customs Service, and International Revenue Service—the Office of the Comptroller of the Currency, and the Financial Information Criminal Enforcement Network (FINCEN)—also plays domestic roles in terms of enhanced research facilities and investigative matters. The ATF in 1989 found that 50 percent of its law enforcement work was drug related, and in fiscal year 1989 it seized nearly 3,000 firearms in drug-related investigations. The ATF has run Project Achilles, which identifies and incarcerates weapons offenders who frequently are violent drug criminals with multiple convictions.

One of the major characteristics of U.S. enforcement measures is the use of task forces, which are run by the Organized Crime Drug Enforcement Task Force (OCDETF) Program. This program uses the expertise of nine federal agencies as well as a number of state and local law enforcement offices in the coordination of investigations and prosecutions of sophisticated and diversified criminal drug-related and money-laundering enterprises. The expertise is all-encompassing, covering financial and tax information and data on trafficking organizations and gang activity. The nine federal agencies are the DEA, Customs, ATF, Coast Guard, U.S. Marshals Service, Internal Revenue Service, FBI, the Justice Department's Tax and Criminal divisions, and the Immigration and Naturalization Service.

The OCDETF is based in thirteen regions: New England (Boston); Great Lakes (Detroit); New York–New Jersey (New York City); Mid-Atlantic (Baltimore); Southeast (Atlanta); Florida–Caribbean (Miami); Gulf Coast (Houston); South Central (St. Louis); North Central (Chicago); Mountain States (Denver); Southwest Border (San Diego); Los Angeles–Nevada (Los Angeles); and Northwest (San Francisco). The OCDETF program is actively assisted by the Law Enforcement Coordinating Committees (LECCs), which are chaired by U.S. attorneys.

Another element of domestic enforcement lies in the area of precursor and other essential chemicals. As the *National Drug Control Survey* (1990) stated: "Much of the cocaine smuggled into this country is processed with chemicals exported by American companies, and nearly all methamphetamine, LSD, and PCP are illegally manufactured using chemicals from domestic suppliers." The U.S. attorney general, under the Chemical and Trafficking Act of 1988, has the responsibility to investigate and prosecute the manufacturers, shippers, importers, or exporters of illegally diverted shipments. Related to this has been a joint Customs–DEA program, Operation Chemcon, which targets high-risk ports.

An additional area of concern for domestic narcotics control is the cultivation of marijuana. U.S. producers have made cannabis a major cash crop, utilizing state and federal parks as well as private residences. The government has sought to reduce such cultivation by enhanced surveillance and crop eradication programs. The key agencies involved are the Forest Service, the National Park Service, the Bureau of Indian Affairs, and the Bureau of Land Management.

Beyond enforcement measures, U.S. government policy entails drug treatment and preventive education. There has been, in recent years, first under the Reagan administrations (1980–1988) and then with the Bush administration (1988–1992), a heavy emphasis on the private sector in this area. However, a fundamental problem is the inability of certain sectors of U.S. society to fund the cost of private facilities for drug treatment. The result is a public sector drug treatment system, largely under the guidance of the Department of Health and Human Services (HHS). The HHS has control over federal block grants. The agency under the HHS that administers this is the Alcohol, Drug Abuse and Mental Health Administration (ADAMHA), which is the home of the Office for Treatment Improvement (OTI). The OTI was established in 1989 to provide leadership and direction for the United States' entire drug treatment system. An additional body that provides drug treatment slots is the Department of Veteran Affairs.

The U.S. government also plays a role in preventive education by assisting communities throughout the nation to develop antidrug programs. The HHS is the primary branch of government involved in this effort and operates through its Office of Substance Abuse Prevention (OSAP) and the National Institute on Drug Abuse (NIDA). ADAMHA also has an educational function in the formulation of effective prevention programs, especially in the form of providing seed money in the form of federal grants.

## INTERNATIONAL POLICY

Based on the foundations of the Anti-Drug Abuse Act of 1988 and the president's September 1989 drug-control strategy, U.S. international policy has four major elements: eradication of narcotics crops, interdiction and law enforcement activities in drug-producing and drug-transitting countries, international cooperation, and sanctions. The first element of U.S. policy for the international narcotics-control strategy is to reduce cultivation and production of illicit narcotics through eradication. In 1989, the United States supported programs to eradicate coca, opium, and marijuana in fourteen countries. These efforts are conducted by a number of government agencies who administer several types of programs. The United States supports eradication by providing producer countries with chemical herbicides, technical assistance, specialized equipment, and spray aircraft. The U.S. Agency for International Development (AID) funds development projects that promote the creation of alternative income for farmers who abandon cultivation of illicit narcotics ($29 million for 1989). U.S. eradication policy receives informational support from the United States Information Agency (USIA), which publicizes the dangers of drug abuse and trafficker violence. Moreover, AID sponsors drug eradication and awareness programs in both Latin American and Asian countries ($13.2 million for 1989).

The second element of U.S. international narcotics control strategy is to help host governments seize illicit narcotics before they reach America's borders. Training of foreign law enforcement personnel constitutes a major part of such endeavors. In 1989, the Department of State funded antinarcotics law enforcement training programs for personnel from more than seventy countries. Furthermore, the Department of State provides host country antinarcotics personnel with a wide range of equipment to perform effectively: DEA agents regularly assist foreign police in their efforts to destabilize trafficking networks. U.S. efforts to promote effective law enforcement against narcotics traffickers also include suggestions to nations on means to strengthen their own legal and judicial systems.

The third element of U.S. international narcotics control strategy is international cooperation. By use of diplomatic initiatives, both bilateral and multilateral, the Department of State encourages and assists nations to reduce cultivation, production, and trafficking in illicit drugs. These bilateral agreements and international conventions have thus far been largely ineffective in reversing the growth of international narcotics trafficking, in part because they lack strong enforcement mechanisms and are not uniformly interpreted by member nations.

U.S. international narcotics control strategy also relies on international cooperation to promote coordinated border operations to interdict traffickers. To this end, the United States has provided technical assistance to coordinated multinational operations in Colombia, Peru, and Ecuador. The United States also participates in multilateral assistance programs through the United Nations Fund for Drug Abuse Control (UNFDAC) and actively enlists the aid and support of other governments for narcotics control projects. UNFDAC currently assists forty-nine developing countries through development, law enforcement, education, treatment, and rehabilitation programs. The 1989 UNFDAC budget totaled $62.5 million, which was derived from voluntary contributions. Furthermore, through the Anti-Drug Abuse Act of 1988, the Treasury Department is mandated to expand access to information on transactions involving specified amounts of U.S. currency through negotiations with foreign countries.

The fourth element of U.S. international narcotics control strategy, initiated by Congress in recent years, involves the application of sanctions against certain drug-producing or drug-trafficking nations. Such sanctions range from suspension of U.S. foreign assistance to curtailment of air transportation to target countries. Current drug sanction legislation requires the president on March 1 of each year to submit to Congress a list of major illicit drug-producing and drug-transitting countries that he has certified to receive U.S. foreign aid and other economic and trade benefits. This action sets in motion a forty-five-day congressional review process during which Congress can override the president's certification.

Certification may be granted because a major illicit drug-producing or drug-transitting country has "cooperated fully" with U.S. narcotics reduction goals or has taken "adequate steps on its own" in tandem with U.S. objectives. A country not qualified on the basis of full cooperation of adequate steps may escape imposition of sanctions if the president certifies that U.S. vital national interests preclude implementation of sanctions on that country.

There is considerable debate about the success or failure of the U.S. drug-control policy. It is estimated that the illicit drug industry generates between $100 and $500 billion annually for criminal organizations. Policymakers face the challenge of deciding the appropriate level of funding required for the nation's international narcotics-control efforts within the context of competing budgetary priorities.

Another challenge confronting the U.S. narcotics-control efforts concerns how to implement policy most effectively. Many argue that current U.S. policy is fragmented and overly bilateral in nature. Many of these analysts suggest that, to achieve success, policy options must be pursued within the context of a comprehensive plan with a multilateral emphasis on implementation. For example, they point out that some studies indicate that interdiction can actually increase the economic rewards to drug traffickers by raising prices for the products they sell. Interdiction as part of a coordinated plan, however, can have a strong disrupting and destabilizing effect on trafficker operations. Some analysts suggest that bilateral and unilateral U.S. policies are ill-suited for solving what is, in effect, a multilateral problem. They cite the need for enhancing the United Nations' ability to deal effectively with the narcotics problem and for more international and regional cooperation and consultation on international narcotics-control issues. They point out, however, that such multinational endeavors are by their very nature difficult to arrange, coordinate, and implement effectively.

## INTERNATIONAL POLICY OPTIONS

Many analysts believe that current efforts to reduce the flow of illicit drugs into the United States have essentially failed and that alternative objectives, policies, programs, and priorities are required. Four major options, which are not mutually exclusive and which could be pursued in various combinations as part of an overall effort, have become the focus of the ongoing debate over U.S. drug-control policy, especially in its international dimension. The options include (1) expansion of efforts to reduce production at the source, (2) expansion of interdiction and enforcement activities to disrupt supply lines and expansion of the role of the military, (3) expansion of efforts to reduce worldwide demand, and (4) expansion of economic disincentives for illicit drug trafficking.

### Reduction of Production at the Source

The first option is an expansion of efforts to reduce production at the source. This involves efforts to reduce the growth of narcotic plants and crops in foreign countries before they are converted into processed drugs. Illicit crops may either be eradicated or purchased (and then destroyed). Eradication of illicit crops may be accomplished by physically uprooting the plants or by using chemical or biological control agents. Development of alternative sources of income to replace peasant income lost by nonproduction of narcotic crops may be an important element of this option.

Proponents of expanded efforts to eliminate growth and production of narcotic crops and substances at the source believe that reduction of the foreign supply of drugs available is an effective means to lower levels of drug use in the United States. Furthermore, they argue that reduction of the supply of cocaine—the nation's top narcotic-control priority—is a realistically achievable option. For example, the Department of State believes that the supply of cocaine being shipped from Latin America to the United States could be reduced significantly if Latin American governments agreed to institute massive herbicidal spraying sufficient to reduce cocaine cultivation by 50 percent in 1993.

Proponents of vastly expanded supply-reduction options, specifically herbicidal crop eradication, argue that this method is the most cost-effective and efficient means of eliminating narcotic crops. They staunchly maintain that, coupled with intensified law enforcement, such programs will succeed since it is easier to locate and destroy crops in the field than it is to locate subsequently processed drugs on smuggling routes or on the streets of U.S. cities. Moreover, because crops constitute the cheapest link in the narcotics chain, producers will devote less economic resources to prevent their detection than to concealing more expensive and refined forms of the product.

Opponents of expanded supply-reduction policy generally question whether reduction of the foreign supply of narcotic drugs is achievable and whether it would have a meaningful impact on the levels of illicit drug use in the United States. They suggest that, even if the supply of foreign drugs destined for the U.S. market could be dramatically reduced, U.S. consumers would simply switch to consumption of synthetic drug substitutes. Thus, they maintain, the ultimate solution to the U.S. drug problem is to reduce the demand at the source and not reduce the supply at the source. Some also fear that environmental damage will result from herbicides. As an alternative, they urge development, research, and funding of programs designed to develop and employ biological control agents such as coca-destroying insects and fungi that do not harm other plants.

Others question whether a global policy of simultaneous crop control is politically feasible since many areas in the world will always be beyond U.S. control and influence. Such critics refer to continuously shifting sources of supply, or the so-called balloon syndrome: When squeezed in one place, it pops up in another. Nevertheless, many point out that the number of large suitable growth areas is somewhat finite and that, by focusing simultaneously at major production areas, substantial reductions can be achieved if adequate funding is provided.

Some also question the value of supply-reduction measures since world production and supply of illicit drugs vastly exceeds world demand, making it unlikely that the supply surplus could be reduced sufficiently to have an effect on the ready availability of illicit narcotics in the U.S. market. Such analysts also suggest that, even if worldwide supply were reduced dramatically, it would first be at the expense of other nations' drug markets. The U.S. market, they argue, would be the last to experience supply shortfalls, because U.S. consumers pay higher prices and because U.S. dollars are a preferred narco-currency.

Many suggest that expanded and effective efforts to reduce production of illicit narcotics at the source will be met by active and violent opposition from a combination of trafficker, political, and economic groups. In some nations, such as Colombia, traffickers have achieved a status comparable to a state within a state. In others, allegations of drug-related corruption have focused on high-level officials in the military and federal police, as well as heads of state. Additionally, some traffickers have aligned themselves with terrorist and insurgent groups and have funded political candidates and parties, pro-narcotic peasant worker and trade union groups, and high-visibility popular public works projects to cultivate public support through a Robin Hood image. Because many groups that benefit economically from coca are so well armed, if the United States were successful in urging foreign governments to institute widespread use of chemical or biological control agents, cooperating host governments could well face powerful and violent domestic opposition from trafficking groups. Heavy military protection, at a minimum, would be required for those spraying or otherwise eradicating. It is possible that U.S. officials, businessmen, and assets might not be immune to terrorist-style attacks by traffickers worldwide.

For some countries, production of illicit narcotics and the drug trade have become an economic way of life that provides a subsistence level of income to large constituencies of masses from whom those who rule draw their legitimacy. "Successful" crop-reduction campaigns seek to displace such income and those workers engaged in its production. In this regard, these campaigns portend real economic and political dangers for the governments of nations with marginal economic growth. Consequently, many analysts argue that the governments of such low-income countries cannot be expected to launch major crop-reduction programs without the substitute income to sustain those whose income depends on drug production.

Those promoting expansion of efforts to reduce production at the source face the challenge of instituting programs that effectively reduce production of narcotic crops and production of refined narcotics without creating unmanageable economic and political crises for target countries. A major area of concern of such policymakers is to achieve an effective balance between the "carrot" and the "stick" approach in U.S. relations with major illicit narcotics-producing and narcotics-transitting countries.

Proponents of a sanctions policy linking foreign aid and trade benefits to U.S. international narcotics objectives argue against business as usual with countries that turn a blind eye to illicit drug trafficking or money laundering. This policy includes a moral dimension that asserts that drug production and trafficking is wrong and that U.S. aid and trade sanctions can provide the needed leverage for nations to reduce production of illicit crops and their involvement in other drug-related activities. They argue that both the moral stigma of being branded as uncooperative and the threat of economic sanctions prod otherwise uncooperative countries into action. They further stress that trade sanctions would be likely to provide highly effective leverage as most developing countries depend on access to U.S. markets.

Opponents of a sanctions policy linking aid and trade to U.S. international narcotics objectives argue that sanctions may have an undesirable effect on the political and economic stability of target countries, making them all the more dependent on the drug trade for income; that sanctions have little impact because many countries are not dependent on U.S. aid; that sanctions historically have had little effect unless they have been imposed multilaterally; and that sanctions are arbitrary in nature, hurt national pride in the foreign country, and are seen in many countries as an ugly manifestation of Yankee imperialism. Finally, an increasing number of analysts suggest that, if sanctions are to be fully effective, they should be used in conjunction with additional positive incentives (subject perhaps to a congressional certification/approval process) to foster antidrug cooperation.

Alternatively, some suggest positive incentives instead of sanctions. They believe that narcotics-producing nations must be motivated either to refrain from growing illicit crops or to permit the purchase or destruction of these crops by government authorities. Many argue that, since the economic stability of the nations supplying illegal drugs depends on the production and sale of illicit drugs, it is unrealistic to expect such nations to limit meaningfully their drug-related activities without an alternative source of income.

It has long been suggested by many analysts that a massive foreign aid effort—a so-called mini–Marshall Plan—is the only feasible way of persuading developing nations to curb their production of narcotic crops. Such a plan would be a multilateral effort with the participation of the United States, Europe, Japan, Australia, other industrialized nations susceptible to the drug problem, and the rich oil-producing countries. The thrust of such a plan would be to promote economic development, replacing illicit cash crops with other marketable alternatives. Within the framework of such a plan, crops could be purchased or else destroyed by herbicidal sprays and biological control agents while substitute crops and markets are developed and assured. Any such program would be coupled with rigid domestic law enforcement and penalties for noncompliance. Thus, it would require a U.S. commitment of substantially increased enforcement assets to be used against both growers and traffickers, and it might require direct U.S. military involvement at the request of the host country.

Critics find much to be concerned about in these positive incentive concepts. They warn of the precedent of appearing to pay protection compensations—providing an incentive for economically disadvantaged countries to go into the drug-export business. They also warn of the open-ended cost of agricultural development programs and of extraterritorial police intervention. Finding markets for viable alternative crops is yet another major constraint.

### Expansion of Activities to Disrupt Supply Lines

A second option is the expansion of interdiction and enforcement activities to disrupt supply lines, including expanding the role of the military. Drug supply-line interdiction is both a foreign and domestic issue. Many argue that the United States should intensify activities designed to disrupt the transit of illicit narcotics as early in the production/transit chain as possible—well before the drugs reach the streets of the United States. This task is conceded to be very difficult because the United States is the world's greatest trading nation; vast volumes of imports daily flow in through hundreds of sea, air, and land entry facilities, and its systems have been designed to facilitate human and materials exchange. These situations have led some analysts to suggest that the military should assume a more active role in antidrug activities.

Congress especially has urged an expanded role for the military in the war on drugs. The idea of using the military is not novel. Outside the United States, military personnel have been involved in training and transporting foreign antinarcotics personnel since 1983. Periodically, there have also been calls for multilateral military strikes against trafficking operations, as well as increased use of elite forces in preemptive strikes against drug fields and trafficker enclaves overseas.

The role of the military in narcotics interdiction was expanded by the fiscal year 1989 National Defense Authorization Act. It was concluded that the Department of Defense (DOD) can and should play a major role in narcotics interdiction. Toward this goal, Congress required the DOD to provide promptly civilian law enforcement agencies with relevant drug-related intelligence; charged the president to direct that command, control, communications, and intelligence networks dedicated to drug control be integrated by the DOD into an effective network; restricted the direct participation by military personnel in civilian law enforcement activities to those authorized by law; permitted the military to transport civilian law enforcement outside the land area of the United States; expanded the role of the National Guard in drug-interdiction activities; and authorized an additional $300 million for DOD and National Guard drug-interdiction efforts. The National Defense Authorization Act was later authorized an additional $450 million for DOD drug-interdiction support activities. Moreover, the DOD was required to examine the feasibility of establishing a National Drug Operations Center for the integration, coordination, and control of all drug-interdiction operations.

Despite the military's obvious ability to support drug law enforcement organizations, questions remain as to the overall effectiveness of a major military role in narcotics interdiction. Proponents of substantially increasing the military's role in narcotics interdiction argue that narcotics trafficking poses a national security threat to the United States; that only the military is equipped and has the resources to counter powerful trafficking organizations; and that drug interdiction provides the military with beneficial, realistic training.

Opponents argue that drug interdiction is a law enforcement mission, not a military mission; that drug enforcement is an unconventional war which the military is poorly equipped to fight; that a drug-enforcement mission detracts from its readiness mission; that a drug-enforcement role exposes the military to corruption; that it is unwise public policy to require the U.S. military to operate against U.S. citizens; and that the use of the military may have serious political and diplomatic repercussions overseas. Furthermore, some personnel in the armed forces remain concerned about an expanded role, seeing themselves as possible scapegoats for policies that have failed, or are likely to fail.

### Expansion of Efforts to Reduce Demand

A third option favored by many is to increase policy emphasis on development and implementation of programs worldwide that seek to increase public intolerance for illicit drug use. Such programs, through information, technical assistance, and training in prevention and treatment, would emphasize the health dangers of drug use as well as the danger to regional and national stability. USIA and AID currently support modest efforts in this area. Some believe that these programs should be augmented, and they advocate a more active role for the United Nations and other international agencies in the development and implementation of such demand-reduction programs.

### Expansion of Economic Disincentives

A fourth option under consideration is the expansion of economic disincentives for illicit drug trafficking. Those who favor this option indicate that the key factor in the international drug market is not the product, but the profit. Hence, they emphasize that any international effort to decrease the flow of drugs into the United States must increasingly address means to seize and otherwise reduce assets and profits generated by the international drug trade.

Policymakers who follow this option must decide whether legislation in countries where they exert influence is too lenient on financial institutions, such as banks and brokerage houses, which knowingly facilitate financial transactions of traffickers. If the answer is ''yes'', national leaders would then take action to coordinate their efforts to enact and apply harsher criminal sanctions to those involved in the movement of money generated by drug sales, including revocation of licenses of institutions regularly engaging in such practices. Finally, those supporting this option favor increased efforts to secure greater international cooperation on financial investigations related to money laundering of narcotics profits, including negotiation of mutual legal assistance treaties (MLATs).

## SOCIETAL REACTION

Considering the wide-ranging parameters of U.S. drug-control policy on both the international and domestic sides, the remaining question is—how has American society responded? No area of the country has been spared from drug abuse and related crime, and estimates of drug users vary between 1.5 and 2.5 million Americans for cocaine and between 500,000 and 750,000 for heroin. Despite media images of crack babies, drug-related violence, and depressed inner cities, the American societal reaction has been one of adjustment. The Drug Abuse Warning Network (DAWN) compiles data on drug-related admissions to emergency rooms and drug-related deaths. According to DAWN data, the emergency-room numbers rapidly expanded during the 1980s: Between 1985 and 1989 cocaine-related admissions rose almost fivefold, overtaking heroin, which had led the way to medical damage for almost two decades.[1] In the last quarter of 1989, cocaine admissions declined by 22 percent and continued to decline into 1990.

In December 1990, NIDA publicized the results of its survey on drug-use trends in the United States. The 1990 NIDA survey of drug use by U.S. households revealed a 45-percent decline in current use of cocaine, compared to data in the 1988 survey. Current use was defined as using the drug at least once in the past month. Current cocaine use among adolescents fell by 49 percent to

115,000 from 225,000 in 1988. These figures included declines in marijuana, alcohol, and cigarettes.

Although the Bush administration used the NIDA survey to emphasize that it was winning the war on drugs, many analysts dispute the survey's accuracy. Moreover, if accurate, it confirmed that drug abuse among better educated Americans was on the decline, but abuse was actually increasing in the country's inner cities for minorities. Related to this is the fact that illicit drugs appear to be still readily accessible despite enhanced interdiction efforts. Another factor is concern that heroin abuse is on the upswing.

Heroin traditionally has been perceived as a drug of the inner city and has been linked to minority-user communities. In the 1970s, heroin use was sharply reduced. However, NIDA data indicated that deaths and emergency-room visits linked to heroin, which had stabilized in the late 1970s, increased by more than 25 percent in the 1980s. While the dismal lives of crack addicts provide a powerful negative image as to what cocaine can do, heroin lingers as a threat. That threat has been enhanced by profits of greater supply, due to bumper crops in Asia and the spread of cultivation of opium and refining in Mexico and Guatemala. An additional factor is that purity levels have increased from the former 10 percent or less to from 35 to 50 percent in such cities as New York and Los Angeles. This means that a more potent form of heroin exists in the 1990s than in the past. As stated by *The Economist*: "High purity and stable prices make it economical for users to smoke rather than inject the drug."[2]

The rise of heroin use in the 1990s, according to some analysts, is to be expected. Traditionally, stimulant epidemics, like cocaine in the 1980s, have been followed by increased sedative use. The heroin epidemic of the late 1960s came shortly after a substantial increase in "speed" or methamphetamine abuse. Smokable heroin, referred to as "chasing the dragon," could help push the use of that drug further. Nevertheless, many analysts suggest that, despite anticipated increases in heroin availability, increasingly widespread heroin use in the United States will simply not materialize. Heroin use traditionally in the United States is not recreationally "cool." It is associated with the Bowery derelict and not the successful Wall Street broker.

The questionable success of U.S. narcotics-control policy has stimulated a debate over legalization of drugs in American society. Proponents of legalization argue that drug-enforcement measures have largely failed and that, like Prohibition in the 1920s, the only way to decriminalize the trade is to make it legal. Through familiarity with drugs, based on freedom of choice, people will learn what is harmful. In time, as with cigarettes, drug abuse will decline because demand will slacken. Opponents argue that legalization will only open the door to greater consumption on a society-wide basis and create huge problems in terms of health care for massive addict populations—the fundamental problem of drug abuse will be greatly augmented as more people will have access to drugs. Although a majority remain opposed to legalization, the debate will continue, especially as the drug-abuse problem continues to linger.

The U.S. government has placed considerable emphasis on the role of the private sector in launching antidrug campaigns. Churches and synagogues have taken an increasingly active role, and the Partnership for a Drug-Free America has launched media campaigns to educate the public on drug prevention. The Partnership has also begun to target minority children. Furthermore, drug prevention is increasingly part of the education process in the nation's school systems.

Considering that drug abuse continues to be a major societal problem confronting American society in the 1990s, the debate continues about whether the U.S. government has committed too few resources to drug treatment and rehabilitation and too much to interdiction and supply country reduction. Linked to this debate are a number of other issues, including drug testing at the workplace, the viability of the private sector to initiate and sustain antidrug use programs, the adequacy of the U.S. health care system, and race relations. The area of race relations increased in significance as the death rate of young black males increased dramatically in the late 1980s and early 1990s.

## CONCLUSION

How serious is the United States' commitment to resolve the drug problem, and is American society willing to bear the cost of an effective war on drugs in terms of potential restrictions on traditionally guarded U.S. freedoms such as the free flow of persons, goods, and funds? Is a federal antidrug budget of roughly $10 billion a year sufficient to contend effectively with a well-established $100 to $500 billion a year criminal enterprise? Is U.S. antidrug policy too cocaine oriented in light of increasing heroin availability? And what is an effective balance between federal supply and demand oriented drug-control policies?[3] These issues appear to be central for the United States drug-control policymakers in the early 1990s. Additionally, U.S. policymakers continue to face related questions: What is the potential impact of foreign supply-reduction operations on U.S. domestic demand reduction? What is the cost effectiveness of such operations, and to what extent should the drug war be fought overseas and to what extent at home?

Increasingly, U.S. and foreign analysis are questioning the effectiveness of U.S. efforts in supplier countries to reduce the availability of illicit drugs and whether it is sound policy to intensify them. More and more, many advocate maximizing efforts and increasing funding to control U.S. demand at home, while interdicting drugs at the border.

## NOTES

Raphael F. Perl is a specialist in International Narcotics Policy with the Congressional Research Service of the Library of Congress in Washington, D.C. The views expressed in this chapter do not constitute an official statement of U.S. policy or of the Congressional Research Service of the Library of Congress.

1. "Drugs: Goodbye Cocaine," *The Economist*, 8 September 1990, 28.
2. *Ibid.*, 33.
3. Increasingly, analysts are suggesting a federal antidrug resource allocation of 60 percent for demand reduction and 40 percent supply reduction instead of the current level of roughly 70 percent supply reduction and 30 percent demand reduction.

## BIBLIOGRAPHY

Bagley, Bruce Michael. "U.S. Foreign Policy and the War on Drugs: Analysis of a Policy Failure." *Journal of Interamerican Studies and World Affairs* 30, 2 and 3 (Summer, Fall 1988): 1989–213.

"Drugs: Goodbye, Cocaine." *The Economist*, 8 September 1990, 28–33.

"Hello, Heroin." *The Economist*, 8 September 1990, 33.

Lee, Rensselaer W. III. *The White Labyrinth: Cocaine Trafficking and Political Power in the Andean Countries*. New Brunswick, N.J.: Transaction Publications, 1989.

Mabry, Donald J. "The Latin American Narcotics Trade and Hemispheric Security." *International Third World Studies Journal and Review* 1, 1 (1989): 33–40.

Office of the President. *National Drug Control Strategy*. Washington, D.C.: U.S. Government Printing Office, 1990.

Perl, Raphael F. "Congress and International Narcotics Control." *CRS Report for Congress*. Washington, D.C.: The Library of Congress, 16 October 1989.

———. "The U.S. Congress, International Drug Policy, and the Anti-Drug Abuse Act of 1988." *Journal of Interamerican Studies and World Affairs* 30, 2 and 3 (Summer, Fall 1988): 19–53.

U.S. Congress. House. *Cocaine Production, Eradication, and the Environment: Policy, Impact and Options*. Report prepared by Raphael F. Perl, Congressional Research Service, on a seminar held 14 February 1990. 101st Cong., 2d sess. Washington, D.C.: U.S. Government Printing Office, 1990.

———. Committee on Appropriations. *Hearings on Foreign Operations, Export Financing and Related Programs Appropriations for 1989*. 100th Cong., 2d sess., 30 March 1988. Washington, D.C.: Government Printing Office, 1988.

———. Committee on Armed Forces. *The Andean Drug Strategy and the Role of the U.S. Military*. Report prepared by Raphael F. Perl, Congressional Research Service, on a seminar held 9 November 1989, 101st Cong., 1st sess. Washington, D.C.: U.S. Government Printing Office, 1990.

———. Committee on Armed Forces. *Narcotics Interdiction and the Use of the Military: Issues for Congress*. Proceedings of a seminar held by the Congressional Research Service, 7 June 1988. Report of the Defense Policy Panel and Investigations Subcommittee of the Committee on Armed Services, House of Representatives, 100th Cong., 2d sess., Washington, D.C.: Government Printing Office, 1988.

———. Committee on Foreign Affairs. *International Narcotics Control Act of 1988*. Report together with additional views to accompany H.R. 4841 . . . including cost estimate of the Congressional Budget Office. Washington, D.C.: Government Printing Office, 1988.

U.S. Congress. Senate. *Drug Money Laundering, Banks and Foreign Policy*. Report prepared by Raphael F. Perl, Congressional Research Service, on a seminar held 27 September, 4 October, and 1 November 1989. 101st Cong., 2d sess. Washington, D.C.: U.S. Government Printing Office, 1988.

U.S. Department of State, Bureau of Public Affairs. *International Narcotics Control Update*. Washington, D.C.: U.S. Department of State Office, January 1990.

U.S. Library of Congress. *The International Narcotics Trade: An Overview of Its Dimensions, Production Sources, and Organizations*. Prepared by William Roy Surrett. Washington, D.C.: U.S. Government Printing Office, October 1988.

# 5

# Canada

DAVID L. CRUM

## INTRODUCTION

Canada does not leap to mind when the topic of discussion is illegal drugs. Nonetheless, it does face significant challenges from the narcotics trade. Canada's problems are twofold. The first is domestic drug abuse. Although Canada's current levels of drug abuse may be moderate by international comparison, the problem seems to be growing, particularly in the use of cocaine. The second is the utilization of Canadian coasts and borders to transship drugs bound for the U.S. market and employment of its financial system to disguise and legitimize the proceeds from narcotics sales in the United States.

## DRUG ABUSE IN CANADA

The magnitude of Canada's domestic drug problem may be smaller than that of its southern neighbor, but it is significant and growing. In the federal government's words: "There is no doubt that there is a very real and substantial problem of alcohol and drug abuse in this country."[1]

Not surprisingly, given its illicit nature, estimates of the total amount of drug traffic in Canada vary widely; however, most figures for the value of illegal drugs sold are in the billions of dollars, perhaps as much as $10 billion annually. A Canadian business group, the Alliance for a Drug-Free Canada, estimates that 10 percent of Canadians use illegal drugs. According to government statistics, the most popular, or most frequently used, illegal drug remains cannabis, or marijuana, and hashish or hashish oil. A 1985 survey showed that 1.1 million Canadians had used cannabis within the previous year.[2] A later poll revealed that 9.5 percent of the residents of Ontario, Canada's most populous province, were regular monthly users of cannabis in 1987.

Perhaps even more worrisome than the existing level of drug abuse is the apparent continuing overall rise in narcotic usage and the increased use of harder drugs, particularly cocaine and its powerful derivative crack cocaine or crack. Although the problem of drug abuse is centered in the cities, no region of Canada seems to be immune, including the rural and remote northern areas. The modern specter of acquired immune deficiency syndrome (AIDS) complicates the picture of harder drugs as some 10 to 15 percent of AIDS sufferers are intravenous drug users.

Some additional feel for the scope of the illegal drug problem in Canada can be gleaned from the crime statistics.[3] Narcotics offenses totaled 67,882 in 1989, of which 40 percent, or 27,142 involved drugs other than cannabis. Total criminal code offenses in Canada rose 1.7 percent between 1988 and 1989; within that total, narcotics crimes shot up 14.2 percent. Moving through the criminal justice process, non-cannabis drug charges and convictions more than doubled between 1980 and 1989. The volume of marijuana and hashish cases apparently is so high that, as of 1989, statistics for cannabis charges and convictions have not been compiled since 1985 due to the prohibitive cost of processing the quantity of data.

Perhaps more serious is the apparent trend toward harder drugs or, more precisely, cocaine. Despite the increase in drug infractions, the number of cannabis offenses was flat in 1989. Marijuana and hashish's share of the total declined from 87.4 percent in 1980 to 60.0 percent in 1989. While the diminishing share of cannabis offenses may well reflect changing law enforcement practices, it seems that the nearly 50-percent rise in cocaine offenses indicates an actual shift in usage, particularly because, in the words of the Canadian Centre for Justice Statistics, the percentage of cocaine infractions, "as a percentage of total drugs, increased dramatically" from 2.3 percent in 1980 to 24.2 percent in 1989. Excluding cannabis, cocaine's share of all drug offenses rose to about 70 percent by 1989. The magnitude of the cocaine increase is highlighted by the fact that heroin's share of drug crimes rose from 0.8 percent to 1.4 percent over the same decade.[4]

## SMUGGLER'S DELIGHT

Illegal drugs can be grown and manufactured in Canada. Some marijuana is cultivated either indoors or, in the more temperate areas such as British Columbia, outdoors. Cannabis grown inside and hydroponically is expected to supply an increasing share of domestic demand. Synthetic drugs such as methamphetamines are manufactured in domestic laboratories. Nonetheless, given its climate, the plants that are the raw materials for most narcotics—the opium and coca plants as well as the majority of cannabis—are not cultivated in Canada. In order to meet the demand for narcotics, traffickers must smuggle the drugs into the country from their Latin American, Asian, and Middle Eastern sources.

In addition to the problem of controlling the running of narcotics into Canada for sale to the local market, Canada faces the challenge of interdicting illegal drugs bound for the United States by way of Canadian territory. Even without taking the relative magnitude of the U.S. drug problem into account, the U.S. population and economy are roughly ten times larger than Canada's. In fact, the majority of many types of the drugs smuggled into Canada is destined for the U.S. market.

This method of transshipment to the U.S. market appears to be attractive to South American exporters of narcotics such as heroin, cocaine, and crack. This is particularly true with the use of the "Canadian connection" by Colombian cartels smuggling cocaine destined for the United States. With the increased efforts of U.S. authorities to seal off its southern borders to drug traffickers using land, sea, or air routes, the northern strategy is attracting the attention of smugglers. Beginning perhaps around 1988, the Canadian route became a regular alternative to the more direct southern approaches.

The breaching of Canada's Atlantic and Pacific Ocean borders by air or sea is simplified by the length and topography of the coast, as well as the scant resources allocated to patrolling those shorelines. The sea borders are policed only sporadically, and the missions of the patrollers—frequently the navy or fisheries ministry—do not always include drug interdiction. Even if more resources were devoted to the task, the long and often rocky and rugged coast would be exceedingly difficult to monitor effectively.

Recalling the days of Prohibition, the eastern Maritime Provinces may be the most popular points of entry. However, the western coast of British Columbia has not been overlooked by drug smugglers. The most popular Pacific Ocean approach is via the Queen Charlotte Islands, an archipelago lying south of the Alaskan panhandle, from which the narcotics are transshipped onto the mainland of British Columbia.

The sea approach from the Atlantic Ocean uses the Maritimes' broken shoreline as cover. The province of Nova Scotia has been used for seaborne drug importation since the early 1970s, with up to thirty attempted shipments per year. Rough weather and police action probably keep the number of successful landings under that level. Typically a larger "mother ship" is kept up to 250 miles offshore while one or more smaller craft—usually fishing craft purchased locally—ferry the drugs to the coast. Cocaine may be smuggled in this fashion, but it seems more cost effective for the bulkier drugs such as marijuana and hashish. The police averaged one capture a year between 1974 and 1986, but since that time were unsuccessful until making two seizures in 1990. Part of the improvement stems from a reinvigorated Royal Canadian Mounted Police (RCMP) program called Coastal Watch which encourages citizen reporting of suspicious activities in the region.

Perhaps the more favored approach into the Maritimes is by airplane to one of the ninety isolated and usually deserted landing strips maintained for lumber companies or fire fighting in the province of Nova Scotia. Perhaps two or three times each month, on the average, long-range turboprop airplanes originating from South America refuel in the Caribbean island of St. Kitts and fly northward over the Atlantic Ocean beyond the range of U.S.–based radar. Their approach into Canada is simplified by the absence of electronic surveillance designed to identify drug flights and of dedicated interceptor planes. The silver lining is that the quantities of contraband carried on each flight are reduced by the extra fuel needed for the long flight.

Once inside Canada, the traffickers find the 5,500-mile U.S.–Canadian border easy to breach compared with the Mexican and Caribbean approaches. On the one hand, the boundary is relatively unguarded. The Canadians maintain no committed force for border patrol duties, and the United States applies substantially fewer resources to this theater than to the southern boundaries. As a result, some remote border crossings are often unmanned. A typical operation could entail the smuggling of drugs into the Maritimes; once in Canada, they would be shipped overland across the sparsely populated border to the neighboring state of Maine where the U.S. distribution network takes over.

Even if border security were massively reinforced, the sheer volume of individuals, motor vehicles, and goods crossing between the two nations would make detection of contraband difficult, and the heightened vigilance could snarl legitimate trade and travel. The United States and Canada benefit from the world's largest bilateral trade relationship. With its continued expansion, under the stimulus of the U.S.–Canadian Free Trade Agreement, opportunities to camouflage illegal shipments will also grow.

The Canadian connection is not just speculation. In March 1989, two Colombians linked to Pablo Escobar, a leader of the Medellín cartel, attracted attention after they crash-landed their twin-engine airplane at a private airport near Fredericton, New Brunswick. Authorities arrested them with 1,100 pounds of cocaine given an estimated New York retail value of $25 million. Later that year, they were sentenced to twenty-two-year prison terms by a Canadian court. In September 1989, Canadian authorities arrested five men linked to the two Colombians who were carrying weapons, a rubber dinghy, life jackets, and other equipment. While there was some initial speculation that their mission was to free the two jailed smugglers, they apparently were preparing to unload contraband from a ship at a prearranged point on the shore.

## DOLLAR LAUNDRY

Canada's proudly maintained image of an internationalist and lawful nation has been increasingly at odds with its emerging reputation as a principal money-laundering center. A March 1990 article in the *New York Times* describing Canada as "one of the world's leading havens for concealing illegal narcotics profits"[5] prompted a sharp reply from the Canadian ambassador to the United States, D. H. Burney. Although Canada has made large, and possibly decisive, strides to curb this activity, the newspaper's description was probably justified.

The flip side of each delivery of cannabis, cocaine, or amphetamine is the payment in cash. As with all large and profitable criminal activities, the amount of cash generated is sizable enough to generate suspicion unless its origins are blurred or disguised as legitimate business income. Estimates of the magnitude of this money laundering range as widely as those of the underlying drug use. However the amounts are even larger because each quantity of narcotics is bought and sold several times over as it passes down the distribution chain.

The global amount of illegal drug profits laundered each year could be anywhere from US $100 billion to as much as $300 billion. If the higher figure, contained in a U.S. Senate report, is true, about $110 billion of the total is generated in the United States. Educated guesses by law enforcement authorities and other sources place the amount of funds laundered at Canadian banks in the billions of dollars. Much of those funds are narcotics revenues generated in the United States. Drug-enforcement specialists estimate that hundreds of millions of dollars are sent from the United States to Canada each year to evade U.S. banking laws designed to stop laundering. Another crude indicator of the scope of the Canadian-based laundering of U.S. drug revenues is the uneven flow of dollars; according to U.S. Senator John Kerry of Massachusetts, U.S. financial institutions sent about $1.2 billion annually to Canadian banks while the reverse flow was about $4 billion.

While the actual magnitude of the money-laundering problem may be unclear, its existence is not mere guesswork. The earliest known instance of major drug-laundering activity in Canada was uncovered in 1983 with the arrest of Luis Pinto in the United States. A Colombian legislator and businessman—as well as a cocaine money launderer—Pinto admitted to a number of financial transactions including the deposit of C$726,000 (US$558,000) in illicit funds in the Royal Bank of Canada.[6]

Since that time, the amount and regularity of funds being laundered through Canada apparently have steadily increased. Besides the money related to drug transactions which are ferried through Canada, U.S. drug-enforcement agencies see more and more cash from Asian heroin and Latin American cocaine shipments being transferred through Canada. The most common methods of bringing funds into Canada are to transport cash physically over the border or to use bank-to-bank electronic transfers.

In 1989, in the largest successful investigation to date, Operation Polar Cap uncovered US$1.2 billion laundered by the Medellín cartel over an eighteen-month period, through the United States, Canada, and Switzerland, including some $12 million via the Swiss Bank Corporation (Canada) in Toronto. The trilateral investigation led to the conviction in the United States of a Panamanian bank, Banco de Occidente, on laundering charges.

Why Canada? It does not appear to have much in common with the established laundering centers of Switzerland, the Bahamas, Luxembourg, Panama, and Hong Kong where banking secrecy and proximity to narcotics-producing regions are the obvious common elements. Nor does it seem to fit in with countries that are reportedly targeted by launderers for increased activity, such as Antigua, Gibraltar, the Netherlands, and Liechtenstein.

While it may lack many commonalities with the above nations, Canada has several characteristics which make it attractive as a laundering center. Some of its "attributes" are the same that attract the transshipping smugglers: proximity to the huge U.S. market, the porosity of the U.S.–Canadian border, and the volume of legitimate financial flows—accompanying the human and merchandise traffic—which serve as an excellent cover for drug transactions. Even without its connection to the U.S. market, Canada's stable currency and government, advanced financial system, free movement of funds, and democratic safeguards on police powers combine to make the country an inviting money-laundering location.

The most controversial attraction of Canada as a laundering center is the disparity between the United States and Canada in the pace and content of the legislation passed to inhibit money laundering. This controversy came out in the open in September 1990, when Senator Kerry publicized a confidential June 1988 report on money laundering prepared by the RCMP and the U.S. Drug Enforcement Administration (DEA). That report noted that "anomalies" in Canadian laws made the antilaundering rules imposed on Canadian financial institutions relatively lax. Even when Canadian laws stiffened, they were outpaced by tougher U.S. legislation. The net effect was to encourage traffickers to use Canadian banks and financial institutions as an alternative to U.S. establishments.

Canadian authorities protested Senator Kerry's accusations and maintained that much of the joint report was outdated by the time he made its existence public. They pointed out that Canada had passed stricter laws in the interim to outlaw money laundering. However, some of the report's authors noted that, although the anomalies may have disappeared, the "hundreds of millions of dollars" in laundered funds continued to flow. While the tightening of Canadian controls over money laundering is detailed below, it is clear that the existence—even if transitory—of a divergence in enforcement mechanisms has rerouted large flows of dirty money through Canadian financial institutions. Canadian authorities may find that it is easier to prevent the use of their nation as a money-laundering center than to uproot established laundering networks.

## THE NATIONAL DRUG STRATEGY

Through much of the 1980s, the Canadian government's response to drug abuse centered on law enforcement. However, as the problem deepened, the limits on the efficacy of enforcement alone became clearer. Even if greater resources were applied to the intervention of illegal importation and trafficking, the results would be subject to the law of diminishing returns.

In recognition of these limitations, the federal government announced its

National Drug Strategy (NDS)—''Action on Drug Abuse''—in May 1987. Under the aegis of Health and Welfare Canada, the broadly based strategy emphasizes prevention and treatment in an effort to widen the government's response. Health and Welfare coordinates the efforts of federal agencies in five areas in addition to enforcement and control: education and prevention, treatment and rehabilitation, information and research, international cooperation, and the catch-all, national focus. The program also targets four distinct segments of the population for special attention: young people, Canada's aboriginal Indian and Inuit people, prison inmates, and health professionals.

NDS tries to address the needs of the public, health professionals, and law officers for information on the drugs themselves, their abuse, and related crime. Under the strategy, the government has set up a national research agenda to better define the factors that influence drug abuse and to examine new methods of treatment and prevention. The government also provides funding for research targeted at drug abuse. Health and Welfare's Bureau of Drug Research has worked to improve and create methods of drug analysis to allow authorities to keep up with new illicit ''designer'' drugs as well as to track better the sources and distribution patterns of confiscated narcotics. Finally, NDS established a task force to improve the national narcotics data base.

Drug abuse in the workplace is approached as an illness. The vehicle for delivering the necessary medical services is an expansion of employee assistance programs. Besides augmenting those programs' benefits, coverage could be extended to include workers' families or the community at large.

Mandatory drug testing remains a controversial tool, and the NDS recommends it only in exceptional cases where public safety concerns predominate. In 1987, routine employer drug tests were deemed a violation of the Ontario Human Rights Code. A spring 1990 proposal for drug testing in the armed forces was strongly opposed by the Canadian Human Rights Commission. And the September 1990 announcement by Toronto-Dominion Bank (which is federally, not provincially, regulated) that it would require drug tests for all new employees faced many critics including the Canadian Labor Congress.

There are some new roles for the law enforcement agencies under NDS. Canada's national, provincial, and local police forces work with regional institutions to educate the public about the dangers of drug abuse. To help fulfill that task, the RCMP increased the number of drug-awareness coordinator positions to include one in each regional division.

However, the primary role of the law enforcement agencies remains control of narcotics imports and apprehension of drug law violators. And there are concerns that inadequate funds are provided for law enforcement, with responsibilities resting primarily on the RCMP's Anti-Drug Profiteering Section. It is true that the government has difficulties in boosting border protection at a time when the military's operating and capital budgets are being reduced to meet overall fiscal goals. The patchwork fixes which often result from working around budget constraints are illustrated by government plans in July 1990 to refit two executive jets for transfer to the Department of Defense for drug smuggling interdiction.

Finally, the NDS commits a major portion of its funding to rehabilitation and treatment. Under Canada's federal system of government, the provinces and territories are deemed directly responsible for developing, administering, and delivering these services. However, to encourage improvements in the area, the central government provides matching funds for the expansion of these local treatment and rehabilitation programs. NDS has included monies for workshops to train drug addiction counselors.

## CLOSING THE DOOR ON LAUNDERING

The heightened awareness of the use of Canada's banks in the laundering of international and domestic drug profits contributed to a steady tightening of laws and policies to prevent this crime.

In January 1989, the Canadian government amended its Criminal Code, the Food and Drug Act, and the Narcotics Control Act through the passage of Bill C–61, Legislation on the Proceeds of Crime. Bill C–61 broadened the powers of the law enforcement agencies to combat drug crime and related laundering activities. For the first time, money laundering itself became a criminal offense as one of several enumerated ''enterprise crimes.'' The police were empowered to ''freeze and seize'' assets of suspected drug traffickers and other criminals.

While the bill was regarded as a positive and necessary first step, there were concerns over Bill C–61's potential effectiveness. Under its terms, the government was liable for losses suffered by persons whose assets were seized improperly or who were acquitted of the underlying crime. Critics argued that this provision discouraged prosecutors from using the new seizure powers except in open-and-shut cases.

In addition, Bill C–61 was contrasted with U.S. laws in an unfavorable light. It did not include any requirement for banks to report suspicious activities; in the United States, such a law was backed up by tough fines for banks which showed ''gross negligence'' in the face of laundering offenses. In addition, the Canadian criminal punishment associated with the newly defined enterprise crimes was incarceration for up to ten years and substantial monetary penalties; this seemed light compared to the U.S. maximum of twenty years and $500,000.

The joint RCMP–DEA report publicized by Senator Kerry in September 1989 seemed to provoke a Canadian response. The day after its revelation, the federal government asked Canadian banks to institute voluntarily procedures to assist in the detection of money-laundering activities. Despite continued criticism from some quarters that a mandatory rule was necessary to ensure compliance, Canada defended this policy for several months.

Finally, in March 1990, the Canadian government changed course and proposed that banks, money exchange houses, and other financial institutions be required to keep records of large cash transactions.[7] The proposed Bill C–89 would include professionals such as lawyers and accountants who maintain large sums in trust accounts for their clients. Records of large cash transactions, usually over C$10,000, would be kept on file by the institutions for at least five years. In addition, any suspicious transactions would be reported directly to law enforcement authorities. These new rules were implemented quickly by the larger banks and, in the latter part of 1990, they were reporting about 100 transactions each month to the authorities.

In defense of Bill C–89, the government argued that the creation of paper trails would aid in the investigation and prosecution of laundering activities. Critics of the bill, which became law in mid–1991, continued to insist that the only effective means of controlling laundering was to institute mandatory reports to the government as is the case in the United States.

On paper, U.S. rules remain stricter than the new Canadian laws. Since 1970, under the Bank Secrecy Act, U.S. financial institutions must report cash transactions of $10,000 or more to the Internal Revenue Service. In addition, U.S. banks must obtain satisfactory personal identification before issuing cashier's checks, bank checks, traveler's checks, or money orders of more than $3,000. Since late 1989, they are required to keep detailed records of the senders and recipients of funds sent by wire transfer. And if the government has reason to focus on a particular bank, individual, or geographical region, the above rules can be greatly tightened. The penalties for noncompliance with the U.S. law are tough: a $10,000 (from $1,000 in 1988) penalty for each transaction, each day, and each branch. In addition, the entire bank may be punished if several of its officials know about aspects of the crime.

While the written rules may be stiffer in the United States, there is some truth in Canada's claims that its more voluntary approach is equally effective. The United States has thousands of commercial banks, but Canada has only sixty-one of which six[8] of the seven national banks dominate the market. These large "Schedule I" institutions have nationwide franchises and maintain close communication on an informal level with banking regulators. Of the fifty-four, mostly foreign-owned, or "Schedule II" banks, the largest is Hongkong Bank of Canada with assets of about C$8 billion. According to Inspector Bruce Bowie, the Ottawa head of the RCMP anti–drug profiteering section, the voluntary bank monitoring of cash transactions, requested by the Canadian government in September 1989, was sufficiently rigorous to force launderers to shift much of their activity to currency exchanges, which did not monitor deposits. Further, the voluntary system may have allowed Canadian banks to highlight suspicious activities rather than overwhelm authorities with quotidian reports.

Canada also has joined in international—both bilateral and multinational—efforts to stem money laundering and drug trafficking. Agreements with the United States are both formal and informal, mirroring the pragmatic and close relationship between the two countries. In October 1989, the U.S. Senate approved treaties with Canada and five other nations to allow mutual inspection of information which could assist in money-laundering investigations and prosecutions, including bank documents, criminal records, search and seizure requests, and depositions. Under the Kerry Amendment to the United States' Anti-Drug Abuse Act of 1988, the United States is mandated to negotiate these treaties to ensure that other countries maintain adequate records on international money movements.

The more informal approach is characterized by the RCMP's creation of drug liaison posts in Miami, New York, and Los Angeles to coordinate efforts with U.S. authorities. This type of interagency cooperation resulted in the July 1990 seizure of about seven kilograms of Indian heroin at New York City's Kennedy International Airport. Agents from the RCMP, DEA, and both customs services worked together to break the Toronto-based ring. With the heroin worth some C$11 million, this was one of the largest interceptions made in North America.

The multinational approach includes initiatives sponsored by the United Nations and by the G–7 group of major Western economies (the United States, Japan, Germany, France, the United Kingdom, Italy, and Canada). The United Nations' Convention against Illicit Traffic in Narcotic Drugs and Psychotropic Substances of December 1988 requires the signatories to prosecute money-laundering offenses under local law. Canada's Office of the Superintendent of Financial Institutions reiterated full support for the Bank of International Settlements' December 1988 code of conduct on money laundering. This statement of principles prompts bank managements to take the steps necessary to prevent their institutions from being used as part of the money-laundering process.

## CONCLUSION: THE GREAT WHITE NORTH?

Canada has a drug problem. Although the level of drug abuse may be moderate by today's standards, the challenge is growing—both in magnitude and severity with the increasing use of cocaine and crack. The government's realization that combatting the problem requires a variety of initiatives—from education to law enforcement to rehabilitation—is a positive strategic step in turning the tide.

Its domestic narcotics problems are shared by many nations, but Canada faces distinctive challenges by virtue of its long border and deep interrelationship with the United States, a nation ten times its size and with a more entrenched narcotics problem. Canada probably can make only a marginal difference in reducing the use of its territory for the transshipment of U.S.–bound contraband without a dramatic increase in expenditures on surveillance systems, ships, and aircraft. Given budgetary constraints and the inadequate response to earlier calls for tighter border controls, such as "sovereignty over the Arctic," such a concerted and expensive effort is unlikely to be forthcoming soon.

An area where Canada can and does make a difference is controlling the invasion of its financial system by money launderers. The steps taken in the past few years have changed the Canadian landscape for the prospective launderer. In the Canadian regulatory context, its control mechanisms may be more effective, albeit more voluntary, than those of the United States. It has turned the corner on this facet of the international narcotics trade, and it will struggle to root out the laundering networks already allowed to take root.

Canada will find it difficult to reverse its domestic addiction and abuse problems, but no worse than other comparable Western societies. The misuse of Canadian banks should moderate as more accommodating havens are found and as the bite of Canada's new laws is demonstrated. Its isolated coastlines and porous southern border may well continue to attract smugglers by air and sea, but with its emerging reputation as a financial haven put to rest, Canada's image should revert to a more serene version of the Great White North.

## NOTES

1. Government of Canada, *Action on Drugs Abuse, Making a Difference* (Ottawa: Minister of Supply and Services Canada, 1988), 5.

2. N.B., Canada's population is 26 million, growing at about a 1 percent rate.

3. Such an analysis needs to take the limitations of the data into account. Official agencies such as the Canadian Centre for Justice Statistics and the Bureau of Dangerous Drugs of Health and Welfare Canada warn that changes in the levels of reported narcotics offenses do not necessarily correlate directly to changes in actual drug use. For example, they could reflect different police priorities and enforcement practices. Nonetheless the figures can be helpful in showing a rough order of magnitude and broad trends.

4. Statistics Canada, Canadian Centre for Justice Statistics, *Canadian Crime Statistics 1989* (Ottawa: Minister of Supply and Services Canada, 1990), 45.

5. Stephen Labaton, "Canada Wants Banks to Record Cash Deals," *New York Times*, 22 March 1990, D2. Also see Scott B. MacDonald, "Anti–Money Laundering Regimes in Europe and Canada," *Comptroller of the Currency Quarterly Journal* 10, 2 (June 1991): 17–21.

6. Although Canadian laws at the time did not allow for the confiscation of the laundered funds, Pinto was assassinated before he could regain access to the money.

7. Interestingly, although apparently not connected, the announcement of this change was made hours after press reports that agents of deposed Haitian dictator, Jean-Claude Duvalier, laundered C$408 million via Canadian financial institutions in 1986.

8. Bank of Montreal, Bank of Nova Scotia, Canadian Imperial Bank of Commerce, National Bank of Canada, Royal Bank of Canada, and Toronto-Dominion Bank. The seventh Schedule I bank, Canadian Western Bank, is a smaller, essentially regional institution.

## BIBLIOGRAPHY

Allen, Glen. "Tracking the Dealers, Canada Adds New Zeal to Its Drug Enforcement." *MacLean*'s, 3 September 1990, 42.

Burney, D. H. "Canada Works to Stop Money Laundering [Letter to the Editor]." *New York Times*, 3 April 1990.

Burns, John F. "Arrests Raise Canada's Fears on Drug Smuggling into U.S." *New York Times*, 16 September 1989, A8.

Gates, Bruce. "Foreign Banks Aim to Fill Domestic Voids." *Financial Post* (Toronto), 11 November 1990, 11.

Gibb-Clark, Margot. "T-D [Toronto-Dominion Bank] to Test Workers for Drug Use." *Globe and Mail* (Toronto), 22 September 1990, B3.

Government of Canada, Health and Welfare Canada, Health Protection Branch, Drugs Directorate, Bureau of Dangerous Drugs. *1989 Narcotic, Controlled and Restricted Drug Statistics*. Ottawa: Minister of Supply and Services Canada, 1989.

Government of Canada. Office of the Superintendent of Financial Institutions. *Annual Report*. Ottawa: Minister of Supply and Services Canada, 1989, 8–9.

Jensen, Holger. "Canada's Crackdown, A New Law Has Led to More Seizures." *MacLean's*, 23 October 1989, 52.

Jensen, Holger, et al. "Hiding the Drug Money, Criminals Are Using Canada to Launder Millions of Dollars in Drug Profits." *MacLean's*, 23 October 1989, 42.

Jones, Colin. "What's in the Suitcase?" *The Banker* (London), April 1990, 12.

Labaton, Stephen. "Canada Seen as Major Haven for Laundering Drug Money." *New York Times*, 28 September 1990, A1+.

———. "Canada Wants Banks to Record Cash Deals." *New York Times*, 22 March 1990, D2.

Malarek, Victor. *Merchants of Misery*. Toronto: McClelland & Stewart Inc., 1989.

Moore, W. John. "Nixing the Cash Connection." *National Journal*, 2 December 1989, 2924–29.

"Ottawa Plans to Clean up Money Laundering." *Canadian Press* (Ottawa), 21 March 1990.

"Police Seize Heroin Shipment." *Globe and Mail* (Toronto), 24 July 1990, A8.

Possamai, Mario. "Hundreds of Millions of Dollars in Drug Profits Slip Through. . . ." *Canadian Press* (Ottawa), 29 October 1989.

"Senate Votes 6 Pacts to Track Drug Money." *New York Times*, 25 October 1989, A14.

Statistics Canada, Canadian Centre for Justice Statistics. *Canadian Crime Statistics 1989*. Ottawa: Minister of Supply and Services Canada, 1990.

Valorzi, John. "Despite a New Money-Laundering Law, Canada Still Continues." *Canadian Press* (Washington, D.C.), 8 February 1990.

Weiner, Eric. "Latin Drug Traffickers Use Canada as New Route." *New York Times*, 26 December 1989, A3.

Yakabuski, Konrad. "Banks Reporting 100 Deals Monthly in Laundry Check." *Toronto Star*, 6 December 1990, F3.

York, Geoffrey. "Ottawa Changes Stand on Promised Sale of Jets." *Globe and Mail* (Toronto), 13 July 1990, A5.

# 6

# Bolivia

EDUARDO GAMARRA

## INTRODUCTION

The explosive growth of the cocaine industry has had widespread socioeconomic and political repercussions in Bolivia. In the past decade, every Bolivian government has faced the consequences of the dramatic boom of this industry. Every aspect of Bolivia's foreign relations, especially with the United States, has been dominated by growing international pressure to deal with the cocaine industry.

Although Bolivia has long been a source of cocaine, it was the increase in demand from the United States and, more recently, Europe and the attraction of huge profits which have led to the present boom in production. Until recently, Bolivia's share of the industry was largely limited to the cultivation of coca leaves and the production of coca paste. Cocaine hydrochloride was mostly produced in Colombia; in the past two years, however, Bolivia appears to have become a leading source of processed cocaine. U.S. government officials claim that, in 1991, Bolivia became the world's second largest producer of refined cocaine hydrochloride. Bolivia is the world's second largest producer of coca leaves and, according to several estimates, cocaine revenue exceeds legal exports. The Bolivian government estimates that approximately $490 million enter the Bolivian economy from the cocaine industry on a yearly basis. Bolivia's profound economic crises of the mid–1980s, exacerbated by the pressures of a prolonged and convoluted transition to democracy, limited the capacity of its governments to deal with the booming cocaine trade. These governments could do even less to resist U.S. pressures to increase repressive activities such as militarizing the counternarcotics campaign. Bolivian governments have agreed, however, to measures which, paradoxically, are intended to destroy the only export that keeps the nation's economy healthy.

Placing the matter into a broader perspective allows for a better explanation of Bolivia's role in the political economy of the cocaine trade. The cocaine industry has provided a source of livelihood not only to traffickers but also to *campesino* coca growers and others who have found work in and around the trade. In the Bolivia of the 1980s, coca and cocaine production became the principal source of income for thousands of people unemployed in the formal and informal economy.

In the mid–1980s, cocaine became the principal pillar of support for the Bolivian economy. Until 1985, the export of tin constituted Bolivia's major link to the world market. Owing to the collapse of the tin market, the closing of the mines, and the imposition of the Nueva Política Económica (New Economic Policy), a draconian austerity plan, large numbers of unemployed workers streamed into the Chapare Valley of the Cochabamba Department where coca growing became their livelihood. Because of the impact of the catastrophic economic crisis, cocaine steadily developed into the major source of foreign exchange for the Bolivian economy.

Bolivia's problem, however, is not only a question of dealing with drug traffickers. In fact, attempting to eradicate coca plantations, the raw material for cocaine, has been the most difficult task facing every Bolivian government in the past decade. The magnitude of the problem facing Bolivia can be understood only by differentiating between coca leaves and cocaine. Nowhere is this point made more clear than in noting the stabilizing effect of traditional coca use on Bolivian and Andean cultures and contrasting this reality with the disruptive and violent phenomenon of cocaine use in the United States.

The cultivation of the coca plant and the use of coca leaves date back to the pre-Columbian civilizations that populated the Andean region. In those cultures, coca leaves were an integral part of a host of sacred rituals that bound together an array of groups in ceremonial solidarity. As a mild stimulant, the coca leaf was used (and continues to be used by all social classes) as a household remedy for a variety of complaints including altitude sickness.

With the coming of the Spanish conquest coca leaves proved to be the most resilient aspect of the Quechua, Aymara, and other Indian cultures subjugated by the Iberians. As mining became the focal extractive industry, Andean Indians were the only labor force that could be employed to perform the hazardous duties of shaft mining. Soon the Spaniards realized that coca leaves were an integral part of the employment contract; in fact, many analysts claim that the coca leaf also had a nutritional value as sustenance for miners who worked long hours without food. A key linkage, which has survived into the 1990s, was quickly established between the mining industry and the multiple uses of coca. In short, the use of leaves reflects more a cultural dimension than an addiction. The coca leaf is central to the rituals of both rural folk and worker groups, such as the miners, who consider a ration of coca leaves to be an integral part of the employment contract.

## THE STRUCTURE OF THE BOLIVIAN COCA/COCAINE INDUSTRY

Owing to the dramatic increase in external demand, coca has become the principal agricultural product in Bolivia. Between 1963 and 1987, production increased 31.5 times, and the area under cultivation increased 20.3 times. During this same period, the Chapare Valley in the Cochabamba Department surpassed the Yungas Valleys of La Paz in total production. In the late 1980s, coca leaf production grew at an even faster rate. Between 1985 and 1988, production grew at an annual rate of 13.4 percent. Coca now represents nearly 30 percent of the national agricultural product and, in the major producer departments of La Paz and Cochabamba, the percentages are 33 and 66 percent, respectively. Clearly, the increase in production of coca was the result of growing external demand for coca paste.

Prior to 1970 most coca leaf production met local demand for chewing, brewing tea, and other traditional uses. By the end of the 1980s, only 16 percent of coca production went to satisfy traditional use of coca. The remaining 84 percent went to service the drug trade.

The Bolivian government estimates that approximately 300,000 persons, or 20 percent of the rural population of La Paz and Cochabamba, are involved in the production of coca. In 1987, the production of coca reached 152,000 tons, which netted $238 million or approximately $1,220 per capita. If these figures are accurate, then peasants in coca-growing regions are comparatively better off than those elsewhere in Bolivia where the annual per capita income barely reaches $500. As a result, the resistance on the part of peasant groups to eradication programs is understandable. As Kevin Healy (1991) and others have noted, the boom in coca production was indeed linked to the magnitude of Bolivia's economic crisis. The deeper Bolivia sank into an economic catastrophe, the greater the size of the coca fields and the greater the size of the population involved in coca production.

Since the early 1980s Bolivia's peasant groups have been vociferous opponents of the attempts to eradicate coca leaf production. Paradoxically the imposition of the Nueva Política Económica in 1985 boosted resistance to government counternarcotics policy as many of the 23,000 mine workers dismissed from state-run mines flocked to the Chapare and other coca-growing regions.

Bolivia's highly organized coca growers' unions, especially the Federación de Trabajadores del Trópico (Federation of Workers from the Tropics), have availed themselves of civil rights guarantees enshrined in the Bolivian constitution to protest legislation and other government attempts to eradicate coca crops. Bolivia's democracy has ensured that peasants work within the system, a pattern sociologists and anthropologists argue accounts for the lack of appeal of guerrilla warfare. This strategy of social contestation has proven to be extremely effective as peasant unions have forged ties with political parties and have extracted significant concessions from the Bolivian government. For example, analyses of the May 1989 electoral results demonstrate the appeal of the United Left (IU) party in the Chapare Valley. In the lowland section of the valley, where coca leaf producers are concentrated, this party obtained 42.3 percent of the vote. On a national scale IU garnered only 7 percent.

The Bolivian government's alternative development program (to be discussed later) is the product of government-union negotiations over the course of the last four years. Although the government has given much lip service to the plan, which calls basically for an integrated rural development alternative, the reality is that interdiction efforts have taken precedent over these proposals. The result has been rampant civil and human rights violations in the coca-growing regions by the elite U.S.–trained counternarcotics police forces known by their UMOPAR (Unidad Móvil de Patrullaje Rural, or Mobile Units for Rural Patrolling) acronym.

In the past five years, conflict between UMOPAR and coca growers has resulted in occasional bloody battles. At least three examples of these confrontations should be noted. On May 27, 1987, five peasants were killed during a skirmish between UMOPAR and peasant groups in Parotani, Cochabamba. In part because of the fallout from this incident, the government signed an agreement with the Bolivian Labor Central (COB) and peasant unions from the Chapare Valley. This accord instituted the so-called Integral Development Plan for the Substitution of Coca (PIDYS), which ushered in the alternative development thesis.

Peasant leaders claimed that violations of promises not to classify coca as a dangerous substance in the PIDYS accord led to a second confrontation. While the Bolivian National Congress debated a far-reaching antidrug law (Law 1008 to be discussed below), peasant opposition to the new drug law culminated in violence on June 27, 1989, when UMOPAR troops fired upon coca growers who allegedly attacked the police unit's headquarters in the town of Villa Tunari, Cochabamba. Five peasants were killed; scores more were injured and arrested.

In 1991, several human rights organizations documented human rights violations by UMOPAR and the Fuerza Especial de Lucha contra el Narcotráfico (FELCN—Special Counternarcotics Force), the two Bolivian outfits charged with interdiction activities. These findings included cases of arbitrary arrests followed by torture and illegal searches and seizures. Coca growers have been extremely active in resisting U.S.–backed interdiction programs. Their federation has been especially active in mobilizing the peasantry in the Chapare to resist government plans to militarize the region. Backed by the COB, the peasants have announced widespread resistance including the establishment of armed groups and the staging of roadblocks and marches.

In short, the worst case scenario is that Bolivia's coca growers could end up in a shooting conflict with the armed forces. Peru's lessons are worth noting: When drug-interdiction and crop-destroying programs targeted peasants, they turned to such groups as the Shining Path, the violent Maoist guerrillas, for protection. In Bolivia, for the moment, the freedom to organize in protest provided by the Bolivian democracy has prevented this situation; however, with the recent arrival of fifty-six U.S. military advisers and the ordering of two army battalions into the Chapare, the prospects for continued peace in the region are diminishing considerably.

## BOLIVIA'S DRUG BARONS

Bolivia's drug lords do not rank with the well-known cartels of Colombia, although the U.S. Drug Enforcement Administration (DEA) claims that the trend in the 1990s is toward the emergence of larger, more powerful, and more violent organizations, particularly in the eastern city of Santa Cruz. Santa Cruz has always had the reputation of being the Bolivian Medellín, complete with its own cartel-like structure known as the "*Corporacion.*"

Without a doubt, in the early 1980s the Santa Cruz drug barons controlled Bolivia's cocaine industry. These barons were, in turn, dominated by Roberto Suárez Gómez, the so-called King of Cocaine, whom many claim was Bolivia's direct link to the Medellín cartel. Suárez and his Santa Cruz associates are assumed to have financed the bloody 1980 coup of General Luis García Meza. García Meza's followers included Italian neo-Nazis, Klaus Barbie, and the infamous "Minister of Cocaine," Colonel Luis Arce Gómez, who was recently sentenced to serve thirty years in a U.S. prison by a federal judge in Miami, Florida. These military officers and their followers provided protection for Suárez and others throughout the Santa Cruz and Beni departments.

Apart from Suárez, the most notable case was that of Sonia and Walter Atalá, a husband and wife drug-trafficking team from Santa Cruz with direct contacts with the Medellín cartel. In 1980, the Atalás obtained protection from Minister of Interior Arce Gómez; as a result, they strengthened the ties between the Bolivian suppliers of paste and the Colombian cartels. The quid pro quo also included offers from Sonia Atalá to Arce Gómez to assassinate leftist politicians. After being discovered by the DEA, the Atalás agreed to testify against Arce Gómez and members of the Medellín cartel in exchange for their enrollment in the U.S. witness protection program.

The collapse of García Meza and the end of military rule did little to disrupt the flow of coca paste from Bolivia. Ironically, the coming of democracy may have also had a democratizing impact on the drug industry. Roberto Suárez faced increased competition from other traffickers who no longer feared a state-supported Santa Cruz monopoly over the industry. Clearly, Suárez's power and influence remained strong, but he also spent much of his time hiding from U.S.–supported initiatives which were accepted by successive Bolivian governments.

Owing to increased competition and joint U.S.–Bolivian counternarcotics efforts, Roberto Suárez's grip over the Bolivian cocaine trade gave way in the late 1980s. His arrest by Bolivian police in July 1988 capped a ten-year effort to end the reign of the monarch of the industry. Suárez's jailing in La Paz, however, did little to disrupt the cocaine production process. In fact, by the time of his arrest, Suárez's nephew Jorge Roca Suárez, also known as "Techo de Paja," had already displaced his uncle and had become Bolivia's principal trafficker. Techo de Paja was less parochial and more entrepreneurial than Suárez. In a few years, he developed direct trafficking routes between Bolivia and Mexico and into Southern California. Many speculated that, because of the crackdown in Colombia, the Santa Cruz *Corporacion*, now headed by Techo de Paja, was destined to become more powerful than the Medellín cartel.

Techo de Paja's empire crumbled on December 14, 1991, however, when he was arrested in a San Marino, California, mansion where, to the surprise of many, he had been living for some time. With his downfall came numerous revelations about the extent to which he had penetrated the Bolivian economy. In fact, the money-laundering mechanisms were shrewdly used by the Bolivian drug barons to clean millions of dollars.

As in other Andean nations affected by the cocaine industry, money laundering has become a very large problem in Bolivia. The preferred mechanisms are real estate transactions and cattle ranching. Roberto Suárez, for example, was involved in cattle ranching. Money laundering has also been carried out in other innovative ventures. According to some reports, in the late 1980s savings and loans operations, radio taxis, aero taxis, furniture factories, shopping malls, discotheques, and even television stations were all related to money laundering.

*Financieras*, or savings and loans operations, have recently been targeted by both the government and the DEA as one of the principal mechanisms for laundering drug money. The most glaring example was the Financiera Integral, Sociedad Anónima (FINSA), a savings and loan agency, which paid its depositors high interests despite having less than $9 million in assets. Moreover, FINSA was also accused of purchasing property from people linked to the drug industry. In late March 1991, the DEA and the Bolivian government closed in on FINSA; however, after a convoluted round, the owners of the savings and loan agency were released and allowed to reestablish their operation.

Critics of the Bolivian economic stabilization success story have also charged that money laundering has been carried out with the complicity of the nation's central bank. Many have noted that one of the most sophisticated mechanisms is the recently established *bolsa de valores*, or stock exchange. Others have pointed to the establishment of a *bolsín* (auction mechanism) in the central bank, a key to exchange rate stabilization, which has also created a means for laundering narco-dollar profits. A recent report from the Central Bank notes that, between September 1985 and March 1991, the *bolsín* sold over $3 billion to banks, the public sector, and individual customers. The government, however, claims that the dollars auctioned to customers came from foreign loans and export revenue.

## JOINT UNITED STATES–BOLIVIAN GOVERNMENT RESPONSES

Throughout the 1980s, successive Bolivian governments have dealt with the coca and cocaine trade through a variety of policies. Responding to U.S. pressure,

Bolivian governments have escalated interdiction operations and have agreed to expand the role of police and the armed forces in these activities. Simultaneously, Bolivian governments have pursued a variety of policies ranging from crop eradication and crop substitution to the development of the highlands and attempts to substitute the entire coca economy. For the better part of the last decade, the interdiction option has tended to subordinate all so-called alternative development programs. This trend is likely to continue throughout the 1990s.

In 1983 Bolivia established, under U.S. guidance, specialized police units, the UMOPAR, to direct counternarcotics operations. The government of Hernán Siles Zuazo (1982–1985) also agreed to eradicate 10,000 hectares of coca in return for $14.1 million in U.S. aid. Siles Zuazo was incapable of carrying out an effective counternarcotics program; in fact, hectarage under cultivation doubled between 1982 and 1985.

Moreover, in June 1984, in a rather pathetic turn of events, several UMOPAR officers were involved in the kidnapping of Siles Zuazo. To demonstrate his government's commitment to combat the drug war, in August 1984, the hapless Siles ordered the army into the Chapare region. Almost immediately critics charged that the publicity that characterized the order had served only to warn the drug lords. The weak government had to confront charges that, like the corrupt military government it had replaced, it was also providing protection to drug traffickers.

A major turning point in U.S.–Bolivian counternarcotics efforts came in July 1986 when the Bolivian government agreed to launch Operation Blast Furnace. Between July and November 1986, six Black Hawk helicopters and 160 U.S. troops provided air mobility to Bolivian UMOPAR forces. The most significant impact was a temporary disruption in coca production. Because no *peces gordos* (big fish) were arrested and only a few kilos of cocaine were confiscated, success was measured mainly by the resolve of both governments to carry out joint counternarcotics operations.

Blast Furnace also ushered in a new era for the Bolivian armed forces which, after the fiasco of their August 1984 entry into the Chapare, displayed little interest in playing a subordinate role to the UMOPAR. After engaging in joint military exercises with U.S. Southern Command troops in April 1986 and promises of military assistance, the Bolivian armed forces became more predisposed to participating in counternarcotics operations. Beginning with Blast Furnace, the navy and air force provided airlift and riverine capability to the UMOPAR forces. No role, however, was envisioned for the Bolivian army.

The burden of the operation fell on the year-old government of Víctor Paz Estenssoro, who had to contain opposition in the Congress and from organized labor. Mainly because of his ruling coalition's control over the Congress, Paz Estenssoro decided his government could afford to challenge opposition to Blast Furnace. As the former leader of the populist Movimiento Nacionalista Revolucionario (MNR) which sponsored Bolivia's agrarian reform in 1953, however, Paz Estenssoro did not want to stir the wrath of *campesino* farmers. Nevertheless, the controversy generated by Blast Furnace was greater than its accomplishments.

Blast Furnace was conceived by the U.S. embassy in La Paz as early as November 1985 without any consultation with Bolivian government officials. Even after President Paz Estenssoro authorized the operation, embassy officials gave little or no consideration to the legal implications under Bolivian law. Significantly, the Bolivian constitution prohibits the presence of foreign troops without specific congressional approval. Blast Furnace initiated a pattern of violation of Bolivian constitutional provisions supported, if not encouraged, by the U.S. embassy in La Paz. The lip service paid to democratic norms did little to prevent the erosion of the legitimacy of counternarcotics operations.

Ideally, Blast Furnace was to involve year-round activities including riverine and airlift support by the United States. Additionally, the operation required extensive intelligence gathering on the location of cocaine laboratories. Because it became mainly a political demonstration on the part of both the U.S. and Bolivian governments, however, riverine operations were never initiated. Moreover, because the U.S. military and its Bolivian UMOPAR allies relied almost exclusively on DEA intelligence, the initial success of the operation may have been jeopardized.

Blast Furnace pursued three objectives. First, cocaine-processing laboratories in the Beni region would be closed down. Second, this action would disrupt cocaine processing and consequently reduce the demand for coca leaves. Third, the price of coca leaves would fall below production prices thus forcing peasants to turn to crop substitution programs. From the Bolivian government's perspective, Blast Furnace would demonstrate its commitment to combatting drugs.

Based on the experience of Blast Furnace, Bolivian and U.S. officials argued that, if the price for the coca leaf could be depressed significantly for a prolonged period, peasants would permanently move to other, more profitable cash crops. They claimed that repressing the trafficker (or middleman) would reduce demand for coca leaves, thus depressing its market price. In fact, during the operations, many campesinos in the Chapare flocked to USAID (United States Agency for International Development) crop substitution programs; however, enough resources to satisfy all the requests were not available. The price of coca leaves fell from $125 to $15 according to some estimates. The Bolivian government also claimed that 800 traffickers had fled the country. As soon as the U.S. troops left, however, the price of coca leaves jumped back to pre–Blast Furnace levels. As noted previously, the total hectarage under cultivation increased concomitantly over the next three years.

The "success" of Blast Furnace prompted calls for a continuation of this strategy. As a result, Operation Snow Cap was initiated secretly in 1987. Special attention was given to avoiding the political backlash associated with joint counternarcotics operations. DEA strategists argued that Snow Cap was meant "to arrange the profile in such a way that it is perfectly acceptable politically, mediawise and every other way in support of what we are trying to do." Directed by the DEA and the State Department's Bureau of International Narcotics Matters (INM), Snow Cap extended a variety of interrelated aerial, waterway, and ground enforcement programs in Bolivia, Peru, and Colombia. Apart from DEA advisors and INM personnel, U.S. Coast Guard and Border Patrol agents also participated. Snow Cap was intended to suppress

> cocaine supply through the destruction of clandestine laboratory facilities, control of precursor and essential chemicals, and interdiction of the drug on land and waterways in conjunction with eradication and economic development programs. A major thrust of this strategy is to improve the resources and expertise of host government forces. (U.S. Congress, House, Committee on Foreign Affairs, 1990, p. 8)

Between 1987 and 1989, the INM leased six Huey helicopters from the Department of Defense (DOD) and loaned them to Bolivia's UMOPAR. In addition, under Snow Cap, UMOPAR troops received U.S. Army Special Forces training which included small-unit tactics, map reading, jungle survival, and communications. According to the DEA, Snow Cap yielded positive results: 30 cocaine laboratories were destroyed between 1987 and 1989; 9.5 metric tons of coca paste and cocaine base were seized; and 12 private airplanes involved in cocaine trafficking were seized.

Other figures contradicted the DEA's claims; for example, a World Bank report noted that Bolivia's coca trade had grown at an annual rate of 35 percent since 1980 and was likely to continue for the remaining years of the 1980s. Despite the efforts of Snow Cap, coca cultivation and processing continued apace. As dissatisfaction with the DEA's role and the effectiveness of Snow Cap mounted, the Bush administration stepped up efforts to either expand the role of the U.S. military or to extract a commitment from the Bolivian government to send the army into coca-growing regions.

As Blast Furnace had demonstrated, the political costs of allowing U.S. troops on Bolivian soil would be great to any government. Thus, Snow Cap became an acceptable substitute both to circumvent the political opposition in Bolivia to the use of U.S. military personnel and to impress the U.S. Congress. By the end of 1989, however, the Bush administration had insisted on increasing the role of U.S. military advisers and on using Bolivian armed forces to carry out interdiction operations.

The Bolivian government pursued a different strategy domestically, although policy was clearly supervised by the United States. A key aspect of this strategy was the July 1988 signing of Law 1008, known as the Ley de Sustancias Peligrosas y el Regimen de la Coca (Law of Dangerous Substance and the Coca Regime). Lauded as the most far-reaching antidrug law in Latin America, Law 1008 called for the voluntary eradication of coca plantations, the demarcation of coca-growing regions that would meet the demand for traditional consumption, and the establishment of thirteen special drug courts to prosecute all drug offenders. Significantly, the new law prohibited the use of herbicides in the eradication of coca leaves.

Alternative development has been the cornerstone of Bolivian policy over the

**Table 6.1**
**Bolivia's Crop Substitution Program: 1990–1995**

| Projected Crop Reduction | | | | Remaining Coca Crops | | |
|---|---|---|---|---|---|---|
| YEAR | TOTAL | CBBA/1 | La Paz | Excess | Tradit. | TOTAL |
| 1989/2 | | | | 43,753 | 12,000 | 55,753 |
| 1990 | 7,500 | 6,600 | 900 | 36,253 | 12,000 | 48,253 |
| 1991 | 7,500 | 6,600 | 900 | 28,753 | 12,000 | 40,753 |
| 1992 | 7,500 | 6,600 | 900 | 21.253 | 12,000 | 33,253 |
| 1993 | 7,500 | 7,083 | 417 | 13,753 | 12,000 | 25,753 |
| 1994 | 7,500 | 7,500 | 0 | 13,753 | 12,000 | 18,253 |
| 1995 | 6,235 | 6,235 | 0 | 0 | 12,000 | 12,000 |
| TOTAL | 43,735 | 40,636 | 3,117 | 0 | 12,000 | 12,000/3 |

1. Includes 110 hectare area in Yapacaní.
2. 1989 is the base year of reference
3. Traditional crops: La Paz 5,000 and Cochabamba 7,000 has.
Source: CONALID, La Estrategia Boliviana Contra el Trafico de Drogas. (La Paz, 1990), Annex III.

past five years. The main long-term objective of the past two governments has been to substitute the coca-cocaine informal economy with a solid and diversified formal economy. This alternative development strategy entails an almost insurmountable task of substituting not only crops but also jobs and income for thousands who have come to depend on the drug industry.

The transformation of the agricultural sector in Bolivia over the course of the past decade is noteworthy. During the past fifteen years, a rapid shift from other agricultural products to coca growing has occurred. In the mid–1980s this shift accelerated as a result of hyper-inflationary pressures and neoliberal policies put forth to stabilize the economy. According to a government estimate, 61,000 families, or 300,000 people, depend directly on the production of coca. In 1989, the production of coca accounted for 12 percent of gross domestic product (GDP). In short, alternative development implies a profound structural change of the Bolivian economy which can be accomplished only with large amounts of foreign aid.

The current Paz Zamora government's Programa Nacional de Inversión de Desarrollo Alternativo has put forth a six-year time table for the "substitution of the coca economy." As Table 6–1 illustrates, between 1990 and 1995, this program intends to eradicate 43,735 hectares of excess coca production. The Bolivian government has also been quick to point to recent success in meeting crop-eradication (see Table 6–2) targets mandated by bilateral agreements with the United States. In the same time period, the economy will lose $385.9 million in production, 175,300 jobs, and $195.6 million in revenue (see Table 6–3). Bolivian government officials claim that 1.8 billion dollars in the same time period will be required to carry out its coca for development project (see Table 6–4) for breakdown). Securing financing for these programs has proven elusive, especially given the U.S. focus on interdiction and militarized solutions.

**Table 6.2**
**Total Eradication of Coca Plantations in Bolivia: 1987–1990**

| | Total Ha. | TOTAL NUMBER OF Ha. ERADICATED 1987 | 1988 | 1989 | 1990 | TOTAL ERADIC. | LEFT TO ERADICATE |
|---|---|---|---|---|---|---|---|
| Trad. | 6,859 | 3764 | 27.80 | 158.6 | --- | 186.1 | 6,672.85 |
| Excess | 53,253 | 1,345.4 | 1,400.5 | 1840.2 | 7,766.1 | 12,352.4 | 40,900.6 |
| Illicit | 598 | - | 47.33 | 440.4 | 40.07 | 527.8 | 70.2 |
| Total | 60.710 | 1,345.8 | 1,475. | 2,439.3 | 7,806.2 | 13,066.4 | 47,643.6 |

Source: Based on data from CONALID, La Estrategia Boliviana Contra el Trafico Ilicito de Drogas. (La Paz, 1990), Annex II.

**Table 6.3**
**Projected Economic Losses Stemming from the Eradication of Coca: 1990–1995 (in 1989 millions of U.S. dollars)**

| COCA AND DERIVATIVES | | | | REMAINING SECTORS | | | TOTAL (1) | | |
|---|---|---|---|---|---|---|---|---|---|
| Period | Prod. | Empl.* | Rev. | Prod. | Empl.* | Reve. | Prod. | Empl.* | Rev. |
| 1990 | 33.0 | 16.3 | 35.3 | 32.1 | 12.8 | -2.4 | 65.1 | 29.1 | 32.9 |
| 1991 | 32.9 | 16.1 | 35.3 | 31.4 | 12.7 | -2.5 | 64.3 | 28.8 | 32.8 |
| 1992 | 32.9 | 16.1 | 35.7 | 31.8 | 13.2 | -2.8 | 64.7 | 29.3 | 32.9 |
| 1993 | 32.9 | 16.2 | 36.3 | 32.3 | 13.6 | -1.6 | 65.2 | 29.8 | 34.7 |
| 1994 | 32.9 | 16.3 | 36.7 | 34.1 | 14.8 | -3.8 | 67.0 | 31.0 | 32.9 |
| 1995 | 27.5 | 13.5 | 31.2 | 32.1 | 13.8 | -1.8 | 59.6 | 27.3 | 29.4 |
| Total | 192.1 | 94.4 | 210.5 | 193.8 | 80.9 | 14.9 | 385.9 | 175.3 | 195.6 |

* in thousands of persons.
1. The gain in revenue in the remaining sectors is owed to a depreciation of the real exchange rate value produced by a reduction in the availability of revenue from the coca economy. This situation could be reverted with foreign aid and investment.
Source: CONALID, La Estrategia Boliviana Contra el Trafico Ilicito de Drogas. (La Paz, 1990), Appendix IV.

One of obstacles to the alternative development strategy is that payments to peasants in exchange for voluntarily eradicating coca crops have been very slow. As coca prices recover, the attractiveness of substitution is not great to peasants who cannot make a living from other crops. Additionally, coca substitutes, such as macadamia nuts, take years to generate profitable returns. Still others have start-up costs; moreover, *campesinos* are not guaranteed a market for new products. In 1990 the Bolivian government presented a list of seventy-five alternative development projects to the World Bank that required $611.4 million dollars in investment. Clearly the potential for carrying out a great number of projects is there; however, financing has been slow to come. Perhaps the greatest obstacle to the alternative development is the absence of markets to which Bolivian agricultural products can be exported. The Bush administration's Andean Trade Preference Act has faced an uphill battle. Strong opposition in the U.S. Congress to any type of agricultural product will block attempts to open the U.S. markets to Andean products.

**Table 6.4**
**Financing Necessary to Carry out Coca Economy Substitution: 1990–1995 (in 1989 millions of U.S. dollars)**

| Period | Investment | F.C.S | Balance of Payments | TOTAL |
|---|---|---|---|---|
| 1990 | 246.7 | 33.7 | 32.9 | 313.3 |
| 1991 | 246.8 | 33.7 | 32.8 | 313.3 |
| 1992 | 246.7 | 33.7 | 32.9 | 313.3 |
| 1993 | 244.9 | 33.7 | 34.7 | 313.3 |
| 1994 | 246.6 | 33.7 | 33.0 | 313.3 |
| 1995 | 196.0 | 28.1 | 29.0 | 253.1 |
| TOTAL | 1427.7 | 196.6 | 195.3 | 1819.6 /1 |

I) Capital stock required to substitute the coca economy.
This table reflects approximate and conservative data; thus, it should be estimated that the financing required for this program would range between $200 and 300 million.
Source: CONALID, La Estrategia Boliviana Contra el Tráfico Ilícito de Drogas. (La Paz: 1990), Annex V.

Moreover, the Bolivian government does not açknowlege that voluntary eradication targets may have been successful only because of temporary low coca prices resulting from both the disruption of trafficking operations in Colombia and a glut in the coca market. Because of the lack of alternative crops, Bolivian *campesinos* who voluntarily eradicated their crops have also planted new coca fields. In late 1990 and early 1991, the price for coca leaves rebounded from the low of $10 to around $47 per hundred pounds. These signs do not bode well for alternative development goals.

The fact remains that, without a great infusion of foreign investment or aid and a coherent and long-term rural development component, Bolivia's Coca for Development thesis is doomed to failure. In the Bush administration, there are few enthusiasts who embrace this approach and perceive it only as an obstacle to a so-called real solution. The U.S. Congress, in turn, continuously regrets Bolivia's decision to ban the use of herbicides for the eradication of coca plantations and finds little political use for alternative development programs. Consequently, Bolivia's only choice has been to accept military assistance and to push ahead with its intention to order the army into the drug fray.

## THE THRUST TOWARD MILITARIZATION

Following the February 1990 Cartagena Summit, where the presidents of Bolivia, Colombia, Peru, and the United States came together to discuss hemispheric responses to the drug crisis, the Bush administration claimed that the first antidrug cartel had been signed. U.S. officials noted that the Bolivians, as well as Colombians and Peruvians, had finally accepted their proposals to escalate repressive activities, including militarizing the battle against drug lords. In turn, the Andean presidents claimed that the Americans had finally acquiesced to their demands for an alternative development policy and had increased economic aid. The Andean presidents and President Bush agreed that responsibility for combatting the drug war should be shared. They also agreed, however, that policy distinctions should be made between consumer, trafficker, and producer nations.

As 1990 wound down, however, the specifics of the Bush administration's Andean strategy was unveiled. The strategy indeed calls for a multifaceted approach to combatting the production and trafficking of cocaine. In a March 1991 report to Congress, the administration noted the strategy's four principal objectives. First, the administration seeks to "strengthen the political will and institutional capability" of the three Andean governments to enable them to attack the cocaine trade. In theory, diplomatic, professional, and training missions will aid these governments in carrying out effective programs to counter the drug trade.

A second objective of the Andean strategy is to improve the intelligence-gathering capability of both law enforcement and military institutions. The strategy calls for assistance to police and military units to ensure that they are "well-equipped, trained, and cooperate in an integrated strategy." For the Bush administration, "[i]t has become clear that the Andean nations can conduct more effective counter-narcotics operations with the involvement of the armed forces; this is especially true where the traffickers and the insurgents have joined forces" (U.S. Congress, House, The Andean Drug Strategy and the Role of the U.S. Military, p. 2).

In short, the Bush administration's principal objective is to involve the Latin American militaries in the drug war to target coca-growing regions, to eradicate coca plantations, to identify and destroy cocaine labs, and to shut down clandestine airstrips throughout the region. Because of the size of the three countries and the remoteness of the regions where drug activity is carried out, the Andean strategy argues that the capacity of law enforcement units to deal with the problem of drug production and trafficking is extremely limited.

Claiming that U.S. military assistance will strengthen democracy in the region, the administration's report to Congress cites five reasons for involving the military in counternarcotics operations. First, the report notes that civilian governments negotiate and approve all military assistance although the details are worked out by military-to-military contacts. Second, the administration argues that a poorly trained and impoverished military is more susceptible to corruption and human rights abuses. Third, U.S. government strategists insist that, if the military is sidelined, it would be critical of civilian counternarcotics efforts and would constitute a grave threat to democracy. Fourth, the report claims that involving the military would augment scarce resources available to fight the war on drugs; consequently, the battle would be carried out in a more effective manner. Finally, the U.S. administration assumes that only with the involvement of the military can a safe and secure environment be provided for economic growth and democracy.

The administration claims it is providing assistance to develop specialized skills for conducting counternarcotics operations, not to create major combat units. In other words, its principal aim is to support the law enforcement activities of both military and police units. Under present policy, the United States forbids the use of counternarcotics assistance for other purposes, such as fighting insurgents. In Colombia and Peru, however, this distinction has been a difficult one to make. Because it is providing the Andean governments with the tools and assistance to defend their political will and sovereignty, the administration argues that U.S. policy is not "militarizing" the counternarcotics campaign in the Andes. This logic is reminiscent of the rationale employed by the United States to bolster military aid to El Salvador throughout the 1980s in the name of strengthening that country's democracy.

An expanded role for the Department of Defense has prompted concern about a possible involvement for the U.S. armed forces in Bolivia and elsewhere in the Andes. The United States is careful to point out, however, that DOD personnel are forbidden to accompany local forces on "actual operations or engage in any activities where hostilities are imminent" (U.S. Department of State, International Narcotics Control Strategy Report). This prohibition does not extend to U.S. civilian personnel, such as DEA agents, who usually accompany Bolivian forces on counternarcotics operations. Because both DEA and local military and police forces have undergone Special Forces military training, counternarcotics operations are indeed militarized.

The third objective of the Andean Strategy claims that

> by strengthening ties between police and military units and creating major violator task forces to identify key organizations, bilateral law enforcement and military assistance will enable the host government forces to target the leaders of the major cocaine trafficking organizations, impede the transfer of drug generated funds, and seize their assets within the United States and in those foreign nations in which they operate. (U.S. Department of State, International Narcotics Control Strategy Report)

The Andean strategy's third objective does not distinguish between civilian and military law enforcement efforts; in fact, the objective of current policy in Bolivia is to subordinate the civilian police to the military's counternarcotics operations. The thrust of the policy, measured by the amount of assistance earmarked for the Bolivian military, is to strengthen the armed forces without serious consideration being given to the long-range impact their strengthening may have on Bolivian democracy.

The fourth objective of the Andean strategy is to expand economic assistance beginning in fiscal year 1991. The Bush administration claims that one half of the \$2.2 billion five-year plan will consist of economic assistance (see Table 6–5).

**Table 6.5**
**Andean Strategy Narcotics-Related Funding: Bolivia 1989–1994**

| | FY 1989 Actual | FY 90 Estimate1 | FY 91 Request | FY 92 Plan | FY 93 Plan | FY 94 Plan | Total 5-year plan |
|---|---|---|---|---|---|---|---|
| Military Assistance2 | $5.8 | $33.7 | $40.9 | $40.9 | $40.9 | $40.9 | $197.3 |
| Economic Assistance | $4.0 | $95.8 | $130.8 | $130.8 | $130.8 | $130.8 | $528.9 |
| Law Enforcement3 | $10.0 | $15.7 | $15.7 | $15.7 | $15.7 | $15.7 | $78.5 |
| DEA Support | $4.0 | $6.6 | $6.6 | $6.6 | $6.6 | $6.6 | $33.0 |
| TOTAL | $23.8 | $96.7 | $159.0 | $194.0 | $194.0 | $194.0 | $837.7 |

1/The obligations projected for FY90 are approximate and adjustments may be made during the course of the year. They include Byrd Amendment reductions.
2.Military assistance includes both Foreign Military Financing (FMF) and International Military Education Training (IMET). FY90 IMET projections are: Bolivia $0.5 million. FY91 projections are Bolivia $0.9 million.
3. The Law Enforcement category for FY 90 includes $38.2 million in International Narcotics Matters (INM) funds as well as a portion ($16.5 million) of the $125 million in FMF appropriated for counternarcotics programs in section 602 of the Foreign Operations, Export Financing, and Related Programs Act for FY 90.

Source: Office of National Drug Control Policy June 20, 1990.

Disbursement, however, is tied to counternarcotics performance, economic policies, and respect for human rights. U.S. economic assistance includes financing for crop substitution and alternative development, drug awareness, administration of justice, balance of payments support, and export promotion.

This final objective, however, appears almost to be an afterthought in the administration's report to Congress. As the House of Representatives Government Operations Committee noted,

> the Committee has become acutely aware of the enormous economic impact the coca economy has had on Bolivia, and the need to develop economic solutions. Yet in the [administration's] rush to win the drug war through military and law enforcement efforts, the Administration has not prioritized these central economic dimensions of the problem. (U.S. Congress, The Andean Drug Strategy, p. 10)

## BOLIVIA'S INTERNATIONAL LINKAGES FOR DRUG CONTROL

Apart from arrangements made with the United States, Bolivia has made several other attempts to secure international cooperation to carry out counternarcotics efforts. In the mid–1980s most Bolivian efforts culminated only in declarations of support from other Latin American nations. This was especially true between the Andean Pact nations, which are the most affected by the cocaine trade. In 1986, however, the Bolivian government signed the Rodrigo Lara

Bonilla accord with member nations of the Andean Pact. Signed in honor of Rodrigo Lara Bonilla, Colombia's Justice Minister who was murdered by drug lords, this agreement was significant because, for the first time, linkages were established between the Andean countries to carry out jointly counternarcotics activities.

In 1988 Bolivian members of the Andean Parliament signed a declaration expressing their commitment to stamp out cocaine trafficking. The declaration was endorsed by members of the U.S. House of Representatives' Select Committee on Drug Abuse and Narcotics Council. A few days later the Andean Parliament signed the so-called Cooperation and Coordination Agreement with the Organization of American States' Inter-American Commission for Controlling Drug Abuse (CICAD).

Bolivia's international counternarcotics commitments are embodied in United Nations' conventions. In 1961 Bolivia subscribed to a UN convention on drug trafficking which brought together in a single document twelve multilateral antidrug treaties signed since 1912. In that agreement, no distinction was made between coca leaves and cocaine: both were described as dangerous drugs. Bolivia also agreed to eliminate completely its production and consumption of coca leaves within twenty-five years. The military governments that ruled Bolivia between 1964 and 1978 ratified the UN convention.

In June 1987, the United Nations sponsored an international conference in Vienna on illicit drug trafficking where a broad plan for future counternarcotics activities was conceived. Bolivia was urged to control its supply of coca; however, the recommendation distinguished between coca leaves consumed traditionally and those used for the production of coca paste.

Representatives from 120 countries, including Bolivia, attended the 15 November–20 December 1988 United Nations Convention against Illicit Traffic in Narcotic Drugs and Psychotropic Substances, in Vienna, Austria. Bolivian Minister of Foreign Affairs Guillermo Bedregal was elected president of the convention. A thirty-four-article declaration, based mainly on the 1961 convention, was the product of this month-long meeting. Four points stand out. First, the convention declared that, on its own, the coca leaf is not a dangerous substance or a drug. While approving the traditional uses of coca, the convention also noted, however, that coca grown specifically for the cocaine industry should be targeted for eradication. Second, the delegates at the convention agreed that violence was not to be employed as a means to reduce coca plantations. Instead, the convention declaration called for integrated rural development programs. Third, the convention called on Bolivia and other drug-producing nations to investigate the fortunes and real estate properties of all people believed to be involved in drug trafficking. Finally, each country was urged to control precursor chemicals, airplanes, and guns used by traffickers.

These four issues, presented by the Bolivian delegation at the convention, were the product of intense negotiations between coca growers and the Paz Estenssoro government. Peasant leaders, however, were still disappointed by the convention's refusal to endorse a ban on chemical products for the eradication of coca leaves. In large measure, the UN Drug Convention set the tone of all future negotiations with European and other Latin American nations. The current Paz Zamora government has also endorsed the UN Drug Convention despite having succumbed to U.S. pressures to increase interdiction efforts.

The Bolivian government has signed several agreements with the United Nations Fund for Drug Abuse Control (UNDFAC) to help fund alternative development programs in the Chapare region. These agreements provided funding for rural electrification, the construction of roads, and the development of a dairy industry in the same region.

## CONCLUSION

Drug consumption in Bolivia has increased dramatically over the last decade; however, accurate figures on the size of the consumer population in Bolivia are unavailable. The figure most often cited—although it is based mainly on nonscientific estimates from the DEA or Bolivian government institutions—is that 240,000 Bolivians, or 4 percent of the nation's population, are addicted to cocaine or its derivatives.

Consumers cross class barriers, but like elsewhere, most prevention and rehabilitation programs reach the upper and middle classes while the poor have no recourse. Ranging from the smoking of *pitillos* by homeless children to the effects of acetone and kerosene on the feet of *zepeadores*, who are hired for pennies to stamp coca leaves into paste, the Bolivian health care system is overwhelmed by the social impact of the drug trade.

A number of programs exist to aid Bolivia in drug prevention; however, the emphasis on interdiction has left little room for such programs. Until the late 1980s poorly prepared charity groups, such as women's associations in the larger cities, were among the most visible providers of assistance in terms of prevention, rehabilitation, and treatment. Other nongovernmental organizations (NGOs), such as religious organizations, have also been at the forefront in prevention programs. They are, however, underfunded and understaffed to deal with the growing numbers of addicts and other victims of the cocaine trade.

Several other very visible and prominent NGOs are involved in preventive programs. These include the Bolivian Red Cross, the Italian Center for Solidarity (UOMO project), the U.S. embassy–funded Drug Awareness Campaign (CESE), and the Bolivian Private Entrepreneurs Confederation's SEAMOS project.

Governmental responses to Bolivia's drug addiction problem has been extremely slow, although, in the late 1970s, a state-run National Institute for Research on Drug Addiction (INIF) was founded. This institution depends on state funding to carry out preventive, treatment, and rehabilitation programs primarily in urban areas. Like many state-run programs, it lacks adequate funding levels. The Preventive Education Department of the National Direction for the

Control of Dangerous Substances carries out the same activities in the rural sector.

In 1988, the government of Paz Estenssoro established a multiagency National Council for the Prevention, Treatment, and Rehabilitation of Drug Addicts (Consejo Nacional de Prevención Tratamiento, y Rehabilitación del Uso Indebido de Drogas). This task force has been continued under the Paz Zamora government. AID and the United Nations have provided some funding to the Bolivian government to conduct a mass media drug prevention and education campaign. England, Germany, and Sweden, among other European nations, have also provided some funding for these programs. In the main, however, the Bolivian drug consumer lacks access to any state-run treatment or rehabilitation facility.

## BIBLIOGRAPHY

Abbot, Michael H. "The Army and the Drug War: Politics or National Security?" *Parameters U.S. Army War College Quarterly* 18, 4 (December 1988): 95–112.

*Andean Anti-Drug Efforts: A Report to the Congress*. Washington, D.C.: Departments of Defense and State, March 1991.

Aquino Huerta, Armando. *Legislación y Procedimiento en Narcotráfico*. La Paz: EDVIL, 1990.

Bedregal Gutierrez, Guillermo, and Ruddy Viscarra Pando. *La Lucha Boliviana Contra la Agresión del Narcotráfico*. La Paz: Los Amigos del Libro, 1989.

Gamarra, Eduardo A. "Bolivia," in *Latin America and Caribbean Contemporary Record*, edited by James M. Malloy and Eduardo A. Gamarra, vol. 7. New York: Holmes and Meier, 1990.

———. "Bolivia," in *Latin America and Caribbean Contemporary Record*, edited by James Malloy and Eduardo A. Gamarra, vol. 8. New York: Holmes and Meier, 1991.

———. "Drugs, Politics and Foreign Policy in Bolivia." Paper delivered at the International Symposium on Money Laundering, Miami, Florida, 26–28 October, 1989.

Gamarra, Eduardo A., and James M. Malloy. "Mass Politics and Elite Arrangements: Elections and Democracy in Bolivia." In *Bolivia after Hyperinflation*, edited by Jerry Ladman and Juan A. Morales. Tempe: Arizona State University, Center for Latin American Studies, forthcoming.

Healy, Kevin. "Structural Adjustment, Peasant Agriculture and Coca in Bolivia." Paper presented at the 16th International Congress of the Latin American Studies Association, 4–6 April 1991, Washington, D.C.

Honorable Cámara de Diputados. *La H. Cámara de diputados discute los antecedentes, el presente y el futuro del Narcotráfico en Bolivia*. La Paz: Cámara de Diputados, 1987.

ILDIS. *Temas de Política Social: Efectos del Narcotráfico*. La Paz: ILDIS, 1988.

Malloy, James M., and Eduardo Gamarra. *Revolution and Reaction: Bolivia 1964–1985*. New Brunswick, N.J.: Transaction Books, 1988.

Menzel, Sewall. "Operation Blast Furnace." *Army* (November 1989): 24–32.

Office of National Drug Control Policy. *National Drug Control Strategy*. Washington, D.C.: U.S. Government Printing Office, 1991.

Pacini, Deborah, and Christine Franquemont, eds. *Coca and Cocaine: Effects on People and Policy in Latin America*. Cornell Latin American Studies Program and Cultural Survival Report 23. Ithaca, N.Y.: Cornell University, 1986.

Presidencia de la República. "Estrategia Nacional del Desarrollo Alternativo 1990." La Paz: Presidencia de la República, 1990.

Serrano Torrico, Servando, ed. *Ley del Régimen de la Coca y Sustancias Controladas*. La Paz: Editorial Serrano, 1988.

U.S. Congress. Committee on Foreign Affairs. House, *Hearings on Operation Snow Cap: Past, Present and Future*. 23 May 1990, 8.

———. Subcommittee on Western Hemisphere Affairs of the Committee on Foreign Affairs. *Hearings on the Andean Initiative*. 6, 20 June 1990.

———. *The Andean Drug Strategy and the Role of the U.S. Military*. Report of the Defense Policy Panel and Investigations Subcommittee of the Committee on Armed Services. January 1990.

———. *United States Anti-Narcotics Activities in the Andean Region*. Committee on Government Operations, Thirty-eighth Report, November 30, 1990. (Washington, D.C.)

United States Department of State, Bureau of International Narcotics Matters. *International Narcotics Control Strategy Report* (Washington, D.C.: Department of State, March 1991).

U.S. Government Accounting Office. *Drug Control U.S. Supported Efforts in Colombia and Bolivia*. Washington, D.C.: Government Accounting Office, 1988, 44.

# 7

# Brazil

LUIZA THEREZA BAPTISTA DE MATTOS

## INTRODUCTION

Brazil is the largest industrial country in Latin America, and although it is the eighth leading economy of the world, it is ranked as the forty-fifth country in terms of the quality of life. During the 1970s and 1980s, this Portuguese-speaking South American country was preoccupied by severe economic and social problems. One of the newest problems, commencing in a sizable fashion in the late 1980s, is the production, consumption, and trafficking of illicit drugs, namely cocaine and marijuana. The country's economic crisis, however, has fueled the drug problem on both the demand and the supply sides. The drug problem is exacerbated by the fact that the country has as it neighbors the biggest producers of drugs in South America.

Since Brazil is the largest country in South America, bordering on all the other nations of the South American continent except Ecuador and Chile, it is the major transshipment country for cocaine produced in Colombia, Bolivia, and Peru, which is transshipped to North American, Middle Eastern, or European markets. Brazil is also a major legal producer of ether and acetone, chemicals that are used to produce cocaine hydrochloride. In some areas of the Amazon jungle the Indians cultivate a variety of cocaine known as *epadu*. The country is also a large producer of marijuana, which is consumed domestically. Marijuana is the most commonly used drug in the country and it is grown in almost all the Brazilian states.

## COUNTRY BACKGROUND

Brazil is the largest tropical country in the world and the fifth largest country in the world. To the north it borders on Guyana, Suriname, French Guiana, and

Venezuela; to the northwest, Colombia; to the west, Peru and Bolivia; to the southwest, Paraguay and Argentina; to the south, Uruguay; and to the east, the Atlantic Ocean. Its borders with the main producing countries of drugs in South America include 1,664 kilometers with Colombia, 2,995 kilometers with Peru, and 3,126 kilometers with Bolivia. Brazil's border with Bolivia is its largest international border.

Brazil is a federal republic with twenty-six states and a federal district, in which the capital is located. Its supreme law is the Federal Constitution, which was published on October 5, 1988. The states have individual constitutions and elected governments. Brazil has only one drug law, Law 6368, which was published on October 21, 1976.

Brazil's estimated population in 1990 was more than 140 million, almost equally divided between men and women. The population is young; nearly 88 million Brazilians are under thirty years of age. Life expectancy is 62.3 years for men and 67.6 for women. The population is composed primarily of white descendants of Portuguese colonizers and other European immigrants, mostly Italian, Spanish, and German. Six percent are black descendants of slaves. Thirty-nine percent are mulattoes. There are also some Orientals, especially Japanese, and the Native Indians who have been reduced to small groups in some parts of the country.

Brazil has one of the biggest external debts in the world, and its government remains preoccupied by its severe economic problems. From the Sarney to Collor administrations, the country has been rocked by bouts of hyperinflation, industrial slowdown, and declining social conditions. Finance ministers have come and gone in rapid succession, creating problems in the continuity of reform measures and complicating a resolution of the external debt problem.

On March 15, 1990, Brazil's first elected civilian president since 1960, Fernando Collor de Mello, became the nation's chief executive. This development was significant because it consolidated the process of democratization that had been under way since 1985 when José Sarney became president after the president-elect Tancredo Neves unexpectedly died. Sarney's sudden rise to Brazil's highest office was unexpected, and his tenure was one of the country's more difficult periods. Sarney did not appear to have a profound concern about the illicit drug trade in Brazil, although the government did watch matters closely. Collor, on the other hand, seemed to be concerned about the drug problem early in his presidency. On April 28, 1990, he jogged wearing a T-shirt on which was written "Drugs: Out of Here," and he started a campaign against the use of illicit drugs. This campaign was his answer to a demonstration made by the mothers of Corumba, the capital of the state of Mato Grosso do Sul which borders on Bolivia. This was the first direct engagement of a president of Brazil in the war against drugs.

## THE NEW CONSTITUTION AND THE DRUG ISSUE

Although Brazil still suffers with economic and social problems, its legislation is very modern and shows a societal concern with illicit drugs. The new constitution, which was promulgated on October 5, 1988, includes provisions on the war against drugs. In the second title, Fundamental Rights and Guarantees, in its first chapter on individual and collective rights and obligations, article 5, in paragraph XLIII, states that trafficking in narcotics and similar drugs is a crime that does not qualify for bail or for mitigation of punishment. In article 5, paragraph II, the extradition of Brazilian citizens is prohibited, except for naturalized citizens who have committed a common crime prior to their citizenship and those against whom there is proof of involvement in trafficking in narcotics and similar drugs. Title VIII of the Social Order, in chapter V, on social communication, in article 220, paragraph 4, provides that commercial advertising of tobacco, alcoholic beverages, agricultural poison, medical drugs, and therapies shall be subject to legal restrictions and will, whenever necessary, include warnings of the injurious effects that can follow from their use.

Title VIII of the Social Order, in chapter VII on the family, the child, the adolescent, and the elderly, in article 227, paragraph 3, contains prevention programs and specialized care for the child and the adolescent addict of narcotics and similar drugs. In title IX, General Constitutional Provisions, article 243 provides for the confiscation of lands in any region of the country on which unlawful crops of psychotropic plants are found. Article 243 provides that all goods of monetary value taken in custody in connection with the traffic in narcotics and similar drugs will be confiscated and that the proceeds therefrom will be used for the treatment of users, the prevention of drug use, and the repression of the drug traffic.

## BRAZILIAN BILLS ON DRUGS

On January 1, 1942, the Penal Code (Bill 2848 of December 7, 1940) established a place for drug-related crimes in article 281. The Penal Code comprises two parts: the general part and the special part. The special part, which defines crimes, has been in effect since 1942. The general part of the Brazilian Penal Code was enacted by Bill 7209, passed on July 11, 1984. Drug-related crimes were governed by the 1940 Penal Code in its special part, in article 281, until 1968. In 1968, decree 385, of December 26, modified article 281 of the Penal Code and established the same penalty for the drug trafficker and the nonaddict drug user. On October 29, 1971, Bill 5726 was revised: It regards the drug addict as a sick person who needs treatment.

Another important piece of legislation is Law 6368, passed on October 21, 1976, which criminalizes the illegal traffic and misuse of any drugs and substances that cause physical or psychological dependence. This law is a very modern law because it focuses on the great value of education in the war against addiction. Indeed, according to article 5: "Teacher training programs will include material about drugs and substances which result in physical or psychic dependence, so that this material will be disseminated observing scientific principles."

Article 5 also establishes that teaching of the disciplines of natural sciences, which are a part of the curriculum of courses of the first level, will include material that explains the nature and effects of drugs and substances that result in physical or psychological dependence. Law 6368/76 establishes a sentence for the drug user (nonaddict).

The crime includes acquiring, keeping, or bringing on one's person, for one's use, any drugs or substances that result in physical or psychological dependence, without authorization or in violation of legal or regulatory determinations. The law exempts any agent, who due to addiction or being under the effect of a substance that results in physical or psychological dependence (no matter what act was practiced at the time), was unable to understand the illicit character of the act. On the other hand, if the agent did not possess, at the time of the action or omission, full capacity to understand the illegal character of the fact, or acted pursuant to this diminished understanding, the sentence may be reduced by from one-third to two-thirds.

## DRUG POLICY

Brazil is a major trafficking country and is the main producer of ether and acetone in South America. Additionally, many clandestine laboratories are being installed in the major cities for the industrial production of illegal drugs, causing an increase in the drug trade. Many of those laboratories have been located and dismantled by the police. Because of the widespread danger posed by the drug trade, the government is very concerned about the problem and is trying to protect especially its youth from the drug scourge. On the domestic level, the National Congress is drafting complementary legislation (ordinary law) to regulate the provisions of the 1988 constitution. A new drug bill has been prepared by a group of experts (jurists) and is being debated by the National Congress.

Law 6368, of October 21, 1976, in chapter I, on prevention, states in article 3: "The activities of prevention, inspection and repression on the traffic and use of drugs or substances that result in physical or psychological dependence will be integrated in the National Prevention, Inspection and Repression System, formed by the set of organs that exercise these functions at the federal, state and municipal levels."

The Executive Branch has established an organization to deal with the mechanisms of coordination and control to be exercised specifically at the federal, state, and municipal government levels.

Decree 85110, of September 12, 1980, created the National System for the Prevention, Supervision and Repression of Narcotics and gave other provisions. It integrates the activities for the prevention, supervision, and repression of the traffic and use of narcotics or substances that cause physical or psychological dependence as well as the activities for the recovery of physical or psychological dependents.

The objectives of the National System for the Prevention, Supervision and Repression of Narcotics are established in article 2:

1. to formulate the national narcotic policy, to associate and provide the compatibility of the national plans with regional, municipal and state plans as well as to supervise its respective execution;
2. to establish priority among the activities of the System, through technical, economical and administrative opinions;
3. to modernize the structure and the proceedings of the administration in the field of prevention, supervision and repression, searching for its constant development and efficiency;
4. to establish continuous and permanent exchange and flow of information among the central organ of the system and international organizations in order to facilitate the decision and planning proceedings and processes;
5. to encourage research, aiming at the development of the inspection and supervision control of the traffic and use of narcotics or substances that cause physical and psychological dependence;
6. to promote, before and with the competent organs, in order to include the teaching and instructions related to narcotics or substances that cause physical or psychological dependence, into the programs and courses for the location of teachers with the purpose of transmitting such instructions and teaching, observing the scientific principles;
7. to promote, before and with the competent organs, the inclusion of specific items into the curriculums and programs of the elementary schools and junior high schools, in the field of science, with the purpose of informing and clarifying the students as to the nature and effect of narcotics or substances that cause physical or psychological dependence.

The National System for the Prevention, Supervision and Repression of Narcotics contains a central organ, known as the Federal Council of Narcotics (CONFEN), which is the sanitary supervision agency of the Ministry of Health. CONFEN is the Organ for the Repression of Narcotics of the Federal Police Department, the Federal Board of Education, the supervision and inspection organ of the secretariat of the federal revenue of the Ministry of Finance, the National Institute of Medical Assistance for Social Welfare (WNAMPS), the Brazilian Legion Foundation for Assistance (LBA), and the National Foundation for the Welfare of Minors, attached to the Ministry of Social Work and Welfare. Every one of these agencies is subject to supervision by the Federal Council of Narcotics in regard to their activities, which are established by CONFEN.

CONFEN is a second-level, deliberative organ within the Ministry of Justice. It receives technical, administrative, and financial assistance from the General Office of the Ministry of Justice. Its head offices are located in Brasilia. Its purposes are to propose national narcotics policy; to plan and carry out the strategy; to coordinate, supervise, control, and inspect all activities related to the traffic and use of narcotics and other substances that cause physical or psychological dependence; and to carry out other functions and activities related to the objectives of the National System for the Prevention, Supervision and Repression of Narcotics.

CONFEN comprises one representative of the Ministry of Justice; one representative of the Ministry of Health; one representative of the Ministry of Education and Culture; one representative of the Ministry of Social Work and Welfare; one representative of the Ministry of Finance; one representative of the Ministry of Foreign Affairs; one representative of the Organ for the Repression of Narcotics of the Federal Police Department; one representative of the Sanitary Vigilance Organ of the Ministry of Health; one jurist of renown with experience in narcotics affairs, who is elected and appointed by the Minister of Justice; and one medical doctor in psychiatry with a significant amount of experience in the field of narcotics, who is nominated by the Brazilian Medical Association and appointed by the Ministry of Justice. Each member of CONFEN has a substitute. CONFEN members and their substitutes are nominated by the organs of the entities to which they belong and are officially appointed by the Minister of Justice.

CONFEN members and their respective delegates are appointed for three years, and they can be reappointed at the discretion of the Minister of Justice. The chairman of the CONFEN is one of the members who is selected and appointed by the Minister of Justice. The chairman, besides his personal vote, has the tie-breaking vote. The chairman is responsible for directing, coordinating, and supervising the activities of CONFEN, particularly representing the council at all and any necessary functions; summoning and presiding at the meetings and ordering the carrying out of decisions; approving the agenda of the meetings; signing, jointly with the council members, the decisions and resolutions of the council; appointing members to constitute committees; promulgating ad referendum of the staff and complementary norms related to the functioning of the council, and the order of the works; promulgating all necessary administrative acts; and practicing and executing all further necessary acts for the complete fulfillment of the objectives of the council.

The responsibilities of the members of CONFEN are to participate and vote at the plenary sittings, to report on the subjects assigned to them, to propose or request information that may be useful for a better appreciation of the subjects under study, and to perform other activities assigned to them by the chairman.

Representatives of interested entities, who contribute to clarifying certain subjects which are of interest to the council, may participate in the discussions and meeting, but they have no right to vote, and they act of and at the opinion of the chairman.

CONFEN has an executive secretariat, which is directed, coordinated, and supervised by the executive secretary and is subordinated to the chairman. In turn, the executive secretary is responsible to elaborate and submit to the chairman the agenda of the meetings; to act as secretary of the meetings; to draw up the respective minutes and to promote the publications of the summaries, compendiums, or extracts of the decisions and resolutions; to prepare the annual report of the activities of the council; to promote and prepare all the correspondence of the council; to issue the certificates prepared and signed by the chairman; and to carry out all other activities assigned by the chairman.

Ordinary meetings of CONFEN are held once each month. Extraordinary meetings can be held when summoned by the chairman or by one-third of its members. The meetings must be held with a legal quorum, which is the presence of the majority of its members.

Decisions may be made by the majority of members present at the meetings. Strict secrecy may be requested by the council at the meetings, when the subjects of the agenda so require. At the meetings, CONFEN may deliberate on the creation of temporary committees to examine specific subjects for the purpose of reaching its goals.

The organs of the federal administration, in cooperation with the National System for the Prevention, Supervision and Repression of Narcotics, must carry out and fulfill all the decisions of CONFEN. The Sanitary Vigilance Organ of the Ministry of Health is another constituent member of the National System for Prevention, Supervision and Repression of Narcotics. Its responsibility is to carry out the supervision and inspection of narcotics or substances that cause physical or psychic dependence.

The Organization for the Repression of Narcotics of the Federal Police Department is responsible to prevent and enforce the laws against the illegal use and traffic of narcotics or substances that cause physical or psychological dependence.

The Federal Board of Education carries out normative orientation and supervision of the subjects concerned in the curriculas and programs of the courses for the training of teachers for elementary schools and junior high schools.

The Supervision and Inspection Organ of the secretariat of federal revenue of the Ministry of Finance carries out the supervision and inspection of the traffic of narcotics or substances that cause physical dependence at borders, ports, and airports.

The National Institute of Medical Assistance for Social Welfare, the Brazilian Legion Foundation for Assistance, and the National Foundation for the Welfare of Minors are in charge of rendering the services of social and medical assistance established in Law 6368, passed on October 21, 1976.

At the state level, there are also councils of narcotics. Only two Brazilian states, Rio Grande do Norte and Tocantins, do not yet have a council of narcotics. At a lower level of government, the creation of municipal councils of narcotics has been encouraged. This establishment of municipal councils would facilitate the adaptation of the national and state policies to the regional and municipal needs. Because Brazil is a big country and because life-styles and needs vary from place to place, the establishment of municipal councils is deemed essential.

## LAW ENFORCEMENT

The main drug-enforcement agency in Brazil is the Federal Police Department (DPF). Customs has the authority to conduct inspections and screenings. At the state level, each Brazilian state has a separate uniformed police organization (called military police, *Policia Militar*, because its members are trained in quarters and their discipline is the same as in the military forces) and a plainclothes police organization. The two police organizations are under the authority of the governor. The effectiveness of these organizations varies from state to state, but they have considerably more manpower than the DPF.

To improve federal-state cooperation in law enforcement, a National Public Safety Council was created in late 1989. This council includes permanent representatives of the uniformed and civil police of each state and the federal police. The organization was convened formally for the first time in January 1990; the minister of justice served as president, and the DPF director general served as the coordinator for operations. The principal objective of the new organization is to unite the country's police resources against organized crime elements and to develop a system to exchange criminal intelligence among the states.

The United Nations Fund for Drug Abuse Control (UNFDAC), which was reorganized into the consolidated UN International Drug Control Program (UNIDCP) in May 1991, began deliveries of equipment to the DPF in 1989 under a $5.5-million enforcement assistance project. Brazil and UNIDCP signed the agreement for this project in 1987, but the project had been dormant since then. Most of UNFDAC's assistance to the DPF will be in the form of commodities, such as vehicles and radios.[1]

U.S. bilateral narcotics assistance to Brazil is principally directed to the DPF, for the conduct of investigations of organized drug traffickers, precursor chemical control, coca eradication, some cannabis eradication, crop reconnaissance and detection, development of a DPF drug-detector dog service, and special training projects for federal and state drug-enforcement officials. A new program with the Brazilian Customs Service provides assistance for enhanced screening in airports and frontier ports of entry using drug-detector dog teams to uncover drug smuggling. Assistance to selected federal, state, and local drug-awareness organizations will continue in order to increase public and governmental awareness of the drug problem.[2]

The major Brazilian cities are experiencing a substantial amount of drug-related violence. In the city of Rio de Janeiro 75 percent of all robberies are committed by minors. Drug traffickers also hire minors. Today, in the state of Rio de Janeiro alone, there are 2 million needy minors, and 200,000 of them are abandoned children. Only 23,000 of them are enrolled in educational or vocational programs, for example, the State Federation for the Education of Minors (FEEM).

Because the Brazilian police are poorly equipped, the government must rely more on human resources than on equipment. Consequently, many joint operations combine the resources of more than one enforcement agency. An example of this occurred in 1987, in a joint operation called "Mosaic Operation," in which policemen of the DPF and of the state of Rio uniformed police organization (altogether, 265 men: 170 DPF policemen, 70 uniformed policemen, and 25 plainclothes policemen) killed Antonio José Nicolau, known as "Toninho" Turco, and his bodyguard in a Rio suburb.

Turco was believed responsible for the distribution of 60 percent of the cocaine consumed in Rio (from eight to fifteen tons per month). Turco, well-known as a criminal figure, had incurred the interest of the U.S. Drug Enforcement Administration and had been involved in crime for many years. In 1958, Turco was involved in a murder, although it was not until 1971 that he suffered his first drug-related arrest. His primary employment had been as a smuggler. Once he discovered that dealing in cocaine could enable him to earn twice as much as smuggling, he became a drug dealer.

The situation with Turco and the drug trade was not without political undercurrents. Turco's son, José Antonio Nicolau, twenty-eight years old when his father was killed, was a member of Rio's House of Representatives. He had received a large majority of the votes in the suburb where his father had his thirty-seven places of drug business.

Darcy da Silva Filho, known as "Cy," took the place of Toninho Turco. He had his headquarters in a slum area called Acari, in a big house with all the best appliances hidden from the outside by the poor surrounding houses. He was called "boss" or "bishop" by the poor population of the slum. According to the police, he might have had one thousand people working in his drug business. Some weeks after Cy's arrest, the police seized many weapons in the slum including an American rifle Colt AR–15 valued at U.S. $20,000. Cy distributed 60 percent of the cocaine consumed in Rio, selling about nine kilograms per day (sold in small packages of one gram each), and he had links to the drug dealers of Medellín and Bolivia.

In January 1990, another big drug trafficker, Isaias da Costa Rodrígues, was arrested in the slum area, Borel, where he had his headquarters. With his arrest, all the big drug traffickers of the slums were in jail, but the narco-traffic business did not diminish. The government of the state of Rio de Janeiro called the arrest of all the main drug traffickers, "Rio, say no to the Medellín cartel."

Despite these significant arrests, the problems of poor equipment continue to dog Brazilian enforcements efforts; in fact, the traffickers often have better equipment and weapons than the police.

Brazil borders on the main drug-producing countries in South America. To protect its borders effectively from the entry of drugs would require more than two million men day and night to patrol the border of the state of Amazon (with Peru and Colombia) and of the states of Mato Grosso do Sul and Mato Grosso do Norte (with Bolivia). These borders make Brazil the major transshipment country for drugs produced in Peru, Bolivia, and Colombia for routing to the United States, the Middle East, and Europe. In 1990 and 1991, Brazil also became part of a new trade of South American cocaine for Southeast Asian heroin, that was conducted by Nigerian middlemen. In the early 1990s, the police added a new concern when they discovered narcotics laboratories in the slums and in some areas near Rio de Janeiro, demonstrating that traffickers are starting this activity in Brazil.

Official Brazilian statistics show that only a small percentage of Brazil's legal production of ether and acetone is diverted to cocaine production. However, the country's stature as a major commercial producer of these chemicals continues to make it an alternative source when traffickers encounter difficulty in obtaining them from the United States and Europe.[3]

Sometimes several gangs engage in drug trafficking in the slums, and its members are always fighting each other for leadership. In some slums there is a drug-related murder almost every day. The poor people who live in the slums are also frightened because, when the police go up the hills to arrest the narco-traffickers, additional casualties result.

Many arrests are made at the Rio de Janeiro international airport. At the beginning of May 1989, a Bolivian was arrested in a taxi on his way to the airport. His criminal organization was going to send 13.594 kilograms of pure cocaine to Europe: Five Chilean women were going to carry the cocaine in their bodies. The women were using repellent in order to confound the drug-detector dogs. The seized narcotics, which were from Bolivia (Santa Cruz de la Sierra) and entered Chile by land and Rio de Janeiro by air, were destined for Frankfurt, Germany, by plane, and from there by train to Milan, Italy, where the drugs would be sold in small packages of 200 milligrams. Each kilogram of cocaine would be sold for U.S. $35,000; the total price of the cocaine seized would be U.S. $490,000. The mules would have received U.S. $6,000 each for their work in transporting the drugs.

Colombian or Bolivian trafficking organizations control most of the drug shipments transiting the country. Sometimes Brazilians are involved in the transaction. The drugs enter Brazil by land and river and are then exported from the airports of Rio de Janeiro, São Paulo, Belém, Recife, and Manaus.

*Epadu*, the Brazilian variety of cocaine, is planted by Indians in areas of the Amazon Jungle and sometimes even in their reservations. Cultivation areas are difficult to locate as they are protected from aerial observation. The DPF, which has conducted extensive ground reconnaissance in the state of Amazonas, indicated in 1990 that cultivation had declined considerably during that year due to eradication programs. However, terrain in the region makes it difficult to know how much *epadu* is produced and where it is located.

The DPF conducted a five-phase coca eradication operation in the state of Amazonas. The actual eradication of coca was preceded by eight months of ground and river reconnaissance to develop targets for operations in these almost inaccessible areas. The Brazilian military provided airlift and logistic support. Along with eradication of cultivations, police conducted civic action programs with Indian tribes to counteract the influence of Colombia traffickers. During these operations, a revised plant-leaf weight yield formula was developed which reduces by half the metric tonnage calculations previously used to estimate coca leaf destroyed. Eradication activity has accounted for the destruction of 330 metric tons of leaf, less than that destroyed in 1988 because the DPF found less coca than it had in previous years. Brazilian law enforcement seizures of cocaine hydrochloride during 1989 totaled 1.7 metric tons, almost 15 percent above the 1988 levels.[4]

In 1988, marijuana seizures included 23,116 kilograms of marijuana; 30,543 kilograms of marijuana seeds; 40,332,186 marijuana plants; and 437 areas planted with marijuana. Eleven clandestine laboratories for industrial production of unlawful drugs were located and dismantled. Seizures in national territory included 5.920 litres of acetone, 8.018 litres of ether.[5] Additionally, in 1988, 2,876 drug dealers were indicted, and 2,755 investigations were conducted.[6]

Article 34 of Law 6368, October 21, 1976, authorizes the forfeiture of vehicles, boats, airplanes, and other means of transport as well as mechanisms, utensils, instruments, and objects of any type used for the crimes defined in that law. After the court pronounces the sentence, which declares the loss of any of the goods referred to, the forfeited assets become the property of the state.

Law 7560 of 1986 established the Fund for Addictive Drug Prevention, Rehabilitation and Control (FUNCAB), which is implemented by Decree 85659 of January 1988. It disposes of goods taken in custody and acquired with products of the drug traffic and related activities. During 1989, seizures of drug trafficker assets included 4 aircraft, 213 vehicles, and some real estate. Not all of these assets will be permanently retained by the government, however, as each case must be confirmed in the judicial process before the federal government can legally dispose of a seized item. A ship, seized in 1987, was sold in 1989. Efforts are under way to define more clearly and improve the forfeiture procedures and to enhance the revenues from seized assets.[7]

There are no confirmed reports of major drug money laundering in 1989, although several allegations are currently being investigated by Brazilian authorities. If detected, drug money laundering could be prosecuted under federal tax laws and the asset seizure provisions of the new constitution.

## DOMESTIC DRUG USE

Marijuana, inhalants, and cocaine are the most widely consumed drugs in Brazil. In the major cities, street kids consume inhalants, usually glue, which contribute to their often violent behavior. Middle-class adolescents start using drugs by inhalants (perfume) and amphetamines. Later they use marijuana; after that, cocaine. According to a survey done in the ten major cities of Brazil, in a group of 100 students, 26 have tried at least once some kind of drug. In Belo Horizonte, the capital of the state of Minas Gerais, 34 percent of the students have tried light drugs at least once. However, it is in Rio where cocaine is used: Among 100 students 2 had once sniffed cocaine. Crack cocaine is still relatively unknown in Brazil.[8]

Cocaine is still a relatively expensive drug. Consequently, it is used more by executives and members of the upper middle class. In February 1990, one gram of cocaine cost the same as one gram of 18-karat gold. According to *Veja* magazine, in an upper-middle-class treatment facility, years ago the executives who work at large companies consumed amphetamines, like "Percitin" used with marijuana, and no patients were cocaine addicts. Today, the majority of the patients are cocaine users.

In October 1988, in Rio de Janeiro, thirty-four people were killed by drug overdose. The majority of these people used cocaine and marijuana; some also used alcohol. In 1985, in São Paulo, in every traffic accident with dead victims the drivers had consumed alcoholic beverages. In the early 1990s, besides alcohol, the experts also found cocaine in three out of every five drivers.

In 1980 all AIDS patients were homosexual. In 1984, needle sharing accounted for 1.34 percent of AIDS cases. In 1989, the percentage caused by needle sharing had risen to 16.94 percent.

On January 27, 1990, a middle-class, twenty-year-old girl died from an overdose of cocaine in a small town in Minas Gerais where she had gone with her boyfriend and other friends to spend the weekend. According to the experts, she had consumed Diazepan, alcohol, and cocaine (at least two grams according to *Veja* magazine), and had smoked marijuana. She had convulsions but was not taken to the hospital immediately because her friends were afraid of being arrested. About two hours later, a neighbor appeared and took the girl to the hospital, but it was too late and she died.

In 1977, Claudia Lessin Rodrigues, a twenty-one-year-old, middle-class student died at a "party" where people were doing cocaine. Her death marks the starting point of the abuse of drugs among upper-middle-class youth. The main person indicted in the crime was a rich man who had double nationality (Brazilian and Swiss) who fled to Switzerland. Twelve years later, in September 1989, he was killed in Switzerland.

One of the most shocking drug-related deaths in Brazil was that of Elis Regina, a very famous Brazilian singer, who died from an overdose of cocaine and alcohol. His death shocked Brazilian society and helped sensitize society to the drug problem.

## PREVENTION

Although economic and social problems are the leading problems of Brazil, the government is responding to the drug problem on both the demand side and the supply side. In less than two months after his inauguration, President Collor started the campaign against drugs. In his speech at the meeting of ministers on the Illicit Use and Production of Narcotics Drugs and Psychotropic Substances and Traffic Therein/Alliance of the Americas against the Drug Traffic, held in Ixtapa, Mexico, Minister of Justice of Brazil Bernardo Cabral emphasized the importance of prevention in the war on drugs, affirming that among all the goals of the international community demand control is the biggest challenge. He explained that the resources to achieve prevention include public awareness campaigns through the media, training of teachers, and making parents and children conscious of the problem.

In 1988, the DECIDIR program comprised professionals in the forefront of education and community who assisted support groups in 120 class hours divided in three phases covering such topics as the psychology of adolescent development and family interaction, drug classification, the role of the school in coping with illicit drug use and of the educator in preventing drug abuse, the anthropological view of drugs and their cultural setting, and reasons leading to drug use.[9]

Through the PREVIDA program, a pilot project was designed and carried out in 1988 at the Brazilia Student Games (JEBs), the sporting event with the largest concentration of Brazilian youth, approximately 5,000 primary (grades 6–9) and secondary (grades 10–12) school students. PREVIDA enlisted the participants' support for integrated prevention action to combat drug abuse, placing emphasis on the welfare of people and life and on the unification of efforts to obtain support from the JEB participants for prevention actions, under an approach for strengthening community health, and to look for alternative uses of leisure time by young people, through training in sports as a means of preventing abuse. DECIDIR trains professors to orient students with respect to the prevention of the unauthorized use of drugs, following procedures that foster decision making and permit the utilization of sports as an integral part of their lives; its syllabus examines such topics as peer pressure, the influence of the mass media, and the establishment of values and personal behavior.[10]

## INTERNATIONAL LINKAGES FOR CONTROL

At the international law level, Brazil signed the Single Convention on Narcotic Drugs, adopted in New York on March 30, 1961, which was promulgated by Decree 54216 of August 27, 1964. Brazil is also a party to the 1972 protocol thereto, as well as the 1971 Convention on Psychotropic Substances which was promulgated by Decree 79.388 of March 14, 1977. Brazil also signed the United Nations Convention against Illicit Traffic in Narcotic Drugs and Psychotropic Substances, which was adopted by the conference on December 19, 1988, in Vienna, Austria. On June 12, the Brazilian Senate approved the 1988 Vienna Anti-Narcotics Convention. On May 23, the Brazilian Chamber of Deputies passed the convention. The Brazilian Executive Branch declared its entry in force in Brazil in June 1991.

In 1987, a memorandum of understanding for the control of unauthorized drug use and drug trafficking and an agreement for the control of unauthorized drug use were signed with UNFDAC. Hence, Brazil has a major 1987 UNFDAC narcotics assistance agreement and the 1983 bilateral drug accord with the United States.

By virtue of all these agreements, the government of Brazil is in compliance with the requirements of the Chiles Amendment. Brazil has also signed many bilateral agreements. Brazil signed agreements on narcotics with Peru in 1976,

Colombia in 1981, Venezuela in 1977 and 1987, and with the United States (1974, 1981, 1982, 1983, 1986). Brazil has also concluded agreements with Guyana and Paraguay on the prevention, control, policing, and suppression of abuse and traffic in narcotics and psychotropic substances. Brazil and the United Kingdom signed an agreement through an exchange of notes as an additional protocol to the Convention on Mutual Assistance for the Suppression of Drug Trafficking concluded with Bolivia in 1977.

In March 1990, representatives of Argentina, Brazil, Colombia, Mexico, Peru, Uruguay, and Venezuela met in Mexico City and reaffirmed their decision to combat the drug traffic respecting the sovereignty and the territorial integrity of the states. Since that time Brazil has sought to work with other Latin American governments in coordinating efforts against illicit drug trafficking. This was reflected, on April 19, 1990, when Brazil, represented by its minister of justice, Bernardo Cabral, signed the Ixtapa declaration condemning once again the crime of drug trafficking in all its forms, recognizing it as an international criminal activity, and reiterating that it is a crime that affects all of mankind and recognizing that the strengthening of international cooperation is the best weapon to combat the drug trafficking.

## CONCLUSION

Although it is the richest and largest country in South America, Brazil faces difficult economic problems and has a very low quality of life. It is a country of contrasts where wealthy people live near poor people, and where street children are being hired by drug dealers and the crime rate is increasing tremendously. Drug abuse is a growing problem, partly due to the emotional instability resulting from the severe economic crisis. Crack cocaine is unknown in the country, but the consumption of cocaine is increasing.

Brazil is the major transshipment country to Europe and to United States for the drugs produced in Bolivia, Colombia, and Peru. Its borders are so vast that they are almost impossible to patrol effectively. Although Brazilian police do not have much equipment to combat the drug trade, the drug enforcement side is working hard counting more on human resources and on the bravery of its members.

## NOTES

1. U.S. Department of State, Bureau of International Narcotics Matters. *International Narcotics Control Strategy Report*. (Washington, D.C.: U.S. Department of State, March 1991), 90–93.
2. Ibid.
3. Ibid.
4. Ibid.
5. See Organization of American States, Inter-American Drug Abuse Control Com-

mission, *Annual Report of CICAD to the General Assembly*, doc. 174/89 (Washington, D.C.: Organization of American States, rev. 26 October 1989).

6. Ibid.

7. See section on ''Brazil'' in U.S. Department of State, *International Narcotics Control Strategy Report*, 91.

8. Ibid.

9. OAS, *CICAD Report*.

10. Ibid.

## BIBLIOGRAPHY


*Almanac, Abril 1990*. São Paulo, Brasil: Almanac, 1990.

Barreto, Menna. *General Study of the New Narcotics Law*. Rio de Janeiro: Editora Rio, December 1976.

Brazilian Foundation Institute of Geography and Statistics, *Annual Statistics of Brazil 1987/1988*. Secretary of Planning and Coordination. 1988.

Cabral, Bernardo (Ministry of Justice). ''Speech to the Meeting of Justice Ministers on the Consumption, Production and Trafficking of Narcotics and Psychotropic Substances.'' Speech presented at Ixtapa, Mexico, 19 April 1990.

CONFEN, *Drug Legislation in Brazil*.

Constitution of Brazil, Official Diary of the State of Rio de Janeiro, Special Supplement. 6 October 1988.

Greco Filho, Vincente. *Drugs: Prevention and Repression*. Speech (On file with chapter author).

Law 6368, 21 October 1976, São Paulo, Saraiva, 1977.

Hungria, Nelson. *Commentaries on the Penal Code*. Rio de Janeiro: Edigão Revista, Forense, 1958.

*O Dial* (Rio de Janeiro newspaper), 30 September 1989.

*O Estado de São Paulo* (São Paulo newspaper), 24 September 1989.

*O Globo* (Rio de Janeiro newspaper), 11 February 1987; 21, 24 September 1989; 7, 25 November 1989; 16 January 1990.

Organization of American States, Inter-American Drug Abuse Control Commission, *Annual Report of CICAD to the General Assembly*. Doc. 174/89. Washington, D.C.: Organization of American States, rev. 3–26 October 1989.

*Ultima Hora* (Rio de Janeiro newspaper), 14 September 1989.

U.S. Department of State, Bureau of International Narcotic Matters. *International Narcotics Control Strategy Report*. Washington, D.C.: U.S. Department of State, March 1991.

*Veja* (magazine), Editora Abril, Ediggo 1117, Ano 23, 14 February 1990.

Vieira, João. *Toxicos*. São Paulo: Forense, 1988.

# 8

# Caribbean Offshore Financial Centers: The Bahamas, the British Dependencies, and the Netherlands Antilles and Aruba

SCOTT B. MACDONALD AND BRUCE ZAGARIS

## INTRODUCTION

The major Caribbean offshore banking centers are located in the Bahamas; the British dependencies of Anguilla, the British Virgin Islands (BVIs), the Cayman Islands, Montserrat, and the Turks and Caicos Islands (TCIs); and the Netherlands Antilles of the Five (Curaçao, Bonaire, Saba, St. Martin and St. Eustatius) and Aruba. The primary problem these countries (the term is used loosely to apply to the dependencies) face in narcotics control is that they have functioned as major transit points in the flow of illegal drugs northward from South America and have provided the financial facilities for the laundering of narco-profits. In addition, although they are not considered major Caribbean offshore banking centers, the British dependencies of Anguilla, the British Virgin Islands (BVIs), Montserrat, the Cayman Islands, and the Turks and Caicos Islands are discussed owing to the similar problems they have encountered with money laundering and drug transitting.[1] Considering the similar nature of the drug control problems confronting these Caribbean nations, they are consolidated into one group in this chapter. At the same time, the authors are aware of the many socioeconomic and political differences between the Bahamas, a sovereign state, and the European dependencies, which remain constitutionally linked to the metropole. It should be added that, although London and The Hague continue to be the symbolic and administrative capitals, the British dependencies and their Dutch counterparts have generally become self-governing with largely elective legislative bodies.

The standard of living in the Caribbean offshore banking center countries is relatively higher than it is in much of the surrounding region. Whereas neighboring Haiti has the dubious distinction of being the poorest nation in the Western Hemisphere with a gross national product (GNP) per capita income of $380

(1988 U.S. dollars) and a life expectancy of fifty-five years at birth, the Bahamas' GNP per capita income is $10,700 and the life expectancy is sixty-eight years. The GNP per capita income of the dependencies, according to the World Bank, is estimated to be in the high-income bracket. Unlike other countries in the region, like the Dominican Republic, Cuba, and El Salvador, the Bahamas and the British dependencies are not plagued by external debt overhang, inadequate infrastructure, and poor or nonexistent health care programs. Although discrepancies exist between the rich and the poor, they are not at all as blatant or as wide as in Haiti or many of the Central American republics. Furthermore, the Bahamas and dependencies have been relatively free from the political turmoil that has characterized the recent history of such countries as Grenada, Suriname, and Nicaragua.

The Bahamas, the British dependencies, the Netherlands Antilles and Aruba share a number of characteristics. As a group, they are small in size and population, and they are limited in natural resources. Anguilla has a population of 6,500 and covers 35 square miles; the BVIs, 12,200 people and 59 square miles; the Cayman Islands, 17,000 inhabitants and 100 square miles; Montserrat, 12,100 people and 39.5 square miles; and the Turks and Caicos Islands, 7,500 inhabitants and 192 square miles. The Netherlands Antilles covers 800 square kilometers and has a population of 204,000; Aruba is 193 square kilometers and has a population of 65,000. The Bahamas, the "giant" in the group, covers 36,098 square miles (13,864 square kilometers) and has a population of 250,000.

The lack of natural resources has meant that the economics of the Bahamas and British and Dutch dependencies are built around tourism, British or Dutch financial assistance, and offshore financial services. The Bahamas, the Caymans, and the Netherlands Antilles, in particular, have developed world-class offshore financial service centers; the other dependencies have sought to duplicate their efforts with varying degrees of success. It is this dimension of the economy, combined with the geographical locations of the island states between the South American coca fields and the North America markets, that has brought the illicit drug trade to the region. In the Bahamas, the inroads of the illicit narcotics trade have resulted in the transit of cocaine and marijuana, the corruption of government officials, local addiction problems, and money laundering. In the TCIs, the drug trade led to the downfall of the dependency's chief minister and to his incarceration in the United States on his conviction of drug charges.

The limited resources of the Bahamas, the British dependencies, and the Netherlands Antilles and Aruba for drug control programs and concern about the negative impact of eroding the secrecy of their economically vital banking sectors have occasionally led to tensions between these governments and those of the United States and the United Kingdom. The Caribbean jurisdictions have found themselves caught between the need to maintain the attractiveness of their offshore financial services and pressure from Washington, London, The Hague, and increasingly intergovernmental organizations to help stem the flow of drugs and to root out drug-related money-laundering activities. The United States' emphasis on supply-side reduction and interdiction has, more than once, resulted in charges of "Yankee imperialism"; British efforts, especially in Montserrat in the late 1980s, have occasioned complaints of "British colonialism." Yet, most of the Caribbean offshore financial centers have become more sensitized to the illicit drug problem. Measures have been taken to make money laundering and transit activities more difficult. The lure of narco-dollars, however, remains an ongoing threat to the national security of these states and a primary concern for enforcement authorities in the Caribbean region as well as in North America and Europe.

## STRUCTURE OF THE INDUSTRY

The major drug-related problem for the Bahamas and British and Dutch dependency governments (and, by extension, the British and Dutch governments) is the use of the region as a transit zone for South American cocaine cartels. In this capacity, the transit states are not producers of any major narcotic, but they function as "pit stops" for traders. A particular state may serve as a base of operations to set up a deal, for aircraft or a ship to refuel, or for the recruitment of personnel required for such activities and protection. Moreover, a number of transit states, such as the Bahamas and the Netherlands Antilles, have the facilities necessary to launder "hot money": well-developed telecommunications, luxury hotels, easy access from major metropolitan centers, strict bank secrecy laws, and low or no taxes.

One of the problems confronting enforcement agencies in North America and Europe in the detection of hot money moving around the world and into legitimate businesses has been bank secrecy laws that are oriented to protect the investor. In some particular tax havens, in the 1970s, through most of the 1980s, and, in some cases, in the 1990s, shell corporations have been available to a foreign investor. Many of these mechanisms have been marketed from the United States in the form of direct mail, seminars, advertisements, videos, and audio cassettes. After the acquisition of a prepackaged shell corporation, the investor deposits money in a bank authorized to conduct business transactions with foreigners. Under the protection of the offshore banking center's secrecy laws, the corporation can transfer money to the local branch of a large international bank, such as Citibank, Chemical Bank, or Marine Midland, or wire transfer funds out of the Caribbean offshore center to an international bank in New York, London, or Luxembourg. Money is then borrowed in the name of another corporation either from the local branch or from the bank in the metropole. The result of this elaborate route is an obscuring of the records of the financial trail between the actual drugs-for-dollars transaction and the investment of the profits into a legitimate business enterprise, luxury goods, or other bank accounts in their countries.

The combination of drug trading and money laundering, as well as the legal side of international offshore banking, has served as an important conduit of capital for some Caribbean jurisdictions. The underlying idea of an offshore financial center is to attract funds from wealthy investors and corporations, who, for a number of reasons usually related to tax considerations, want to utilize vehicles in those countries with incentives to attract investors into their international financial sector. That capital has helped each state's development in terms of economic expansion, employment generation, fees, transfer of skills, and an increase in the overall standard of living. There has also been a downside: When drug-related funds have been invested and when significant drug transitting has occurred, political corruption, problems of domestic addiction, rising crime rates, and, in certain instances, political uncertainty have ensued.

The transit-laundering nexus of the Caribbean offshore banking centers has been an important link in the inter-American drug trade chain. Without the use of the Caribbean's bases, penetration of the U.S. market would be more difficult. It should be remembered that many of the Caribbean jurisdictions offer legal financial facilities, which attract a wide range of customers, from large corporations raising Eurobonds to lawyers and dentists seeking tax breaks. Unfortunately, the same factors that attract legal investors also attract drug dealers.

## THE BAHAMAS

The Bahamas flourished in the 1980s as part of the transit system in the inter-American drug trade for several reasons: its proximity to the United States; the archipelago nature of its geography, which makes enforcement difficult; and the structure of its banking system. Since independence from the United Kingdom in 1973, the Bahamas aggressively pursued the development of offshore banking and international financial services. In the late 1980s, it continued to be the leading Caribbean financial center, ahead of such other countries as the Cayman Islands and Panama. The banking sector, therefore, was an important economic sector. Any attacks (in the form of criminal allegations or erosion of bank secrecy) were perceived as a threat not just to the banking center, but also to the nation's overall economic well-being. As one British financial publication noted in 1987: "Preservation of secrecy is widely held by the government and the business community to remain absolutely critical for the continued success and growth of the Bahamas as a leading international financial centre."[2]

The Bahamas function as an important transshipment point and laundering center for drug money, a role that has diminished considerably since the heydays of the 1980s. As early as 1974, the government was aware that drug smuggling was an emerging problem. This changed, however, in the late 1970s. As the Bahamas Commission of Inquiry report noted, "The degree of violence was increasing and the foreigners were often armed with the most sophisticated weapons and had up-to-date systems of communication."

The 700 islands of the archipelago were convenient stopping points for *narcotraficantes*, such as Carlos Lehder, who were flying from South America. While the South Americans traded in cocaine and hashish, boats from Jamaica arrived in Bahamian waters, carrying marijuana. Difficult to patrol for government authorities, many islands came to offer refueling facilities for traffickers. A number of islands, such as the Exumas, Grand Bahama, and Cat Island, became known as locations for drug deals. Bimini, in particular, became a major smuggling point. The Bahamas Commission of Inquiry report commented: "Because of the very large sums of money involved, it is clear that many officials in Bimini succumbed to corruption and many of the local inhabitants took an active part in the transshipment of drugs."

Because the flow of drugs was to North America and not to the islands and because the transshipment of drugs brought a considerable inflow of capital, which helped keep the economy moving forward, official Bahamian reaction to these developments in the 1970s was not as fact as the U.S. government would have liked. This inflow of dollars was monitored, in part, by the Central Bank of the Bahamas. From 1977 to 1983 the amount of U.S. dollars transferred from the only bank in Bimini to the Central Bank or deposited in the United States on the behalf of the Central Bank increased from $544,360 in 1977 to $12.3 million in 1983. Considering that Bimini's population is 2,000 and that the legal economy is based on tourism, it was dubious that the inflow of money came from licit activities or that wealthy relatives were suddenly sending money. The answer was the laundering of drug money. The proceeds of the cocaine trade, according *The Economist* (The Caribbean: Open Palms Among the Palms, p. 11), were estimated to account for one-tenth of the country's economy.

Although the drug trade made a number of Bahamians wealthy, it also made the relationship with the United States problematic. In September 1983, an NBC television report alleged that Prime Minister Lyden Pindling and other high-ranking government officials were receiving $100,000 a month to protect a drug distribution operation run from the islands by fugitive U.S. businessman Robert Vesco. This disclosure created a degree of friction between the Bahamas and the United States thus forcing Pindling to create a blue ribbon royal commission to investigate the allegations of bribery and to examine other charges of corruption.

While the commission was being created, another incident marred relations with the United States and cast even greater doubt on the Bahamian prime minister's integrity. Samuel Leroy Miller, chairman of the National Progressive Committee, and John J. Rolle, a high-ranking Bahamian immigration officer, were arrested leaving a sting operation with a large amount of cash. The meeting had been held with agents from the U.S. Drug Enforcement Administration (DEA), who were posing as cocaine dealers, and the money was part of a payment that eventually was supposed to total $300,000. For this sum, the two Bahamians promised protection in their country for the traffickers.

The incident was embarrassing for Pindling on two accounts: Rolle was an official of the state, and Miller was a longtime political ally of the prime minister and an outspoken critic of the heavy-handedness of U.S drug policy in the Bahamas. Additionally, the timing roughly coincided with the formation of the royal commission. Although the commission acquitted Pindling, it did take note that the prime minister's bank accounts reflected deposits of $3.5 million in excess of his salary between 1977 and 1983. Moreover, it noted that a number of Friendly Island Commissioners, the representatives of the central government on nearly all the country's islands, "claimed they either had no direct knowledge of drug trafficking or never received any complaints regarding such activity. . . . We find that to be quite remarkable and we do not believe that they were being candid with us . . . they could not help but know what was going on in relation to drug trafficking. We have concluded that there must have been a degree of acquiescence on their part."

The commission also addressed charges that Colombian drug *capo* Carlos Lehder used Norman's Cay. It found that from 1978 to 1982, the Colombian had used the island as a transshipment base for cocaine and that local enforcement figures were paid "substantial bribes." The commission stated, "Based on the evidence of many witnesses it is clear that the government and senior law enforcement officers were well aware of the fact that drugs were being smuggled through the Bahamas to the United States of America in very significant amounts and that some percentage of the drugs was remaining in the Bahamas and being used by Bahamians."

The scandals that rocked the Bahamas and the public debate that followed failed to topple Pindling from his office. Though five ministers were either sacked or resigned, Pindling maintained the support of most of the members of his ruling Progressive Liberal Party (PLP), which had a comfortable majority n the parliament. Despite the lingering stench from the scandals and new allegations of cocaine transshipment and official involvement, Pindling's party won another election in 1987. Pindling survived politically because during his terms in office, more than eighteen years as of 1987, the Bahamas enjoyed political stability and underwent robust economic growth, especially in the 1980s. Moreover, the perception that the United States was seeking to unseat the prime minister stirred local nationalism.

In the 1980s, when the illicit narcotics trade moved into the Bahamas in a major way, the island-state's economy outperformed almost all other Caribbean nations. Even during the recession in 1981 and 1982, economic growth continued at a pace of 1 percent. In 1983 the country began to pull out of the recession, and by 1984 and 1985 gross domestic product (GDP) expansion was at 3 percent and better. With the exception of 1982, the construction sector was hardly affected by the recession; it grew by 6.3 percent and 6.5 percent in 1984 and 1985, respectively. Though difficult to prove, it is probable that at least some percent of that growth was drug related. A Bahamian government report noted on this trend in Bimini: "Another sign of the sudden increase in the availability of money was the rapid increase in the construction of new buildings by people whose regular source of income had not changed in any way" (Bahamas Commission of Inquiry, p. 14). The drug trade, therefore, helped maintain the economy's expansion, and despite a growing internal outcry over corruption, Pindling maintained a majority of the population's political support. Apart from economic reasons, the ruling party remained in office as a result of the nationalistic backlash to U.S. pressure against Pindling.

There was a downside to the massive influx of narcotics in the Bahamas. Drug addiction and drug-related crimes increased as well as prostitution. When the drug trade first emerged in the Bahamas, few perceived that it would become a major domestic problem. By the mid–1980s, however, medical experts in the Bahamas had noted that the amount of cocaine freebasing exceeded anything outside of Colombia.[3] David Allen, a Bahamian psychiatrist and a voice of drug education in the Bahamas, blamed cocaine freebasing for the unprecedented level of crime in the country. By the late 1980s, the Bahamas had gradually come to acknowledge that the offshoots of the drug trade were all in evidence: drug addiction, suicides, an erosion in family units, child abuse, and a rise in violent crime.

The Bahamian government, concerned about the unsavory reputation it received from the allegations of drug related corruption and money laundering, moved in 1989 and 1990 to provide a cleaner image. The royal commission's inquiry and overall negative media images in North America and Europe had also contributed to the movement of funds and companies to other offshore centers, such as the Caymans or Luxembourg. By 1989, the Bahamas' place as a world leader in offshore banking had fallen considerably. In 1983, the Caribbean nation was the third largest in the world, exceeded only by the United States and the United Kingdom, accounting for $157 billion in foreign liabilities and a market share of around 7 percent.[4] By 1989, the Bahamas banking share of offshore business had slipped to eleventh place; its world market share was now around 3 percent.

Among the new laws enacted to strengthen its international financial sector are the International Business Company (IBC) Act, the Trust (choice of governing) Law Act, the Ship Fee Reduction and Stipulation, and a Stamp Act, which reduces the applicable stamp duty on various transactions. Within nine months of the enactment of the IBC act, more than 1,800 new international companies had registered under the act.[5] The new success is its international financial sector has confirmed to Bahamians the need to protect and nurture this sector, which is the second most important sector and has long been the second major employee, revenue earner, and educator of professions. Reno Brown, chief executive officer (CEO) of the Royal Bank of Scotland, a leading private international bank, underscored the need for the Bahamas to maintain its confidentiality laws and its political stability to ensure its position in the international financial sector.

Relations with the United States over the drug and money-laundering issues have not always been tension free. In April 1987, U.S. Senate hearings were highly critical of the Bahamas, and there was an effort to suspend U.S. assistance. The Bahamian response was to deny a U.S. extradition request then pending against Nassau lawyer and associate of Pindling, Nigel Bowe. The U.S.–Bahamian relationship was further soured in 1987 by revelations that the Miami,

Florida, police in 1984 had planned a sting operation that was cancelled by the State Department, despite claims that there was ample evidence to arrest and try Pindling. One of the low points of the U.S.–Bahamian tussle occurred when the U.S. ambassador's special parking place in Nassau was revoked.

Despite the tensions in relations between Nassau and Washington, there have been areas of cooperation. In March 1985, Operation "Blue Lightening" was launched, in which thirty islands were blockaded by U.S. Coast Guard and Customs forces while raids were conducted by Bahamian police and soldiers. The raids resulted in the capture of 6,500 pounds of cocaine and 17 tons of marijuana worth $1 million as well as a number of boats and aircraft. Furthermore, a mutual legal assistance treaty (MLAT) was signed between the United States and the Bahamas. As of the early 1990s, the Bahama is actively cooperating with the United States on improving drug interdiction and on reducing the scope of money-laundering operations.

Bahamians point out that several internal measures have been unilaterally taken to guard against criminal elements in its international financial sector. For instance, according to Hermann-Josef Hermanns, who works with NatWest International Trust Group in Nassau, the government of the Bahamas a few years ago did not renew the licenses of several Bahamian financial entities in order to eliminate these undesirable entities from the international financial sector (Interview with Bruce Zagaris, January 4, 1991). In addition, the Association of International Banks and Trust Companies in the Bahamas has promulgated a code of conduct that requires persons in the international financial sector to follow a know-your-customer set of principles.

Furthermore, the Bahamas government has acted to combat illicit drug activity by enacting the most comprehensive asset forfeiture law of any developing country. The law, limited to drug-related forfeiture, enables the Bahamas to give assistance to foreign governments, provided the property of Bahamian nationals is not involved. One of the cases in which the United States has sought Bahamian assistance is forfeiting drug proceeds is the Carlos Lehder case, in which a notorious Colombian drug kingpin was operating and literally controlling the sparsely populated Norman's Cay in the southern Bahamas. By the time U.S. courts had convicted Lehder and had requested forfeiture assistance under the U.S.–Bahamian MLAT,[6] which had awaited the ratification and exchange of instruments by the United States for several years, the Bahamian government informed the United States that it had given all the assistance possible; it had itself confiscated the assets of Lehder, the bulk of which was real estate, and there was nothing else left to forfeit or share with the U.S. government. Apparently, the U.S. government has been satisfied with the response and actions of the Bahamian government in this case.

Still another pending case is the extradition of Nigel Bowe, a criminal defense attorney, who represented several narcotics traffickers. Bowe's extradition was requested by the United States for narcotics conspiracy. After many appeals, the Privy Council has found that the extradition treaty applies, and the case is now pending. Bahamian courts will eventually determine whether Bowe can be extradited under the requests, after which further appeals are likely.

Although there is no precise data on the amount and scope of the money-laundering operation in the Bahamas in the early 1990s, some analysts believe there was a moderate decrease in such activities and in the movement of U.S. currency through Bahamian banks. Partially due to U.S. pressure and partially due to a local desire to clean house for business purposes, the Bahamian government and banking industry have adopted a wide-ranging set of operating and reporting regulations which make money laundering more difficult. Still, the conditions for money laundering of drug profits remain, especially as the new regulations are largely self-managed. Moreover, money laundering is not a crime in the Bahamas.

International enforcement relations between the Bahamas and the United States clearly are as good as they have been for some time. Progress has been made in interdicting narcotics. The conclusion of an MLAT and its implementation, as well as the conclusion of an extradition treaty, bode well and have established a degree of trust between the two governments in law enforcement. The troubled area that remains is in fiscal and money movement cooperation. The United States would like the Bahamas to go much farther in committing itself to cooperate and in overriding its bank secrecy. The Bahamas government, however, has an important stake in maintaining confidentiality in both its tax and banking policies. Tension may well occur in these areas should the United States unilaterally press too hard on this issue.

## THE BRITISH CARIBBEAN DEPENDENCIES

### Overview

In the 1970s and early 1980s the British Caribbean dependencies either established or further developed offshore financial centers. Business had increased in that period, in part, due to the recycling of petro-dollars. An an example of this is observable with the movement of Mexican petro-dollars into the Cayman Islands. Mexico's shift from net oil importer to net oil exporter in 1975 brought a flood of dollars into the country. Although much of that capital went into large government development programs and for the purchase of an increasing volume of imports (partially paid for by commercial bank loans from the United States), large sums of petro-dollars were, according to R. T. Naylor, "being drained out again by asset stripping in both private and public companies—leaving the spectacle of rich entrepreneurs managing virtually bankrupt enterprises buried under dollar-denominated debt."[7] One route for these fleeing funds was to the United States, but the other "favored by money seeking to hide its origin as well as destination, was through secret bank accounts in peekaboo centers such as the Cayman Islands. From there, the funds were placed in trust with U.S. institutional investors, who in turn invested them in real estate in the American

Southwest."[8] Although the Mexican petro-dollar recycling came to an end in 1982, the flow of funds such as these clearly helped stimulate growth in the British dependencies for financial services protected by strong bank secrecy laws.

Although the movement of Mexican funds through the Cayman Islands was not illegal in a strict sense of the word, the rapid development of offshore financing did bring drug traffickers and their profits to these islands in the early 1980s. It has been only in the late 1980s that countermeasures have been taken to deal with the problem of the laundering of narco-dollars. In 1989, the accounting firm of Coopers and Lybrand, under contract to the British government, conducted an extensive review of the offshore financial centers in the British dependencies and confirmed the need for better regulation by both British and local authorities (Report of Mr. Rodney Gallagher of Coopers and Lybrand on the Survey of Offshore Finance Sectors in the Caribbean Dependent Territories [House of Commons, London: HMSO, January 19, 1990]). Consequently, in 1990, the five dependencies adopted or were in the process of adopting legislation akin to the United Kingdom's Drug Trafficking Offenses Act. Additionally, information-sharing agreements have been put in place with the United States and the United Kingdom.

## Anguilla

Despite many allegations and inquiries about drug money laundering, there have been no reported major financial scandals involving offshore institutions registered in Anguilla. Started in 1981, Anguilla's offshore business in terms of deposits by nonresidents grew at an average of 90 percent in the 1981–1987 period.[9] In 1989, forty-two offshore banks were registered on the island.

The high degree of confidentiality and minimal requirements for registration and licensing made Anguilla an ongoing concern about the potential for drug money laundering. This situation resulted in some erosion of the island's bank secrecy, when in March 1987 the United Kingdom, acting on the behalf of Anguilla, signed an information-exchange agreement that allowed U.S. federal authorities to have access to accounts where laundering of illicit funds is suspected. An important exclusion to this agreement was tax evasion, which is not recognized as a criminal act in Anguilla. Another ongoing point of concern on the drug front related to currency movements is that Anguilla has no exchange controls despite its membership in the East Caribbean Central Bank. One last point is that there is some drug use on the island, largely the smoking of cannabis, but it is not regarded as a major social or health problem.

## British Virgin Islands

The British Virgin Islands are relatively new to offshore finance, but they have been helped by their close proximity to the United States, Puerto Rico, and the U.S. Virgin Islands. From a slow start in the early 1980s, the number of companies registered has expanded at a quick pace; about 13,000 companies were registered at the end of 1988. Banks have also been attracted to the BVIs, but not on the same scale as in other offshore centers. At the end of March 1989, eleven financial institutions held licenses under the banking act; about thirty trust companies (these do not require banking licenses) were incorporated by the end of 1988.

During the late 1980s and early 1990s, the BVIs have recognized the value of the offshore financial sector, both in terms of a diversification of economic activity and as a contribution to local government revenue. There is a widespread recognition on the part of the authorities of the benefits of improved regulations and supervision of offshore companies and of ensuring that the sector is not tainted by allegations of criminal activity, such as drug-related money laundering. The BVIs, like many other such centers, are not without prior mishaps. In the BVIs, drug trade involvement surfaced in 1986, when it was revealed that one company, the Financial Management and Trust, was formed to launder narco-dollars. This led to the downfall of Chief Minister George Romney, who had been the trust's major shareholder. Although Romney was not involved in criminal charges, his naivete left a strong impression on the dangers of offshore finance and the need to be alert. This also helped set the stage for the BVIs to sign an information-exchange agreement with the United States in 1987. Unlike the Caymans and other offshore centers, the BVIs do not provide an institutionalized legal framework designed to provide confidentiality in respect to international financial transactions.

## Cayman Islands

The Cayman Islands, with the largest offshore financial center in the British dependencies, has representation of forty-six of fifty of the world's largest banks, many of which participate in the daily Eurobond business that is an estimated $2 billion daily. Over 18,000 companies have registered for various reasons. Consequently, the Cayman Islands has worked hard to maintain a good reputation. The Cayman Islands has an MLAT and narcotics agreements with the United States and regularly amends legislation regarding the activities of banks, insurance companies, trusts, and company management.

In 1983, the United States clashed with both the Cayman Islands and Canada over an incident involving the Canadian-owned Bank of Nova Scotia. U.S. authorities had long argued that bank secrecy was being used by U.S. tax evaders and drug smugglers to launder billions of dollars through Caribbean offshore finance centers, such as the Bahamas. In the particular case involving the Bank of Nova Scotia, the bank refused to compromise the confidentiality of its customer. In August 1983, the Canadian bank was forced to give a Florida grand jury records belonging to a client of its Cayman office after being threatened with a $50,000-a-day fine imposed on the bank's Florida branch. The Cayman,

Canadian, and British governments condemned this action as an infringement of Bahamian sovereignty and contrary to international law.

The MLAT signed with the United States in 1986 came after the Bank of Nova Scotia and other incidents. Although a number of institutions left the Caymans in the aftermath of the MLAT, the island-state's offshore financial sector did not collapse. Some analysts, for example, Tony Thorndike, even felt that the "sector benefitted from the loss of the less reputable while many more institutions were attracted by the Cayman's 'clean image'."[10] Moreover, the clean image was an attraction to offshore companies and banks departing from Panama in the 1987–1989 period. In fact, Cayman authorities refused licenses to a number of Panamanian banks of questionable background. As of March 1988, the Caymans had gained 450 new companies that had transferred out of Panama.

The significance of the offshore financial sector to the Cayman Islands' economy cannot be overstated. Upheld by the bank secrecy act of 1976, the government has spent considerable sums to maintain and upgrade all electronic facilities. Moreover, in the mid–1970s, when direct air services to Miami were threatened, the government stepped in and created Cayman Airways. Although Cayman Airways has run at a loss and is maintained by government subsidies, it guarantees easy travel to the Cayman Islands' clients. Furthermore, in extending the nature of the Caymans' attractiveness to outside investors, there are no exchange controls and no income, company, estate, or capital gains taxes.

## Montserrat

Montserrat's offshore financial center has been rocked with problems in the early 1990s, and only recently have measures been taken to improve its reputation. Montserrat's venture into offshore financial came in the mid–1980s as part of an effort to diversify the island's economic foundations. The offshore banks were barred from conducting business with local firms and individuals, and most transactions were done by telephone, mail, or fax. In 1988, bank registration and renewal fees earned the government $762,577 or 5 percent of its revenue. Regulatory and supervisory controls, however, were poor.

By 1989, the British and U.S. governments were investigating a number of companies that operated out of the island for fraud, drug-related money laundering, and other criminal activities. In 1990, the British government intervened in local administration and revoked the licenses of 250 of the island's 350 banks. New regulatory legislation was pending in 1991.

The British government's intervention in Montserrat's affairs was not without political fallout. The island's chief minister, John A. Osborne, who was also the finance minister responsible for bank supervision, indicated that London was intentionally seeking to embarrass Montserrat to hobble efforts to achieve greater autonomy based on racial prejudice. What was especially irritating was the November 1989 visit by Tim Sainsbury, the British foreign office minister responsible for the Caribbean, during which Osborne was informed that control of offshore finance was to be shifted from the finance minister's control to the governor, who is the local representative of the Queen.

### The Turks and Caicos Islands

The Turks and Caicos offer another example of problems with offshore businesses and money laundering. In the mid–1980s, the expansion of offshore finance was perceived as a means of diversification and, for some, a way to new riches. Unfortunately, one of those seeking to make money through offering the TCI as a transit point to Colombian *narcotraficantes* was the chief minister, Norman Saunders. Although allegations of drug trafficking increased considerably in the early 1980s, it was not until 1984 that British authorities cooperated fully with the United States. In March 1985, a sting operation in Miami caught Chief Minister Saunders and a member of his cabinet. The British government was forced to intervene. After being forced to dismiss the entire government in July 1986 and conducting an inquiry that barred certain politicians from public office and resulted in new constitution, local government was restored with the March 1988 elections.

The offshore financial center of the TCIs remained relatively rudimentary in the early 1990s. The lack of a developed social and physical infrastructure and the absence of specialized knowledge of financial ordinances have prevented the industry from expanding beyond the activities of company formation. Many of the companies formed are on behalf of other offshore financial centers where taxes and company formation expenses are higher or the laws are less flexible. In such cases, the majority of business remains in the other offshore financial centers, while the TCIs undertake only company formation and management activities. Following an earlier banking sector scandal, there has been an effective moratorium on the issue of bank licenses since 1985.

As the Turks and Caicos enter the 1990s, it is likely that the drug trade will continue to be a security concern. The many islands of the dependency, their proximity to the United States, and the lack of economic activity as well as the large profits to be made make the drug trade an alternative form of economic activity.

### Agreements with the United States and the United Kingdom

On November 9, 1991, the United States exchanged notes with the United Kingdom, extending the MLAT with the Cayman Islands to the British Virgin Islands, the Turks and Caicos Islands, and Anguilla. The U.S.–Cayman Island MLAT was signed on July 3, 1986, and took effect on March 9, 1990.[11]

The United Kingdom had to deal with the Helms understandings that were adopted by the United States as part of the ratification of the MLATs. The understanding had language "to prevent the granting of assistance to foreign officials who engage in, encourage, or facilitate the production or distribution of illegal drugs.'' The United Kingdom put on its ratification an understanding of its own, rejecting the Helms resolutions and specifying that the United Kingdom regards the U.S. understandings only as interpretive and not as modifying the understandings and substantive obligations under the treaty. The United Kingdom further states that the understandings of the United States did not form part of the treaty and did not bind the other party. The United Kingdom also sent the United States a note endorsing the statement of the head of its delegation in Parliament that it is wrong for a contracting party to make an understanding after the conclusion of a treaty and that the United Kingdom would proceed with the understanding that the United States made this understanding without seeking to modify the obligations within the treaty.

The signing of a mutual legal assistance treaty between the British Virgin Islands and the United States is significant for the BVIs because their financial services sector provides approximately 20 percent of the territory's GDP although most of it is international business companies and not offshore banks.[12] Apparently debate occurred in the BVIs' legislature in which some legislators expressed concern that the MLAT could adversely impact on investor confidence in the BVIs' offshore financial services sector. Montserrat was eligible for the extension, but it is not included yet because it did not pass the legislation required. The slowness of Montserrat to act, combined with the problems it encountered earlier in money laundering, has raised the ire of both British and U.S. law enforcement officials.

The extension of the MLAT to the three territories will enable the United States to obtain cooperation in important criminal cases, and it signals important continuing political progress in cooperation on criminal matters between the United States and the United Kingdom insofar as the U.K. retains responsibilities and control of its territories. Only six years ago, enormous tension existed over the enforcement of extraterritorial subpoenas by the United States in key Caribbean dependencies of the United Kingdom.[13]

The United Kingdom has had a program of concluding MLATs providing for asset seizure and cooperation in investigations arising from matters covered by the Drugs Trafficking Offenses Act of 1986. The MLATs cover assistance by one country to another country in the confiscation of proceeds, the enforcement of confiscation orders from abroad for offenses concerning drug trafficking, including banks' receipt of moneys that should reasonably be suspected are the proceeds of crime. For instance, the United Kingdom has concluded such agreements with Italy and recently with Guyana and Argentina. It has also finished negotiating an agreement with Panama, a country at loggerheads with the United States because the United States wants a much broader agreement—one that will cover tax and insider trading crimes. The United Kingdom has also been negotiating, and is nearing an agreement, with Brazil, Uruguay, and other key countries.

Another mechanism that the United Kingdom has utilized for criminal co-operations is the ship rider agreement, whereby the United States and the other signatory countries waive the right of entry of police vessels of other countries in their territories, provided their officials are on board and have the power of arrest. It enables the vessels of other countries to patrol and arrest violators carrying contraband, and it helps prevent smugglers who cleverly can outfox the law enforcement officials of the smaller countries, knowing that thereafter they should have free sailing. Although the BVIs and the U.S. Coast Guard have a ship rider agreement, there is discussion of extending it to include the U.S. Customs Service.

## THE NETHERLANDS ANTILLES AND ARUBA

The existence of offshore corporations, tax breaks, and secrecy-protected financial services dates back to World War II in the Dutch dependencies. When the Netherlands was overrun by German forces in 1940, the head offices of many Dutch companies were transferred to Curaçao. This was done to prevent their takeover by German authorities as well as their confiscation as enemy assets on the part of the Allies in nonoccupied areas. Though such companies as Royal Dutch Shell and Philips left Curaçao at the end of the war, a foundation of legal and financial expertise had been established, not to mention a greater tax base. For nominal taxes, the Netherlands Antilles offered an attractive registration location to non-Antillean companies.

Another attraction that brought foreign companies and investors was the 1964 treaty between the Netherlands Antilles and the United States that provided reduced withholding taxes on dividends and an exemption of withholding taxes on interest and royalties. Over time, the Netherlands Antilles became an important offshore financial center for U.S. and European companies participating in the $600 billion Eurobond trading business. Use of the Netherlands Antilles fueled an enormous Eurobond business, which was based on the exemption from a 30-percent U.S. federal withholding tax on interest payments paid by U.S. corporations on their securities issues. The Eurobond market access helped maintain offshore registrations and provide the Netherlands Antilles with an annual fee income of over $100 million, which accounted for 25 percent of the government's total revenue.

The relative political stability of the Netherlands Antilles was another factor in attracting offshore investors. Despite the riots of 1969 in Curaçao, the islands were generally peaceful. The constitutional arrangement helped guarantee a continued Dutch presence, especially in terms of economic assistance. When the Netherlands emerged from World War II, it had two groups of colonies: those in the Caribbean, the Netherlands Antilles and Suriname; and those in Southeast Asia, the Dutch East Indies. The Dutch East Indies soon became the independent nation of Indonesia. The Dutch constitution that emerged in 1954 created a tripartite kingdom that was broken down between Holland, Suriname, and the Netherlands Antilles. Aruba was then part of the Netherlands Antilles. In 1975,

Suriname became independent, leaving the Netherlands with only the Caribbean dependencies. Unlike much of the region, the Netherlands Antilles rejected independence, preferring the constitutional arrangement that gave them local elective self-government which had responsibility over all areas, except defense and foreign affairs. Moreover, the Antilles were always represented by a minister in the governments in The Hague.

By the mid–1980s, the Netherlands Antilles had become a leading offshore financial center, with over 40,000 registered companies (most from the United States). The business was largely based in Curaçao, but it was developing in Aruba. The bulk of the business continued to be in Eurobonds. When dark clouds began to form around the 1964 tax treaty with the United States, which the U.S. Treasury Department regarded as a serious source of lost tax revenue, drug money and other hot money began to taint the center's clean image. The expropriation by the Spanish government of the large conglomerate, RUMASA, in 1983 brought awkward questions about the use of a Curaçao shell company.

The ability to combine the use of bearer shares in owning Antillean corporations and the secrecy laws facilitated the use of the Antilles by unsavory persons such as drug dealers and fellow travelers (tax evaders and arms traffickers). This meant that there was hardly any trail for those investigating drug money-laundering operations to follow. The result was noted by Naylor, "It [the Netherlands Antilles] became a favorite haunt not only for tax evaders and flight capitalists but also for drug dealers and arms traffickers seeking to shift their money into legitimate investments in the U.S."[14]

While the Netherlands Antilles became a money-laundering and transit state for the Colombian cocaine cartels, Aruba left the Netherlands Antilles to achieve its long desire to achieve *status aparte* on January 1, 1986. This meant that Aruba would no longer be in what it perceived as a Curaçao-dominated federation and would have a separate status. Though the achievement of *status aparte* was accomplished with the understanding that Aruba would also achieve full independence in 1996, the island's population remains opposed to such a future and prefers to stay part of the Dutch kingdom, taking Suriname's old place in the tripartite constitution. Aruba's changed circumstances coincided with the closing of the Lago oil refinery, which negatively affected around 40 percent of the state's labor force and put the economy in a steep recession. Hence, Aruba began to operate its offshore banking at a time of local economic dislocation and when drug money was flowing into the Caribbean region.

To the respective governments in the Netherlands Antilles and Aruba the situation was difficult in the late 1980s in terms of the drug trade and money laundering. On one hand, there was concern about the movement of drugs and money laundering through the region, but on the other hand the local economies were hard pressed. Some local analysts felt that erosion of Antillean and Aruban bank secrecy would drive away legitimate as well as undesirable business. A complicating factor was the deterioration of relations with the United States in 1987 and 1988.

While the United States was pushing for stronger cooperation with the Netherlands Antilles and Aruba on enforcement and interdiction, the U.S. Treasury slashed Antillean revenues by unilaterally terminating the 1964 tax treaty on January 1, 1988. The matter, however, was soon turned over to the U.S. Congress for final determination as a result of the uproar caused by many U.S. pension and insurance companies that had purchased around $32 billion in bonds and were threatened with large losses. While this matter was being sorted out, the Netherlands insisted that the Antilles sign a new treaty with the United States which increased the tax on European dividends by a substantial 250 percent. The overall loss of business cost the Netherlands Antilles government over $100 million a year. Robertico Croes, the former head of the External Affairs Section of the government of Aruba, noted that the U.S. action "reportedly removed the financial means of the Antillean government to combat the drug traffic."[15] Even the eventual outcome of the issue, in which the U.S. government announced only partial termination of the treaty and allowed a tax exemption on interest, hurt. Simultaneously, the U.S. Congress enacted a law that enabled new Eurobond offerings to occur without using the Netherlands Antilles. At least the continuation of the interest provisions allows a transition and enables the Antilles to continue receiving revenue and some employment from existing Eurobond deals. Of more importance for the U.S. Congress, the continuation of the interest provisions allows U.S. multinationals to continue the preferential structuring of such Eurobond deals.

Relations between Aruba and the United States in terms of drug control policy improved in the late 1980s and early 1990s in contrast to U.S.–Netherlands Antillean relations. Aruba's closer cooperation and coordination on drug interdiction were praised by Vice President George Bush when he wrote a personal letter to Prime Minister "Henny" Eman in June 1988, commending the government of Aruba for its "resolute" action in the extradition of a drug dealer to the North American country.

Aruba has sought to be a regional Caribbean voice in antinarcotics efforts. Representatives from Aruba attended a conference held in Barbados in March 1988, and Aruba hosted a conference in September, at which it promoted the concept of cost-sharing with its allies in the war on drugs. In 1990, Aruba became one of the driving forces behind the implementation of the anti-money laundering recommendations of the G–7 Financial Action Crime Task Force. It hosted a regional meeting during the year.

The Netherlands Antilles has responded to requests for greater cooperation. In October 1987, Venezuelan President Jaime Lusinchi visited Curaçao and signed an agreement with his Antillean counterpart to provide police training with a special emphasis on narcotics interdiction. That same month, the U.S. Immigration and Naturalization Service (INS) was allowed to open a preinspection facility in Curaçao, staffed with INS personnel. The facility would both assist enforcing U.S. immigration laws and developing Curaçao's tourism.

## CONCLUSION

The international drug trade remains one of the major problems confronting the national security of the Caribbean offshore banking centers. Though the threat should not be overstated and other concerns clearly exist, the drug trade and related money-laundering activities threaten to undermine and pollute the nature of each society. This pollution is characterized by bribery of officials, including law enforcement officers, drug abuse, and an increasing turn to illicit economic activities instead of licit activities. In combatting the drug trade in all its manifestations, the unbridled power of organized traffickers requires outside assistance. This is being accomplished through regional cooperative efforts, including the Inter-American Drug Abuse Commission (CICAD) of the Organization of American States, the Caribbean subregional Interpol group, the UN Committee for the Prevention of Crime and Treatment of Offenders in Latin America, and the Regional Police Training Center in Barbados, and through closer enforcement efforts with the United States, Canada, the United Kingdom, the Netherlands, France, and Venezuela. At the same time, Caribbean sensitivities must be considered and clearly defined, especially in efforts with the United States. Enforcement efforts do not always keep pace with the power and dynamism of some organized crime groups and with their abilities to use the latest technologies and their sophisticated and ruthless abilities to move illegal narcotics and launder their profits.

On an overall basis, progress has been made in attacking the drug threat throughout the Caribbean; however, many *lacunas* (gaps) remain, especially since many countries continue to foster legal environments where money laundering is not considered a criminal activity. Consequently, the drug trade and related money laundering are likely to continue as security and social concerns in the region.

A key element of any solution must be that it comes from the region. Trinidad and Tobago's then Prime Minister A.R.N. Robinson has called for two initiatives for an international criminal tribunal to try selected crimes that might otherwise be difficult to try (i.e., when multiple members of organized crime or high-level government officials are charged). Another initiative is the call by Jamaican Prime Minister Michael Manley for a regional strike force to assist governments in supplementing regional police forces. Two other initiatives come from regional intergovernmental organizations. CICAD is preparing uniform money-laundering legislation, has enacted model laws against the sale of precursor chemicals, and has made several recommendations as part of its legal plan of action against narcotics trafficking. The Caribbean Financial Action Task Force agreed to consider the forty recommendations of the Financial Action Task Force of the G–7 countries plus twenty-one additional recommendations. The challenge to the Caribbean region (especially the offshore banking centers) in the 1990s, in terms of international narcotics control, lies in the ability to come together and agree on some common policies that are not dictated by the metropolitan countries. In the early 1990s, Caribbean antinarcotics and anti–money-laundering efforts are divided among different organizations, national governments, and territories. Greater regional unity on the matter would enhance outside technical assistance and financing from extraregional sources giving credibility to the policies in the face of the power of organized crime groups.

## NOTES

Scott B. MacDonald is an official of the Office of the Comptroller of the Currency, but the views expressed here are solely his own and do not represent those of that agency or the U.S. government in any capacity.

1. Other Caribbean jurisdictions, such as Bermuda and Barbados, have banking centers. These jurisdictions are not discussed here due to limited space and their comparative lack of money-laundering problems to date.

2. "Bahamas: Still a Flourishing Offshore Centre," *Latin American Times* (London), 29 April 1987, 29.

3. Nicki Kelly, "Cocaine Money Breeds Trouble in the Bahamas," *Financial Times* 19 July 1983, 5.

4. Canute James, "The Bahamas Acts to Reverse Decline in Offshore Banking," *Financial Times*, 28 November 1989, 31.

5. For additional background information on the Financial Secretariat, see "Financial Services Secretariat Launched in Nassau," *Bahamas Financial Insight*, Executive Director, Financial Services Secretariat, Ministry of Finance, Nassau, Bahamas. September 1990.

6. For a discussion on the substance of the U.S.–Bahamas MLAT, see Bruce Zagaris, "U.S. and Bahamas Conclude Mutual Legal Assistance Treaty," 3 *International Enforcement Law Reporter* 10, 345 (October 1987).

7. R. T. Naylor, *Hot Money and the Politics of Debt* (London: Unwin Paperbacks, 1987), 61.

8. Ibid, 62.

9. Tony Thorndike, "Anguilla," in *The Latin American and Caribbean Review* (Saffron Walden, England: World of Information, 1988), 126.

10. Thorndike, "Caymans," in *Latin American and Caribbean Review*, 143.

11. For additional information on Cayman laws to combat money laundering, see Bruce Zagaris, "Cayman Islands Strengthens Its Efforts against Money Laundering," *International Enforcement Law Reporter* 6, 53 (February 1990).

12. For information on the international financial sector in the British Virgin Islands, see M. Langer, "The British Virgin Islands Copes with Loss of Its U.S. Treaty," in *Practical International Tax Planning* (New York: Practicing Law Institute, 1991); also Noel Barton, "British Virgin Islands," in *Tax Havens Encyclopedia*, ed. Barry Spitz (London: Buttersworth, 1991).

13. See Bruce Zagaris and Constanine Papavizas, "Recent Decisions by United States Courts on the Exercise of Subpoena Powers to Secure Evidence Abroad in Criminal Matters," in *International Criminal Law: A Guide to U.S. Practice and Procedure*, V. Nanda and C. Bassiouni, ed. (New York: Practicing Law Institute, 1987), 301–29.

14. Naylor, *Hot Money*, 282–3.

15. Robertico Croes, ''Netherlands Antilles,'' in *Latin America and Caribbean Contemporary Record*, vol. 7, 1987–88, ed. James M. Malloy and Eduardo Gamarra (New York: Holmes and Meier, 1990), B421.

## BIBLIOGRAPHY


Anderson, Jack, and Dale van Atta. ''Federal Agents Probing Anguillan Bank.'' *Washington Post*, 4 October 1990, D6.

Bahamas Commission of Inquiry. *Report of the Commission of Inquiry Appointed to Inquire into the Illegal Use of the Bahamas for the Transshipment of Dangerous Drugs Destined for the United States of America, November 1983–December 1984*. Nassau, the Bahamas: The Bahamas Commission of Inquiry, 1984.

''The Caribbean: Open Palms Among the Palms,'' *The Economist* (October 11, 1986).

Croes, Robertico. ''Netherlands Antilles.'' In *Latin America and Caribbean Contemporary Record*, vol. 7, 1987–88, edited by James M. Malloy and Eduardo Gamarra, B415–32. New York: Holmes and Meier, 1990.

James, Canute. ''The Bahamas Acts to Reverse Decline in Offshore Banking.'' *Financial Times*, 28 November 1989, 31.

———. ''Barclow Clowes Scandal Prompts Row over UK Colony.'' *Financial Times*, 7 December 1987, 12.

Kelly, Nicki. ''Cocaine Money Breeds Trouble in the Bahamas.'' *Financial Times*, 19 July 1983, 5.

''Montserrat: Stormy Weather.'' *The Economist*, 9 December 1989, 41.

Naylor, R. T. *Hot Money and the Politics of Debt*. London: Unwin Paperbacks, 1987, 1989.

Sanders, Ronald. ''The Drug Problem: Social and Economic Effects—Policy Options for the Caribbean.'' *Caribbean Affairs* 3 (January/March 1990): 18–28.

Thorndike, Tony. ''Bahamas.'' In *The Latin America and Caribbean Review*, 130–33. Saffron Walden, England: World of Information, 1988.

———. ''Caymans.'' In *The Latin America and Caribbean Review*, 142–44. Saffron Walden, England: World of Information, 1988.

———. ''The Future of the British Caribbean Dependencies.'' *Journal of Interamerican Studies and World Affairs* 31, 3 (Fall 1989): 117–40.

———. ''Netherlands Antilles.'' In *The Latin America and Caribbean Review*, 180–83. Lincolnwood, Ill.: NTC Business Books, 1987.

Treaster, Joseph B. ''On Tiny Isle of 300 Banks, Enter Scotland Yard.'' *New York Times*, 27 July 1989, A12.

Turks and Caicos Islands. *Report of the Constitutional Commission 1986*. London: Her Majesty's Stationery Office, Command 111, April 1987.

Walter, Ingo. *The Secret Money Market: Inside the Dark World of Tax Evasion, Financial Fraud, Insider Trading, Money Laundering and Capital Flight*. London: Ballinger Publishing Company, 1990.

Zagaris, Bruce. ''The Caribbean Basin Tax Information Exchange Agreements Program of the United States: Eat Softly and Carry a Big Stick.'' *International Bureau of Fiscal Documentation Bulletin* (March 1989): 115–18.

# 9

# Colombia

SCOTT B. MACDONALD

## INTRODUCTION

One image of Colombia is that of silk-suited, jewelry-dripping drug lords, surrounded by bodyguards, who have few qualms about terminating rivals, members of the judiciary, and law enforcement officers. This viewpoint carries with it the idea that Colombia's political leadership is corrupt, its institutions are morally bankrupt, and its police and legal system are hopelessly ineffective. Although Colombia is one of the most pivotal countries in the global drug trade, especially in the commerce of cocaine, the country's enforcement agencies and political leadership have fought a long and bloody war against the drug *capos*. This struggle recently, particularly since the late 1980s and early 1990s, has been marked by bombings, assassinations, and kidnappings. Among the victims have been several of Colombia's supreme court judges, two attorney generals, three presidential candidates, and many policemen, journalists, and innocent bystanders. Despite this level of violence linked to the drug trade, Colombia's 30 million people continue to be democratically governed, and the country's economy remains one of the best managed in Latin America.

Colombia is strategically located between the coca-producing nations of Bolivia and Peru and the routes through the Caribbean and Central America that lead to the lucrative North American and European markets. In the 1990s, this location is also strategic for supplying drugs to a newly emerging market in the Far East.

## THE STRUCTURE OF THE COLOMBIAN DRUG INDUSTRY

Colombia's history is not as closely entwined with coca as those of Bolivia and Peru, where native American populations made extensive use of the plant.

Despite this, Colombia's pre-Conquest Amerindian population did cultivate small amounts of coca and considered it sacred. During the colonial era and the early days of the republic, coca consumption was limited to the relatively small Amerindian communities and generally was not regarded as socially acceptable by Europeans. By the mid-twentieth century, coca production was limited to regions around the sources of the Chicamocha River in Santander and in the department of Cauca, which were inhabited by the Páez and Guambiano Indians.

The stimulus to expand Colombia's cocaine industry came in the 1950s, initially from Cuba. Prior to the Castro revolution, Cuba was infamous for its corruption, gangsterism, and ties to the U.S. Mafia. During the dictatorship of Fulgéncio Batista (1952–1959), the Cuban Mafia was a significant force in importing small amounts of cocaine from South America. In this commerce, cocaine was purchased from small refineries in Bolivia and Peru. The Colombians largely functioned as couriers for the Cubans.

When Fidel Castro came to power in 1959, the Cuban Mafia fled the island-state. Many emigrés relocated in the United States, especially in Florida, and some of them had developed a cocaine habit. Consequently, the Cuban Mafia resumed its cocaine trade, but this time into the United States. It soon became apparent that the rest of the United States offered a lucrative market. By the 1960s, the Cuban Mafia was heavily involved in the drug trade.

The expansion of the drug business in the United States occurred in the 1970s. Colombian drug dealers, closer to the source of cocaine than their Cuban business associates, soon saw opportunities for expansion. In the late 1970s, Colombian criminal groups ruthlessly eliminated many of their Cuban competitors as well as other Colombians competing in the same area. South Florida in particular was the scene of many gangland killings. By the early 1980s, Colombian criminal groups had risen to the top of the Latin American drug trade servicing North America.

Colombia's drug industry is dominated by the trafficking of cocaine and marijuana; money laundering of drug proceeds occurs to some extent in the financial system. Although Colombia is a coca producer, with an estimated harvestible cultivation of 38,400 hectares in 1991, it is in the area of cocaine refining, transporting, and marketing that the country's criminal organizations have been and continue to be the most successful.[1] Colombia's coca leaf production places it a distant third behind Bolivia and Peru, but well ahead of Ecuador. In terms of Colombia's standing in worldwide net production of marijuana, it is number two behind Mexico (excluding net U.S. domestic production).

## Cartels

Two loosely organized criminal cartels have dominated Colombia's drug trade: one operates out of the city of Medellín, and the other out of Cali. The Medellín cartel, which emerged in the 1970s under the guidance of Pablo Escobar, Jorge Luis Ochoa, José Rodríguez Gacha, and Carlos Lehder, came to control about

80 percent of all cocaine entering the United States. The Medellín cartel helped to revolutionize the South American cocaine trade, modernizing transportation from mules (couriers) to large aircraft and seafaring boats. They were able to establish trafficking networks that included Panama, Central America, and Mexico as well as Suriname, Cuba, and the Bahamas. The Medellín cartel was active in the development of its own enforcement establishment—a well-armed, highly trained one. Weapons were often state-of-the-art, and instructors were recruited from the ranks of international mercenaries, including former British and Israeli soldiers. It has also been alleged that the Medellín cartel established a working relationship with some of Colombia's leftist revolutionary groups who often shared the same remote, rough terrain with their refining and transport operations.

The Medellín cartel in its heyday of the 1980s became active in Colombian politics, helping to sponsor candidates to local and national governments. Carlos Lehder even founded a neo-Nazi party, the Movimiento Civíco de Liberacion Nacional, which among other things advocated the legalization of marijuana. Escobar's public profile was high. In March 1982 he was elected to the Colombian congress as an alternative representative from Antioquia, which briefly ensured his immunity from arrest. As a delegate, he was able to use the congress as a launching pad for attacks upon the 1979 extradition treaty with the United States as well as attacks on any of those members of congress in the legislative body who were antinarcotics. The treaty with the United States was strongly disliked by drug kingpins, such as Escobar, because if justice was served and he was extradited to the North American country, the chances of using bribery or threats would be substantially reduced. This is not to say that the Colombian legal system lacked the courage to tackle the issue, but that the *narcotraficantes*, through political means, bribery, or assassination, have greater leverage in their domestic arena than in the United States.

The Medellín cartel was well-known for its flashiness and grandiose public gestures. For example, when Escobar was not in congress or conducting narcotics business, he played philanthropist: His donations launched a program called "Medellín without Slums," which resulted in the construction of many new homes and a hospital for the poor. Escobar's estate in Puerto Triunfo, the Hacienda Napoles, was noteworthy. Over the entrance gate, the drug *capo* mounted an airplane, which allegedly was his first smuggling vehicle. The most ostentatious display, however, was Escobar's own private zoo, which included ten hippopotamuses, four giraffes, two elephants, and a number of exotic animals. The estate had twenty-four artificial lakes, a country house that was capable of serving one hundred guests, and a swimming pool flanked by a statue of Venus and a mortar emplacement.

The cockiness of the Medellín cartel ultimately resulted in a collision with the Colombian government. Simply stated, the Medellín cartel had become too powerful, too conspicuous, and too greedy. By 1984, they were blatantly arrogant about their wealth and had few qualms about using their influence. This substantially threatened the state and mocked the concept of government by law.

The government response began as early as October 1983 when it was announced that the *narcotraficantes* had infiltrated professional soccer: Six of fourteen clubs in the country were owned by people linked to drugs. Minister of Justice Rodrigo Lara Bonilla also publicly stated that traffickers were major stockholders in Bogotá's Millionarios team. Other allegations were more extensive, implicating owners of Medellín's Atletico Nacional and Cali's América team, as well as professional bicycling, boxing, and auto-racing teams. Lara Bonilla also insisted that the 1979 extradition treaty with the United States be used.

The *narcotraficantes* found Bonilla a major problem. The justice minister, who was operating with the support of the president, was actively taking the war to them. On April 30, 1984, a two-man hit team killed Bonilla on his way home. When it was quickly revealed that the assassins had been hired by the Medellín cartel, a major crackdown was launched against the drug lords, many of whom fled to Panama. That neighboring nation had in the past been used as a safe haven and a place to launder drug profits. Additionally, Panama offered luxurious hotels and fashionable restaurants, and the ruling armed forces, then dominated by Manuel Noriega, were corrupt and heavily involved in smuggling drugs and guns. Though negotiations to allow the drug *capos* back into Colombia were snubbed by the Betancur government, the Medellín cartel was forced to rethink its strategies. In time, as the intensity of government enforcement efforts slackened, the *capos* gradually returned to Colombia.

The Medellín cartel, however, could not resist, once again, throwing around its weight. Eventually it moved back onto a collision course with the government after a number of assassinations including on July 31, 1986, Supreme Court Justice Hernando Baquero Borda, who was involved in revising the Colombian–U.S. extradition treaty of 1979; on November 17, 1986, police Colonel Jaime Ramírez Gómez, commander of a number of major antinarcotic campaigns; and on December 17, 1986, *El Espectador's* editor Guillermo Cano Isaza, an outspoken opponent of the drug trade. As assassination attempt was made on Colombia's ambassador to Hungary, Enrique Pareja González, in Budapest. Pareja had succeeded Lara Bonilla as justice minister. Another major assassination came on October 11, 1987, when a leading leftist politician and former guerrilla leader, Jaime Peredo Leal, was shot and killed. Although the Medellín cartel was hurt by the capture and extradition of Carlos Lehder in 1987, it was able to plan and execute the assassination of Attorney General Carlos M. Hoyos Jiménez on January 25, 1988.

The culmination of assassinations of major public figures came with the assassination in July 1989 of the front-runner presidential candidate, Luis Carlos Galan, a strong anti–drug trade advocate, who was a former colleague of Lara Bonilla. Since then, Colombian government pressure on the Medellín cartel has been intense. Despite their declaration of war against the government and their murder of 420 policemen in 1990, the Medellín cartel's operations were disrupted: Rodríguez Gacha was killed in a shoot-out; the international assets of that drug *capo* were seized; and Fabio and Jorge Luis Ochoa both surrendered to the authorities, in December 1990 and in January 1991, respectively. The biggest prize was the surrender in June 1991 of Pablo Escobar. This hardly means that Colombia's war on drugs is over, but the Medellín cartel is considerably weakened in the early 1990s.

The other cartel in Colombia operates out of the city of Cali. Though the Medellín cartel has usually dominated the headlines and has controlled the lion's share of cocaine entering the United States, the Cali people gained control of New York City's cocaine market. Less brash and less inclined to be nouveau riche, the Cali cartel has expanded operations in the late 1980s and 1990s at the expense of the Medellín cartel. The Medellín's occasional efforts to attack the Cali group have been largely unsuccessful.

The Cali cartel is allegedly led by José Santacruz Londono and brothers Miguel and Gilberto Rodríguez Orejuela, who are described in the local press as businessmen. The Cali cartel functions more as a hierarchy among that city's and region's *narcotraficantes*, rather than a single organization. With no criminal charges against them in Colombia, they own a number of legal business ventures, including a drugstore chain, real estate, construction companies, and radio stations. Although the Cali cartel has been discreet at home, many enforcement agencies point to them as the key factor in the expansion of cocaine into the European, Asian, and Middle Eastern markets. Rather than confronting the Colombian government in a head-on confrontation, as the Medellín cartel did, the Cali cartel has been content to work within the existing political system. Whereas the Medellín *capos* threatened to disrupt society and jeopardize the country's long-standing tradition of democracy, the Cali cartel was quiet.

In the 1990s the future appears to belong to the the Cali cartel as the major force in the underground empire of drug trafficking in Colombia. It should be added that, although the Cali and Medellín cartels have played a predominant role in Colombia's drug trade, other, smaller criminal organizations exist and are involved in the export of cocaine and other drugs.

The change in the structure of Colombia's drug industry in the early 1990s potentially portends the end of cartel dominance and the rise of new, yet more compact organizations. While Colombian law enforcement put Escobar in prison and otherwise compromised the Medellín cartel's operations, new groups have emerged in medium-sized cities, such as Pereira, Barranquilla, and Monteria. Representing a challenge to the older cartels, these newer groups are oriented to shipping via the Pacific Ocean instead of the traditional Caribbean and Central American routes. One analyst opined in early 1991, "we are seeing the democratization of the industry, partly because Escobar is no longer powerful enough to impose order, and partly because new routes are needed, and new people are finding ways to get things done."[2]

One of the newer criminal groups was noted in April 1991, when Colombian police discovered twelve tons of cocaine, one of the largest busts in Colombian enforcement history. Neither the Medellín nor the Cali cartels was involved, but a new, hitherto unknown group, the so-called Cartel of the Coast was. Some analysts identified the leaders of this group as Dario Mendoza and Luis Geronimo Berocal. Colombian police thought that the Cartel of the Coast was mainly a transit operation, which dealt with the movement of cocaine from Bolivia and Peru.

Even within the ranks of the Cali cartel, the process of fragmentation of organizational dominance appears to be a major trend. Long regarded as a stable, low-profile operation, the lower tier of dealers, *narquitos*, began indicating in 1991 that they wanted more autonomy from the ruling families. Part of the reason for this is related to the decline of the Medellín cartel's centralized dominance over the industry. Some of the most widely recognized *narquitos* are brothers Iván and Fabio Urdinola, who were active in the northern Cauca Valley. The Urdinolas, then in their early twenties, had experienced working with Escobar and were reputed to be more prone to violence. It was thought that the assassinations of six members of the Zuniga family, in June 1991, were the handiwork of their rivals, the Urdinolas.

One of the major issues about the drug trade in Colombia concerns the actual amount of money that returns to the country. The process of drug delivery to North America and the return of drug dollars to Colombia is referred to as La Vuelta (The Round). While there is a broadly based consensus that drug money is laundered in Colombia, how much and how it enters the country have given considerable room for discussion. Two schools of thought dominate this issue. The first school of thought is represented by Colombian economist Miguel Urrutia, director of Fedesarrollo, a private think tank, based in Bogotá. Urrutia contends that the drug trade has had an overall negative impact on the Colombian economy. Along these lines, the narco-profits are largely laundered through the purchases of contraband, sometimes, but not always, in the form of luxury goods. The annual average amount of drug money returning to Colombia is from $200 to $300 million. The ongoing strength of the contraband trade, partially caused by the past rigidness of the foreign exchange regime (set amounts of foreign exchange were allowed to be held by Colombians), created an underground economy that continues to be conducive to the trade in narcotics and the laundering of its profits. Contraband bought by drug money, he argues, helped destroy the textile industry in Medellín: Drug money was used to buy cheaper foreign textiles, which were then smuggled into the country where it undersold locally made items. Urrutia has also noted that the money involved in this is lost to government revenues as it is not taxed. Furthermore, the related violence of the drug trade has driven away foreign investment.

The second school of thought agrees with the negative impact of the drug trade, but contends that a larger amount of money is laundered in the country through the banking system, money exchange houses (*casas de cambios*) and precious metal dealers. Couriers and third country currency exchanges have also been used. According to estimates from the Banco de República, the amount of drug money returning to Colombia could have ranged from $600 to $800 million in 1989. Other estimates range upward to $4 billion, which is probably too high. The consensus appears to be in the range of from $500 million to $1.5 billion, which, at the upper end, would make drugs comparable to coffee as a major export.

Most analysts concur that the large percentage of drug money stays outside of Colombia, usually in offshore banking centers. Beyond the investment of drug money into the contraband trade, other elements of hot money investment have included the real estate sector (with perhaps up to 3 to 4 percent of arable land owned by traffickers), especially agricultural land. Some of these funds are also expected to go into construction. This movement of funds into agricultural land and construction has been negative rather than positive to the economy owing to the lack of use of the former and the dislocation caused by the rapid pattern of drug baron investment in the latter.

## GOVERNMENT RESPONSE

The Colombian government has conducted an ongoing war against the *narcotraficantes*—a war that has been characterized by some major successes and many tragic episodes, such as the assassinations of supreme court judges, a minister of justice, and numerous policemen. The major bureaucratic organization for narcotics control is a multiministerial policy-making body, the National Council of Dangerous Drugs (CNE). It is chaired by the Ministry of Justice; the minister of justice and the commander of the National Police coordinate Colombia's antidrug effort. Despite disagreements on policy, this body more or less produces and is responsible for the implementation of drug-suppression efforts. The Colombian armed forces have also played an important role in the drug war.

Colombia's accomplishments in the 1990s in narcotics suppression have been impressive. First and foremost, the effectiveness of the Medellín cartel has been weakened considerably with the death of Rodríguez Gacha, the imprisonment of two of the Ochoas, and the earlier extradition of Carlos Lehder. Second and equally important, efforts to seize drugs and eradicate crops have continued to make inroads. In 1990, according to the U.S. International Narcotics Matters annual report, over seventy-seven metric tons of cocaine hydrochloride were seized—a substantial increase over 1990 seizures—and over nine tons of cocaine base. Additionally, government enforcement agents destroyed more than 700,000 gallons of essential chemicals (ether and acetone), 339 cocaine labs, 5 morphine labs, and in 1990 over 125 airstrips; seized 37 aircraft; and arrested more than 7,000 people. Eradication efforts were also extended to cannabis; in 1990, 500 metric tons of marijuana were destroyed.

The government of President Cesar Gaviria, who entered office in 1990, has conducted a strong campaign against the drug trade. At the same time that security forces have maintained pressure on the Medellín cartel, another important policy has been to negotiate with the *capos*. The message has been straightforward: In exchange for surrender, extraditions would end and prison sentences would be reduced, perhaps cut in half. This new policy was embodied in Government of Colombia Decree 3030, issued on December 14, 1990. Under this decree, a trafficker would have to confess to at least one trafficking (or, in the case of a terrorist, one terrorist) charge and would then be imprisoned in especially designated locations.

Although the Gaviria government has provided an opening to negotiations with the *narcotraficantes*, it has also maintained a position that they should be tried in Colombia. Along these lines, President Gaviria established "faceless courts" with eighty-two selected judges, who will try cases on paper anonymously in an effort to reduce intimidation. Many analysts think that this change in policy—trial but no extradition—led to the surrenders of the Ochoas and Escobar. Moreover, conviction rates in those courts were close to 70 percent, up from less than 10 percent in normal courts.[3]

The Colombian government tried not to abandon extradition to the United States altogether. A politically hot issue in Colombia, touching upon the nerve of nationalism, the Gaviria administration wanted to keep the door open to this possible mechanism if other options failed. In 1990, for example, fourteen traffickers were extradited to the United States under the authority of a decree issued by former President Barco under the constitutionally granted state of siege authority. The decree replaced the 1979 U.S.–Colombian extradition treaty, which was found to be "inoperable" by the Colombian Supreme Court in 1986. After the new administration came into office, Gaviria and his justice minister have followed a policy in which the areas for extradition are more limited. Moreover, to launch the new initiative for negotiations with the Medellín cartel, Gaviria imposed a moratorium on extradition for the last three months of 1990.

The Gaviria administration's legal efforts were stymied by the writing of a new constitution, which went into effect on February 2, 1992. The assembly writing the constitution refused to support the principle of special courts and opted to leave the decisions to the new congress. Although the courts could be maintained through interim legislation from July 5 to February 2, it was expected that the new congress would be opposed to any continuation of the special courts once in session. The new constitution also bans extradition. In an interview with the French publication, *Le Point*, President Gaviria commented about the banning of extradition: "It must be understood that extradition is very unpopular here. It is a cause to which the narcotraficantes have committed much of their bloody attention. Personally, I consider it a very useful option, but it is against the sentiment of the population."[4]

One of the major areas that has been decimated by the war on drugs is the Colombian judiciary. No other country in recent memory has witnessed the brutal elimination of the majority of its supreme court, which occurred in November 1985. A number of cocaine traders awaited trial and extradition to the United States in the supreme court in the Palace of Justice in Bogotá. The Betancur government had shown considerable resolve in bringing this group to trial. The arrests and trials had advanced despite corruption, threats, and assassinations of government officials. On November 6, 1985, M–19, a leftist guerrilla group stormed the Palace of Justice and took 400 people hostage, including the president of the supreme court. After a tense twenty-eight-hour seige by the Colombian military, the building was stormed. In the aftermath of the final assault, 100 people died, including most of the guerrillas and almost the entire supreme court.

Although the issue of linkages between *narcotraficantes* and Colombia's guerrilla groups is hotly debated, the M–19 assault destroyed most of the drug dealer files, and four judges waiting to hear drug-related cases were among those killed by the M–19. Other assassinations of members of the judiciary followed: on July 31, 1986, Supreme Court Justice Hernando Baquero Borda, who was involved in revising the Extradition Treaty of 1979 was shot and killed; and on January 25, 1988, Attorney General Carlos M. Hoyos Jiménez was murdered with two of his bodyguards on his way to the Medellín airport.

The difficult straits faced by the Colombian judiciary have caused the government to reform certain elements of the legal system. Having faceless judges review cases, a system implemented in December 1990, was undertaken by the Gaviria administration to buffer judges from the threat of silver or lead—bribery or assassination. The eighty-four well-protected judges will operate in five major cities to try drug dealers. In a more simplistic manner, security has been improved for members of the judiciary. It should also be added that the December 1990 decree expanded the legal authority of the police to investigate crimes without direct judicial supervision.

The Colombian government's response to the drug trade also encompasses economic policy. The Gaviria administration moved in the early 1990s to liberalize the economy, opening up the system to greater investment opportunities through privatization and stimulation of the country's three stock exchanges. The idea is that, if the legal economy functions well, the attraction of the illicit economy will be that much less.

In Colombia money laundering is not a criminal act. Despite that factor, the Colombian government in the early 1990s became more aware of the issue of money laundering, and efforts are being made to provide for a cleaner banking system. While the government has yet to fully develop adequate financial criminal investigative capacities, Colombian banks have been encouraged to maintain their own standards on knowing their customers. Part of this stems from the fact that Colombian banks have branches in the United States where money laundering is considered a criminal act. In the late 1980s, a number of Colombian banks came under scrutiny for possible money-laundering infractions as with the Bancode Occidente, which caused some tension between the U.S. and Colombian governments. However, Colombian officials worked with U.S. officials and with Colombian banks to make a cleaner banking environment. Moreover, the Banco de la República has legal authority to record information on cash transactions in foreign currencies, which it has been doing for several years. Additionally, in 1991, Colombia changed its foreign exchange law, ending the Banco de la República's monopoly on foreign exchange transactions in an effort to reduce the need for businesses to resort to black market (often narco-used money exchanges. In the same year, Colombian banks were instructed to completely identify those Colombian nationals who make foreign currency transactions of US$10,000 or more.

Although money laundering is not a crime, Colombia's legal regime is potentially stringent on drug trafficking. Law 30 provides sentences of up to twelve years for individuals involved in the production, selling, acquiring, and financing of controlled substances. Substance abuse is also punishable by sentences of up to four years. Additionally, Article 47 of Law 30 allows asset forfeiture.

Under Colombian law (Article 51), users of cocaine and other drugs who have become addicts, as determined by a medico-legal finding, must be admitted to a psychiatric or similar establishment, public or private, for recovery. The law also provides that the authorities may place the drug addict in the care of his or her family or send the person, under the family's responsibility, to a clinic, hospital, or health facility for the necessary treatment, which will last as long as recovery demands.

## SOCIETAL REACTION

The violence and power of the *narcotraficantes*, the threat posed by this group to Colombia's political system, and the growing problem of domestic drug abuse have caused considerable concern within Colombian society. At the beginning of the 1980s, this was not an area of great concern; many Colombians regarded drug addiction as a *gringo* problem. By the mid–1980s, however, as the supply for cocaine expanded rapidly and enforcement measures tightened access to the North American markets, larger amounts of this drug showed up on the streets of Bogotá, Cali, and Cartagena. According to the U.S. State Department's *International Narcotics Control Strategy Report* of March 1986, more than 600,000 Colombians had "serious" addiction problems. According to the National Health Ministry of Colombia, the estimated number of people smoking *basuco*, a cocaine derivative, in early 1987, the time of the last national survey (as of mid–1991), was more than 400,000. Another estimate put the number of Colombians abusing drugs at 1.2 million.

The 1987 Colombian survey examined Colombia's four major cities; the results were highly alarming to a society already under seige from the drug *capos* in the area of law and order. The main findings of the study, beyond the increased usage of *basuco* was that marijuana, readily available throughout much of the country, was the first drug of choice, followed by *basuco*. Use of heroin was almost nonexistent. Although another national survey is due to be conducted in either late 1991 or 1992, the National Drug Council believes that the situation remains largely unchanged.

The increasing awareness of the drug problem as a domestic concern has helped stimulate a greater response from both the public and private sectors. A greater emphasis is being given in demand reduction and for the treatment of drug misusers. In the early 1990s, Colombia developed an excellent drug education program in the country's school systems. This was developed through the cooperation of the Ministry of Education, the Colombian Institute for Family Welfare, and the Bogotá municipal government. These bodies have been supported by a wide-ranging number of private organizations and businesses. One such antidrug initiative was an antidrug poster campaign sponsored by a private bank. Other initiatives have included the establishment, by a private foundation, of an antinarcotics game for children, aimed at enhancing their awareness of drugs.

Another negative impact on the drug trade on Colombian society has been in regard to the country's small Amerindian population. The cocaine industry gradually has made inroads into what had been the remote, isolated locations of the country where the Indian world survived. In the 1980s, when the cocaine boom began, the Indians found their traditional life-styles disrupted by the entry of the drug lords and their sometimes guerrilla allies, like the Armed revolutionary Forces of Colombia (FARC). As Richard Craig noted, "In several instances, traditional Indian communities have undergone forced draft changes almost overnight."[5] This has meant the transformation of villages into violent boomtowns, a transition from subsistence agriculture to rural wage employment in the cocaine factories (or marijuana plantations), and the imposition of new materialistic consumption patterns. Moreover, the Indians have often found themselves caught in the middle of range wars between various drug barons.

Despite growing awareness of domestic problems with drugs, survey research in 1991 indicated that a plurality of Colombians continue to assign responsibility for the drug war to consuming rather than producing countries.[6] At the same time, a large number of Colombians remain convinced that their country has done more than the United States to combat drug problems. These societal attitudes must be considered by the Colombian government in formulating national policy.

## INTERNATIONAL LINKAGES FOR CONTROL

Colombia is an active member in the international effort against the international drug trade. It is a signatory of both the 1961 United Nations Single Convention on Narcotic Drugs and the 1971 United Nations Convention on Psychotropic Substances. The 1988 United Nations Convention against Illicit Traffic in Narcotic Drugs and Psychotropic Substances was signed but not ratified as of late–1991. Colombia has also participated in the various efforts of the Organization of American States (OAS) in combatting the illicit drug trade and drug money laundering.

One of the more significant efforts undertaken by the Colombian government was to host the Cartegena Summit in February 1990. An important meeting with the presidents of Colombia, Bolivia, Peru, and the United States, the summit was held with the objective of coordinating antinarcotics strategies, ranging from demand and supply reduction options to improving local financial investigative capacities.

One of the major areas of difficulty in Colombia's foreign drug policy is extradition. The U.S.–Colombian Extradition Treaty of 1979 has engendered an ongoing domestic dispute within Colombia, while the United States has often pressed for more usage of extradition. For many Colombians, the shipping of its citizens abroad to face legal proceedings was and is a difficult road to travel. According to Mark Andrew Sherman, "Colombians object to having their fellow citizens extradited and tried in the United States, a nation whose culture and legal tradition differ markedly from those of Colombia, and whose people are the primary users of cocaine."[7]

Colombian irritation about U.S. pressure was reciprocated by concerns that the South American country's legal system was paralyzed by the drug trade's corruption and violence. The extradition issue, therefore, took on the dimensions of Colombian national pride and U.S. righteous indignation. The Colombians were further incensed by seeing the film of Marian Barry, the mayor of Washington, D.C., using cocaine who was then able, in Colombian eyes, to escape justice.

A particular incident that hardened the U.S. position about the problematic nature of the Colombian legal system was the 1987 release of Jorge Ochoa from detention in a Colombian prison, presumably as the result of bribery. Colombian apologists noted that "the same commentators uniformly fail to give any credence to the fact that Ochoa was released pursuant to an affirmative judicial finding of unlawful detention following his petition for a writ of habeas corpus."[8] What was right or wrong morally, what was correct or incorrect under the law of the land was blurred as an issue before the fact that one of the most wanted *narcotraficantes* in the United States walked out of a Colombian prison. Both the Colombians and the Americans felt justified by their views.

The Barco administration did use the extradition tool in August 1989, when Colombia resumed extradition of the United States of suspected drug traffickers. The striking down of the Colombian government's authority to use extradition in 1991 was not taken well by the United States. Moreover, the ability of Escobar to negotiate his surrender, which put him in a special prison, was criticized by U.S. authorities, as well as by many European governments. Despite differences such as these, Colombia's relations with the United States and European countries largely have been positive.

## CONCLUSION

Colombia's role in the global drug trade is not likely to diminish dramatically in the 1990s. The government has taken considerable measures to stem the tide of drugs and has paid the price in large numbers of deaths of policemen and judges. Colombian society also appears to be repulsed by the heavy-handed actions of the Medellín cartel and has rallied around the government. The struggle, however, has been long, and there is a certain war weariness that makes the search for other options, such as negotiations, attractive. Although some analysts doubt the ability of negotiations to succeed in bringing the drug barons in from the cold and reducing the scope and influence of the drug trade, it should be remembered that similar discussions with the country's guerrilla groups have been relatively successful. If negotiations fail to stem the tide, it appears that the traffickers will have the option of Rodríguez Gacha: to die in a shoot-out with the police or to trade until a rival puts one out of business. This option means for Colombian society further violence and bloodshed.

## NOTES

Scott B. MacDonald is an official of the Office of Comptroller of the Currency, but the views expressed here are solely his own.

1. U.S. Department of State, Bureau of International Narcotics Matters, *International Narcotics Control Strategy Report, March 1991* (Washington, D.C.: U.S. Department of State, March 1991), 101.
2. Douglas Farah, "Upstart Traffickers Vie with Top Colombian Rings," *Washington Post*, 11 April 1991, A37.
3. Douglas Farah, "Colombia Turns to Courts as Anti-Drug War Founders," *Washington Post*, 2 June 1991, A26.
4. "En couverture, Cesar Gaviria, Président de la République," *Le Point*, 29 June 1991, 18.
5. Richard B. Craig, "Illicit Drug Traffic: Implications for South American Source Countries," *Journal of Interamerican Studies and World Affairs* 29, 2 (Summer 1987): 23.
6. United States Information Agency, "Andean Public Opinion on the Drug War: Most See Increased U.S. Drug Use But No Tie to Trafficking," *USIA Research Memorandum* (Washington, D.C.), October 18, 1991, p. 1.
7. Mark Andrew Sherman, "Colombian Constitutional Assembly Endorses Ban of Extradition of Nationals," *International Enforcement Law Reporter* 78 (May 1991): 177.
8. Mark Andrew Sherman, "United States International Drug Policy, Extradition and the Rule of Law in Colombia," *NOVA Law Review* 15 (Spring 1991): 666.

## BIBLIOGRAPHY


Bagley, Bruce M. "Colombia and the War on Drugs." *Foreign Affairs* 67, no. 1 (Fall 1988): 70–92.

Castillo, Fabio. *Los jinetes de la cocaina*. Bogotá: Editorial Documentos Periodisticos, 1988.

Collett, Merrill. "The Myth of the 'Narco-Guerrillas.' " *The Nation*, 13–20 August 1988.

Craig, Richard B. "Domestic Implications of Illicit Colombian Drug Production and Trafficking." *Journal of Interamerican Studies and World Affairs* 25, 3 (1983): 33–45.

———. "Illicit Drug Traffic and U.S.–Latin American Relations." *Washington Quarterly* 8, (Fall 1985): 105–124.

———. "Illicit Drug Traffic: Implications for South American Source Countries." *Journal of Interamerican Studies and World Affairs* 29, 2 (Summer 1987): 1–34.

Dermota, Ken. "Cali Picks Up Drug Slack." *Washington Times*, 8 April 1991, A1, A10.

Eddy, Paul, with Hugo Sabogal and Sara Walden. *The Cocaine Wars*. New York: W. W. Norton & Company, 1988.

Gómez, Hernando José. "Notas sobre el tamano del Narcotrafico y su impacto economico." *Revista Ecónomia Colombiana* (Bogotá), February 1990.

Lee, Rensselaer W. III. *The White Labyrinth: Cocaine and Political Power*. New Brunswick. N.J.: Transaction Publishers, 1989.

MacDonald, Scott B. *Mountain High, White Avalanche: Cocaine and Power in the Andean States and Panama*. New York: Published for the Center for Strategic and International Studies by Praeger, 1989.

Organization of American States. *Comparative Study of the Legal Regime on Drug Control in Ten South American Member States of the Organization of American States*. Washington, D.C.: Prepared for the Secretariat for Legal Affairs, General Secretariat of the Organization of American States, 1988.

Shannon, Elaine. *Desperados: Latin Drug Lords, U.S. Lawmen, and The War America Can't Win*. New York: Viking, 1988.

Sherman, Mark Andrew. "Colombian Constitutional Assembly Endorses Ban of Extradition of Nationals." *International Enforcement Law Reporter* 78 (May 1991): 174–78.

Tanzi, Vito, ed. *The Underground Economy in the United States and Abroad*. Lexington, Mass.: Lexington Books, 1982.

Treaster, Joseph B. "Surrender of Cocaine Smuggler Isn't Expected to Have Large Effect." *New York Times*, 21 January 1991, A15.

Urrutia, Miguel. "Cost-Benefit Analysis of the Drug Trade for Colombia." Paper prepared for the Project on Hemispheric Cooperation for the Prevention of Drug Abuse and Trafficking, Washington, D.C., April 1990.

United States Department of State, *International Narcotics Control Strategy Report, March 1992* (Washington, D.C.: US Department of State, March 1992).

United States Information Agency, "Andean Public Opinion on the Drug Wars: Most See Increased U.S. Drug Use But No Tie to Trafficking." *USIA Research Memorandum*, 18 October 1991. Washington, D.C.

Yarbo, Stan. "Drug Barons Dangle Olive Branch." *Christian Science Monitor*, 27 November 1990, 5.

# 10

# Mexico

BRUCE ZAGARIS AND SCOTT B. MACDONALD

## INTRODUCTION

Mexico's drug industry has three components: the production and export of heroin and marijuana and the transshipment of cocaine from the Andean region to the United States.[1] The drug trade has become a local problem in terms of addiction, corruption, and other related socioeconomic problems. There has since the 1980s been a growing preoccupation by Mexican society and its government with the drug problem. The Salinas administration in particular has taken significant action both in Mexico and in its regional policy.

## BACKGROUND

Mexico began to develop noticeable narcotics activity during World War II with opium poppy cultivation and refining. Its heroin industry had become well-established by the late 1940s after it began to produce morphine for medical purposes during World War II at the request of the U.S. government. By the 1960s Mexico's narcotics business was based largely on heroin and marijuana, although some cocaine was smuggled through the country from South America. Most of its heroin came from Turkey via Marseilles, France, into Vera Cruz, Mexico City, and then north to the United States in trucks or small planes.

In the 1960s, Mexico's marijuana production underwent a boom period. It was produced primarily by thousands of small farmers in the northern Sierra Madre mountains. The farmer would harvest and bring it into town on pack donkeys. The dealers would buy, usually at $4 per kilo (2.2 pounds). The dealers, some with links to the big family organizations, had cash, small warehouses, and contacts with the local police. The grey-green marijuana leaves and flowers were moistened with sugar water, packed, and redried in one-kilo blocks, which were wrapped in cellophane or newspaper and allowed to accumulate until there were enough to prepare a truckload for shipment. In the United States, in 1969, a kilo could fetch between $75 and $150. Some marijuana was reduced to the more potent hashish, which sold for from $500 to $650 per kilo.

In 1969, growing frustration by the United States over the flow of narcotics from Mexico reached a crescendo. Mexico's Federal Judicial Police, who had jurisdiction over narcotics violations, numbered only 264 agents and had few aircraft for observation. They lacked facilities (i.e., spraying planes) for crop eradication.

In September 1969, the Nixon administration launched Operation Intercept. Two thousand customs and patrol agents were posted along the border in what was announced as "the largest peace-time search and seizure operation by civil authorities."[2] The U.S. government declared Tijuana "off limits" to U.S. military personnel. The United States hinted that other border towns, including Juarez and Nogales, would be next. However, Operation Intercept failed to intercept even one major shipment of heroin or marijuana, and the unannounced border blockade was perceived by Mexico as an affront to its national honor. Mexico's vocal discontent jeopardized the Nixon administration's desire to improve relations with Latin America. Finally, the two governments concluded an agreement whereby the United States provided Mexico with $1 million to eliminate plantations for both opium poppies and marijuana. Operations were conducted in the rugged Sierra Madre mountain states of Durango, Sinaloa, and Chihuahua. The Mexican army seized a 250-acre marijuana farm in the southern state of Oaxaca.

In 1972, the collapse of the French Connection, due to the banning of opium production by the Turkish government, led to the establishment of Mexico as one of the major sources of heroin for the United States. In the late 1970s some estimates put the Mexican share of U.S. imports of heroin and marijuana at over 80 percent. As a result, the United States and Mexico renewed efforts of cooperation, beginning with Operation Condor, in which the Mexican government pushed crop eradication and better enforcement. During this time, periodic arrests by Mexican officials of U.S. citizens for illegal possession of drugs or for commerce in drugs became inflammatory, partly because of the dislike by Americans of languishing in Mexican prisons.[3]

During the mid–1980s the dramatic expansion of Mexico's external debt, based in part on borrowing to exploit its energy and the lower oil prices in the 1980s, the inflationary spiral in Mexico, and its advance trade balance, and worsened by two earthquakes in 1985, forced Mexico to reschedule its external debt for the second time and made its people even more vulnerable to the lure of illicit narcotics. During this same period the U.S. demand for drugs escalated. Mexico's *narcotraficantes* also benefited from stricter eradication programs in Colombia and Peru, the preoccupation of Mexico's government with the direct economic conditions caused by the debt crisis, and corruption within the country's law enforcement system.

In the late 1980s, an increasing amount of heroin was produced in Mexico, and at least 40 percent of the marijuana used in the United States in 1985 and 1986 was produced in Mexico.[4] Traffickers from South America increased their utilization of Mexico as a convenient transshipment point for cocaine. These items were transported by people crossing the frontier on foot, trucks, mules, and aircraft.

Many of the Mexican *narcotraficantes* are horizontally and vertically involved, controlling production, transportation, smuggling, enforcement, and marketing to distribution areas. The only areas not operated are street sales, which are left to native dealers. In many respects the business of producing marijuana has not changed since the 1960s, with the exception of refining and transporting the merchandise.

In the late 1980s Mexico's illegal drug industry was much more resilient than it was in decades past. It was heavily oriented to exports, not domestic consumption. Similar to Bolivia and Colombia, the Mexican *narcotraficantes* have become important players in the legal economy. Mexico's drug trade was estimated to be worth at least from $1 to $2 billion annually in terms of sales and possibly from $300 to $350 million in capital inflow into Mexico. Considering the difficult economic situation of the country since 1982, the economic importance of the *narcotraficantes* cannot be overlooked.

In 1985, Mexican–U.S. drug relations endured a crisis which still is smoldering. Renewed U.S. interdiction efforts off the Florida coast led Colombian drug producers to forge a new alliance with Mexican organizations to ship cocaine through Mexico despite the greater length and the greater cost. The Mexican organization was to receive approximately 10 percent of each shipment in return for storage and protection.

On February 7, 1985, Drug Enforcement Administration (DEA) agent Enrique Camerena Salazar and his Mexican pilot, Alfred Zavala Avelar, were murdered. Camerena had been kidnapped by four gunmen in broad daylight after departing from the U.S. consulate in Guadalajara. Demands were made by U.S. Attorney General William French Smith and DEA chief Francis "Bud" Mullen. Even President Reagan personally communicated with President de la Madrid requesting assistance.

On March 6, 1985, the tortured bodies of Camerena and Zavala were found at a remote ranch sixty miles southwest of Guadalajara. One of the persons believed responsible was Rafael Caro Quintero, a notorious trafficker who was intercepted two days later by Mexican federal and state police led by Armando Pavón who had been alerted by the DEA. Quintero bribed his way to Costa Rica. Subsequently, Armando Pavón admitted that he had accepted a $275,000 bribe to allow Caro Quintero's plane to leave Guadalajara airport.[5] Pavón was sentenced to a jail term in Mexico City.

In April 1985, Caro Quintero was captured, along with four heavily armed bodyguards, in Costa Rica by local authorities acting on a DEA tip. Found with the *narcotraficantes* was the kidnapped seventeen-year-old daughter of a wealthy Mexican businessman, who is also the brother of an official in the PRI (Partido Revolucionaro Institutivo or Institutionalized Revolutionary Party). Caro Quintero was returned to Mexico, where he was tried and sentenced to prison.

Soon after Quintero's arrest, Ernesto Fonseca, a major trafficker sought in the case, was arrested with twenty-three other persons, many of them federal enforcement agents.[6] Although Fonseca admitted to trafficking, paying bribes, and involvement in planning Camerena's kidnapping, he denied murdering the DEA agent and accused Miguel Felix Gallardo, another notorious trafficker. The United States became frustrated with the slowness of the Mexican investigation into Camerena's murder. The Mexican government became embarrassed, especially during a period when the PRI was already under attack in Mexico for corruption and fraud.

In April 1986, Glenn Miles, a U.S. Customs Service patrol officer, was killed by traffickers on the U.S. side of the border, adding more fuel to the cross-border tensions.[7] In June 1986, the hearings on whether Mexico and other countries should be certified as properly cooperating in international narcotics policy brought media attention. In particular, the annual narcotics report of the U.S. State Department's Bureau of International Narcotics Matters stated that Mexico perhaps was again the leading exporter of marijuana to the United States and the single largest source of heroin.[8] It was predicted that Mexico would produce between twenty-one and forty-five metric tons of opium in 1986 and approximately 3,000 metric tons of marijuana.[9]

In June 1986, during President de la Madrid's visit to Washington, D.C., a subcommittee of the Senate Foreign Relations Committee, over which Republican Senator Jesse Helms presided, became the next irritant. Earlier the U.S. Congress made accusations about corruption in Mexico, including claims that former Mexican presidents were involved in billion-dollar corruption schemes and that the former police chief of Mexico City, a crony of President Portillo (1976–1982), was reputed to be heavily involved in the drug trade. During the Helms hearings, allegations ensued over official corruption in Mexico, the drug trade, immigration, and the questionability of its claims to being a democratic country. Helms himself made accusations. The testimonies of John Gavin, former U.S. ambassador to Mexico, and U.S. Customs Commissioner William Von Raab were highly critical of Mexico's antidrug efforts. The fact that the hearings coincided with de la Madrid's visit created undue embarrassment to the Mexican government.

Reagan and de la Madrid did agree to work together on the drug trade, and de la Madrid pledged greater cooperation. The Mexican government began a new antidrug campaign during the meeting in Washington. The new operation involved twenty-five helicopters and a large crop-dusting plan, financed by the United States, and targeted marijuana production in northern Mexico. Spraying was extensive and was intended to continue through February to catch the 1987 opium poppy harvest.

Improved relations were marred when, during the meeting of the two heads of state in Washington, police in Guadalajara detained a DEA agent, Victor Cortéz, and tortured him. Although he was released, Attorney General Edwin Meese protested to his counterpart, Attorney General Sergio García Ramírez, and the narcotics issue did not go away during the rest of 1986.

During October 1986, a major antidrug campaign in Mexico resulted in the arrest of the brother of a former governor of the state of Sonora. Gilberto Ocana García was charged with drug trafficking in connection with the marijuana fields he owned. Additionally, the Mexican government publicized its antinarcotics work over the past three years. Mexican documents revealed that the Mexican army and navy and the attorney general's office had assigned 45,000 men to the effort: 90 percent of the marijuana and poppy producing capacity was destroyed, and 18,792 people, both nationals and foreigners, were arrested.[10] In the three-year effort, the army lost 318 men; the navy, 25; and the attorney general's office, 43.

One incident that illustrates the casualties sustained by Mexican law enforcement was the November 1985 slaying of twenty-one Mexican policemen in southern Mexico by *narcotraficantes*. The police intercepted a major shipment of marijuana on land. A firefight ensued with the traffickers who were well equipped. Although a number of police were killed in the fight, the majority surrendered when they exhausted their ammunition. They were then taken to a river where they were tortured and shot. Only a few of the original force survived.

## MEXICO'S SOCIETAL RESPONSE

Although drug abuse is not such a major societal problem as it is north of the border, concern is growing in Mexico. One national survey of drug addiction noted that 4.3 percent of Mexicans have tried drugs at least once. By another estimate, Mexico City has 200,000 young addicts; the highest rates of drug abuse are found in the northwestern states of Baja California, Sonora, and Sinaloa. The drug of choice is marijuana, primarily because of its low cost and availability. That stated, marijuana consumption has not reached alarming proportions, and heroin abuse is low in epidemiological terms. Cocaine use is not wide, although it is readily available in a few circles in the upper socioeconomic levels. The consumption of hallucinogens and other psychotropic substances is not yet a cause of concern.

Drug abuse appears to be most widely prevalent among unemployed youth between the ages of seventeen and twenty-four. Consequently, federal, state, and local authorities and private sector organizations are attempting to create new employment options as well as maintain support for sports, recreational, and educational programs. Mexican organizations, both of the public and private sector, are also pushing antidrug use campaigns: "Yes to life" and "No, no to drugs." Mexican authorities are, moreover, attempting to broaden the reach of rehabilitation programs. An example of this was the opening of the first university drug rehabilitation center at the University of Nuevo Leon in early 1991.

Much of the antinarcotics approach on the societal front is linked to the economy's performance. Mexico's external debt management problems in the 1980s clearly reduced the level of funding that would be available for social programs, such as drug abuse education, while also helping to generate unemployment. Conditions in the state of Jalisco reflect this: as of January 1991, around 80 percent of the state's municipalities lacked prevention or educational programs against drug abuse. Additionally, sports centers and playing fields are few in number. Jalisco has high unemployment and there is some concern that disaffected and idle youth may turn to drugs.

## MEXICAN GOVERNMENT POLICY DURING THE SALINAS ADMINISTRATION

In December 1988 President Salinas underscored that the antinarcotics policy was a national priority.[11] He promised to strengthen governmental structures, amend the law to increase the penalties for drug traffickers, augment the corresponding human, financial, and material resources to that end. The Salinas administration has a commendable record of committing resources to the drug problem, battling corruption, reorganizing government resources on antidrug policy, and leading the formation of a Latin American drug policy.

## GOVERNMENT STRUCTURE FOR DRUG POLICY

### Office of the Attorney General

The Office of the Attorney General is in charge of investigating and pursuing drug-related health crimes involving narcotic drugs and psychotropic substances, which constitute a federal offense. Appointed and serving at the discretion of the president, the attorney general is responsible for the Federal Public Prosecutor's Office. The attorney general brings federal crimes before the federal courts, with the assistance of the Federal Judicial Police who are under his orders. He also advises the federal government on policy (i.e., proposes and helps draft legislative proposals).

### The Armed Forces

The Secretariat of National Defense has the job of guaranteeing national security, intervening to provide assistance to the civilian population, and carrying out civic actions and social services in fulfillment of the orders issued by the president in his role as commander in chief.

The Mexican Army assists the Federal Public Prosecutor's Office and the

Federal Judicial Police in locating and destroying illicit cultivations. It destroys clandestine laboratories and drug networks which traffic, distribute, sell, and consume narcotics and psychotropic substances. The armed forces arrest drug traffickers only when they catch them in the act of growing, distributing, or using, as stipulated in the constitutional provision that allows any person to arrest a criminal and his accomplices and place them at the immediate disposal of the federal public prosecutor.

The agents of the local Public Prosecutor's Office in each of the states of the Mexican Republic, as well as the Judicial Police agents assigned to them, collaborate with the Office of the Attorney General of the Republic to assist in the procurement of federal justice.

From the perspective of public health, the prevention and treatment of drug addiction are the province of the Health Secretariat through the National Council on Addictions, which is chaired by the secretary of health.

## REINVIGORATION OF GOVERNMENTAL STRUCTURES

### Establishment of the Assistant Attorney for Investigation and Combat of Drug Trafficking

On December 23, 1988, the Mexican president promulgated new regulations for the organic law of the Office of the Attorney General for the purpose of reinforcing its structure through the establishment of an Office of Assistant Attorney General for Investigation and Combat of Drug Trafficking. The office has the authority to investigate and pursue health crimes involving narcotics and psychotropic substances. The new office has four new departments: Criminal Procedures for Crimes Involving Narcotics and Psychotropic Substances, International Relations, Narcotics Investigation, and the Campaign against Production of Narcotics. Under these departments are nine area offices and one special division.

### Expansion and Specialized Training of Human Resources

Since the beginning of the Salinas administration, 1,200 positions have been budgeted for agents of the Federal Judicial Police, to be assigned exclusively to the fight against drug trafficking, and 344 positions for agents of the Federal Public Prosecutor's Office specializing in narcotics and psychotropic substances. Twenty branch delegations of the Permanent Campaign against Drug Trafficking and fifteen supervisory units have been established to investigate and combat drug trafficking. In 1989, the Office of the Attorney General had 117 operational bases throughout Mexico, which are divided into 344 sectors and 1,331 subsectors. The Secretariat of National Defense, which is organized into thirty-six military zones in Mexico, assigned in 1989 22,440 men (25 percent of the total armed forces on active duty) to the fight against drug trafficking, with special plans and operations during seasons for the planting and harvesting of drug-producing crops.

### Expanded Budgetary Resources

The Mexican government has been continually expanding the financial resources allocated to combatting drugs. Between December 1, 1982, and November 30, 1988, the Office of the Attorney General and the Secretariat of National Defense were directly allocated a budget of $631,730,509,000.00 Mexican pesos ($1,445,399,300,000.00 American dollars) to combat the production and trafficking of drugs.

In 1988, the antidrug budget of the Office of the Attorney General was $44,613,000,000.00 Mexican pesos ($102,074,000,000.00 American dollars). In 1989, the Attorney General's Office allocated over 61 percent of its budget for this purpose, a total of $122,600,000,000.00 Mexican pesos ($280,508,800,000 American dollars), which represented a budget increase of 174 percent compared to the previous year.

### Expanded Material Resources

In 1989, the Office of the Attorney General had the following aircraft and related equipment to combat drug trafficking: 55 Bell 206 helicopters, used chiefly for spraying; eleven Bell 212 helicopters, which are used for the protection of operations and for the transport of police and military personnel; twenty-nine Cessna 206 airplanes, used for reconnaissance and verification of illegal crops; and six airplanes for transporting campaign personnel. The logistical support is made up of 418 land vehicles, including tank trucks, trucks, and pickups.

### New Legislation

On December 14, 1988, the Salinas administration submitted to the Mexican Congress a package of proposed amendments to the Federal Criminal Code for the purpose of increasing the penalties for drug-related offenses and firearms offenses and of reducing the time required for federal judicial procedures thereby expediting trials.

*Organized Crime*

The maximum prison sentence was increased from six to eight years for offenses committed in conjunction with a criminal association and criminal organizations. In the case of crimes committed by current or former police officers, the penalty was increased by an additional 50 percent. In addition, such offenders would be dismissed from public employment and disqualified from holding any other public positions for a period of up to five years. The penalty for offenses committed by gangs, known as temporary criminal associations, was increased to up to 50 percent more for the offenses committed. In the case of a gang member who is or was a public employee, the penalty was increased by up to two-thirds of the relevant penalties for the offenses committed. Such persons would be removed from office and disqualified from holding other public positions for a period of up to five years.[12]

### *Health Crimes*

Revisions to the criminal code specified in stricter terms the circumstances under which a clear distinction could be made in cases in which drug traffickers are using *campesinos* to sow, cultivate, or harvest cannabis or marijuana plants. To merit more lenient treatment by the criminal justice system, such conduct must occur in circumstances of social isolation.[13]

Maximum penalties for crimes against health, especially in the case of different types of narcotics and psychotropic substances, were increased from fifteen to twenty-five years in prison. Fines were also increased and set on the basis of multiples of minimum daily wages so as to automatically rise with inflation.

Various additional amendments were made to stiffen penalties for narcotics offenses; for example, when the offense is committed by public servants entrusted with prevention or investigation of drug-related offenses, or when minors or incompetent individuals are used to commit the offense. In addition, when the act is committed by professionals, technicians, auxiliaries, or personnel related to the different branches of health care who utilizes this situation to commit the offense, the rights or functions of such persons to practice their profession or skill will be suspended for five years and they will be disqualified for a further period equivalent to the prison sentence. When the proprietor, holder, lessee, or usufructuary of an establishment of any type uses the establishment to commit an offense of this nature or permits it to be used for such purposes by third parties, the establishment will be permanently closed.

### *Corrupt Offenses*

The penalties for the offenses of abuse of authority, intimidation, and bribery were increased by 50 percent when the offenders are members of a police force or the customs or immigration services. In addition, such offenders will be dismissed from their posts and disqualified for a period of up to eight years from holding another public position.[14]

### *Procedural Reforms*

The term in which a defendant must be sentenced was reduced from fifteen to ten days following the completion of the hearing. The time during which the public prosecutor must present written conclusions after the close of proceedings was limited to a maximum of thirty days when the file exceeds 200 pages.

## Campaigns against Drug Trafficking

During the period from December 1, 1988, to September 20, 1989, the Mexican government waged campaigns against drug trafficking. The official statistics of the Mexican government show the following:

**PLANT SEIZURES**

| | Number of Plantings | Area in hectares |
|---|---|---|
| Poppy | 38,334 | 2,927 |
| Marijuana | 30,454 | 2,851 |
| Total | 68,788 | 5,778 |

| **Drug Seizures** | |
|---|---|
| Cocaine | 21,984.3 kg. |
| Marijuana | 374,574.8 kg. |
| (dried and packaged) | |
| Heroin and opium gum | 541.8 kg. |
| Total | 397,100.9 kg. |

| **Vehicle Seizures** | |
|---|---|
| Land vehicles | 2,587 |
| Aircraft | 55 |
| Seacraft | 5 |
| Total | 2,647 |

Furthermore, the judicial authorities arrested and held for trial 8,039 persons; 4,538 judicial proceedings were in process; 22 air incidents occurred; 15 public servants were killed in action; 20,671 flying hours of flight personnel were spent on reconnaissance, spraying, and verification; and the area covered by reconnaissance flights was 772,612 kilometers.

During the past administration, from December 1, 1982, to November 30, 1988, the Mexican authorities eradicated 307,536 illegal plantings, with a surface area of 34,871 hectares. Mexican authorities seized 726.9 kilograms of heroin and opium gum, 33,176.6 kilograms of cocaine, and 9,669 kilograms of marijuana. In addition, Mexican authorities dismantled 47 laboratories and seized 6,414 vehicles, 75 vessels, 125 aircraft, and 9,978 weapons. Also, 70,460 persons were arrested and held for trial by the judicial authorities, charged with drug-related crimes, and 43,895 trials were started. During this period 47 federal agents lost their lives in actions against drug trafficking.

### Border Operations

Two major border operations were mounted to combat drug trafficking in Mexico. On April 1, 1989, the Office of the Attorney General initiated a special operation in the north of Mexico. The operation combined the efforts of the Mexican Army, the Federal Highway Police, and state and municipal authorities pursuant to the provisions in the respective Federal-State Development Agreements and Action Coordination Agreements. The operation occurred in an area 120 nautical miles south of the border of the United States in the states of Baja California, Sonora, Chihuahua, Coahila, Nuevo León, and Tamaulipas, states which border on the United States. Actions also took place in the states of Baja California Sur and Sinaloa. The statistics, in terms of plantings destroyed; drugs, vehicles, and weapons seized; laboratories dismantled; and arrests and arraignments made, are significant. Additionally, several criminal organizations were dismantled, for example, the organization led by Adolfa Jesús Constance, ''El Padrino,'' in Matamoros, Tamaulipas was dismantled in April 1989. The authorities also arrested Ramón Salcido Bojórquez, who was responsible for several murders in California; he was extradited to the United States.

On August 15, 1989, the Mexican government (Office of the Attorney General) started a special operation in the south of Mexico aimed at discouraging drug-related activities. The operation also combined federal with state and local authorities pursuant to provisions in the respective Sole Development Accords and Action Coordination Agreements. This operation has been implemented in the states of Chiapas, Campeche, Quintana Roo, and Tabasco, which share borders with Guatemala and Belize. In addition, the operation is being conducted in the states of Guerrero, Morelos, Oaxaca, Puebla, Veracruz, and Yucatán. Sixty checkpoints have been established, while operating twenty-four hours a day at strategic locations in the above-mentioned states.

## INTERNATIONAL ACTIVITIES

### Cooperation with Multilateral Organizations

The Mexican government participated actively in the drafting, in Vienna, Austria, of the United Nations Convention against Illicit Traffic in Narcotic Drugs and Psychotropic Substances (thereafter referred to as the UN Drug Convention), and signed the convention on February 16, 1989. The Mexican government especially contributed to the following provisions in the convention: a comprehensive approach to the problem, including demand, and the aspects of supply and transit of narcotics and psychotropic substances; respect for sovereignty, for the principle of nonintervention and for the internal rule of law of states; the stance against replacement of national jurisdiction by the law enforcement agencies of other countries; and the stance against supervision or certification of punitive provisions on the part of states.

Mexico actively participates in specialized international agencies, such as the Commission on Narcotic Drugs of the United Nations Economic and Social Council and the International Narcotics Control Board of the United Nations Fund for Drug Abuse Control and Drug Division.

At the regional level, Mexico's presence has been reinforced in the Organization of American States through its participation in the Inter-American Drug Abuse Commission (CICAD). It is one of the three governments that are drafting the uniform laws on money laundering.

Mexico and the United Nations Fund for Drug Abuse Control concluded a memorandum of understanding on August 16, 1988, and an agreement on February 16, 1989, authorizing the use of US $15 million in Mexico for activities aimed at implementing comprehensive rural development and community sanitation programs in the states of Guerrero, Michoacán, and Oaxaca in order to discourage drug production in areas where planting has been critical or reoccurring.

This contribution initially came from the government of Italy. Its fundamental purpose consisted of providing peasants with options for legal work and, consequently, legal income. The program plans public works, including the establishment of power plants, rural schools, agribusinesses, production units, and drinking water.

## Bilateral Cooperation with the United States: The Mutual Legal Assistance Treaty and the Bilateral Drug Convention

Despite the multitude of cross-border criminal transactions, the mechanisms for law enforcement cooperation between the two countries have not kept pace with the propensity and celerity with which criminals perpetrate crimes and consciously manipulate legal, cultural, political, and economical differences between the two countries for their own advantages. Indeed, so great are the differences that organized criminals exploit the gap to operate their syndicates. Many rackets combine moving people, drugs, money, planes, vehicles, and guns. Depending on the experience, expertise, and circumstances of law enforcement cooperation, some groups concentrate on one or more of these ''commodities'' at different times.

The Mutual Legal Assistance Treaty (MLAT) and the Bilateral Drug Convention are important because both instruments are so new that a discussion of them helps both government officials and private sector counsel to understand the extent to which criminal organizations will utilize them. Until now, the absence of mature law enforcement instruments has resulted in self-help measures and actions that arguably may violate the laws of the other country. For instance, for years the U.S. government has pressured the Mexican government to allow U.S. officials to conduct on Mexico soil a variety of law enforcement activities. Indeed, U.S. law enforcement officials have long been present and actively conducting activities in Mexico. Still, other requests, such as to make hot pursuit against criminals or suspected planes with narcotics into Mexico, have been rejected.

After a long and intensive negotiation lasting several years, the MLAT was signed on December 9, 1987, approved by the Mexican Senate on December 29, 1987, and published in the Official Gazette of the Federation on January 8, 1988. The U.S. Senate Foreign Relations Committee approved the MLAT on July 25, 1989, and the U.S. Senate finally voted to approve its ratification on October 24, 1989. In the Senate, the vote of approval to the resolutions of ratification on all pending MLATs included language in the form of an understanding proposed by Senator Jesse Helms (R–N.C.) "to prevent the granting of assistance to foreign officials who engage in, encourage, or facilitate the production or distribution of illegal drugs." This language, publicly directed at the alleged role of certain Mexican officials, apparently blocked the exchange of instruments to the MLAT. Finally, on May 3, 1991, the MLAT went into force.

The MLAT provides a wide variety of new mechanisms for cooperation in criminal matters. Mutual assistance includes: (1) the taking of testimony or statement of witnesses; (2) the provision of documents, records, and evidence; (3) the execution of requests for searches and seizures; (4) the serving of documents; and (5) the provision of assistance in procedures regarding the immobilizing, securing, and forfeiture of the proceeds, fruits, and instrumentalities of crime. Recently enacted U.S. legislation and the Drug Convention allow equitable sharing of forfeited property with a foreign government to reflect that government's contribution in narcotics investigations leading to seizure or forfeiture.

An MLAT has many advantages over letters rogatory and Interpol, which are the main mechanisms of law enforcement cooperating in the absence of an MLAT. MLATs are designed to enable law enforcement authorities to obtain foreign evidence in a form admissible in the requested party's courts. Letters rogatory are written requests from a court in one country to a court in another country for assistance in obtaining evidence. Letters rogatory generally are slow and relatively inefficient because the requests must go through many bureaucratic steps, including courts in both countries, foreign ministries, justice ministries, and, in some instances, embassies. The procedure is time consuming, cumbersome, and inefficient, and it often results in information that cannot be introduced in court. In contrast, MLATs are made directly for one competent authority or Justice Ministry to the other. MLATs provide an obligation for contracting parties to assist upon request, with certain exceptions, as when the request relates to a political or military offense. In contrast, execution of letters rogatory is only a matter of comity.

One of the issues during the U.S. ratification of the MLAT was that, unlike some U.S. MLATs, the U.S.–Mexican MLAT authorizes, but does not guarantee, the right of cross-examination of deposition testimony taken in Mexico. The U.S. position is that, whenever possible, MLATs should guarantee this right since the right to confront and cross-examine witnesses is a right guaranteed under the Fifth Amendment to the U.S. Constitution. However, Mexican officials advised U.S. negotiators that direct and cross-examination of witnesses by U.S. prosecutors and defense counsel rather than Mexican officials would violate Mexican law and render the treaty unratifiable in Mexico. The U.S. government believed that the benefits of an MLAT with Mexico clearly outweighed the disadvantages of the inability of Americans to examine witnesses directly.

An innovative provision contained in some recent U.S. MLATs obligates the signatory governments to consult, as appropriate, to develop additional specific agreements or arrangements, formal or informal, on mutual legal assistance. They may agree on practical measures as may be required to facilitate the treaty's implementation. The proposed Mexican–U.S. MLAT provides that the signatory governments will meet at least every two years in order to review the effectiveness of the MLATs implementation and to agree on "whatever individual and joint measures are necessary to improve its effectiveness." The requirement of a review and the establishment of working groups provides for a mechanism whereby law enforcement officials can review the need for improved measures to adjust to whatever circumstances exist in criminality and enforcement techniques in each of the countries. For instance, one of the most dynamic results of the Italian–U.S. MLAT has been periodic meetings of joint working groups, which have developed a series of major law enforcement programs on arms trafficking, organized crime, drug trafficking, and terrorism. As a result of the working groups, the two governments are exchanging information and technology, have cross-training of law enforcement agents in the two countries, and have begun other exchange programs involving magistrates and judges. The working groups have reviewed the results of organized crime trails and have considered how to continue to support their efforts against organized crime. Hence, the inclusion of a provision to establish a working group and review mechanism is essential to continued improvement in law enforcement cooperation. The inclusion of this provision in the Mexican–U.S. MLAT provides a potential dynamic mechanism for improved law enforcement cooperation and flexibility to meet changing circumstances of cross-border criminality.

*Mexico–U.S. Narcotics Cooperation Agreement*

In a potential watershed development, the governments of Mexico and the United States have concluded an agreement to cooperate in combatting narcotics trafficking and drug dependency, which was signed on February 23, 1989, and entered into force on July 31, 1990. The role of the United Nations Fund for Drug Prevention, particularly the UN Drug Convention and the Comprehensive and Multi-disciplinary Plan of Future Activities in the Control of the Improper Use of Drugs, are acknowledged at the beginning of the agreement.

The agreement aims at attacking the narcotics and drug dependency problems from four major areas: prevention and reduction of the illicit demand for narcotics and psychotropic substances; control of supply; suppression of illicit traffic; and treatment and rehabilitation. Perhaps the most important provision is the requirement that the signatory parties adopt the necessary measures to fulfill the obligations of the agreement, "including legislative and administrative measures, in conformity with the fundamental provisions of their respective internal legal systems." In broad terms, the agreement also safeguards the national integrity of each signatory country. It obligates the signatory parties to fulfill their obligations under the agreement pursuant to the principles of self-determination, nonintervention in internal affairs, legal equality, and respect for the territorial integrity of states. It also specifies that the signatory parties are not allowed by the agreement to exercise and perform in the other signatory's jurisdiction the function or authority exclusively entrusted to the authorities of that other signatory party by its national laws or regulation. The agreement obligates the signatory parties to consult in advance with the other members of the commission on actions that one of the parties may intend to undertake, which may affect the other party in a manner inconsistent with the objects and purpose of the agreement.

The agreement provides that cooperative measures will be undertaken within a framework of joint responsibility and will be defined by the parties according to their budgetary capabilities, through a Memorandum of Understanding. Seven specific areas are set forth for programs that are intended to accomplish the following:

1. Reduce demand through prevention, treatment, and public awareness activities.
2. Eradicate narcotics cultivation and establish programs for substitute crops.
3. Identify and destroy narcotics processing labs and facilities.
4. Regulate the production, importation, exportation, storage, distribution, and sale of inputs, chemicals, solvents, and other chemical precursors whose use is diverted to the unlawful preparation of narcotics and psychotropic substances.
5. Establish systems for exchanging information on combatting narcotics trafficking and drug dependency.
6. Draft such new legal instruments as the parties consider appropriate for combatting narcotics trafficking and drug dependency.
7. In general, undertake all activities that are considered relevant to achieving better cooperation between the parties.

Institutionally, a principal engine of the cooperation will be the establishment of a United States–Mexico Permanent Mixed Commission of cooperation against narcotics trafficking and drug dependency (the commission), which will begin to operate within six months from the entry into force of the agreement. It will be composed of the coordinating operational and consultative authorities of the parties. The parties will designate the operational authorities. The consultative authorities will be the foreign ministries of the parties. The commission will meet every four months, with the principal mission of formulating recommendations to its governments on the most effective form in which the cooperation under the agreement can be provided. For their implementation, the commission's recommendations will require the approval of each of the governments. The approval will be formalized diplomatically through Memoranda of Understanding which must be executed by the operational coordinating authorities of the commission. Annually the commission will prepare a report on the implementation of the agreement. It will describe the status of the cooperation between the parties and will constitute the joint basis for both governments in evaluating the efforts of the parties in combatting narcotics trafficking and drug dependency.

The agreement will enter into force when the governments of the parties notify each other through diplomatic channels that they have completed all their respective constitutional requirements and procedures. The agreement continues indefinitely but can be terminated by either party at any time, provided notification is given through diplomatic channels in writing, in which case the agreement will terminate ninety working days from the date of delivery of such notification. The signatory parties can revise the provisions, and such revisions will take effect when the governments of the parties notify each other through diplomatic channels that they have completed their respective constitutional requirements and procedures.

The agreement does not specifically cover money laundering related to narcotics trafficking nor does it cover forfeiture of assets. Nevertheless, the agreement is so broad both in scope and with its commission, that it could decide to tackle both matters within the commission's work (i.e., by way of joint programs to exchange information and audit returns of suspected traffickers). The establishment of a commission may well be a watershed in narcotics cooperation. In other criminal cooperation areas, working groups have provided a dynamic element that facilitates intensive cooperation and enables governments to find innovative solutions to new and sometimes unforeseen crime problems. The commission also provides for both countries to bring together persons who will develop personal relationships and commitments to solving narcotics problems. In the past, such relationships have blossomed and developed, often surpassing the nationalistic and domestic blinders that limit cooperation, prevent growth in cooperation, and even cause cooperation to die.

Some critics may charge that the United States should not do business with a government that has not cooperated in the past or that is indelibly corrupt. It is correct that, without the will to administer agreements, such agreements are worthless. However, even if one government is not willing or is unable to implement an agreement, the existence of an obligation to cooperate under international law can itself cause pressure and ultimately bring down a government. Without an agreement binding a signatory party, both countries lose a potential source of persuasion. Additionally, governments change. This agreement will continue to exist and succeeding governments, as well as members of the commission, may make a positive difference. The agreement appears to represent a conscious, determined effort by the new Salinas administration to strengthen bilateral cooperation. The United States should welcome these kinds of initiatives wholeheartedly. Indeed, strong forces in Mexico are and will continue to undermine this initiative. To succeed, the Mexican government and bilateral mechanisms will require all the political support they can muster.

### Bilateral Cooperation with Other Countries

Mexico has signed bilateral agreements to cooperate against illicit narcotics trafficking with Venezuela (July 10, 1989), Colombia (July 11, 1989), and Guatemala (August 18, 1989). Additionally, Mexico is discussing the possibility of concluding similar cooperation agreements with Belize, Costa Rica, Spain, Great Britain, and Peru.

## DRUG DEPENDENCE CARE

Although drug abuse is not currently a serious problem in Mexico, specific work is being done in areas such as research, education, promotion of community involvement, medical care, and legislation, under the coordination of the National Council against Addictions, chaired by the secretary of health.

The Office of the Attorney General is represented on the National Council. Through an anti–drug dependence program called ADEFAR, the attorney general has established committees that operate in every city in Mexico. Government authorities preside over the ADEFAR committees. Their membership includes parents, teachers, neighborhood groups, organizations, civil groups, and health, education, law enforcement, and public security institutions. Currently, 1,150 ADEFAR committees operate in Mexico, and 22,951 subcommittees do preventive work in high-risk areas.

## CURRENT MEXICAN GOVERNMENT DRUG INITIATIVES

In 1991, the Mexican government undertook additional initiatives to combat illicit narcotics trafficking, including new structures in its government, regional diplomatic initiatives, and ongoing operations on cases.[15]

The new approaches of the Mexican government include enhanced cooperation abroad and within Mexico, both within the federal government and between the federal and state governments. It includes improving access to new technology in three areas: more reliable interdiction; improved efforts to combat money laundering; and better use of human resources, especially in sophisticated crimes.

Efforts toward improved cooperation include strengthening links with the rest of the world, in other words, with international organizations and governments, such as the United States and Central America, which has become a significant problem owing to the increased growing of illicit narcotics, especially poppies.

Intelligence is very important in operations to combat narcotics operations, and Mexico is developing a national intelligence center. Mexico will improve its technology to strengthen interdiction on sea, land, and air, to combat money laundering, and to penetrate and suppress organized criminal groups.

On February 1, Mexico opened a new police academy to train police attached to the Office of the Attorney General. Although Mexico has an existing police academy, it does not concentrate on training personnel for specific narcotics skills. Additionally, on February 1, the Office of the Attorney General underwent a reorganization to enable it to improve its response to the narcotics problem.

The increased cooperation between the United States and Mexico includes ongoing undercover operations. Law enforcement officials are allowing the operation to proceed in order to penetrate the criminal organization.

With respect to the intelligence operation, three objectives exist: The first is to interact quickly with agents of foreign governments on reports on movements of planes, boats, and cars transporting narcotics. In this regard, Mexico has established facilities in Monterrey and Acapulco for telecommunications to enable Mexico to cooperate with U.S. law enforcement officials in El Paso, Texas. In addition, Mexico has nine helicopters and will soon have a total of twenty-one helicopters and special planes to interdict drugs. Currently, Mexico is training crews to operate the planes. During the week of January 14–19, 1991, Mexico seized two planes with huge amounts of cocaine, using the new cooperative approach.

The other two objectives of intelligence are to combat money laundering and to ascertain and penetrate the criminal networks in Mexico in a more systematized manner. Mexico has recently made significant advances on the latter objective.

To strengthen international cooperation, Mexico has just created a task force to attack money laundering aggressively within the Office of Procurador General. It still requires more legal support.

Concerning the proposed United States–Mexico MLAT, which both countries have ratified but Mexico has not yet exchanged instruments of ratification due to the Helms reservations, some officials believe that the treaty should be completely renegotiated; others believe that the Mexican Attorney General, the Minister of Foreign Affairs, and the Mexican Senate must try to find a means to solve this obstacle.

With respect to cooperation in the context of Central American integration, at the meeting held on December 15–17, 1990, in Puntarenus, Costa Rica, of the five presidents of Central American countries and Panama on economic integration, narcotics was only a secondary topic. However, cooperation against illicit narcotics trafficking has become more important. The amount of poppies in Guatemala has tripled in the last five years, and Mexican enforcement efforts have driven organized traffickers to countries such as Belize for landing strips to transport narcotics. Regional cooperation is characterized by officials in the Mexican government as very primitive, partly because Central American governments believe that narcotics trafficking is primarily a U.S. problem and partly because they lack the money to take action. Mexico can help these countries by exchanging ideas. In fact, Dr. Jorge Carrillo Olea, the general coordinator for combatting narcotics trafficking, is traveling to Central America to attempt to begin a dialogue about cooperation against illicit narcotics trafficking.

In December 1990, a Commission of Narcotics was created by the Group of Three—Colombia, Venezuela, and Mexico. It intentionally will be small in order to be dynamic. The group will next meet in Cuernavaca, Mexico. At present, it is difficult to know both the attitude and the capability of Colombia and Venezuela to exchange intelligence. However, the governments must begin to explore cooperation.

In May 1991, the Mexican Office of the Attorney General opened its second office overseas—an observation office in Costa Rica with responsibility for Central America—partly to concentrate on the narcotics problem. Mexico is considering the establishment of a third office in South America.

In response to allegations of human rights difficulties of persons imprisoned on narcotics charges, the Mexican government has established an office of human rights in the Office of the Attorney General. A former official of the Mexican Supreme Court heads the office, and Mexico is committed to prevent deprivations of human rights.

## CONCLUSION

The history of Mexico as a major producer and transshipment point for illicit narcotics trafficking—along with its relatively difficult economic circumstances for a large number of its people, the enormous demand for illegal drugs in North America, the relative ease of transporting contraband, and the great profits derived from the illicit narcotics trade—makes the task of combatting illicit narcotics trafficking difficult and costly. In the past, the bilateral tensions between the United States and Mexico have been reflected in the frustrations of the United States in its inability to bring to justice quickly the assassins of Enrique Camerena. The Camerena case was only the tip of the iceberg; the United States is frustrated by its inability to control effectively the influx of illegal narcotics. The use of foreign scapegoats is an expedient and politically convenient manner in which to justify the failure of U.S. policy. Despite the occasional setbacks, which undoubtedly will recur, the Mexican and U.S. governments have achieved progress in cooperation, as manifested by the signing of a bilateral narcotics cooperation agreement, a tax information exchange agreement, and a mutual legal assistance treaty (which is not yet in force), and by the number of arrests and seizures made of drugs and plants that were part of the illegal cross-border narcotics traffic.

The Salinas government is devoting substantial new resources toward combatting illicit narcotics trafficking. Just as important, Mexico is aggressively searching for new approaches and is actively reaching out to other governments and international organizations to cooperate. Of great significance should be the potential for improved regional cooperation in the context of the Mexican initiative since other Latin American countries will be able to understand the Mexican legal system and its culture and to identify with Mexico which has shared the problems of their status as supply and transshipment companies. In fact, although drug cooperation between Mexico and North American countries has improved and will continue to improve, the most important result of the Mexican government's initiative is likely to be the crystallization of a Latin American approach. Some Latin American governments, despite promises of aid, money, planes, and guns, do not pay heed to the U.S. emphasis on the use of the military to stop growing illicit narcotics. This is illustrated by the rejection by the Fujimora government in Peru of U.S. foreign assistance in narcotics. Eventually, Mexico may well be a leader of Latin American drug policy and an intermediary between Latin America and North America, especially since its negotiation of a free trade agreement and other economic integration agreements, including a free trade agreement with Venezuela and Colombia and one with the Central American countries, will lead irretrievably to closer enforcement and narcotics cooperation, similar to the Schengen Convention within the European Economic Community. The Schengen Convention has established both an information system and a permanent drug work force.[16]

## NOTES

The authors are grateful for comments on the manuscript by Gustavo Gonzàlez Báez and Miguel Angel Gutierrez Canto, Office of Minister for Narcotics Affairs, Mexican Embassy in Washington, D.C.

1. For a background to the history of Mexico's drug trade, see Scott B. MacDonald, *Dancing on a Volcano: The Latin American Drug Trade* (New York: Praeger, 1988), on which this account relies heavily.
2. *New York Times*, 9 September 1969, 1.
3. Abraham Lowenthal, *Partners in Conflict: The United States and Latin America* (Baltimore: Johns Hopkins University Press, 1987), 8.
4. *Latin American Times*, December 1987, 12.
5. Mary Thornton, "Suspect in DEA Slaying Said to Live Well in Mexico," *Washington Post*, 22 February 1986, A1.
6. James Mills, *The Underground Empire: Where Crime and Governments Embrace* (Garden City, N.Y.: Doubleday & Company, 1986), 1155.
7. Mary Thornton, "A Murder at the Border of No-Man's Land," *Washington Post*, 13 April 1986, A3.
8. Quoted in Mary Thornton, "Mexico Is Top U.S. Source of Heroin," *Washington Post*, 22 February 1986, A20.
9. Ibid.
10. Jesús Yanez Orozco, "The Right against Drug Trade," *Voices of Mexico* (September–November 1986): 52.
11. United Mexican States Office of the Attorney General of the Republic, *Mexico's Efforts in the Fight Against Drug Trafficking* (Mexico City: Government of Mexico, 1989).
12. Mexican Penal Code, Articles 164 and 164 bis.

13. Ibid., at Article 195.

14. Ibid., at Article 312 bis.

15. This section is essentially taken from Bruce Zagaris, "Mexican Government Outlines New Drug Policy Initiatives," *International Enforcement Law Reporter* 7, 2–5 (1991). It summarizes a briefing on 24 January 1991 by Dr. Jorge Carillo Olea, the General Coordinator for Combatting Narcotics Trafficking.

16. For a discussion of the application of the Schengen Agreement to drug trafficking, see Bruce Zagaris, "Schengen Convention Points Way to Enhanced EC Criminal Cooperation," *International Enforcement Law Reporter* 7, 26 (January 1991).

## BIBLIOGRAPHY

Lowenthal, Abraham. *Partners in Conflict: The United States and Latin America*. Baltimore: Johns Hopkins University Press, 1987.

MacDonald, Scott B. *Dancing on a Volcano: The Latin American Drug Trade*. New York: Praeger, 1988, 1990.

Mills, James. *The Underground Empire: Where Crime and Governments Embrace*. Garden City, N.Y.: Doubleday & Company, 1986.

Secretaría de Relaciones Exteriores. *El problema del narcotráfico: Visión internacional*. Mexico City: Secretaría de Relaciones Exteriores, 1989.

Shannon, Elaine. *Desperados: Latin Drug Lords, U.S. Lawmen, and the War American Can't Win*. New York: Viking, 1988. This is primarily a DEA perspective on the Camerena incident.

United Mexican States Office of the Attorney General of the Republic. *Mexico's Efforts in the Fight against Drug Trafficking*. Mexico City: Government of Mexico, September 20, 1989.

Zagaris, Bruce, ed. *Developments in Mexican–U.S. Law Enforcement Cooperation: What the Practitioner Needs to Know*. ABA Criminal Justice Section April 20, 1990. A Report for the ABA.

# 11

# Panama

LAURA VÁSQUEZ AND BARBARA JAHANSOOZI

## INTRODUCTION

As was vividly demonstrated in December 1989, with Operation Just Cause and the capture of Panamanian strongman Manuel Antonio Noriega by U.S. armed forces for his alleged involvement in the drug trade, the Republic of Panama has played a significant role in the trafficking of narcotics from South America. As with other countries involved in this illicit commerce, Panama's prominence derives from the country's unique geographical location. Panama lies between the Pacific Ocean and the Caribbean, on the narrowest part of the Isthmus of Panama which links Central America and South America. It can be stated that, while those countries involved in coca and cocaine production are endowed with an appropriate soil conducive to cultivation, Panama is endowed with a geographical position that has traditionally made it an important transshipment point for all types of goods. Thus, Panama's role in the inter-American drug trade is primarily as a transshipment point for illicit narcotics on their way to the U.S. market. Other factors that have enhanced Panama's role in the international drug trade include the Latin American country's banking system, which was based on tough secrecy laws, as well as the corruption of certain elements of the country's elite, in particular the armed forces.

## COUNTRY BACKGROUND

Although this chapter is concerned mainly with Panama's role in the international drug network, in order to fully understand the country's role in this commerce, one must briefly examine the historical background. Though drugs and money laundering are historically a new departure for the use of Panama as an entrepôt for contraband trading, the country's development from its earliest colonization included smuggling. Under the Spanish, the colony survived as a trade and communications center linking Madrid's colonies on the western portion of South America with their rich deposits of precious metals to their motherland in the Iberian Peninsula. With the discovery of silver in modern-day Peru and Bolivia, Panama's importance to its mercantilist motherland was augmented as it became the main terminus on the coveted mineral's journey from South America to Europe. Notes one author, "[A] century before the English settled Massachusetts, Panama was the crossroads and the marketplace of the great Spanish Empire, the third richest colony of the New World."[1]

Spain's adherence to a mercantilist trading system created an adverse reaction within the New World. Many hardy entrepreneurs took to contraband trading, smuggling to other parts of Europe or to other European colonies in the Americas. The tradition of smuggling, therefore, was well established by the seventeenth century, despite the decline in the mines and Spanish power. In the nineteenth century, with the opening of the West Coast of the United States and the California Gold Rush, Panama's fortunes revived. Panama once again became a primary transshipment point for the treasure, but in a slightly different way than in the days of the Spanish galleons. Initially, transport across the isthmus was conducted by rail; however, in the early twentieth century, the Panama Canal was built.

The Panama Canal has greatly enhanced Panama's position as a trade crossroads. It has been estimated that some 5 percent of the world's trade in goods passed through the Panama Canal in the 1980s, and the canal contributed 5 percent to Panama's gross domestic product.[2] It is only natural, with such a huge volume of trade, that a certain amount of smuggling occurs, especially when one considers the smuggling tradition that permeates the region.

The precedent for Panama's involvement in narcotics trafficking and related money laundering can be traced to the 1950s and 1960s. As far back as 1955, Panamanian strongman General José Antonio Remón Cantera was implicated in the drug trade. There are indications of concern in the Eisenhower administration over Remón's involvement in the trade, and efforts by the administration to discourage Remón's illicit activities. General Remón was assassinated in 1955 by an unknown assailant; most theories implicate the drug Mafia.

Panamanian strongman General Omar Torrijos, who seized power in a 1968 coup, is also known to have been involved in illicit activities: smuggling arms from Cuba and South America through Panama to assist in the overthrow of the Somoza dynasty in Nicaragua. In addition, it is also widely accepted that Torrijos had connections and dealings with major figures in the South American drug Mafia during his regime. As Frederick Kempe noted, "After the Torrijos coup, Panama began replacing pre-Castro Cuba as a magnet for Mafia money laundering, drug racketeering, arms smuggling, and various other contraband operations."[3] The Torrijos regime, along with Manuel Noriega (who was then head of Panama's military intelligence), was targeted by the Nixon administration for their involvement with the drug trade as well as for alleged ties with international communism through Castro in Cuba. Nixon had declared drug abuse a "national emergency" in the United States and had prioritized the elimination of drug trafficking as a partial solution to the problem.

In addition to his personal drug use, Torrijos' brother Moises is also known to have been involved in illicit drug trafficking through Panama. He and Noriega were implicated in a 1971 seizure of 154 pounds of heroin carried by the son of a Panamanian government official holding a diplomatic passport.[4]

Panama's position as a center of international finance and a haven for money laundering was ensured by Torrijos and his 1969 Minister of Planning Ardito Barletta. Following bank reform laws in the late 1960s and early 1970s, which emphasized stringent secrecy and limited restrictions on bank transactions, the number of banks conducting business in Panama grew from only 12 in 1967 to over 120 in 1987. Thus, Torrijos transformed Panama into the "Switzerland of Latin America." Under Torrijos, according to one author, "[i]llicit funds flowing to Panama grew commensurately and dummy corporations multiplied like rabbits."[5]

In the 1990s, the role of the banking industry in Panama and the bank laws that helped foment the expansion of that industry in the prior twenty years were points of tension between the Panamanian and U.S. governments. Much disagreement existed over the economic benefits of Panama's position as a center of finance and offshore banking. There is little doubt that the finance industry infuses large amounts of needed capital into Panama's economy and generates much needed employment. Opponents of Panama's banking secrecy laws in the United States argue that the laws as they have existed (prior 1991) only served as a cover for money-laundering activities, and that Panama will continue to be a center for drug activity in Latin America and the Caribbean until the laws are changed and financial institutions are prudently supervised. They contend that the proliferation of foreign financial institutions in Panama limits the nation's economic autonomy as all economic decisions are scrutinized by the international financial community and that dependence on international capital only makes the country vulnerable to capital flight in the event of major political or economic disturbance, such as the U.S. sanctions in the 1980s and the fall of the Noriega government.

## THE NORIEGA YEARS

After Torrijos died in a mysterious plane crash in 1981, General Manuel Noriega assumed leadership over the Panamanian government. General Noriega's involvement in the drug trade had a history in Panama long before the U.S. military intervention in 1989. Even before 1989, proposals were made by U.S. officials in the Nixon administration for Noriega's assassination as a political solution to the problems of drug trafficking in the isthmus. Nevertheless, despite suspicions of his involvement in the drug trade and other shady dealings, Noriega rose through the ranks of the Torrijos regime to become the third man in line, behind General Ruben Dario Paredes, to take over Torrijos' position after his death. After Torrijos' demise, the reins of power were handed to Paredes, who was eventually forced out by Noriega. Paredes had begun to dismantle many of the dictatorial trappings of the Torrijos state and to move toward a more open, pluralistic polity. Noriega put a stop to all of this and consolidated power in his hands, ruling through a series of figurehead civilian presidents.

Under Noriega, Panama's involvement in the drug trade increased considerably. In 1984, rumors abounded through the country that Colombian *narcotraficantes*, with whom Noriega had an agreement, were working in a large laboratory in the Darien jungle along the border. According to Guy Gugliotta and Jeff Lean, in *Kings of Cocaine*, although the laboratory was discovered by the Defense Forces, the Medellín cartel was able to communicate with Noriega on a European trip, to reach an agreement through the good offices of Cuba's Castro, and to receive most of their equipment back. However, it was doubtful that they returned to Panama to refine cocaine.

During the same year, Noriega supported the presidential bid of Nicolas Ardito Barletta, and although there is considerable evidence of the elections having been rigged, many were willing to overlook that evidence because Barletta appeared to be one of the first civilians to run the country in several years. Hopes for a full-scale return to democracy were crushed, however, when Barletta's figurehead presidency became subject to the vagaries of the Noriega regime. Two weeks after the headless body of anti-Noriegusita Dr. Hugo Spadafora was discovered just over the Panamanian border in Costa Rica in September 1985, Barletta was forced to resign.

Spadafora's death rallied renewed vigor into the civilian opposition to the Noriega regime. The deceased, a former minister of health in the Torrijos government, had been active in fighting against the Somoza regime in Nicaragua. Since Torrijos' death, Spadafora, like many in the growing civilian opposition forces, realized the threat Noriega presented to Panama. After publicly accusing Noriega of links with the international drug trade, Spadafora was brutally murdered, and his decapitated body was found in a U.S. mail sack near the Costa Rican border. The last time he was seen, shortly before his death, Spadafora was in the company of three officers from Noriega's defense forces. His death became a major rallying point for the opposition, and calls were made for a complete investigation into the murky circumstances surrounding his death. When Barletta announced that a meaningful investigation into the murder would be conducted, he was forced out of office.

With Spadafora's murder and increasing abuses by the Noriega regime, accusations increased and, in turn, so did repression. Colonel Roberto Díaz Herrera was the first from within the governmental structure to publicly challenge Noriega. Accusations of the regime's abuses had been made before by many people, for example, by newspaper columnists such as Sanchez Borbon who was consistently harassed for his anti-Noriega statements until he was forced to flee the country in July 1986.

In 1986 the *Wall Street Journal* reported that U.S. officials were accusing the PDF Panamanian Defense Forces (PDF) of involvement in drug and arms trafficking, as well as in money laundering. Similar accusations continued from within and without Panama. With the impetus provided by Herrera and other outside opponents, pro-democratic forces organized the National Civic Crusade, which staged daily protests, strikes, and demonstrations and demanded Noriega's ouster as well as investigations into all those involved in the abuses of his corrupt regime.

Noriega responded harshly to the growing opposition. His abuses included the violent repression of public protests and demonstrations and government censorship, including the closure of all opposition newspapers and the prohibition of any type of broadcasting concerning the increasing political unrest in the country. However, as political protests and resistance mounted, stories of unwarranted and random arrests without charges abounded.

On July 23, 1987, the United States stopped all military and economic aid to Panama and shortly thereafter terminated Panama's sugar quote—the commodity on which the wealth of figurehead president Eric Arturo del Valle's family was based. The U.S. measures were welcomed by most opposition groups. Noriega, in an attempt to regain popular support and to deflect attention from his regime's abuses, appealed to the nationalist anti-American sentiments that traditionally existed among the younger, more politically active forces in Panamanian society. He accused the U.S. government of fomenting unrest in order to provide an excuse to maintain control over the canal after 1999, when the canal is due to revert to full Panamanian jurisdiction. Other maneuvers to curry support included the accusation that the United States destabilized Panama to undermine its position as an international banking center, hoping that the banks would move to Miami. Most efforts, however, fell flat, and the country continued to become polarized between those for and those against the Noriega regime.

## THE U.S. INTERVENTION

The end of the Noriega regime came on December 20, 1989, when the United States militarily invaded Panama. Just as the first president of Panama, Aresemana, was installed by U.S. forces, so was the first president in the aftermath of the invasion, Guillermo Endara. The general perception of the reason for the invasion was that the United States felt a pressing need to stem the flow of drugs that all diplomatic options had failed. In the ten months that followed the invasion, the U.S. military responsibilities in Panama were expanded: Joint patrols were conducted throughout the country by Panamanian police teams and about 200 U.S. military policemen to preserve public order.

The economic sanctions placed on Panama by the Reagan administration had the heaviest impact on the business community, which had played a major role in the opposition to the Noriega regime. As a result of those sanctions, it was estimated that the Panamanian economy may have shrunk by as much as 30 percent.[6] The economic situation, moreover, did not improve in the immediate aftermath of the invasion: Unemployment ranged between 25 and 35 percent; underemployment was equally high; and basic supplies were low. The government of Panama added to the problem when it fired 10,000 employees in an effort to streamline its payroll. Joblessness and an inexperienced new police force fuelled a crime wave in cities that resulted in the business establishment's having to hire armed security guards. In addition to growing numbers of robberies in urban areas, the level of drug trafficking through Panama's remote countryside and coastlines remained high or had even grown in size and scope since the invasion as a result of poor government surveillance and heavy unemployment.[7]

After the invasion, the U.S. government pledged a $1 billion aid package to Panama. Nearly half the package consisted for restored trade privileges and credits, rather than new money. The U.S. Congress then cut the other half of the aid package by 15 percent. All but $84 million in the aid package was given to Panama in 1990. The receipt of the final amount was made contingent upon the signing of a treaty that would allow U.S. officials increased access to local banking records in an effort to end the laundering of drug money.

## RESTRUCTURING PANAMA'S INSTITUTIONS

A two-pronged approach to changing Panama's position in the world of drug trafficking was envisioned by U.S. and Panamanian officials after the invasion. To eliminate all traces of the Noriega regime, the new government announced a restructuring of Panamanian institutions and law enforcement agencies with a goal of safeguarding against the use of Panama for continued drug transshipments. Restructuring also attempted to remedy abuse of the Panamanian financial system to prevent the movement and laundering of drug money. Particular attention was paid to the Panamanian Customs Service and to the anti-democratic armed forces. One of the objectives of the U.S. invasion was to convert the PDF into a lightly armed civilian police that would uphold the constitutional government.

Panamanians were deeply skeptical over the decision, made by their government immediately after the invasion and supported by the United States, to build the 12,000-member Fuerza Publica, a national police force, almost entirely from decommissioned soldiers from Noriega's military. To most Panamanians the incorporation of soldiers into a new police force, maintaining a military-style command structure, represented a contradiction to the government's publicly stated desire to demilitarize society.[8] By the end of October 1990, all officers above the rank of major were dismissed and 57 percent of majors, 40 percent of captains, and 28 percent of lieutenants were retired.[9]

The new Fuerza Publica is now composed of about 10,000 men who work in eight-hour shifts and return to their homes when off duty rather than remain in military barracks, as they did under the Noriega regime. Most of the Fuerza Publica are armed with only sidearms or shotguns; some special-duty units are equipped with Taiwanese-made assault rifles modeled after the M–16. Criticism of the new force has centered on their inability to stop the growth of street crime in Panama City and other urban areas as well as the spread of narcotics-related activities in the countryside.

The Customs Service, once integrated under Noriega's military command structure, was reorganized as a civilian agency responsible for seizing all forms of contraband, including illegal drugs. But with a limited budget, the agency was reportedly pressed for manpower and equipment to keep up with its routine work of collecting duties and enforcing tariffs, leaving few resources for launching major campaigns against drug trafficking. According to one foreign diplomat, "The government is just outmanned, outgunned and outmaneuvered."[10]

Panamanian officials attribute their country's strategic location and its long border with Colombia to having a significant impact on the magnitude of drug smuggling. The invasion and ouster of Noriega failed to stem the tide entirely. Since the invasion, drug trafficking still continues through Panama. Along the northern border with Costa Rica, after the invasion, customs agents were reported to be patrolling on foot for a lack of vehicles. Inspection stations near the Panamanian border, at the periphery of the city of David, were manned by unpaid workers hoping to be hired when more money would become available. In other parts of the country, the customs service has no personnel at all.

Efforts made by the new Customs Service to limit the flow of drugs through Panama included targeting transit points along well-known trafficking routes. Those points in Panama were the Tocumen Airport, the smaller Paitilla executive airport in the center of Panama City, and remote Atlantic coastal towns which have served small cocaine-laden vessels in the past.[11]

## RESTRUCTURING THE FINANCIAL SYSTEM

Although President George Bush and other U.S. officials have characterized the U.S. overthrow of General Noriega as a major victory against drug trafficking, many law enforcement officials claim that Panama has been far more important as a money-laundering center for billions of dollars in drug profits than as a drug transshipment point. Economic sanctions by the Reagan administration, leading to a general strike and the shutdown of the banking system in March 1988, contributed to capital flight from Panama during the last days of the Noriega regime. This dried up local liquidity and triggered a freeze on local deposits. Bank deposits in the country shrank from approximately $40 billion in 1987 to $13 billion in 1988.[12] U.S. officials concerned with Panama's role in the drug trade believed Panama's importance as a money-laundering center was diminished after the invasion as drug traffickers allegedly moved their money to other locations, such as the Cayman Islands, the Bahamas, Uruguay, and Europe.

International banking was an important factor in Panama's economy before 1988, when the United States imposed economic sanctions against Panama. The industry at that time employed about 8,000 people and handled billions of dollars with few restrictions or requirements concerning the identity of the depositor or the source of funds. After the invasion, both Panamanian and U.S. officials were concerned with revitalizing the economy. Concerns about the nature of Panama's banking sector, however, remained on the U.S. side. This led a U.S.–Panamanian mutual legal assistance treaty (MLAT).

Negotiations over the MLAT began almost immediately following the invasion of Panama in December 1989 and the installation of the Endara government. In August 1990, a preliminary draft was initialed. However, the Endara administration rescinded its support for the accord under intense pressure from Panamanian bankers. The Panamanian Banking Association, which represents some 110 to 120 offshore banks in the country, eventually supported the agreement. At first the executives of these banks opposed the MLAT, stating that it would neutralize the benefits of the secrecy laws that enabled Panama to attract money in competition over other regional offshore financial centers catering to confidentiality, such as the Cayman Islands and the Bahamas. Eventually, these concerns were muted, and the Endara administration was able to move ahead with the agreement.

On April 2, 1991, the governments of the United States and Panama announced that they had reached an agreement over an MLAT that had been stalled over an impasse on the scope of crimes covered among other topics. The two governments officially signed the MLAT on April 11, 1991.[13] Although the MLAT will make Panama less attractive to some offshore business, most of the persons who would want bank secrecy will accept the limitations on Panamanian secrecy imposed by the agreement. Many persons who would not accept the limitations would take their money elsewhere and this would not benefit Panama's offshore sector.

What helped pressure the Panamanians into accepting the MLAT was the freezing by the U.S. Congress of $84 million of $420 million in economic assistance to Panama since early 1990 and Panama's dire economic straits. In particular, the United States insisted that the treaty apply to criminal tax evasion investigations. The proposed MLAT, which still must be ratified and the instruments of ratification exchanged before it takes effect, apparently covers tax evasion, embezzlement, and insider trading of securities.

Despite the breakthrough, the United States will still find penetrating Panamanian confidentiality laws difficult because that country's corporation laws enable persons owning companies to use bearer shares. Hence, the U.S. Justice Department, Drug Enforcement Administration, and members of the U.S. Congress have urged the Bush administration to seek changes in Panama's corporation laws. However, Panamanian officials rejected such prompting, arguing that these laws are a matter of Panamanian sovereignty and are therefore not negotiable.[14]

The agreement has significance because it formalizes arrangements whereby U.S. investigators have access to banking information on customers suspected of money laundering or drug trafficking. Currently, all cash transactions over

$10,000 are automatically reported to Panama's banking commission and then to U.S. authorities, if requested.[15]

The Panamanian offshore banking community was strongly opposed to the MLAT with the United States. It contended that inclusion of criminal tax evasion within the treaty would unfairly disadvantage Panama compared to other offshore jurisdictions with secrecy laws. Consequently, the United States apparently agreed to condition the application of the tax evasion provision to the existence of clear evidence that the tax evasion was part of a drug money-laundering investigation. This is essentially the compromise contained in the U.S.–Bahamanian MLAT which provides an Article 2(2) than an "offense for the purposes of this Treaty does not extend to any matter which related directly or indirectly to the regulation, including the imposition, calculation and collection of taxes except any matter pertaining to monies shown to be derived from any activity within the provisions of paragraph 1 of the foregoing definition."[16]

This article of the MLAT with the Bahamas applies to crimes which are punishable by one year's imprisonment or more and which arise from, relate to, result from, or otherwise involve: (1) illegal narcotics or drug activity under Article 36 of the Single Convention on Narcotic Drugs, 1961, as amended by the 1972 Amending Protocol to the Single Convention on Narcotics Drugs, 1961; (2) theft, including the obtaining of money or property by false pretenses, representations, or promises and including the commission of embezzlement; (3) a crime of violence; (4) fraud or the use of fraud; and (5) a violation of a law relating to currency or other financial transactions as an integral element contributing to the commission of any offense covered by the paragraph.

It should also be added that the Endara government passed, in February 1990, Decree Number 41, which was approved by the National Assembly in August. This decree required all banks to maintain records of all cash transactions over $10,000 and provided for heavy fines to be imposed on any banks that were found to be involved with money laundering. This decree, similar in its requirements to U.S. Currency Transaction Reports (CTRs), represents an attempt on the part of the Panamanian government to deal with the issue of money laundering.

## RESTRUCTURING THE JUDICIAL SYSTEM

Since the ouster of the Noriega government in December 1989, the new Panamanian government has struggled to reconstruct a justice system free from the influences and abuses of more than two decades of military dictatorship. Yet, the constitution of the country, which has not changed, establishes the armed forces, or their equivalent, as a branch of the government, coequal with the executive branch. The Legislative Assembly, as of 1991, had not written a new constitution to replace the existing one, penned by Omar Torrijos, and the laws of the dictatorship remain on the books. One such libel law provides for an individual to be jailed for five years based on a simple accusation. Rewriting the constitution of Panama will be critical to establishing and maintaining a democracy in the country.

The president of Panama's Supreme Court, in the aftermath of the ouster of Noriega, Judge Carlos Lucas López, was given the mandate to rebuild the judicial system. The new chief justice, upon receiving his new post, was quick to note that Panama's criminal justice had been "totally destroyed."[17] In Panama City, the Supreme Court building had been sacked by looters and damaged by fire, and hundreds of court records had been destroyed. The central courthouse in Colon, the country's second largest city, was badly burned and the court's archives destroyed. Documents in many outlying court offices and regional capitals were destroyed by fleeing members of the old government. Because of the corruption and overall rot in the old regime's judiciary, one of the first actions of the Endara administration was to replace all nine members of the Supreme Court, along with sixteen out of twenty appeals court judges and 70 percent of the lower court judges.

The new Supreme Court, stripped even of its typewriters in looting, began operations in the cramped eleventh floor of the National Bank in Panama City. Police investigations were not able to cope with the growth in new crimes nor adequately treat the reopening of cases of people long detained. Although efforts were made to reform the legal system, no jury trials were held a year after the invasion (as of early 1991). With the loss of millions of pages of trial documents and a backlog of more than 17,000 cases left by the deposed government, rebuilding brought the judicial system virtually to a halt, leaving thousands of people stranded in prison. Many people have been waiting trial for years longer than the maximum sentence they could receive if convicted. The Panamanian penal system was also characterized by overflowing prisons, leading to a number of escapes and violence. In all likelihood, it will take several years for the Panamanian penal system to recover from the past abuses and from the chaos resulting from the fall of Noriega.

## SOCIETAL RESPONSE

When discussing Panamanian society it is important to remember that the Latin American country is relatively small. Its total area is approximately 77,082 square kilometers and has a population of less than 2.5 million. In general, Panamanian society looks upon the drug trade as a major evil. Drug abuse does exist in the country, and it has grown in recent years, but the problem of the drug trade is regarded as a problem whose primary cause is seen to be the demand by the United States and Europe.

With the use of U.S. troops in 1989 to combat the drug trade in Operation Just Cause it would be impossible to say that the drug trade has not touched most Panamanians. Although the U.S. troops were welcomed by many Panamanians as the ultimate effort to remove Noriega and the abuses of his regime, much controversy remains about the legacy that the U.S. intervention left. Noriega was disliked by most Panamanians, but he was also seen by many as a dictator partially created by the United States who thus had a responsibility to assist in his removal from power. Many now argue that Washington must also actively participate in the country's reconstruction through increased aid and trade credits, as well as following through on rebuilding the lives of those most directly affected by the invasion. Specifically, many argue that the United States must act quickly to rebuild the neighborhoods that were destroyed in the invasion, including the El Chorrillo area. Although the United States has housed many of the families who lost their abodes in the invasion, there remains a sentiment that further compensation is due them.

Most important, post-invasion efforts in Panama are centered on restructuring the judicial and police forces. The political structures are also in serious need of reform, but many argue that this can come only with the next elections. When President Endara was democratically elected on May 5, 1989, many officials from the Noriega regime still remained in positions of authority and are regarded as obstructing movements toward restructuring. In addition, many Panamanians feel an increasing frustration and impatience with the slow pace of reform and recovery.

Panamanian society is also afflicted by the fact that, despite the invasion and fall of Noriega, drug trafficking continues with its disruptive impact on society. In 1990 and 1991, there were indications that the ouster of Noriega removed a centralizing power in the traffic and that, in the ensuing vacuum, some of the smaller Mafioso leaders have begun to vie for control of their particular stake in the country's drug traffic as well as in other criminal activities. The increase in violence may also stem from the diminished capacity of the Panamanian police forces following their overhaul in the aftermath of the invasion.

## CONCLUSION

The role of Panama as a transshipment point for drug trafficking and as a conduit for the movement of money, which will probably continue in the future, is not entirely dependent upon the country's geographical location. Continued demand for drugs in the United States and a growing demand in Europe ensure Panama's prominence as a transshipment center. As in the past, Panama will probably continue to act as a crossroads of the world.

Panama's involvement in the drug trade is also contingent upon the alleviation of the country's economic and political problems in the early 1990s. The restructuring of the judicial system, the reorganization of the police forces, the need for a new constitution, and the question of U.S. aid promised to Panama are all important to stabilizing the country and diminishing opportunities open to drug traffickers and money launderers.

## NOTES

Barbara Jahansoozi is an official of the Drug Enforcement Administration but the views expressed in this chapter are her own and do not in any fashion represent those of the U.S. government.

1. *Panama: A Country Study* (Washington, D.C.: Federal Research Division, Library of Congress, 1989), 3.
2. Ibid., 42.
3. Frederick Kempe, *Divorcing the Dictator: America's Bungled Affair with Noriega* (New York: G. P. Putnam's Sons, 1990), 75.
4. Ibid., 79.
5. Ibid., 74.
6. "U.S. Insists that Panama Ease Bank Secrecy Laws," *Los Angeles Times*, 1 February 1990, A8.
7. "U.S. Troops in Panama Put down Rebellion," *Washington Post*, 6 December 1990, A1.
8. "Panama's Courts Stalled by Chaos," *New York Times*, 6 September 1990.
9. "Meanwhile Back in Panama," *Time*, 26 November 1990.
10. "Panama: A Year Wasted," *Washington Post*, 22 December 1990, A12.
11. "The U.S. and Panama to Assist U.S. on Drug War," *New York Times*, 11 January 1990.
12. "U.S. Insists that Panama Ease Banking Secrecy Laws," *Los Angeles Times*, 1 February 1990.
13. For background on the signing, see "U.S. and Panama Sign Drug Treaty," *Washington Post*, 12 April 1991, A34.
14. For additional information, see Clifford Krauss, "Panama–U.S. Accord Set on Bank Records," *New York Times*, 3 April 1991, D1.
15. Patrick Coone, "Panama and U.S. to Unlock Bank Secrecy," *Financial Times*, 5 April 1991, 3.
16. Quoted from "U.S.–Panama Agree on Mutual Assistance Treaty," *International Enforcement Law Reporter* (April 1991): 129–31.
17. "Panama, A Year Wasted," A15.

## BIBLIOGRAPHY

Eddy, Paul, with Hugo Sabogal and Sara Walden. *The Cocaine Wars*. New York: W. W. Norton & Company, 1988.

Gugliotta, Guy, and Jeff Lean. *Kings of Cocaine: Inside the Medellín Cartel—An Astonishing True Story of Murder, Money, and International Corruption*. New York: Simon and Schuster, 1989.

Kempe, Frederick. *Divorcing the Dictator: America's Bungled Affair with Noriega*. New York: G. P. Putnam's Sons, 1990.

MacDonald, Scott B. *Dancing on a Volcano: The Latin American Drug Trade*. New York: Praeger, 1988.

———. "Getting Caught in the Medusa's Hair: International Banking and Money Laundering.'' Paper presented at the International Symposium on Money Laundering, Miami, Florida, 26–28 October 1989.

Millet, Richard L. ''The Aftermath of Intervention: Panama 1990.'' *Journal of Inter-american Studies and World Affairs*. 32, no. 1 (Spring 1990): 33–67.

# 12

# Peru

LAURA VÁSQUEZ

## INTRODUCTION

Coca, known as "white gold," is the natural precursor to cocaine and is Peru's main link to the international drug trade. With Peruvian coca and cocaine exports estimated at between $600 million and $1.2 billion annually, coca has in the early 1990s become one of this Andean country's main exports to North America. Coca cultivation in Peru is estimated to account for 60 percent of the world's cocaine supply, and most, if not all, of Peru's coca exports are destined for the U.S. market. It is estimated that in Peru 200,000 peasants rely on coca cultivation for their living.

## BACKGROUND

The Republic of Peru is located on the eastern portion of the South American continent, neighboring Ecuador, Colombia, Brazil, Bolivia, and Chile. The third largest nation in South America, it covers approximately 497,093 square kilometers. Peru is divided into three geographical regions. The coastal zone contains a third of the population and most of the country's largest cities, including Lima, the capital. Over half of Peru's population of approximately 21.2 million people lives in the mountainous region of the Andes. Most of the coca is grown in the *selva* (jungle) region of the eastern slopes of the Andes, an area of tropical forest and jungle which also forms part of the tropical forests of the Amazon basin.

Peru's population is made up of Amerindians, mestizos (mixed white and Indian), and whites. While Spanish and Quechua (spoken by the native Indian population) are the official languages, many of the native Indians also speak Aymara. There is a great division between the poorer, less educated Indians, who live mainly in the sierra region and the wealthier, predominantly white population.

## THE STRUCTURE OF THE INDUSTRY

Most of Peru's coca cultivation occurs in the eastern portion of the country near the Amazon river basin in an area known as the Upper Huallaga River Valley. This region has been described as an area "where the hillsides are steep, sandy, wet and well drained."[1] Tingo María, the major urban trade center in the coca-growing region, is located deep in the mountainous jungles of central eastern Peru. In Tingo María, also known as "Snow City," unlike in many other villages found in the poverty-stricken highlands of the Andes, conspicuous consumption abounds. According to one analyst, due to the prevalence of coca in the region, "the heavily forested Upper Huallaga is awash in cocaine money."[2]

The Upper Huallaga Valley is also known as the *Ceja de la Selva* (the eyebrow of the jungle), and the region's jungle is reportedly one of the richest, most biologically diverse and beautiful rain forests in the world—but all of that is threatened by coca. The ecological destruction of the Upper Huallaga Valley by the coca trade has caused the beautiful valley to assume an additional nickname—"the Valley of Death."

Peru's coca industry is divided between the local coca farmers, who sell the coca leaves to the middlemen, who are often Colombian and representatives of the Medellín and Cali cartels. Although refining of coca into coca paste is done in Peru, the chemical refining to cocaine has usually been done in laboratories in Colombia. In the early 1990s, there have been reports of cocaine laboratories in Ecuador, Brazil, and Suriname.

While the Upper Huallaga remains the main area of coca cultivation in Peru, eradication and interdiction efforts of the past few years have caused coca cultivation to spread farther into the Amazon basin, to the Central Huallaga as far as Juanjui, Bella Vista, and Picote and the lower Mayo Valley, further endangering the region's natural resources.

Despite the increasing importance of coca in Peru's export profile in the last twenty years (since the early 1960s), coca itself has had a long history in Peru. Coca is a part of Peru's heritage.[3] Archaeological evidence has suggested coca use among the region's Indian population as early as 1800 B.C., and it is argued that almost all of the ancient Andean cultures' activities included coca use. Coca has been cultivated by the traditional Indian population of the Peruvian Andes for centuries. Even in the early 1990s, it remains an important part of the life of the indigenous Indian population, who for centuries have used coca in their everyday life "to ward off hunger and fatigue."[4] Additionally, coca can take on added importance for the Indian when it is used in traditional and religious ceremonies or as a medium in traditional medicinal treatments wherein (according to traditional beliefs) coca can at times taken on or induce supranatural powers for the user.

With the arrival of the Europeans to the region in the sixteenth century, the value of coca in the traditional societies was soon appreciated. Earliest attempts by the Spanish to profit from the prized coca leaf included failed attempts at taxation. Coca used by the Andean Indians was then discouraged by the sixteenth-century Spanish throne because coca use was feared to be corrupting the Iberian ruling class. Like today, these earlier attempts to control the drug failed, and the Spanish soon learned that, instead of trying to control the coca, coca's importance in the local Indian's everyday and religious life could be used to their advantage. The Spanish learned to manipulate coca and even before the sixteenth-century silver boom, the coca trade was reported to be the "most profitable enterprise in the kingdom," which "made many men rich."[5]

The Spanish conquistadors' main interest in the region in the colony's early days was to be found in the rich ores in the surrounding regions, and their main interest in the local Indian was in his usefulness as a ready laborer in the mines. The Spaniards learned to cultivate coca for use among Indians and reap a profit, establishing *cocales* (labor-intensive haciendas) in the regions surrounding the silver mines, which would produce large amounts of coca for distribution as part of the monthly salaries of the Indian labor force in the silver mining areas.[6] Coca was recognized among the Spanish, not for its religious value, but for its use in making the Indian a more docile, less demanding, more productive worker in the mines.[7]

Nevertheless, despite the enduring presence of coca in the life of the traditional Indian of Peru from colonial times to the present, the industry's structure in the region has changed dramatically in the past few decades. The most important change is in the development of international linkages. Although 40,000 acres of coca are still produced legally in Peru (under the auspices of the Empresa Nacional de la Coca, or ENACO, the official agency for the legal coca trade's supervision) for a limited internal traditional consumption, as well as for export as an anesthetic, most of Peru's coca is destined for illegal export to the industrialized world (especially the U.S. market), where demand for cocaine—the white powder and its variants which are produced by a long process of chemical alteration of the coca leaf—has risen to crisis proportions since the 1970s. The importance of coca in Peruvian heritage is recognized by the fact that limited amounts of coca can still be bought legally in the Indian marketplaces of Peru, where packets of coca leaves are sold for use in making coca tea as well as for their palliative value as remedies for headaches, altitude sickness, and digestive disorders.

Coca cultivation became the obvious alternative when a government-sponsored program during the Belaúnde administration (1963–1968), called the Huanuco–San Martín colonization project, which encouraged migration to the Peruvian Andes from the crowded coastal cities, failed. The government had hoped that the mountainous region on the eastern slopes of the Andes would provide an outlet for the overcrowded coastal cities and sponsored migration to the area for the cultivation of tea, coffee, and tobacco from which the new colonists were to make a living.[8] The program's direction under the subsequent military government of General Juan Velasco Alvarado was changed as the administration emphasized collective and cooperative farming efforts. The colonization project was further undermined by the military government's increasingly heavy international debt burden, and eventually, due to a lack of official funding, the program became defunct. The new migrants to the region were left without sufficient government support. In addition, due to the area's nutrient-poor soil, the government-sponsored plantations had failed to yield a crop amenable to the sustenance of the new colonists; the only crop that seemed to survive and flourish in the region was the hardy coca plant. Thus, the colonists turned to coca, and Tingo María became a center for coca cultivation and the production of coca paste and became the starting point for the long journey that takes the cocaine we see in the streets of U.S. cities from its basic elements found in nature.

## ENVIRONMENTAL IMPACT

Although coca has caused havoc and irreparable damage to the lives of those who have fallen under its spell in the United States as well as conditions of violence and instability throughout Latin America, perhaps the most serious destruction caused by the international drug trade has been its effect on the producing areas' natural resources. The drug user's fleeting pleasure is indirectly responsible for tremendous damage to some of the world's richest, most beautiful natural areas.

The first environmental impact of coca cultivation is deforestation. It has been estimated that 700,000 hectares of rain forest are deforested every year for coca cultivation and related activities—clearing trees for the construction of clandestine airstrips and coca-processing laboratories and the planting of subsistence crops for coca producers.[9]

The Peruvian economy underwent severe economic problems in the 1980s and early 1990s, and the costs of ecological consciousness are too high to be recognized by those who participate and depend on the destruction of Peru's forests for their livelihood. Low prices for alternative agricultural products, poor infrastructure and transportation, and the government's inability to effectively address the menace of the *Sendero Luminoso* (Shining Path) insurgency have made legal farming in Peru economically obsolete.

In the Peruvian countryside peasant farmers have found that coca production pays more than five times as much as any legal crop, and these farmers, fighting for a meager existence, are estimated to be stripping approximately three acres of the Upper Huallaga forest daily to make room for coca fields, laboratories, and airstrips. Given the choice between feeding one's family and protecting the environment, there is no doubt which path to follow.

It is estimated that coca has caused the deforestation of 1.7 million acres of the Amazon rain forest and 14 percent of the Upper Huallaga forest in Peru. Whole mountainsides have been cleared for coca cultivation, a problem worsened by the movement of production deeper into the jungle due to government eradication efforts and *Sendero* terrorism. Coca production is also appearing in the lowland, where the coca is planted under a cover of trees to avoid detection. As a result, each plant produces less. This spurs the coca farmer to plant more coca and thus increase the amount of land used for each crop, exacerbating the environmental crisis in the region.[10]

Coca cultivation has even moved into many national parks, forests, and protected areas, such as the Tingo María National Park, Manu National Park, and the Apurimac National Forest, which claim some of the highest biodiversity in the world.[11] Eradication efforts have had limited effects in stemming the trade and have resulted in the constant movement of production and further deforestation. Additionally, the coca plant is particularly hazardous to the region's environment as it is planted on steep slopes which are sensitive to rapid soil erosion.

Environmental degradation is exacerbated by the coca farmers themselves who are reported to use large amounts of harmful chemical fertilizers to maximize their coca yields and their profits, and to protect their fields with toxic pesticides including paraquat. During the rainy season, the overworked soil in the Upper Huallaga Valley, replete with poisonous pesticides, is swept into area rivers, where the chemicals, in turn, endanger the rivers' systems throughout Peru. This alters pH levels and reduces the water's oxygen content, which is necessary to supply life.

The rivers of the Upper Huallaga are further threatened by the dumping of chemicals used in the preparation of coca paste. Among others, these chemicals include millions of gallons of kerosene, hydrochloric and sulfuric acid, lime, carbide, acetone, and toluene. Many species of fish and other types of aquatic creatures have already disappeared from Peru's rivers, and, according to some analysts, many streams are dead biologically from the pollutants associated with the drug trade.[12] In the Upper Huallaga, a vicious cycle has been created, and short-term economic needs to feed hungry people make the long-term destruction of the valley's ecology seem remote and unimportant. Economic necessity results in environmental degradation, and, as the economic conditions worsen, so does the environmental degradation.

Considerable concern was raised in the United States over the issue of the coca trade and the environment in Peru in 1988 when the Reagan administration made plans to spray the herbicide tebuthiuron (called Spike) in Peru in an effort to eradicate coca production. The controversy grew when it was discovered that sixteen hectares of coca had already been treated with the herbicide in Peru. Some analysts in the United States contended that the experiment in the Upper Huallaga was done with minimal preliminary laboratory experimentation and with little regard for the possible damning effects that the herbicide might have on the region's environment, not to mention the possible health effects on the local population. Environmentalists pointed out that the use of Spike is illegal in the United States and it should not be used in ''areas where soil movement by water erosion and/or natural or mechanical means is likely,'' as in areas where coca is cultivated.[13] In addition, the chemical family to which Spike belongs is known to have cancerous effects. The debate, however, became academic when the Spike program was cancelled when Elanco Products, a division of Eli Lilly, decided to discontinue selling the product due to possible repercussions to the environment in Peru and any possible implication in any natural degradation that might occur with the product's use.[14]

Some argue that, environmentally, it is better to eradicate coca with herbicides than to allow its cultivation and production and the associated threats to the environment to continue. This author is of the opinion that, despite any attempts to eradicate the production of coca, the trade will thrive as long as the market in the United States allows such exorbitant profits to be made, and thus such efforts only exacerbate the environmental degradation as the coca farmers move deeper into the jungle, as well as into other countries, to continue their trade. (It has been reported that the drug trade has moved to the Amazon region of Brazil, where efforts at controlling it are even more difficult due to the remoteness and difficulty of the terrain.)

## SOCIETAL IMPACT

In the 1970s there was not much concern about the production of coca for the U.S. market in Peru. The problem was seen as a *gringo* problem. The coca trade was perceived as only one part of a burgeoning underground economy in Peru as well as a stimulus to the faltering economy. Unlike the United States, Peru did not have a significant drug abuse problem. This, however, in the early 1990s, changed with the signs of increasing consumption in Peru along with associated problems, including increasing crime rates and corruption in enforcement agencies. Furthermore, Peru's judicial system was overloaded with cases, due to increased crime and limited resources. Court dockets were months behind, and jails were overcrowded to the point of crisis.

## THE GOVERNMENT'S RESPONSE

It was in the 1970s that cocaine became the drug of choice among an elite set of drug abusers in the United States, who could afford the high-priced drug. Addiction rates steadily grew throughout the decade, and the United States began to pressure a number of countries to control their production of cocaine. In 1978, the government of Francisco Morales Bérmudez seriously sought for the first time to control illicit coca production in Peru, and he passed Decree Law 22095 which prohibited coca cultivation except where sanctioned by the government.

Following soon thereafter came the first in a series of joint operations between the United States and Peruvian forces in Operation Verde Mar, which sought to eradicate and destroy the existing coca plantations in the Upper Huallaga Valley. This first operation provided an idea of the difficulties involved: Only 60 of an estimated 12,000 hectares of coca in the region were destroyed.[15] As the area under cultivation grew out of control, the Bérmudez administration declared a state of emergency in certain parts of the Upper Huallaga, and government forces moved in to destroy coca crops, to confiscate the land associated with cultivation, and to arrest farmers and landowners who refused to cooperate. Nevertheless, these first efforts at eradication failed; the reduction in the supply of coca in Peru only increased the price of unrefined coca leaves in the black market. The increased profits made coca an even more attractive alternative crop for farmers who were facing increasing difficulties in the cultivation and marketing of legal crops in the region.

### Crop Substitution

Recognizing the difficulties involved in asking farmers to grow another type of crop when coca is so profitable, efforts have been made by the Peruvian government to organize crop substitution programs. Under the Proyecto Especial Alto Huallaga (PEAH) program, sponsored by Peru and the U.S. Agency for International Development (AID), the cultivation of food and cash crops was encouraged during the 1981 to 1985 period. PEAH also instituted programs in the coca-growing region to conduct environmental research, to expand services to the coca farmers, to train agro-scientists, to offer short- and medium-term credit to the coca farmers in the process of conversion, to redistribute land more equitably, to maintain roads and highways, and to supply potable water and sanitation facilities to the area. The PEAH project was by most accounts a failure in tempting the region's farmers to turn to crops other than coca. It was even alleged that loans made under the PEAH program were actually used to plant new crops of coca. The peasants planted legal crops on the land incorporated into their agreement with the PEAH program, but these legal crops failed to generate enough income to repay the loans. Thus, in order to be able to repay the loans received through PEAH, many farmers clandestinely planted coca to repay their debt.

The main attraction of the Upper Huallaga *cocalero* to coca is the discrepancy in earning power between coca and legal crops. Figures highlighting the preciousness of coca as compared to alternative crops abound. According to a number of estimates, a farmer in the Upper Huallaga who relies on legal crops for his income can expect to earn $1.90 a day, but a coca farmer or one who works on the coca plantations can make $15 a day.[16] A hectare of coca can reportedly earn up to $7,000; the same size plot of a legal crop could earn at most $600. It is noted that coca will bring in three times as much as coffee planted on the same ground. Some analysts even argue that the 200,000 peasants who are estimated to grow coca in the Upper Huallaga would "starve if they were forced to grow other crops."[17]

Nevertheless, like most other issues discussed in relation to the drug trade in Peru, there is some disagreement over the relative profitability of coca. Other analysts argue that "many alternative crops like cocoa, coffee and tropical nuts are at least as profitable as coca, if not more so."[18]

It is important to note that efforts at crop substitution are easier said than done. The soil of the Upper Huallaga is reportedly of marginal quality, poor in nutrients and highly acidic. The soil that nurtures coca does not easily support such suggested alternative crops as coffee, tea, bamboo, cacao, and palm oil. Coca reportedly makes better use of the existing soil in the region than alternative crops, and it is not as susceptible to disease as are other more fragile crops. Alternative crops, such as coffee, tea, and palm oil trees, take years to establish before they become income earning. The fertility of the Upper Huallaga for coca production was summarized by a Peruvian peasant: "God made this valley for coca. I plant coffee: it gets knee high and it dies. I plant cacao and it turns yellow. Coca—that's all that grows."[19]

In addition, the marketing of legal crops would require the introduction or renovation of an effective infrastructure which would facilitate the movement of the region's crops to the marketplace (roads, transport, and maintenance). With the cultivation of coca, the crop is moved to the market by the international drug traffickers who have established a complex network of airstrips and middlemen in the region. The middlemen are responsible for the payment to the coca farmers and for the movement of coca and coca paste from the Upper Huallaga to the refineries and ultimately to the marketplace in North America and Europe.

In 1991, President Fujimori called for greater access to international markets for the Peruvian farmer in order to enhance viable alternatives for the *cocalero* of the Upper Huallaga. For these measures to work, investment in the region is required as well as a reassessment of international quotas on coffee (such as the negotiation of a new international coffee agreement), enhanced trade benefits under the U.S. General System of Preferences, increased technical assistance from developed countries, increased trade concessions for legal exports from producing countries to the United States (as called for in the Cartegena Accord of February 1990), and a linkage between the international debt and crop substitution program (as suggested by Fujimori).

The Fujimori administration also returned to the idea of crop substitution. Peruvian experts have called for the issuance of legal land titles as part of the reforms aimed at legitimizing the *cocalero*. This measure would permit the growers to raise alternative crops on land they now would legally own as opposed to coca farming squatting. Peruvian economist Hernando de Soto noted that "alternative crops require investment, credit, large scale production and formal contracts, none of which are possible if farmers are not legally linked to their land."[20] De Soto favors an overhaul of the obsolete land titling and registration system, which was originally copied from the nineteenth-century Spanish system.

### Eradication

Eradication efforts, hand in hand with crop substitution efforts, such as the PEAH project, attempt to introduce alternatives to coca farmers. The Peruvian government's Eradication and Control of Coca Leaf Planting in the Upper Huallaga (CORAH) program was introduced in 1983 with the assistance of the U.S. Department of State's Bureau of International Narcotics Matters. The aim of this program was the total eradication of coca production in the Upper Huallaga. The program offers the Peruvian coca farmer $300 to destroy one hectare of coca, but the coca itself is worth $7,000.

The CORAH program hires *matahojas* (leaf killers) to pull the illegal coca from the land. The leaf killers are protected by armed escorts from the Unidad Móvil de Patrullaje Rural (UMOPAR), a specially trained antinarcotic strike unit, while they are destroying the coca fields. Despite this armed protection, organized attacks by the peasants in the Upper Huallaga (possibly in cooperation with *Sendero Luminoso* forces) against the *matahojas* are not unusual, and dozens of the leaf killers have been killed: Between 1982 and 1988, thirty-two eradication workers and six development officials were killed in eradication efforts.[21]

By most accounts, the CORAH program has been a rather limited effort compared to the massive amounts of coca that are being grown in the region. It is reported that in 1987 only one half of 1 percent of the total coca crops in the region were affected by the program's actions. Although in 1988 the program was given additional funding and resources (heavier UMOPAR protection and helicopter airlifts, power trimmers), due to the increased insurgency activity by the *Sendero Luminoso*, the operation was able to take only a very small bite out of a very large industry in the Upper Huallaga. According to some estimates, for every hectare that has been eradicated in the 1980s, 15 new hectares have been planted. Thus, eradication does not seem to be an effective solution to Peru's coca problem.

## Interdiction

Another approach used by the Peruvian government, with U.S. assistance, has been the interdiction of coca coming out of the Upper Huallaga. Operation Condor, which began in 1985, was one of the first interdiction campaigns to be launched in Peru. A cooperative effort between UMOPAR and U.S. pilots and Drug Enforcement Administration (DEA) officials, Condor's primary goal was to reduce coca prices, with the reasoning that, if coca prices were low, alternative legal crops will become more feasible options for the Peruvian coca farmer. The operation, which used helicopters from the Peruvian Air Force as well as Twin Bell 214 helicopters from the United States, consisted mainly of air raids that targeted cocaine processing laboratories and traffickers' airstrips.

In its first years, Operation Condor was credited with limited success; it reduced the price of coca leaves in Peru by 50 percent. However, in subsequent years, the operation was less successful because of the increased security risk to the agents involved due to the growing violence in the Upper Huallaga related to the activities of the *Sendero Luminoso* forces. Thus, the supply of coca and coca paste leaving Peru steadily increased in the late 1980s.

Another important joint Peruvian–U.S. interdiction program was Operation

Snowcap, which was launched in 1987. This three-year, $24 million program involved nine Latin American countries in which DEA agents were assigned to 3-to-4-month rotations accompanying police forces in Latin American countries in efforts to eradicate and interdict drug operations in the countries.[22] In late 1990, the DEA reported that its participation in antidrug efforts in Operation Snowcap in Peru would be reduced. DEA agents would gradually turn over supervision of drug raids in Peru to national forces.

The use of military and paramilitary operations to address the cultivation and trafficking of coca in Peru has been a point of contention between U.S. efforts in the region and the Peruvian government in the late 1980s and early 1990s. Moreover, there is a conflict within official Peruvian structures between the antidrug police efforts and the role of the Peruvian military in coca-producing areas, especially the Upper Huallaga, with little coordination between the two groups in their efforts. The Peruvian army's main task is to deal with the terrorist threat of the *Sendero Luminoso*, which has virtually paralyzed the Upper Huallaga. Thus, if there is a perceived insurgency threat in the region, the military is called in, and the antidrug forces, which have usually antagonized local coca farmers, are removed, which helps increase coca production.

While the national police force focuses on the drug trade, a clear distinction is made in official channels between the *Sendero Luminoso* guerrilla threat and those parties involved in the illicit drug trade. But this distinction has not always been so clear. U.S.–Peruvian–sponsored paramilitary efforts at eradication and interdiction were partially suspended in 1989 due to heightened security risks as the *Sendero Luminoso* gained a stronghold in the region. In early 1990, the operations were renewed with new vigor, and coca seedbeds became the new targets.

Joint U.S.–Peruvian interdiction and eradication efforts were enhanced in September 1989 with the construction of the Santa Lucia air base, a fortified base built with U.S. financial assistance in the heart of the Upper Huallaga. The base is manned by DEA agents, and the interdiction flights are conducted by civilian pilots employed by a private company contracted by the U.S. State Department (National Air Transport, Inc.). In 1990, the air base was a growing security concern for Peruvian authorities because of growing resistance from local *cocaleros*, and in April the *Sendero Luminoso* attacked the base with rocket-propelled grenades.

The effectiveness of the Peruvian police and of the military control of the region is further hampered by alleged corruption within these forces. Edmundo Morales noted that "the ones who benefit the most economically from the cocaine trade are those charged with fighting it."[23]

Noting the failure of Peru's eradication and interdiction efforts to control the coca trade, the Fujimori administration has rejected further military aid from the United States, calling instead for development assistance, debt relief, and efforts aimed at providing the *cocaleros* with alternatives. Despite this, the Peruvian

Ministry of the Interior signed a $5 million interim agreement for law enforcement assistance in 1991 with the United States.

One of the great complicating factors in the government's response to the drug trade is the involvement of the *Sendero Luminoso*. It is highly likely that the Maoist guerrilla insurgency represents the greatest threat to the Peruvian state. The *Sendero Luminoso* has initiated a campaign to destabilize the government which has affected all parts of the country. *Sendero* violence has affected life in Lima as well as in the countryside. It is estimated that 15 percent of Peru's population live under *Sendero*-controlled areas.[24]

The likelihood that the *Sendero Luminoso* and the *narcotraficantes* have joined forces in Peru, to create a drug-insurgency nexus of narco-terrorism, has generated considerable debate among analysts of the region. Some argue that the link between the *Sendero Luminoso* and the drug-trafficking organizations in the Upper Huallaga Valley represent the strongest narco-terrorist alliance in Latin America; others contend that these type of connections between disparate movements are unlikely and any such ties are necessarily tenuous. Due to the *Sendero*'s highly secretive nature, as well as the secretive nature of the drug trade, it is difficult to establish a clearly defined and long-lasting relationship between the two groups.

Such connections have been traced by some analysts back to a 1983 incident in which three members of the Peruvian Civil Guard were murdered in Nuevo Progresso by the *Sendero* insurgency, allegedly protecting drug activity in the region.[25] In 1984 a guerrilla offensive ousted the U.S.–trained antinarcotics service from the Tingo María area.

The crux of any relationship between the *Sendero Luminoso* and the drug cartels in Peru is said to consist of protection by the guerrillas for some Peruvian coca plantations from destruction by official antinarcotics forces in the high *selva* for money and arms from the drug-trafficking organizations.[26] In return, the *narcotraficantes* receive protection from government destabilization as well as increased production from *Sendero*-run coca cultivation because of the organization's puritan values and work ethic. A former Peruvian judge, Gabriela Tarazona-Sevillano noted that "the growth of narcoterrorism in the coca growing regions of Peru has paralleled the expansion of coca cultivation in the Upper Huallaga."[27] She also contends that, as coca cultivation spreads, narco-terrorism does the same.

A key element in the argument for *Sendero* involvement is that eradication and interdiction programs have alienated coca growers and made them into *Sendero* supporters. In 1991, the Upper Huallaga Valley was a stronghold for the Maoist guerrillas; it has been described by some as a "state within a state." Despite the seriousness of the government's efforts at controlling the drug trade, the destabilizing terrorist tactics of the *Sendero* present more of a threat to the Peruvian state than does the narcotics trade.

If estimates of such a relationship between the drug traffickers and the *Sendero* are accurate, the *cocaleros* are forced between a rock and a hard place, having to rely on the *Sendero* for protection from the authorities who wish to close down their profitable trade as well as protection by *Sendero* from the drug traffickers themselves who, as a warning to others, are reported to execute a *cocalero* who does not deliver the promised crop. While the *narcotraficantes* have the most sophisticated equipment and weapons at their disposal to evade the official forces, the *cocalero* remains vulnerable to incarceration and crop destruction.

Connections with the drug trade may also hold certain attraction for the *Sendero* in its efforts to the challenge U.S. imperialism. While cocaine consumption is not a problem in Peru (although consumption of a cocaine cigarette, *pastillo*, has been rising in recent years), the drug trade helps *Sendero* generate funds for the procurement of weapons and has helped create a group of people in the coca farmers that are sympathetic. According to Alan Riding, ''You'll have imperialists cutting down coca trees in front of a crying peasant woman. . . . Mao could not have thought of anything better.''[28]

It is also reported that the *Sendero* has increasingly moved into other areas beyond protection of the coca grower. In particular, it has been speculated that they have participated in cocaine paste production and distribution as well as in currency exchanges.

Those who argue against the existence of a relationship between Peru's guerrillas and *narcotraficantes* point to the fact that very little is known about the *Sendero Luminoso*. What is known is that the guerrillas hold strong puritan values and practice a disciplined life-style in which drug use is not tolerated. Thus, proponents of this view argue that a meaningful connection between the *Sendero* and the drug cartels is unlikely in Peru.

Another area of concern to drug enforcement officials in Peru is money laundering. With an external debt of over $21 billion (year-end 1991) and inflation that has frequently soared out of control, Peru began the 1990s in desperate need of capital. Consequently, the narco-profits of between $600 million and $1.2 billion annually represent an important source of capital for Peru. While the illegal coca trade is only one part of a burgeoning underground economy that has grown in the Andean country in the 1980s and into the 1990s, it is estimated that it employs 60 percent of the population and is responsible for 40 percent of Peru's gross national product (GNP). According to some estimates, the hard currency entering Peru through illegitimate channels has reached some 20 percent of the country's GNP; foreign exchange earnings from the country's copper industry are estimated at 1.4 percent of the GNP.

Money from the drug trade not only provides the coca farmers and the trafficking middlemen with a source of income, it has also substituted for foreign investment and bank loans which have been wary of the weak Peruvian economy since the early 1980s. The effects of the drug trade on the Peruvian economy are reportedly obvious to the casual observer. One can find in the informal markets in Peru thriving exchange houses, knowns as *cambistas*, which can be an individual with thousands of U.S. dollars on display for exchange at the unofficial rate (higher than the official rate). Although no exact figures exist, it is felt that over 80 percent of the dollars on that market were originally generated through the illicit drug trade.

It does not appear that the narco-money that enters Peru remains, despite reports of conspicuous consumption by the coca-producing farmers. According to official Peruvian sources, drug money is laundered in Peru directly by the traffickers who reportedly insert U.S. dollars into producing areas where the dollars are ultimately exchanged for Peruvian currency at local banks. Banks involved in money laundering, in turn, send money to overseas accounts in Switzerland, Florida, the Cayman Islands, and Colombia. Other money-laundering strategies include the movement of dollars into Bolivia where they are exchanged for bolivianos which are often then returned to Peru and exchanged for the local currency.

Peruvian authorities can do little about drug money laundering. Money laundering is not a criminal act in the country, and any change in that law would require a constitutional amendment.[29] Considering the difficult political and economic problems facing Peru in the early 1990s, combatting money laundering, which brings in capital, has not been a priority. The Peruvian government has the authority to seize assets in cases where there is possession or use of an illegal drug, but in 1989 there was only one known case in which the law was implemented and assets were seized.[30] A key problem faced by all of Peru's enforcement agencies is a lack of the ability to conduct financial criminal investigations.

Gabriela Sevillano-Tarazona argues that, in some areas, the *Sendero Luminoso* has also become involved in the drug trade's money laundering. She describes the regulation of the currency exchange in Xion, an area controlled by the *Sendero Luminoso*, in which the Colombian cartels come to the area with U.S. dollars to be exchanged for Peruvian currency. *Sendero Luminoso* designates certain individuals with whom currencies can be exchanged: No others are permitted. *Sendero Luminoso* forces receive a certain percentage of the exchanges for providing a steady flow of business.[31]

## INTERNATIONAL CONTROL LINKAGES

Former Peruvian President Alan García is known to have been a major proponent of regional cooperation in addressing the drug trade in the Andean countries. Thus, despite the fact that he almost boycotted the Cartagena Drug Summit held in February 1990, García attended the meeting with the presidents of the United States, Colombia, and Bolivia. García felt that the Cartagena agreement was vague and lacked substance; nevertheless, Peru was a signatory, reflecting a commitment to international cooperation in the war on drugs. The Cartagena Declaration committed each of the signatory countries to a comprehensive, multilateral effort in addressing the common problem of the drug trade in the region.

The February summit was a symbolic success in terms of being a united effort and a first step toward more regional cooperation among the participants. It was also significant in that, for the first time, the emphasis of U.S. negotiators was not on eradication, interdiction, and military involvement in the drug war, but on development projects (including crop substitution and the addressing of the socioeconomic disturbance faced by the Andean nations) for the region as a more indirect yet perhaps more effective way of dealing with the drug trade. The accord emphasizes the U.S. commitment to help finance economic activities to stimulate alternative sources of income that will reduce the Andean countries dependency on coca cultivation. Furthermore, during the Cartagena meeting, the United States and Peru signed an agreement for the inclusion of drug traffickers in the extradition treaty of 1989. Peru also signed an agreement with Bolivia for the exchange of tax records, bank statements, and other information that might assist cases investigating drug trafficking and prevent drug money laundering.

Cooperation between the Peruvian government and the United States in fighting coca production has, as noted elsewhere in this chapter, consisted mainly in interdiction and eradication efforts to stem the flow of drugs entering the North American nation. However, these tactics are slowly changing. In the 1980s, the drug problem in the United States was viewed mainly as a supply-side problem. If the supply of drugs could be stemmed, the problem would then be ameliorated. Latin American countries saw the problem from a different angle—as a problem of demand. If demand were reduced in the United States for illicit drugs, the problem would decline. As noted in the Cartagena Accord, the attitudes are slowly changing. Bilateral efforts at interdiction and eradication are giving way to efforts at crop substitution, economic development, and economic assistance. President Bush has made symbolic tribute to the ideas of the promotion of trade between Latin America and the United States with his Enterprise for the Americas Initiative. Nevertheless, there is a long way to go in reducing trade barriers in the United States (as well as the world market) for goods from coca-producing countries.

In a potentially important breakthrough in antidrug cooperation, on May 15, 1991, the United States and Peru announced the signing of an agreement on antidrug cooperation that emphasizes, inter alia, economic development to coca-growing farmers.[32] The agreement has importance first because it breaks the political impasse between the two governments. The agreement provides that the United States will support economic development to facilitate diversion by Peruvian farmers. The agreement also recognizes that the Peruvian peasants are not criminals and should have an input in any decisions concerning their economic future. The agreement signifies a change from the earlier U.S. strategies that focused on forced eradication of the coca crop and treated the farmers as criminals.

On May 14, Peruvian President Alberto Fujimori announced to the Peruvian Congress that both parties will abide by the principle of coresponsibility. On May 15, Bob Martinez, the U.S. drug czar who visited Peru as part of a five-nation South American tour, stated that the agreement will be complemented during the next six months by separate agreements on military, police, and economic assistance. As a result of the agreement, the United States will provide Peru with up to $60 million in economic aid this year for development projects and crop substitution. The figure could reach up to $100 million in 1992 although the Fujimori coup in April 1992 has jeopardized that.

Before the agreement can be successfully implemented, the coca growers must agree and cooperate. Because the agreement was negotiated in secret, the cooperation of the growers may be problematic. In addition, the left, which is very strong, and the organized criminals, also extremely strong, are expected to oppose the agreement.

The political and policy ramifications have significance because the two governments have been deadlocked since September 1990 when Fujimori rejected an initial U.S. offer of $34 million in military aid.

## CONCLUSION

During the 1980s tensions in the Andean region escalated as to how to address the international drug trade and the internal production of coca. It is obvious to all parties that the trade would not exist were it not for the strength of the market for cocaine and its derivatives in North America and Europe. It is the strength of this market alone that drives the drug trade in the Andean region. Nevertheless, the existence of the trade has produced substantial distortions in local economies, fueled corruption in Peru, and contributed to internal political instability.

The Fujimori administration has publicly committed itself to continue the battle against the illegal cultivation and transport of coca in Peru. Besides the illegal cultivation of coca and trafficking, the Fujimori government confronts a wide range of serious internal problems, including restructuring and regenerating the faltering economy, the terrorist threat of the *Sendero Luminoso*, and corruption in official channels.

For the short-term future, the agreement between the United States and Peru should provide a new cooperative initiative that responds to the Peruvian government's request for development aid in the war on drugs, especially as the *cocaleros* need realistic employment options. Along these lines, the new agreement favors the development of voluntary substitute crops and infrastructural improvements, such as roads and bridges to help facilitate the movement of legitimate crops to market. Fujimori also has embarked upon reforming the state's structure, seeking to make it more efficient, and has called for land titling, investment, and crop substitution programs. Furthermore, Fujimori has asked Peru's international creditors to write off part of the country's large foreign debt to help the Andean nation combat the drug trade. The April 1992 coup by the Peruvian president, however, leaves a big question about the outcome of such programs.

## NOTES

1. Scott B. MacDonald, *Dancing on a Volcano: The Latin American Drug Trade* (New York: Praeger, 1988), 61.

2. Edmundo Morales, *Cocaine, White Gold Rush in Peru* (Tuscon: University of Arizona Press, 1989), xvi.

3. Stephanie Joyce, "Snorting Peru's Rain Forest," *International Wildlife* (May–June 1990), 1.

4. Morales, *Cocaine, White Gold Rush in Peru*, xvi, 19.

5. Lyle N. McAlister, *Spain and Portugal in the New World, 1492–1700* (Minneapolis: University of Minnesota Press, 1984), 222.

6. James Lockhart and Stuart B. Schwartz, *Early Latin America: A History of Colonial Spanish America and Brazil* (New York: Cambridge University Press, 1985), 277.

7. Gabriela Tarazona-Sevillano with John B. Reuter, *Sendero Luminoso and the Threat of Narcoterrorism* (New York: Praeger Publishers, in conjunction with the Center for Strategic and International Studies, 1990), 7.

8. Ibid., 101–4.

9. U.S. Congress, Senate, Committee on Governmental Affairs, Permanent Subcommittee on Investigations, *Cocaine Production, Eradication and the Environment: Policy, Impact and Options* (Washington, D.C.: U.S. Government Printing Office, August 1990), 5.

10. Ibid., 14.

11. Ibid., 5–6.

12. Ibid., 13.

13. Senate, *Cocaine Production, Eradication and the Environment*, 157.

14. Ibid., 149. (Taken from Greenpeace, "Briefing Paper, State Department's Coca Eradication Spray Program in Peru," June 1988.)

15. Tarazona-Sevillano with Reuter, *Sendero Luminoso and the Threat of Narcoterrorism*, 109.

16. Joyce, "Snorting Peru's Rain Forest," 23.

17. "Bush Says US Will Boost Economic Aid," *Latin American Regional Reports, Andean Group Report*, 8 March 1990, 2.

18. "Property Rights Key to Coca Eradication in Peru," *Latin American Regional Reports, Andean Group Report*, 8 March 1990, 4.

19. MacDonald, *Dancing on a Volcano*, 61.

20. "Peru: Fujimori's Anti-Drugs Plan," *Latin American Regional Reports, Andean Group Report*, 15 November 1990, 8.

21. Cynthia McClintock, "The War on Drugs: The Peruvian Case," *Journal of Interamerican Studies and World Affairs* (Summer/Fall 1988): 130.

22. James Brooke, "U.S.–Peruvian Teams Renew Drive on Coca," *New York Times*, 18 March 1990, A6.

23. Morales, *Cocaine, White Gold Rush in Peru*, xix.

24. Eugene Robinson, "Peruvians Choose a President amid Deepening Crisis," *Washington Post*, 10 June 1990, A21.

25. Tarazona-Sevillano with Reuter, *Sendero Luminoso and the Threat of Narcoterrorism*, 123.

26. MacDonald, *Dancing on a Volcano*, 63.

27. Tarazona-Sevillano with Reuter, *Sendero Luminoso and the Threat of Narcoterrorism*, 123.

28. Alan Riding, "Rebels Disrupting Coca Eradication in Peru," *New York Times*, 26 January 1989, A6.

29. Tarazona-Sevillano with Reuter, *Sendero Luminoso and the Threat of Narcoterrorism*, 123.

30. U.S. Department of State, Bureau of International Narcotics Matters, *International Narcotics Control Strategy Report* (Washington, D.C.: U.S. Department of State, March 1990), 62.

31. Tarazona-Sevillano with Reuter, *Sendero Luminoso and the Threat of Narcoterrorism*, 121.

32. For further information, see "Peru–U.S. Sign New Drug Cooperation Agreement, *International Enforcement Law Reporter* 7, 5 (May 1991): 173–74.

## BIBLIOGRAPHY

Brooke, James. "U.S.–Peruvian Teams Renew Drive on Coca." *New York Times*, 18 March 1990, A6.

———. "U.S. Pilots in Peru Join Battle against Forces of Coca Trade." *New York Times*, 12 April 1990, A1.

Craig, Richard. B. "Illicit Drug Traffic: Implications for South American Source Countries." *Journal of Interamerican Studies and World Affairs* (Summer 1987): 1–34.

Joyce, Stephanie. "Snorting Peru's Rain Forest." *International Wildlife* (May–June 1990): 21–23.

Lockhart, James, and Stuart B. Schwartz. *Early Latin America: A History of Colonial Spanish America and Brazil*. New York: Cambridge University Press, 1985.

McAlister, Lyle N. *Spain and Portugal in the New World, 1492–1700*. Minneapolis: University of Minnesota Press, 1984.

McClintock, Cynthia. "The War on Drugs: The Peruvian Case." *Journal of Interamerican Studies and World Affairs* (Summer/Fall 1988): 126–42.

MacDonald, Scott B. *Dancing on a Volcano: The Latin American Drug Trade*. New York: Praeger, 1988.

Morales, Edmundo. *Cocaine: White Gold Rush in Peru*. Tucson: University of Arizona Press, 1989.

Riding, Alan. "Rebels Disrupting Coca Eradication in Peru." *New York Times*, 26 January 1989, A6.

Robinson, Eugene. "U.S. Drug Efforts Runs into Latin Resistance." *Washington Post*, 14 September 1990, A22.

Tarazona-Sevillano, Gabriela, with John B. Reuter. *Sendero Luminoso and the Threat of Narcoterrorism*. New York: Praeger Publishers, in conjunction with the Center for Strategic and International Studies, 1990.

U.S. Congress. Senate. Committee on Governmental Affairs, Permanent Subcommittee on Investigation. *Cocaine Production, Eradication and the Environment: Policy, Impact and Options*. Washington, D.C.: U.S. Government Printing Office, August 1990.

U.S. Department of State, Bureau of International Narcotics Matters. *International Narcotics Control Strategy Report*. Washington, D.C.: U.S. Department of State, March 1990.

# 13

# The Southern Cone

SCOTT B. MACDONALD

## INTRODUCTION

The Southern Cone countries of Argentina, Chile, Paraguay, and Uruguay usually evoke images of the pampas, the Andes, llamas, and the sophisticated cities of Buenos Aires, Santiago, and Montevideo. Involvement in the international narcotics trade does not immediately come to mind. Yet the Southern Cone countries are key transit states through which money laundering occurs, cocaine is transported, and chemical precursors are purchased and smuggled out of the country. Uruguay, due to its status as a regional financial center, has become involved with the international drug trade as a money-laundering entrepôt. It should also be added that Paraguay evolved in the late 1980s both as a producer of marijuana and as a money laundering center, especially after the U.S. clampdown on Panama in 1989.

Argentina, Chile, Paraguay, and Uruguay form part of the network that connects the cocaine trade that spans the Andean mountains and extends into North America and Europe in one direction and into the Southern Cone of South America in the other direction. Smuggling in one form or another has existed since colonial times, but the flow of drugs and narco-profits is a relatively new phenomenon. It stems from the rise of Bolivia and Peru as major coca-producing and exporting countries largely in the 1980s. This situation has led to a reassessment of drug policies in Argentina, Chile, Paraguay, and Uruguay and has made regional and international cooperative efforts for drug control more urgent.

## COUNTRY BACKGROUNDS

Argentina, one of the largest countries in Latin America, covers 2,767,000 square kilometers and borders Bolivia, Brazil, Chile, Paraguay, and Uruguay.

The country has a population of 31.5 million, which is well-educated and concentrated around the capital, Buenos Aires. Per capita income, according to the World Bank, was $2,390 in 1987, which made it the highest in Latin America behind oil-producers Venezuela and Trinidad and Tobago. Life expectancy at birth is seventy-one years.

Argentina is both developed and underdeveloped; it shares many characteristics with European society, yet political and economic problems continue to keep the country at a lower level of development. This South American country is one of the most industrialized of the major countries of the Third World, and a higher proportion of its population is urban than in many European countries. Additionally, the working class is highly organized and constitutes two-thirds of the work force. However, Argentina remains, according to Juan E. Corradi, "a peripheral capitalist society, a nonmetropolitan country, a Latin American nation, a fitful republic."[1] In the 1990s, however, Argentina appears to have regained its sense of destiny as the government of President Carlos embarked on far-reaching economic reforms. It has been suggested that the fitful nature of the republic may well be over.

Buenos Aires, one of the region's largest harbors, provides ready access to the South American interior by way of the Río de la Plata. It also provides ready access to Uruguay's capital and financial center, Montevideo, across the Rio de la Plata. Transport by air to Europe and North America is readily available, enhancing its attraction to those involved in illicit activities with drugs and narco-proceeds.

Chile is also relatively developed in comparison to many other countries in Latin America, Africa, and Asia. It shares borders with Argentina, Bolivia, and Peru and covers 757,000 square kilometers. Its population was 12.5 million in 1987, with 85 percent living in urban areas. The capital is Santiago, home to 44 percent of all Chileans. The per capita income in 1987 was $1,310, and the life expectancy at birth was seventy-two years of age.

Chile underwent a long period of dictatorship in 1973 after the elected government of Salvadore Allende fell to a coup. The country's leader became General Augusto Pinochet, who used a combination of far-reaching economic reforms and political repression to transform Chile into a capitalist society. Pinochet ruled directly from 1973 to March 1990 when he turned the government over to Patricio Aylwin, a Christian Democrat elected in the December 1989 elections. Although most Chileans indicated their desire for Pinochet to leave the political stage in the 1989 plebiscite, the country made considerable economic strides in the years under military rule. In the early 1990s, Chile's rate of inflation (27.1 percent in 1989) was one of the lowest in the region, especially when compared to Argentina's 4,955 percent, Peru's 2,775 percent, and Brazil's over 1,000 percent in 1989. Moreover, Chile's external debt management in the late 1980s resulted in net debt reduction.

Chile's involvement in the inter-American drug trade has been minimal and largely tied to Peruvian and Bolivian *narcotraficantes* seeking alternative routes to Australia, North America, and Europe via either Santiago or the northern ports, such as Arica and Iquique. Although the strong-arm tactics of the military government were sore spots in terms of human rights violations, they were helpful in keeping a tight reign on the spread of the drug trade into the country. Since the return of democratic government, there has been increased consumption of heavy drugs in the northern provinces, indicating that Chile is developing its own internal demand problem.

Paraguay covers approximately 406,752 square kilometers and has a population of 3.8 million. Compared to Argentina, Chile, and Uruguay, Paraguay is less developed. In 1988, it had a gross national product (GNP) per capita of $1,180 and an adult literacy level of 12 percent of the entire population. Paraguay's legal economy is dominated by agriculture, but its illegal economy, based on smuggling between the various states that it touches, has provided its own dynamic. The ongoing nature of Paraguayan smuggling has clearly opened the door to the trafficking of illicit drugs, guns, and precusor chemicals and the laundering of narco-profits.

Paraguay emerged in 1989 from the long dictatorship of General Alfredo Stroessner (1945–1989). The February 1989 coup resulted in the first democratic elections in several decades and in the inauguration of President Andrew Rodríguez. One of the corrupting aspects of the Stroessner regime was the semi-official condoning of contraband trading on the part of the armed forces, which ranged from basic consumer goods to illicit drugs—a difficult legacy left to the democratically elected government, especially during a period of economic downturn.

Uruguay sits at the mouth of the Rio de la Plata river and is sandwiched between Brazil to the north and Argentina to the south. Much of the country's existence has been a struggle to maintain its independence vis-à-vis the two larger nations as well as to take advantage of its strategic location in terms of trade. Uruguay covers 176,215 square kilometers and has a population of 3.08 million (1989 estimate). The standard of living is relatively high in comparison with much of Latin America, standing at $2,733 in 1989. The economy is dominated by offshore financial services, agriculture, and tourism.

Uruguay reemerged as a democracy in the 1980s after a long period of military government, which had been preceded by economic crisis and terrorism. The experience with military government (1973–1985) was much like that in Argentina and Chile, with the suspension of constitutional rights and disappearances of enemies of the state, both real and perceived. In 1985 democracy was restored, and in March 1990 President Luis Alberto Lacalle became the second consecutive civilian to win an election and assume the office. The main concern for Uruguay's leaders in the 1990s is how to streamline the economy and make it more competitive than its neighbors. In particular, the banking sector is regarded as a potential economic engine of growth: The offering of a comprehensive array of financial services is hoped to make Uruguay into the Singapore of South America. Although the verdict on that has yet to be made, the future of the country's population will be dictated by its ability to take advantage of its major comparative advantage, its location. With that advantage come the problems posed by the flow of narco-money through the financial center.

## ARGENTINA

### The Structure of the Drug Industry and Trade

Argentina is a transit state, which provides an operation zone for the purchase of precursors needed for cocaine production and functions as a trade route from Bolivia to Europe and North America. A number of cocaine seizures made in 1991 at the Ezeiza International Airport, which services Buenos Aires, revealed the following destinations: Brussels, Madrid, Lisbon, Rome, and Zurich, and the nationalities of those arrested included Argentines, Bolivians, Colombians, Chileans, and Uruguayans. Additionally, Argentina is a key link in the process of laundering "hot" drug money into legal tender or assets either in the country or through Uruguay via Argentina. The major reason for Argentina's emergence as a transit state in the global drug trade is its geographical proximity to Bolivia and, to a lesser extent, Paraguay (a producer of marijuana).

Another reason for Argentina's emergence as part of the international drug trade has been the steady dollarization of its economy in the 1980s and early 1990s. Dollarization, the process in which the local currency is increasingly regarded as valueless and the U.S. dollar is the preferred tender, comes from the country's severe economic problems related to past mismanagement and the external debt crisis. The national currency, the austral, was introduced in 1985, replacing the Argentine peso which was made worthless by hyperinflation in the early 1980s. The austral, however, fared little better. It rose from 1.257 to the U.S. dollar in 1986 to 652.500 in July 1989. By February 1990, it further depreciated against the dollar to 3,000 australes to one U.S. dollar. Consequently, the U.S. dollar increasingly became an accepted and preferred form of payment. By 1991, commercial banks in the country even offered large-dollar accounts, acknowledging their general use in the economy. As Argentine money (usually in dollars considering the low value of the austral) left the country in the form of capital flight in the mid– and late–1980s, drug money in dollars joined the flow from Bolivia.

In the early 1990s Argentina's illicit drug industry operates primarily out of the northwest and in Buenos Aires. While the Argentine and Bolivian criminal organizations are involved in the transit process, there has also been the production of cocaine hydrochloride in underground laboratories inside Argentina. Argentina produces the chemicals that are used to produce cocaine, and, with access to cheap Bolivian coca leaves, the potential for production expansion exists. Much of the smuggling of precursors is done by train; the chemicals move across the border under false documentation or an intentionally different name. No doubt bribery also helps turn a few heads in the other direction.

An additional factor in the structure of the Argentine drug industry is that the chewing of coca leaves is legal throughout Argentina and is widely practiced in those regions bordering on Bolivia. Large amounts of coca leaf are already imported from Bolivia for chewing.

Another dimension of the drug trade in Argentina is its penetration into the ruling class. In early 1991 the Spanish magazine *Cambio 16* released a story linking Arima Yoma and Karim Yoma, two in-laws and close associates of President Menem to Andres Ignacio Cruz de Iglesias, who was arrested after a shipment of cocaine was seized in Cape Verde. According to a leaked Spanish government report and *Cambio 16*, Cruz revealed that Arima Yoma, a personal secretary and sister-in-law to Menem, acted as a "camel": She travelled to New York and picked up cash that drug dealers had paid for drugs from Latin America. As George Melloan noted, "She had no trouble going through customs at the Buenos Aires Airport, Mr. Cruz told *Cambio 16*, because her ex-husband, Col. Ibrahim, was effectively in charge of customs there." The money was then taken across the Rio de la Plata to Uruguay, where it was banked, and payment was made available to the Colombian drug barons.

The scandal resulted in Arima Yoma's firing and the launching of an investigation under an Argentine judge. At the same time, a scandal close to the presidency sensitized many Argentines to the ability of the *narcotraficantes* to corrupt members of the government. It also brought unwanted attention to the growing "Argentine Connection" of drug money laundering and transit trade.

### The Societal Response

Drug abuse is not identified as the leading social problem in Argentina. However, there are indications that it is worsening as the number of drug addicts increases. In 1989, one Argentine estimate put the number at 100,000 who were addicted to some kind of drug. The Peronista government of President Carlos Menem was increasingly concerned in 1989 and 1990 with the rise in trafficking, the deteriorating situation with drug control efforts in Bolivia, and the potential threat to the social stability in the northwestern provinces. Those provinces have already been hard hit by the country's economic crisis, and the lure of huge profits for some and the escape of drugs for others is obviously a social problem that will have to be addressed by the government in Buenos Aires.

Although Argentina's economic crisis in the 1980s was severe and conditions have only begun to improve in the 1990s, efforts to deal with drug abuse are being made by private organizations. Most resources are allocated to Buenos Aires. The major public and private organizations for drug education are APPUE (the Argentine equivalent of the U.S. parents anti-drug organization, PRIDE) and CENARESO (the official national center for drug rehabilitation). Schools and parents groups are targeting drug awareness lectures.

## The Government's Response

The Argentine government's response to the rise of the drug trade was slow for four reasons. First and foremost, Argentine civilian governments since the reestablishment of democracy in 1985 were more concerned with political survival and the creation of a civil society. This meant guaranteeing that democratic government lasted through electoral changes, while the military was brought under control. Bringing the armed forces to reign also carried with it the need to bring to trial those officers involved in human rights violations during the "dirty war" in the 1970s and early 1980s. Several coup attempts against President Raúl Alfonsín (1983–1988) underscored the testiness of the issue within the armed forces.

While political survival was a driving force for the Alfonsín administration in the context of civilian-military relations, the second reason for the slow government response was (and continues to be) the ongoing nature of the economic crisis. The 1980s were regarded as a "lost decade" for the South American country in terms of economic development. Current account deficits, budget deficits, widely swinging levels of inflation (at times over 1,000 percent), a crushing external debt of around $60 billion (1991), and fluctuating commodity prices for what and beef, the two major exports, conspired to make sharp cuts in per capita income and the overall standard of living. The resulting social turmoil, in which labor unions fought austerity programs and companies and individuals sent their capital overseas (often via Uruguay), only complicated matters. Economic policy became a hotly contested issue in Argentine politics, leaving little time for drug-control policy.

The third reason for the slow Argentine response was the incremental nature of the drug trade's penetration of the economy and society. Although the problems of illicit drug transit and drug abuse existed earlier in the 1980s, it was in the latter part of that decade that it became a concern. On the external side, U.S., Latin American, and European efforts to interdict the flow of drugs through Colombia and Panama took several years to have an impact. However, the intensified war in Colombia in 1989–1990 and the U.S. embargo of Panama from 1987 to 1989 (and invasion in December 1989) forced changes in the regional structure of the drug trade. The alternative routes from Bolivia through Argentina, Brazil, and Uruguay, which were not as heavily used at the beginning of the decade, picked up activity when the routes were constricted in Panama and Columbia.

A fourth and final factor was that, at the end of the 1980s, the Bolivian *narcotraficantes*, who traditionally were coca cultivators, decided that they did not need the Colombian middlemen for every transaction. Instead Bolivian *narcotraficantes* turned to cocaine production and marketing. The Bolivians soon developed their own networks through Argentina, Brazil, and Uruguay. In some cases, they developed business relationships with the local criminal groups. The economic crisis and near-dollarization of the Argentine economy in 1989–1990 coincided with the rise of the Bolivian *narcotraficantes*, who also used dollars. By the early 1990s this combination was regarded as a growing concern for the Argentine government.

Despite the wide-ranging problems confronting the government, efforts have been made to combat the drug trade. President Menem in 1989 called for capital punishment for drug dealers and formed a narcotics secretariat within the presidency headed by the founder of the Chamber of Deputies Narcotics Committee, E. Alberto Lestelle. The secretariat indicated that the Menem administration took the issue more seriously than its predecessor. The mandate of the narcotics secretariat is to improve coordination and cooperation among enforcement and prevention agencies. Additionally, it seeks to improve cooperation between public and private prevention and rehabilitation efforts. It should be stated that the authority of the secretariat is limited due to its lack of authority over other antinarcotics bodies.

A tougher antinarcotics law was passed in September 1989 by the Argentine government. Although the new law was introduced three years after being proposed, it reflected a tough stance on combatting international drug trafficking. Under the new law, the areas touched upon include provisions for asset seizure with proceeds going into antinarcotics efforts, criminalization of possession of small amounts of narcotics for personal use, and controls on precursor chemicals. At the same time, the new law allowed the decriminalization of coca chewing throughout the country and the removal of plea bargaining provisions (proposed earlier).

Another part of the new law includes measures with which to deal with money laundering. The new law provides for from three to twelve years in prison for providing space for the production, distribution, storage, or use of narcotics as well as the closing of businesses acquired where such activities occur. Also, this law stipulates penalties of from two to ten years in prison in addition to a fine for investment, sale purchase, or transfer of assets or profits produced or acquired through trafficking. Currently there are no legal controls on precursors.

The Argentine enforcement system involved in combatting drug trafficking includes four federal agencies, under three separate ministries, and twenty-two provincial police forces. Federal judges set policy for and coordinate all drug investigations. The Border Guards, under the control of the Defense Ministry, are mandated to protect the country's borders up to 100 kilometers into Argentina and to provide security at the international airports. They share jurisdiction with Customs, which conducts investigations involving smuggling and is under the Ministry of Economy. The Argentine Federal Police, subordinate to the Ministry of the Interior, have greater resources for conducting narcotics investigations than other agencies, especially in Buenos Aires. The Coast Guard has responsibility for patrolling the country's waterways and for the security of seaports, where it shares narcotics enforcement responsibilities with Customs. The key ports under surveillance are Buenos Aires, La Plata, Mar del Plata, Bahia Blanca, and Rosario (inland).

Each province in Argentina has a provincial police force which is responsible for most police duties under its jurisdiction. Although each province has an antinarcotics unit, most lack training, resources, and expertise.

## International Linkages for Control

On the international front, Argentina is a signatory of the 1988 United Nations Convention against Illicit Traffic in Narcotic Drugs and Psychotropic Substances and the Organization of American States (OAS) Inter-American Committee against Drug Abuse Treaty. Argentina did sign the Chiles Amendment with the United States as well as a mutual legal assistance treaty (MLAT) in December 1990. It has bilateral narcotics cooperation agreements with Bolivia, Paraguay, Peru, Uruguay, and Venezuela.

Since 1989 Argentina's national drug strategy has made relations with Bolivia a priority because successful antidrug efforts in Bolivia are increasingly having a spillover effect in northern Argentina. On May 31, 1991, for example, federal police discovered a clandestine kitchen laboratory 700 kilometers from the Bolivian frontier in Salta Province. It was estimated that 1,300 kilos of coca leaves were seized by Argentine enforcement agents. The laboratory, according to the Argentine newspaper *Clarín* (June 21, 1991) was in a test stage and not fully operational.

Enhanced Argentine concerns about Bolivian traffickers led to a bilateral narcotics assistance treaty, which was signed between representatives of the two countries on April 18, 1991. The Argentine Congress ratified the treaty on May 10, 1991, and enacted it into law. Under the treaty, a mixed Argentine-Bolivian commission will be formed to function as a coordinating body in demand reduction, crop eradication, and narcotics trafficking suppression efforts. Furthermore, both countries commit themselves to information sharing on the export of precursor chemicals as well as reciprocal support in the investigation and judicial actions related to money laundering.

Argentina also provided assistance to the Colombian government in its war against the cartels. Another example of Argentina's international cooperation in dealing with the drug trade has been with Colombia: In late 1989 Argentina donated three Pucara aircraft to the Colombian government. The Pucaras, armed with cannon and machine guns, were meant to be used to seek out coca fields and support antidrug operations.

The relationship with the United States has been of significance in the international cooperation against the drug trade. In 1989 the Argentine government recognized the need for improved and expanded training of enforcement and prevention officials and turned to the United States for assistance. There was an effort to help the development of an integrated narcotics information system, sharing of information among enforcement agencies, and the usage of joint investigations.

## CHILE

### The Structure of the Drug Industry and Trade

Chile has three interrelated concerns with the drug trade: local production of marijuana and the abuse of over-the-counter legal drugs and glue, the growing role of Chile as a transit point for the cocaine trade, and money laundering. Although Chile does not produce cocaine, it borders both Peru and Bolivia, where shipments destined for Australia, Europe, and North America originate. Northern Chile, in particular the two ports of Arica on the Peruvian border and Iquique farther south, has become a ''cocaine corridor'' for *narcotraficantes* operating out of Bolivia and Peru. Chile is a small producer of marijuana. There is legal production, used by local industry involved with fiber goods, and an illicit production, smoked by the local population.

Chile first became significantly involved in the cocaine trade in 1963–1964. According to Chilean police data, in 1964 approximately 19,820 kilograms of cocaine were seized, and 192 people were arrested for trafficking. Between 1963 and 1973, Chile's cocaine industry was driven by its capacity to function as an important transit point. Furthermore, Chilean chemists, known as some of the best in the business, helped push Chile into being part of the processing business, as reflected in the amounts of cocaine seized: 28,360 kilograms in 1968, 32,470 in 1969, and 39,260 in 1973.[2] In the last year, however, many of the chemists were arrested and extradited to the United States.

Chile's role in the cocaine trade declined after 1973 and 1974. The emergence of the military regime under Pinochet may have allowed the national police to monitor more carefully those they believed to be involved in the drug trade. Given the tense political environment in Chile during the early years of the military government, smuggling drugs was as accessible as any smuggling to scrutiny because of the government's concern about arms imports to support radical leftist groups. Moreover, the Colombian drug organizations had other, more accessible transit locations, such as Panama, Ecuador, Paraguay, and Uruguay.

It was not until the 1980s that the cocaine trade became a major activity in Chile. Although Chilean authorities readily admit that, for every 10 shipments caught, probably 100 pass, police records of drug-related arrests and kilograms of cocaine seized provide an indication of the growth of the problem (see Table 13.1).

Those detained on drug charges included violations for other drug abuses as well; but, in any event, the data indicate that the problem expanded in the 1980s. Although most of those arrested were Chilean citizens, the majority of foreigners arrested were Peruvian and Bolivian.

Chile's banking sector has a good reputation for being efficient as well as clean of money laundering. However, in the late 1980s and early 1990s, money laundering emerged as a concern in the northern part of the country. In particular,

**Table 13.1**
**Drug-Related Arrests and Seizures in Chile**

| Year | Cocaine Seized (Kg) | Traffickers Arrested |
|---|---|---|
| 1979 | 12,490 | 1,412 |
| 1980 | 22,840 | 1,452 |
| 1981 | 29,480 | 1,329 |
| 1982 | 9,300 | 1,455 |
| 1983 | 46,150 | 1,476 |
| 1984 | 20,690 | 1,353 |
| 1985 | 24,080 | 1,489 |
| 1986 | 32,110 | 1,305 |
| 1987 | 32,280 | 1,188 |
| January 1 to July 15, 1988 | 27,285 | 632 |

a free-trade zone in the city of Iquique was increasingly used by those seeking to convert hot drug money into legal tender. In the free-trade zone, money laundering is facilitated by the utilization of bearer bonds which can be bought in any sum. Because the bearer bonds are negotiable instruments, they have been involved in the conversion of large amounts of cash into an equivalent financial instrument, which is easier to manage and manipulate. The Chilean authorities have noted that *narcotraficantes* frequently use the bearer bonds to purchase large quantities of goods, which they later sell across the border as a means of generating legal tender.

Another method of converting drugs into money has occurred with the trading of mussels in Chile's north for cocaine. Mussels have been extensively fished in the country's north, but in the late 1980s efforts were made to conserve the mollusk. However, demand for mussels remains high. Inventive drug traffickers from Peru and Bolivia began trading in 1989 with Chilean fishermen who received cocaine for a shipment of mussels, which they (the Chileans) then smuggled into Chile either for transshipment or for domestic use. The mussels are either consumed in Peru or Bolivia or processed and sent back to Chile as a finished product.

Money laundering was also made relatively easy by the absence of a disclosure requirement on large financial transactions and by the existence of a legal parallel foreign exchange market in which transactions are not recorded. The latter mechanism allows any amount of money to be exchanged. Additionally, there is no requirement that those using the parallel market identify themselves, making it difficult to trade large transactions to their source. The banking system is more sophisticated than many others in Latin America, and laundering operations are not thought to be extensive.

### The Societal Response

Chilean society has not been as receptive to drug usage as those in other parts of Latin America or in the United States. In the early 1990s all sectors of Chilean society condemn drug usage. However, although information is scarce, there are indications that a certain amount of drug usage is seeping into society. One of the problems confronting health authorities is the need for systematizing available information to have a better understanding of the problem and to develop the appropriate countermeasures.

### The Government's Response

Although Chile's cocaine traffic is not on the same level as that of Bolivia, Peru, and Colombia, Chile shares with other Latin American countries concerns about future developments in the inter-American trade. Consequently, the government's reaction has been to increase cooperation with the Peruvian police and with such international organizations as Interpol. Bolivia's higher level of political instability has presented problems in the past, however, and Chile had, throughout most of the decade, no regular contacts with Bolivia's police. The two countries do not have diplomatic relations.

The newly elected civilian government that took office in March 1990 confronted many of the same problems that confronted their Argentine counterparts. On one hand, there was concern about human rights abuses, which might be perceived in the course of an investigation, and, on the other hand, there was little desire for the drug trade to spread into Chile.

Chile's antidrug enforcement effort has four components: the *Carabineros* (National Police), the National Investigation Police (Policia de Investigaciónes de Chile), the Coast Guard, and Customs. The *Carabineros*, the main interdiction unit, are under the administrative authority of the Ministry of Defense. Beyond the limited role played by the Coast Guard, which is a branch of the Chilean Navy, the military role is minimal and expected to remain that way. Coordination of antidrug efforts was not a priority in the 1980s, largely because of the relative unimportance of the narcotics issue and the relatively low usage of the country by *narcotraficantes*. However, that appears to be in the process of changing in the 1990s as more drugs are entering the country. Consequently, a Drug Control Office has been given greater significance, and the four law enforcement agencies have representatives in this body.

One of the areas under discussion in Chile is what to do about the sale of chemicals that can be used as precursors in cocaine production. As of early 1990 there were no restrictions on the purchase of precursor chemicals from the wide range of companies operating in Chile that manufacture, export, and import these chemicals. Moreover, the Chilean Army manufactures ether and is authorized to sell it to the private sector. Although no new legislation has been passed (as of December 1991), there is a move in the Chilean Congress to introduce legislation that will apply controls to precursors.

Another area of discussion is money laundering: Does Chile need more stringent laws? Currently, Chilean law requires solid proof of identity as a prerequisite to opening a bank account. Moreover, all transactions are recorded with reference to the customer's national identity number, which makes all bank transactions traceable. Another key law is Article 20 of the General Banking Law, which stipulates that all foreign exchange transactions equal to $50,000 must be reported to the central bank. Also, it is customary for Chilean banks to track foreign exchange transactions in excess of $10,000. While these laws and regulations clearly hamper money-laundering operations, Chilean law protects bank secrecy. Moreover, the information gathered is not open to sharing with foreign law enforcement authorities, which impedes international investigations.

### International Linkages for Control

Chile has ratified the 1988 South American agreement on psychotropic and narcotics substances. This includes provisions for controlling traffic in precursor chemicals, which is currently under discussion in Chile. As already noted, Chile has sought to develop better relations with Argentine enforcement authorities. While there is some cooperation with Peruvian authorities, Chilean-Bolivian relations have historically been tense due in part to a long-standing border dispute. The lack of cooperation on the frontier with Bolivia, one of the major producers of coca, raises serious questions about any future joint border efforts to curtail both drug trafficking and money laundering. A positive development was an invitation by the Bolivian National Police, under the auspices of the U.S. Embassy in La Paz, for two Chilean *Carabineros* to attend an advanced antinarcotics course in 1991.

## PARAGUAY

### The Structure of the Drug Industry and Trade

Paraguay's rugged terrain is highly conducive to marijuana cultivation, and the country's location is ideal for smuggling. As Carlos Miranda noted in 1990, "Paraguay was and is a player in the major leagues of international smuggling, and military officers skimmed off much of the cream."[3] Considering the country's dominance by the military and the long rule of General Stroessner, corruption at high levels in the government allowed the drug trade to flourish. However, Stroessner's process of co-optation went one step further—military officers were allowed to benefit from corrupt practices like contraband as a reward for staying out of the country's politics. According to Miranda, "Stroessner 'legalized' the right of the military officers to engage in practices whose profits filled their pockets."[4] This included the drug trade and money laundering. Paraguay was a busy location for heroin trafficking in the 1960s and 1970s.

In the post-Stroessner period the drug industry in Paraguay is dominated by the growth of marijuana and the transshipment of cocaine. The former is grown primarily in the rugged terrain of Amambay and Canendeyu departments on the frontier with Brazil. In addition, smaller areas of cultivation have been noted in

Concepcion and Alto Parana departments. Cocaine transshipments increased considerably in the late 1980s and early 1990s due to intensified antidrug campaigns in Colombia and, to a lesser extent, in Bolivia. Although there are no accurate figures on the extent of cocaine trafficking, it is estimated to be between 500 and 1,000 kilograms per month, according to the U.S. Bureau of International Narcotics Matters (*International Narcotics Control Strategy Report*, March 1990).

In addition to being a producer of marijuana and a transit point for cocaine, Paraguay has been used as a place to launder drug money. This is, in part, due to the lack of currency controls: There are no restrictions on the flow of foreign or domestic currency into or out of Paraguay. Another attractive element for money launderers is that there are no restrictions on holding dollar accounts. Additionally, there are no restrictions on foreign ownership of real or corporate property. As one U.S. government study noted in 1990, "The combination of liberal banking laws—banking confidentiality is respected and dollar accounts are allowed under GOP banking regulations—and a sophisticated financial structure (Paraguay's relatively small economy is served by 24 banks and numerous exchange houses) makes Paraguay an attractive country for money laundering operations."[5]

Paraguay's president, following the 1989 coup, General Andres Rodríguez, was also alleged to have some involvement in drug money laundering. As the owner of the foreign exchange house, Cambios Guarani, he came under considerable scrutiny when he was running for the presidency. Rodríguez vigorously denied all charges of drug smuggling and money laundering, and no new claims involving the nation's chief executive in illicit activities have appeared. In fact, in July 1990, President Rodríguez relieved two generals from their commands for allegedly allowing *narcotraficantes* to transit cocaine through areas under their command after a plane crashed carrying 500 kilograms of cocaine.

### International Linkages for Control

Paraguay's international antidrug efforts are underscored by President Rodríguez's antidrug policy, which has been emphasized by the country's ongoing commitment to work with the United States and other nations. In October 1989, he endorsed President George Bush's antinarcotics campaign at the United Nations General Assembly. Bilateral efforts with the United States have included a joint program of eradication of illegal marijuana cultivation and cooperation between Paraguay's narcotics police (DINAR) and the U.S. Drug Enforcement Administration, Department of Defense, and Department of State. Additionally, Paraguay signed an amendment to the 1987 bilateral antinarcotics agreement with the United States, in August 1989, which provided for the expansion of U.S. material support for DINAR.

Paraguay has also been active on a regional basis. In 1989, it hosted the planning conference for the Seventh International Drug Enforcement Conference

(IDEC). Other regional efforts included joint investigations and seizures with Argentina and Brazil. Moreover, in September 1990, Paraguayan officials made the biggest cocaine seizure in the country's history, netting some 323 kilograms of cocaine and $210,000 in U.S. currency. The seizure came from a Bolivian registered aircraft which landed at a military airfield near the Bolivian border. Paraguay was a signatory of the 1988 UN Drug Convention, but it has not yet ratified the convention.

## URUGUAY

### The Structure of the Industry and Trade

Uruguay's role in the international drug trade is that of a money-laundering center. The emergence of an open banking system with a government that places an emphasis on tight bank secrecy and allows dollar-denominated accounts has helped position Uruguay as a key financial entrepôt, much like the offshore banking havens in the Caribbean. Uruguay's highly developed financial center includes thirty-five banks and twenty-two investment companies. It also has South America's only free currency exchange system, with seventy-five major exchange houses in Montevideo alone. The combination of these factors, as well as the absence of legal provisions for asset forfeiture and no criminal law that prohibits money laundering, makes Uruguay an attractive spot for *narco-traficantes*.

What has helped considerably is Uruguay's location between Argentina and Brazil. This has meant that the economic dislocations in those countries have made Uruguay a welcome port for investors sorely tested by uncertainty at home. Additionally, the option of secret bank accounts in Montevideo has an appeal to many wealthy Latin Americans wishing to avoid paying taxes. The scope of Uruguay's usage was indicated in 1989 when one burst of hyperinflation in Argentina allegedly sent $600 million in flight capital to Montevideo. The protection of bank secrecy and the accepted movement of flight capital have made the detection of narco-proceeds difficult and have enhanced Uruguay's role in the regional drug trade.

### International Linkages for Control

The use of Uruguay as a money-laundering center became a political issue between that country and the United States in 1989. Operations C-Chase and Polar Cap, undertaken with the cooperation of Uruguayan officials, uncovered evidence of extensive use of the Southern Cone country's financial institutions for drug money laundering. For example, Operation Polar Cap unveiled that one trafficking organization may have moved over a billion dollars in narco-profits from the United States through Uruguay. In December 1989, Uruguay cooperated with the United States and extradited a currency exchange dealer identified by Polar Cap investigations as an alleged money launderer.

The political tension between the United States and Uruguay is rooted in the government's commitment not to erode its bank secrecy. Two bills to combat money laundering were introduced in 1989, but both failed to be voted into law.

## CONCLUSION

The Southern Cone countries share many of the same problems in controlling the international drug trade through their respective territories. While actual production of coca or other illicit narcotics is not a concern, transitting and money laundering clearly are, and they pose difficult questions about enforcement. In responding to the challenge, these governments are legally and constitutionally ill prepared. Compartmentalization of authority over areas of legal and nonlegal issues makes it difficult to deal with a problem that cuts across many areas, ranging from financial institutions to border controls, sniffer dogs and precursor chemicals. Additionally, drug abuse appears to be a growing problem that could generate into a major health concern.

The Southern Cone countries are relatively new to the problems associated with containing drug usage, unlike other countries, such as Colombia, Thailand, or Turkey. There is likely to be a learning curve for enforcement agencies in each case. This does not necessarily mean that Argentina, Chile, Paraguay, and Uruguay will be engulfed by illicit drugs or that the drug Mafias will penetrate and come to dominate the political-economic structures of the countries. What it does mean is that the problem will probably grow before it is better dealt with later in the decade. Furthermore, the four countries have other, more pressing, concerns, such as Argentina's bouts with hyperinflation and its inability to service its large external debt and Chile's and Paraguay's struggles to shift from authoritarian to democratic forms of government.

## NOTES

1. Juan E. Corradi, *The Fitful Republic: Economy, Society, and Politics in Argentina* (Boulder, Colo.: Westview Press, 1985), 2–3.
2. Data provided in a presentation by General Fernando Paredes Pazarro, then General Director of the Investigation Police of Chile in Santiago, Chile, on 19 July 1988.
3. Carlos R. Miranda, *The Stroessner Era: Authoritarian Rule in Paraguay* (Boulder, Colo.: Westview Press, 1990), 151.
4. Ibid., 150.
5. U.S. Department of State, Bureau of International Narcotics Matters, *International Narcotics Control Strategy Report* (Washington, D.C.: U.S. Department of State, March 1990), 61.

## BIBLIOGRAPHY


Adams, Nathan M. "The Hunt for Andre." *Readers Digest*, March 1973, 224–59.

Barham, John. "Uruguay." *Financial Times Survey*, 15 October 1990, 1–6.

Corradi, Juan E. *The Fitful Republic: Economy, Society, and Politics in Argentina*. Boulder, Colo.: Westview Press, 1985.

Government of Chile, Policia de Investigaciones de Chile. "Conferencia a los asesores del congreso de los Estados Unidos," Santiago, Chile, 19 July 1988.

Lee, Rensselaer W. III. *The White Labyrinth: Cocaine and Political Power*. New Brunswick, N.J.: Transaction Press, 1989.

MacDonald, Scott B. *Dancing on a Volcano: The Latin American Drug Trade*. New York: Praeger Publishers, 1988.

———. *Mountain High, White Avalanche: Cocaine and Power in the Andean States and Panama*. New York: Praeger Publishers, with the Center for Strategic and International Studies, 1989.

Melloan, George. "Drugs—The Argentine Connection." *Wall Street Journal European Edition*, 26–27 April 1991, 8.

Miranda, Carlos R. *The Stroessner Era: Authoritarian Rule in Paraguay*. Boulder, Colo.: Westview Press, 1990.

Montalvo, Tina. "Paraguay: Paying for the Coup." *Latin Finance*, March 1989, 51.

Morris, Felipé, with Mark Dorfman, Jorge Pedro Ortiz, and Maria Claudia Franco. *Latin America's Banking Systems in the 1980s: A Cross-Country Comparison*. Washington, D.C.: The World Bank, May 1990.

Nash, Nathaniel C. "For Argentines, There's No Place Like Uruguay." *New York Times*, 7 February 1991, A4.

Organization of American States, Inter-American Drug Abuse Control Commission. *Comparative Study of the Legal Regime on Drug Control in Ten South American Member States of the Organization of American States*. Washington, D.C.: Organization of American States, 1988.

Robinson, Eugene. "Leader's In-Laws Named in Argentine Scandal." *Washington Post*, 30 April 1991, A18.

Serra, Alfredo. "La verdad sobre la droga en la Argentina." *Somos*, 4 January 1985, 29–39.

U.S. Department of State, Bureau of International Narcotics Matters. *International Narcotics Control Strategy Report*. Washington, D.C.: U.S. Department of State, March 1990.

World Bank. *World Development Report 1989*. New York: Oxford University Press, 1989.

# III

# Country and Regional Studies: Europe

# 14

# Western Europe and the European Community

BRUCE ZAGARIS

## INTRODUCTION

Following international trends, the growth of drug trafficking in Western Europe has achieved levels not expected ten years ago. For example, Europe has approximately half a million heroin addicts, and countries traditionally free from the drug scourge, such as Germany, are now penetrated by the traffic. Additionally, some member states, like Spain and Italy, are becoming crossroads for drug trafficking. Only 10 percent of the cocaine pouring into Spain is consumed there; the remainder is directed to other European countries. Most of this European drug traffic is dominated by the Naples-based organized crime group called the Camorra.

This chapter discusses the European institutions that are dealing with cooperation against drug trafficking, the steps that are being taken, and the implications for business. Until now, European cooperation has been long on declarations of intentions and short on actual implementation. However, the coalescence of integration in the wake of the Single European Act, the ratification of the December 1988 United Nations Convention against Illicit Traffic in Narcotic Drugs and Psychotropic Substances (hereafter referred to as the UN Drug Convention), and declarations of cooperation at the G–7 summits, in addition to other developments, cause dynamic legislative and regulatory activity in the European Community (EC) in the fight against illicit narcotics trafficking.

The battle in Europe is fought primarily, but not solely, by the EC. Indeed the Council of Europe, which includes, for instance, the Nordic countries and other governments outside the EC, is a key player. The new regulatory regime will have profound impact on business and travel within the EC. This chapter summarizes these trends. and the implications for the growth of the European

Community, the growth of the Western European Community with the entry of new democracies from Central and Eastern Europe into the Council of Europe, and the emerging regime of international cooperation against crime.

## EUROPEAN COMMUNITY

Since drug-related criminality has spread throughout Europe, European institutions are the most suitable means to stop certain aspects of this plague. The basic goal of the Treaty of Rome, establishing the EC, is to suppress economic and trade barriers among the twelve member states: Belgium, Denmark, France, Germany, Greece, Ireland, Italy, Luxembourg, the Netherlands, Portugal, Spain, and the United Kingdom. This movement was accelerated by the signing of the Single European Act on July 1, 1987, which is aimed at completing a Europe without frontiers. By 1993, goods, services, and persons will freely circulate within the territory of the EC.

The removal of trade and economic barriers within the EC will obviously accelerate the growth of cross-frontier criminal activities, in particular drug trafficking. This phenomenon will directly affect EC and European integration. In a report published in September 1986, the European Parliament indicated that "the problem of drug abuse affects general areas of European policy including external relations, trade customs, law and order, health, social affairs, education and citizens' rights." Therefore, the EC has a unique interest in dealing directly with drug trafficking.

In the present situation, however, enforcement mechanisms against the trafficking of illicit narcotic substances are found primarily at the member-state level. There is neither a community criminal body of law nor enforcement agencies to implement a community response to drug trafficking. The Treaty of Rome promotes *economic* integration among member states. Because political integration does not expressly fall within the competence of the EC, the regulation of criminal law at the community level cannot yet be realized.

Although strong direct community enforcement measures have not yet been undertaken, member states and community institutions themselves have been working, within the limits of their competence, to achieve a common response to the growing menace of drug trafficking. Each of these community institutions has taken steps to join the movement. The following developments show how the different institutions of the EC act in forging a policy of the community on regulating and preventing drug trafficking.

### The EC Council

The EC Council led the action of the community against drugs at its meeting in The Hague on June 1986. The heads of states agreed to collaborate with the commission to combat drug addiction. The council pointed out that international cooperation already exists, in particular within the Pompidou Group of the Council of Europe. The Pompidou Group, named after former French President Georges Pompidou, was formed in 1971 to organize the problems of drug abuse and illicit drug traffic from a multinational perspective. Twenty countries are represented in the group, including all twelve EC member states. On December 1986, the council agreed on the need to work in close cooperation with the Pompidou Group to cooperate to stop and prosecute those who criminally traffic in illegal drugs; to coordinate legal action and, in particular, ensure that the assets of someone convicted of illicit trafficking in one EC country will be liable to confiscation throughout the EC; and to intensify cooperation between police and customs authorities. In addition, the heads of states requested a report to the next EC Council with recommendation for action by the EC and its member states.

This first community step toward cooperation in the fight against drugs signified an expansion of the EC field of action in a manner unforeseen by the drafters of the Treaty of Rome. The heads of states agreed to set up *legal* cooperation among themselves and to organize the beginning of a European jurisdiction for the forfeiture of assets coming from drug offenses.

More recently, the EC Council has taken significant action to curb money laundering as a result of its commitment to sign the UN Drug Convention, but it has moved even beyond drug-related laundering. On December 17, 1989 the EC finance ministers agreed on a ''common position'' on a framework directive on money laundering.

The proposal for a Council directive on the prevention of the use of the financial system for the purpose of money laundering was submitted by the EC Commission to the Council of Ministers and the European Parliament (EP) on March 23, 1990. In the EP, the proposal was referred to the Committee on Legal Affairs and Citizens' Rights, which appointed Geoffrey Hoon as its rapporteur. The report prepared by Mr. Hoon was adopted at the EP's plenary session on November 22, 1990.

The EP's opinion was taken into account by the EC Commission, which subsequently submitted a revised proposal. On the basis of this revised proposal, an agreement in principle was reached by the Economic and Finance Ministers (ECOFIN Council) on December 17, 1990.

The directive was approved in final on June 10, 1991 and will come into effect on January 1, 1993. It is discussed below.

### The EC Commission

The EC Commission also has been active in the anti-drug policy. On November 1986, it adopted a program for a comprehensive proposal on the fight against drugs in the community, which stated that the antidrug policies had become urgent and, to be fully effective, had to be organized on a community-wide basis. An appropriation of 2,250,000 European currency units (ECU) has been earmarked for the program. The action envisaged by the commission is mainly prevention, treatment, rehabilitation, and research. However, it also provides for the setting up of a European information system on the drug problem supported by a European data bank. The communication does not provide details on the specific uses intended for the data bank.

## The European Parliament

The European Parliament set up an inquiry committee on the drug problem in the member states of the community. It reported in September 1986 that a lack of coordination existed among European countries and that a European strategic plan was required. The report's recommendations are intended to be "complementary to and integrated into the activities of existing bodies" acting on an international level. It emphasizes that the international network of drug traffickers must be dealt with at the international level through international legislation. The report pointed out the unique role the EC must play in this international action because of its superior economic and political forces, which enable it to persuade the world community to support such policies as crop substitution, coordination of drug and international economic policies, and the control of precursor chemicals. Finally, the report urges new strategies by the commission and the Council of Europe that will emphasize policy and customs cooperation such as (1) the setting up of a European Community task force, modeled on the existing U.S. Task Force Program, to coordinate a European-wide fight against drugs; (2) tighter customs control at the community's external frontiers because of the progressive dismantling of customs and control barriers within the community; and (3) the establishment of a computer network between the different EC nations whose networks are not currently compatible.

In October 1986, the European Parliament passed a resolution on the drug problem in which it urges the Council of Europe to adopt a draft resolution on concerted action against the drug problem. The draft resolution undertakes (1) to introduce effective measures for dealing with the laundering of money coming from drug crimes, especially the issuance of a community directive on currency transaction reporting; (2) to amend existing customs regulations to provide for the seizure of goods related to drug trafficking; and (3) to ensure that each member state has a central drug intelligence agency and to facilitate exchanges of information between such drug agencies through an efficient computer information system. In addition, the resolution expresses the council's intention to establish strict controls on community exports and imports of known chemicals and precursors used in manufacturing illegal drugs. Finally, the council asks the commission to organize the European conference to study all the implications and effects of drug use in order to assess, inter alia, the activities of criminal organizations.

## The Trevi Group

The Trevi Group, which focuses on the fight against terrorism, drug trafficking, and organized crime, has taken further steps toward stronger criminal cooperation in combatting drug trafficking. The group met on May 11–12, 1989, to examine the possibility of establishing a bureau to coordinate information and eventually to take action on public safety. In this regard, Spain proposed the creation of a European information technology space (laws and regimes for European information technology) for the identification and control of criminals, particularly terrorists and drug dealers. An informal meeting of the ministers of justice of the European Community was held on May 26, 1989, in San Sebastian, Spain, under the impetus of the Spanish minister of justice. Among the most significant accomplishments was the opening for signature of an EC convention on international criminal cooperation reflecting the recent agreement on the simplification and modernization of extradition procedures. Moreover, the ministers reached an agreement on the confiscation of funds from illegal transactions, primarily from drug deals.

## EC Money-Laundering Directive

On June 10, 1991, the EC Council of Ministers unanimously adopted the EC directive on money laundering. The directive prohibits money laundering of funds derived from drug trafficking *and other criminal offenses*, unlike the UN Drug Convention and the Financial Action Task Force recommendations, which deal only with drug-related laundering.

Under the directive, money laundering is defined as intentional conversion or transfer of property while knowing that the property is derived from criminal activity "for the purpose of concealing or disguising the illicit origin of the property or of assisting any person who is involved in the commission of such to evade the legal consequences of his action." The directive also states that knowledge or intent may be "inferred from objective factual circumstances."

The directive specifies enhanced know-your-customer requirements. It requires banks and other credit and financial institutions to obtain identification from customers when they open accounts or when they undertake a transaction of 15,000 ECUs (about $18,000) or more. The directive includes certain exceptions for pension plans. Germany had sought a higher threshold of 25,000 ECUs and France a lower threshold of 10,000 ECUs. Member states will be able to impose stricter rules, although obviously the adverse economic impact of such an action may limit such action.

Following the recommendations of the G–7 Financial Action Task Force, the directive provides for enhanced record keeping. In particular, financial institutions must keep copies of the customer identification records for at least five years after their relationship with the customer has terminated.

Under the directive, attention is given to suspicious transactions. Active cooperation between financial institutions and competent authorities will be ensured by a system of reporting suspicious transactions. Financial and covered institutions must review with special attention any transaction that appears by its nature to be related to money laundering. Banks must pay special attention to transactions with third countries that do not apply comparable standards against money laundering to those established by the EC or to other equivalent standards established by international fora and endorsed by the EC.

The directive also gives assistance in relieving employees or directors of a bank who in good faith report information concerning a suspected money laundering to authorities. They will not be responsible for breaching restrictions on disclosure of information.

The directive requires financial institutions and covered institutions to develop special training programs to enable employees of financial institutions to detect money laundering and to inform them how to respond to suspected cases.

The directive covers certain branches of credit institutions with their headquarters outside the EC.

The directive expressly states that the EC, while adopting the strictest standards in the world, will continue to participate in the work of the Financial Action Task Force on Money Laundering and help ensure that equivalent standards are applied in other areas of the world. The EC has an incentive to have equivalent standards apply worldwide; otherwise, they will lose business.

A key feature of the directive is that the EC Commission will explore associating the new democracies in Eastern Europe with the agreement so that similar measures criminalizing the laundering of proceeds from trafficking will apply in those countries.

The directive is still not as stringent as U.S. money-laundering legislation, which relies heavily on the collection of information on a routine basis when transactions pass a threshold of only $10,000 (almost one-half the threshold in the EC) by a host of professionals and financial institutions, who must then forward such information to the U.S. Department of Treasury.

The directive will add to the pressure internationally for action against money laundering; for example, the Caribbean and jurisdictions that cater to flight capital will be under new pressures to act. If the Caribbean countries take action, it makes sense that they should do so as a group; otherwise, money launderers and persons moving money for legitimate purposes and seeking anonymity will take advantage of the countries that do not have such legislation.

Indeed the real nuances will develop when EC members begin to implement the directives. Several solicitors, accountants, and financial institutions have criticized the framework directive as too broad—both because it embraces optimally serious crimes and because it covers financial institutions.[1] At the time of its adoption, the United Kingdom, France, Spain, and Luxembourg were the only countries in which money laundering was a crime. This announcement, therefore, is significant because it would require all members of the EC to criminalize money laundering. The United Kingdom is also leading a proposal to establish a task force on money laundering, which is expected to become institutionalized.

In sum, both European governmental officials and community officials are now undertaking efforts to regulate at a European level the trade of narcotic or narcotic-related substances and the money derived therefrom and to organize a common police and customs action. The growth of community law related to these products will directly affect the movement of goods, services, and persons within the community, which are the primary areas of intervention of the EC. The completion of the Single European Market in 1992, realizing a supplementary transfer of sovereignty from the states to the EC, will strengthen the powers of the community. Even though it cannot yet issue direct criminal provisions, its regulatory powers are likely to have a significant impact on the operation of businesses involved in the production or distribution of chemical and pharmaceutical products along with effects on the corporations involved in the transportation of goods and persons. Furthermore, the community can induce the member states to take criminal measures by means of directives and regulations.

## THE COUNCIL OF EUROPE

### Overview

The aim of the Council of Europe (COE), created in 1949, is to achieve greater unity within its members, to safeguard and realize the ideals and principles they have in common, and to facilitate their economic and social progress. The Council of Europe is an organization of cooperation, not of integration like the European Economic Community (EC), for its goal of unity—not of union—is achieved through agreements and common action. The interests of the COE encompass economic, social, cultural, scientific, legal and administrative matters, and human rights.

The COE has been the European organization that has led in international criminal cooperation. Eighteen COE treaties have been concluded in the past thirty years on extradition and judicial assistance. Among the most important are the 1957 Extradition Convention, amended in 1978; the 1959 Mutual Assistance Convention, amended in 1978; the 1970 International Validity of Criminal Judgments Convention; and the 1972 Transfer of Proceedings Convention.

### Cooperative Arrangement on Antinarcotics Policy between COE and EC

Overlapping jurisdiction and rivalry between the COE and EC has caused lacunae in some of the substantive enforcement efforts. In an exchange of letters dated June 16, 1987, the secretary general of the COE and the president of the EC Commission agreed to strengthen the cooperation between the two European bodies. The agreement provides for the advisability of the insertion, in any new draft European convention prepared by the COE, such as the convention on the confiscation of Funds from Illegal Drugs, of a clause allowing for the European Community to become a contracting party to the convention. The commission may also be invited to participate in meetings of the Committee of Ministers o questions of mutual interest. Finally, high-level meetings between the officials of the two European organizations will be arranged to examine questions of mutual interest and to consolidate cooperation, particularly in the field of legal affairs. Pursuant to this exchange of letters, an interdepartmental working party was established to follow cooperation developments.

On March 1989, the commission sent a communication to the European Council on Relations between the EC and the COE. The communication explains that the two organizations have different political aims, fields of activity, and working methods: The Council of Europe is an organization of intergovernmental cooperation, operating by means of conventions and recommendations; the European Community is an organization of integration, endowed with sovereign powers delegated to it by the member states. The communication states the goals for cooperation to ensure the complementarity of activities of the two organizations to avoid duplication or overlapping of effort. Finally, the commission will continue to look into possible EC participation in the conventions of the COE in areas covered by the EC's powers.

Therefore, the emphasis the commission puts on the limits of the cooperation between the two European organizations will probably lead to a separate and parallel development of their actions to combat drug trafficking. The COE will continue to operate on a cooperation basis, working on the drafting of conventions and on their implementation by its twenty-one member states. Pursuant to the exchange of letters of 1987, the COE will, for each of the new draft conventions, consider the appropriateness of inserting a clause allowing the EC to become a party to the convention. The last draft convention elaborated by the COE, the Comprehensive European Convention on Inter-State Cooperation in the Penal Field, does not include such a provision, which means that cooperation between the COE and the EC on extradition and mutual assistance has been temporarily deferred. The COE and the EC are still working out the best modes of cooperation.

## European Laundering Convention

The Draft Convention of Laundering, Search, Seizure and Confiscation of the Proceeds from Crime (hereafter the Laundering Convention) was prepared by a select committee of experts on July 25, 1990, and was adopted by the Committee of Ministers of the Council of Europe on September 10, 1990.[2] On November 8, 1990, twelve governments signed the Laundering Convention on the first day it became open for signature: Belgium, Cyprus, Denmark, Germany, Iceland, Italy, the Netherlands, Norway, Portugal, Spain, Sweden, and the United Kingdom. Finland and Switzerland signed shortly afterwards, and France and Ireland are expected to adopt it too. This kind of response signals tremendous success for antilaundering laws.

The convention contains some far-reaching provisions that have the potential to revolutionize international cooperation and the overall development of the regime of regulating international money movement. In particular, although the convention is based on the December 1988 UN Drug Convention, it allows signatory countries to criminalize laundering for non–drug-related matters. Significantly, the participants in the drafting and potential signatories include countries outside the Council of Europe. In addition to the experts from sixteen Council of Europe countries, the group included experts from Australia, Canada, and the United States, as well as Interpol, the United Nations, the International Association of Penal Law, the International Penal and Penitentiary Foundation, and the International Society of Social Defense. The Laundering Convention also contains important substantive developments, such as allowing the criminalization of negligent money laundering, and for explaining that hiring defense counsel is not meant to constitute a laundering offense.

The convention has four chapters: the first explains the use of terms; the second sets forth measures to be taken at a national level; the third defines the obligations and parameters of international cooperation; and the fourth contains final provisions.

The momentum for the preparation of the convention first occurred at the fifteenth Conference of the European Ministers of Justice in Oslo, Norway, on June 17–19, 1986, when the penal aspects of drug abuse and drug trafficking were discussed. In particular, the ministers discussed the need to combat drug abuse by smashing the drug market, which was often linked with organized crime and even terrorism, by freezing and confiscating the proceeds from drug trafficking. As a result of the meeting, the first resolution was adopted, in which the ministers recommended that the European Committee on Crime Problems (CDPC) should examine "the formulation in the light *inter alia* of the work of the United Nations, of international norms and standards to guarantee effective international cooperation between judicial (and where necessary police) authorities as regarding the detection, freezing and forfeiture of the proceeds of illicit drug trafficking." The CDPC at the thirty-sixth Plenary Session in September 1987 proposed, and the Committee of Ministers authorized, the creation of a select committee of experts on international cooperation in regard to search, seizure, and confiscation of proceeds from crime. At the extraordinary Conference of the Pompidou Group in London in May 1989, the ministers urged the Council of Europe to expedite the work of the committee, and thereafter its work was expedited.

## EUROPEAN FOREIGN POLICY

The European Community has exercised its competence to establish links with third states within the scope of the Treaty of Rome. Under Article 229 of the treaty, the commission can maintain relations with the organs of the United Nations and generally with all international organizations to undertake commitments on cooperation in combatting money laundering. The EC has specifically acted in leading the negotiation of and the signing of the 1988 UN Drug Convention and in establishing a financial action task force to deal with the exchange of currency flow information related to money laundering in the G–7 summits. Article 5 of the Treaty of Rome gives the EC the authority to make rules that will preempt commitments in treaties that both it and the member countries sign.

### UN Drug Convention

The 1988 UN Drug Convention requires the EC, as an entity, to fulfill to the limit of its authorities the commitments of the convention. Several important provisions pertain to money laundering. For instance, Article 3 sets forth offenses and requires the signatory countries to criminalize such offenses. Among the offenses are the laundering of money coming from drug crimes and the acquisition or use of property derived from such crimes. Article 5 provides for the confiscation of proceeds derived from any of the offenses established in Article 3, which includes not only money laundering, but also a broad range of other drug and drug-related offenses.

Article 6 provides for extradition. The signatory parties agree to include each of the offenses within the U.N. Drug Convention as extraditable offense in any extradition treaty existing and to be concluded between parties. Article 7 provides for mutual assistance, which may include taking evidence or statements from persons, effecting service of judicial documents, or executing searches and seizures. An important provision is that a requested party cannot refuse to render mutual legal assistance on the basis of bank secrecy. Finally, Article 8 obligates the signatory parties to consider the possibility of transferring to one another proceedings for criminal prosecution of those offenses established by the convention.

The probable accession of the EC to the convention will not signify that its provisions will apply de facto in the twelve member states. As already mentioned, the EC does not have competence to enact rules of criminal law binding on the states. Therefore, the enactment of regulations is not possible; however, a council directive could require member states to at least enact quasi-criminal provisions and other sanctions implementing the convention. By whatever mcans, the EC displays, by acceding to the UN Drug convention, its intention to become actively involved in the fight against drug addiction in Europe and its will to be more than just a public forum for debate.

### G–7 Summits

Significantly the EC is a participant distinct from the EC member states in the G–7 summits. In the summit, which was concluded in France on July 16,

1989, it signed communiqués that address money laundering, which call for the initiation of a financial action task force from summit participants and other interested countries. Its working orders are to assess the results of cooperation already undertaken to prevent the utilization of the banking system and financial institutions for money laundering and to consider additional preventive efforts in this field. France called the first meeting, and its report was completed by April 1990. In addition, the G–7 summit participants agreed to conclude further bilateral or multilateral agreements and to support initiatives and cooperation, where appropriate, including measures to facilitate the identification, tracking, freezing, seizure, and forfeiture of drug crime proceeds. In the context of its authority to bring about a European monetary union, the EC will be formulating a central currency and regulations for a Central Bank. Hence, the EC will have ample authority and opportunity to implement its agreement on the G–7 summits and the financial action task force.

## Other Intergovernmental Organizations

The EC participates and coordinates policies of its member states in other intergovernmental organizations that have important policy and operational roles in combatting money laundering. For instance, it participates in Interpol and in the G–10 Group (Bank for International Settlements).

At the Interpol General Assembly meeting on April 18–21, 1989, a resolution was adopted on forging an agreement on gathering and sharing international currency flows. The resolution recommends that governments take action to record and, where appropriate, report financial information connected with, arising from, or relating to, narcotics transactions and organized and other crimes, including suspicious and large currency transactions and large currency exchanges involving domestic and foreign currency.

The EC has also participated in the Basle Committee on Banking Regulations and Supervisory Practices, which consists of the central bank governors of the major industrialized countries. In December 1988, a Statement of Principles was adopted by the Basle Committee. It establishes a code for banks to verify the true identity of the beneficial owners of accounts and refuse transactions, avoid suspicious transactions, cooperate fully with law enforcement authorities, and adopt policies to ensure adherence to the code by their employees.

All of the above organizations, in which the EC participates, require the EC to take action to implement the commitments. As these agreements move into the implementation stage, the EC will begin to utilize its authority as the central banker and as the policymaker in enforcing cooperation in illicit money movement, especially when it is connected to specifically proscribed activities such as narcotics trafficking, terrorism, and organized crime.

## CONCLUSION

Until now the EC officials have restricted the action of the EC to the coordination of police and customs measures, leaving the member states free to join the COE conventions on cooperation on extradition and mutual assistance. However, the recent publication of the commission proposal for the signing of the 1988 UN Drug Convention Against Illicit Traffic in Narcotic Drugs and Psychotropic Substances displays the intent of the commission, if not the EC, to involve the community in legal cooperation with other states. The various abovementioned documents also demonstrate an intent by the various EC organs to initiate action to combat the drug menace. The bases from which to establish legal and even criminal measures to implement new policies to combat narcotics trafficking may already be in place. For instance, the European Parliament, in recommending now antinarcotics trafficking measures, cites as bases the duty of the EC to regulate areas of life affected by the problem of drug abuse: external relations, trade and customs law, law and order, health, social affairs, education, and citizens' rights. This same phenomenon, pointing to the dangers to society resulting from drug abuse, has occurred in other countries, such as the United States and Canada, as reasons to impose additional governmental regulation on the lives and freedoms of persons.

The UN Drug Convention includes provisions of great importance on money laundering, conspiracy, forfeiture, and adjective (procedural) enforcement aspects. The four following points summarize the provisions of the conventions:

1. Article 3 sets forth a series of offenses and requires member states to criminalize those offenses. Parties must criminalize the following behavior: the production, preparation, transport, or delivery of any drug or narcotic substance contrary to the 1961 convention; the laundering of money from drug crimes; and the acquisition or use of property derived from the foregoing offenses.

2. Article 5 provides for the confiscation of proceeds or narcotic substances derived from the offenses established in Article 3.

3. Article 21 provides for new functions for the Commission on Narcotic Drugs of the Economic and Social Council of the United Nations to supervise implementation.

4. Articles 5–8 provide broad mutual assistance. One form of mutual assistance that is provided for in Article 6 is extradition: The signatory parties agree to include each of the offenses within the UN Drug Convention as an extraditable offense in any extradition treaty existing and to be concluded between parties. Article 7 provides for mutual assistance, which may include taking evidence or statements from persons, effecting service of judicial documents, or executing searches and seizures. An important provision is that a requested party cannot refuse to render mutual legal assistance on the basis of bank secrecy. Finally, Article 8 obligates the signatory parties to consider the possibility of transferring to one another proceedings for criminal prosecution of offenses established by the convention.

The accession of the EC to the convention does not signify that its provisions will apply de facto in the twelve member states. As already mentioned, the EC is not able to enact rules of criminal law binding on the member states. Therefore, the enactment of regulations is not possible. However, a council directive could require member states to at least enact quasi-criminal provisions and other sanctions implementing the convention. However, the EC will demonstrate, by acceding to the UN Drug Convention, its intention to become involved directly in the fight against drug abuse in Europe, and its will to be more than just a public debating forum.

The effects of the new cooperation against drug trafficking will be profound. Criminal cooperation will be greatly enhanced. Extradition and, especially, mutual assistance in the investigation and prosecution of drug cases will be improved considerably. The EC's directives and regulations, to implement the recommendations of the European Parliament to combat narcotics trafficking, will apply across the community. For instance, on February 20, 1989, the EC's Council of Foreign Ministers adopted a binding regulation on the export of eight so-called precursor substances that can be used in the manufacture of chemical weapons. The same type of regulations will be adopted on the export of precursor substances that can be used in illicit narcotics trafficking and in the manufacturing of psychotropic drugs. In addition, as customs officials are required to tighten control and detection of goods that may carry narcotics, harsher penalties will be imposed on persons engaged in illicit trafficking. Consumers of illicit narcotics will increasingly experience criminal problems when they cross borders and find themselves also subject to forfeiture and financial penalties even though they are in a foreign country.

In foreign policy, the ability of the EC to support crop substitution programs in supplier countries, trade preferences for supplier countries, and various programs to influence supply and demand of illicit narcotics drugs will increasingly impact on international narcotics policy. The EC's influence stems from both its economic importance and its dominant political role, such as at the G–7 summits. It is also very influential in Interpol and in the United Nations Fund for Drug Abuse Control.

Other countries have begun to follow the lead of the EC. Most notably, the U.S. Congress, in December 1989, enacted legislation urging the president to provide economic assistance for crop substitution and to coordinate U.S. trade with its narcotics policy. However, until now, the U.S. Executive has not fully followed the EC lead on linking antinarcotics policy to trade preferences for supplier countries. The most concrete commitment to coordination of drug and economic policies was made by President Bush in February 1990 at the Andean Drug Summit.

An important effect of European cooperation against illicit narcotics trafficking and psychotropic substances will be the adoption of uniform laws in EC and COE member states. These laws will establish new criminal offenses, such as money laundering as well as establish new procedural laws, such as in the identification, freezing, seizing, and forfeiture of the proceeds and instrumentalities of crime based on either the Italian or United Kingdom model laws. For example, the European Committee of Experts, under the auspices of the Pompidou Group, has prepared the European Laundering Convention in regard to the International Cooperation in Respect of Search, Seizure and Confiscation of Proceeds of Crime. As discussed above, the convention requires signatories to enforce confiscation orders of other signatories and to initiate confiscation actions of their own. Another development in European cooperation is that EC member states will unify sentences for certain offenses. Together, the uniform laws will bring some profound changes in criminal practice.

Eventually, the EC is likely to adopt measures that common carriers must adopt or face penalties. At present, however, the absence of these measures contrasts with the harsh "Supercarrier Initiative" of the United States, which require carriers to spend enormous resources to secure the carrier and its employees from illicit drugs. Violations result in forfeiture of vessels and severe fines. For instance, as a result of finding three containers of marijuana on board the Evergreen in April 1987, the U.S. Customs Service imposed a fine of over $59 million against Evergreen for its culpability in transporting the drugs and not discovering them. After petitions and considerable work by attorneys, the entire penalty was remitted. However, most vessels have not been so fortunate.

The easier regulatory regime in the EC enables EC carriers to operate more economically in the regional and world market. From a business planning perspective, carriers are wise to arrange their operations to be subject only to the EC regime. Practically, this may mean avoiding U.S. ports unless the cargo is significant. Enforcement cooperation against trafficking by air has resulted in the establishment of an independent cooperation group to exchange intelligence and promote cooperation. Many EC governments have agreed to exchange information on passenger lists; however, objections by Lufthansa have blocked a more formal agreement.

One of the most important areas in which EC drug policy will be felt is in international politics. Some global interactions are initiated and sustained entirely, or almost entirely, by governments of nation states. Other interactions, such as narcotics deals and laundering the proceeds of narcotics or other illicit international transactions, involve both governmental and intergovernmental actions. To combat international narcotics trafficking successfully is to view the law enforcement community as an actor in a world politics paradigm and contrast it with the state-centric paradigm, that is, to confer on intergovernmental organizations increased roles vis-à-vis those of the nation-state. To the extent the EC is not able to decide whose jurisdiction it should be to ban the export of precursor drugs or to require common carriers or financial institutions to police effectively the abuse of their enterprises for trafficking and laundering, organized criminals will exploit such gaps to achieve their goals and legitimate business can occur with fewer regulations and costs. The decision of the EC to sign and participate in the implementation of the UN Drug Convention signals its determination to view the drug policy in the context of the world politics paradigm. The sophistication of many of the EC member countries and its experts and their memberships in many important international nongovernmental organizations (INGOs), such as the Association International de Droit Penal, will help them involve INGOs and facilitate the establishment and development of long-term alliances among the law enforcement community (e.g., a type of pattern of an elite network that leads to dynamic integration growth).

## NOTES

An earlier version of this chapter appeared as Bruce Zagaris and Ange Fantauzzi, ''Breaking the Connection,'' *Security Management* 34 (June 1990): 47–52. However, as the chapter relates, two significant developments have already occurred—the European laundering convention and the draft money-laundering framework directive. The fact that they were done by different organizations—the Council of Europe and the European Community—indicates the importance of both in the drug policy.

1. For additional background on action taken by the EC against drug trafficking and money laundering see Bruce Zagaris and Ange Fantauzzi, ''Breaking the Connection,'' *Security Management* 34 (June 1990): 47–52; on antidrug trafficking, Bruce Zagaris and Bornheim, ''When the Walls Come Tumbling Down,'' *Security Management* 34 no. 5 (May 1990): 69–74; and on anti–money laundering, Bruce Zagaris and Ange Fantauzzi, ''The External Impact of European Unification,'' *1992 The External Impact of European Unification*, 8 September 1989, 9–12 and Scott B. MacDonald, ''Anti-Money Laundering Regimes in Europe and Canada,'' *Comptroller of the Currency Quarterly Journal* (Summer 1991): 6–11.

2. For background on the adoption of the Laundering Convention by the Committee of Ministers, see Council of Europe's Anti–Money Laundering Convention Is Adopted by the Committee of Ministers,'' *International Enforcement Law Reporter* 6 (September 1990): 308.

## BIBLIOGRAPHY

Carlson, Scott, and Bruce Zagaris. ''International Cooperation in Criminal Matters: Western Europe's International Approach to International Crime.'' *Nova Law Review* 15 (Spring 1991): 551–80.

''The Drugs Situation in Europe after 1992.'' *International Criminal Police Review* (July-August 1990): 25–32.

''European Community Adopts Regulations on Exporting Precursors.'' *International Enforcement Law Reporter* 5 (April 1989): 150.

European Parliament, Committee on Inquiry into the Drug Problem in the Member States of the Community. *Report on the Result of the Inquiry*, Strasbourg: European Parliament, September 1986.

Exchange of letters between the Council of Europe and the European Community concerning the Consolidation and Intensification of Cooperation. *Official Journal of the European Communities*, no. L273135, 1989.

*The Fight against Drugs in the Community*, BULL. EC Bulletin 11–1986.

MacDonald, Scott B. "Anti–Money Laundering Regimes in Europe and Canada." *Comptroller of the Currency Quarterly Journal* (Summer 1991): 6–11.

United Nations. Proposal for a Council Decision of the United Nations Convention against Illicit Traffic in Narcotic and Psychotropic Substances, concluded in Vienna, Austria, on 20 December 1988, COM (89) 26–26 January 1989.

Zagaris, Bruce, and Markus Bornheim. "International Cooperation against Money Laundering in the European Integration Context." 1992—*The External Impact of European Unification* (3 November 1989): 13–16.

Zagaris, Bruce, and Ange Fantauzzi. "Breaking the Connection." *Security Management* 34 (June 1990): 47–52.

# 15

# The Netherlands

GOVERT FRANK VAN DE WIJNGAART AND
SARAH BARBER

## INTRODUCTION

The Dutch approach toward drug abuse is a novel one. Compared to many of its neighbors' policies, it can be viewed as lenient and liberal; however, the Dutch have a well-researched, pragmatic national program for dealing with drug abuse and its inevitable social ramifications that, in many ways, is the envy of other comparable, highly industrialized nations. Dutch drug policy must be seen in relation to its social and cultural context. Because basic facts about the Netherlands are an important part of that context, before we begin to outline the Dutch policy on the health care, social services, penal code, and national attitudes that fuel its approach to drug policy, a brief outline of the Netherlands is helpful.

## BACKGROUND

The Netherlands (''low lands'') is a small, densely populated, highly developed country, situated in Western Europe on the North Sea. Politically speaking, the Netherlands is a constitutional monarchy with a parliamentary system. The seat of government is in Den Haag (The Hague), and Amsterdam is the capital. The most densely populated area is the ''Randstad'' conurbation in the western part of the country which comprises Amsterdam, Rotterdam, Den Haag, and Utrecht.

Economically, the most important activities are commerce, shipping, and transit trade. For many years Rotterdam has been the world's busiest port.

The modern history of the country can be traced back to 1581, when it became an independent republic, the ''Republic of the Seven United Netherlands,'' in which the most important part was being ''Holland.'' The Golden Age of the nation was the seventeenth century: The Dutch made a fortune trading around the world and continuously appropriated colonies. At the beginning of the nineteenth century, the Netherlands were annexed by France under Napoleon. After Napoleon's defeat, the country was remodeled into a monarchy by England and Germany. Until World War II, the Netherlands was one of the largest colonial powers.

Being a prosperous and independent country, the Netherlands gained a reputation as a port of distress for political refugees. After the Germans had violated Dutch neutrality in World War II, the Netherlands started to develop the role of a conscientious and critical ally in the Western world. Since the early 1960s the Netherlands has experienced an influx of foreign guest-workers from the Mediterranean area, in particular, from Morocco and Turkey.

The Netherlands is a social welfare state. It offers to its population an excellent health care system which is available to every citizen. The National Assistance Act entitles every citizen to financial help when it becomes impossible to support himself or herself. Likewise, under the National Health Insurance Act, every inhabitant of the country is entitled to medical, pharmaceutical, dental, and hospital treatment. However, in an era of rising medical costs, the Dutch system, like its European state-run counterparts, is having a difficult time financially sustaining the level of medical care available to its people.

## DRUG HISTORY

Drug use in the Netherlands has been present since the early twentieth century when small Chinese communities in the cities of Amsterdam and Rotterdam continued their traditional use of opium, which originated in China. The Dutch who used opium or morphine were physicians, nurses, pharmacists, and "artists." Another group of opium users included those who had problems giving it up after it had been prescribed by their physicians. It was only in the 1960s that the use of opium filtered into other groups of society, especially into certain groups of middle-class "way-out" youth. According to Geerlings (1975), there were several hundred Dutch opium addicts in the early 1970s.

Before 1972 the use of heroin was very limited. Although heroin was a highly desirable substance in the eyes of regular opium users, the supply was rather inconsistent and insufficient. At the end of the 1960s heroin was sometimes brought in by American and other hippies from abroad while visiting Amsterdam. However, after the summer of 1972, it became relatively easy to buy heroin in the Netherlands. An analysis of the heroin showed that it was pure and must have originated from large, well-equipped laboratories.

The departure of Americans from Vietnam meant that an important market for dealers had disappeared, and in its place a new market in Western Europe was developed. Three large Chinese syndicates from Hong Kong and Singapore found their way to the gateway of Europe—the Netherlands, an excellent intermediate station to other countries, especially the German Federal Republic where many U.S. soldiers were stationed.

After 1975, heroin again became difficult to obtain. The price rose, and police efforts were increased, causing large amounts of the substance to be seized, thus further depressing the available supply. In 1977 the number of heroin addicts was estimated at 5,000. Most of the heroin came from the Golden Triangle of Thailand, Burma, and Laos. Today, much of the heroin comes from Afghanistan, Iran, and Pakistan.

At present, the number of drug addicts in the Netherlands is estimated to be between 15,000 and 20,000. More than 50 percent of all addicts reside in the four major cities, by far the greatest number—about 5,000—in Amsterdam. More and more heroin addicts take a wide variety of drugs, especially tranquilizers and alcohol. Research indicates that persons who have few possibilities of improving their socioeconomic situations increasingly become addicted to heroin.[1] These people may have little education, may be unemployed, and may experience an adverse housing situation. Among ethnic minorities in the Netherlands, particularly those of Moluccan and Surinamese origin, the proportion of drug addicts is relatively high. It is not difficult to see the parallels between the drug-using populations of the Netherlands and the United States' own characteristic demographics of drug use.

Drugs other than heroin, such as hashish, have also been viewed as causing problems in the Netherlands. The use of hashish spread during the 1960s, but few individuals went on to try harder drugs. Amphetamines have been a source of concern as well, but after a surge in their use in the early 1970s, abuse has been declining. Today, addiction to heroin alone is seldom encountered. Until recently, cocaine use was increasing as well, often alternated with heroin use.

## DRUG PROGRAMS

The Dutch began formal aid to those suffering from the effects of drug abuse as early as 1930. The focus at the time was on alcohol, as drug abuse per se had not materialized. The private initiative started in the 1930s was a means of providing aid to alcoholics not only in terms of rehabilitation, but also in dealing with their legal problems. In 1953 the Federation for the Care of Alcoholics (FZA) was established to facilitate cooperation between organizations providing assistance to alcoholics on the national level. The FZA specialized in clinics for the treatment of alcohol and drugs. In 1988 it restructured itself into the Netherlands Institute of Alcohol and Drugs, which now plays an important role in collecting and disseminating information, in developing expert knowledge, and in training professionals throughout various municipalities.

In forty-five municipalities there are a little over a hundred special facilities for young people, some of which are specifically aimed at drug users. These projects, which employ around 500 professionals, can be categorized as prevention projects. The most of them in 1985 amounted to fifty million ($26,095 million) guilders. Inpatient facilities for alcohol and drug addicts are located throughout the country. They have a maximum capacity of just over 800 beds. Some specialize in alcohol treatment and others in the treatment of drug addiction. A third category is open to both alcohol and drug addicts.

The whole relief system is financed through the government, and admission and services are free. In addition the number of (often small scale) institutions is increasing. These institutions, which often have religious backgrounds, acquire their money from various sources. They are characterized by a combination of initial care, treatment, aftercare, and other help that might be needed afterward. Admission and services for these are also free.

The Netherlands started to utilize methadone in 1968. Initially this took place with little organization on a small scale. In the middle of the 1970s, however, official methadone programs were established. These programs formulated new objectives and new methods of implementation. Generally speaking, there are two kinds of methadone programs in the Netherlands: One emphasizes the reduction of the use of opiates (reduction to abstinence); the other emphasizes the stabilization of use, or maintenance. In the latter case, regulations control the intake of other drugs.

In the major cities the phenomenon of the ''methadone bus'' has been known since the end of the 1970s. It is generally believed that concentrations of addict-clients can be associated with the increase in petty crime, aggression, and the attraction of receivers and dealers. The advantage of a methadone maintenance program, distributed from a mobile bus, is that it does not cause any great annoyance to people in a specific area. Hence, the optimal capacity of a dispensing program is between 20 and 25 clients. It is open only to registered clients on a regular basis after central intake and selection; methadone is not given to unknown transients.

A bus program has many advantages over an immobile program in a health center or clinic. The bus can reach people in certain neighborhoods who are otherwise hard to contact. The number of clients in a specific location can be kept small to prevent fringe crimes. The expenses of a mobile bus are less than those of an immobile clinic on private property, especially in prosperous areas.

Methadone has proved itself a valuable instrument for establishing contact. Within this system, concomitant social assistance is tailored to the needs of the client, both with regard to content as well as intensity. Assistance varies from incidental contracts concerning minor problems, to referral to intensive treatment services.

## PENAL CODE AND DRUGS

After the Hague Convention, the first Dutch opium act was enacted in 1919. This law has been changed a number of times; the most recent alteration occurred in 1976 when a distinction was made in the law between high-risk drugs and low-risk drugs, which include ''traditional hemp products,'' or hashish and marijuana. In a move toward international enforcement, the Netherlands ratified the 1961 Single Convention on Narcotic Drugs of New York in which trafficking and possessing drugs of any kind, except for medical or scientific purposes, are punishable offenses.

The first signs of growing drug use in the Netherlands, which appeared in the 1950s, consisted mainly of cannabis abuse. The courts began to take action in 1955, when public prosecutors began to demand eighteen months imprisonment for the possession of 1,400 grams of marijuana. In 1956, several citizens were sent to prison for periods of more than a year. For example, in a marijuana case in 1957, the public prosecutor demanded a thirty-six months' imprisonment; the actual sentence given was twelve months. In the following years, both the sentence demanded and the sentence handed down were still more than one year. Convictions and sentences of more than one year continued throughout the 1960s.[2]

Although criminal law had not played a part in preventing individual drug use, at the end of the 1960s, a reconsideration of the prosecution policy was advocated by a growing number of experts and official agencies. They insisted on a decrease in punitive measures aimed at the use of cannabis products, or for a deletion of these products from the Opium Act. Their recommendations were based on the theory that protecting people from the dangers of certain substances by means of punishment is an insufficient motive for interfering with a person's privacy. Not all supporters of a policy revision decided in favor of deletion of these substances from the Opium Act; some wanted to prevent the Netherlands from becoming a trading center for cannabis as long as other countries had not adopted the same attitude, and others wanted to prevent the unwanted situation of not having any restrictions toward cannabis at all.

The amended Opium Act of 1976 separated "drugs presenting unacceptable risks," such as heroin, cocaine, amphetamines and LSD, from "traditional hemp products," such as hashish and marijuana. In addition, the possession of illicit drugs is subject to a less severe penalty than is international trafficking. The act reflects the view of the Dutch government that criminal law should play only a minor part in preventing individual drug use. Although the risks to society must be taken into account, it is the Dutch philosophy that every possible effort must be made to ensure that drug users are not caused more harm by criminal proceedings than by the use of the drug itself. The Dutch legal system takes into account the prevention and treatment of the individual, as well as the social risks involved in the use of drugs.

Drug abuse did not emerge as a social problem in the Netherlands until the late 1960s. Initially, the police and judiciary dealt severely with drug users, but increasing doubts arose as to the value of criminal proceedings in such cases. These doubts and the growing significance of the problem led the government to appoint experts from various disciplines to form a working party on drugs. The working party's recommendations, published in 1972, have largely determined the direction of present-day Dutch drug policy. Since that time, drug policy has had two main aspects: the enforcement of the Opium Act on the one hand, and a policy of assistance to addicts on the other. The central objective is to prevent and deal with the risks that drug abuse presents to the addicts themselves, to their immediate environment, and to society as a whole. In 1974, an interdepartmental steering group was set up to coordinate the national-level activities of the various ministries involved. The first government policy document, specifically focusing on aid to drug addicts, appeared in 1977. Since then the national government has formulated a number of policy principles:

1. That a multifunctional network of medical and social services be built up at a local or regional level to provide assistance in ways that are appropriate to particular problems.
2. That assistance be made more accessible.
3. That social rehabilitation of drug addicts and former drug addicts be promoted.
4. That greater and more efficient use be made of nonspecialist facilities that can provide assistance to drug addicts, such as primary health care facilities including general practitioners, and youth welfare facilities.
5. That various aid facilities be coordinated more effectively.
6. That the role of information should not be overestimated.
7. That the risks of drug abuse should be part of a general health education campaign rather than a separate issue.

In the Netherlands much attention is focused on the individual drug user. Dutch policy also takes into account the perceived interest of the addict's parents. In 1980 the "Junkiebond," a kind of union for users, was set up by a group of concerned hard drug users. The direct cause of this was a local plan to force addicts to abstain from drug use. Although the national authorities have always taken a negative view about the forced hospitalization of drug addicts, the Junkiebond observed the ever-increasing problems and the deteriorating situation of addicts, and cited these and other reasons as the cause for their foundation.

The starting point of the Junkiebond is to look after the interests of the drug users. The most important thing is to combat the deterioration of the user, such as improving housing and the general situation of the addict. Their philosophy is that drug users themselves know best what their problems are. The work of Junkiebond involves consultations with government offices about matters like the distribution of methadone, the availability of free sterile syringes, the policy of the lawmakers and police, and housing problems. The ability of such a group to exist and cooperate for mutual benefit with government officials is a prime example of the level of tolerance and open-mindedness of the Dutch government.

Another initiative, like Junkiebond and the methadone bus program, which has had a positive impact on the problem of drug abuse in the Netherlands, has been a successful program providing for the free exchange of needles and syringes. These needle-exchange programs, developed in cooperation with the Junkiebond, have provided a way for drug users to stay in relatively good shape and for society as a whole to run fewer risks from diseases such as hepatitis and, in Amsterdam, AIDS. The number of exchanged needles and syringes rose from 100,000 in 1985 to 700,000 in 1987.[3] In 1988, some 720,000 needles and syringes were exchanged at eleven different locations. On the basis of both quantitative and qualitative data, no evidence has been found that needle-exchange programs have led to an increase in drug use.[4] But the question remains whether these experiences and achievements can be generalized to other countries. One expert claims that certain constraints exist: "It is questionable whether findings from Amsterdam can be generalized to other cities, since the needle exchange is embedded in a particular drug helping system and carried out within a specific social political climate."[5] Findings from the evaluation of the needle-exchange schemes in England and Scotland, however, show a similar outcome.[6] What the success of these policies would be in countries where law enforcement measures have led to the marginalization and criminalization of drug users is unknown.[7]

## DUTCH PERSPECTIVE AND COMPETING PERSPECTIVES

In the Netherlands, higher priority is given to activities of trying to control the demand for drugs than to those of trying to control the supply of drugs. It is estimated that 5 or perhaps 10 percent of all illegal drugs are seized by the authorities. Better prospects, according to the Dutch government, lie in trying to reduce individual or collective demand. The Netherlands has instituted a number of measures aimed at reducing demand. Interestingly enough, some studies have shown that publicity is ineffective in preventing the problems of drug abuse, particularly where it has the effect of sensationalizing the dangers of drugs. Publicity of this kind is likely to be one-sided and is therefore not used by the Dutch government. Such publicity, it is felt, may even encourage drug use.[8] The use of educational programs in the schools, usually as part of an overall health program meant to diminish the allure daring drugs evokes among the young, have been successful.

The basis for much of the Dutch programs for dealing with the problems of drug abuse has been their unique perspective. In comparison with the approaches in the United States and in most other countries, the approach in the Netherlands is best described as "normalization"; the United States and other European countries usually try to control illicit drug use through "deterrence." The two approaches can be defined as follows: the deterrence approach claims that the best way to prevent the problems arising from the use of drugs is to try to eliminate their use altogether; the normalization approach states that the problems arising from drug use are not inevitable and are intensified rather than alleviated by attempts to eliminate their use.

### Deterrence Approach

In the view of those who support the deterrence perspective, the serious consequences (both physical and social), which may be associated with the use of certain substances, stem from the intrinsic properties of the drugs themselves. Drugs ''create'' problems in a direct, causal way. This belief in the direct efficacy of drugs enables protagonists of the deterrence perspective to assert further that drugs can be ordered according to their harmfulness into a clear-cut hierarchy. Moreover, because this perspective is closely associated with the legal sanctions that have been instituted against drug use, it goes on to assert that this hierarchy corresponds to the current legal status of the drugs in question. If the police and the courts take a severe attitude toward a certain substance, it can be assumed that the drug in question is indeed a very dangerous one. Heroin is the substance that most commonly falls into this category.

According to the deterrence perspective, the effect of a drug is primarily understood in terms of its physiological work. This in turn can be understood in terms of a deterministic or mechanistic type of causality. Central to this model is addiction, which is seen as a physiologically determined compulsion to reuse the drug in increasing quantities.

The deterrence view asserts, in general, that the problems associated with drug use are caused by that use, rather than being only, as the normalizing view tends to see them, the side effects of it. These problems include deterioration of personality and mental state; deterioration of relationships; loss of work motivation; and a general shift in values toward an antisocial, irresponsible, aimless, and generally nihilistic attitude to life. Also, on the deterrence perspective, drug use is not just a problem for the individual concerned, but has repercussions for the well-being of society as a whole. The deterrence theory advocates the following policy toward drug users: (1) the users must be obliged to give up drugs, normally through criminalization of drug use; (2) drug use can be deterred by simply cutting off the supply, at least until it becomes impossible to obtain; (3) at the same time, steps must be taken to discourage any who might be tempted to become drug users. Deterrence advocates view the opposition, namely the normalization groups, as those who simply refuse to see the seriousness of the problem and who are over-permissive.

### Normalization Approach

In contrast with the deterrence view, the normalization perspective sees the effects of a given substance not as determined by a simple physiological mechanism, but as a complex interaction of physiological and nonphysiological factors. The most important mediating factors, which are social and psychological, have to do with the personality of the use, the culture, the situation, and the meanings ascribed to particular actions within this context. Thus, the same substance in different contexts of use can have quite different effects, both primary as well as secondary.[9]

Regarding the primary effects of drugs, it is known that subjective expectancies play an important role in determining the effect of a particular substance. The current physical and mental state of the user can also produce wide variations in drug effects. Alcohol is a prime example of this. Apart from the factors of expectancy, mood, and setting, cultural and historical factors are important in mediating the effects of drug use. The proponents of normalization reject the idea that the effects of drugs are directly physically determined. Because of this, they also reject the idea of a clear-cut hierarchy of "dangerousness." Some drugs considered very dangerous are often "safely" used, but such use tends to be invisible because the users never become problem cases and moreover never have to hide their habit from public view. Conversely some "safe" substances can—if unwisely used—be very dangerous. Because they do not believe in such a concept as the dangerousness—in an absolute sense—of a drug, supporters of this view reject the idea of a correlation between dangerousness and legality. The misuse of a substance such as alcohol (or tobacco) is responsible for personal and social destruction on a wide scale, but these substances, currently at least, are not restricted outside the Arab world.

## IMPLICATIONS OF THE DUTCH EXPERIENCE

To what extent can the insights gained from the Dutch experience be applied to the situation in other countries? Throughout this chapter the emphasis has been on understanding drug use in the context of its specific cultural and historical situation. Such understanding, by its very nature, cannot be simply extrapolated to other social contexts.

There is absolutely no guarantee that attempts to imitate Dutch drug policy in other countries would meet with success. Crucial elements of the Dutch context would appear to be the following: a strong belief in equal rights; a belief in the possibility and legitimacy of social intervention; and a sound system of welfare and health care provisions. By comparison, some aspects of the American situation, which appear to be important determinants of the nature of the drug problem in that country, do not apply in the Dutch context. R. Draper argues that it is hardly possible to isolate drug policy from foreign, economic, and social policy. He concludes that, while good social policy is not a panacea for drug problems, it does contribute to their solution.[10]

In containing drug problems it is important to recognize that the criminal status of drug use is a major factor in causing problems for addicts and the community in general. However, we agree with B. K. Alexander (1990) that the transition from the present situation to a more measured response to drugs should be a gentle one.[11] It would seem unwise to make too many (new) drugs publicly available in a short time, because time is required for society to "domesticate" new drugs from general usage and to adapt to a new way of thinking.

An indication of the popularity of the normalization approach can be seen from the conclusions of the meeting at Tilburg in 1988 between U.S. and European experts:

1. Legal and illegal drugs have several basic similarities. The distinctions drawn between them today are a result of various historical conditions. The distinctions are not based on the innate character of the various substances.
2. The results of the system of prohibition and of severe penal measures against the totally forbidden substances are poor compared to the costs. The "control costs" are mounting and threaten internal peace and the preservation of central values of human rights in many countries.
3. The international community must commence now the work of analyzing the possibilities to bring the total prohibition within this field to an end and to create instead control systems similar to those used vis-à-vis other potentially harmful substances.
4. The conference suggests a considerable reduction in the punishment level. The use of capital punishment for drug dealing ought immediately to be brought to a stop. Personal use and the possession for that use should not be punished.

International treaties should promote the creation of alternative forms of control to those which are applied today with such limited success and with such severe costs.

## CONCLUSION

The Dutch drug policy is indeed unique and significant. The situation of the Netherlands, a country traditionally with ample international commerce and visitors, is important since it has been an important consuming and transit country. Most important, its innovative drug policy bears further study and application by the world community and some countries. In particular, the emphasis on normalization rather than deterrence and of prevention and treatment over control of supply has met with success. The de facto decriminalization of soft drugs (cannabis) and normalization ("recreational use" by the generation of the 1960s and others, domestication of use, and, in public areas, passive acceptance by the general public) have achieved success: They have not led to more use of these soft drugs. Just as important, the prioritization of treatment over control has facilitated a better quality of life for the entire Dutch society since persons with drug problems have not been driven underground where they become more debilitated by using dirty needles or becoming infected with AIDS. The results of the system of prohibition and of severe penal measures against the totally forbidden substances are poor compared to the costs. Examples of these control costs are consolidation of organized crime, the undermining of the principals of legality and due process, and the diversion of scarce law enforcement resources. The large amount of money circulating in the drug trade threatens international economic and political stability. The humaneness of the Dutch drug policy and the failure of the repressive approach of other countries have brought an influx of drug addicts seeking help to the Netherlands, thereby skewing the statistics. In any event, the total number of regular, dependent, hard drug users indicates that the level of use is slightly lower than in other countries and has stabilized with few new cases being reported. The condition of users and of the population as a whole is very much better, in terms of social integration and access to welfare services.

The key to the unique Dutch drug policy lies in the combination of its emphasis on long-term prevention, a policy that requires an expenditure of resources to support activities to control demand; a commitment to treat rather than merely punish persons who are not able to control their use; and strong programs for those who ask for help.

## NOTES

1. See O. Janssen and K. Swierstra, *Heroinegebruikers in Nederland-Een typologie van Levensstijlen* (The Hague: RUG Groningen, 1982).
2. J. D. van der Meulen, ''Drugs en het strafrecht,'' in *Soft Drugs*, ed. C. Wijbenga, 35–36 (Amsterdam: Van Gennep, 1969).
3. G. van Brussel and E. Buning, ''Public Health Management of AIDS and Drugs in Amsterdam,'' in *Problems of Drug Dependence*, ed. L. S. Harris, 295–301 (Rockville, Md.: NIDA Research Monograph 90, 1988).
4. Ibid.
5. E. C. Buning, *Effects of Amsterdam Needle and Syringe Exchange*. (The Hague: Dutch-American Debate, 1989).
6. Stimsom et al., 1988, cited in Buning (1989), p. 7.
7. Buning, *Effects of Amsterdam Needle and Syringe Exchange*, 7.
8. For further information, see H. Nowlis, *Drugs Demystified: Drug Education* (Paris: UNESCO, 1980).
9. N. E. Zinberg, *Drug, Set and Setting* (New Haven, Conn.: Yale University Press, 1984).
10. R. Draper, ''Balancing of Supply and Demand,'' Proceedings 16th International Institute on the Prevention and Treatment of Drug Dependence (Lausanne: ICAA, 1987). Paper presented at proceedings.
11. B. K. Alexander, *Peaceful Measures—Canada's Way out of the 'War on Drugs'* (Toronto: University of Toronto Press, 1990).

## BIBLIOGRAPHY

Alexander, B. K. *Peaceful Measures—Canada's Way out of the 'War on Drugs'*. Toronto: University of Toronto Press, 1990.

Brussel, G. van, and E. Buning. Public Health Management of AIDS and Drugs in Amsterdam.'' In *Problems of Drug Dependence*, edited by L. S. Harris. Research Monograph 90, pp. 295–301. Rockville, Md.: NIDA, 1988.

Buning, E. C. *Effects of Amsterdam Needle and Syringe Exchange*. The Hague: Dutch-American Debate, 1989.

Buning, E. C., R. A. Coutinho, G.H.A. van Brussel, G. W. Van Saoten, and A. W. van Zadelhoff. ''Preventing AIDS in Drug Addicts in Amsterdam.'' *The Lancet* (21 June 1986): 1435.

Draper, R. ''Balancing of Supply and Demand.'' Proceedings, 16th International Institute on the Prevention and Treatment of Drug Dependence. Lausanne: ICAA, 1987. Paper presented at a conference.

Geerlings, P. J. ''Hulpverlenign aan drugsverslaafden.'' (Assistance to drug addicts). *Maandblad Geestelijke Volksgezondheid* 30 (1975): 549–57.

Janssen, O. and K. Swierstra. *Heroinegebruikers in Nederland-Een typologie van Levensstijlen*. The Hague: RUG Groningen, 1982.

Meulen, J. D. van der. ''Drugs en het strafrecht.'' In *Soft Drugs*, edited by C. Wijbenga, 7–41. Amsterdam: Van Gennep, 1969.

Nowlis, H. *Drugs Demystified: Drug Education*. Paris: UNESCO, 1980.

Zinberg, N. E. *Drug, Set and Setting*. New Haven, Conn.: Yale University Press, 1984.

# 16

# Sweden

SARAH BARBER

## INTRODUCTION

Unlike many of the other countries that have been featured in various chapters of this book, Sweden does not produce many illicit narcotics. Nor is Sweden a noteworthy transit country of the narcotics trade. However, it is a consuming country, albeit on a much smaller scale than, say, the United States. Sweden is a country intensely interested in the rehabilitation of drug abusers and in social welfare, in general. Partly what makes Sweden an especially interesting study within the framework of this handbook on narcotics control is its humane approach to dealing with the problems associated with narcotics trafficking and production in very practical terms: its impact on the individual within society. A general understanding of the Swedish approach can be more readily understood in the context of its history and place in the international community, as well as its unique national philosophy.

## BACKGROUND

Sweden, with its population of 8.5 million, is an independent and affluent nation. With a history of political neutrality, Sweden has been something of an enigma to other European countries. At the outbreak of both world wars, Sweden declared its neutrality, although it allowed Germany to send troop trains through Sweden in order to reach the fronts during Germany's occupation of Norway and Denmark during 1940. Sweden itself has not fought any wars since 1814. In an effort to continue its neutrality, Sweden has refused to join the North Atlantic Treaty Organization (NATO) feeling that such a move would threaten its policy of impartiality in international conflicts. Sweden does have, however, mandatory military service for all males and a strong military force for defensive purposes. Its air force has been particularly strong, although other areas of defense, namely an effective navy, nave not enjoyed similar success.[1]

While choosing to practice a philosophy of nonalignment, Sweden is very internationally oriented. A strong supporter and participant in the United Nations, Sweden has participated in peacekeeping efforts, including sending Swedish troops to the Middle East. International trade is especially important to Sweden, since it relies heavily on exports to other countries. Sweden joined the Organization for Economic Cooperation and Development (OECD) just after World War II. In the past, Sweden had declined to apply for membership in the European Community (EC), on the basis that the Treaty of Rome contains supranational policies, but it applied for membership in the early 1990s.[2] While not participating in the European Community, Sweden has nonetheless fostered its international trade sector by playing an important role in the formation of the European Free Trade Association (EFTA), which was created in 1960. Sweden has also actively supported the General Agreement on Tariffs and Trade (GATT), in addition to signing a free trade agreement with the EC in 1972. Sweden is, despite its resistance to enmeshment in the political affairs of other countries, very sensitive to international commerce and trade; it has firmly established itself as an economic power while remaining very nationally oriented in its approach.

This philosophy of self-reliance in an increasingly interconnected world can be seen in its national policy of a social welfare state. Sweden enjoys an extraordinarily high standard of living, with the government subsidizing to a large extent education, health care, and other social concerns such as care of the elderly and day care. Part of this formula of a welfare state is high taxes. Swedes accept this in order to support their high standards, although large segments of the population are clamoring for a reexamination of some aspects of the welfare state due to the high taxes. The national elections of 1991 reflected the desire to limit any further expansion of the welfare state when the conservative coalition was successful.

## PENAL SYSTEM

In Sweden, the criminal justice system must be viewed in the context of the social factors involved. Unlike many other countries, Sweden's penal code does not come into play much for narcotics offenders, but its policy is indicative of the influence of social welfare policy throughout its society. The Swedish rehabilitation, probation, and training programs must be seen as part of the state's overall social welfare program.[3] Criminal cases are handled by a judge and five lay assistants in an informal, conversational type of hearing during which a defendant is given ample time to speak. As in the United States, indigent defendants are provided counsel by the state. Most of the sentences that are handed down are much less severe than those given in the United States. For example, the average prison sentence in Sweden is around five months.[4] There is special emphasis on probation and on other forms of noninstitutional deprivations of freedom. In part, the criminal system is able to function in this manner because of the homogeneous nature of its population and its small size. The Swedish view of society presumes it should function as a whole and not as a group of individuals with competing interests. Their concept of society is similar to that of family; there is little emphasis on the punitive nature of punishment, and the goal is rehabilitation and return to society.

In criminal cases, the public prosecutor has to institute (in theory at least) an action against every offender. In reality, there has been an increasing tendency for prosecutors to use their discretion and not prosecute if the offender is willing to pay a fine.[5] Special consideration is given to an evaluation of the social conditions that might explain the offense based on medical or social authorities' reports, called personal case studies. Also prevalent through the Swedish penal system is the presence of ombudsmen. An ombudsman's function is to supervise the activities of the state municipal authorities to ensure that they fulfill their duties and obligations toward the public as set in the law and statutes of the country.[6] Elected by Parliament, they are active on behalf of government agencies, private agencies, banks, companies, and so on, as well as the public at large.

With so much emphasis on protecting the rights of the individual, it is not surprising that narcotics offenders are more likely to be given treatment than prison time. Currently, drug abusers can be treated in fifteen outpatient wards, with another 100 beds in the drug addict wards of hospitals, and treatment homes with an additional 230 beds. Punishment for violation of the Narcotic Penal Law was strengthened in 1968, at which time the maximum penalty for serious crimes was increased from four to six years in 1969, and then from six to ten in 1972 in response to the increased instances of abuse.

## NARCOTICS STRATEGY AND HISTORY

Since it is a social welfare state, Sweden's government has been involved intimately in combatting the problems of drug abuse, and these problems have strong national backing. Sweden has attempted to deal with the problem of drug abuse among members of its population primarily through targeting groups which they feel are most vulnerable to becoming involved in drug abuse or illicit trade. Sweden started gathering statistics on the incidence of drug abuse, especially among the young, around the early 1960s. Because the Swedes have tried novel approaches to drug abuse, these statistics can give a means for measuring their success, but only a general one for, as statisticians know, many factors can affect the outcome of surveys, and many of them are unrelated to what is being measured. For instance, in the assessment of the case of drug abuse, the classification of causation may be difficult (e.g., whether increased enforcement efforts result in the arrest and detention of more people on drug charges, with little or no actual increase in the actual level of drug abuse, or whether there is simply more drug abuse activity, and hence more arrests, despite any increase in enforcement). Sweden has been very aggressive in implementing new legislation as well, and these changes in the law will of course have an impact on the results of any statistics that might be gathered.

Sweden's statistics on drug abuse are broken down into two different categories. First is the category of occasional abuse, and these measures have been obtained through surveys of schoolchildren in the ninth form (fifteen to sixteen years old) and military conscripts (usually around eighteen). Sweden's research shows that, in the early 1970s, approximately 15 percent of ninth-form pupils reported having tried drugs. The proportion declined during the mid–1970s and amounted to between 7 and 8 percent in 1975.[7] This percentage remained constant until the early 1980s, where it dropped to 5 percent in 1983 and 3 percent in 1987.[8] These results seem to indicate that experimental or occasional drug use was more prevalent in the 1970s than in the 1980s, at least for school-age children. The figures belie the efforts Sweden has made to use school education as a weapon against drug abuse, especially among the young. Their philosophy is that frank talk and correct information can prevent much drug abuse. This brief history provides the background for further discussion of the Swedish approach to handling drug problems which many nations now find themselves facing.

Despite the success of early intervention programs in the Swedish school system, the statistics on hard-core drug abuse, the other category that has been the subject of considerable research in Sweden, show that this side of the drug problem is much more virulent and difficult to eradicate. During the latter half of the 1960s, drug abuse in Sweden, as in the United States, increased sharply. Available data indicate that this surge in drug abuse levelled off somewhat during the early 1970s. Indicators, such as the number of narcotics cases reported to the police, the reported offenses against the criminal code on narcotics, drug seizures, sentencing, and summary convictions, suggest that during the 1970s there was a slight rising trend. One of the most comprehensive drug abuse surveys done in Sweden in 1979 by the Commission on the Extent of Drug Abuse (UNO) estimated the number of hard-core drug abusers at somewhere between 10,000 and 14,000.[9] Of these, it was estimated that nearly 1,500 injected drugs daily. Nearly 80 percent of this hard-core drug abuse was centered in major metropolitan areas within Sweden.[10] A study conducted in 1984 on the number of drug abusers in Stockholm dictated that the number (3,000) had not changed appreciably from the UNO estimates in 1979.[11] Nevertheless, indications are that the number of hard-core abusers in urban areas has increased.

Using the same measures mentioned above, namely drug arrest rates and summary convictions, a rise in drug abuse occurred between 1980 and 1982. Clearly though, extraneous factors may have contributed to the increase as well. For instance, new guidelines for the dismissal of charges as well as increased law enforcement personnel and technical resources have led to more drug seizures, more suspects, and the uncovering of more crimes. Whether or not the entire increase can be accounted for by these changes is difficult to say. Drug abuse decreased during 1983 and 1986, but the level of drug abuse still exceeds the 1979 levels, indicating that the problem is not going away. There are signs, according to a report by the Sweden Council for Information on Alcohol and Other Drugs (CAN) that there has been an increase in the supply of amphetamines during the past several years.

Sweden's most successful and strongest efforts have been to educate the young; they have reduced the numbers of young people who experiment with drugs and become drug abusers. Conversely, there appears to be an increase in the degree of abuse, showing that those who might have been occasional users, namely adults, may have increased their consumption to the extent that they can be labeled as hard-core users. The increase in central nervous system stimulant use, primarily amphetamines, is not surprising, since it has been the drug of choice in Sweden among intravenous drug abusers during the entire time under examination, from the 1960s to the present. Heroin has also played a role in hard-core abuse since the 1970s, although the recruitment of new heroin users has been quite low. It appears that most drug abuse occurs among multidrug users, which makes it difficult to isolate certain age groups or certain drugs as being especially resistant to prevention and rehabilitation efforts.

Additional concern has been voiced in many countries that are dealing with significant drug problems over the consumption of psychopharmaceutical drugs, which are usually obtained by prescription. Here, however, the news for Sweden has been encouraging. After a peak in 1971, abuse of psychopharmaceutical drugs has been on the decline.[12]

The early developments in Sweden, primarily before 1965, on the drug abuse problem is simply not readily available due to the lack of research. What is available comes from the Committee on Treatment of Drub Abuse, which has attempted to chart the early development of drug use in Sweden. Opiates, namely opium, morphine, and heroin, were used only to a limited extent before 1965. Abuse was much more common among members of the medical profession and individuals who obtained morphine for pain relief from a physician and, as a consequence, became addicted. As much as 10 percent of the early opiate abusers may have come exclusively from the medical profession. These drug-dependent physicians in turn provided patients with prescriptions for opiates, which helped spread the abuse of opiates to new populations.

The main characteristic of the drug abuse situation in Sweden is the prominence of the abuse of central nervous system (CNS) stimulants. Originally introduced for medical use, abuse soon became extensive. The first synthetic CNS stimulant produced was amphetamine, and it was introduced in 1935 within the medical field as phedrine and benzedrine. A prescription was not needed, and these drugs were available as over-the-counter remedies; nearly 230,000 pills were sold in 1938. They became available by prescription only in 1939, and there was a corresponding decrease in their use. By 1942, however, nearly 6 million pills were being sold each year, and nearly 3 percent of the adult population had used them. While this early abuse of stimulants was private, its character slowly evolved to a more sinister kind of abuse, as it spread to new groups. Two more stimulants, phemetralin and preludin, were introduced in 1955 as weight reduction aids. They were greeted enthusiastically and soon occupied a large portion of the illicit drug market, until the drugs were classified as narcotics in 1959. Cannabis or hashish was also originally used for medical purposes. The cannabis preparations were used as tranquillizing agents until 1950. Prior to 1965, there was very little abuse, but then its use spread among the young and soon became the most commonly used narcotic drug. LSD and other hallucinogenic drugs, including cocaine, were used very little before 1965, according to the Committee on Treatment for Drug Abuse.

Other areas of abuse have been on the increase. Barbiturates were commonly abused until their potential for dependency was fully recognized. It appears that the year 1965 brought a change in the level of and the attitude toward drug abuse in Sweden. Drug abuse was becoming common enough that it was finally recognized as a serious social and medical problem. Thus, the formation of the Committee on Treatment for Drug Abuse in 1965 can be seen as an outgrowth of this increasing concern. National resources were effectively mobilized with the Narcotics Regulation Act of 1964,[13] which regulated the manufacture, sale, and transfer, as well as possession of, narcotics. Introduced shortly afterward in 1968, the criminal code on narcotics defined narcotic offenses and the legal ramifications for violations of the code. The period between 1965 and 1969 is seen as the period during which "contemporary" drug abuse was firmly established. The abuse of cannabis spread among the young, and CNS stimulants became common among heavy abusers who injected the drugs. The first survey done in 1967 set the number of drug abusers at 3,000 in Stockholm and about 6,000 for the entire country.

The amount of experimental drug abuse is well documented for the period starting in the 1970s through the beginning of the 1980s. Again, these figures were obtained through surveys of schoolchildren in the ninth form and from military conscripts. In 1971, 14 percent of the boys in the ninth form reported having tried drugs, compared to 7 percent in 1975. For girls, the percentage who had tried drugs dropped from 17 percent in 1971 to 8 percent in 1975. During the first few years of the 1980s, the figures were stable for both groups. In the mid–1980s, the numbers decreased for both boys and girls, until in 1986 the numbers were 5 percent and 3 percent, respectively.[14] The number who reported having tried drugs only once were slightly higher for both groups.

The development of heavy drug abuse in Sweden is harder to measure, as the measures are easily influenced by outside factors, making accurate statistics very difficult. According to the measures available, it is clear that serious drug abuse increased during the 1960s and seemed to have stabilized during the early 1970s. However, by the end of the 1970s, it appears drug abuse was again on the rise. UNO's estimates on the number of heavy drug abusers in all of Sweden in 1979 was between 10,000 and 14,000.[15] Of these, 7,500 were intravenous drug abusers, and 1,500 were daily abusers. The three major urban areas accounted for 60 percent of the total abuse and for 80 percent of the heaviest abuse.

Drug abuse trends in Sweden beginning in 1979 seem to indicate an increase in abuse among the older population. The number of reported offenses against the Criminal Code on Narcotics more than doubled between 1979 and 1980, and the number of reported drug cases increased from roughly 7,000 to 11,000.[16] Several changes during the early 1980s may help account for the increase. New guidelines for waivers of prosecution, issued by the Crown Prosecutor in 1980, which restricted the possibilities for dismissing charges, may have led to an increased tendency to intervene in petty drug crimes and to an increase in the number of reported drug offenses. The addition of police personnel and technical resources may very well have resulted in the greater number of seizures and more crimes detected. The most significant increase occurred in the number of amphetamine seizures from 852 to 2,142, or 151 percent, for 1979 to 1982; cannabis seizures rose by 49 percent during the same period. However, beginning in 1982, there is a marked decreasing tendency. In an encouraging sign, the number of narcotics offenses decreased from 68,500 in 1982 to 29,000 in 1988.

As mentioned before, the CNS stimulants are the predominant drugs used by intravenous drug abusers, which has been the case since the 1960s. Throughout these studies, the amount of CNS stimulants confiscated has been higher than the amount of heroin. Of the intravenous drug abusers, nearly 80 percent use CNS stimulants and only 30 percent use heroin. Of course, there is some overlap between the two groups. Since the 1970s, the number of heroin seizures has increased, and heroin is now the most common drug among opiate abusers. While heroin abuse is still present, the recruitment of new users has decreased steadily. Today, few persons under the age of twenty-one have been convicted of opiate-related drug offenses. As of 1989, only 5 percent of those convicted for opiate-related drug offenses were under twenty-one.[17] Although the most popular drug, cannabis, is still used occasionally or experimentally by young people and by socially well-adjusted groups, much of this abuse goes undetected. In 1987, cannabis was involved in 61 percent of all convictions, and CNS stimulants were involved in 35 percent. During recent years some seizures of cocaine have occurred, and the number is increasing. This may mean that the substance is in use among the traditional groups of drug abusers, but the overall incidence of this drug remains extremely low. During the fifteen to twenty years in which extensive data are available on drug abuse, it is clear that different age groups have become involved in the drug trade. The number of youth who have experimented with drugs has dramatically decreased by about two-thirds from 1971. Convictions for heavy drug abuse among the young have also shown a steady decrease, indicating that Sweden's school-based drug education programs are meeting with some success. However, the abuse of cannabis, which was previously confined to youth, now exists among older age groups as well. Individuals over the age of twenty-four account for an increasing proportion of cannabis convictions. In 1987, the group between twenty-five and thirty-nine increased to 54 percent of the convictions. It seems the older generations are bringing their drug habits along into adulthood, similar to the trend observed for CNS stimulants and opiates. As the demographics of the drug abuse problem change, the challenge to nations committed to combatting drug abuse is to recognize and adapt to these new trends.

An area of increasing concern in the battle against drugs has been the increase in psychotropic substances being abused. These substances are used as antidotes to mental disturbances and organic nervous diseases. They can be prescribed, for instance, for insomnia, uneasiness, anxiety, depression, and psychosis. The most common forms are sedatives and tranquillizers, and, in 1988, nearly two-thirds of all psychotropic substances prescribed fell into one of these two groups. However, abuse of sedatives and tranquillizers has been on the rise, and it is forming the new group of social-medical problems of the drug industry. In Sweden, the heaviest consumption of these drugs occurred during the 1960s, as was stated at the beginning of this chapter. However, since these drugs are often prescribed for perfectly legitimate medical reasons, statistics on actual abuse are difficult to obtain or even estimate. There is no really clear definition of what constitutes abuse of these substances. The number of abusers of sedatives in 1977 was estimated at 16,000 for urban areas, and estimates for the country as a whole show 75,000 heavy users. While these substances are of great value in many psychiatric contexts, they have also given rise to serious problems. In 1986, nearly 800 people died in Sweden as a result of poisoning by psychotropic substances.

## NATIONAL RESPONSE

The Swedish National Board of Health and Welfare (NBHW) is responsible for state efforts in combatting drug abuse with information programs.[18] Part of Sweden's success with its drug campaign is done at the city and county levels which complements national efforts. Drug education has included narcotics-related work within different trade school programs, adult education, and military service. The other prong of the effort has been programs in drug information, which are mostly preventive in nature. The primary goals set forth by Sweden against alcohol and narcotics abuse are as follows:

1. To reduce alcohol consumption.
2. To create a society completely free from nonmedical use of narcotics.
3. To work to eliminate all sniffing of glue and solvents.

These measures can be further divided into three groups: (1) primary prevention, which includes drug information and general preventative work aimed at both youth and adults before problems arise; (2) efforts aimed at people in the risk zone for abuse, such as in housing areas with social problems, and

(3) tertiary prevention, which is the care and treatment of abusers. The primary goals for drug information are to increase debut age, reduce alcohol consumption, and oppose all nonmedical use of drugs. Secondary goals are to increase knowledge about the effects of drugs and to affect attitudes and behavioral changes among the young to an antidrug culture. According to a report on strategies for drug information by the NBHW, the content of the drug information should vary for different target groups. Particularly stressed is information about all forms of drugs and their social, physical, and psychic effects. For children and youth, one of the basic objectives for the information is to stimulate open discussions about feelings, relationships, and values. Developing young people's feelings of self-worth in order to resist peer pressure is a major objective. Another important element in this informational effort is to focus on increasing knowledge about alcohol and narcotics laws, a special emphasis that is notably absent from other national programs on drug education.

These programs are carried out under the direct supervision of NBHW's steering group which is the coordinating organ for drug information and includes among its representative members: (1) the NBHW, (2) the National Police Board, (3) the National Board of Education, and (4) the Federal of County Government. The NBHW is responsible for coordinating drug information among the various governmental groups. An information newsletter is one of the links in this program; another link is a catalog of narcotics informational material, which is brought up to date regularly. The NBHW also distributes an "idea paper" with information about local projects receiving state support. Other projects are highlighted in "theme reports." Another government project has been the novel approach of establishing audiovisual centers for drug education; these centers inexpensively accommodate all interested parties, whether they are national or local associations. At the county level, special coordinating groups have been formed to deal with preventive work. Much of this work is done through conferences sponsored by the CAN and the NBHW.

One of the original aims of this strategy was to attempt to achieve continuity in narcotics information. Ideally, these programs would follow individuals from preschool through elementary school and high school, "teen centers", university, military service, and advice centers for new parents or those with teenagers. But this aim has proved to be inefficient, since many people are members of several of these groups. Thus, the approach has been to divide the efforts into a variety of target groups. Influencing children at an early age has been important, but a great deal of effort has been focused on helping teenagers to cope, and they along with their parents constitute the largest, most important target group. Nonetheless, alcohol and drug education often begins in preschool in an effort to create an open attitude toward alcohol and drugs and to allow children to express their fears and experiences. Once children progress to elementary and junior high school, the information becomes much more substantive, and, in addition, there is a particular emphasis on the legal restrictions on use.

Perhaps the comprehensiveness of the Swedish educational system for drug information can be best appreciated when it is understood that, according to Swedish social service law, the Social Welfare Committee is to "work to prevent and counter abuse of alcohol and other dependency-producing substances. Special attention should be paid to efforts for children and youth. The Social Welfare Committee shall forward the information to the authorities, organizations and individual, and through outreach activities, increase knowledge of the damaging effect of abuse and about available assistance."[19] Hence, there is a legal responsibility to disseminate drug information in local communities and to help ensure that all important target groups are reached by this information. The law outlines proposed methods of cooperation with schools, cultural boards, and police. Special programs are available for inmates in various penal institutions and drug-dependency treatment facilities.

National campaigns against drug abuse are carried out every two or three years. From 1980 to 1982, the Swedish Ministry of Health and Social Affairs conducted two nationwide campaigns against alcohol and narcotics abuse: the first, Action against the Dangers of Alcohol—Stop Sales to Minors, occurred in April 1980; the second, Action against Drugs, aimed primarily against cannabis use, began in autumn 1981.[20] The main focus of the campaigns was to stimulate discussion and debate at the local level. The campaigns, which used the mass media to reach as many people as feasible, particularly young people, were meant to establish a rapport and a different attitude toward drugs among the population. Most public reaction has been positive, as the high level of participation on all levels testifies.

## NARCOTICS LEGISLATION

Sweden's Penal Law on Narcotics (1968) makes it a punishable offense to manufacture narcotics, to engage in the purchase or sale of narcotics, or to have narcotics in one's possession.[21] In the same year, an ordinance was passed which prohibited the importing or carrying on of trade in hypodermic syringes or needles without a special license. More recently, in 1988, Sweden passed an act on the treatment of alcohol and drug misusers which provides guidelines for treatments designed to help individuals discontinue drug abuse. The most startling provision in the act, however, is the provision that treatment can be coerced if it is necessary to stop the abuse.[22] Forced treatment is allowed if the abuser seriously endangers his or her own physical or mental health, if he or she runs an obvious risk of destroying his or her own life, or if it is feared that he or she will inflict serious damage on himself or herself or someone with whom he or she has a close relationship.[23] Doctors are required to report patients whom they have been unable to help, if attempts at treatment have failed. Compulsory care may last from two to four months. This nonvoluntary care has been constantly under debate, and it is under review at the present. The goal of the Swedish program is to limit compulsory treatment and to promote voluntary measures.

Narcotics offenses in Sweden fall into three categories: petty offenses, offenses, and serious offenses. The maximum prison sentences for these categories are six months, three years, and from ten to sixteen years, respectively. A separate law on the smuggling of narcotic substances prescribes penalties ranging up to ten years' imprisonment.

## INTERNATIONAL COOPERATION

Sweden's international efforts to help combat narcotics trafficking have included working together with other Nordic states on criminal matters. Extradition matters are less complex among the Nordic states because of the similarity of their legislation.[24] Extradition from one state to another may not take place if the crime in punishable in the requesting state by a fine only, but it is permitted when imprisonment is dictated by the legislation of the requesting state but not that of the requesting state.[25] As with other international extradition agreements, the extradition of nationals is technically not allowed; nevertheless, a national of the requested state will be extradited if the offense is one which, by the law of the requested state, carries a sentence of four years or more, and if the fugitive has been living in the requesting state for at least two years.[26] Thus, extradition is allowed only for the more serious narcotics offenses and for the smuggling of narcotics. Also, depending on the requesting state's laws, extradition would probably be denied by Sweden if the fugitive were to face the death penalty. Within the United Nations, Sweden has participated in international agreements to control narcotics trafficking by signing, on December 20, 1988, the Convention against Illicit Traffic in Narcotic Drugs and Psychotropic Substances, which is now awaiting ratification by the Swedish government.

## CONCLUSION

Sweden's approach to narcotics emphasizes prevention through education and treatment and reflects its social welfare state. The comprehensiveness of the drug information campaign is impressive. Sweden has criminalized the manufacture, purchase, sale, or possession of narcotics. Swedish criminal legislation mandates forced treatment in certain cases.

## NOTES

1. Stig Hadenius. *On Sweden* (Helsingborg: Swedish Institute—Schmiots Boktryckeri AB—1990).
2. Janet Porter, ''Sweden's Role in a New Europe,'' *Journal of Commerce*, 5 March 1991, 10.
3. Lloyd K. Moyer, ''The Mentally Abnormal Offender in Sweden: An Overview and Comparison with American Law,'' *American Journal of Comparative Law* 22 (1974).
4. Ibid.
5. Alvar Nelson, ''Sweden's New Penal Code of 1965: Criminality Is a Manifestation

of Individual Deviance Curable by Treatment and Care,'' *American Journal of Comparative Law* 21 (1973).

6. Ibrahim Al-Wahab, *The Swedish Institution of Ombudsmen: An Instrument of Human Rights* (Trych: Central-Trycheriet AB, Boras, 1979).

7. Swedish Council for Information on Alcohol and Other Drugs, *Report 89: Trends in Alcohol and Drug Use in Sweden* (Stockholm: Swedish Council for Information on Alcohol and Other Drugs, 1989).

8. Ibid.

9. Ibid.

10. Ibid.

11. Ibid.

12. Swedish Institute, *Alcohol and Narcotics in Sweden* (Stockholm: Swedish Institute, 1988).

13. National Council for Crime Prevention, *Current Swedish Legislation on Narcotics and Psychotropic Substances* (Stockholm: National Council for Crime Prevention, 1990).

14. Swedish Council for Information on Alcohol and Other Drugs, *Report 89*.

15. Ibid.

16. Ibid.

17. Ibid.

18. National Swedish Board of Health and Welfare, *Strategies for Drug Information* (Stockholm: National Swedish Board of Health and Welfare, 1987).

19. Swedish Institute, *Alcohol and Narcotics in Sweden*.

20. National Swedish Board of Health and Welfare, *Strategies for Drug Information*.

21. National Council for Crime Prevention, *Current Swedish Legislation on Narcotics and Psychotropic Substances*.

22. ''The Care of Alcoholics, Drug Abusers and Abusers of Volatile Solvents'' (Special Provisions) Act, October 1989.

23. Ibid.

24. M. Cherif Bassiouni and Ved P. Nanda, *A Treatise on International Criminal Law*. (Springfield, Ill.: Charles C. Thomas, 1973).

25. Ibid.

26. Ibid.

## BIBLIOGRAPHY

Al-Wahab, Ibrahim. *The Swedish Institution of Ombudsmen: An Instrument of Human Rights*. Trych: Central-Trycheriet AB, Boras, 1979.

Bassiouni, M. Cherif, and Ved P. Nanda. *A Treatise on International Criminal Law*, Springfield, Ill.: Charles C. Thomas 1973.

''The Care of Alcoholics, Drug Abusers and Abusers of Volatile Solvents'' (Special Provisions) Act, October 1989.

Hadenius, Stig. *On Sweden*, Helsingborg: Swedish Institute (Schmiots Boktryckeri AB, 1990.

Moyer, Lloyd K. ''The Mentally Abnormal Offender in Sweden: An Overview and Comparison with American Law.'' *American Journal of Comparative Law* 22 (1974): 22.

National Council for Crime Prevention. *Current Swedish Legislation on Narcotics and*

*Psychotropic Substances.* Stockholm: National Council for Crime Prevention, 1990.

National Swedish Board of Health and Welfare. *Strategies for Drug Information.* Stockholm: National Swedish Board of Health and Welfare, 1987.

Nelson, Alvar. "Sweden's New Penal Code of 1965: Criminality Is a Manifestation of Individual Deviance Curable by Treatment and Care." *American Journal of Comparative Law* 21 (1973).

Porter, Janet. "Sweden's Role in a New Europe." *Journal of Commerce*, 5 March 1991, 10.

Swedish Council for Information on Alcohol and Other Drugs. *Report 89: Trends in Alcohol and Drug Use in Sweden.* Stockholm: Swedish Council for Information on Alcohol and Other Drugs, 1989.

# 17

# The United Kingdom

LOREN CAIN

## INTRODUCTION

This chapter covers the United Kingdom of Great Britain and Northern Ireland. Although some minor differences in regulatory approach exist among England, Scotland, and Northern Ireland, similar efforts have been taken to control a rising drug problem. The most extensive drug problems in the United Kingdom occur in some of the major cities. However, the scale and nature of drug abuse varies considerably from region to region. In Northern Ireland, for example, the indications are that it remains a relatively minor problem in comparison with other parts of the United Kingdom and, for that matter, in the Republic of Ireland.[1]

Until the early 1990s, the United Kingdom's role in the drug trade was one of being a consumer nation and occasionally an area for the transshipment of drugs to other European nations. Heroin comes to the United Kingdom mainly from Southwest Asia; cocaine from South America; and cannabis from Africa, the Middle East, and the Caribbean. A growing problem appears to be the manufacture of amphetamines, and the United Kingdom has become a source country as well as a consumer of these drugs.

The types of drugs commonly abused in the United Kingdom are those that are common elsewhere: the opiates (e.g., heroin, morphine, methadone, dipipanone, pethidine, buprenorpnine); stimulants (e.g., cocaine and amphetamines); tranquillizers (e.g., benzodiazepines, such as valium, temazepam, and ativan); sedatives and hypnotists (e.g., barbiturates, such as tuinal); and hallucinogens (e.g., LSD and cannabis).

## BACKGROUND

The United Kingdom's legal framework to control drug abuse has developed over a long period of time. Jeffrey Bishop noted, "Drugs of addiction were common in England long before there existed any control over their use."[2] Following is a review of some of the more important pieces of legislation since the first law, the Pharmacy and Poisons Act, was passed in 1868. This legislation gave a small measure of control over opium and its derivatives by prohibiting the sale of this narcotic by anyone other than a chemist or druggist. The Pharmacy and Poisons Act remained in effect until 1908 when it was amended to include opium and all of its preparations containing 1 percent or more of morphine. The sale of cocaine was also restricted for the first time by this amendment.

In 1909 the representatives of thirteen countries, including the United Kingdom, met at the Palace Hotel in Shanghai to explore solutions to the opium problem. This Opium Commission was desired by the United States, which had recently obtained the Philippines and its opium trade, and was chaired by the chief of the American delegation, Charles Henry Brent, the Episcopal bishop of the Philippines.[3] Nine resolutions to control opium use and trade were unanimously passed by the delegates. These resolutions were mild (by today's standards) and for the most part dealt with the suppression of opium smoking and trading. This set the stage for the First International Opium Convention which met at The Hague in 1911, again at American insistence and again chaired by Bishop Brent. This convention differed from the Shanghai Conference as it led to an international treaty rather than merely an agreement. This convention required the nations to control morphine, heroin, any new derivative that proved dangerous, and cocaine.[4]

World War I interfered with the immediate implementation of the treaty's provisions; however, in 1916, it was found that cocaine was being peddled to and by prostitutes in London. Also, several cases of cocaine's being given to Canadian soldiers were reported by the police.[5] In response to this, the Defense of the Realm Regulations prohibited the gift or sale of any sedatives, narcotics, or stimulants to members of the armed forces. This was later expanded to include civilians and allowed possession of these drugs only by "authorized" persons. Morphine abuse was not yet considered dangerous, and morphine was not included.

On September 1, 1920, Britain passed the first Dangerous Drugs Act which attempted to establish a system of control over the import, export, and handling of opiates and cocaine. These were considered to be the most dangerous drugs, or at least the most readily accessible to control. This was an important development in Britain legislation as it was the first act of domestic and social legislation to be passed as a result of an international agreement, the Hague Convention.[6]

In the following years, various international conventions were held which resulted in changes to keep legislation in conformance with these conventions.

One result was that in 1947 the first synthetic narcotics were brought under control. These had been developed during World War II when traditional sources of morphine and other painkillers were jeopardized by wartime conditions.

In 1964, for the first time, legislation unrelated to any international treaty was introduced. The Drugs (Prevention and Misuse) Act was applied to amphetamines and related drugs and made the unauthorized possession of these drugs an offense. This was followed by the 1970 Misuse of Drugs Act which replaced all previous acts. The old acts were thought to be inadequate or too inflexible to cope with changing patterns of drug use. Previous acts that preserved a distinction between narcotics and other drugs were regarded as outmoded. The 1970 act had four main aims: (1) to distinguish between possession and trafficking, (2) to operate without consulting international bodies in order to bring new drugs under control quickly, (3) to stamp out overprescribing by banning doctors from prescribing specific drugs if it was shown that they had been prescribing irresponsibly, and (4) to create a council to advise the Home Secretary on policy matters.[7]

Under the 1970 act, drugs were divided into three classes, and a severity of punishment was assigned to each class. Most important is Group A, which includes most of the drugs that are controlled internationally. Two exceptions to this are cannabis and cannabis resin which, with other important central nervous system stimulants, are included in Group B. Group C includes the less potent central nervous system stimulants. Some penalties were hardened, such as those for LSD and amphetamines, and some were lightened, such as those for heroin and cannabis. The maximum penalties for abuse are as follows: Group A, seven years in prison; Group B, five years; and Group C, two years. A distinction was also recognized between the possession of an included drug and its trafficking. The penalty for trafficking a Group A drug is fourteen years in prison, or a fine, or both. A tribunal system was introduced which has the authority to remove a doctor's right to prescribe certain drugs. The maximum penalty for continuing to prescribe is a fine and/or fourteen years in prison.[8]

The United Kingdom's policies toward the drug addict have developed and changed along with the legal structure. The British view of addiction has been described as more humane than that of some other countries, like the United States. It has also been cited as an example of legalization's shortcomings. Both viewpoints have their merits and their flaws. One important difference is that the number of British addicts is much smaller than the number of American addicts. This can be why the two societies, the United Kingdom and the United States, perceive the addiction problem differently. It also underscores the difficulty in making comparisons between the approaches to drug addiction and policy taken in the two countries.

For approximately forty years, the general medical belief was that drug addiction was a manifestation of a disease frequently associated with nervous instability and frequently requiring treatment and not merely a vice demanding punishment.[9] It could be viewed as a sickness or as a by-product of an individual's environment, but not as a criminal act. British Professor Alfred Lindesmith collected a list of thirty-three different terms, all of which have been used to describe the personality of the drug taker. The list contains such varied terms as "passive psychopath," "hostile," "weak," "paranoid," and "essentially normal." Lindesmith notes that this aspect of research may be said to be in a state of confusion.[10]

A basic belief in the United Kingdom was that the treatment of the addict, though exclusively the responsibility of doctors, should be predicated on a realistic view of what can and what cannot be enforced in the criminal code.[11] In 1924, a committee under the chairmanship of Sir. Humphry Rolleston met "to consider and advise as to the circumstances, if any, in which the supply of morphine and heroin . . . to persons suffering from addiction to those drugs may be regarded as medically advisable."[12] The report of this committee was the basis of British government policy regarding addicts for the next forty-two years in the United Kingdom.

The Rolleston Committee defined an addict as "a person who, not requiring the continued use of a drug for the relief of the symptoms of organic disease, has acquired, as a result of repeated administration, an overpowering desire for its continuance, and in whom withdrawal of the drug leads to definite symptoms of mental or physical distress or disorder."[13] Although varying factors may be present, they felt that drug addiction should be regarded as a manifestation of a disease, not just an indulgence. The committee recognized that it may not be possible to cure all addicts and that under any method of treatment "relapse, sooner or later, appears to be the rule."[14] It also rejected the idea that doctors should be required to report cases of addiction.

In 1959 evidence that the drug problem was increasing led to considerable concern that a new epidemic of drug abuse was pending. In response to this, Sir Russell Brain was appointed to head a new commission to find remedies. in 1961, however, the Brain Commission reported that the addict population was stable and that the controls in place were adequate. It discounted the views that addiction had increased even though the numbers of 1960, which had just been released, showed an increase in young male heroin addicts. It also reiterated the attitude that addiction was a mental disorder rather than a criminal behavior. As the number of addicts was still small, it was not considered practicable to establish specialized institutions for the treatment of drug addicts, which could best be done in the psychiatric ward of a general hospital. Britain entered the 1960s with a system which allowed any doctor to prescribe as many dangerous drugs as he or she wished, justified on the grounds of treatment, but with few legal sanctions or requirements except minor ones such as keeping a register.[15]

The Brain Commission was reconvened in 1964 to address the problem of a continued increase in the number of drug addicts. Again primarily concerned with heroin and cocaine, it did not include other narcotics that were used in the treatment of diseases. The commission felt that insufficient control of drugs might lead to the spread of addiction, as was then happening. At the same time, severe restrictions which kept addicts from getting drugs legitimately would lead to a growth of an organized traffic in illegitimate drugs. This time the commission proposed providing treatment centers for addicts which would restrict supplies, provide advice if a person's addiction were questionable, and require doctors to notify the Home Office of new addicts.[16] This was a major change as it was the first time in British history that most doctors lost the right to prescribe heroin and cocaine for addicts.

With the implementation of these recommendations into law, treatment centers began to reduce overprescribing which had been the black market's main source of 100-percent pure heroin.[17] In spite of these efforts, the number of addicts who have gone to treatment centers and have been reported to the Home Office continue to increase. According to the Home Office's "Statistical Bulletin", dated March 19, 1990, the number of new addicts notified to the Home Office in 1989 was slightly less than 6,000. This is in line with an increasing trend throughout the 1980s, which reached a peak of over 6,000 addicts in 1985, and dropped slightly in 1986 and 1987. The vast majority of these new addicts (87 percent) used heroin, although increases in cocaine follow the same upward trends.[18] Unfortunately, these numbers indicate only those who have gone to treatment centers and not those who obtain drugs on the black market.

## COCAINE AND CRACK

The *New Statesman and Society* reported in 1989 that cocaine and crack were beginning to make inroads into Europe's illicit drug markets.[19] It went on to note that this situation was by the design of Colombia's Medellín and Cali drug cartels which were looking to Europe since the U.S. market for cocaine was saturated. Although some British government agencies reported a rise in those seeking help with cocaine-related problems, the number of known users remains low. British customs officers intercepted a total of 424 kilograms of cocaine in 1989 and 325 kilograms in 1988.[20] In early 1991, 540 kilograms of cocaine were seized in Scotland, apparently headed for London. These seizures may indicate two trends: Interdiction efforts are effective and improving, and large amounts of cocaine are being smuggled into the United Kingdom to satisfy a growing market.

By 1989, Steve Tippell of the Southward Community Drug Project had witnessed an increase in cocaine use in local housing estates in the United Kingdom, usually in empty flats and boarded-up property. According to Tippell, "It's a new but developing problem and with cocaine prices as low as £40 [$70] a gram the market is booming. Two years ago, one in ten of the people coming to us was using cocaine. Now it's one in five, with a larger proportion using it as crack."[21]

Crack, a cocaine derivative, is appearing more commonly, especially in British cities, in the early 1990s. Street dealers in 1989 sold "rocks" for £30, which could then be broken into smaller amounts costing from £5 to £8.[22] This gives crack the image of being a cheap drug, which is wrong. Crack's effects are intense but short lived, lasting from between ten and fifteen minutes. The subsequent crash leaves the user with depression, anxiety, and a craving which the user knows can be alleviated only by a further hit. Many users go on binges or runs, which last for several days, smoking continuously until the drugs and money are gone.

Powell also reports that the connection between crack and the human immune deficiency virus (HIV) infection poses a threat. The latest craze of combining oral sex and crack smoking (known as masterblasting) has grave implications for the spread of acquired immune deficiency syndrome (AIDS). In the crack houses, prostitutes, who may be drug users themselves, offer masterblasting services to others. Crack users commonly suffer from blistered lips from using pipes to smoke the drug, which leads to a high risk of infection[23]

The use and trafficking of cannabis and other hallucinogens for recreational use is illegal in the United Kingdom. It is known that Britain has become a source country as well as a user of such synthetically produced drugs as LSD, MDMA, and amphetamines. However, the extent of use of these drugs is not known. British customs' seizures for 1989 show that seizures of cannabis increased by 14 percent to over 50 tons, following a 170-percent increase in 1988.[24] This increase is most likely a result of increased shipments to Britain and better interdiction methods. Seizures of synthetics have occurred in small amounts. The extent of use of any of these drugs in Britain is not known.

## GOVERNMENTAL REACTION

The British government's strategy for dealing with drug abuse involves simultaneous action on five fronts:

1. Improving international cooperation in order to reduce supplies from abroad.
2. Increasing the effectiveness of police and customs enforcement.
3. Maintaining effective deterrents and tight domestic controls.
4. Developing prevention publicity and education.
5. Improving treatment and rehabilitation.[25]

The Home Office has the responsibility to coordinate these measures with other governmental offenses and departments. It is a complex problem, and the strategy is to reduce both the supply of and the demand for drugs, to help drug abusers seek treatment, and to keep young people from becoming involved with drugs. Several actions have been taken to fulfill these goals.

### International Cooperation

In April 1990 the British government, in association with the United Nations, organized an international summit against drugs which met in London. The result of the World Ministerial Summit to Reduce the Demand for Drugs and to Combat the Cocaine Threat was the adoption, by consensus of 124 countries, of a declaration to give higher priority to the prevention and reduction of illicit drug demand at the national and international levels. In her address, Prime Minister Margaret Thatcher stressed that reducing the demand for drugs would put the dealers out of business and added: "There is no glamour in drugs, only depravity and despair."[26] Princess Anne said that asking producers in developing countries to stop growing coca leaves was like asking Scots to stop growing barley or the French, grapes. Along these lines, Princess Anne posed the question: What had to be decided in the developed world was what we would be willing to pay for such commodities as coffee and cotton, which could serve as substitute crops.[27]

Other international activities include cooperative efforts with the United States, the successor states of the Soviet Union, the Council of Europe, and the Commonwealth Caribbean nations. Drug liaison officers have been stationed at these and other British diplomatic posts. These officers assist local officials and share information with them, resulting in significant drug seizures and arrests.[28] The Overseas Development Administration provides funds to support drug–related developmental projects in drug-producing and drug-transitting countries. In addition, the Home Office has a program to assist drug-related law enforcement projects overseas; for example, equipment and training have been provided to a number of drug-producing and drug-transitting countries in Asia, Africa, the Caribbean, and South America.

### Police and Customs Enforcement

The National Drugs Intelligence Unit is an effort to ensure that police and customs work together to deter and detect drug-trafficking organizations. The unit gathers, collates, analyzes, and disseminates intelligence from Britain and abroad on drug trafficking, including financial intelligence about funds suspected as having been derived from drug trafficking. Its staff is drawn from police forces throughout the country and from customs, which provides a link between the two enforcement services. This staff has doubled since it was established in 1985.

Her Majesty's Customs and Excise Service has primary responsibility for preventing and detecting the illegal import or export of controlled drugs, the investigation of organizations and individuals engaged in international drug smuggling, their prosecution, and the identification of any proceeds of such crime. The government has increased the number of investigators and has improved technical resources to fulfill this responsibility. The success of these efforts is demonstrated by the increased amounts of drugs that have been seized.

The police are responsible for dealing with offenses of manufacture, supply, and possession. Police action against drug traffickers and dealers is organized on three levels. Nine Regional Crime Squads in England and Wales and the Scottish Crime Squad deal with major traffickers. Second, there are seventeen drug wings in the eight Regional Crime Squads outside of London, three in the Scottish Crime Squad, and the Metropolitan Squad in London.[29] Furthermore, each police force has a number of officers who are dedicated to the drug effort within their areas. These forces all have received additional personnel and funding in line with the increased emphasis placed on drug control in recent years.

A result of this program has been an increase in the number of persons dealt with for drug offenses. In 1988, about 30,500 persons were found guilty, cautioned, or paid a penalty in lieu of prosecution for offenses involving controlled drugs, which was an increase of 16 percent from 1987.[30] Of these, about 5,000 were arrested for drug-trafficking offenses. The majority of offenders were dealt with for offenses involving cannabis. The number of offenses involving other drugs, such as amphetamines, cocaine, and heroin, approximated 6,200 in 1988, unchanged from 1987.

An unforeseen result of increased trafficking and police efforts has been the apprehension of African women who have been used as couriers to smuggle drugs into the United Kingdom. Yvonne Roberts noted that they have no money or friends, so time in jail is time alone, with no contact with families.[31] According to 1987 numbers, over 100 women, mostly from Nigeria and Ghana, were in prison because they had acted as drug couriers. Cocaine and heroin go into these countries from the Golden Triangle, Pakistan, or South America on the way to the United Kingdom. There is no general awareness of cocaine or heroin in Nigeria or Ghana, so the women probably did not know what they were carrying or its value, and were unaware of the risks. It was out of desperation to cope with everyday economic problems that some women became couriers. Roberts also noted that these women, who are not members of drug cartels and may have carried small amounts of drugs, remain in prison. There is little deterrent effect in their home countries since their sentences are not publicized there.

## Programs to Treat and Rehabilitate Drug Users

Treatment for drug dependence is mainly provided on an outpatient basis, and an increasing number of family doctors also treat addicts. Many hospitals provide specialist treatment for drug abusers, mainly in psychiatric units, or have special drug treatment units. The government is advised on a wide range of matters relating to drug abuse and related social problems by the Advisory Council on the Misuse of Drugs. A number of nonstatutory agencies work with and complement the health service provision: advice and rehabilitation services including residential facilities, for example, are provided mainly by voluntary organizations. Support in the community is handled by the probation service and the local social services departments.

Over £17.5 million was provided for local treatment and rehabilitation projects over a six-year period from 1983 to 1989 through health authorities in England for the further expansion of services for drug misusers. This included £1 million to enable services to respond to the spread of HIV infection among drug abusers.

Similar projects are in progress in Wales, where £4.2 million has been provided for voluntary groups and health authorities since 1985. A separate program in Scotland has provided more than £4 million for locally based drug projects since 1985.[32]

The government established a drugs advisory service to advise district health authorities on the development of facilities in their areas. Funds have been made available for local educational authorities in England, Wales, and Scotland to discourage drug misuses through publicity campaigns and community action.

The Standing Conference on Drug Abuse (SCODA) is the national coordinating body in England and Wales for the nonstatutory organizations in the field of drug abuse. Its aims are to assist the development of existing organizations, to advise on and support the establishment of additional services, to encourage field research into problems of drug misuse, and to provide a forum for the exchange of information and views on the changing patterns of drug misuse. The Scottish Council for Community and Voluntary Organizations, the Wales Council for Voluntary Action, and the Northern Ireland Council for Voluntary Action perform similar functions.

### North Western Region

The North West Regional[33] Drug Training Unit, based in Manchester, is a member agency of SCODA. The following description of the practical efforts to help those who misuse drugs and to prevent others from using drugs is typical of the programs in other areas. The majority of services are provided locally by a range of agencies including those from the independent sector. However, the regional specialists provide treatment and assistance to those with particular problems associated with drug misuse and training, advice, and expertise to those working in local services.

The region recognized that a major difficulty of helping those with drug problems is making the initial contact and maintaining links. The reluctance by people to use services may be related to the illicit nature of drug misuse, and the type, style, and location of services available. Users may also have a negative image of the services. The region has developed a mental health implementation plan, Focusing on Care, which states its service principles and also addresses these concerns:

1. The value and dignity of the individual are [sic] stressed in their approach and a user of the service should have these qualities enhanced and not diminished.
2. The strengths and abilities of the user should be acknowledged and built upon to help resolve or mitigate their problems.
3. The positive aspects of the user's social relationships should be preserved and developed while using the service.
4. The user is able to retain a sense of control over his life and his use of the service.

5. All aspects be regularly reviewed in order to assess its effectiveness, relevance, and its place within a range of services. This evaluation should include the views of users.
6. The family and friends of a user who may be affected by his/her problems receive consideration and use of appropriate services.
7. [The service should ensure that] the region has established a Regional Drug Research Unit.

This unit provides an information gathering service regarding the extent and nature of drug misuse, trends from one year to the next, and the utilization of services. This information helps the region evaluate its work and ensure that it is responsive to the needs of the service's users.

The Regional Drug Dependence Service has its administrative base, inpatient beds, and part of its outpatient facility at Prestwich Hospital. People with particular problems of a substantial or complex nature, who cannot be fully supported locally, can make use of these services. One of the major areas is that of specialist inpatient treatment of drug misusers which is undertaken in a self-contained unit separate from the other psychiatric services available at the hospital. It incorporates both a detoxification unit and a rehabilitation facility, and it accommodates a range of more general drug-related admissions.

### Community Drug Team

The region is divided into various districts, all of which have a Community Drug Team (CDT). The members of the CDT have a particular expertise to deal with the drug problems locally. They may come from the independent sector, which provides complementary services and helps ensure that the CDT has clear service aims and objectives. General practitioners have a responsibility to provide health care for patients with drug-related problems. The CDT sees to it that close links are maintained with these doctors to ensure that appropriate care is available. In this way, local areas have access to regional expertise and knowledge, and the region gains more information about drug misuse at the local level.

Training on drug issues plays an important part in enabling workers in all professions to respond effectively to drug misuers. The region's training philosophy goes beyond necessary technical aspects and addresses the attitudes held by service workers. These attitudes include the beliefs that (1) drug abusers have the same rights and responsibilities as other members of the community; (2) those working with drug users should work in ways that encourage individual responsibility but guarantee those rights; (3) those working with drug users are prepared to reevaluate their own attitudes toward these people and assist others to do so; (4) training encompasses the clinical, ethical, and political issues associated with drug use.

General practitioners and other primary health care staff were encouraged to play a major role in care and treatment of drug abusers. The Guidelines of Good Clinical Practice in the Treatment of Drug Misuse (issued to all doctors in October

1984 by the Chief Medical Officer) emphasized that all doctors have a responsibility to care for both the health needs of drug misusers and their drug-related problems. HC (88) 26—Services for Drug Misusers—Curbing the Spread of AIDS and HIV Infection—drew attention to a report from the Advisory Council on the Misuse of Drugs on measures to prevent the spread of HIV infection among injecting drug abusers, and from them to a wider population. This circular remains a key source of advice, and its value was emphasized in the Resource Assumptions and Planning Guidance Circular, HC(88)43.

Drug misusers are a major risk for infection with HIV, which gives rise to AIDS. The government has taken steps to warn drug abusers of the dangers they face and to emphasize the need to use the treatment services. A number of needle- and syringe-exchange schemes have been created in the recognition that, while abstinence remains the ultimate aim, steps must be taken to reduce the risks of AIDS being spread by drug misusers who are not willing to give up injecting. Such schemes encourage the return of used needles and syringes to ensure their safe disposal and to provide counseling covering both drug misuse problems and the risk of acquiring and passing on the HIV infection. Pharmacists may also sell needles and syringes to drug misusers, and general practitioners may issue injecting equipment to drug misusers as part of their treatment of patients with drug problems.

In January 1990, advice on cleaning injecting equipment was issued to a variety of agencies working with drug abusers. This guidance, drawn up in consultation with the Expert Advisory Group on AIDS, recognized that in certain situations some drug misusers would be unable or unwilling to use sterile equipment. Cleaning would not protect absolutely against HIV infection—it could only help reduce the risk.[34]

## MONEY LAUNDERING

In April 1990, then Chancellor of the Exchequer John Major announced the publication of the report of the Financial Action Task Force on money laundering. Following the July 1989 Group of Seven Paris Summit, this task force was created to review existing measures against money laundering and to recommend improvements in member countries. The report had three main sections: an assessment of the extent and nature of the problem, a review of existing legal and administrative measures against money laundering, and forty detailed recommendations for further action. In presenting the report Major stated that money laundering "is an international problem which cannot be tackled by individual countries in isolation. The commitment by the major industrialized countries to strengthen international cooperation in the fight against money laundering is therefore all the more welcome."[35]

The report recommended implementing the 1999 United Nations Convention against Illicit Traffic in Narcotic Drugs and Psychotropic Substances (UN Drug Convention), improving the laws and administrative practices related to institutions dealing with large amounts of cash, and strengthening international cooperation. The Drug Trafficking Offenses Act of 1986 already made drug money laundering an offense and gave the police and customs strong enforcement powers. Provisions included in the Criminal Justice Act of 1990 strengthened these powers and set the stage for ratification of the UN Drug Convention.

The Drug Trafficking Offenses Act of 1986 contains provisions for the investigation of suspected drug-derived assets prior to arrest, the freezing of assets on arrest or issuance of a summons, and confiscation of these assets following conviction. It creates an offense of assisting a drug trafficker to retain the benefits of his proceeds. This law is aimed at those who launder drug money, and the offense is punishable by a maximum of fourteen years' imprisonment, a fine, or both. This offense is committed by anybody who, knowing or suspecting that another person is a drug trafficker, either holds or controls the proceeds of drug trafficking, or puts funds at the trafficker's disposal, or gives the trafficker help in investing those proceeds.

Under this act financial institutions may themselves be prosecuted if they fail to report transactions which they suspect of being linked to money laundering. This act established a suspicion-based transaction reporting system which does not require a report based only on the currency amount of a transaction. Most members of the task force favored keeping this type of reporting system. The Bank of England has written to Britain's 550 domestic banks to warn that they risk losing their licenses if they fail to install or maintain adequate controls to prevent money laundering.[36]

The Criminal Justice (International Cooperation) Act of 1990 makes it an offense for a person, who knows or has reasonable grounds to suspect that property is derived wholly or in part from the proceeds of drug trafficking, to conceal, disguise, convert, transfer, or remove that property from the jurisdiction of the courts for the purpose of assisting any person to avoid prosecution for a drug-trafficking offense or for the making or enforcement of a confiscation order.

The adoption of the standard principle of "know your customer," as stated by the Basle Committee on Banking Regulations and Supervisory Practices in December 1988, represented a step toward preventing the use of the financial system for money-laundering purposes. The statement has been enforced by the Bank of England and circulated to all institutions authorized under the Banking Act. The statement, which asserts that public confidence in financial institutions may be undermined through their association with criminals, sets out the following basic principles:

Customer identification: a reasonable effort should be made to determine the true identity of the customer when a relationship is established by opening an account or providing any other service including safe custody and safe deposit box facilities.

Compliance with legislation and law enforcement agencies: business should be conducted in conformity with high ethical standards and local laws and regulations pertaining to financial transactions. Institutions should cooperate fully with national law enforcement authorities to the extent permitted without breaching customer confidentiality.

Record keeping and systems: institutions should implement specific procedures for retaining internal records of transactions and establish an effective means of testing for general compliance with the Statement.

Staff training: attention should be given to staff training and ongoing education in the institution's procedures to facilitate the recognition and reporting of money laundering in accordance with UK statutes.[37]

The national reception point for disclosures under the above acts is the National Drugs Intelligence Unit (NDIU). The NDIU, which is staffed jointly by police and customs officers, is situated at New Scotland Yard. The NDIU also acts as national and international advisors on money laundering and maintains an up-to-date list of trained officers. The NDIU offers practical guidance and assistance to the financial sector on the subject of money laundering.

## CONCLUSION

The United Kingdom unfortunately suffers from a growing drug abuse problem. Because the trade is illicit, the number of addicts is not known. Even though clinics must maintain records of those reporting to them for treatment, many misusers, especially of cocaine, never go to a clinic and cannot be counted. The British experience results from the premise that heroin, morphine, codeine, and other opiates have a legitimate place in medicine. Although not all general practitioners can still prescribe these drugs as they were previously allowed, they may still choose from a variety of approaches in dealing with their addict patients. Through certified clinics, the physicians and patients may choose psychotherapy, oral methadone, or even injectable heroin which may be forbidden in a number of countries, such as the United States. This approach applies only to specific drugs; recreational users cannot apply to a clinic or a doctor for their drugs.

The United Kingdom has been and continues to be very involved with international efforts to halt the trade in illicit drugs. This involvement has been consistent since the Shanghai Conference in 1909 and continues with the recent United Nations conferences in London. British domestic legislation has been changed as necessary to include the provisions of resulting international agreements. The government cooperates at various levels with other countries and international organizations to control the trafficking of drugs. It also participates in schemes to encourage drug-producing countries to turn to other types of income-producing commodities.

British policy recognizes that eliminating the illicit drug trade requires the elimination of the desire for drugs at home. To this end, various educational programs have been initiated with the goal of keeping people, especially the young, from experimenting with drugs. Other programs to help the drug addict have been established at public and private levels. These programs, which recognize the value and rights of the individual, try to eliminate the addict's physical and psychological need for drugs.

The United Kingdom has joined international efforts to prohibit the laundering of profits earned from the trafficking in illicit drugs. Legislation also allows for the seizure of assets that are derived from this activity. Banks in the United Kingdom are required to report any suspicions of money laundering to the proper authorities, and penalties can be severe for failure to report. However, unlike some other countries, the United Kingdom does not favor a mandatory requirement for all transactions over a certain amount.

The United Kingdom has no miracle cure for its drug misuse problems. However, governmental and private efforts are being made on the international, national, and local levels and on all fronts: education, prevention, rehabilitation, and interdiction. Domestically, the treatment approach used with the individual misuser of drugs is practical. But efforts to apprehend illicit drug traffickers and to enforce laws against the illicit use of drugs have been strengthened. Whatever the final solution may be, it will undoubtedly be a result of the United Kingdom's comprehensive approach to the issue and its international cooperation and leadership.

## NOTES

1. Home Office, Her Majesty's Government, *United Kingdom Action on Drug Misuse: The Government's Strategy* (London: Home Office, Central Office of Information, 1990).
2. J. Bishop, "Commentary on the Management and Treatment of Drug Addicts in the United Kingdom," in *The Drug Addict as a Patient*, ed. Marie Nyeswander et al., 149 (London: Grune and Stratton, 1956).
3. Horace Freeland Judson, *Heroin Addiction in Britain* (London: Harcourt Brace Jovanovich, 1974), 13.
4. Ibid, 14.
5. Philip Bean, *The Social Control of Drugs* (London: Martin Robertson & Company, 1974), 28.
6. Ibid, 23.
7. Ibid, 88.
8. Ibid, 89.
9. Ibid, 68.
10. Ibid, 4.
11. Judson, *Heroin Addiction in Britain*, 21.
12. Ibid, 19.
13. Ibid, 20.
14. Ibid.
15. Ibid, 34–35.
16. Bean, *The Social Control of Drugs*, 80.

17. Marc Kusinitz, *Drug Use around the World: The Encyclopedia of Psychoactive Drugs—Series 2* (London: Chelsea House Publishers, 1988), 68.
18. Home Office, *Statistical Bulletin*, Issue 7/1990 (London: Her Majesty's Government) 19 March 1990.
19. Robert Powell, "Sound the Smoke Alarms," *New Statesman and Society*, 21 July 1989, 23.
20. Home Office, *United Kingdom Action on Drug Misuse*, 4.
21. Powell, "Sounding the Smoke Alarms," 24.
22. Ibid.
23. Ibid.
24. Home Office, *United Kingdom Action on Drug Misuse*, 11.
25. Ibid, 6.
26. "Developed Nations Promised Aid to Curtail Drug Demand," *United Nations Chronicle* (September 1990): 62.
27. Ibid, 63.
28. Home Office, *United Kingdom Action on Drug Misuse*, 8.
29. Ibid, 12.
30. *Britain 1990: An Official Handbook* (London: Central Office of Information, 1990), 149.
31. Yvonne Roberts, "To the Slaughter," *New Statesman and Society*, 13 October 1989, 10.
32. *Britain 1990*, 150.
33. See North Western Regional Health Authority, "Responding to Drug Misuse in the North Western Region: A Framework for Services," (Manchester, U.K.: Gateway House, November 1990.)
34. Home Office, *United Kingdom Action on Drug Misuse*, 21.
35. David Lascelles, "Money Laundering under Siege," *Financial Times*, 20 April 1990, 30.
36. John Evans, "British Banks Get Warning on Laundering," *American Banker*, 17 November 1989, 21.
37. *Money Laundering, Guidance Notes for Banks and Building Societies*, (London: British Government, December 1990) 7.

## BIBLIOGRAPHY

Bean, Philip. *The Social Control of Drugs*. London: Martin Robertson & Company, 1974.

Cooper, Mary H. "The Business of Drugs." *1990 Congressional Quarterly* (Washington, D.C.: U.S. Government Printing Office, 1990).

Dolan, Edward, Jr. *International Drug Traffic*. New York: Franklin Watts, 1985.

Government of the United Kingdom. *Statistical Bulletin*, Issue 7/90. London: Home Office, 19 March 1990.

———. *United Kingdom Action on Drug Misuse: The Government's Strategy*. London: Home Office, Central Office of Information, 1990.

Hamony, Ronald, ed. *Dealing with Drugs*. San Francisco: Pacific Research Institute for Public Policy, 1987.

Judson, Horace Freeland. *Heroin Addiction in Britain*. London: Harcourt Brace Jovanovich, 1974.

Kusinitz, Marc. *Drug Use around the World: The Encyclopedia of Psychoactive Drugs—Series 2*. London: Chelsea House Publishers, 1988.

McCuen, Gary E. *The International Drug Trade*. Hudson, Wis.: Gary E. McCuen Publications, 1989.

Naylor, R. T. *Hot Money and the Policy of Debt*. New York: Linden Press and Schuster, 1987.

# 18

# The Union of Soviet Socialist Republics

RENSSELAER W. LEE III

## INTRODUCTION

Narcotics trafficking is a worldwide phenomenon that affects socialist as well as capitalist societies. While most people associate the Soviet Union with alcohol abuse rather than drug abuse, an ever increasing number of Soviet citizens are becoming addicted to drugs. Most of their drugs are produced and supplied domestically by elements of the Soviet criminal underworld. The growth of narcotics industries is symbiotically related to other important changes in the Union of Soviet Socialist Republics: the growth of organized crime, the acceleration of contacts with the West, the emergence of a nonstate economic sector, and the breakdown of the Soviet "empire."

## BACKGROUND

The Soviet Union is one of the largest countries in the world and has the third largest economy, behind only the United States and Japan. Despite the country's great size, covering some 22,402,200 square kilometers (twice the size of the United States), and its powerful military capacity, the Soviet Union is a deeply troubled country, and it confronts serious problems of both a political and economic nature. President Mikhail Gorbachev, since 1985, has sought to restructure Soviet society and the economy through his programs of *glasnost* and *perestroika*. Despite efforts to reform the economy, the Soviet Union entered the 1990s in a state of considerable uncertainty about its future. The development of a rapidly growing drug trade could well be one offshoot of the various changes occurring in the Soviet Union.

## SIZE AND CHARACTERISTICS OF THE ILLEGAL DRUG MARKET

Soviet public health and internal affairs organizations have identified approximately 118,000 Soviet citizens who engage regularly or occasionally in the nonmedical use of narcotics; more than half of these registered users are classified as "addicts" and are receiving medical treatment. Yet, Ministry of Interior (MVD) sources say that the official statistics are just the tip of the iceberg—that there are, in reality, 1.5 million Soviet citizens who use drugs or have tried them.[1] However, a recent multiregional survey conducted in the Soviet Union suggests that there are 1.5 million people just in the age category of fourteen to seventeen who have used drugs on at least one occasion; extrapolating from this figure, we can guess that as many as 15 million Soviets have tried some narcotic substance at least once in their lifetimes.[2]

The typical Soviet drug user is a male, blue-collar worker, who is thirty years of age and lives in a major city such as the capital of a union republic, oblast, krai, or autonomous republic. About six times as many men as women consume drugs in the Soviet Union; in the United States, the ratio of male to female drugs users is less than 1.5 to one.[3] The amount of narcotics use among people who work in the countryside seems to be small—less than 5 percent, according to most surveys—but this result may reflect an urban bias in the sampling procedures. (Illicit drug crops grow in agricultural locations, so why wouldn't Soviet peasants themselves consume opium, marijuana, or hashish?) In addition, there is some survey evidence that Soviet drug users come from families that have above-average incomes by Soviet standards—perhaps we are observing an analogy here with patterns of drug abuse in the United States two or three decades ago.

Consumption of drugs varies greatly by region. For example, according to Ministry of Health statistics, the rate of addiction in Soviet Central Asia, where opium cultivation and consumption are deeply ingrained in the local culture, is 60 percent higher than in the Russian Republic and 165 percent higher than in the Baltic Republics. In 1989, in Turkmenia, the rate of 103 addicts per 100,000 people was almost five times the national average of 22 per 100,000. It is worth noting, however, that the republic with the second highest rate of drug addiction is the Ukraine, with 38 registered addicts per 100,000 people.[4] Moreover, the pattern of substance abuse varies substantially throughout the Soviet Union. People in the north European parts of the country are far more likely to consume amphetamines and toxic substances not classified as narcotics (glue, gasoline, weed killer, acetone) than are people in the southern regions and the Soviet Far East, where plant-based drugs are more readily available. The rate of "toxicomania," for example, is twice as high in the Baltics as in the four Central Asian Republics. In other words, the poisons that people ingest in the Soviet Union are largely a function of geography.

It is important to point out that the Soviet Union is a narcotics-producing as well as a narcotics-consuming nation. Indeed, the country is virtually self-sufficient in narcotics as it is in so many other commodities. One MVD source in Moscow reports that more than 98 percent (by value) of the drugs consumed in the Soviet Union are of domestic origin. Imports of substances, such as cocaine and heroin, are increasing but still represent a negligible part of the market.

The Soviet Union itself possesses a gigantic base of raw materials for the production of narcotics: millions of hectares of mostly wild hemp, including as many as 4 million hectares in Kazakhstan, Azerbaijan, the Ukraine, and southern European Russia.[5] The variety of poppy called *maslichny* (oil-bearing), which grows in the Ukraine and southern Russia, has a lower opium content than the Asian strain, but it is widely cultivated and is sufficiently potent to constitute a significant factor in the Soviet substance abuse problem. This is underscored by the tremendously high rate of drug abuse in the Ukraine. By all indications, the Soviet Union has the potential to be a significant exporter of drugs; currently, however, the main role played by the Soviet Union in the international narcotics market is that of a transit country. As much as 20 to 30 tons of illegal drugs passes through Soviet territory each year en route to customers in the West. Most of these drugs are shipped by narcotics Mafias operating in the Golden Crescent or Golden Triangle countries. The majority of this illicit cargo travels in sealed containers aboard freight trains; at present, the Soviets lack the man-power or the technology to search more than a tiny fraction of the 150,000 containers that pass through the country each year.

The main drugs of choice, the most commonly used drugs in the Soviet Union by far, are marijuana and hashish (hashish is much more popular in the Soviet Union than it is in the United States). The other most popular drugs are opium; morphine; koknar, an evil brew made by grinding up the stems of poppies that contain opium; and ephedrone, and amphetamine extracted from ephedrine, a readily available prescription drug. Narcotic substances are often procured on the black market, but a considerable proportion—more than 30 percent according to some MVD estimates—are collected, manufactured, prepared, or stolen by the addicts themselves. In addition, roughly 2 to 3 percent of illegal drug supplies leak into the market from pharmaceutical enterprises, medical storehouses, and hospitals. In important respects, the Soviet illicit drug market is less "capitalistic" than its counterpart in the West—drugs are frequently obtained rather than bought.

How much Soviet consumers spend to support their habit is pretty much a mystery. Official estimates of the annual retail value of the Soviet narcotics trade range from 3 billion rubles to 14 billion rubles; MVD projections fall at the low end of the scale, while estimates from the Committee of State Security (KGB) are at the high end.[6] How these estimates are derived is not clear. The differences apparently reflects widely varying assumptions about drug users' expenditures to support their habits. Some analysts believe that the MVD's estimate is much too low, even taking into account the noncapitalistic features of the Soviet narcotics market. A minimum credible figure—based on the official estimate of

1.5 million addicts and users—would be from 7 to 8 billion rubles. This number was reached by calculating expenditures for drugs by chronic addicts as opposed to those by occasional users. Yet, 7 to 8 billion rubles must be considered a nominal or hypothetical figure because Soviet statistics on drug abuse are not particularly reliable.

## Market Dynamics

At first glance, the Soviet drug problem would not appear to be a problem, at least by U.S. standards. A few obvious comparisons can be drawn. The 1.5 million officially acknowledged Soviet drug users represent an infinitesimal part of the total Soviet population: less than 1 percent. In contrast, in the United States in 1990, according to the National Institute for Drug Abuse, 27 million Americans (11 percent of the population) used some illicit drug at least once a year. Similarly, the Soviet drug market of 3 to 14 billion rubles ($100 million to $500 million at the current tourist rate of exchange) is small in obsolete terms compared to the estimated $40 billion market in the United States; however, the percentage of (1989) GNP may be larger in the Soviet Union (0.04 to 1.9 percent) than in the United States (07.7 percent). Furthermore, arrests related to manufacturing, possessing, or trafficking in narcotics account for only about 1 percent of all Soviet arrests, compared to about 9 percent in the United States. It should be added that U.S. drug-law violators account for about 10 percent of the 800,000 inmates in state prisons and local jails and more than 33 percent of the 440,000 inmates in federal prisons.[7]

The extent of drug trafficking and drug abuse in the Soviet Union thus is extremely modest by U.S. standards, but such problems nonetheless are creating significant anxiety for Soviet law enforcement and public health officials. Several factors explain the state of Soviet affairs.

First, the use of drugs in the Soviet Union is increasing rapidly. Between 1984 and 1990, the number of registered addicts in the Soviet Union jumped more than 90 percent—from 35,254 to 67,622. President Gorbachev's ill-conceived antialcohol campaign (1985–1987) may well have driven many young people to use drugs. The main concern of the antialcohol program was to reduce consumption of alcohol and regain lost productivity in the work force. In some parts of the country, the increase in drug use was especially rapid; for example, almost 200 percent in the Ukraine and almost 400 percent in Byelorussia.[8] By contrast, consumption of the most widely used drugs in the United States, marijuana and cocaine, has actually declined since the mid–1980s. Although not very significant by American standards, the number of recorded drug offenses in the Soviet Union increased 36 percent between 1988 and 1990. In addition, according to a 1990 MVD briefing, drug addicts commit as much as from 30 to 40 percent of residential burglaries and 80 to 90 percent of pickpocket thefts.[9] This is hardly surprising in a country where the average price of a gram of opium is higher than the average Soviet worker's monthly wage. Moreover, between the mid–1970s and the 1980s, research conducted in the Republic of Georgia over eighteen years suggests that the profile of users is changing: Better educated, they are more likely to have finished high school and even to have attended college; they are better off economically; and they are more frequently women.[10] All of these trends are obviously worrisome for Soviet officials.

Second, the Soviets view the expansion of drug abuse and drug trafficking as stark symbols of the disintegration of their society. *Glasnost* and *perestroika* have furnished fertile soil for the growth of organized crime in general and of narcotics trafficking in particular. As social and political controls break down and the union crumbles, the power and influence of the criminal world are concomitantly amplified. Relatively large narcotics trafficking organizations, comprising twenty or thirty or more members, are emerging and are exhibiting signs of internal specialization. Such criminal syndicates have their own leaders, procurers, manufacturers, distributors, security guards, paid informants, money launderers, and muscle men. The trafficking organizations are well-equipped with transportation, weapons, and communications equipment—in fact, they may well be better equipped than the Soviet police who pursue them. Furthermore, many of these criminal syndicates operate over wide geographical territories; for example, a drug syndicate based in Tashkent or Baku might support distributors in Moscow, St. Petersburg, or even Vladivostok. Also, the Soviet authorities are beginning to observe evidence of criminal organization in the ways in which drug crops are cultivated, especially in Central Asia. Such crops are grown ever increasingly in remote mountain or desert regions, on plots of land that are carefully camouflaged and sometimes even protected by armed guards.[11]

Even more troublesome, these trafficking organizations, like the rest of the criminal underworld, have succeeded in developing external ties with police, government officials, and even Communist party cadres at the district level and higher government echelons. Drug-related corruption is rampant in Central Asia, especially in the two republics of Turkmenia and Uzbekistan. Of course, the cultivation of drug crops is traditional in Central Asia; and the relative poverty of the region, the clannish structure of the society, and certain elements of Islamic culture all contribute to the phenomenon. But serious cases of corruption also plague the European sector of the Soviet Union. According to one MVD source, in 1987, one of the few heroin laboratories discovered in the Soviet Union was detected in Riga, the capital of Latvia. The ensuing investigation disclosed a network of official protection that extended to party and MVD organs at the union republic level.[12]

To be certain, the drug traffic in the Soviet Union has not penetrated the society and the political system to the extent that it has in many other parts of the world. We do not yet see Soviet drug dealers behaving like South American cocaine lords—buying off top political and military leaders, maintaining private armies, issuing communiqués to the media, or conducting negotiations with governments. We do not see a clear linkage between drugs and national separatist movements, as in Burma or Pakistan, or between drugs and anti-state terrorism, as in Colombia and Peru. Still, the Soviet leadership in looking at the expansion of the Soviet market for narcotics and the increasing sophistication of the criminal organization response to this market is apprehensive.

## GOVERNMENT RESPONSE

Having discussed the structure of the Soviet illicit drug industry and the scope of the country's drug abuse problem, what are the Soviets doing to control their drug problem and how effective are such efforts?

Most of the drug-fighting burden in the Soviet Union is being borne by four organizations: the MVD, the KGB, the State Customs Administration, and the Ministry of Health. The MVD, the lead drug enforcement organization in the Soviet Union, has responsibility for eradicating illicit crops, seizing drug shipments, arresting drug criminals, and investigating criminal organizations that peddle narcotics. The MVD has a subunit: the Administration for Combatting the Illegal Narcotics Trade, which is roughly analogous to the United States' Drug Enforcement Agency. The MVD also maintains a network of research institutions that study problems of social deviance including drug abuse and drug trafficking. In addition, the MVD is in the business of treating drug addicts. Soviet law provides for the compulsory institutionalization of addicts under certain circumstances, and the MVD maintains a network of facilities, so-called work therapy centers or work education centers, which perform this function. Compulsory treatment seems designed more to punish addicts than to rehabilitate them; few addicts are cured in these centers, and some apparently do not survive the experience.

The KGB also investigates criminal organizations that deal in drugs, especially larger organizations that transcend union republic boundaries or that have apparent ties with trafficking organizations abroad. The KGB, moreover, has a mandate to investigate all cases of drug contraband uncovered by the Soviet Customs. In addition, cases of drug-related corruption (such as bribing of officials and vote buying) fall within the KGB's sphere of responsibility. There is considerable duplication between the KGB's responsibilities and those of the Ministry of Internal Affairs. The organizations are bureaucratical rivals, competing for a larger share of the same anticrime budget. A number of analysts, both Soviet and non-Soviet, indicate that there is little love lost between the two organizations. The KGB, according to its own spokesmen, has entered the narcotics field because the MVD lacks the resources, the competence, and the experience to cope with the problem, and also because the MVD is highly susceptible to corruption by narcotics Mafias, especially in major drug source regions, such as Soviet Central Asia.[13] (Note: The KGB is now being restructured, but it will apparently retain its domestic responsibilities in the fight against corruption and organized crime.)

The role of the Soviet Customs, as one might suspect, is to detect and to seize illicit drugs that cross Soviet frontiers. However, criminal investigations that are precipitated by drug seizures are handled by the KGB and the MVD. The Ministry of Health has various responsibilities: maintaining statistics on drug abuse, treating addicts, conducting research in the sources or preconditions of addiction, and organizing education and prevention activities.

Many other organizations are also involved, on both the supply and demand sides, in the Soviet fight against drugs. The Procuracy, for example, prosecutes drug cases, supervises and coordinates the work of other drug-fighting agencies, and conducts regional surveys on the incidence of drug abuse. The Soviet military provides helicopters and pilots for crop eradication campaigns. The Ministry of Foreign Affairs negotiates "framework" agreements for antidrug cooperation with foreign countries. The State Committee of Industrial and Agricultural Production (GOSAGROPROM), which cultivates hemp (i.e., marijuana) for industrial purposes, is attempting to develop new varieties of hemp with a low narcotic yield. (Prior to 1987, there was also legal cultivation of oil-bearing poppies; GOSAGROPROM got out of this business because it could not successfully guard its poppy fields against thefts by desperate addicts.) Finally, there are other Soviet organizations, such as the Konsomol, the Ministries of Education and Culture, the Russian Orthodox Church, "Znanie," and various voluntary societies (such as the All-Union Society for Saving Children and Juveniles from Drugs and the Russian Fund to Combat Drug Addiction), which are engaged to a greater or lesser extent in disseminating information about the dangers of drugs.

In general, Soviet antidrug efforts have yielded poor results. The Soviets, who have for years deluded themselves that drug addiction was a problem peculiar to capitalist societies, lack both the experience and the resources to deal with the problem. The MVD currently allocates only 900 employees to the Soviet war against drugs. Demand-reduction activities—"antinarcotics propaganda"—are sporadic and weakly organized. Despite several highly touted campaigns to eradicate illicit crops in Soviet Central Asia, opium production appears to be increasing rapidly in that region to serve the growing market in the European part of the Soviet Union. Central Asia opium production increased 400 percent between mid–1989 and mid–1990, according to one unofficial MVD estimate. Drug trafficking is becoming more organized, and more interregional; and, of course, more and more Soviets appear to be coming under the influence of drugs.

What about the future? The Soviet drug abuse and drug trafficking will probably get worse in the years to come. Westernization, internal economic reform, and the loosening of Moscow's hold over the union republics will all play a role in this process. One factor is the movement toward increased convertibility of the ruble. As one Moscow MVD official recently observed, "If ruble convertibility is achieved, a tremendous flood of drugs could pour toward us."[14] By the mid–1990s, full convertibility may well be a reality in the Soviet Union. If traffickers can sell drugs to Soviet customers in exchange for dollars, or francs, or marks, they undoubtedly will make some effort to penetrate that market. The possibility that foreign Mafias might introduce massive quantities of relatively cheap drugs such as crack absolutely terrifies Soviet officials.

The second future trend is the privatization of economic activity within the Soviet Union. Some other nearly 200,000 cooperatives now in existence have clearly served as a convenient legal cover for drug money laundering. Sometime in the early 1990s, cooperatives and Soviet-foreign joint ventures will be able to freely exchange rubles for foreign currency in specially designated currency houses. This new development will doubtless be welcomed enthusiastically by drug Mafias both in the Soviet Union and abroad, especially as Soviet bank regulators are inexperienced with private sector banking in general and with money laundering in particular (in the Soviet Union as of March 1991, there were only 10 bank supervisors for 3,000 banks compared to 3,000 examiners for the 4,000 banks that report to the Office of the Comptroller of the Currency in the United States).

The third future trend is the rapid expansion of trade, travel and economic ties with Western countries (and also with countries in the Far East), which will widen the drug pipeline. As one Russian Federal Republic MVD official said, it will "broaden the basis of the penetration of narcotics from abroad."[15] Also, the international pipeline will be a channel for the transfer of Western Mafia expertise—such as refining technology, distribution methods, and concealment techniques—to the Soviet criminal world.

The fourth trend is the weakening of central power or the breakup of the Soviet Union into separate nations that populate the Eurasian landmass. This will enormously complicate the enforcement of drug laws. For example, in the reconfigured Soviet Union, it is not clear which functions will be allocated to Moscow, which will belong to the union republics, and which will be the responsibility of ethnic minority groups (such as Tatars, Buryats, and the like) in the major union republics. Clearly, organized crime and drug trafficking are by nature interregional and require law enforcement strategies with the same reach.

In addition, the indifference or hostility of local populations to drug control and the pervasive drug-related corruption are arguments for strong central control. But a Muscovite solution may not work, especially in Central Asia where the largely Islamic population is apt to view narcotics-control campaigns as an instrument of Russification. Furthermore, narcotics production or smuggling could become an attractive proposition economically for the region, particularly if, as the price of greater national independence, Soviet Central Asia loses some of the 8 billion rubles worth of subsidies that it now (as of 1990) receives from Moscow. (The five central Asian republics are also the five poorest in the Soviet Union [1989] with per capita incomes ranging from 45 percent to 75 percent of the national average.) For political and economic reasons, drugs seem likely to become a serious issue in relations between Moscow and the Central Asian republics: Central Asia could become to European Russia what Latin America is to the United States. MVD officials interviewed in Moscow in September 1991 anticipate a significant expansion of narcotics production in Soviet Central Asia as the breakup of the Soviet Union accelerates.

## INTERNATIONAL LINKAGES TO DRUG CONTROL

The Soviet Union is faced with a growing narcotics threat; it lacks the experience and the resources to cope with this threat; and it has made a strategic decision to seek antinarcotics assistance from the West. In the past three years, the Soviets have signed antidrug cooperation agreements with six Western countries, including the United States; they have joined the United Nations Fund for Drug Abuse Control; and most recently, they have joined Interpol. With respect to the United States, Soviet customs and MVD officials participate in training seminars organized by the Drug Enforcement Administration (DEA). In 1990, Soviet customs officials witnessed the joint DEA–U.S. Customs seizure of a drug-smuggling ship on the high seas off the coast of Florida.[16] Also in August 1990, DEA officials were invited on a helicopter tour of the gigantic marijuana fields that are located in the Chu Valley in Kazakhstan. But not all exchanges involve law enforcement. For example, the Ministry of Health (specifically its All-Union Narcology Institute) has an ongoing research project with the National Institute for Drug Abuse to study the biological preconditions (that is, the genetic predeterminants) of drug abuse.

The Soviet wish list—what they hope to get from the West and the United States in the drug-control area—is vast. They want, for example, chemical herbicides or biological control mechanisms that can destroy opium and poppy plantations without ruining the environment. They want better technology for detecting illicit crops and drug shipments. They want Western advice on how to rationalize their legal codes against drugs. They want to draw on Western police experience in identifying the members of criminal organizations and in tracking the flow of illegal drug money. They want foreign help to develop, test, and patent drugs that seem to show promise in treating drug addicts. They want the United States to fund, equip, and advise centers for antinarcotics propaganda in various union republics. And one top Soviet narcotics expert even proposed establishing a joint American-Soviet computerized information center that would collect and analyze all data about narcotics abuse, drug-related offenses, and narcotics Mafias in the Soviet Union.

The Soviet dilemma of turning to its former, and perhaps once again future, rival for help with its drug problem poses a difficult question for the United States. Should a U.S.–Soviet relationship be developed against the international narcotics trade? First, such a relationship would widen U.S. access to the Soviet system and enhance its ability to comprehend the momentous political and social changes now occurring in the Soviet Union. This is particularly true if the United States could establish cooperative links with the MVD and other relevant Soviet ministries in the individual union republics. One informal suggestion by Soviet officials is the possibility of an antidrug cooperation agreement between the United States and Latvia, the United States and the Russian Republic, and the United States and Georgia. Such proposals would imply an expanded U.S. official or quasi-official presence in Soviet territory; however, as of early 1991 the United States does not even maintain a narcotics representative at the embassy in Moscow. Second, the Soviet Union, by virtue of its size, geographical location, and potential for cultivating drug crops, could become a significant exporter of narcotics by the end of the century. Already the Soviet Union plays an important role in transshipping drugs westward from Southeast and Southwest Asia. Without doubt, developments in the Soviet narcotics market need to be closely observed.

## CONCLUSION

The Soviet Union is both a producer and a transit state for narcotics. It is probable that in the future these problems will increase, especially in light of the uncertain political environment in the future. The Soviet Union's geographical location near major drug-producing countries, such as Afghanistan, and its own capacity for opium and marijuana cultivation greatly enhance the nature of the drug problem as a threat to national security. Soviet law enforcement agencies as well as the country's social infrastructure will be hard-pressed to deal with the problem, and international assistance will be needed. The dilemma for Western countries, especially the United States, will be that cooperation on the drug war front has the potential to appear to strengthen organizations that form part of the repressive apparatus of the Soviet state.

## NOTES

1. A. Illesh, "Skol'ko u Nas Narkomanov," *Izvestia*, 29 August 1990, 6.
2. This inference is based on the results of a survey conducted by Dr. Anzor Gabiani in 1988–1989 in Latvia, the Ukraine (L'vov Oblast), the RSFSR (Gorkiy and Novosibirsk oblasts, Primorskiy and Stavropol Krais), and the cities of Moscow; Tashkent. (Hereafter referred to as the Gabiani survey.)
3. Anzor Aleksandrovich Gabiani, *Na Kraiu Propasti* (Moscow: Mysl, 1990). See Chapter 2. Also see Gabiani survey and National Institute for Drug Abuse, *National Household Survey on Drug Abuse: Population Estimates 1988* (Washington, D.C.: U.S. Government Printing Office, 1989), 17.
4. Date provided by the All-Union Research Center on Medical-Biological Problems of Narcology, USSR Ministry of Health (hereafter Narcology Institute), August-September 1990 and September 1991.
5. A. Urvantsev, "From Competent Sources: Will We Curb the Drugs Business?" *Pravda*, 23 November 1990, 6.
6. V. Kryuchkov, "Znaem li my vsiu pravdu o tenyevoi ekonomike?" *Pravda*, 18 August 1990, 2.
7. Federal Bureau of Investigation, *Crime in the United States* (Washington, D.C.: U.S. Government Printing Office, August 1990), 172. A. Pokrovskiy, "Krysha dlya Narkomanov," *Izvestia*, 17 February 1990, 6. Ethan Nadelmann, "U.S. Drug Policy: A Bad Export," *Foreign Policy* (Spring 1988): 99.
8. Narcology Institute.

9. "Government to Combat Narcotics Abuse," TASS Moscow 1956 GMT, 14 February 1990.

10. Gabiani, *Na Kraiu Propasti*, Chapter 2.

11. Interviews with USSR Ministry of the Interior (MVD) and RSFSR MVD officials. Moscow, August-September 1990. See also, "O Sostoyanii Bor'by Nezakonnym Oborotom Narkotikov v. SSSR." Report of Soviet delegation to the first European Conference, Heads Law Enforcement Organs for the Struggle against Drugs. Moscow, November 19–23, 1990.

12. Interview with Latvian MVD official. Moscow, August 1990.

13. "Kontrrazvyedka: Protiv Spersslužhb i Organizovennoi Prestupnosti," (interview with vice-head of KGB V. F. Gruskko), *Pravda*, 26 August 1990, 2; V. Kuleshov, "Details for *Izvestia*: In the Dock—A Narcotics Gang," *Izvestia*, 12 February 1990, 6.

14. Urvantsev, "From Competent Sources."

15. Interview with RSFSR MVD official. Moscow, September 1990.

16. A. Bylov, "USSR—Ssha Vmestye protiv Narkotikov," *Izvestia*, 2 February 1990, 4.

## BIBLIOGRAPHY

Bylov, A. "SSSR—Ssha Vmestye protiv Narkotikov." *Izvestia*, 2 February 1990, 4.

Gabiani, Anzor Aleksandrovich. Na Kraiu Propasti. Moscow: Mysl, 1990.

"Government to Combat Narcotics Abuse." TASS Moscow 1956 GMT, 14 February 1990.

Illesh, A. "Skol'ko u Nas Narkomanov." *Izvestia*, 29 August 1990, 6.

"Kontrrazvyedka: Protiv Spetssluzhb i Organizovennoi Prestupnosti." (Interview with vice-head of KGB V. F. Gruskko.) *Pravda*, 26 August 1990, 2.

Kryuchkov, V. "Znaem li my vsiu pravdu o tenyevoi ekonomike?" *Pravda*, 18 August 1990, 2.

Kuleshov, V. "Details for *Izvestia*: In the Dock—A Narcotics Gang." *Izvestia*, 12 February 1990, 6.

Levin, Brois Mikhailovich, and Mikhail Borisovich Levin. "Narkomania i narkomany." (Moscow, unpublished manuscript, 1988).

Levin, M. "Itak Narkomania." *Ogoniok* 23 (1988).

Nadelmann, Ethan. "U.S. Drug Policy: A Bad Export." *Foreign Policy* (Spring 1988): 83–108.

Neuhauser, Kimberly. "The Market for Illegal Drugs in the Soviet Union in the Late 1980s." *Berkeley-Duke Occasional Papers on the Second Economy in the USSR*, Paper no. 23, November 1990. University of Berkeley and Duke University.

Urakov, N. G., V. E. Pelipas, and L. D. Miroshnichyenko. "Dinamika raspostranyennosti narkomaiy v SSSR" (Dynamics of the spread of narcotics addiction in the USSR). *Voprosy Narkologii* (1989): 50–54.

Urvantsev, A. "From Competent Sources: Will We Curb the Drugs Business?" *Pravda* 23 November 1990, 6.

# IV

# Country and Regional Studies: Asia and the Middle East

# 19

# Afghanistan

SCOTT B. MACDONALD

## INTRODUCTION

Images of Afghanistan in the 1980s were usually those of an occupied country, fighting a bloody civil war to regain its independence. From the Soviet invasion in 1979 until the Soviet withdrawal in 1989 this was indeed the case. Afghanistan, however, entered the 1990s in the throes of an ongoing civil war between a still Soviet-supported regime in Kabul, the capital, and the various rebel groups, known as the *mujahidin*. While war has dominated Afghanistan's development for more than a decade, weak central authority and the traditional Afghan ability to smuggle have combined to make conditions highly conducive for the spread of the illicit drug trade. Add to this soil that is fertile for poppy cultivation and corruption of both Pakistani and Iranian officials, and one begins to understand why Afghanistan began the 1990s as the world's second largest producer of opium (behind Burma) and hashish (behind Lebanon). It is also a significant producer of cannabis.

## BACKGROUND

It is no understatement that Afghan society has been influenced by the country's rough physical environment. Located at a crossroads where the civilizations of China, India, and the Middle East overlap, Afghanistan has been the scene of numerous invasions and movements of people. At the same time, its austere and imposing terrain has meant that those groups of peoples who now constitute the modern Afghan nation have developed in a highly independent fashion. Afghanistan's geography is largely defined as mountainous; the western offshoot of the Himalayas, the Hindu Kush, with peaks often higher than 20,000 feet, covers more than half of the country. Consequently, more than half of the country can be described not only as mountainous, but also as barren and difficult to inhabit. The other half consists of rich river valleys and plateaus, where the bulk of the country's population and agricultural sector are located, and of border regions which are desolate and dry.

Afghanistan's geography has also been a factor in the development of its society. The crossroads nature of the region has meant that there has been a considerable intermixing of ethnic groups as well as the isolation of others. This is reflected in the fact that there are more than thirty distinct languages native to the country, with four major language families of which Farsi is probably the most widely used. Most of the nearly half of the population who speak Pushtu are located in the eastern part of the country along the border with Pakistan. Other major language groups include Baluchi, an Iranian tongue; Turkish languages, which are spoken among the country's Tajiks, Khirghiz, and Turcomans; and Arabic and Brahui, related to the Dravidian group of India, which are spoken by several small groups. The mixture of languages reflects the tremendous diversity of ethnic and tribal groups in the country, ranging from the Pushtuns (roughly divided into ten major tribes), to Tajiks (descended from Turkish and Mongol invaders from Central Asia), Turcomans, Hazaras, the Baluchis.

Data concerning the standard of living in Afghanistan is sparse due to the country's acute political instability. Suffice it to say, Afghanistan is probably one of the poorest countries in the world in terms of per capita income, literacy, and life expectancy at birth. What social infrastructure that had been in place before the Soviet invasion in 1979 was effectively negated in the war-torn 1980s. Massive population disruption resulted in large refugee communities in Pakistan and, to a lesser extent, Iran. the period of armed struggle in the 1980s in Afghanistan also contributed to the traditional problem of central authority versus the tribes. As has occurred many times prior the 1980s, the tribes have refused to accept central authority over the direction of their affairs.

The same factors that undermined the country's social fabric also destroyed Afghanistan's already weak economy. The nature of the war—of a Soviet occupying force and its local allies sitting in the major cities and sallying forth for periodic offenses against rebel forces in their mountain valley bases—was somewhat reminiscent of the failed British occupation in the 1840s. Ultimately the Soviets left Afghanistan, having fought a long, frustrating war without a total victory. They left behind a largely devastated country, where the cultivation of poppies and smuggling of opium and heroin emerged as a major industry.

Although opium has long existed in Afghanistan as a narcotic for consumption, usage was never widespread or socially disabling as it was in neighboring Iran (then Persia) or China during the Ch'ing dynasty. Prior to the 1970s, Afghan opium production was linked to events in Iran. Though opium had been cultivated and used in Iran since the eleventh century, its usage became a major problem in the early twentieth century. Addiction rates grew at a rapid pace, until in the 1950s it was estimated that the country had over a million addicts. This led the

Shah's government to ban poppy cultivation in 1955. As local supply disappeared, entrepreneurial Afghans stepped into the breach, making use of traditional smuggling routes. In 1969, the Iranian government changed its policy and allowed a limited amount of opium cultivation. This was meant to be carefully supervised, and only government-recognized addicts were given coupons that provided them access to the state's opium supply.

Despite the partial reactivation of Iran's poppy crop, Afghan opium production continued to grow with Iran as its major market in the early 1970s. Afghan traffickers found the movement of opium into Iran relatively easy and well worth the effort, despite the death penalty if caught for drug smuggling. Clashes with Iranian law enforcement forces along the Afghan-Iran border were frequent.

Afghanistan's experience with the modern international drug trade commenced in the 1970s when large numbers of Westerners descended on the Asian country to "drop out" and "turn on" inexpensively. At one stage, before the 1973 coup, it was estimated that between 5,000 and 6,000 hippies lived in Kabul.[1] After the coup, the new government tightened both visa and drug controls, forcing many Western drug users to depart. The Afghan view about drug use and trafficking in the early 1970s was summarized by Linette Albert, "Few Afghans indulge in drugs to any marked degree, and authorities regard the police problems associated with drug-taking and trading as a Western headache and a Western expense."[2] The situation was to change radically by the early 1980s.

Afghanistan's rise to the big leagues of illicit narcotics production and trafficking came from a tremendous increase in external demand. While the Iranian market was the major incentive for Afghan traffickers in the 1960s and early 1970s, the rest of the world accounted for a relatively small percent of total opium production. Small amounts transited Pakistan, making it to Western Europe and North America. Those two markets were largely supplied by heroin from the Golden Crescent countries of Southeast Asia. The situation changed when the governments of Vietnam and Laos fell in the early and mid–1970s, disrupting a link between the Golden Triangle supply of Burma, Thailand, and Laos and the United States. Moreover, a prolonged drought in the late 1970s and early 1980s reduced the ability of the Golden Crescent to supply world heroin demand. The combination of these factors placed a greater demand o the Golden Crescent countries, especially Afghanistan and Pakistan.

The traditional market for Afghan opium farmers was soon disrupted, which added another factor in the changing structure of the international heroin trade. The initial chaos that followed in the wake of the Shah's fall from power in 1979 and the rise of the Islamic fundamentalist forces temporarily disrupted enforcement in that country and helped stimulate local opium cultivation. The Iranian market for Afghan opium shrank at roughly the same time that traditional smuggling routes to Iran were blocked by Soviet forces in their occupation of Afghanistan.

By 1980, Afghan narcotics traders were confronted by a radically changed international market. Shorn from the Iranian market and with years of record

**Table 19.1**
**World Opium Production (1987–1990)**

| Country | 1987 | 1988 | 1989 | 1990 |
|---|---|---|---|---|
| | (in metric tons) | | | |
| Burma | 925-1230 | 1065-1500 | 2625 | 2780 |
| Afghanistan | 400-800 | 700-800 | 585 | 500-800 |
| Laos | 150-300 | 210-300 | 375 | 300-450 |
| Iran | 200-400 | 200-400 | 300 | 200-400 |
| Pakistan | 190-220 | 190-220 | 130 | 118-128 |
| Mexico | 45-55 | 45-55 | 85 | 85 |
| Lebanon | - | - | 45 | 45 |
| Thailand | 20-45 | 23-33 | 50 | 40 |
| Guatemala | - | - | 14 | 6 |

[Source: U. S. Department of State, Bureau of International Narcotics Matters, International Narcotics Control Strategy Report (Washington, D.C.: March 1990), p. 18]

crops behind them, Afghan traffickers soon learned to refine opium into heroin and discovered new outlets in Europe and North America. The latter was usually accomplished through Pakistani middlemen, especially in the United States, Canada, and Germany.

## STRUCTURE OF THE NARCOTICS INDUSTRY

Although Pakistan lead Afghanistan in opium production in the 1970s, Afghanistan rapidly gained ground in the 1980s. After the initial disruption caused by the Soviet invasion in 1979, Afghan peasants returned to poppy cultivation. The nature of the Soviet occupation, moreover, contributed to the development of the illicit economy due to the policy of trying to starve the *mujahidin* by destroying food crops. As Afghan agriculturalist Mohammad Qasim Yusufi noted in 1988, "Because of war conditions, agricultural production factors such as labour force, fertilizers, irrigation water, improved seed varieties, agricultural machinery, proper farming and management, and maintenance of land have been greatly disrupted on one hand, and the government pays very little or no attention to the agricultural sector of the country on the other."[3] He also added that most of the country's highly educated personnel on agricultural matters left the country in the 1980s, and all Western and Muslim country assistance was stopped. The combination of these factors was the suppression of the legal agricultural economy and, in a number of cases, in those places beyond Soviet control, a turn to opium cultivation. As a finished product, heroin brought profits that were used to purchase weapons and food in Pakistan.

Table 19–1 provides insights into the pecking order of opium production in the 1987–1990 period.

Afghanistan's mountainous terrain, especially its river valleys, are ideal for opium production. Analysts estimate that in 1990 around 40 percent of Afghanistan's opium crop was cultivated in the Helmand River Valley, which is an integral part of the Golden Crescent. A rebel-controlled region, the Helmand River Valley is in the country's southwest, bordering both Iran and Pakistan.

The Helmand River Valley opium base provides insight into the structure of the Afghan narcotics industry. Because of the civil war, especially during the Soviet intervention, large parts of the country fell out of the Kabul government's control. Various U.S. and Pakistani-backed and equipped factions of *mujahidin* emerged to fight the Soviets and their Afghan allies. This has meant that the groups involved in drug trafficking, usually tribes, went from carrying single-shot rifles to automatic weapons and light artillery. The firepower of traffickers, therefore, came to equal that of government authorities on both sides of the Afghan-Pakistani border.

The *mujahidin* also established some form of local administration in the areas where they held sway. These local administrations were responsible for local security, logistics and crop cultivation, and any type of social services that could be provided. Crop cultivation, especially that of opium, was felt to be important by some analysts because of the narcotic's ability to raise the cash required for the war effort. Poppies are planted, pruned, irrigated, and harvested by guerrilla groups, peasants, and criminal organizations. The by-product is then smuggled across the porous Pakistani border. At the same time, it should be emphasized that not all *mujahidin* groups or tribes are involved in the narcotics trade.

In the Helmand River Valley it is alleged that *mujahidin* leaders and poppy growers use middlemen, including other *mujahidin* factions, such as the radical Hizbe-Islami party, and some Pakistani military officials who coordinate the guerrillas' arms supplies.[4] These middlemen operate on both sides of the border, though the Pakistani city of Peshawar functions as an essential smuggling hub.

An important element in the structure of Afghanistan's narcotics trade is the large refugee community in Pakistan. The brutal nature of the Soviet occupation led to a massive exodus of Afghans to nearby Pakistan. As the process commenced in the early 1980s, many Afghans settled in Pakistan. Some married locally; others purchased shops in the bazaars, started their own business, or simply transferred their trade from Kabul to Pakistan. Others embarked upon the region's other traditional cross-border activity. As noted by Edward R. Girardet, "The refugees have infiltrated two vital areas of the economy in the frontier region—the arms business and the profligate smuggling or consumer goods and drugs."[5]

The opium and heroin flow from Afghanistan transits Pakistan, India, and then Sri Lanka by overland and air routes. Another route transits Pakistan to Hong Kong and Malaysia and then to North America by ship. Other routes transit Iran, Turkey, and Lebanon by land and then to Europe by land or by sea through the Indian Ocean to the Red Sea, through the Suez Canal, and on to key markets in Europe and North America. It should be added that Afghan drug smugglers have also managed to help meet Europe's demand for hashish, especially the variety known as "black" hashish.

The ongoing incentive for Afghan narcotics traffickers is profit. There is a difference between wholesale and retail prices—the price the opium farmers ask and receive for their crop in Afghanistan and what dealers in Europe and North America receive for sales at street value. As Roger Lewis explained in 1985, "One kilo of heroin purchased for £4,000 (US $7,000) on the Pakistan/Afghan border may be sold as such in Britain for £20,000 (US $35,000) to £25,000. If the kilo is sold in separate ounces it can realize between £28,000 (US $43,700) to £42,000. Dilution or 'cutting' may increase the profits even further, although reduction of heroin content by more than half is far less common in Britain than in the United States."[6]

## SOCIETAL REACTION

Drug abuse is not regarded as a major problem in Afghanistan. There are no accurate estimates of opium or heroin use, although access to such narcotics is relatively easy. It is difficult to measure the level of drug abuse when basic survival is at issue as it is in the case of many Afghans in the early 1990s.

During the Soviet occupation, drug abuse among Soviet troops was a well-known problem. One analyst noted in 1985, "Like the American troops in Vietnam, the Russians are turning to drugs through disillusionment with their Asian involvement."[7] The same analyst noted that the Soviets were forced to reduce the tour of duty for their troops in an effort to cut down on exposure time to narcotics abuse. They also sought to put tighter controls on military ordinance that was often traded for narcotics. Soviet troops put into a hostile country, often in remote posts, found heroin (usually smoked), opium, and marijuana available. The heroin was of extremely high quality, usually with a purity of 60 percent, but at times up to 90 percent. What began as an intervention in 1979 continues in the 1990s in the streets of Moscow, St. Petersburg, and Rostov, though much of what supplies the Soviet market is produced in the Soviet Union. It is also likely that the political and economic instability in the former Soviet Union, especially after the failed coup in August 1991, will enhance the environment for the drug trade.

## INTERNATIONAL LINKAGES OF DRUG CONTROL

No discussion of the Afghan narcotics trade would be complete without covering international linkages to drug control. Sadly, though opium production is illegal in Afghanistan, the law means little because the central government lacks effective control over most of the country. Additionally, the United States, the People's Republic of China, and Pakistan spent much of the 1980s supporting opposition forces, which some analysts believe are active in narcotics cultivation and trafficking. The Kabul government's closest partner in drug control probably remains the Soviet Union, due to the movement of Afghan narcotics across the frontier.

Afghanistan's preeminence in the world narcotics trade has meant that the

United States denied it certification in 1990, which prohibited any granting of economic assistance. The reasons for certification denial were stated as such: "There is no indication that the regime in Kabul has taken any action to suppress opium cultivation and heroin refining . . . we are concerned about opium poppy cultivation in areas controlled by Mujahidin commanders. We fear . . . that once hostilities end, refugees will turn to poppy cultivation during the period of economic disruption as they seek to rebuild a livelihood interrupted by 10 years of war."[8]

Afghanistan's opium-poppy cultivation is a major concern to the United States and Canada in the 1990s. Some analysts feel that, as cocaine usage in North America peaks in the late 1980s and early 1990s, there will be greater demand for heroin, as drug abuse cycles often turn from stimulants, like cocaine, to depressants, like heroin. The view was underscored in a testimony before the U.S. Congress by Assistant Secretary of State Melvyn Levitsky in 1990: "We are seriously concerned with the potential for heroin to again become a major drug of abuse in the United States, especially if and when the crack phenomenon begins to abate."

Any major effort to reduce the production of narcotics in Afghanistan will have to be implemented along with a disarmament of the tribes that constitute the backbone for *mujahidin* forces. As Alex Brodie, BBC correspondent in Islamabad, Pakistan, commented in 1985, the "heroin trade can only be stopped with the agreement of the tribes. If that were forthcoming, the pressure might have to be taken off hashish and opium. If the chiefs ban heroin, the government might have to back off on other issues. But it will have to be done by negotiation, because, as a Pakistani official put it: 'To disarm the tribes these days, you'd need the Pakistani, the Afghan and the Russian armies.' "[9] This situation raises many questions. For the United States, support for Afghan rebel forces has diminished as the Soviets have removed their troops. Therefore, to the many Afghans still resisting the government in Kabul, the international drug trade continues to be a certain way of making the necessary capital for the procurement of weapons. In the meantime, Afghan heroin continues to flow into the United States and Europe.

## CONCLUSION

Afghanistan is a major narcotics-producing country, which plays a significant role in the international opium and heroin markets. Considering the ongoing nature of the country's civil war, it is unlikely that government efforts to enforce laws already on the books will amount to much. Consequently, it is probable that one of the major concerns for international narcotics suppression will be Afghanistan's opium crops. The Golden Crescent, including Iran and Pakistan, will remain a problem in the 1990s. An additional concern relates to the potential for political instability in Pakistan, which was marked by a coup in 1990 and strong anti-Western sentiment in 1991 due to the U.S.–led war against Iraq.

Any weakening of antinarcotics efforts in Pakistan will clearly help augment the flow of narcotics from Afghanistan.

## NOTES

1. Linette Albert, ''Afghanistan: A Perspective,'' in *Afghanistan in the 1970s*, ed. Louis Dupree and Linette Albert (New York: Praeger, 1974), 257.

2. Ibid.

3. Mohammad Qasim Yusufi, ''Effects of the War on Agriculture,'' in *The Tragedy of Afghanistan: The Social, Cultural and Political Impact of the Soviet Invasion*, ed. Bo Huldt and Erland Jansson (London: Croom Helm, 1988), 212.

4. John Jennings, ''Afghanistan: Efforts to End Opium Cultivation Hit New Snags,'' *Far Eastern Economic Review*, 14 June 1990, 22.

5. Edward R. Girardet, *Afghanistan: The Soviet War* (New York: St. Martin's Press, 1985), 207.

6. Roger Lewis, ''Serious Business—The Global Heroin Economy,'' in *Big Deal: The Politics of the Illicit Drug Business*, ed. Anthony Henman, Roger Lewis, and Tim Maylon (London: Pluto Press, 1985), 9.

7. Brian Freemantle, *The Fix: Inside the World Drug Trade* (New York: A Tom Doherty Associates Book, 1985, 1986), 179.

8. U.S. Department of State, Bureau of International Narcotic Matters, *International Narcotics Control Strategy Report, March 1990* (Washington, D.C.: Department of State, March 1990), 18.

9. Quoted from Tim Maylon, ''Love Seeds and Cash Crops: The Cannabis Commodity Market,'' in *Big Deal*, ed. Henman, Lewis, and Maylon, 89–90.

## BIBLIOGRAPHY


Dupree, Louis, and Linette Albert, eds. *Afghanistan in the 1970s*. New York: Praeger, 1974.

Forbis, William H. *Fall of the Peacock Throne: The Story of Iran*. New York: Harper and Row, Publishers, 1980.

Freemantle, Brian. *The Fix: Inside the World Drug Trade*. New York: A Tom Doherty Associates Book, 1985, 1986.

Girardet, Edward R. *Afghanistan: The Soviet War*. New York: St. Martin's Press, 1985.

Henman, Anthony, Roger Lewis, and Tim Maylon, eds. *Big Deal: The Politics of the Illicit Drug Business*. London: Pluto Press, 1985.

Jennings, John. ''Afghanistan: Efforts to End Opium Cultivation Hit New Snags,'' *Far Eastern Economic Reform*, 14 June 1990, 22–23.

Newell, Richard S. *The Politics of Afghanistan*. Ithaca, N.Y.: Cornell University Press, 1972.

President's Commission on Organized Crime. *American's Habit: Drug Abuse, Drug Trafficking, and Organized Crime*. Washington, D.C.: U.S. Government Printing Office, March 1986.

U.S. Congress. Senate. ''Testimony of Assistant Secretary of State Melvyn Levitsky, Bureau of International Narcotics Matters, Department of State, before the Subcommittee on East Asia and Pacific Affairs and the Subcommittee on Terrorism and Narcotics, Senate Foreign Relations Committee, 9 March 1990.

U.S. Department of State, Bureau of International Narcotics Matters. *International Narcotics Control Strategy Report, March 1990*. Washington, D.C.: Department of State, March 1990.

# 20

# The Islamic Republic of Iran

SCOTT B. MACDONALD AND
BARBARA JAHANSOOZI

## INTRODUCTION

The place of the Islamic Republic of Iran in the international narcotics trade is that of a major producer of opium, a key transit state for Afghan and Pakistani heroin, and a consumer of heroin and opium. The fall of the Pahlavi dynasty in 1979 and the ensuing chaos that marked the birth of the Islamic Republic in the early 1980s provided ideal conditions for the spread of opium cultivation and abuse. Iran had emerged by the early 1990s as one of the world's leading opium producers, behind only Burma, Afghanistan, and Pakistan. Iranian authorities have sought to deal with the problem, but they have been confronted with other priorities, such as the 1980–1988 war with Iraq, which have severely limited the capacities of any antinarcotics campaign. With the termination of hostilities with Iran, it is possible that, in the early 1990s, the Islamic Republic will begin to explore greater regional cooperation in fighting the drug war.

## BACKGROUND

Iran is located in the Middle East and shares borders with the Soviet Union in the north, Afghanistan and Pakistan to the east, Turkey and Iraq to the west, and the Persian Gulf states to the south. The country covers 636,293 square miles (1,648,000 square kilometers), and the majority of its population (52 percent) of 49 million is urban based. The terrain is mountainous and, in parts, desert-like. The official language is Farsi (also called Persian), but Turkic languages are spoken as well. The average life expectancy at birth is sixty-three years. The economy is dominated by the hydrocarbon sector, although agriculture is important.

Data on Iran's standard of living, educational levels, and economy since the Islamic Revolution and the Iran-Iraq War (1980–1988) have been sparse. Many analysts think that the overall standard of living fell substantially in the 1980s, due to the heavy costs of conducting a war against Iraq, reconstruction of wartime destruction, and the precipitous fall in oil prices in 1986. Domestic political turmoil throughout the decade also contributed to the economic downturn. According to Dilip Hiro, Iran's per capita income fell from 114,000 rials in 1978 to 55,000 in 1988 (or from $1,425 to $688).[1] It was not until the end of the decade that Iran appeared to have returned to a relative sense of political stability. In the meantime, the country's narcotics problem grew despite renewed enforcement efforts.

There is nothing new about drug cultivation and abuse in Iran. According to William H. Forbis, "Opium may have been introduced into what is now Iran by the Sumerians sixty centuries ago; in any case, the Arabs, who fed opium to their camels as well as to themselves, brought the drug with them in the course of their conquest."[2] Despite the debate on the exact date that opium was introduced to Iran, what is certain is that the poppy was well-suited for the country's dry climate. During the Safavid dynasties in the sixteenth and seventeenth centuries, opium was often mixed with wine.

Opium became part of Iran's cultural fabric. This was exemplified by the fact that it was the Persians who developed the standard opium pipe. Moreover, opium was used for medicinal purposes for almost any ailment, including the teething pains of children, menstrual pains for women, and insomnia for men. In the nineteenth century, Iran emerged as one of the world's biggest opium exporters. This was further stimulated by the invention of the hypodermic needle in 1853, which soon made morphine, an opium derivative, a widely used medical sedative in the West. One of the major buyers of Iran's opium was the British East India Company, part of which was sold to China. The incentive to export, which began in 1853 in a large way, was simple: Iran wanted European products and had to raise the foreign exchange to pay for them. The heavy demand in Europe and Asia made opium an excellent export crop. Another stimulus for opium production came in 1898 when heroin was first derived from morphine.

Opium continued to play a central role in the Iranian economy in the early twentieth century. By 1924 opium production earned Iran a fourth of its export income (apart from oil) and supplied the government with a tenth of its annual revenue. The first Pahlavi ruler, Reza Shah, was known to enjoy an occasional pipe of opium. The first Pahlavi Shah also sought to regulate poppy growing, seeking to gain better control of the crop with an eye to enhanced revenues. Incidentally, one of the major buyers of Iran's opium in the 1920s and 1930s was the Japanese Imperial Army, which used it as a weapon to destabilize and control the Chinese. By the mid–1950s, Iran supplied as much as three-fifths of the world's legal opium, averaging around 100 tons a year.

Iranian society paid heavily for the country's premier role as a world leader in the opium market. Although Iranians did not take to using the needle for heroin and morphine, opium smoking was very popular. When world markets collapsed with the advent of World War II, the country was inundated with the narcotic. The result was noted by Forbis: ''World War II, cutting off exports, flooded Iran itself with the drug, causing the most widespread addiction in history. The Anti-Opium and Alcohol Society in 1943 counted a million addicts, twelve hundred opium dens, and five thousand opium-induced suicides a year.''[3]

After the war, Iran resumed its opium exports. The problem of domestic abuse, however, continued. Some analysts contend that Iran was on its way to becoming a country of opium addicts. Finally, in 1955, the government took a major step in drug control: It prohibited all opium poppy cultivation. The ban eliminated a $60 million yearly farm industry, cut $30 million off of Iran's legal exports, and reduced the number of addicts by two-thirds.[4] Afghan and Turkish drug traffickers soon were busy smuggling opium into Iran. The borders soon resembled the American Wild West, with Iranian gendarmes frequently clashing with smugglers.

Despite halfhearted efforts on the parts of Afghan and Turkish governments for cooperation, the Iranian government increasingly fought a losing battle. Eventually, it was felt that the policy of banning poppy cultivation was a failure. In 1969, the Shah's regime once again allowed poppy cultivation. This time, however, poppy cultivation was to be carefully regulated, and the government was to distribute opium to addicts, who would be required to register. The certified addicts had to be sixty years of age. In tandem with these measures, new and more stringent penalties for traffickers were imposed, and programs were created to rehabilitate nonregistered addicts.

The partial legalization of opium was a failure. First and foremost, coupons given to registered addicts soon became the foundation of a new black market. large numbers of unentitled people soon had to access to state opium, a situation greatly assisted by official corruption. Second, the limited crop of opium left a lacuna in demand that continued to be met by Afghan, Pakistani, and Turkish opium contraband. Third, addiction rates began to rise again. In 1975, 169,512 persons were registered as opium addicts; those taking illicit narcotics ranged between 200,000 and 500,000. By 1979, it was estimated that between 500,000 and 700,000 Iranians, then about 1.5 percent of the population, were addicted.

When the Shah's government fell in 1979, the illicit narcotics trade initially benefited. Although the newly established Islamic Republic was strongly opposed to drug abuse, it was saddled with a plethora of challenges that demanded attention. The problem, therefore, was one of priorities. The Islamic Republic had to fight to gain control of the country from a multitude of forces, ranging from royalists to the Marxist Mujahedin-e Khalq. Additionally, Kurdish and Azeri separatists provided strong challenges in the northeast, while the seizure of the U.S. Embassy contributed to international isolation. It was in this realm of struggling to assert central authority that the Islamic Republic confronted the country's drug problems. The situation was further complicated by the outbreak of the Iran-Iraq War, which soon became a question of regime survival.

**Table 20.1**
**Iran's Opium Production: 1986–1990**

| Year | Metric Tons |
|---|---|
| 1986 | 200-400 |
| 1987 | 200-400 |
| 1988 | 200-400 |
| 1989 | 300 |
| 1990 | 200-400 |
| 1991E | 200-400 |

Source: U.S. Department of State, Bureau of International Narcotics Matters, International Narcotics Control Strategy Report, March 1991 (Washington, D.C.: Department of State, 1991), p. 215.

Iran entered the 1990s as one of the world's leading producers of opium, with an estimated half million addicts and ongoing transits of heroin, hashish, and opium from Afghanistan and Pakistan to the West. Table 20–1 provides data on Iran's opium production.

## POST-REVOLUTIONARY IRAN

The Islamic Republic's response to the drug problem has not achieved its goals. In 1980 Hojatoleslam Khalkhali was given the responsibility of eradicating the country's drug traffic. In shifting to an Islamic society after the revolution and basing its legal system on a severe moral code, numerous campaigns or crusades were conducted in Iran by the authorities in attempts to deal with what had become a visible internal crisis in the new republic. The drug problem in Iran was perceived by Iranian officials to have three dimensions requiring attention.

The first dimension was the problem of addiction. The monarchy left Iran with addicts possessing coupons exchangeable for rations of opium before the revolution. The new government decided it would not continue distributing opium to registered addicts. A second dimension of the drug problem in Iran was felt to be the problem of illegal trafficking of drugs within Iran's cities and national borders. Stories were frequently told of individuals who were selling drugs, either opium or heroin, in the alleys and streets of Iran's towns. The third dimension of the drug problem was identified as the problem of drugs transitting from Pakistan and Afghanistan through the Islamic Republic of Iran, intended for sales in other locations, but often being consumed in Iran. With the dimensions of the problem identified, Iranian officials responded with educational and medical programs before they criminalized drug use and implemented severe penalties both for the use of drugs and the distribution of drugs.

Official statements indicate that drug addiction increased after the revolution and afflicted all sectors of society with little discrimination in sex, age, or class. The size of the addiction problem presented the Islamic government with a major challenge, and, after a decade, efforts to control the spread of addiction have not been greatly successful. A ban on alcohol, increasing unemployment, and the breakdown of political control in the first years of the Islamic revolution were seen as significant factors contributing to an increase in drug smuggling.[5] During the eight-year war with Iraq, drug abuse was reported to have risen alarmingly.

In an article appearing in the Teheran newspaper *Keyhan* in September 1980, Hojatoleslam Khalkhali's crusade against narcotics, an antidrug and antiaddiction program, was explained. The antiaddiction crusade of the Ministry of Health offered to all addicts fifty years and older, who had not yet used government treatment services, a program to break their addiction, including free hospitalization and treatment. This offer of treatment, made for six months, terminated on September 22, 1980. The supervisor of the central coordinating staff of the antiaddiction campaign admitted that those seeking treatment were finally not hospitalized, but were given medicine. As of March 20, 1981 (the Iranian New Year), if someone was an addict he or she would be considered a criminal and had to expect punishment. As late as 1989 news services noted that whole villages, especially on the eastern drug routes from Pakistan and Afghanistan, were addicted to drugs. In cities, heroin was reported to be very easily purchased.

Drastic measures seemed to signal the failure of previous efforts to wipe out a growing addiction problem. Khalkhali stated in 1980 that he did not believe in medical rehabilitation, or in treating drug addicts with drugs.[6] Medical specialists at the Ministry of Health believed in the physical and mental treatment of addicts. The chief of the antinarcotics crusade was quoted as saying: "The environment in which an addict breaks his habit must be a restricted environment, such as a camp or even a prison, not connected with any place4."[7] This point of view also included putting an addict to work rebuilding damaged roads or farming to keep the addict under control while breaking his or her habit. By the end of the decade (1989), an Islamic revolutionary commander, Serajeddin Mousavi, was quoted as saying: "From now on we [Iranian officials] will not deal with drug addicts as miserable persons, but rather as enemy infiltrators in society."[8]

Under the law that became effective on January 1989, addiction to narcotic drugs became a criminal offense in Iran, and alleged addicts were sent to special labor camps in remote areas until cured. Later that same year, reports surfaced that as many as 55,000 drug addicts at one time were rounded up to be sent to labor camps in several provinces. An additional 150,000 registered drug addicts were soon to follow.[9] Numerous reports in the world news services gave repeated accounts of roundups of people alleged to be addicts who were sent to labor camps. Other sources claimed that addicts interned in labor camps were used to mine the traditional eastern border drug routes of Iran.

The difference of opinion about the treatment of addicts and traffickers expressed in the Islamic Republic during the early 1980s foreshadowed a law that was passed at the end of the decade. On December 5, 1988, the Expediency

Council, established by Ayatollah Khomeini to speed up legislation snarled in Iran's bureaucracy, announced a new law which took effect on January 1, 1989. Under the new legislation, addiction became an offense punishable by internment in a labor camp until cured. Addicts were told to register with the government to receive help or face criminal penalties. Any drug trafficker caught in possession of thirty grams of heroin, morphine, cocaine, hashish, or chemical derivatives of morphine or with five kilograms of opium would be sentenced to death and his property confiscated. Drug smugglers would be tried immediately after their arrest and would be executed within fifteen days if convicted. Any person found guilty of addicting another would be sentenced to a minimum of twenty years' imprisonment. Civil servants caught with any amount of heroin would be dismissed from government service for life and face other punishments.[10]

Law enforcement measures and operations directed against narcotics traffickers after the passage of the January 1989 law were also reported together with measures taken against insurgents. Members of the Iranian opposition living outside of the country asserted in 1989 that several hundred individuals executed for violating the nation's drug law were actually already in jail for political charges such as favoring a secular government over the ruling clergy and plotting to overthrow the government of Iran.[11] Although Iranian officials denied these charges, suspicions of Iranians persist.

In efforts aimed at eliminating the distribution of drugs within Iran and the transit of drugs through Iran, Khalkhali's special crusading group against narcotics—together with the municipal police, Islamic Revolutionary Guards (IRG), and the Gendarmerie of the Islamic Republic—waged campaigns against smugglers throughout the 1980s.[12] Even the Iranian Air Force gave occasional support.

In combatting the trafficking of drugs in Iran, major law enforcement efforts have been concentrated along the eastern border. During the early 1980s the chief of the Office of the Anti-Narcotics Crusade was quoted as saying that the crusade was effective against drug distribution and that, owing to great fear on the part of smugglers, narcotics had decreased. "A number of the big smugglers were executed, a number have fled or are in hiding. The only smugglers that are active at the present moment are border smugglers. This is because the borders are open and are not watched. Surveillance is nearly zero."[13] The chief of the Office of Anti-Narcotics Crusade went on to add that approximately 80 percent of the narcotics problem at that time arose from the openness of the borders. In 1988 there were reports of the IRG's battling with large gangs of alleged drug smugglers in the Iranian desert and border areas—both sides used machine guns and rocket-propelled grenades. In several operations, helicopter gunships of the army airborne division were called out to assist the IRG.

Due to the self-imposed isolation of Iran, reports of drug seizures and arrests of traffickers cannot be verified. According to official statistics, as reported by the Iranian news services, during 1989 the IRG alone found and seized a total of 38 metric tons of drugs, and arrested over 19,000 drug traffickers. The IRG alone reportedly opened 940 centers throughout the country from which they fight the drug problem. Other reports have attributed numerous operations, seizures, and arrests to the Gendarmerie.[14]

During the 1980s in Iran, heroin use became more widespread among addicts. Some estimates indicate that heroin use rivaled the use of opium, which had been used by the upper class as well as the lower classes during the reign of the Pahlavis. In addition to the use of heroin and opium, seizures of hashish were reported. The U.S. Department of State estimated in its March 1990 *International Narcotics Control Strategy Report* that Iran may have as many as 2 million users of heroin and an unknown number of opium users. In the early 1980s, Khalkhali guessed that there were more than 2 million addicts in the country. Iranian government agencies admit that it is not possible to get exact statistics.[15]

Most of the drug addicts in Iran are men. They range in age, with an older age group linked to opium smoking. Although many became addicted to drugs during the years of the Shah's regime, a younger generation of addicts appears to have evolved. Anecdotal evidence also indicates that by the early 1990s it has become more difficult to buy drugs outside of the major urban areas.

One of the key agencies in the Islamic Republic's struggle against the illicit drug trade is the Office for Propagation of Virtues and Prevention of Sins. Established shortly after the fall of the Shah, its mandate is to eradicate moral degeneracy. The initial targets were prostitution and drugs. As to the former, Teheran's red-light district was torn down in May 1980; approximately 1,000 prostitutes were "rehabilitated." The drug problem has been tackled by ongoing propaganda about the ills of drug use.

Government agencies with drug-enforcement responsibilities prior to the 1979 revolution were the Gendarmerie and the National Police. Both agencies worked under the Ministry of the Interior. The Gendarmerie was a police force with jurisdiction in towns and villages with populations of less than 5,000 people. The National Police were also responsible for such matters as passport procedures and the issuance of identity cards and drivers' licenses. Since the revolution, both agencies have undergone complete reorganizations according to Islamic guidelines. The Gendarmerie was purged of five colonels and its commander, who was executed in late summer 1980. Some areas of responsibility, which fell under the jurisdiction of the National Police, were absorbed by the IRG.[16]

The IRG was not formed specifically to carry out drug-enforcement operations in Iran but has undergone changes in its mission during the tumultuous 1980s. Ayatollah Khomeini created the IRG, or Pasdaran, by decree on May 5, 1979. Formed to oppose counterrevolutionary threats from leftist elements in Iran or from loyalists to the former regime, the Pasdaran assisted the ruling clergy in the daily enforcement of Islamic codes and morality. The Iranian constitution provides for the defense of Iran's territory and independence by the military and gives the responsibility of preserving the revolution to the Pasdaran. This in turn gave the new regime an armed basis of support. Today, Islamic revolutionary committees, called *komitehs*, are police stations or centers located in the cities of Iran, and the Pasdaran work in the *komitehs*.[17] In June 1990, the Iranian

Parliament passed a bill merging the Islamic revolutionary *komitehs* with the police and Gendarmerie to create a strong force with which to fight drug traffickers.[18]

Iran is not regarded as a major money-laundering center. The country's banking system has undergone considerable changes since the revolution in 1979. The Islamic Republic now presides over a nationalized banking system, largely consolidated into nine banks. The regulatory environment is guided by the tenets of Islamic banking, which do not allow the collection of interest (regarded as a form of usury). Tight foreign exchange laws were imposed in 1987 to dampen the flight of capital, protecting the country's foreign exchange reserves. Although money laundering of drug profits under these conditions is not impossible, it is doubtful that large-scale operations are active. Simply stated, drug traffickers can find other, easier places to launder their profits than in the Islamic Republic.

Government authorities claim that drugs enter their country from Afghanistan, Pakistan, and the Soviet Union but add that, in Iran, the cultivation of poppies for the production of opium has stopped.[19] Although the cultivation of poppies was officially banned in Iran in 1989, opium from the Helmand province of Afghanistan has long been a major source of supply for Iranian addicts.[20] In the *International Narcotics Control Strategy Report*, published in March 1991 by the U.S. Department of State, it was noted that the production of opium in Afghanistan has declined sharply since 1988. It has recently been thought, however, that, despite the ban on poppy cultivation, this activity may have increased in the last few years in the remote areas of Iran.[21]

As of early 1991, the Iranian newspaper *Keyhan* reported hat Iranian security forces were taking new measures to check the flow of narcotics coming from Afghanistan and Pakistan. With the passage of the new law, Iran launched a campaign against insurgents and narcotics traffickers in the southeastern province of Baluchestan, bordering Pakistan. Clashes between security forces and gunmen reportedly occurred in that area when enforcement efforts were stepped up. Another measured called for the uprooting of border villages and moving them farther inland to deprive traffickers of shelters. It was unknown how many border villages were to be relocated.[22]

## INTERNATIONAL LINKAGES

Iran's relations with its neighbors in terms of drug control have been complicated by war with Iraq and apprehension about the Soviet occupation of Afghanistan in the 1980s. There has been some cooperation with Pakistan. The estimated 200 to 400 metric tons of opium produced in Iran is not felt to be adequate to meet local demand, which continues to leave the door open to Afghan and Pakistani opium and heroin.

Relations with Pakistan and Turkey have improved in the late 1980s and early 1990s, opening the door to greater cooperation in regional narcotics control. Teheran is the headquarters of the Economic Cooperation Organization (ECO), which has three members: Iran, Pakistan, and Turkey. The ECO's purpose ultimately is to create a free market founded upon the three countries' joint population of 220 million and foreign trade turnover of more than $70 billion.[23] A meeting was held in June 1990, which was attended by the foreign ministers of the three nations. The movement toward an ECO free-trade area is a positive one for regional economic integration; however, although an ECO free-trade area will help facilitate quicker movement of goods, it will also heighten the prospects for easier transitting of illicit narcotics and will necessitate better regional enforcement.

Relations with the Soviet Union and its successor states have improved markedly since the Soviet troop withdrawal from Afghanistan in February 1989. This clearly addressed one of Teheran's most persistent grievances vis-à-vis its northern neighbor. When Azeris in the Soviet Union created considerable political turmoil in 1990, especially in the region along the northern border, the Rafsanjani government did not fall prey to some of those who felt moral support and weapons should have been provided to their coreligionists. Considering the growing linkages in trade between the two countries, the Iranians and Soviets also share concerns about the region's narcotics trade. The Soviet Union is acknowledging the spread of drug use and the transitting of narcotics. In the future, it is possible that this will be a key area of joint action.

Relations with the United States in terms of antidrug efforts are not positive. Iran was denied certification in 1989 and 1990 because of its lack of cooperation with U.S. authorities. Considering disagreement over other issues and deep mutual suspicion, the lack of cooperation in drug matters is not a surprise.

## CONCLUSION

The Islamic Republic of Iran's problems with narcotics use and trafficking are likely to continue into the medium term. However, the growing stability of the Islamic Republic and the improved state of relations with the successor states of the Soviet Union, Turkey, and Pakistan, and, to a lesser extent, with Afghanistan, holds out the possibility of greater cooperation in narcotics control on a regional basis. A key element is the maturing of the Islamic Republic, which entails a movement back into the mainstream of international relations. This provides new options for cooperation in combatting a problem that extends beyond the country's frontiers. The Islamic Republic's internal policies vis-à-vis drug abuse will also be affected by the level of regional cooperation.

## NOTES

1. Dilip Hiro, "Iran in the 1990s," *Middle East Insight* 7, 5 (1990): 45.

2. William H. Forbis, *Fall of the Peacock Throne: The Story of Iran* (New York: Harper and Row Publishers, 1980), 178.

3. Ibid, 179.

4. "Results of Anti-Narcotic Efforts Reviewed," *Keyhan* (Teheran), 10 September 1980, 5.

5. "Seventeen Hanged as Iranians Intensify Drive against Drugs," *New York Times*, 8 January 1989, 28.

6. Ibid.

7. Ibid.

8. "Iran's Drug Addicts Take Last Legal Fix," *Reuter Library Report*, 22 July 1989.

9. "Iran Rounds up 55,000 Addicts to be Confined in Labor Camps," *Chicago Tribune*, 23 July 1989, 21.

10. "Iran in Brief: Anti-Drug Law Goes into Effect," British Broadcasting Corporation, Summary of World Broadcasts, 23 January 1989.

11. "Iran Puts Addicts in Its Labor Camps," *New York Times*, 22 July 1989, 8.

12. "Results of Anti-Narcotic Efforts Reviewed," 5.

13. Ibid.

14. "Islamic Republic Implementing a Harsher Anti-Drug Effort," *Iran Times Newspaper Archives*, March 1989, 4–6.

15. "Results of Anti-Narcotic Efforts Reviewed," 5.

16. *Iran, A Country Study: Area Handbook* (Washington, D.C.: Library of Congress, 1978), 290.

17. Ibid, 267–71.

18. "Iran: Security Force to Merge with Two Units," *Los Angeles Times*, 11 June 1990, 21.

19. U.S. Department of State, Bureau of International Narcotics Matters, *International Narcotics Control Strategy Report* (Washington, D.C.: U.S. Department of State, March 1991), 213.

20. "Iran Still Pumping out Lots of Opium," *Iran Times Newspaper*, 8 March 1991, 15.

21. Ibid.

22. "Iran Rounds up 5,400 in Anti-Drug Sweep," United Press International, 28 February 1990.

23. Salamat Ali, "Pakistan, Turkey, Iran Revive Economic Organisation," *Far Eastern Economic Review*, 5 July 1990, 24.

## BIBLIOGRAPHY

Ali, Salamat. "Pakistan, Turkey, Iran Revive Economic Organisation." *Far Eastern Economic Review*, 5 July 1990, 22–25.

Arjomand, Said Amir. *The Turban for the Crown: The Islamic Revolution*. New York: Oxford University Press, 1988.

Daneshkhu, Scheherazade. "Iran Fails to Foil Its Money Changers." *Financial Times*, 26 July 1990, 4.

Forbis, William H. *Fall of the Peacock Throne: The Story of Iran*. New York: Harper and Row Publishers, 1980.

Hiro, Dilip. "Iran in the 1990s." *Middle East Insight* 7, 5 (1990) 44–46.

———. *Iran under the Ayatollahs*. London: Routledge and Kegan Paul, 1987.

Hunter, Shireen T. "Iran and the Soviets: The Chill Is Gone." *Middle East Insight* 7, 1 (1990): 17–23.

Keddie, Nikki R. *Roots of Revolution: An Interpretive History of Modern Iran*. New Haven, Conn.: Yale University Press, 1981.

McLaughlin, Gerald T. ''The Poppy Is Not an Ordinary Flower: A Survey of Drug Policy in Iran.'' *Fordham Law Review* 44, 4 (March 1976): 701–72.

McMorris, David D. ''Demographic Setting and Education.'' In *Iran: A County Study: Area Handbook*. Washington, D.C.: Library of Congress, 1978.

U.S. Department of State, Bureau of International Narcotics Matters. *International Narcotics Control Strategy Report*. Washington, D.C.: U.S. Department of State, March 1990.

World Bank. *World Development Report 1990*. New York: Oxford University Press, 1990.

# 21

# Pakistan

SUSAN S. HARDESTY

## INTRODUCTION

Pakistan in the last dozen years has been rocked by the upheaval of its neighbors, beginning with two key events in 1979. Both the Islamic revolution in Iran and the Soviet invasion of Afghanistan have had profound effects on the political and social fabric of Pakistan. The war in Afghanistan, as well as the eight-year Iran-Iraq war (1980–1988) created chaos in the region and made Pakistan's antidrug efforts an exercise in swimming against the tide. Internal Pakistani politics were in flux during the 1980s with the transition from a military to a civilian government and the assassination of President Mohammed Zia ul-Haq in 1988 in a midair plane explosion. The election in 1988 of Prime Minister Benazir Bhutto was followed by her dismissal in 1990 by President Ghulam Ishaq Khan, amid corruption charges made by her opponents, and the return of a conservative ruling party supported by the military under Prime Minister Nawaz Sharif.

Pakistan's roles in the world drug trade are as a major processing and transshipping center for heroin and as a significant supplier of opium and hashish. Pakistan has long been a source of hashish (the second largest source after Lebanon), but Pakistan has emerged as a major supplier of opium only in the last thirty-five years. However, Pakistan's opium contribution is dwarfed by the opium produced in Afghanistan and Iran. Over the past five years, Pakistan has produced roughly 16 percent of the Southwest Asian heroin.[1] The larger role for Pakistan has been its clandestine laboratories and its rugged, inaccessible smuggling routes along its western border. Most of the Southwest Asian heroin is refined in or shipped through Pakistan.[2] The heroin produced in Southwest Asia represents a large share of the heroin consumed in the United States, varying from 52 percent in 1982 to 25 percent by the end of the decade.[3]

## BACKGROUND

Pakistan, a bit larger than the state of Texas, is ringed by Iran to the west, Afghanistan to the north, China and the territory disputed with India, Kashmir, to the northeast, India to the east, and the Arabian Sea to the south. Pakistan shares with Afghanistan a rugged boundary in the Hindu Kush mountains, a continuation of the eastern Himalayas. To the south and east lie the plains of the Indus River Valley, which make up about a third of the country and contain Pakistan's most populated areas and richest agricultural lands. This area boasts one of the world's longest irrigation systems. In the east is the Thar Desert, and in the southwest is the arid Baluchistan Plateau, which borders Iran, a region characterized by ranges of low mountains and hills.

The area that is now Pakistan has given rise to a half a dozen ancient civilizations and cultures. Pakistan, which has a population of 114 million people, has a diverse ethnic makeup which reflects the history of the invasion and settlement of the Indian subcontinent. An estimated three million Afghan refugees came to Pakistan during the 1980s. Punjabis constitute the largest ethnic group, approximately 66 percent of the population; the Pushtus, 8.5 percent. The Sindhis account for 13 percent of the total population, but also for a majority in the Sind province of the lower Indus Plain, one of the four provinces in Pakistan, along with Baluchistan, the Punjab, and the Northwest Frontier Province (NWFP). The NWFP, which includes federally administered but politically autonomous tribal areas, is home to the Pushtu (also known as the Pathan), who inhabit both sides of the Pakistani-Afghan border.

Although English is spoken for business and government, Urdu is the official language. Regional languages include Punjabi, Sindhi, Pushto, Baluchi, Brahvi, and Hindko, among many others. The raison d'être for the separation of Pakistan from India in 1947 (then known as East Pakistan with what became Bangladesh in 1972 as West Pakistan) was to provide a separate state for Moslems from the predominantly Hindu India. Therefore 97 percent of Pakistanis are Moslems, the majority of which are Sunni; economically significant minorities (Ismailis, Memons, and Bohras) are Shi'a Moslems, which are most strongly represented in the Sind Province.

Pakistan's economy is based on agriculture; the main crops are rice, wheat, cotton, and tobacco. Pakistan reports that agriculture, including processed agricultural products, makes up 23 percent of the gross domestic product (GDP), employs 50 percent of the labor force, and makes 70 percent of export earnings. Pakistan is pushing industrialization, especially in heavy industries, and reports that industry contributes 18 percent to the GDP and employs 13.4 percent of the labor force.[4] Industries include textiles, food processing, chemicals, leather products, carpets, sporting goods, surgical appliances, engineering goods, and petroleum products. Natural resources include natural gas, iron ore, rock salt, and some crude oil reserves. In 1988 Pakistan's gross national product was $39.4 billion and per capita income was $370, with a real growth rate of 4.9 percent.[5]

Major trading partners include Saudi Arabia, Japan, the United States, the United Kingdom, West Germany, China, and Kuwait (before the Gulf War).

Before Pakistan became a separate nation in 1947, opium was supplied by the Opium Monopoly of British India.[6] Upon independence, Pakistan set up its own licensing monopoly but still imported opium from India, producing only 10 metric tons per year itself. Domestic production did not begin to increase until 1955, when India ratified the 1953 Opium Protocol and ceased exporting opium to Pakistan. Licensed cultivation increased, and unlicensed cultivation began. Pakistani opium then began to be exported to Iran and Afghanistan. In 1971–1972, the reduction of opium production in Turkey provided the impetus for a major increase in Pakistani production. Some of the same characters out of business in Turkey in the French Connection turned up in Pakistan looking for a new source of opium. Beginning in 1975 heroin processing labs were being set up along the Afghan-Pakistani border in the Northwest Frontier Province, an area known for its traditional smuggling routes. Its inaccessible mountain reaches provide an ideal area for poppy cultivation and clandestine, mobile heroin laboratories. High opium prices in 1978 resulted in a record opium crop in the 1978–1979 growing season. Falling prices, bad weather, and efforts by Pakistan and the international community have reduced Pakistan's opium cultivation since 1978. Since the pinnacle, opium cultivation figures have imitated a roller coaster, depending on weather and law enforcement. The number of hectares cultivated jumped 300 percent from 1984 to 1988, but are expected to reach only half the 1988 level in 1991.[7] However, processing of opium into heroin has increased in Pakistan. The turmoil in Afghanistan after the Soviet invasion led to increased poppy cultivation there. Afghan poppy is processed in the labs across the border in Pakistan, along with Pakistani poppy. With the continued civil strife in Afghanistan, since the Soviet pullout, poppy cultivation is expected to continue at high levels in Afghanistan, making it very likely that processing in Pakistan will also continue.

## STRUCTURE OF THE NARCOTICS INDUSTRY

A major impediment to halting opium cultivation in Pakistan is the lack of political control the government of Pakistan exercises in portions of the NWFP. The legally autonomous tribes straddle the Pakistani-Afghan border. Many tribes have been involved in smuggling various contraband items, not necessarily drugs, for centuries over traditional routes. The tribes in this region are legendary for their ability to produce counterfeit copies of anything from furniture to weapons. The government of Pakistan urges and cajoles tribal leaders to ban the growing of poppies, but it has few options to enforce a ban in such a remote, relatively inaccessible region. In fact, government control and a poppy growing ban have been established in areas where development projects have begun, especially those that have included the building of new roads. However, even when roads are built, some areas continue to be politically inaccessible. Because of past efforts by the government of Pakistan, opium cultivation had shifted from traditional areas outside the NWFP to the tribal areas of Khyber, Bajaur, Mohmand, Malakand, Swat, Gadoon, and the Dir Districts in the Northwest Frontier Province. Many of these areas, or portions of them, have come under the poppy ban in recent years, but their adherence to the ban depends on continued enforcement and successful alternative development.

While Pakistani opium cultivation is a major source of opium for heroin processing, the contribution of Afghanistan and Iran is much greater. However, almost all of the Southwest Asian opium, including the opium from both Pakistan and Afghanistan, is processed into heroin in the approximately 100 clandestine laboratories (some estimates are as high as 200 laboratories) in the Khyber Agency, the remote areas of Mohmand, and Baluchistan. Therefore, processing and transshipment of opium and heroin are Pakistan's greater contribution to world heroin supply.

Many smugglers who were once known for supplying hashish, now smuggle heroin. Southwest Asian heroin processed in Pakistan is smuggled across Afghanistan, Iran, and Turkey to Western Europe in sealed trucks (transport international Rotier or TIR) along the Balkan route. Such trucks are allowed to pass through several countries under a customs seal and are not inspected until the final destination. This trafficking is dominated by Turkish and Iranian organizations.[8] Another major smuggling route is across the Pakistani-Indian border.[9] Heroin and hashish are also smuggled by international trafficking organizations based in Karachi in boats called dhows across the Arabian Sea to the United Arab Emirates en route to Europe and the United States. In the late 1980s Pakistan began to be flooded with Nigerian couriers who carried small amounts of heroin concealed in body cavities, or in craft items, or in auto parts. Other couriers have employed a wide array of concealment methods. Heroin is also shipped through the international mail system in cargo as varied as magazines, fruit, religious artifacts, and many other items.

Corruption among Pakistani authorities is blamed for the lack of progress in closing down laboratories and in stopping major traffickers. Poorly paid police officers are susceptible to bribes, and more senior enforcement officials reportedly receive protection money from major traffickers.[10] Some have charged that Pakistan has a situation similar to Panama's under Manuel Noriega, where drug trafficking was sanctioned and even conducted by the military. Frontier guards, army officers, and members of Pakistan's military intelligence agency, Inter-Services Intelligence, are allegedly involved themselves in trafficking as well as protecting drug traffickers.[11] A Congressional study termed major traffickers "untouchable," with policemen at the bottom of a caste system featuring the drug traffickers at the top.[12] In 1990 two alleged drug traffickers from the NWFP were elected by tribal councils as representatives in the National Assembly.

Pakistan is not a large center for money laundering. In fact, it is nearly impossible to ascertain how much drug money is in Pakistan because of the use of black and informal markets. Some estimate that there are large sums of money from the drug trade in the informal markets, but it is generally believed that major traffickers keep their funds overseas.

## GOVERNMENT RESPONSE

Pakistan's response to the drug situation has been mixed. Pakistan has taken many tough steps to reduce poppy cultivation, but its efforts to move against the heroin laboratories and major traffickers leave much to be desired. Pakistan ratified the 1953 Opium Protocol and the 1961 Single Convention on Narcotic Drugs. On February 10, 1979, the government of Pakistan issued the Enforcement of Hadd order prohibiting opium cultivation and bringing drug laws into conformity with Islam, which prohibits any intoxication. The law bans production, possession, processing, manufacture, sale, and use of all intoxicant drugs. The poppy ban was intended to be enforced in phases, with the ban being applied gradually as development projects were introduced into poppy growing areas.[13] In 1983 Pakistan strengthened its narcotics laws and penalties and passed asset seizure laws in 1985.[14] In 1988 Pakistan and the United States signed the Tribal Areas Agreement, which provided for U.S. development assistance in Bajaur and Mohmand Agencies and called for a gradual introduction of the ban on opium production over a five-year period.[15] Asserting control over the tribal areas has been difficult, but where new roads were built and government services extended, the Pakistani government has enforced the ban on poppy cultivation. In 1990 Pakistan was successful in maintaining the opium ban in Bajaur and Mohmand, Malakand, Swat, Gadoon, and the southern subdistricts of Dir. It extended the ban to the Panjkora Valley and in areas of Bajaur and Mohmand where the ban had not been enforced before. Also in 1990, Pakistan signed the 1988 United Nations Convention against Illicit Traffic in Narcotic Drugs and Psychotropic Substances, and it is drafting a strengthened asset seizure law. The government of Pakistan has also upgraded the Office of the Narcotics Control Division to the ministry level.[16] In 1989 Pakistan agreed to set up five elite antinarcotics investigative units to address the problem of poorly trained antinarcotics police officers. Two of the five units have been established but have not been put into action because authorizing legislation has not yet been passed.

The government of Pakistan has been less vigorous in closing down the clandestine heroin laboratories; only a handful are closed each year. The definition of "closing down" a laboratory is also in question, as this action may only entail turning in some equipment to the Tribal Jirags, or Committee of Elders, leaving the processor free to restart his laboratory a short time later. No chemicals, opium, or heroin need be turned in, nor must customers or supply sources be named. Repeat offenders may be forced to pay a moderate fine.[17]

As mentioned above, government officials have been accused of corruption and of abetting drug trafficking, with the result that few large seizures are made. However, in October 1990, members of the Frontier Corps made the largest single drug seizure ever made—two tons of high-quality heroin worth about $500 million. The response of the Pakistani government to this seizure was less than enthusiastic, lending credence to charges of government collusion. The seizure was kept secret for weeks, and the chief of the Frontier Corps was transferred from his post.[18] The U.S. Drug Enforcement Administration (DEA) has given the government of Pakistan lists of major drug traffickers, many of which could be found in accessible parts of Pakistan, but few have been arrested. The United States had long sought extradition of a number of traffickers from Pakistan to the United States, to no avail. However one trafficker, Malik Saleem, was extradited in May 1989 on hashish trafficking charges in Miami, Florida, and is now imprisoned in the United States.[19] Other U.S. extradition requests are pending.

## SOCIETAL REACTION

The Pakistan Narcotics Control Board estimates that Pakistan now has over 2 million drug addicts, 1.2 million of whom are addicted to heroin. The U.S. Department of State estimated that there were more than 1 million users of heroin in Pakistan in 1990. The distinction between addicts and users is an important one in Pakistan, an area where drugs traditionally have been easily available. While heroin addiction is clearly a growing problem that was nonexistent in Pakistan as recently as 1980, some skeptics have cautioned that the figures on Pakistani addicts appear inflated. They point out that it is in the interest of Pakistan to have the world community believe that Pakistani heroin is consumed domestically and is not a source of supply for the West in order, at the same time, to attract donor funds for treatment and education projects. Pakistan reports that there are thirty drug treatment centers available with both inpatient and outpatient programs.[20] Demand reduction programs to educate the public about the dangers of drugs were begun, particularly under Prime Minister Benazir Bhutto's government.

## INTERNATIONAL LINKAGES OF DRUG CONTROL

International efforts for drug control have been carried out by the United Nations Fund for Drug Abuse Control (UNFDAC). UNFDAC began in 1971 as a trust fund to finance, coordinate, plan, and evaluate narcotics-control efforts around the world. UNFDAC's Buner Agricultural Development Project, begun in 1976 in the Buner subdivision of the Swat District, was the first major poppy control project undertaken in Pakistan. The project used a crop substitution policy based on voluntary participation. Its limited success highlighted the need for the enforcement of the poppy ban in development projects.[21] UNFDAC is funding several projects in Pakistan, including a development project in the Dir District, and a demand reduction project aimed at developing antinarcotics efforts at the community level. The Dir project has been heavily criticized as a mismanaged affair with little impact on reducing poppy cultivation.[22] In December 1990 the

UN General Assembly voted to restructure the UN groups working on drug issues and integrated UNFDAC with the Division of Narcotic Drugs and the International Narcotics Control Board.

The United States contributes money to UNFDAC and also directly sponsors numerous projects in Pakistan. U.S. efforts are handled by three agencies: the State Department's Bureau of International Narcotics Matters (INM), the Agency for International Development (AID), and the DEA.[23] INM's goal to control narcotic supply in source countries by crop eradication and national bans on cultivation of narcotic plants. Economic development of the host country is not the focus of this strategy, but it may encourage development as a secondary result. INM funded two projects in the early 1980s: the Agricultural Outreach Project and the Malakand Area Development Project. Both aimed at the suppression of poppy cultivation, with infrastructure development, but without efforts to develop alternative income sources for farmers growing poppy. INM has also funded projects in Bajaur and Mohmand focusing on road building to extend the authority of the Pakistani government. INM is currently considering a similar project in the Khyber Agency, which is the only major poppy growing area without a development project.[24]

AID's primary focus is on economic development. AID has used a number of approaches to narcotics control in its projects in Pakistan. Whether or not projects were directly related to narcotics reduction, it has inserted "poppy clauses" into its project agreements, requiring denial of benefits to poppy growing farmers and village communities. AID had inserted poppy clauses into more than a dozen projects begun in the early 1980s. It has funded several major crop substitution and integrated rural development projects in Pakistan, including the Tribal Areas Development Project and the Northwest Frontier Area Development Project. Both contain numerous subprojects. Finally, AID has started public education programs for demand reduction.

In March 1986, following the transition from military to civilian rule and a concomitant surge in poppy cultivation, government eradication efforts were met with violent resistance, and the Pakistani government became less willing to eradicate the poppy crops.[25] This experience has pointed out the need for government enforcement to avoid undercutting the goals of INM's and AID's projects.

DEA's role is to provide expertise, training, and technical assistance to Pakistani law enforcement officials. It provides no funding to Pakistan for projects as do INM and AID. DEA assists in investigations and helps the Pakistani government develop programs to eradicate narcotic crops, to locate clandestine laboratories and export routes, and to interdict drug shipments. DEA has conducted its own "controlled delivery investigations," in which traffickers are set up and arrested outside of Pakistan, in countries where prosecution is more likely to take place. Several Pakistani traffickers have thus been arrested in the United States and in Saudi Arabia. DEA opened its first office in Pakistan in 1972 and now has fifteen agents with offices in Karachi, Islamabad, Lahore, and Peshawar. DEA continues to do its own survey to ascertain the size of the poppy crop, since, as noted earlier, many estimates tend to be inaccurate, optimistic, or a political exercise.[26]

Despite DEA's success with the controlled delivery investigations, and some large heroin seizures, DEA operations in Pakistan have often been frustrating for the agents. Legal procedures are ill-defined in Pakistan, and law enforcement techniques are hampered by difficulty in obtaining information that would be simple to find in the United States, such as an arrest record. DEA has provided the Pakistanis with long lists of major traffickers and locations of heroin labs. The results have been disappointing, with few major traffickers arrested and even fewer sentenced. As noted previously, the small number of laboratories reportedly closed down is a meaningless figure as the operators merely turn in some supplies and can resume business in short order.

The United States' efforts and interests in providing Pakistan with economic and military aid have been stymied and tempered by other aspects of U.S. policy toward Pakistan. The United States has long been concerned about the prospect of Pakistan's acquiring nuclear weapons capability, especially given the history of Indian-Pakistani disputes and in light of India's membership in the nuclear "club" in 1974. In 1979 the United States cut off economic and military aid to Pakistan under the provisions of the Symington amendment (PL 94–329), prohibiting foreign aid to countries taking steps to build nuclear weapons, because of Pakistan's efforts to acquire technology to enrich uranium. However, U.S. interests in augmenting then-President Zia's support of the Afghan rebels in resisting the Soviet invasion put nonproliferations objectives on the back burner. Pakistan became the base for Afghan resistance, as well as the base of operations for U.S. covert aid to the rebels. It was in this context that President Zia rejected President Carter's aid offer in 1980, calling it "peanuts." In 1982 President Reagan waived the aid cutoff. The U.S. policy of supporting Pakistan because of its role in assisting Afghan rebels reportedly resulted in a disinclination to investigate reports of heroin trafficking by the very Afghan rebels it was supporting, as well as by Pakistani military officers, and by members of Pakistan's military intelligence agency, Inter-Services Intelligence.[27]

The president of the United States is required to certify that Pakistan does not possess a nuclear device and that U.S. aid will reduce the risk of their acquiring one under the Foreign Assistance Act (PL 99–83) passed in 1985.[28] Evidence mounted that Pakistan, aided by China, was pushing ahead with its nuclear program in a revealing conviction in U.S. courts of a Pakistani involved in illegally exporting to Pakistan U.S. metals that are needed to produce nuclear weapons.[29] In October 1990, with the Soviet troops gone from Afghanistan and such convincing evidence of a Pakistani push to develop a nuclear capability, President Bush failed to make this certification, once again freezing aid to Pakistan.[30] However, the president did certify, under the Anti-Drug Abuse Act (PL 99–570 and PL 100–890), that Pakistan was cooperating with the United States and was taking steps on its own toward preventing illicit drug production, trafficking, and money laundering. This certification will allow INM and AID programs related to drug reduction to go forward. DEA is unaffected by the aid freeze because it does not provide funding to Pakistan. The exact breakdown of projects affected by the conflicting policies was not yet available.

The U.S.–led Gulf War against Iraq also led to strains in the U.S.–Pakistani relationship. Although Pakistan sent the fourth largest group of Moslem troops, popular sentiment toward Iraqi President Saddam Hussein led the Pakistani government to insist that their soldiers be used to protect Moslem holy sites, away from direct conflict with Iraq.[31]

## CONCLUSION

Pakistan should be given credit for reducing the size of its domestic poppy crop and for its efforts to prevent the return of poppy crops in areas where it had been banned. There has been no return to the record crop of 1978. Still, Pakistan could do a much better job of closing heroin laboratories, arresting major traffickers, and enforcing the poppy ban throughout the country. While that would surely have a positive impact on the worldwide heroin situation, its magnitude is unclear. Even if Pakistan were to close down all of the estimated 100 heroin laboratories, a significant portion of the processing would likely move across the border into the chaotic situation in Afghanistan. Restoration of order and assertion of government control in Afghanistan would do much to stem the tide of the opium coming into Pakistan, but is is unlikely that civil strife in Afghanistan will end soon. It is also unlikely that Pakistan will muster the political courage to close the laboratories and arrest the major traffickers, which leaves a bleak outlook for improvement in the Southwest Asian heroin situation in the near future.

Given this poor prognosis, it appears to be an inopportune time for the United States to weaken its economic support for Pakistan. Pakistan is the only one of the three major Southwest Asian opium suppliers with which the United States can work to control heroin supplies at all; it has no leverage at all with Afghanistan or Iran. The United States has an interest in supporting the reductions in cultivation that have taken place in Pakistan and in helping to prevent a massive increase in poppy cultivation. Preserving the progress achieved in Pakistan is an important policy goal, while the United States waits for the opportunity to curtail opium production in the rest of Southwest Asia. Evaluations of projects in Pakistan cited those projects that had long-term economic development as their focus on those most successful in preventing the return to poppy cultivation. Those that merely relied on crop substitution with government enforcement of the poppy ban were more likely to be areas that would revert to poppy cultivation in the face of reduced government resolve. While the aid ban allows direct antinarcotics programs to continue, it may be reducing the programs that have proved the most successful in the past. In balancing its policy goals in Pakistan, the United States will have to consider whether its antinuclear proliferation strategy will be furthered as much as its antinarcotics efforts will be damaged by the aid cutoff.

## NOTES

1. This figure was calculated from data in U.S. Department of State, Bureau of International Narcotics Matters, *International Narcotics Control Strategy Report* (Washington, D.C.: U.S. Government Printing Office, March 1991).

2. U.S. Congress, House, Committee on Foreign Affairs, *U.S. Narcotics Control Programs Overseas: A Continuing Assessment*, Report of a Staff Study Mission to South America, the Mediterranean and the Middle East, and Southwest Asia, March 1986–January 1987 (Washington, D.C.: U.S. Government Printing Office, 1987). Hereafter referred to as Staff Assessment.

3. U.S. Department of Justice, Drug Enforcement Administration, *Worldwide Heroin Situation Report* (Washington, D.C.: U.S. Government Printing Office, January 1990), 42.

4. Embassy of Pakistan, Information Division, *Pakistan—A Profile* (Washington, D.C.: Government of Pakistan, 8.

5. *Information Please Almanac Atlas & Yearbook 1991*, 44th ed. (Boston: Houghton Mifflin Co., 1991), 242.

6. Information for this section was gathered from several sources including interviews with DEA agents formerly stationed in Pakistan; Krishna Kumar, Ernest Carter, and Stan Samuelson, *A Review of AID's Narcotics Control Development Assistance Program*, U.S. Agency for International Development, AID Evaluation Special Study no. 29 (Washington, D.C.: U.S. Government Printing Office, March 1986), Appendix B; and U.S. Department of State, *International Narcotics Control Strategy Report*.

7. Figures for production, yield, and eradication are notoriously inaccurate, often exercises in political posturing. Only the figure for hectares under cultivation is considered to be even somewhat accurate. However, even that can be misleading since aerial photographs sometimes have not been made because of the possibility of planes being shot down near the Afghan border—precisely the area where much of the poppy is grown.

8. Unless otherwise indicated, trafficking information found in U.S. Department of Justice, Worldwide Heroin Situation Report, 13–21.

9. U.S. Congress, House, Hearings before the Committee on Foreign Affairs, *Review of the 1990 International Narcotics Control Strategy Report, March 1, 6, 8, 13, and 15, 1990*.

10. U.S. General Accounting Office, *Drug Control, U.S. Supported Efforts in Burma, Pakistan, and Thailand*, GAO/NSIAD–88–94 (Washington, D.C.: U.S. Government Printing Office, February 1988), 29.

11. James Rupert and Steve Coll, "U.S. Declines to Probe Afghan Drug Trade, Rebels, Pakistani Officers Implicated," *Washington Post*, 13 March 1990, A19.

12. U.S. Congress, House, Staff Assessment, 29.

13. Kumar, Carter, and Samuelson, *A Review*, Appendix B.

14. Government of Pakistan, Ministry of Information and Broadcasting, *Pakistan Fights Narcotics Menace*, Islamabad, May 1989, 5.

15. National Narcotics Intelligence Consumers Committee, *The NNICC Report 1989,*

*The Supply of Illicit Drugs to the United States* (Washington, D.C.: U.S. Government Printing Office, June 1990), 52.

16. Robert C. Bonner, Administrator, Drug Enforcement Administration, U.S. Department of Justice, ''Statement before the Task Force on International Narcotics Control,'' Committee on Foreign Affairs, U.S. House of Representatives, 5 March 1991, 24.

17. National Narcotics Intelligence Consumers Committee, *NNICC Report*, 51.

18. Kamran, Khan, ''Pakistan Plays down Seizure of 2-Ton Heroin Cache, Observers Say Government's Handling of Case Indicates Collusion by Some Officials,'' *Washington Post*, 24 December 1990.

19. U.S. Congress, House, *Review of the 1990 International Narcotics Control Strategy Report*.

20. U.S. Department of State, *International Narcotics Control Strategy Report*, 224.

21. Kumar, Carter, and Samuelson, *A Review*, B–20, B–21.

22. U.S. Congress, House, *Review of the 1990 International Narcotics Control Strategy Report*, 249.

23. Unless otherwise indicated, information for this section was taken from Kumar, Carter, and Samuelson, *A Review*, and U.S. General Accounting Office, *Drug Control*.

24. U.S. Department of State, *International Narcotics Control Strategy Report*, 222–23.

25. U.S. Congress, House, Staff Assessment, 28.

26. For DEA's crop estimates see U.S. Department of Justice, *Worldwide Heroin Situation Report*.

27. Rupert and Coll, ''U.S. Declines.''

28. Pat Towell, ''Bhutto, on Visit, Moves to Ease U.S. Worries over Policies,'' *Congressional Quarterly Weekly Report*, 10 June 1989, 1415–16.

29. ''Foreign Aid Authorization Bill Stalls,'' *Congressional Quarterly Almanac* (1987): 168.

30. Carroll J. Doherty, ''Mideast Countries Top List in '92 Budget Request,'' *Congressional Quarterly Weekly Report*, 11 March 1991.

31. Steve Coll, ''Pakistan Seeking New Identity as Alliance with U.S. Falters,'' *Washington Post*, 8 February 1991.

## BIBLIOGRAPHY

Bonner, Robert C., Administrator, Drug Enforcement Administration, U.S. Department of Justice. ''Statement before the Task Force on International Narcotics Control, Committee on Foreign Affairs, U.S. House of Representatives,'' 5 March 1991.

Coll, Steve. ''Pakistan Seeking New Identity as Alliance with U.S. Falters.'' *Washington Post*, 8 February 1991.

Doherty, Carroll J. ''Mideast Countries Top List in '92 Budget Request.'' *Congressional Quarterly Weekly Report*, 11 March 1991.

Embassy of Pakistan, Information Division. *Pakistan—A Profile*. (Washington, D.C.: Government of Pakistan, 1989).

''Foreign Aid Authorization Bill Stalls.'' *Congressional Quarterly Almanac* (1987) 168.

Government of Pakistan, Ministry of Information and Broadcasting. *Pakistan Fights Narcotics Menace*, Islamabad, May 1989.

*Information Please Almanac Atlas & Yearbook 1991*, 44th ed. Boston: Houghton Mifflin Co., 1991.

Khan, Kamran. ''Pakistan Plays down Seizure of 2-Ton Heroin Cache, Observers Say Government's Handling of Case Indicates Collusion by Some Officials.'' Washington Post, 24 December 1990.

Kumar, Krishna, Ernest Carter, and Stan Samuelson. *A Review of AID's Narcotics Control Development Assistance Program*, U.S. Agency for International Development, AID Evaluation Special Study no. 29. Washington, D.C.: U.S. Government Printing Office, March 1986.

National Narcotics Intelligence Consumers Committee. *The NNICC Report 1989, The Supply of Illicit Drugs to the United States*. Washington, D.C.: U.S. Government Printing Office, June 1990.

Rupert, James, and Steve Coll. ''U.S. Declines to Probe Afghan Drug Trade, Rebels, Pakistani Officers Implicated.'' Washington Post, 13 March 1990.

Towell, Pat. ''Bhutto, on Visit, Moves to Ease U.S. Worries over Policies.'' *Congressional Quarterly Weekly Report*, 10 June 1989, 1415–16.

U.S. Congress, House. Committee on Foreign Affairs. *U.S. Narcotics Control Programs Overseas: A Continuing Assessment*. Report of a Staff Study Mission to South America, the Mediterranean and the Middle East, and Southwest Asia, March 1986–January 1987. Washington, D.C.: U.S. Government Printing Office, 1987.

U.S. Congress, House. Hearings before the Committee on Foreign Affairs. *Review of the 1990 International Narcotics Control Strategy Report, March 1, 6, 8, 13, and 15, 1990*.

U.S. Department of Justice, Drug Enforcement Administration. *Worldwide Heroin Situation Report*. Washington, D.C.: U.S. Government Printing Office, January 1990.

U.S. Department of State, Bureau of International Narcotics Matters. *International Narcotics Control Strategy Report*. Washington, D.C.: U.S. Government Printing Office, March 1991.

U.S. General Accounting Office. *Drug Control, U.S. Supported Efforts in Burma, Pakistan, and Thailand*, GAO/NSIAD–88–94. Washington, D.C., February 1988.

# 22

# Turkey and India

CAROLINE S. WEST

## INTRODUCTION

Although geographically distant, Turkey and India are the world's two traditional producers of legally sold opium. Together, the two countries command at least 80 percent of the United States' licit opium market, as well as a major portion of the world market. The opium poppy, which grows profusely in the soil-poor regions of Turkey and India, has been an integral part of Turkish and Indian societies for nearly five thousand years. Yet, it was not until the second half of this century that the cultivation and sale of opium poppies caused immense concern in the international arena.

Turkey and India have taken measures to prevent the illegal cultivation of opium as well as the diversion of government-controlled opium into illicit markets. While Turkey has had overwhelming success in both areas, current estimates are that at least half of the legally produced opium in India is diverted into the illicit heroin market. In addition to controlling domestic production, both Turkey and India are working to curb the flow of narcotics through their borders from Middle Eastern, Asian, and African countries to European and American markets. Once again, success has been mixed.

## TURKEY

### Background

The Turkish proverb, "We come from the East, we go to the West," which recalls the original migration of the Ottoman Turks from Asia to Anatolia in the eleventh century, remains an accurate representation of the Turkish quest for westernization. Even facing their defeat in World War I, reformers maintained,

"There is no second civilization, civilization means European civilization, and it must be imported with both its roses and its thorns."

This view, asserted by an Istanbul journalist in 1913, became the primary policy of Turkey's founder, Mustafa Kemal Ataturk. In 1923, Ataturk abolished the sultanate and caliphate and established the Republic of Turkey, the last remnant of the great Ottoman Empire. For 600 years the Ottoman Turks ruled vast expanses of northern Africa, southeastern Europe, and western Asia. Modern Turkey, isolated by high mountains on all but the western front, is bordered by the Soviet Union, Greece, Bulgaria, Iran, Syria, and Iraq.

Consequently, the importance of Turkey's role as a staunch Western ally cannot be understated. At the end of World War II, Turkey became a charter member of the United Nations. From that point on, the country's main strategic role—as perceived by Western allies—was to block Soviet expansion in the Middle East. To further this aim, the 1947 Truman doctrine initiated large-scale U.S. military and economic aid to Turkey. The western alliance established, Turkey joined the North Atlantic Treaty Organization in 1952. In addition, Turkey is a party to the Organization for Economic Cooperation and the Council of Europe and is an associate member of the European Community.

Despite the strong ties to the West, Turkey has retained its Middle Eastern–Islamic traditions. The result is a dynamic coexistence of past and present. Dankwart A. Rustow, author of *Turkey: America's Forgotten Ally*, remarked, "Middle Eastern–Islamic and modern Western customs are closely related. . . . The afternoon prayer call from the urban minaret is likely to have been taped and electronically amplified" (pp. 26–27). Indeed 98 percent of Turkey's nearly 57 million citizens are Moslem, and the two major ethnic groups are Turks (85 percent) and Kurds (12 percent).

Tensions have long existed between the ethnic groups, and active right and left extremists have caused long periods of violence and unrest. The Republican People's Party, established by Ataturk in 1923, ruled until 1950 when the Democrat Party came to power. The period from 1950 to 1960 was fraught with growing economic problems and political tensions which resulted in a military coup. A new constitution was written, and the civilian government was restored when the Grand National Assembly (GNA) convened in October 1961. From 1961 to 1965 no party won a majority, but in 1965 and 1969, the Justice Party won a sizable majority and ruled alone. However, disruptions of public order and terrorism increased as left- and right-wing extremists took to the streets. The Justice Party, unable to cope with the violence, was replaced by a military regime led by Nihat Erim in 1971. Shortly thereafter, the military regime imposed a complete ban on opium poppy cultivation.

By the early 1970s, the right and left extremists had developed a successful arms-for-drugs network that operated along the Bulgarian and Syrian borders of Turkey and on the Black Sea coast. One illustrative example of the connection between extremists and drugs was the career of teenager Mehmed Ali Agca, the would-be assassin of Pope John Paul II in 1981. In 1979, Agca had been jailed for the murder of one of Turkey's leading liberal journalists. After escaping from jail through his right-wing connections, Rustow noted, "Agca apparently spent some months . . . with the opium-and-weapons-smuggling gangs operating the route from Turkey through Communist Bulgaria and Yugoslavia to Western Europe" (p. 81). In the early 1980s, the Turkish government began to clamp down on these overland narcotics and weapons smuggling routes.

Despite Turkey's turbulent political and ethnic history, combined with its traditional cultivation of opium, its people have been spared a serious drug addiction problem. Berki Dibek, a counselor at the Embassy of Turkey in Washington, D.C., attributes the lack of addiction problems to the close-knit family structure and the strong religious and moral values. However, the concern of educators and medical personnel that it could become a serious problem was voiced in the March 1991 *International Narcotics Control Strategy Report* issued by the U.S. State Department. Most current problems with heroin addiction are found among the Iranian immigrants, but the 1991 United Nations Commission on Narcotic Drugs found that heroin and cocaine abuse seems to be increasing. Abuse tends to occur in the eighteen-to-twenty-five-year-old age group; 5 percent of the abusers are women.

## Narcotics Production

The word "opium" is derived from the name of the Anatolian city of Afyon, one region where the poppy has been cultivated since 3000 B.C.. The poppy plant, grown in a soil inappropriate for other crops, has sustained the lives of the Anatolian farmers for thousands of years, according to Dibek: "In many areas it is the only source of income for farmers. Oil is extracted from its seeds and used for cooking and pastries, and the residue of the seeds is used as animal feed." Consequently, the poppy crop has always been of substantial economic importance to Turkey.

In 1933, the first restrictions on opium production were imposed when Turkey became a party to the International Opium Convention. The Turkish Grain and Opiates Board (TMO) was established in 1938 to further centralize and control opium production. The TMO has control over all production, purchase, stock, standardization, and export of poppy straw. They also regulate the import and distribution of drugs for domestic medical requirements and the production of all kinds of narcotic drugs. Until poppy cultivation was banned in 1971, according to Dibek, the TMO exported the world's best-quality poppy gum with the highest morphine concentration obtainable by lanced production. During that period Turkey controlled 50 to 55 percent of the licit world opium market.

Yet in the late 1960s and early 1970s, amid domestic political strife, Turkish opium production came into direct conflict with growing U.S. concerns about the proliferation of heroin. AT that time, approximately 150 tons of opium were grown legally in forty-two of the sixty-seven provinces in Turkey every year. Due to grossly inadequate controls, it was estimated that at least 100 tons of opium gum were produced illegally every year and that 80 percent of the heroin on the streets of the United States was derived from Turkish opium. Fearing the cancellation of U.S. aid, the government of Turkey responded by imposing a total ban on opium poppy cultivation. In return, the United States gave Turkey $35 million in temporary financial assistance to help the Anatolian farmers shift to other cash crops.

The resulting political and economic havoc caused a strain in international relations. Because the ban was implemented shortly after a military regime had been installed in the country, the Turkish people felt that the government ''was not nationalistic enough and had sold out Turkish interests,'' said Henri Barkey, an expert in Turkish-American relations. In addition, Barkey said, the United States' heavy-handed treatment of the issue only served to ''fuel the controversy more.'' According to Barkey in ''The Making of a Lukewarm Alliance: Turkish-American Relations in the Post-War Era,'' the ban became a major campaign issue of the 1973 elections as the parties ''vowed to repeal this 'act of bribery and shameful agreement' with the U.S. The unpopularity of the ban provided the civilian politicians with the means by which to punish the military for its 1971 intervention.''

Not surprisingly, the ban on poppy cultivation was revoked in March 1974, shortly after the Republican People's Party and their coalition partners won the national elections. During the three years that the ban was in force, the government of Turkey estimated that 1.5 million people were adversely affected and, in the Afyon region alone, economic losses totaled approximately $400 million. Attempts to grow substitute crops in the poor soil were unsuccessful.

Additionally, the ban had no effect on the volume of the global heroin trade. The gap left by the elimination of Turkish opium in the market was quickly filled by illegal cultivation in Latin American and South Asian countries, such as Mexico, Afghanistan, and Myanmar, formerly known as Burma.

## Narcotics Control

Following the 1974 easement permitting poppy cultivation, a new form of processing was initiated: the concentrated poppy straw (CPS) method. Traditionally, the opium gum is collected by ''lancing'' the poppy capsules before they are ripe, allowing raw opium to drip from the cut. The raw opium is then collected and can be refined into approximately twenty different alkaloids, including morphine, codeine, thebaine, and noscapine. The raw opium gum also can be easily converted to heroin. Under the new CPS method, however, dried unincised capsules are converted through an expensive industrial process to morphine base, thereby guaranteeing the unavailability of raw opium gum for heroin production.

Using the CPS method, as well as strictly enforced licensing procedures, the government of Turkey has managed to eradicate illicit cultivation. Poppy growers in the eight provinces where cultivation is currently authorized must apply annually for licenses from the TMO. After the licenses are issued, the TMO inspects the fields, and any excess cultivation is destroyed. Stiff penalties are imposed for any incised capsules found in the field. In addition to TMO controls, the Turkish National Police, the Jandarma (a paramilitary organization), and the Turkish Customs Office are committed to narcotics interdiction. The entire poppy straw yield is then purchased at a fixed rate by the state and processed at the Bolvadin Alkaloid Factory in Afyon.

The facility, which began commercial production in 1981 and is the largest of its kind in the world, has a capacity of 20,000 tons of poppy straw per year. The Bolvadin factory has yet to operate at full capacity; in 1990, it processed only 3,500 tons of raw material due to the effects of a severe drought. In order to make more efficient use of the alkaloid factory, Turkey is expanding its poppy cultivation. From 1981 to 1988, Turkey increased the harvested area of poppies form 8,500 to 18,200 hectares. However, the poppy straw yield per hectare has not risen appreciably. Worried that increased production could cause a glut in the market, Assistant Secretary of the Bureau of International Narcotics Matters Melvyn Levitsky urged before the U.S. Congress that Turkey use the alkaloid factory to produce nonnarcotic alternatives, such as bella donna and licorice.

There is little or no diversion from licit cultivation, and Turkey has been "uniquely successful" in controlling illicit poppy cultivation, according to the 1990 *International Narcotics Control Strategy Report*. The study noted several reasons for the high success rate. First, the Turkish government pays a better price for the poppy straw than the farmers could earn by incising the pods and trying to compete with the opium gum smuggled into Turkey. Second, the return does not justify the labor required to collect opium gum. Finally, the incised pods are extremely visible and farmers do not want to incur the stiff penalties imposed by the Turkish government.

## Narcotics Trafficking

Although Turkey is no longer a source country for heroin, it continues to be a significant drug conduit—a land bridge between the Middle East and Europe. Heroin, morphine base, and, to a lesser extent, hashish, enter Turkey from Pakistan, Afghanistan, and Iran. According to the Drug Enforcement Administration (DEA) in Ankara, fully processed heroin is usually smuggled into Turkey from Afghanistan and Pakistan; morphine base originates in Iran. The morphine base reaches Turkey, often on horseback or muleback, across the 300-mile-long mountainous Iran-Turkey border. In Turkey, the Iran-manufactured morphine base is processed into a potent heroin which commands higher wholesale prices. While the majority of narcotics enter across the Iranian border, lesser amounts transit the Syrian border. It was reported in the *New York Times* that, "Turkey, no longer a producer, has instead become the principal country from which hashish, heroin, and unprocessed opium or morphine or heroin base are dispersed to dealers and finally to Western users."

The trafficking problem in Turkey is exacerbated by the estimated 250,000 bonded in transit (TIR) trucks that pass through the country every year. Each TIR truck, which is permitted to cross international borders without customs inspection, takes from sixteen to twenty hours to search. In addition, heroin and morphine base are often transported by Turkish guest workers who have a legitimate reason to drive between Turkey and Western Europe.

The government of Turkey has been fully cooperative in working to curb this serious problem, and its specialized police forces are committed to drug interdiction. Turkey has cooperated with international efforts to fight narcotics smuggling, and was one of the first signatories of the United Nations 1988 Convention against Illicit Traffic in Narcotic Drugs and Psychotropic Substances. Turkey is also party to the 1961 UN Convention on Narcotic Drugs and the 1971 Convention on Psychotropic Substances. Recent bilateral agreements between Turkey and Denmark, Spain, the United Kingdom, Austria, and the Soviet Union will facilitate drug interdiction. In addition, the United States, Germany, and the United Nations Fund for Drug Abuse Control have provided the Turkish National Police with equipment and training in order to improve both resources and officer caliber. As a result, seizures and arrests continue to increase substantially every year. Such seizures include three TIR trucks that were stopped outside of Istanbul in January 1990 in which 100 kilograms of heroin and 70 kilograms of morphine were found. In 1989, nine heroin laboratories were seized. There are no reliable estimates about the amount of heroin produced or the number of laboratories operating. These primitive laboratories, generally set up for individual load conversions, tend to be protected by terrorists who finance their organizations through heroin trafficking. Also in 1989, the Turkish Coast Guard seized 6.5 tons of hashish off the coast near Antalya. As the sea becomes a more viable means of trafficking, the Coast Guard, established in 1985, will assume a larger role. The Coast Guard checks 70,000 vessels annually, and patrols 8,300 kilometers of coastline.

The remote borders of Turkey, populated predominantly by the Kurds, pose additional problems for the Turkish National Police and the Jandarma. One specialist in Kurdish relations noted, "Smuggling in these regions is fairly well established . . . it is an open field and there is a lot of money to be made." Aram Nigogosian of the University of Pennsylvania remarked that there tend to be more roadblocks and greater security in Kurdish populated areas due to the ethno-political tensions. Yet, he said, "Technically there should be a lot more interdiction, but I don't see it happening." It has been noted that the Kurdish population on both sides of the Turkish-Iranian border is heavily involved in smuggling narcotics into Turkey. The Kurds also control much of the heroin supply system in Turkey.

### The Licit Opium Market

The Turkish ban on poppy cultivation from 1971 to 1974, combined with poor worldwide poppy straw and opium gum yields, caused a shortage of the opium required to satisfy U.S. legal morphine and codeine requirements in the mid–1970s. Even when Turkey resumed production under the CPS method, it had lost its place in the licit opium market and was at an extreme disadvantage. By the late 1970s, since other countries had begun selling opium on the world market, an oversupply of the raw narcotic material existed. Understandably, the United States and the international community were concerned. In 1979 and 1980, the United Nations Commission on Narcotic Drugs adopted resolutions to support the traditional narcotic raw material producing countries—Turkey and India. The intent of these resolutions was "originally to help India and Turkey dispose of their narcotic raw material surpluses and to guarantee them substantial foreign markets in the face of increasing competition from nontraditional nations," said Gene R. Haislip, deputy assistant of the DEA before the House of Representatives Subcommittee on Crime.

It was in this context that in 1981 the United States promulgated the "80/20 Rule." Under this rule, at least 80 percent of the U.S. opium imports—a major part of the world market—is reserved for Turkish CPS and Indian opium gum exports. The remaining 20 percent is divided between the five nontraditional CPS producers arising as a result of the opium shortage of the 1970s: France, Poland, Hungary, Australia, and, to a lesser extent, Yugoslavia. With the help of the guaranteed U.S. market and aggressive price increases of as much as 70 percent, Turkey is beginning to regain its share in the world market.

## INDIA

### Narcotics Production

While Turkey has made substantial progress in controlling illicit narcotics production and has had some success with interdiction, the situation in India is grave. Current U.S. State Department reports estimate that as much as half of the opium legally cultivated in India is likely to be converted to heroin. A recent Interpol investigation has also determined that quantities of heroin produced in India are now being exported worldwide. In addition, India has become an increasingly important transit point for illicit drugs of all kinds—heroin, cannabis, and hashish—produced in Asia and Africa. Mass quantities of gold, silver, foreign currencies, and weapons are also smuggled through India's porous borders. While estimates about the seriousness of the problem that India is facing may seem inflated or exaggerated, the reality is that the numbers are probably on the conservative side. Former member of the Parliament of India and former Ambassador to England N. G. Goray remarked that the true extent of production and trafficking is most likely 50 percent higher than the reported numbers. "There is a lot of underground activity. [The government] tries to regulate the opium cultivation but without much success . . . [and] the heroin keeps on coming. As far as real success? No, not really."

On the other hand, a counselor at the Embassy of India in Washington, D.C., commented that discussions about Indian opium would have to be about "licit production because there is no illicit production." Overall, the government of India considers licit diversion to be less of a problem than the heroin smuggled in from other countries, reported the U.S. State Department. The subject is clearly sensitive, but the question remains: Why hasn't the government had success in controlling the diversion of legal opium into the illicit market? The primary reason is that India is the only major legal poppy cultivator to still use the lanced method of production, by which heroin can be easily processed. More than 95 percent of all the licit raw opium gum in the world comes from India—more than $8 million a year's worth bought by the United States alone.

However, that amount—based on Indian government prices of from $14 to $16 per kilogram of opium—is nothing when compared to the current black market prices of $150 per kilogram. Thus, major quantities of opium gum pass through farm gates or "opium gates," crude heroin laboratories that operate near legal growing areas. This diversion does not seem to be a result of theft or misdirection of legally harvested raw opium, but rather from underreporting of licit crop yields or unlicensed cultivation. Wherever this diversion may originate, the State Department (1988a) noted that "the problem primarily lies with a lack of resources and governmental effort to prevent leakage from among the 140,000 quarter-acre plots spread over non-contiguous areas in several states."

Poppies for licit production are grown in only three states—Madhya Pradesh, Rajasthan, and Uttar Pradesh—and all are under the control of the Narcotics Commissioner. The commissioner determines the acreage which will be licensed for planting and oversees the entire process of production, from collection to export. The commissioner is also responsible for India's two manufacturing facilities for processing opium, neither of which can be considered efficient. In addition, despite efforts to bring the total amount cultivated more into line with market conditions, India has an estimated 2,000 metric tons of unsold—surplus—raw opium. The stockpile may drop to 1,450 metric tons in the spring of 1991, due to a drought in other licit poppy growing areas, including Turkey. Nevertheless, this stockpile clearly represents a need for better planning and control. Although there is no indication that any of this stockpile has been diverted to the illicit market, its very presence worries narcotics officials.

The raw opium cultivated legally in India, some of which inevitably plays a role in the world heroin supply, has a guaranteed market—the United States—as a result of the 80/20 Rule. "The idea that the United States is subsidizing Indian heroin production has sparked growing outrage in Congress, with many other lawmakers wanting to allow American pharmaceutical companies to shop elsewhere for their opium supplies," reported the *Los Angeles Times*. Some pharmaceutical companies, such as Johnson & Johnson International, say that they would be glad to oblige, stating that the 80/20 Rule forces companies to buy a "commodity that they do not want from a country that cannot prevent diversion." Truly, opium and CPS are very different commodities. Turkish CPS, for example, produces morphine and traces of codeine, but not other alkaloids, such as thebaine and noscapine, which can be derived from raw opium or from alternate forms of CPS processing. While the demand for noscapine has greatly diminished recently, there continues to be a demand for thebaine. Australia and France, which employ a slightly different form of CPS, can also produce these two alkaloids. These two countries, which could conceivably handle a larger market share and have excellent records regarding diversion, are relegated to the minority due to the 80/20 Rule. During a House of Representatives Subcommittee on Crime, Raymond Stratmeyer, vice president of Johnson & Johnson International, testified, "When Turkish CPS is unavailable, the 80/20 Rule forces J&J to buy opium from India when it would prefer to buy CPS from Australia or France. There is widespread opium diversion at the farmgate in India and increasing manufacture of heroin. There are no such problems in countries producing CPS."

Despite these valid concerns, the State Department has recommended that the 80/20 Rule be extended for another three years. More than a million Indian peasant farmers are dependent on the labor-intensive opium industry for survival, and if the United States were no longer buying, they would continue to sell elsewhere—regardless of whether the sale was legal or illegal. "With all the farmers who depend on opium [production], the Indian government would have a hard time if this subsidy disappeared," said one U.S. official to the *Los Angeles Times*. "That is what worries them—and us—the most."

In the long run, the United States hopes to help India combat this problem by convincing this traditional producer to convert to the CPS method, as has Turkey. The House Subcommittee on Crime hearings determined that even a partial conversion would help reduce diversion and would simplify enforcement and regulation. In addition, as buyers worldwide find CPS more attractive and affordable, it would help India remain competitive in the market. Conversion to CPS would help India by giving it the means to meet its own requirements for narcotic alkaloids, which at this point must be imported from others. India cannot begin to undertake the complex and expensive conversion process until it has both ample funds and political stability—and that may take a while.

Regulation and control difficulties are further exacerbated by the current chaotic political situation in India. President Ramaswami Venkataraman had the new prime minister, Chandra Shekhar, removed from office in March 1991. It was only five months ago that Shekhar replaced former Prime Minister Vishwanath Pratap Singh without an election. Government departments, intelligence agencies, and state administrations are now being fully restaffed in order to remove both Singh and Shekhar appointees and supporters. While martial law has been imposed in some states, legislative deadlocks have occurred in others. In many cases, governmental confusion has prevented officials from reaching the villages in which poppies are grown to distribute seed and licenses. Ultimately, any realistic attempts to resolve increasing narcotics production and trafficking are impossible in such domestic political turmoil.

Central to the fall of Singh's government was his opposition to Hindu radicalism and a proposition to undo caste discrimination through affirmative action quotas. The final blow to his government was an apparent inability to keep peace between the 83-percent Hindu majority and the 11-percent Muslim minority. President Venkataraman's decision to install a government led by a party with a small minority in Parliament had worried many political analysts, and it has broadened into a concern about the future of constitutional government in India, reported Barbara Crossette in "Indian Premier Has a Problem: He's Seen as Gandhi's Shadow." Former Prime Minister Shekhar's hastily assembled party, the Janata Dal-Socialist, held sixty seats—a small minority—in the 525-seat lower house of Parliament. Many believed that former Prime Minister Shekhar was no more than a front for the Congress Party led by the former prime minister, Rajiv Gandhi, who was assassinated in May 1991. Amid a scandal regarding corruption in military purchases during the late Gandhi's term in office, Gandhi was defeated at the polls in 1989 and replaced by Singh. Despite this defeat, Gandhi's party still holds 195 seats, a majority in the Parliament. Ultimately, these four major changes in the central government have had a devastating effect on India's ability to actively enforce narcotics controls.

## Narcotics Trafficking

Indian's endemic political turmoil and extreme religious and ethnic tensions are not the only reasons why the Indian Connection is becoming so strong. On the other side of the Himalaya Mountains and the Thar Desert, India has neighbors such as Myanmar, formerly Burma, China, Bangladesh, Nepal, and Pakistan. Not only are these some of the poorest countries in the world, but they are also some of the largest cultivators of illegal opium and producers of heroin. India and Pakistan, along with Iraq and Afghanistan, form the Golden Crescent, which produced more than 3,000 tons of illicit opium in 1990, double what it grossed two years ago. The combination of record-shattering opium crops, unstable political conditions, and the lack of effective international cooperation has made the subcontinental region a safe—and profitable—haven.

India and Pakistan have been called perennially suspicious neighbors. Recently, however, former Prime Minister Shekhar made some attempts to improve relations between the two countries. Regardless, the Indo-Pak political instability and the crackdowns in the northern border states of Kashmir and Punjab, where Sikh terrorists operate, have made the more southern Indian border state of Rajasthan the drug-traffickers' paradise. The most vulnerable areas in Rajasthan are Barmer and Jaisaimer, which are underdeveloped and remote. Using the "ship of the desert"—the camel—large quantities of narcotics are smuggled into Barmer from Sukkur in Pakistan. This is but one of many preferred routes that carriers use to transport narcotics from Pakistan into Rajasthan. Most of the carries are local youths who know the terrain and the numerous entry points. From Rajasthan, the narcotics are delivered to the two major transit points: Bombay and New Delhi. The narcotics reach the West by air and, increasingly, by sea. According to Interpol, from 1984 to 1987, all the non-Europeans arrested in Europe for carrying drugs, with the exception of Pakistanis, had travelled from Bombay or New Delhi.

Positive results in narcotics interdiction are similarly difficult to obtain along the Indo-Burmese border as long as opium warlord Khun Sa continues to do business without opposition in Burma and Laos. "Little cooperation is possible with the Government of Burma which has little interest in or capability to prevent smuggling across the Indo-Burmese border," said the U.S. State Department in its 1991 *Narcotics Control Strategy Report*. Heroin traffic along the virtually unpatrolled, desolate 340-kilometer border of the state of Manipur has risen from almost nothing to approximately 20 percent of all the heroin entering India. From the opposite side of the border, shipments of acetic anhydride, one of the ingredients necessary to refine heroin, are smuggled from India to laboratories in Burma. This cross-traffic also serves to fuel the drug trade. Additionally, it has been reported that Burmese drugs runners are trying to convince Manipurian villagers to cultivate poppies illegally in order to solidify the trafficking. Not only have more than 150,000 poppy plants have been destroyed in recent months, but at least 1,500 people have been arrested on drug-related charges.

Prior to the removal of India's Singh government in November, several proposals were made and partially implemented in order to control the flow of illicit narcotics along both the Indo-Pak border and the Indo-Burmese border. Along the Punjab border, some of these measures included doubling the strength of the armed forces and fencing and installation of floodlights. In Kashmir, army and paramilitary forces were deployed, and they brought the smuggling of drugs and arms under control, reported the Calcutta *Statesman* in October 1990. H. P. Bhatnagar, director general of the Border Security Force, said that security had been doubled in the Rajasthan area and that portions of the border would be fenced. Increased security patrols were also proposed in Manipur. Yet, as of March 1991, little has been done. The government restructuring, a result of the political upheaval, has also had an impact on the narcotics interdiction offices. There have been several changes of senior officials and shortages of personnel. Reported the U.S. State Department (1991), "Counter-narcotics efforts in India have suffered from a lack of adequate resources, effective policy coordination and vigorous implementation."

Because of the heavy use of India as a transit country, drug addiction and the number of AIDS cases are rising fast. There are no reliable statistics regarding opium and heroin addiction. The U.S. State Department estimates that the number of opium addicts is between 1 and 5 million, and most live in rural areas. The current estimates for the number of heroin addicts is between 750,000 and 1 million. It is reported that there are at least 100,000 people addicted to "brown sugar"—the India-produced heroin—in Bombay alone. These addicts include urban workers, middle-class people, and children. in 1985 a friend of former Prime Minister Gandhi complained before Parliament that Bombay drug dealers were selling heroin-coated milk lollipops in order to hook children. The government of India, concerned about this skyrocketing problem, supports detoxification and rehabilitation centers. Unfortunately, success is hampered by what the State Department (1991) termed ''bureaucratic rivalries and professional differences.'' Private organizations have been more effective, but all lack adequate funding. India and the United Nations Fund for Drug Abuse Control (UNFDAC) agreed in 1987 to a $20 million five-year plan that addresses all facets of the drug problem. In addition to monitoring licit opium cultivation and training additional enforcement personnel, the project also targets preventative education on drug abuse, dependence treatment, and rehabilitation. Unfortunately, UNFDAC officials had to freeze some of the available money because India had not acted on portions of the project. Other multinational efforts that India is a party to include the 1961 UN Single Convention on Narcotic Drugs, and its 1972 Protocol Amendment, and the 1971 UN Convention on Psychotropic Substances.

## CONCLUSION

Although Turkey has managed to enforce controls on its licit opium production, it remains a significant narcotics transit country. During the Gulf War in early 1991, the U.S. State Department noted that the majority of commercial traffic through Turkey ceased. This increased security along the borders with Iraq and Iran has also forced many traffickers temporarily to use alternate routes.

On the other hand, a difficult path lies ahead for India. The political situation in India changes daily, causing confusion at all levels of the government. Although Singh began many necessary domestic reforms to help the country recover from Gandhi's corruption-riddled government, his year in office was not long enough for any of these reforms to have gained any stability. The same can be said for Shekhar's short-lived term in office. In addition, the recent assassination of Gandhi has shocked the country. Truthfully, there is no working government in India at the present time. Given these domestic conditions, it is doubtful that any opium cultivation controls and narcotics interdiction programs, either on national or international levels, will be effectively implemented until the government stabilizes. In other words, the currently bad situation in India is likely to get worse.

## BIBLIOGRAPHY

Akoin, Varol. ''Turkish Measures Force Detour in Drug Traffic.'' *New York Times*, 17 September 1986.

Ali, Salamat. ''Going for Gold: Contraband Flood Fuelled by Drug Money.'' *Far Eastern Economic Review*, 29 December 1988.

———. ''Moving to Centre Stage: The Middleman in the Drug Trade Is Turning Producer.'' *Far Eastern Economic Review*, 28 December 1990.

———. ''South Asian Paradise: Business Is Booming for Illegal Trade in Drugs and Goods.'' *Far Eastern Economic Review*, 29 December 1988.

Barkey, Henri J. Interview. (Professor of International Relations, Lebigh University, Bethlehem, Pa.) 1 March 1991.

———. "The Making of a Lukewarm Alliance: Turkish-American Relations in the Post-War Era." In *Soviet and American Relations with Turkey, Iran, and Afghanistan: Advances and Setbacks*, edited by Stephen Dale and Alam Payind. New York: Unwin and Hyman, forthcoming.

Chawla, Ashok. Interview. (Economic Consular, Embassy of India, Washington, D.C.) 3 March 1991.

Clad, James. "Valley of Violence: The Deep Chasm between Kashmiri Muslims and India." *Far Eastern Economic Review*, 24 May 1990.

Crossette, Barbara. "Indian Premier Has a Problem: He's Seen as Gandhi's Shadow." *New York Times*, 24 December 1990.

———. "India's Parliament Falls into Chaos." *New York Times*, 28 December 1990.

———. "India's Premier Blazing a Foreign Affairs Trail." *New York Times*, 30 December 1990.

———. "Premier of India Meets Sikh Leader." *New York Times*, 29 December 1990.

Dibek, Berki. Interview. (Counselor, Embassy of Turkey, Washington, D.C.) 25 February 1991.

Fisher, Kevin. "Trends in Extraterritorial Narcotics Control: Slamming the Stable Door after the Horse Has Bolted." *New York University Journal of Law and International Politics* 16 (Winter 1984).

Gopal, Ajit S. "Heroin Explosion in India." *Free Press Journal*, (Bombay, India), 29 September 1990.

Goray, N. G. Interview. (Former member of parliament and Indian ambassador to England, Bombay, and India.) 5 March 1991.

Haislip, Gene R. (Deputy Assistant Administrator, Office of Diversion Control, Drug Enforcement Administration). Testimony. "The Licit Importation of Opium." Hearing before the Subcommittee on Crime of the Committee of the Judiciary, House of Representatives, 27 February 1990.

Howe, Marvine. "Its Poppy Crop Curbed, Turkey Becomes Drug Conduit." *New York Times*, 11 May 1980.

Jehl, Douglas. " 'Indian Connection' Poppies Throw Curve at U.S. Drug Policy." *Los Angeles Times*, 19 March 1990.

Kamm, Henry. "Drug Flow Through Turkey Defies Control." *New York Times*, 17 July 1986.

Levitsky, Melvyn (Assistant Secretary of State). Testimony. "The Licit Importation of Opium." Hearing before the Subcommittee on Crime of the Committee of the Judiciary, House of Representatives, 27 February 1990.

National Narcotics Intelligence Consumers Committee. *The NNICC Report 1989: The Supply of Illicit Drugs to the United States*. Washington, D.C.: U.S. Government Printing Office, June 1990.

Nigogosian, Aram. Interview. University of Pennsylvania, Philadelphia, Pa., 6 March 1991.

"Rajasthan Border 'Drug-Traffickers' Paradise." *The Statesman* (Calcutta, India), 31 October 1990.

Rustow, Dankwart A. *Turkey: America's Forgotten Ally*. London: Council on Foreign Relations Press, 1989.

Stavrou, Nikolaos A. "The Politics of Opium in Turkey." In *Drugs, Politics & Diplo-*

*macy, the International Connection*, edited by Luiz R. S. Simmons and Abdul A. Said. Los Angeles: Sage Publications, 1974.

Stratmeyer, Raymond J. (Vice President, Johnson & Johnson International). Testimony. "The Licit Importation of Opium." Hearing before the Subcommittee on Crime of the Committee of the Judiciary, House of Representatives, 27 February 1990.

Turkish Opiates Board. "Turkey's Policy on Poppy Cultivation and on Matters Related with International Cooperation in Controlling Drug Abuse." *Narcotics Control in Turkey*. Ankara: Ministry of Foreign Affairs, Ministry of the Interior, Ministry of Health and Social Assistance, and Ministry of Finance and Customs, 1987.

United Nations Economic and Social Council. *Report of the Commission on Narcotic Drugs*. Vienna: United Nations, February 1990.

———. *Report of the Commission on Narcotic Drugs*. Vienna: United Nations, February 1991.

United Nations International Narcotics Control Board. *Report of the International Narcotics Control Board for 1988*. Vienna: United Nations, 12 January1989.

U.S. Department of State, Bureau of International Narcotics Matters. *International Narcotics Control Strategy Report*. Washington, D.C.: Department of State, March 1989.

———. *International Narcotics Control Strategy Report*. Washington, D.C.: Department of State, March 1990.

———. *International Narcotics Control Strategy Report*. Washington, D.C.: Department of State, March 1991.

U.S. Department of State, Bureau of Public Affairs. *India*. Washington, D.C.: U.S. Department of State, 1988.

———. *Turkey*. Washington, D.C.: U.S. Department of State, 1988.

# 23

# The Golden Triangle: Burma, Laos, and Thailand

DEBRA A. LIANG

## INTRODUCTION

The Golden Triangle—so named for the vast wealth generated by its scattered yet plentiful fields of opium poppies—occupies a 150-square-mile area where the borders of Burma, Laos, and Thailand meet. Burma (now called Myanmar) is the world's largest producer of opium poppies; Laos is the third largest grower. This relatively small region accounts for nearly three-quarters of the world's raw opium supply and is the source for almost 50 percent of the heroin reaching the United States and Western Europe.[1] What are the origins of opium cultivation in Southeast Asia and why has it remained such a resilient and thriving industry?

Many circumstances have combined to make the Golden Triangle a hub of opium production, heroin refining, and drug trafficking. The most fundamental is the region's geography, which is extremely hospitable to a successful drug industry. The Golden Triangle is endowed with waterways and mountain ranges that transect the three countries. These topographical traits facilitate more efficient transportation and communication systems. Favorable climatic conditions are also conducive to cultivation.

## BACKGROUND

Of the countries that constitute the subcontinent of Southeast Asia, Burma is the largest and also one of the most sparsely populated. It is bordered on the northwest by Bangladesh and India, on the northeast by China, and on the southeast by Laos and Thailand. Its long coastline is washed by the Bay of Bengal and the Andaman Sea. Burma's two principal rivers are the Irrawady and the Salween. Nearly half the country is covered by tropical rain forests. The landscape is dominated by the Kumon mountain range in the north, the western mountains, and the Shan Plateau in the Shan State in the east (where most of the narcotics activity takes place). The Shan State, whose 62,500 square miles of land area makes it almost as large as Washington state, produces an estimated 2,625 tons of opium every year—more than half the world output. Three-fourths of the population inhabits the central delta regions where the Irrawady and Sittang rivers flow into the Andaman Sea.

Burma, like most developing nations, remains almost wholly dependent on agriculture even though its land is rich with unexploited mineral resources. Rice and tropical hardwoods are its leading legal exports. The military government of General Saw Maung (1988–present) is rife with inefficient and corrupt officials. Ordinary consumer goods are virtually inaccessible except on the black market, which is as large as (if not larger) than the legal economy.

The landlocked, Communist-run People's Democratic Republic of Laos is bordered by China, Vietnam, Kampuchea, Thailand, and Burma. Like all other tropical countries in Southeast Asia, it endures a monsoon season from May to October, which alternates with a dry season that runs from November to April. Slightly larger than Great Britain, Laos is scattered with dense forests, but perhaps the two most distinguishing features that characterize this country are the Mekong River and the Annamite mountain range.

These two topographical characteristics have proven helpful allies to the drug industry in Laos: the river for the relative ease of transport it provides and the mountains for the isolation they afford. The Mekong River, which originates in Tibet, flows southeastward along the borders of Laos and Burma, cuts farther inland, and continues down along the Thai-Lao border. Forty percent of the population inhabits the lowlands, where the river and its tributaries provide good conditions for the cultivation of rice (the nation's primary food staple). Rice is also raised without irrigation along the hillsides. The Annamite mountains also originate in Tibet and cover approximately 90 percent of Laos' 91,428 square miles. In the hills of the northwest, two of the four major ethnic groups—the Hmong (or Meo) and the Iu Mien (or the Yao)—raise most of the poppy crop. In the upper regions of these countries and along the deltas lies the alkaline, mineral-rich soil necessary for healthy crop production.

The roots of the opium trade in Southeast Asia go back to the early eighth century, when Arab and Turkish merchants first introduced opium to the Chinese, who used it for medicinal purposes until the early seventeenth century. It is believed that Formosans (now Taiwanese) began mixing opium with smoking tobacco for pleasure around 1620. This practice grew increasingly popular as it spread to Fujien and Guangdong provinces. By the 1660s, methods of opium smoking became more refined, and the practice quickly became fashionable among the leisure class. Soon thereafter, the "hobby" proved not to be socio-economically specific, and people from all walks of life partook in the pastime—from the impoverished to the noble classes.[2]

With the escalating demand for opium in China, domestic cultivation of poppies in Sichuan, Yunnan, Fujien, Zhejiang, and Guangdong provinces boomed, the imports rose along with it. By 1729, concern about the extent of opium use led the imperial government to prohibit the sale and smoking of the drug. In 1796, importation and cultivation of opium poppies was outlawed entirely. By the early nineteenth century, opium smuggling was such a lucrative business that large private firms (especially British interests, which accounted for over one-third of the opium in China at one point) conducted cash-only, under-the-table trade with the Chinese. According to Immanuel C. Y. Hsü's *The Rise of Modern China*, drug use expanded even farther into mainstream society and branched out from young men of rich families to government officials, merchants, literati, women, servants, soldiers, and even Buddhist monks, nuns, and priests. Illicit opium-dealing organizations (or *yao-k'ao*) came into existence, and the dealers often maintained relations with the underworld as well as with the Shansi bankers for transmission of funds. Chinese society's dependency on opium eventually created such a high demand that there was a rapid rise in opium imports to the country—a situation that immediately caused the demise of the favorable balance of trade between the Chinese government and the foreign traders.

The largest expansion of the opium market, however, occurred after World War II, when large numbers of Chinese—many of them members of the defeated Kuomintang (KMT) or Nationalist Party—fled their homeland to escape Mao Zedong and his victorious Communists. Most of the refugees settled in Taiwan, but many Chinese from Yunnan Province sought refuge in Burma, where they reestablished themselves and intermarried. Some of them became quite active in the narcotics trade. Hill tribes in Burma had begun cultivating opium poppies in the end of the sixteenth century. They produced the poppies in limited quantities and used the drug purely for medicinal and recreational purposes. Over time, the hill tribes came to rely on the poppy trade to support themselves and the insurgencies they were waging against the central government. Subsequently, with the Chinese influence, opium was produced increasingly as a business venture.

The Golden Triangle is a complex region in which two familiar forces influence the narcotics industry: politics and economics. At the heart of this complicated structure lies a welter of contentious ethnic groups which provide, however inadvertently, a favorable matrix for the political economy of opium. Some groups not only produce opium, but also receive revenue by taxing the opium that moves through their territories or taxing the land on which the opium is produced. Among the more prominent groups are the Shan, whose Shan United Army (SUA) is led by Chang Qi-fu (also known as Khun Sa) and the Kachin with their Kachin Independence Army (KIA) in northern Burma.[3] Smaller groups include the Wa (Wa National Army) and the Kokang. These four are the most heavily involved, although there are certainly others—some of them fractious subgroups of the larger tribes.

In Laos, as in Burma, various insurgent groups rely on opium trading to sustain them. The country's severe poverty, combined with the rapidly growing insurgent problem, has spurred the Laotian government's recent efforts to boost the highland peoples' standard of living by encouraging them to move down to the lowlands where rice growing is easier and where schools and medical clinics are more accessible. Some observers, however, believe that the government's true motive for persuading these groups to move down is to dampen the insurgencies by luring the hill tribes into a more controlled environment. Opium is grown by only the Lao Soung (Hmong and Yao) and Lao Theung (indigenous inhabitants of Laos), all of whom live and farm at altitudes of 1,000 meters or higher.

The politics of this region are as complicated as the multitude of divergent groups that occupy it. The many ethnic minorities are widely spread from the river valleys to the higher elevations of the mountains. The region's political boundaries, which stem from the days of European colonization, take no account of ethnicity. Since independence in 1948, Burma has been wracked by strife between the central government and a plethora of ethnic and ideological insurgent groups which control many of the country's opium cultivation areas. This infrastructure, combined with the topographical nature of the area, allows for greater separatism among the groups, and therefore they make less effort toward political cooperation. This desire to maintain group independence from one another encourages the political economy of the drug industry. Because there is no controlling force (i.e., government) that is able to monitor, let alone willing to control or even serve as a proponent of cohesion among these groups, the ethnic minorities are able to carry on with the industry, much to their economic advantage.[4] To complicate matters, the Burmese government has also been cooperating with the Wa and Kokang groups in an effort to suppress the Karen insurgents, who are not involved in producing, trafficking, or taxing opium. About 500,000 Karens, who are largely Christians and animists, live in rebel-held territory near the Thai border, when they occupy a third of Burma's Karen State and some adjacent areas. They have been fighting for their independence since 1949.

## STRUCTURE OF THE DRUG INDUSTRY

While the ethnic minorities are divided into fragmented groups, there is yet a larger matrix to which they belong. It is difficult to divide neatly the various groups and to separate them into their own categories, but it is important to understand that these various sections of the political environment exist within the framework of the opium industry. The four types of organizational bodies that help to define this complicated arrangement are ethnic insurgents, revolutionary movements, warlord organizations, and syndicates and consortia.

In Burma, most of the ethnically divided groups of the region are involved with insurgent activities in order to gain some form of independence or autonomy from Rangoon (now Yangon). Some groups claim political reasons for their actions, but most of them pursue narcotics interests for private gain.

Revolutionary movements became involved in the drug industry in order to raise funds to acquire munitions. These groups seek to overthrow the central government by means of force, and they are often seen as ethnic insurgents. The expatriated KMT is a case in point. Initially, after the late 1940s, the KMT's fanatical anti-Communist stance kept them active as freedom fighters in southern China, Burma, Laos, and northern Thailand. However, as the aging KMT generals nursed their fading hopes of regaining their homeland, they began to find new methods that would enable them to return to China. As one Nationalist general put it, "[T]o fight the evil of communism, you must have an army; and any army must have guns. To buy guns, you must have money. In these mountains, the only money is opium."[5]

Ironically, probably the most prominent revolutionary force that was involved with the drug trade was the Burmese Communist Party (BCP). Originally, the BCP opposed opium cultivation, but it turned to narcotics as a source of funding after Chinese support waned in the late 1970s. By 1988, the BCP controlled about 80 percent of Burma's opium cultivation. The BCP broke apart in the spring of 1989 as ethnic factions splintered off to join the Wa and Kokang groups, which continue to be involved with narcotics trafficking.

The Golden Triangle is also the home of private armies whose main purpose is the illegal production and distribution of narcotics. Unlike ethnic insurgencies or revolutionary groups, warlord organizations like the SUA have no goals other than making money in an illicit industry. By 1978, SUA warlord Khun Sa controlled 70 to 80 percent of the opium trade in the Golden Triangle; it remains the leading drug-trafficking organization along the Thai-Burmese border. Khun Sa, who claims that his organization was formed to fight for the autonomy of Burma's Shan State, maintains a vast administrative infrastructure to support his operations.

Khun Sa, whose name means "prince prosperous" in the Shan dialect, was given this moniker as a boy, long before drug dealing raised him to truly princely prosperity. Born to an ethnic Chinese father and a Shan mother, he has a long history of cooperation with government officials on both sides of the Thai-Burmese border, who in turn have allowed his opium caravans to pass unhindered. From 1964 to 1967, he led a division of the Burmese government–sponsored anti-insurgent militia, known as the Ka Kwe Ye (KKY), which fought insurgents for the government in return for Rangoon's tolerance of its drug dealing. Established in 1963, the KKY was given the right to use all government-controlled roads and towns in the Shan State for opium smuggling in exchange for fighting anti-Rangoon rebel forces in the area. The KKY was abolished in 1973 when the regional commanders became too powerful for the government to control. Khun Sa gained fame in 1977 when he proposed to the U.S. government that he would hand over his entire opium crop and aid U.S. antinarcotics officials if he was awarded $300 million over a six-year period. The U.S. government rejected the offer. In March 1990, a federal grand jury in New York indicted him on ten separate counts of drug trafficking stemming from the seizure of more than a ton of heroin in Bangkok, Thailand, on February 14, 1988. There is no hope that the indictment will lead either to his arrest or to a decline in the drug industry of the Golden Triangle.

Another prominent drug kingpin is Lo Hsing-han, who like Khun Sa, began as a commander for the KKY in the Kokang area. With Khun Sa's usefulness plummeting in Rangoon's eyes, it is believed that Lo Hsing-han's star is rising rapidly. Other newly emerging drug warlords (the Pheung brothers, Liu Go Shi, Hong Lau San, Zhang Zhi Ming, and Lin Ming Xian) are also quickly gaining notoriety along the Burma-Chinese border.[6]

Even more intricately organized groups involved with the drug industry are the syndicates. These companies maintain a regular business that organizers trade, owns shares in refineries, finances opium purchases, is responsible for transportation costs, handles refining operations, and even provides the precursor chemicals necessary for heroin refining. Syndicate companies are usually well connected politically; their operations and facilities are safe from police raids and other narcotics-control activities.

The cultivation of opium poppies and the refining and trafficking of heroin are intricate businesses that rely on a sophisticated, yet essentially simply, network of experienced, low-paid workers. Cultivators typically plant opium poppies from September to March. After harvest, rice and maize crops may be planted. This provides the farmer with both cash and food crops almost year round.

Burma is by far the world's largest cultivator of opium poppies. It produces four times as much opium as Afghanistan, the world's second largest producer. The major areas of opium production remain beyond the control of Burma's central government (the Shan State and the Kachin State, both in northern Burma). Burma also hosts many refineries that turn raw opium into various grades of processed opiates, including heroin. Refineries typically are small, scattered, well camouflaged, and located close to a source of water. They are often portable, but they range from temporary huts to more elaborate permanent installations with storage and living quarters for guards and refinery personnel. The major refineries in Burma are located near the Thai border, in the Wa and Kokang areas along the Chinese border, and in the areas controlled by the KIA. Principal trafficking routes for the processed heroin run through Thailand to India, Bangladesh, and southern China. All of these countries have relatively uncontrolled borders with Burma. The Burmese regime has benefited from the breakup of the BCP, a former Wa ally, and it has reportedly accommodated SUA, WA, and Kokang activities in the north while devoting the Burma Army's energy to quelling the insurgent Karen National Union (KNU) in the south.[7] Opium cultivation is also largely controlled by the Third Chinese Irregular Force (CIF).

U.S. narcotics officials report that Mandalay is becoming a hub for Burma's drug traffic. Chemicals (mainly acetic anhydride, which is needed to convert raw opium into heroin) are smuggled into the city from India and then transported to refineries. Mandalay has a relatively well-developed communications system and an airport, as well as good rail and road links to the Shan State.

Laos has a communications system that is highly unreliable even by the relatively primitive standards of Southeast Asia; facts and figures, if they can be had at all, are often uncertain. Opium production in Laos was estimated at 375 metric tons in 1990. Production is heaviest in the country's northern highlands, where hill tribes have cultivated opium for over 150 years, first for medicinal and recreational purposes and then as a cash crop. Opium addiction rose sharply over the following years, and it remains one of the major problems the government faces. The opium addiction rate is officially recognized as 50 percent in some mountain villages. Suppression efforts in Thailand (and previously in neighboring Burma) have pushed major trafficking operations into Laos, where traffickers have been able to grow and refine opium in areas that are not easily accessible to authorities. It is difficult to contain drug production in Laos, especially because the lure of profits (for both producers and traffickers) has led to the involvement of senior Lao civilian and military officials. High-level involvement of officials in the Lao government continues to hinder constructive cooperation with the United States.

Thailand is the smallest producer of opium in the Golden Triangle. Its crop is less than 2 percent of that produced in all of Southeast Asia. Most Thai opium comes from the mountainous regions in Chiang Mai and Chiang Rai Provinces, with scattered cultivation in Mae Hong Son and Nan Provinces. Once considered a major opium-source country, Thailand has reduced its production of illegal opiates in recent years. It remains important to the drug industry, however, because its relatively sophisticated communications and transportation systems make it the prime conduit for Southeast Asian heroin on its way to the international market. It is estimated that as much as from 70 to 80 percent of all Golden Triangle heroin passes through Thailand en route to target nations.

Corruption forms a significant obstacle to Thailand's drug enforcement efforts—as it does in most major drug-producing and drug-conduit countries. Corrupt civilian and military officials actively and passively assist the drug-trafficking organizations of the Golden Triangle. Thailand's expansion of trade with Burma seems to have facilitated narcotics-smuggling activities. The growth of cross-border trade and security links also promotes ties among groups that smuggle drugs and increases the potential for narcotics-related corruption. Authorities along the borders often turn a blind eye on the insurgent and trafficking groups from Burma who frequently use the Thai side of the remote and ill-defined border as a safe haven for their activities.

Thai corruption is largely connected to the logging interests the government has in Burma. In 1988, following a government ban on logging in an effort to stem deforestation, former Royal Thai Army (RTA) commander General Chavalit Yongchaiyudh visited Rangoon on a goodwill mission that opened the door to a surge of logging contracts between Thai companies and the Burmese government's Timber Corporation.[8]

In order for the logging companies to operate in rebel-controlled areas, the Thais are attempting to appease both the Rangoon government and the insurgents. The situation is precarious, as the insurgent forces strongly oppose the Burmese government. Rangoon receives some counterinsurgency aid from the Thai government in exchange for logging contracts. Meanwhile, insurgent groups appear to tolerate logging in areas they control in return for Thai military compliance in permitting heroin to enter Thailand across the Thai-Burmese border. U.S. drug enforcement personnel, the RTA, and the Thai Border Police monitor the border, but interdiction and enforcement are relatively ineffective along the extremely porous border.

In China, opium cultivation in the southwest is partially controlled by the government, which harvests the poppies for what it says are exclusively medicinal uses. It is believed, however, that much more illicit cultivation than is reported occurs in the tribal areas of Yunnan Province, which are directly adjacent to the opium-growing region of Burma. Although China is active in the cultivation of opium, it is not listed in the U.S. Department of States' *International Narcotics Control Strategy Report* as an opium producer. As far as addiction in the country is concerned, the rate is growing. (It is still slow in growing, however, due to an antidrug campaign led by the police of Kunming City in Yunnan Province.) Chinese officials report that drug smuggling across Chinese territory is rampant. Kunming is a transit point where heroin shipments stop briefly en route from the Golden Triangle to Hong Kong and Macao, from whence they are smuggled to the West. The border between Burma and China is ill defined, which enables drug producers to construct remote, fortified opium-growing complexes that are beyond the reach of both Rangoon and Beijing.[9]

For thirty years after Beijing (under Mao) launched its campaign against illicit narcotics in the 1950s, Chinese society was practically drug free. In the 1950s, Communist Party leaders were venerated by society, and consequently obeyed (some say to the detriment of the country's economy and, to a certain extent, to its cultural heritage). But recently, the party's ideological sway has weakened, and drug abuse is more common. There is a ready market for heroin in Yunnan. Natives of Yunnan in the countryside consider drug use to be socially acceptable. This is understandable if one remembers that Yunnan Province was once a major producer of opium before the British promoted the drug in China during the last century. Also, many Chinese, especially in the countryside, do not understand the hazards of hard drugs because drug use has not yet entered mainstream Chinese society and therefore has not received the attention that it otherwise would.[10]

It is difficult to determine exactly how much opium is grown each crop year, although estimates can be made. Communications are limited in these remote areas, and accurate statistics are not easily gathered. It is evident that opium production, even allowing for fluctuations in yields over the past decade, is rising almost exponentially. An actual decline in output was reported in the crop years between 1978–1979 and 1979–1980 because of a drought that struck the region; the 1989–1990 crop has been the largest yield in history, thanks to better-than-normal weather and growing conditions. Also, recently, estimates have been increasingly accurate with data analysis and figures on eradication effectiveness.

## INTERNATIONAL LINKAGES

In 1989, worldwide opium production jumped 50 percent to more than 4,200 metric tons. Over the past four years, opium production has doubled while street prices for heroin in the United States have fallen and purity has risen. Smokable heroin (sometimes mixed with cocaine) has become increasingly popular with the international drug user, perhaps due to growing fears about the danger of contracting AIDS from hypodermic needles. Also, those who are psychologically needle-shy are finding heroin agreeable in its smokable form.

For the last few years of its term, the authoritarian Ne Win government in Burma (1963–1988) stressed counternarcotics programs mainly to undercut the financial base of various insurgencies. Between 1974 and 1988, the United States gave Burma more than $80 million in counternarcotics assistance. This includes twenty-eight helicopters, eleven fixed-wing crop-spraying planes, large amounts of herbicide, and pilot-training assistance for aerial eradication programs. By the summer of 1988, street demonstrations against the Ne Win government led to a massive government crackdown on internal dissent, and the government shifted priorities toward internal control and repression. Opium eradication efforts virtually ceased in 1989.

The program was suspended in 1988 after the State Law and Order Restoration Council (SLORC), headed by General Saw Maung, took power. Its self-proclaimed leaders deemed its existence necessary to ensure "peace" in the face of social unrest, but there was no mistaking the fact that SLORC was simply a reincarnation of Ne Win's rule with a new acronym—it was and remains a repressive military regime with no clear social program other than suppressing the prodemocracy protests that had become more and more frequent.

In response to the government crackdown, the United States withdrew its antinarcotics assistance programs. According to some analysts U.S. support for eradication efforts had proved ineffective because enforcement actions would need to be combined with economic development to achieve long-term narcotics reductions. Additionally, the U.S. State Department's enforcement-based assistance does not encourage a settlement and fails to address the economic problems. To be sure, the biggest hindrance to the program's effectiveness was the lack of the Burmese government's active participation. But the same analysts highlighted a much more serious problem in U.S. antidrug programs overseas: the State Department's narrow focus on enforcement and interdiction rather than on a broader approach including economic development and efforts at curbing demand. This is surprising given the apparatus the State Department has at its disposal for policy development and execution.

The Bureau of International Narcotics Matters (INM) is responsible for managing the U.S. government's multiagency effort to reduce the flow of illicit drugs from abroad and for the overall coordination of the State Department's international narcotics role. The State Department is the leading agency for international drug control matters in the United States and, in conjunction with U.S.

ambassadors and narcotics officials in source countries, it coordinates the activities of other agencies involved in drug-control efforts overseas.

In Laos, the State Department had allocated $500,000 to aid an anticipated eight-year program to develop substitute crops and economic development projects in the two big opium-growing regions during FY90. Another $500,000 was requested for FY91 for an expansion of the program to include demand reduction efforts and infrastructure development projects that would establish conditions in that country for alternative, non-opium-based economic development.

Of the three countries in the Golden Triangle, the Thai government probably has the friendliest relations with the United States. It is for this reason, however, that the prospect of establishing drug-control programs with the Thai government encountered a great deal of frustration when foreign officials discovered rampant corruption among Thai officials. According to the 1989 INCSR, "strengthened relationships between Thai military and civilian officials and traffickers in Burma and Laos significantly constrain effective disruption of narcotics production and trafficking in the area."[11]

Efforts could be aided by devoting more resources to increase interdictions; more important, Thai resolve to improve the effectiveness of ongoing law enforcement programs and to eliminate corruption is paramount. Once narcotics have cleared the Thai-Burmese border, Thailand's extensive transportation network makes interdiction difficult as drugs are quickly moved toward exit points. These points are increasingly difficult to control because the Thai export sector has undergone significant expansion. The growing use of containerized shipping has made it much easier to ship larger quantities of heroin from Thailand. According to the INCSR, legal and law enforcement mechanisms in Thailand need "significant improvement."

Concurring with the conclusions of the INCSR, the Drug Enforcement Administration (DEA) notes that Thai prosecution of suspected narcotics traffickers has been seriously hampered by the absence of effective conspiracy and asset seizure laws. A law combining both of these elements has been in the planning stages for over six years, and was submitted to the Thai Parliament in May 1990. In addition to the lack of asset seizure and conspiracy laws, Thailand has no money-laundering laws. About 50 percent of *licit* cash transactions do not go through money exchanges—this makes tracking illicit cash transactions virtually impossible. Thai legislators are currently negotiating a draft bill that would allow for the seizure of drug traffickers' assets. It provides that anyone who transports or shelters materials for drug trafficking or who receives money or other assets from the offender will be liable to punishment, and assets of third parties would be subject to seizure if those assets were obtained through drug trafficking. Money laundering is usually conducted in Hong Kong and Singapore since the financial institutions in these cities—by dint of their complexity and the sheer volume they handle each day—are better able to conceal transactions than those in the countries that make up the Golden Triangle. Ironically, Singapore boasts of having the most stringent antinarcotics laws in the world.

Currently, INM funds a three-pronged program in Thailand that focuses on the following: (1) a narcotics law enforcement project to provide assistance to law enforcement agencies and to aid them in their infrastructure development, (2) crop control assistance programs, and (3) a drug abuse prevention project. Four million dollars have been requested for this program for FY91.

Part of the State Department's heroin strategy led to a Bush administration study of the heroin threat to the United States that will serve as the basis for future U.S. battles against heroin. Heroin interdiction and opium eradication, although necessary elements of an effective narcotics-control strategy, may not be sufficient to staunch the flow of heroin across European and North American borders. In addition, many opium production areas are simply beyond reach. Another obstacle (as mentioned earlier) is the corruption in the transit countries. While the bulk of the heroin leaving Southeast Asia goes through Thailand, countries such as Laos, China, Hong Kong, and Nigeria are becoming significant players in transit operations.

## BURMA

Serious economic, political, and social problems impede the narcotics-control program in Burma. The Burmese economy is so underdeveloped that some analysts speculate that it would take decades to reverse the economic decline ushered in by the military dictatorship led by General Ne Win and now by his hand-picked successor, General Saw Maung, who was installed in September 1988.

From the colonial era under the British up until World War II, Burma was the world's leading exporter of rice, producing three-and-a-half million tons a year for export—half the rice traded on international markets. Burma was rich in fertile farmland, a product of the Irrawaddy delta. There is no doubt that the native Burmese were repressed under British rule (1886–1947), yet industry thrived. Burma was a major supplier of crude oil to other Asian nations; now it cannot produce enough oil to meet its own needs. In early 1987, the Burmese government requested that the United Nations give it least-developed country (LDC) status, which would qualify it for additional aid.[12] It is now considered to be one of the forty existing LDCs (Laos is also included) according to UN criteria.

Since a robust economy with a thriving export sector is a primary requisite for inducing opium poppy farmers to enter crop substitution programs, the hopes that Burma could embrace such programs are dismal. Even if Burmese farmers wanted to grow other crops, they would be unable to get their produce to market promptly because of the inadequate transportation system and an underdeveloped market infrastructure. At a minimum, the military regime would have to devote itself to a massive economic reform program before narcotics-control efforts—including alternative crop development, enforcement, and eradication projects—could be effective. Yet, the regime considers economic reform tantamount to political instability, and, as such, it is anathema.

Until the United States suspended assistance in 1988, Burma was the State Department's second most expensive antidrug program in the world. This statistic only serves to reflect Burma's distinction as being the world's largest opium producer and narcotics exporter. U.S. aid was suspended in September 1988 in response to the military regime's violent suppression of popular, antigovernment demonstrations for political and economic reform. With the suspension of U.S. aid, Burma discontinued most of its drug-control programs and, since that time, Burmese authorities have generally ignored the problem. In fact, the regime has sought to strengthen relations with major drug-producing and drug-trafficking organizations in the Golden Triangle in an effort to crack down on other ethnic insurgents such as the Karen. The U.S. antinarcotics program will likely remain inactive until the serious economic, political, and domestic problems in Burma are resolved.

Suspended in 1988, the INM had funded Burma's antinarcotics assistance program, yet U.S. officials complained that the program was only marginally effective because they were not permitted to monitor the program's results adequately or to observe how herbicide-spraying aircraft were being used by the Burmese. One report noted that government officials refused to spray areas not thoroughly secured by their ground troops, which left more than 90 percent of the opium crops untouched. (The government does not control large areas of the country where thousands of tons of opium are grown and refined.) Reported eradications amounted to a fraction of the estimated harvest, and seizures accounted for less than 1 percent of the total production. There have also been allegations that Burmese military officials used the aircraft provided by the State Department for purposes other than drug control, including eradication of subsistence crops in areas controlled by insurgent groups. Since the program has been discontinued, opium production in Burma has more than doubled from about 1,200 metric tons in 1988 to an all-time high of 2,600 metric tons in 1989.

The United States needs to continue a working-level dialogue between embassy officials in Rangoon and their Burmese law enforcement counterparts. These law enforcement officials should also prepare plans for effective drug interdiction and eradication efforts in the future.

## LAOS

Cooperation between the United States and Laos has improved markedly within the past few years. In 1989, Laos took several steps to begin cooperation with the United States on narcotics control, which led to its certification (eligibility for U.S. aid), for the first time ever, in 1990. In September 1989, Laos and the United States entered into a bilateral agreement on a crop control project. That year also marked the first time a U.S. national-interest wavier was not granted to the country. For the first time since the 1970s, Laotian officials participated in U.S.-sponsored drug-training programs. Two Congressional delegations concerned with narcotics control visited Laos in 1989 and 1990. In addition, high-level State Department and DEA officials visited Vientiane to discuss cooperation on narcotics control, including the need for concrete enforcement measures that should be undertaken by joint action of the Laotian government and military officials. In January 1990, the United States and Laos signed a wide-ranging narcotics-control agreement that commits Laos to enforcement cooperation.

One of the U.S. aid packages launched an $8.7-million program (to be used over a projected six-year period) intended to encourage substitute crops such as sesame, coffee, and mulberry trees (for silk) in high-altitude regions. U.S. funds will also go toward the construction of three dams designed to increase irrigated paddy lands by 50 percent in hopes of luring opium growers out of the hills. Two of the dams will be devoted to hydroelectric power generating. Two new roads (with a combined length of 103 kilometers) will also be constructed in order to help farmers get their new crops to market. This new project, however, is being implemented in an area not considered to be a significant opium-producing region of the country. There are at least six other provinces in Laos that contribute to the bulk of the country's opium production. One reason the Laotian government selected the Houa Phan region as the area for the program is that there is no insurgency problem there—unlike the situation in the Golden Triangle region of Laos. The Houa Phan program, which was agreed to by the U.S. and Laotian governments in late September 1989, seems to indicate that the insurgency problem in Laos has been serious enough to prevent the government from going after the opium where it is grown in the greatest quantities. Until two years ago, Laotian government officials insisted that drugs were not a problem in their country; the fault lay with "the demand in decadent Western societies." But in November 1989, a Laotian delegation attended a regional antinarcotics seminar for the first time, in no small part because Laotian officials have decided that the fight against drugs can provide a balm for their people's desperate poverty. By UN estimates, Laos is one of the ten poorest countries in the world with a per capita income of $160.

As for the United States, the project reflects a genuine desire to improve relations with Laos. Even if the Houa Phan plan does little for the effort against drugs, it may improve the United States' position in Indochina, clearing the way for a rapproachment with Vietnam.[13] Improved relations with Laos may also open up regions beyond Houa Phan to provinces where U.S. missions are eager to search for remains of American soldiers listed as missing in action during the Vietnam conflict.

In addition, the Laotian government reportedly has passed a new criminal code that includes penalties ranging from two to ten years in prison both for selling opium and for refining or trafficking heroin and other drugs. As encouraging as all of these agreements sound, however, the United States continues to receive reports that the Laotian military and government officials are themselves plying the drug trade and notes that no enforcement or eradication efforts have, as yet, been undertaken by the Laotian government. The lure of relatively quick and easily obtained profits is a difficult temptation to resist, especially for officials in impoverished nations such as Laos. The high-level involvement of military and civilian officials in the government programs (e.g., the military's Mountainous Area Development Corporation) continues to undermine constructive cooperation with the United States. It is difficult to balance corruption and ongoing trafficking activities on one hand with the beginnings of cooperation on the other.

## THAILAND

Significant increases in opium production and heroin refining in the Golden Triangle (especially in neighboring Burma) have alarmed U.S. government officials, who have focused their attention on Thailand as both a major trade route and as a source of booming production. Expansion of trade with Burma has only served to facilitate narcotics-smuggling activities. Official cross-border links for trade and security purposes promote ties with drug smugglers. These relations, in turn, lead to potentially increased narcotics corruption among relevant officials. The United States has urged the Thai government to enact long-pending asset seizure and conspiracy legislation through high-level contacts both in Bangkok and Washington, D.C. U.S. drug-control and crop substitution programs continue to be implemented in Thailand, although extremely good growing conditions produced the largest opium crop in recent years (about 50 metric tons). Thailand's significance in the region's transnational drug industry, however, still remains as an importer of opiates. Ironically, the nation's addicts consume more illicit narcotics than the country produces, thereby making Thailand a net importer of opium and heroin.

The Thai government continues to support programs aimed at reducing demand and improving treatment, both of which have received more attention recently. Drug abuse in Thailand is becoming a major problem that is only now beginning to receive the recognition it needs in order to justify the development and implementation of drug-control programs. The two elements of an INM-funded program in Thailand are law enforcement and crop control, in order of importance.

The foremost narcotics-control problem in Thailand is cross-border trafficking of Burmese heroin through Thailand to the world market. Since 1972, the INM has spent about $50 million in Thailand to help the Royal Thai government carry out law enforcement, crop control, and demand reduction programs. As a result of the Thai government's efforts during the past two decades, illicit opium cultivation has been reduced to about one-fourth of the 1960s levels (when production in Thailand peaked). Although narcotics-related arrests had increased in 1988 to an estimated 55,000, drug seizures were down.

One major problem with U.S. efforts in Thailand is that the U.S. government has not expressed sufficient concern with Thai corruption and its adverse effects on drug-control programs. Senior U.S. officials have been advised to accentuate whatever positive aspects there may be of Thai efforts to control narcotics in order to avoid friction between the two governments. This policy is not conducive to a candid approach seeking Thai cooperation in a meaningful interdiction program that would disrupt trafficking through Thailand.[14] Embassy officials in Bangkok, reporting on the narcotics situation in Thailand, did not accurately reflect more candid reporting by U.S. officials. The incongruities are only now being addressed. Thailand is the only key drug-producing nation in the international community that has offered to cooperate with drug-enforcement officials.

Despite persuasion by U.S. government officials, prospects for effective Thai asset seizure and narcotics conspiracy statutes remain less than optimistic. New statutes are being negotiated, but their enactment is not seen as likely in the immediate future.

An area that is gaining new importance in drug trafficking is the lightly patrolled dense forest on the Indian-Burmese border. Drugs are transported from Burma and Thailand to Katmandu, Calcutta, Bombay, and New Delhi, and then are flown to target destinations in the West. Although most of the heroin entering India comes from Afghanistan and Pakistan, it is reported that about 20 percent of the total now enters from the northeast. It is a two-way trade: Heroin comes into India, and acetic anhydride (a heroin-refining compound) is smuggled back into Burma. Some of the refining factories are located only fifty to sixty miles east of the border.

## THE INTERNATIONAL IMPACT OF THE GOLDEN TRIANGLE

After remaining stable for several years, heroin abuse in the United States is again on the upswing. The Bush administration's antidrug policy, however, has centered on reducing the production and availability of cocaine, and, therefore, has devoted its attention to Latin America. Significantly, there is increasing evidence of a definite linkage between domestic heroin and cocaine consumption. Drug abuse counselors have warned of the growing trend among addicts of using the two drugs in tandem—addicts take heroin to come down from the cocaine high. This is particularly true among those addicted to the more powerful crack form of cocaine. The growing appeal of the combination results from heroin's prolongation of the cocaine high while slowing down the "racing" feeling of crack and reducing the anxiety, depression, and paranoia that would otherwise occur when the crack high wears off.[15]

The prevalence of heroin use in the United States and Europe had never reached alarming proportions in previous decades because it never made serious inroads among those who engaged in social or casual drug use. This is not surprising given heroin's devastating effects, its limited availability, and, some would argue, a widespread psychological aversion to using hypodermic needles. The possibility of contracting AIDS has further discouraged heroin use by injection (which is the commonplace method). A new smokable form of relatively pure heroin has made its appearance among more and more casual drug users of late, threatening to vitiate traditional objections to heroine use and raising the potential for introducing heroin to a new generation. It is for this reason that monitoring programs must be established to measure the potential impact of the crack cocaine epidemic on heroin use. Heroin no. 4 (''white'' heroin, which is 90 percent pure) is typically injected, and it is preferred by U.S. and European addicts who sometimes mix it with crack cocaine in a smokable form. Brown (or ''red'' heroin no. 3, which is 60 percent pure), is smokable and consumed mainly in Asia. Given this newer, more convenient way of consuming heroin and its high level of purity in smokable form, drug experts and DEA officials fear that the United States may be poised on the brink of a heroin epidemic. Heroin production estimates indicate that the supply definitely exists to fuel such an epidemic. Total production of opium reached 4,209 metric tons in 1989, which is up from an estimated 1,458 metric tons in 1985. While one could endlessly cite statistics and search for evidence to establish a direct causal link, one would equally be hard pressed to deny that the growing drug industry in Southeast Asia is more than a significant factor in escalating heroin abuse in not only the United States, but also in Western and Eastern Europe and in Asia.

The National Narcotics Intelligence Consumers Committee (NNICC) believes that Southeast Asia has replaced Southwest Asia as the major regional source for heroin entering the U.S. market. The DEA supports this conclusion based on extensive monitoring and ''signature'' programs (a chemical analysis of heroin seized in the United States to determine its origin). A signature program administered recently shows that 46 percent of the samples analyzed were of Southeast Asian origin. Similarly, a 1989 monitoring program analysis of street purchases by DEA undercover agents indicated that over 90 percent of the purchases analyzed were of Southeast Asian origin.

Another alarming aspect of heroin trafficking in the country is the increase both in total heroin seizures and the size of the shipments. Annual domestic heroin seizures quadrupled between 1981 and 1989. While several kilograms once constituted a major domestic seizure, four seizures of Southeast Asian heroin in the past two years have weighed between 71 and 373 kilograms. A single shipment of 1,086 kilograms (destined for the United States) was seized in Bangkok in February 1988.

In addition, the dynamics of the heroin trade in the United States shifted in the 1980s after successful law enforcement strikes against organized crime left a void in the heroin distribution market in the United States. The emergence of the Chinese as drug barons in recent years has been due partly to the prosecution of the major Italian organized crime syndicates, which traditionally ran heroin trade from Southwest Asia into the United States. International organized crime syndicates in Hong Kong operate in tightly knit triads. These networks maintain connections in Chinese communities (through ethnic Chinese triads) in Bangkok, New York, San Francisco, Los Angeles, Amsterdam, and a host of other cities.

Despite law enforcement activities conducted in cooperation with other nations, the enormity of the problem continues to grow. Heroin-related hospital emergencies in the United States increased annually from 1980 to 1988 (reversing the trend during the 1970s, when heroin-related hospital emergencies generally decreased). Heroin-related emergency room notices received by the Drug Abuse Warning Network increased 26 percent from 1985 to 1988. Most of the upswing occurred on the East Coast. New York State and federal officials say that at least 200,000 of the estimated 500,000 heroin addicts in the nation live in New York City alone.[16]

Western Europe is the other prime destination for Southeast Asian heroin. Zurich, Switzerland, is one example of a city with a serious drug problem. Hardcore users gather in Platzspitz Park, or ''needle park'' as it is commonly known, and engage in an open spree of buying, selling, and using drugs. Drug use in this bizarre setting has been tolerated for many years by city officials, who believe that drug use should be regarded as a sickness rather than a crime. Over time, Zurich's drug policy has evolved from one of strict police enforcement, which drove the illicit market from one part of the city to another, to one of containment, which channelled the drug use away from the city's main streets and into this out-of-the-way park. Neighborhoods once plagued by petty crime and the sight of blatant drug abuse benefited from the containment policy, but statistics show that the overall crime rate has remained constant.[17]

Alarmingly, overall heroin use is also rising as a result of four major factors: (1) a significant increase in availability, (2) a dramatic increase in heroin purity, (3) more intense drug use habits, and (4) more convenient methods of ingestion.

This drug-consumption problem is not unique to the United States. As 1992 approaches, the question of a borderless Europe is making its way to the forefront of the political and economic agendas of the European Community (EC). The Single European Act of 1987 allows for the eventual free movement of people, goods, and services among members of the EC. The removal of physical barriers, immigration controls, and customs checks may enable drug traffickers to transport illicit drugs unhindered.[18]

Currently, a number of EC organizations—including the Schengen Group, the Pompidou Group, the TREVI Group, and the Rhodes Group—are considering solutions to the multitude of potential security problems that will be created by a borderless Europe. Some measures that have been suggested to combat the flow of drugs once the internal border controls have been eliminated include expanded international police cooperation, a broader network of information exchange, a common visa policy among EC countries, expanded judicial cooperation, common extradition standards, and a strengthening of security controls along the outer borders of the EC.

The concept of a borderless Europe is intriguing, but it is doubtful that the EC can effectively implement such a plan. Although the advantages of a more unified Europe seem strong, the problems that the participating countries will ultimately face may work to Europe's disadvantage. The United States' ability to control drug trafficking within its own borders will hinge upon how well the EC is able to handle these problems (as Europe may also prove to be a reliable conduit for illicit drugs).

Thailand will remain a focus of concern for the West because of the comparatively greater access to that country's interior enjoyed by international drug-control agencies. These concerns are threefold and can be categorized by explaining the individual situations in each producer country:

1. Burma remains the most serious challenge to the international community as there is a pressing need to develop effective and closely monitored drug-control programs while seeking to forge cooperative agreements with a regime over which the United States has limited influence.
2. Laos presents the United States and Western Europe with the most viable opportunities for cooperating in drug-control programs. In 1989, the Laotian government met all the conditions set by the U.S. government on narcotics cooperation, and, as a result, has begun to make considerable progress on interdiction and related programs.
3. Thailand holds the most promise for active participation in drug-control programs; however, officials from the West must encourage the Royal Thai government to monitor its drug industry closely and to control corruption. These points were mentioned in the certification agreement between the Thai and U.S. governments.

The United States and Western Europe have limited or no access to the source countries where 90 percent of the heroin consumed in the West originates. Countries producing the greatest amounts of opium are those in which the INM does not have a narcotics-control program (Afghanistan, Burma, Iran, and Laos). Their three more broadly based narcotics-control objectives are to support Thai efforts to improve law enforcement operations aimed at seizing illegal drugs and dismantling heroin refineries, to eliminate domestic planting of opium crops, and to foster drug abuse prevention and treatment activities.

Another concern for the United States and Europe is the amount of drugs produced in the region that are "spilling over" into lesser-developed countries. International governments are concerned that the possible expansion of the heroin-smuggling trade to such countries as Malaysia, China, Bangladesh, and India (which are all experiencing an increase in trafficking and abuse) will require more international resources devoted to countries outside the Golden Triangle. In order to target both major producing countries and the countries through which trafficking occurs, the United States is considering seven policy initiatives with regard to heroin production, abuse, and transit.[19]

Although the United States has actively sought to deter the drug industry in this region, the global nature of the heroin threat needs more participation by other developed countries and by the producer and trafficker countries themselves. Countries that are most able to share the burden of drug control include members of the Organization for Economic Cooperation and Development (OECD) or the Group of Ten. Some rather indirect—and, therefore, more palatable—options include increased emphasis on joint measures aimed at monitoring financial transactions and refining conspiracy laws in order to target money launderers and to better detect and seize traffickers' assets. These policy options may act as a small deterrent to drug-trafficking operations, but they would, in reality, have little impact on diminishing what may amount to a vast, transnational drug industry headquartered in Southeast Asia.

According to a March 1990 report released by the U.S. Senate Committee on Foreign Relations, there exist other indirect policy options that hold more promise for effective drug control. These include encouraging the United Nations Fund for Drug Abuse Control (UNFDAC) to expand current programs in order to make them more effective in major producing and trafficking regions; giving financial support to regional organizations (like ASEAN) based on cost-effectiveness in the high-priority countries; and encouraging regional organizations to assume greater responsibility for playing a more active role in suppressing heroin production and trafficking (especially since ASEAN members are most affected by the ever-increasing amount of heroin available on the Southeast Asian market). The United States would like to assist in developing and strengthening narcotics-control programs within major producing and trafficking countries, yet the overall sentiment is that these governments should be held more responsible for the progress in increasing the flow of drugs. The certification process is an important instrument in making countries accountable for their part in controlling the international drug trade. However, the annual certification report has been a source of considerable public debate in recent years largely because some members of Congress think that the State Department has not been tough enough with countries where the drug trade flourishes.[20]

Another important element in successful narcotics control is raising public awareness of drugs in producer, trafficking, and consumer countries. Governments can pass antidrug laws and institute drug-enforcement programs, but without widespread public cooperation, these efforts are unlikely to succeed. Improvements in international and regional public diplomacy programs that focus on all aspects of the opium and heroin problem and help to raise public awareness of how it affects consumers and producers alike should be implemented. Programs like these exist in Thailand, but Laos and Burma have not begun any such initiatives. Successful efforts to convince other nations that heroin is a major menace demanding a vastly greater degree of international cooperation could result in the gain of additional resources through expanded World Health Organization programs or even through the creation of a common OECD fund devoted to a comprehensive international solution to the spreading heroin problem. The United States has already undertaken initiatives with Japan on the Asian heroin front, and the issue was taken up at the 1989 Economic Summit held in Houston, Texas. This is at least a step in the right direction, since these nations now recognize the importance of providing a higher profile for drug control in the region by using concrete actions to support countries willing to attack the problem and by gaining greater access to and influence in countries that are currently unable (or unwilling) to assist in a worldwide heroin-control effort.

Since 1972, the State Department has spent over $660 million worldwide—primarily in Latin America and Asia—for drug control. For FY90, in an effort to reduce the flow of foreign-produced drugs entering the United States, the INM requested $115 million to fund programs that are designed to assist foreign countries in reducing cultivation, production, and trafficking of illicit drugs within their borders.

## TREATMENT

With the growing number of heroin addicts in the global community, the need for treatment centers and clinics is rising in importance on the international wealth and welfare agenda. The largest population of addicts exists in producer countries (Thailand, Burma, and Laos) and their target regions (the United States, Western Europe, and now parts of Eastern Europe). The prevalence of addiction is also growing in transit areas such as Africa, China, and Hong Kong. According to UN statistics (''On the Shipment Path: A Growing Need for Treatment Centers.'' *Incite*, 1990), Thailand has about 300,000 addicts and Hong Kong has about 40,000. Burma claims to have a mere 9,000 addicts, but this figure leaves researchers incredulous.

To be sure, before a treatment center can be of any benefit to a society, it must have clients. Thus addicts must surmount the herculean challenges of recognizing their problem and realizing that they must seek treatment. This seems to be the biggest hurdle to overcome. Without a sufficient number of patients to treat, centers encounter more difficulty raising money. But in some cases, even though centers are filled to capacity with addicts in need of care, they still remain inadequately funded and must eventually resort to ''warehousing'' instead of client-centered treatment.

In some countries, the mere existence of treatment centers is an acknowledgement of a drug abuse problem in their country, something that leaders of developing countries often wish to deny. In Thailand, for example, a small monastery ninety miles from Bangkok houses a treatment program that boasts a 70 percent success rate in getting addicts off heroin permanently. Founded more than thirty years ago, the Tum Krabok monastery's treatment methods include herbal steam baths, a week of hard labor, and ingestion of an emetic herbal mixture that patients must take every morning ''to purify the system.'' But perhaps the most significant aspect of this treatment center lies in the spiritual dimension—it changes addicts' attitudes toward drugs and toward themselves.[21]

The Thai government reportedly runs about 134 treatment centers across the country, and private groups manage about 22 others (many of them are small-scale operations that are located in the slums around Bangkok and run by former addicts). Few, if any, are very successful in getting addicts off drugs for even a short amount of time. Hong Kong has a higher percentage of addicts who enroll in treatment programs. As one of the major transit countries for Southeast Asian heroin, Hong Kong has a large addict population. The city has three main treatment programs that have three equally different methods for treating drug abusers. One system is designed for those who have been convicted of an offense and who have consequently been sentenced to jail. It is run by correctional officials, and those who agree to enroll in the program are sent at a judge's discretion for a year in lieu of imprisonment. This year is then followed up by another year of counseling.

Those who voluntarily decide to seek help may enroll in a private detoxification program run by the Society for the Aid and Rehabilitation of Drug Abusers. The clients in this private organization's program spend time in a colony located on Shek Kwu Chau island (about twelve miles southwest of Hong Kong in the South China Sea). Small and mountainous, the island is an idyllic setting for a gradual detoxification of its patients by using methadone, a synthetic narcotic that blocks the effects of heroin. After a period of detoxification, work therapy is provided. The addicts construct and maintain their own buildings and grow their own food. It is the society's intention to rekindle in their patients a feeling of self-worth by having the addicts create something for which they can be responsible. Peer counseling lasts for several weeks and, once back in Hong Kong, clients are encouraged to continue counseling for a minimum of two years.

Hong Kong's third program, and by far the largest, is a methadone maintenance program. For about US $.12 a day, addicts can get a supervised dosage of methadone that allows them to gradually withdraw from heroin. Some 7,500 addicts are enrolled in this program, and many drug abuse counselors think it is the most realistic program available.

Another factor that drug treatment centers must contend with is the AIDS virus, whose most prevalent form of transmission is through shared hypodermic needles. These centers must learn to handle not only an addict dependent on heroin, but also one who is infected with the virus. A doctor from the University of Zurich opened an AIDS prevention clinic in Platzspitz Park in 1988, which is supported by the city and other organizations. It supplies free needles, condoms, and meals. It also provides emergency services for overdose victims. Some of the clinic's social workers help to guide addicts into drug treatment programs, but often they are unsuccessful in persuading the serious addicts to reform. An estimated 35 percent of heavy drug users in Zurich are infected with the AIDS virus.

In the West, drug treatment programs of all kinds are not hard to come by, but they also admit to low success rates. Drug rehabilitation programs frequently find that crack cocaine users mix the drug with heroin leading to a "polydrug" addiction, which is much more difficult to treat than addiction to a single drug.

## CONCLUSION

The Golden Triangle is the world's largest producer of opium, and consequently it has a significant impact on the global drug market and its money-laundering operations. As demand for illicit drugs continues to rise in industrialized as well as in developing countries, supply will also continue to escalate. The Golden Triangle's drug industry (especially in Burma) enjoys such close ties to local authorities that local and foreign intervention to curb production and trafficking have few hopes for any lasting success. This complex industry, which lies in the heart of a very volatile part of the world, will require close attention from the global community.

The drug trade has survived for centuries, and it is not likely to disappear anytime soon. Not least among the reasons for this is the current lack of demand for an international solution to the drug problem; with the possible exception of Thailand, the countries which form the Golden Triangle are of no geopolitical significance to the West. In its understandable preoccupation with the cocaine problem, the Bush administration has strayed unwittingly into underrating the threat posed by heroin to U.S. national security.

Until heroin is perceived as a serious threat to the domestic stability of a country such as the United States, it will not receive significant international attention. Western governments have but scraped the surface of the volcanic layers of the international drug problem, but any steps, however small, are in the right direction.

## NOTES

1. U.S. Congress, Senate, Committee on Foreign Relations, 7 March 1989.

2. This brief outline of the history of opium in Asia is heavily indebted to Immanuel C. Y. Hsü's excellent treatment of the subject in *The Rise of Modern China* (New York: Oxford University Press, 1983, 3d ed.), especially pp. 168–93.

3. For a detailed account of the Kachin Independence Organization, see their "Opium Statement" produced by the Central Committee for the Kachin Independence Organization, 1987.

4. See Jon A. Wiant, "Narcotics in the Golden Triangle," *Washington Quarterly* (Fall 1985): 125–40.

5. Economist Intelligence Unit (London), *Country Study of Thailand*. A publication of *The Economist*, 1989.

6. See Bertil Lintner, "Triangular Ties" and "The New Dealers," *Far Eastern Economic Review*, 28 March 1991, 22–26.

7. For greater detail, see the U.S. Congress, Senate, Committee on Foreign Relations, "Narcotics Trafficking in Southeast Asia," 9 March 1990.

8. According to the corporation's records, by February 1989, twenty concession areas had been leased with an estimated revenue of $112 million for the Timber Corporation. The company agreed to enter into contracts only with those Thai interests recommended by the Thai authorities concerned. Many of these firms have major shareholders who are

in the RTA or in the governing political party. There is a great deal of commingling between Thai and Burmese interests. For example, a relative by marriage of Chavalit is the principal stockholder in one of the major firms operating in Burma. Also, the largest shareholder in the first firm to receive a concession in Burma is a former member of parliament with connections to the ruling party's coalition partner. Chavalit eventually resigned his position as deputy prime minister. He was given the position for fear that he would carry out a coup as he was a vocal critic of government corruption. On 24 February 1991, Thailand's military leaders launched a successful coup against the Chatichai Choonhavan government, and martial law was declared. He was accused by the military of tolerating corruption and interfering with the armed forces. The United States has suspended $16 million in military and economic aid that was intended for development projects.

9. James L. Tyson, "China Takes on 'Golden Triangle'," *Christian Science Monitor*, 13 December 1990.

10. Also see Nicholas D. Kristof, "Heroin Spreads among Young in China," *New York Times*, 9 March 1991.

11. U.S. Senate Committee on Foreign Relations, 7 March 1989.

12. See Stan Sesser, "A Reporter at Large: A Rich Country Gone Wrong," *New Yorker*, 9 October 1989, 55–96.

13. For more details about the Houa Phan region and U.S. policy, see Jinny St. Goar, "Poppy Diplomacy," *Far Eastern Economic Review*, 24 May 1990, 40–42.

14. U.S. Senate Committee on Foreign Relations, 9 March 1990.

15. Gordon Witkin, "Return of a Deadly Drug Called Horse," *U.S. News and World Report*, 14 August 1989, 31–32.

16. Evelyn Nieves, "Tainted Drug Kills 4 More, Officials Say," *New York Times*, 4 February 1991, B1, B2; Joseph B. Treaster, "Craving for Better High Is Fatal Synthetics' Lure," *New York Times*, 4 February 1991, B2.

17. Joseph B. Treaster, "Help Is at Hand, but the Mad Revelry Grinds On," *New York Times*, 27 September 1990.

18. For greater detail, see Gerald Soloman and Bruce George, *North Atlantic Assembly Political Committee Report* (Washington, D.C.: North Atlantic Assembly, November 1990), 1–27.

19. For the seven policy initiatives mentioned, refer to the U.S. Senate Committee on Foreign Relations, 9 March 1990, p. 7.

20. Michael Isikoff, "Opium, Cocaine Crops Rose Sharply in 1988," *Washington Post*, 2 March 1989, A3.

21. For further information, see "The Perilous Swim in Heroin's Stream," *Insight*, 5 February 1990, 8–17.

## BIBLIOGRAPHY

Ching-hwang, Yen. *A Social History of the Chinese in Singapore and Malaysia 1800–1911*. Singapore: Oxford University Press, 1986.

*Drug Control Programme in Singapore*. Singapore: Government of Singapore, 1990.

George, F. J. *The Singapore Saga*. Singapore: Fernandez Joseph George Publishers, 1985.

Naylor, R. T. *Hot Money: And the Politics of Debt*. London: Unwin Paperbacks, 1987.

Pan, Lynn. "Fraternal Is as Fraternal Does," *Far Eastern Economic Review* (April 25, 1991): 34.

Posner, Gerald L. *Warlords of Crime, Chinese Secret Societies: The New Mafia*. New York: Penguin Books, 1988.

*Selected Financial Centres: Summary of Banking and Tax Regulations*. Toronto, Canada: Price Waterhouse, 1988.

Sesser, Stan. "Reporter at Large: Singapore, A Nation of Contradictions." *The New Yorker* (January 13, 1992): 37–68.

Trebach, Arnold S. *The Great Drug War: And Radical Proposals that Could Make America Safe Again*. New York: Macmillan Publishing Company, 1987.

Trocki, Carl A. *Opium and Empire: Chinese Society in Colonial Singapore, 1800–1910*. Ithaca and London: Cornell University Press, 1991.

Turnball, C. M. *A History of Singapore 1819–1975*. Singapore: Oxford University Press, 1977.

United States Department of State, Bureau of International Narcotics Matters. *International Narcotics Control Strategy Report March 1991*. Washington, D.C.: United States Department of State, 1991.

Walter, Ingo. *The Secret Money Market: Inside the Dark World of Tax Evasion, Financial Fraud, Insider Trading, Money Laundering, and Capital Flight*. New York: Harper Business, 1990.

# 24

# Singapore

SCOTT B. MACDONALD

## INTRODUCTION

Singapore is a highly developed city-state surrounded by larger, less developed countries. Located on the Strait of Malacca, it occupies a geostrategic position that few other nations possess. Consequently, Singapore's economy is based on a combination of manufacturing, financial services offered through its offshore banking sector and stock market, and its function as a regional transportation hub for shipping and air transport. Many of the same factors that have made Singapore attractive to companies from around the world have also made the city-state attractive to money launderers and drug smugglers. Singapore is well known for its tough stance on drug traffickers. However, its location south of the Golden Triangle countries—Burma, Laos and Thailand—puts it in a neighborhood where drugs are accessible. Additionally, money laundering is not a criminal act in Singapore, and it is suspected by some analysts that the country's offshore financial sector is used as a transit point in the laundering process of drug money. To a lesser extent, Singapore's transportation hub has attracted some transit traffic, using either the harbor or the international airport.

## BACKGROUND

When Singapore received its independence in 1966 after it left an abortive federation with Malaysia, the prospects for its success were not promising. A former British colony, founded by Sir John Raffles in the early 1800s, Singapore was a predominantly Chinese island in a Malay world, with Malaysia due north of the Strait of Jahore and Indonesia due south. Despite considerable misgivings about Singapore's ability to survive as an independent country, the country's leadership met the developmental challenge and converted what was potentially an economic backwater into one of the world's most successful examples of capitalism.

Singapore in the 1990s is one of the New Industrializing Economies (NIEs) of the Pacific Basin, a status shared with Hong Kong, South Korea, and Taiwan. This means that it has moved ahead of most of the developing world in terms of economic and social indicators. Anyone travelling to Singapore from any number of countries in the region is struck by the city-state's modernity as exemplified by its multitude of skyscrapers, excellent system of telecommunications, and overall efficiency. Singapore's per capita income, life expectancy, and literacy rates are higher than those of its immediate neighbors, including Indonesia, Malaysia, and the Philippines.

Although Singapore is not a drug producer and currently not a major consumer, its history is interwoven with one of the world's more nefarious episodes in the traffic of narcotics—the China opium trade of British merchants. In the very foundations of the colony, the international drug trade hovered over the future nation's emergence as a trade hub. Singapore became a convenient port on the route from opium produced in another British colony, India, and nearby Persia. At the same time, Chinese traders sailed to the Malacca Strait settlement bringing cargoes of sugar, fine raw silk, porcelain, damasks, brocades, satins, and musk. They returned to southern China laden with manufactured goods from the West as well as with opium.

As the colony became more settled at the turn of the century, its demands for labor attracted large numbers of Chinese coolies, many of whom indulged in smoking opium. The British colonial administration was largely indifferent, and opium smoking and its sale were allowed. In fact, Singapore had an opium factory, which was a lucrative commercial enterprise for local Chinese merchants. The main customers for smokable opium were the Chinese workers on Singapore's pepper and gambier farms. The revenues from the sale of opium, according to some analysts, could be said to have underwritten the empire building and paid for Singapore's emerging role as a major trade entrepôt in Southeast Asia.

The attraction of opium smoking in the early years of Singapore's existence as a British colony should not be understated. In the nineteenth century most Europeans regarded opium smoking as a bad habit which, in the words of historian C. M. Turnball, was "soothing and soporific, evil if taken to excess."[1] It was estimated in 1848 that 20 percent of the entire population and more than 50 percent of the Chinese adults were opium addicts.[2] Rich Chinese, who had access to high-quality opium, were not seriously affected, as were their poorer countrymen whose financial status meant that they could only afford opium refuse, which carried with it health problems. It was not until 1906 that an Anti-Opium Society was founded and 1908 that a government commission examined the problem. In 1910, the colonial administration assumed control of local cultivation and the sale of opium. This was done to maintain a better quality of opium and to reduce the number of health problems related to smoking the refuse. British authorities also burned the refuse.

Opium smoking continued as a problem in Singapore well into the twentieth century. Opium still accounted for almost half of the colony's revenue in the mid–1920s. With the restoration of British control in the aftermath of World War II, it was decided that something finally had to be done to reign in the problem. In 1946, the Opium and Chandu Proclamation was implemented, which made opium possession and the possession of opium-smoking utensils a criminal act. This was followed in 1955 by the creation of the Opium Treatment Centre. Additionally, legislation was passed that required all opium abusers arrested to be admitted for rehabilitation treatment. Antidrug education campaigns and the increasing legal pressure against opium smoking led to a sharp decrease in narcotics use. According to Singaporean sources, opium addicts fell from an estimated 40,000 in 1946 to a low of 7,000 in 1970. Additionally, opium smoking was largely limited to an older generation of adults, who began to die off in the 1980s.

While the Chinese and British brought opium use to colonial Singapore, the Indians who came to the colony introduced cannabis smoking. This remained on a limited scale until the 1960s when it became more widespread. Although some cannabis smoking continues in the 1990s, Singaporean authorities do not regard its use with the same alarm as they do use of the other major narcotic—heroin.

Heroin did not become a problem in Singapore until the 1970s. Considering Singapore's location due south of the heroin-producing Golden Triangle, the narcotic was easily accessible. Additionally, the so-called hippie culture of the time helped stimulate a curiosity to try new drugs. As a Singapore government report noted: "Heroin found its way into discotheques, bowling alleys, back-lanes, shopping centres and working places. Even schools were not spared. The spread of heroin was so swift that it reached epidemic proportions within a span of a few years."[3] This was reflected by the number of heroin arrests, which shot up from 4 in 1972 to 5,682 in 1976.

The government's response to the heroin epidemic was effective. The heroin addict population was estimated at 13,000 in 1977, which amounted to 3 percent of the males between the ages of fifteen and twenty-four years. After an examination of the drug strategies of other countries, Singapore adopted a conservative program with supply and demand components. The former, based on the arrest and incarceration of as many drug traffickers as possible, is in line with the efforts of many other countries; the efforts made on the demand reduction side are still controversial.

## DEMAND REDUCTION PROGRAM

Singapore's demand reduction program was and still is aimed at arresting as many addicts as possible and committing them to undergo treatment and rehabilitation. As a government study notes: "To ensure identified abusers undergo rehabilitation and treatment without delay, they are committed by executive authority and not court order. After rehabilitation and treatment, they were placed on compulsory supervision and aftercare."[4]

Since the Singaporean drug rehabilitation program is still operational in the 1990s, it is worth discussing further. The central component of the program is a system of Drug Rehabilitation Centers (DRCs). The drug addict is admitted to a DRC by executive authority in the director of the Central Narcotics Bureau (CNB). Under Singaporean law addicts are identified either through a urine test or through medical observation and examination by two doctors. The period of time spent in a DRC can vary from six to thirty-six months depending on the number of admissions and the patient's progress in the program.

In the DRC, the addict undergoes a five-stage process: detoxification, recuperation and orientation, indoctrination, physical fitness, and work program. At the end of this cycle, the DRC inmate is placed on a day release scheme (DRS). This program, started in September 1979, continues to function as a halfway house. Those placed on a DRS are allowed to work outside of the program, but they must return after working hours. Random urine tests are conducted to make certain that the inmate is making progress. If there is a relapse, the inmate is pulled out of the DRS and sent back to the DRC and forced to undergo the entire program again. Those who complete the DRS are released to undergo two years of statutory supervision. During the period of supervision, the supervisee is expected to attend counseling sessions conducted by volunteer aftercare officers (VAOs). The volunteers are recruited and trained by a nongovernmental organization known as the Singapore Anti-Narcotics Association, which works closely with supervision officers.

In 1987, the DRC program was reviewed and modified. Two additional rehabilitation programs were added: the Exit Counselling Programme (ECP) and the Intensive Counselling Programme (ICP). The ECP, introduced in April 1988, is oriented to first-time addicts who wish to take a "short, sharp, shock" treatment. The addict deemed as having the necessary motivation undergoes detoxification and then is channelled for two weeks of intensive drug education and counseling. The successful candidate is placed on special supervision, while the special counseling continues. If he or she remains drug free, the supervision order, which is valid for two years, is revoked after only one year. If a candidate fails at any point of the ECP, he or she is sent back to DRC where the cycle is restarted.

The ICP, implemented in October 1988, is streamlined for those DRC inmates who are repeaters but are motivated to change. It lasts two months and consists largely of intensive group and individual counseling for the purpose of inculcating the discipline required to avoid drugs. Through the formation of self-help groups, inmates share their experiences and learn from them. After a successful ICP, the participants are placed on the modified and improved four-month DRS. After that, they are placed on special supervision for two years, but, if they remain drug free, their supervision order will be revoked after one year. Any relapses send the failed inmate back to the five-stage DRC program.

It is important to clarify that Singaporean law provides for compulsory institutional treatment and rehabilitation, but addicts are not charged in court. This is done to avoid criminalizing addicts. As the Singaporean government states, "The DRC is not a prison and addicts are sent by executive authority and not by the judiciary."[5]

Singapore's treatment program for addicts was complemented by harsher penalties for narcotics trafficking. Under the Misuse of Drugs Act of 1973, the mandatory minimum sentence for trafficking in very small quantities of heroin is five years and five strokes of the cane; and for cannabis, three years and three strokes of the cane. A second component of going after traffickers was the introduction of the death penalty in December 1975. Offenses of trafficking, importing, and exporting involving more than fifteen grams of diamorphine (heroin) or more than thirty grams of morphine or manufacturing a controlled drug will warrant the sentence upon conviction.

Singapore's drug control policy, which was largely introduced in the 1970s and modified in the 1980s, has been relatively successful. The number of addicts fell from 13,000 in 1977 to 6,000 in 1983. However, the compulsory nature of the rehabilitation program and its ongoing supervisory program have made some analysts critical because of the lack of basic civil rights of the addict in a "democratic" society. What has been debated is that Singaporean authorities treat drug addicts like an "infectious agent" and rehabilitate the addict through quarantine—a period of time during which the addict loses his or her personal liberties. As Arnold Trebach noted, "Addicts are spared the stigma of a criminal conviction because they are simply arrested, given a urine test, and, if they do not pass, are placed in the rehabilitation center without a formal trial."[6] To those who favor the Singaporean model for the United States, Trebach added, "They were offering quick-fix police-state solutions to a delicate and distressing problem requiring patience, toleration, humane treatment options, and adherence to the rinciple that even suspected drug users, like suspected robbers, had rights in a ocracy."[7]

gapore uses other means to control drug trafficking and abuse: denial of ts, use of narcotic detector dogs, computers at entry/exit points, and rine test machines (IUTs). For the first, all drug offenders are denied for a period upon release from prisons or DRCs. The only exceptions who successfully complete ECP and ICP supervision. This is done to ir travel movements to prevent them from conducting new drug traf- use. Sniffer dogs are used extensively at the harbor, the Mails and ion, and the airport to detect narcotics. Computers are used at im- hecks to identify drug offenders and suspects, who can be searched d to take a urine test. Finally, IUT machines have been installed at oints and all police stations. Identified foreign addicts are refused he country; locals are sent immediately to the DRC.

Singapore's drug-control policies have made it a place to be avoided by many traffickers and, for locals, a place not to take drugs. However, both drug use and drug dealing continue. According to Singaporean government data, in 1988, 5,451 abusers were arrested along with 484 traffickers. The main narcotic seized was cannabis, which amounted to 138.2 kilograms in 1988, followed by seizure of 52.4 kilograms of heroin.

The most popularly abused narcotic in Singapore in the late 1980s was heroin number 3, which is about 20-percent purity. Most heroin enters the country from the Golden Triangle; cannabis comes from Thailand and Indonesia. One of the best known criminal organizations involved in trafficking of drugs is the Ah Kong Triad, which is based in Singapore's large Chinese community. It was active in the expansion of the heroin market in the Netherlands in the 1970s and continues to be a player in the transshipment of Southeast Asian narcotics into Europe.[8] Singapore also appears to be on the transit line for Nigerian criminal organizations moving heroin from Southeast Asia through Africa and to either Europe or the Americas.

## MONEY LAUNDERING

One of the great strengths of the Singaporean economy is its financial sector. Highly efficient and with a solid reputation, the city-state's offshore finance is well protected by bank secrecy laws, and its comparative advantage vis-à-vis many other nations is its absence of foreign exchange controls. Singapore is the largest offshore banking center in the Asian-dollar market (the Pacific equivalent of the Eurodollar market). With the majority of well-known international banks with offices in Singapore, a significant volume of capital flows in and out of the country on a daily basis. Considering the location near the Golden Triangle, some analysts feel that drug money laundering takes place. R. T. Naylor commented in 1987, "Singapore bank-loan officers were notorious for their greasy palms, and Singapore banks equally notorious for evading restrictions imposed by the regulatory authorities."[9]

Singapore is expected to gain considerable offshore finance business
Hong Kong reverts to the control of the People's Republic of China in
This raises a number of questions about whether or not the city-state is p
to deal with a large inflow of capital, some of which is potentially h
linked to Chinese triads involved in the international heroin trade. De
some perceive as a reluctance to weaken bank secrecy, the Singap
ernment indicated in 1991 that it was considering new measures to
better control over potential penetration of money-laundering organi
the same time, Singaporean authorities are prohibited from sharing
with foreign law enforcement agencies. Moreover, the asset forfeitur
of Singapore's anticorruption law have not provided an entree for s
related assets.

The supervisory authority for banks and banking activities in Sing

Monetary Authority of Singapore (MAS). The MAS supervises, reviews, and inspects the financial sector through its Banking and Financial Institutions Department. Under this mandate, the MAS has the following powers: to monitor compliance with the Banking Act and the notices and guidelines issued by the MAS to the banks, to conduct inspection of the banks, to make regulations in regard with the provisions of the Banking Act, and to prescribe the kinds of information to be submitted by the banks. Although there are no exchange control regulations in Singapore, banks must disclose all foreign exchange contracts that they enter into in their monthly returns to the MAS.

## INTERNATIONAL LINKAGES TO DRUG CONTROL

Singapore is committed to international cooperation in fighting the international trade in illicit narcotics. The city-state has provided funds and expertise to the United Nations Fund for Drug Abuse Control (UNFDAC) and is a signatory to the United Nations Single Convention on Narcotics Drugs of 1961 and as amended by the 1972 Protocol. Singapore is also a signatory of the United Nations Convention against Illicit Traffic in Narcotic Drugs and Psychotropic Substances of 1988.

Singapore's General Narcotics Bureau has maintained close working relations with national drug enforcement agencies in the Association of Southeast Asian Nations (Brunei, the Philippines, Indonesia, Malaysia, Singapore, and Thailand). Relations have also been good with other regional and international agencies, such as the International Criminal Police Organization (Interpol), the United Nations Division of Narcotics Drugs, the International Narcotics Control Board, and the Colombo Plan Bureau Drug Advisory Programme.

Relations with the United States on the international drug issue have been relatively positive. Although the U.S. (as well as the British) government would prefer to see tighter anti–money-laundering laws, relations were solid enough for Singapore to extradite an American citizen wanted in the United States on drug charges. This was the first time that Singapore had done so; prior to the extradition, the city-state had argued that it lacked a conspiracy statute that would permit the government to charge persons not in actual possession of drugs at the time of the arrest. The Singapore court system ruled that the U.S. conspiracy charge was consistent with Singapore's statute of aiding and abetting, which allowed the government to grant the request for extradition.

## CONCLUSION

Singapore's experience with the narcotics problem has been one based on its location near the Golden Triangle and of its being a small society capable of rapidly mobilizing to deal with potential epidemics of drug abuse. It is likely in the future that it will increasingly come under pressure to tighten its controls on the offshore banking sector with an eye to making money-laundering operations more difficult. The looming change of control over Hong Kong is likely to put ever greater pressure on Singapore, especially as triad organizations search for other bases of operation. Singapore, with its highly protected bank secrecy, is likely to be attractive despite the vigilance of the country's enforcement agencies. At the same time, Singapore maintains one of the more drug-free societies in the world, a notable achievement considering its location so close to three major source countries.

## NOTES

1. C. M. Turnball, *A History of Singapore 1819–1975* (Singapore: Oxford University Press, 1977), 64.
2. Ibid.
3. Government of Singapore, "Drug Control Programme in Singapore," Singapore Embassy in Washington, D.C., no date, received in 1991, 2.
4. Ibid, 3.
5. Ibid, 6.
6. Arnold S. Trebach, *The Great Drug War: And Radical Proposals that Could Make America Safe Again* (New York: Macmillan Co., 1987), 130.
7. Ibid.
8. See Gerald L. Posner, *Warlords of Crime, Chinese Secret Societies: The New Mafia* (Harmondsworth, England: Penguin Books, 1988).
9. R. T. Naylor, *Hot Money and the Politics of Debt* (London: Unwin Paperbacks, 1987), 223.

## BIBLIOGRAPHY

Ching-hwang, Yen. *A Social History of the Chinese in Singapore and Malaysia 1800–1911*. Singapore: Oxford University Press, 1986.

George, F. J. *The Singapore Saga*. Singapore: Fernandez Joseph George, 1985.

Government of Singapore. "Drug Control Programme in Singapore," provided by Singapore Embassy in Washington, D.C. No date given, received 1991.

Posner, Gerald L. *Warlords of Crime, Chinese Secret Societies: The New Mafia*. New York: Penguin Books, 1988.

Price Waterhouse. *Selected Financial Centres: Summary of Banking and Tax Regulations*. Toronto: Price Waterhouse, 1988.

Trebach, Arnold S. *The Great Drug War: And Radical Proposals that Could Make America Safe Again*. New York: Macmillan Co., 1987.

Trocki, Carl A. *Opium and Empire: Chinese Society in Colonial Singapore, 1800–1910*. Ithaca, N.Y.: Cornell University Press, 1991.

Turnball, C. M. *A History of Singapore 1819–1975*. Singapore: Oxford University Press, 1977.

# V

# International Organizations and Drug Control Policy

# 25

# The Organization of American States and Drug Control in the Americas

MICHAEL J. DZIEDZIC

## INTRODUCTION

As an embodiment of the collective will of over thirty sovereign states, the Organization of American States (OAS) is a creature of consensus. Effective action by the organization to deal with any regional concern necessarily awaits multinational convergence around a common course of action. With regard to the transnational drug trade, consensus was a considerable period in gestation. The OAS's quest to join the battle against the *narcotraficantes* was initially impeded by a divergence in perceptions and policy preferences between drug-consuming and drug-producing states. Only after it became clear that the operations of transnational drug "cartels" (TDCs) were a real or potential menace to all member states did the essence of a drug-control regime begin to take shape. This chapter traces the emergence of that regime as it is manifested both in hemispheric accords and in the form of a permanent OAS commission to address this matter.

## THE QUEST FOR CONSENSUS

The initial barrier to OAS action against narcotics trafficking was a schism between drug-exporting and drug-consuming nations. As the world's predominant market for illicit drugs, the United States was held accountable for the pathologies associated with the drug phenomenon. Indeed, regional producers of marijuana, opium, and coca leaf were not especially sympathetic to appeals for action since the deleterious consequences appeared to be largely isolated to the United States. As former Peruvian President Alan García (whose country is responsible for the production of about two-thirds of the world's coca crop) observed, drug cartels constitute Latin America's first successful multinational corporations. That a portion of the hard currency generated by this activity was flowed back into the economies of drug-producing states (and that employment has also been engendered as a result) has not always been a major cause for concern among those south of the Rio Bravo.

Since the negative implications of drug abuse seemed to be concentrated in the United States, drug-producing states were clearly disinterested in being compelled to bear much of the burden associated with a counterdrug campaign. Nor was it their preference to have the drug war fought primarily on their soil. Thus the typical Latin American perception was that the drug problem was essentially a North American concern, and the preferred policy option was that the United States clean up its own house by reducing demand. There was little sympathy for diverting scarce national resources to cope with a phenomenon that had been visited upon developing Latin American nations by degenerate behavior in the United States.

These perceptions and policy preferences were not shared by the United States, of course. Both production and consumption of illicit drugs were regarded as morally reprehensible, but the more tractable solution seemed to be to attack the problem "at its source." In particular, this meant seeking to eradicate drug production, although interdicting the flow into the United States was also a desirable option. These policy preferences were manifested in budget allocations which devoted roughly 70 percent of spending to supply-side programs and only 30 percent to demand reduction in the United States.

Eradiction and interdiction programs, however, can be implemented effectively only with the cooperation of producing and transit states. U.S. initiatives in these areas were not often embraced with great enthusiasm throughout the region for reasons of divergent national interests. In addition, Latin American sensitivities toward potential infringements of their national sovereignty tended to become aroused. U.S. frustrations were exacerbated by growing indications that narcotraffickers had infiltrated high government offices and had compromised vital institutions of law and order. One response to this was to establish a "certification" process whereby drug-producing nations that failed to cooperate fully with the United States were to be denied U.S. assistance.

Thus, from the U.S. perspective, drug-control efforts were vitiated by the corruption of officialdom in drug-producing and drug-transitting states; Latin American leaders, on the other hand, viewed the problem essentially as one of decadence in U.S. society leading to a $100 billion national drug habit. Whereas the United States preferred to attack the problem at its source through eradication (and interdiction), drug-producing states viewed the source of the problem as U.S. demand and insisted upon greater exertions to control drug abuse. These opposing perceptions and policy preferences did not constitute fertile soil for the emergence of a regional drug-control regime. Yet, as narcotrafficking became more entrenched throughout the Americas, especially with the burgeoning of the cocaine trade during the 1980s, the basis for collective action began gradually to develop.

Differences between drug-producing and drug-consuming states began to narrow during the latter part of the 1980s when it became clear that Latin American nations were liable to suffer dearly from the ravages associated with the drug trade. The deepening tragedy in Colombia was an object lesson for all nations in the region. After an attorney general, a justice minister, multiple Supreme Court justices, innumerable policemen and soldiers, and ultimately a leading presidential candidate fell prey to narco-terrorism in Colombia, it became abundantly clear that the United States was not the only prospective victim of this transnational phenomenon. Indeed, the consequences were so extreme that this activity came to be recognized as a bona fide threat to regional security.[1]

The financial resources and firepower at the disposal of TDCs meant that national law enforcement agencies were severely underfunded and outgunned. Magnates of the drug cartels preferred insidious means, seeking first to suborn officials responsible for enforcing drug laws. If this failed to produce desired results, force could always be used. Thus, pertinent law enforcement or military officials were inevitably offered a succinct choice between *plata o plomo* (essentially a bribe or a bullet). In any event, the longer that drug cartels were allowed to operate relatively unmolested, the more thoroughly they could insinuate themselves into the very agencies of law and order that were the nation's only defense against them. In addition, there was the chilling potential for narcoterrorists to form a marriage of convenience with subversive groups, thus compounding the challenge to national security. Not wishing to see the Colombian experience replicated in their own countries, statesmen in Latin America began to explore the possibility of concerted hemispheric action to combat the scourge of narco-trafficking.

Divergent perceptions about the nature of the problem narrowed further as it became clear that drug abuse was not solely a North American affliction. Especially in coca-growing and cocaine-processing areas, consumption of *basuco* (a cheap, smokable form of semi-refined cocaine) became a mounting concern. At the same time, recognition began to grow in the United States that curtailing domestic demand was a sine qua non of the war on drugs. Stimulated by Nancy Reagan's "Just Say No" campaign and accentuated by the Bush administration's National Drug Control Strategy, the United States began to undertake the sort of demand reduction measures Latin American officials had been requesting. Thus, the previous gap between fundamental policy preferences has been narrowed considerably. A regional consensus has emerged in support of a simultaneous assault on both supply and demand, and the tendency to engage in mutual recriminations has been suppressed. Most would now agree that no longer is there a "geography of blame" dividing the region.

## THE EMERGING INTER-AMERICAN DRUG CONTROL REGIME

As this consensus was being molded, the OAS began to enjoy increasing scope for promoting hemispheric cooperation to combat narco-trafficking. Initial impetus was provided by the Declaration of Quito in August 1984. The product of a summit meeting involving the presidents of Bolivia, Colombia, Ecuador, and Venezuela (as well as representatives from three other countries), this declaration exhorted the international community to declare drug trafficking a crime against mankind and to establish a fund to provide assistance to developing countries afflicted by this malady. The Quito Declaration served as a springboard for the OAS to take up the issue at its fourteenth regular General Assembly session held in Brasilia in November 1984. At that gathering, member states adopted a resolution declaring drug trafficking a ''crime that affects all of mankind'' and resolved to convoke an Inter-American Specialized Conference on Traffic in Narcotic Drugs in 1986.[2] Specific items to be considered at this conference were economic alternatives for coca production, demand reduction measures, mechanisms to facilitate regional cooperation, and creation of a special fund as a source of assistance for member states affected by narco-trafficking.

Convened in April 1986 at Rio de Janeiro, this conference constituted a watershed for the OAS as an actor in the counterdrug effort. The Program of Action of Rio de Janeiro that emerged from this hemispheric gathering was notable for two reasons.[3] First, it constructed a framework of recommended actions for member states to follow in their own efforts to cope with the drug problem. Second, it brought the OAS itself directly into the counternarcotics campaign.

Concerning the first aspect of the Program of Action, delegates reached with respect to principles that would guide national conduct. A primary consideration was the goal of socioeconomic development. Attendees concurred that actions to counter use and trafficking in drugs should be consistent with this objective, and that a solution to the problem would necessarily entail progress toward developmental goals. Participants also exhorted governments to respect human rights, democracy, the environment, and national sovereignty. Conferees further recognized that narco-trafficking itself placed these values in jeopardy. Accordingly, nations committed themselves to cooperate in pursuit of the main objectives of the Program of Action, which were ''to reduce the demand for drugs, prevent drug abuse, and effectively combat unlawful production of and trafficking in drugs.''[4]

In subsequent chapters, the Program of Action recommended that OAS members take a host of specific actions. To reduce demand for illicit substances, the program recommends that governments assign this objective their top priority, that they conduct studies of the causes and extent of drug abuse in their individual countries, and that they promote prevention, treatment, and rehabilitation programs. To address the supply side, states were urged to exchange information about trafficking organizations and their activities and to consider developing common legislation to attack TDCs in the areas of money laundering, seizure of assets, and control of precursor chemicals essential for the manufacture of illicit substances. With regard to production, the program approved of crop substitution ''under appropriate conditions,'' as well as eradication of these crops by environmentally acceptable means "as defined by each state." Finally, the program endorsed certain general measures such as the establishment of a central agency to coordinate each nation's drug effort.

The second major accomplishment of the Program of Action was to begin the process of mobilizing the resources of the OAS for concerted action on the drug front. Although the recommendations cited above represented a multilateral consensus about how the drug problem ought to be addressed, they relied totally upon action by individual member states for their implementation. To give the program greater practical effect, the conference recommended that the next General Assembly create a commission to coordinate the exertions of member states in this regard. To be known as the Inter-American Drug Abuse Control Commission (CICAD), this entity could also submit proposals of its own for the purpose of increasing the effectiveness of this nascent drug-control regime. In addition, the Program of Action called for the General Assembly to consider creating a regional fund to support these activities. It asks the Inter-American Juridical Committee (CJI), moreover, to explore issues such as extradition; cooperation among judicial, police, and customs organizations; and harmonization of national laws dealing with drug trafficking. Other relevant Inter-American Specialized Organizations were also requested to lend support within their particular areas of competence.

The OAS took a further stride toward the goal of producing an effective drug-control regime in April 1986 when it signed a cooperative agreement with the International Association of Penal Law (AIDP). Under this agreement, the OAS would receive support from AIDP in the following areas: training for staff members on criminal law matters, drafting of a model penal code for Latin America, and formation of a group of experts to assist the OAS in combatting criminal activities, including drug trafficking, in the Americas.

In November 1986, the General Assembly of the OAS convened its sixteenth regular session in Guatemala City. Among the more salient items on its agenda were the creation of CICAD and the approval of its statute. Not only did the General Assembly bring CICAD into existence, it chose to do so with as much fanfare as possible. To accompany the birth of the new hemispheric body, the assembled foreign ministers and heads of delegation promulgated the Declaration of Guatemala: The American Alliance against Drug Trafficking. In this declaration, the need for collective action to counter the transnational operations of drug traffickers was underscored. The signatories declared drug trafficking to be "a crime of broad international scope that must be combatted by all the member states" and pledged their total support to the efforts of CICAD.[5]

The commission brought into being at Guatemala City was comprised of representatives from eleven member states elected by the General Assembly for a term of three years. The activities of the commission are guided by the principles and objectives of the Program of Action of Rio de Janeiro. An autonomous consultative and advisory group, the commission is charged with assisting member states in pursuing the recommendations of the Program of Action, preparing an annual report for the General Assembly, and establishing cooperative affiliations with other international organizations involved in counternarcotics activities. To carry out its functions, the commission is aided by an executive secretary and staff; the expenses of this administrative apparatus are borne by the OAS. The commission convenes twice a year to review the activities of its secretariat and provide guidance.

It is the executive secretary and staff who conduct the daily business of CICAD. In particular, they assumed responsibility for tasks assigned to the OAS General Secretariat by the Program of Action. Among these are the following:

1. Creation of a data bank of information on drug production, trafficking, and abuse throughout the hemisphere for use by all member states.
2. Establishment of regional training centers in the areas of drug abuse prevention, treatment, rehabilitation, and law enforcement.
3. Creation of a documentation center to serve as an inter-American library on drug-related topics.

The evolution of CICAD and its progress in pursuit of these and additional drug-control functions are reviewed below.

## THE EVOLUTION OF CICAD

Prior to the initial session of the commission, the CICAD secretariat made substantial progress in developing draft rules of procedure for the organization and guidelines for the three statutory programs assigned to it by the Program of Action. In April 1987, scarcely five months after its inception, the eleven commission members (representing Argentina, the Bahamas, Bolivia, Brazil, Colombia, Guatemala, Mexico, Panama, Peru, the United States, and Venezuela) met to chart the future course of the organization.

Proposed guidelines for the Inter-American Data Bank specified the nature of its prospective data base. Two basic types of information were to be incorporated.

1. Statistics and reports on all phases of the drug trade (i.e., production, processing, trafficking patterns and routes, and effects of consumption in member states).
2. A compilation of legal measures and agreements, in existence or proposed, to deal with the problem, including national laws, model legislation crafted by committees of experts, and international accords on the subject.

The commission also approved the secretariat's proposed guidelines for inter-American training centers specializing in education, treatment, and law enforcement. The essential initial step was to canvass member countries to determine what public and private training facilities were already in existence in each of these categories. The intent was to determine which of these might be suitable as potential regional training centers.

The final statutory program, the Inter-American Documentation Center, was slated to be in operation by late 1987. Included within its holdings would be information on prevention, diagnosis, treatment, and rehabilitation of drug dependency. In addition to the statutory programs mandated by the Program of Action, the commissioners also considered other measures that might be undertaken. Foremost among these was drug prevention through education and community mobilization. Among other activities contemplated by CICAD were several that had initially been commended to the CJI for consideration (i.e., cooperation among national law enforcement entities and harmonization of national laws dealing with trafficking and abuse). Considering its exceedingly limited financial resources, CICAD placed a premium on cooperation and coordination with existing international and nongovernment organizations. Thus, it considered the possibilities of working with the CJI to draft model antidrug legislation, with the United Nations Committee for the Prevention of Crime and Treatment of Offenders in Latin America (ILANUD) to improve cooperation among regional law enforcement agencies, and with the Pan American Development Foundation (PADF) to stimulate involvement of private organizations in drug prevention programs.[6] Particular emphasis was placed on the need to coordinate CICAD activities with relevant UN agencies and other international and regional entities to avoid duplication of effort and to promote the complementarity of their respective programs.

CICAD's ability to carry out a more ambitious program was severely hamstrung by the financial crisis afflicting the OAS. The organization's ability to sustain its general programs had been seriously eroded because of its inability to collect full contributions from member states. Funding for CICAD's entire operation in 1987, therefore, was a mere $775,000. In hopes of alleviating this constraint, CICAD reiterated a recommendation made in the Program of Action that a special fund be created to which voluntary contributions could be made in support of CICAD's activities.

By the time of CICAD's second regular session in September 1987, the secretariat had begun to take action on a number of programs. As anticipated, the Inter-American Documentation Center had come into existence. Movement toward placing the Inter-American Data Bank in operation was stymied, however, by lack of resources to hire a permanent staff. The secretariat had made considerable progress, nevertheless, on designing the data base so that it could eventually be accessible to national subscribers throughout the region. Less success could be reported toward the establishment of inter-American training centers. Although the secretariat had conducted a limited survey of existing training facilities, work had not advanced to the stage where any recommendations could be made regarding which of these might prove suitable as potential regional centers. Once again, funding stringencies had thwarted further progress.

Even though financial constraints had precluded CICAD from fully implementing its three statutory programs, it was still determined to consider other priority programs that might be undertaken when conditions were more favorable. During its second session, the commission approved the following lines of action:

1. Education against drug abuse.
2. Mobilization of private and community organizations to prevent drug abuse.
3. Legal development.

The last project, legal development, would involve initiatives to harmonize national narcotics laws, improve law enforcement cooperation, and develop model legislation in areas such as money laundering and asset seizure.

All of these prospective programs would have to be placed on hold, however, because of CICAD's impecunious circumstances. Budgetary allocations for 1988 were $900,000, the bulk of which ($650,000) would be consumed by the administrative costs of sustaining the CICAD secretariat. The remaining $250,000 was largely devoted to the organization's three statutory programs, leaving virtually no latitude for more expansive operations.

A degree of hope for fiscal relief was provided during CICAD's second session when the OAS Permanent Council approved creation of the Specific Fund (also known as Fund 85). Monies for this fund were to come from voluntary contributions by OAS member governments and other donations. The purpose of the Specific Fund was to permit CICAD to undertake priority lines of action for which direct OAS budgetary support was inadequate.

Prior to CICAD's third regular session in March 1988, the secretariat made great strides in establishing productive linkages with other international organizations having an interest in the drug problem. The purpose was not only to promote coordination of common programs but also to activate an additional source of funding for CICAD's embryonic lines of action. CICAD and the United Nations Division of Narcotic Drugs (DND) agreed in principle to conduct annual programming sessions to coordinate activities in the region and to develop a joint calendar of events to avoid scheduling simultaneous meetings. CICAD asked the Commission of the European Communities to pick up a significant share of the financial burden for the data bank and documentation center projects, and the Canadian government expressed interest in aiding the formation of an inter-American training center for police officers. Symbolic of the emphasis placed on establishing these linkages, the March session was well attended by representatives from a host of regional and international organizations.

During the third regular session, the secretariat reported that the Pan American Health Organization had agreed to provide the findings of its twenty-city epidemiological study into the Inter-American Data Bank. Action pertaining to the training center concept was confined to providing about a dozen fellowships for the purpose of police training, monitoring of prescription drugs, and prevention of drug abuse.

A new activity approved by the commission during this session was the formation of a working group to study the economic implications for developing nations of their involvement in the drug trade. The working group was to include interested countries; the World Bank, the Inter-American Development Bank, and regional economic organizations would also be invited to participate.

The major development among CICAD's priority lines of action was the scheduling of a hemispheric conference to initiate the legal development project. This conclave was slated to be held in May 1988 at the headquarters of ILANUD in San José, Costa Rica. The purpose of the conference was to identify specific topics CICAD ought to address in drafting model legislation and in conducting workshops and training programs to facilitate law enforcement cooperation.

The May 1988 meeting in San José was profoundly influenced by the anticipated United Nations Convention against Illicit Traffic in Narcotics Drugs and Psychotropic Substances, which was due to be signed in Vienna, Austria, in November. Once in effect, the convention would commit states to a broad array of antidrug measures (e.g., in the areas of money laundering, asset seizure, precursor chemicals, and seizure on the high seas). Accordingly, the conference at San José made expediting the ratification of the UN Drug Convention a top priority. Through this action alone, an enormous step would be taken toward harmonizing antidrug legislation throughout the region. Other priorities were established at the San José meeting:

1. To improve the safeguarding and presentation of evidence and the sharing of criminal information.
2. To fortify the judicial process.
3. To develop adequate sanctions against drug traffickers.
4. To generate public support for necessary legal measures.

With regard to the development of model legislation, the conferees recommended that a committee of experts be convened to address the topics of money laundering, asset seizure, and control of precursor chemicals. An additional group was to study the advisability of declaring drug trafficking to be a crime against humanity.

In addition to setting the Legal Development Project in motion, the CICAD secretariat also launched its Demand Reduction Project in May 1988. This took the form of a workshop held in Montevideo, Uruguay, for education, public health, and drug-control officials from the Andean and Southern Cone regions. The focus of the session was preventive education with the aim of incorporating the subject of drug abuse prevention into the curriculum of all schools in the hemisphere. CICAD undertook the action in coordination with the Inter-American Council for Education, Science, and Culture (CIECC). Three additional workshops were scheduled for Brazil, the Caribbean, and Mexico–Central America. Assuming sufficient funding would be forthcoming for these gatherings (primarily through contributions to the Special Fund), the secretariat anticipated producing a detailed plan for approval by the commission by summer 1989.

In addition to preventive education (which involved working with government agencies), the secretariat sought to reduce demand by mobilizing support within the private sector. Having received funding for this program via a donation from the U.S. government, the secretariat planned a series of seminars and workshops for members of the media, community organizations, and business groups.

At CICAD's fourth regular session in August-September 1988, the commission approved the recommendations made by the San José conference on legal development. To implement the envisioned action items, however, CICAD would need to secure the requisite funding. The commission directed the secretariat to solicit contributions and also to coordinate its actions with the UN, the CJI, and the ILANUD.

As usual, the commission also received a report on the status of the organization's three statutory programs. The documentation center had published a catalog of its holdings and was engaged in developing a network of similar centers throughout the region. The data bank was still in the design stage, but progress had been made on developing a uniform system of record keeping so that data could be input in standard form by all member states. Lagging farther behind was the training center project, although contacts had been made with certain key institutions, and negotiations were under way to determine what courses they could provide.

The secretariat could also report progress in establishing cooperative accords with counterpart organizations such as the South American Accord on Narcotic Drugs and Psychotropic Substances, the Inter-American Commission on Women, the Andean Parliament, and CARICOM (Caribbean Common Market and Community). In spite of its accomplishments, however, CICAD expressed grave concern about the growing magnitude of the drug plague throughout the hemisphere and the inadequacy of its own resources to confront the problem. CICAD recommended to the OAS General Assembly that it reaffirm its commitment to the counterdrug effort and that member states be urged to give special consideration to supporting CICAD by contributing to the Special Fund. Furthermore, the commission recommended that a special ministerial meeting involving all member states be convened in 1989 to evaluate current efforts to cope with the drug problem. At its 18th General Assembly session, held in November 1988, the OAS passed resolutions putting into effect each of these recommendations.

During CICAD's next year of operation (through September 1989), all three of its priority lines of action—education for prevention, community mobilization, and legal development—went into full swing.

With the motto "The Chance to Grow: Education in the Campaign against Drug Abuse," the Education for Prevention Project completed three additional regional meetings (i.e., in the Caribbean, Mexico–Central America, and South America). These sessions were aimed at generating interest in a regional drug prevention program and forging consensus about objectives and the activities that ought to be undertaken. The stage had thus been set for a meeting of education ministers from throughout the hemisphere. Slated for early 1990, this conclave would be used to launch a comprehensive program involving training centers for teachers, production of audio visual support materials, and a mechanism for exchanging information and experiences.

The companion drug education project, "Community Mobilization through Public Awareness," got off the ground with a regional workshop on public awareness in January 1989. Over sixty media specialists analyzed marketing techniques for putting the antidrug message across. Subsequently, CICAD sponsored a series of seminars for journalists, newsroom decision makers, and owners of media. The community mobilization aspect of this project came into being with a training program for 500 parents in slum areas of Lima to help them discourage drug abuse among their children.

The third line of action, the Legal Development Project, was not as active as the others owing to a lack of funding. Nevertheless, a workshop aimed at producing more effective law enforcement techniques, better protection of evidence, and enhanced multilateral cooperation was held in July 1989 with the assistance of the Canadian government (with a subsequent workshop slated for July 1990). Furthermore, the secretariat laid the groundwork for the first meeting of experts to draft model legislation for the control of precursor chemicals used in the production of illegal drugs. To fund the project's activities, the U.S. government had authorized (but not yet appropriated) $1 million. In addition, the executive secretary approached the Italian government with a proposal for a $5 million grant spread over a five-year period.

Developments among the three statutory programs included linking the documentation center with similar entities throughout the region under the rubric of the Inter-American Information System. To promote this regional network, for which CICAD would serve as the clearinghouse, the secretariat convened a meeting of prospective participants in October 1988. This gathering concluded with an agreement to establish such an information system using a uniform classification scheme. Subsequently, the secretariat carried out preliminary measures, including establishing the staffing requirements. To underwrite the expenses associated with establishing his information network, CICAD secured a grant for $250,000 from the Commission of European Communities. The initial stage of bringing the data bank into operation also took place during the year, using a computerized information storage system.

As had been the case since its inception, CICAD continued to be plagued by financial shortfalls. Funding from the OAS was sufficient to maintain a staff of only thirteen. CICAD's budget for non-personnel expenses, moreover, had been slashed from $700,000 to $400,000 during the year, owing to the OAS's continuing financial crisis. Contributions to the Specific Fund, amounting to $1 million, had enabled CICAD to carry out its three priority lines of action, at least on a partial basis. In the hope of increasing its support among OAS members, CICAD expanded its membership to twenty states during the year (i.e., Antigua-

Barbuda, Argentina, the Bahamas, Bolivia, Brazil, Chile, Colombia, Costa Rica, the Dominican Republic, Ecuador, Guatemala, Jamaica, Mexico, Nicaragua, Panama, Paraguay, Peru, the United States, Uruguay, and Venezuela). Once again, in its recommendations to the OAS General Assembly, the commission made an urgent appeal for member states to contribute additional resources to CICAD's programs.

CICAD commissioners met to review the organization's activities during the September 1989–March 1990 time frame at their seventh regular session. Concerning CICAD's three statutory programs, one highlight was the formulation of a four-year program to develop a uniform statistical system for the data bank. To fund this initiative, the secretariat had made a solicitation to the Italian government for a grant of $865,000. The documentation center had published its second catalogue and had begun establishing cooperative arrangements with relevant agencies in member states for the exchange of information. The training center program had continued to languish due to inadequate funding. This had precluded engaging in any new training activities during the period. Future support would be targeted specifically at training relevant to the organization's priority lines of action. In the short term, rather than seeking to create a number of regional training centers, CICAD would rely on existing national facilities throughout the hemisphere. Based on its accumulated experience with these institutions over the longer term, CICAD would consider establishing permanent relationships. This could eventually include creation of training centers with genuinely regional enrollment.

Regarding CICAD's priority lines of action, two noteworthy developments had taken place within the drug abuse prevention area. The Community Mobilization Project, using funding provided by the U.S. government, had scheduled an inter-American teleconference for May 1990. Linking thirteen states throughout the Americas, the purpose was to stimulate efforts in both the public and private sectors to mobilize public opinion against drug abuse. The Education for Prevention Program had taken several initiatives to curb drug use among street children of the region. In collaboration with the Inter-American Children's Institute, it had conducted youth encounter programs in Ecuador and Paraguay, and, using funding supplied by the Inter-American Development Bank, it had launched a survey of drug abuse among street children in Bogotá, Colombia; Caracas, Venezuela; Cochabamba, Bolivia; Lima, Peru; and São Paulo, Brazil.

The surpassing accomplishment of CICAD's March 1990 session was the submission and approval of model regulations for the control of precursor and essential chemicals (and other items) involved in the production of illicit drugs. The product of six months of work by a CICAD-sponsored group of experts, this model legislation built upon the framework created by the 1988 UN Drug Convention. Article 12 of the convention calls upon the international community to take steps to prevent the diversion of such chemicals. The purpose of the model regulation was to stimulate OAS members to adopt consistent, effective legislation on the subject. The draft developed by the group of experts would require producers, exporters, importers, and users of drug-related chemicals (and other relevant items) to register with government officials, to obtain a license for each international transaction, and to maintain a record of these dealings. Anyone involved in the transnational movement of these substances would also be required to report suspicious activities to competent authorities. Member states were encouraged to designate a point of contact for international cooperation in this matter. The approval of this model legislation by CICAD provided a promising context for the forthcoming ministerial meeting scheduled for April 1990.

In spite of CICAD's efforts to nurture this embryonic drug-control regime, the "Meeting of Ministers on the Illicit Use and Production of Narcotic Drugs and Psychotropic Substances and Traffic Therein—Alliance of the Americas against Drug Traffic" convened under a dark cloud in Ixtapa, Mexico. Only a few days prior to this gathering, Machain, a suspect in the murder of Drug Enforcement Administration (DEA) agent Enrique Camarena, had been kidnapped and taken to the United States where he was turned over to waiting DEA agents. This ostensible affront to Mexican national sovereignty, the very country where the ministerial meeting was to take place, could have dealt a harsh blow to the spirit of cooperation vital for the success of such an international undertaking. Owing to the Alvarez Machain incident, Mexican President Salinas de Gortari was compelled to lecture about the poisonous effect that unilateral violation of national sovereignty can have on efforts to create effective regimes of multilateral cooperation. In spite of this inauspicious start, however, delegates to the conference were able to put the urgent need for cooperative action ahead of concerns about U.S. interventionism (with the Mexican delegation, in fact, playing a crucial role in facilitating consensus).

Ironically, the Ixtapa meeting turned out to be one of the more successful regional undertakings since the Rio de Janeiro meeting that gave birth to the Inter-American Program of action and CICAD. The most noteworthy accomplishment was the boost Ixtapa gave to the creation of common pan-American legislation for the control of precursor and essential chemicals. Conferees endorsed the proposed model legislation provided to them by CICAD and issued a mandate for similar action to be taken regarding money laundering and asset seizure. These measures, of course, are totally reliant on subsequent action by member states, both to adopt such legislation themselves and to enforce it effectively.

In addition to actions in the realm of legal cooperation, the assembled ministers underscored the vital nature of CICAD's work in the area of education for prevention (both in schools and in the workplace) and expressed their firm resolve to seek ratification of the 1988 UN Drug Convention throughout the hemisphere. Indeed, the conferees reached agreement that OAS states should go beyond the minimum requirements established in the UN Drug Convention whenever possible. They also directed CICAD to study measures to curtail trafficking in weapons and explosives often associated with the drug business and to investigate the matter of crop and income substitution.

The April ministerial meeting was followed immediately by a meeting of senior education officials in May 1990 in Quito, Ecuador. Jointly sponsored by CICAD and CIECC, the formal title of the gathering was the "Hemisphere-Wide Meeting on Programming and Implementation of the Inter-American Plan of Action: Education in the Campaign against Drug Abuse." The purpose was to consider the plan of action developed in previous subregional workshops conducted under CICAD auspices between May 1988 and July 1989. During the session, the delegates approved the plan of action with only minor amendments.

A goal of the action program is to ensure that the subject of drug prevention is incorporated into the curricula of schools throughout the hemisphere. The plan extends beyond the confines of the schoolhouse, however, to encompass a broad array of social institutions. As stated in the document:

> Comprehensive prevention education, understood as social education, covers a broad educational base that promotes human values and comprises: formal and non-formal education, community life, the world of work, the mass media, and other facets of society.[7]

To achieve this ambitious agenda, the plan of action calls for development of curricular materials and associated educational aids, teacher training (through the use of fellowships, exchange programs, regional training centers, traveling teams, and demonstration projects), research, and outreach programs for the community, the media, and the family. The linchpin of the program will be the exchange of information and experiences. CICAD will be accomplished primarily through the Inter-American Drug Information System and via subsequent regional workshops and seminars. Implementation of the program has been turned over to the individual member states, with CICAD and CIECC serving a supportive and evaluative function.

## CONCLUSION

During its first three and a half years of its existence, CICAD laid down a sturdy foundation upon which to erect an inter-American drug-control regime. In spite of the organization's chronic financial difficulties, cooperative mechanisms were installed for the purpose of information sharing, preventive education, community mobilization, law enforcement cooperation, and control of precursor and essential chemicals. In taking stock of these achievements, it is instructive to consider two questions about the role of CICAD and the OAS generally:

1. Can any more be done?
2. Will these efforts be sufficient to bring drug trafficking under effective control?

On balance, the initiatives already undertaken by CICAD are much more substantial than its list of outstanding projects. Certainly it has an unfinished agenda (e.g., the Inter-American Training Center Project and model legislation dealing with money laundering and asset seizure). There are a number of projects, moreover, that have yet to get off the ground because of insufficient funding (e.g., the study of the economic implications of the drug trade for producing countries and the examination of approaches to crop and income substitution). CICAD's raison d'être, however, is not to conduct studies. Rather, it is to facilitate multinational collaboration against the illicit drug trade. In this respect, it has successfully opened five avenues of hemispheric cooperation:

1. Sharing data about the magnitude of the drug trade in the region and for facilitating access to documents that may help member nations understand and deal with this phenomenon.
2. Developing preventive education programs for school children and in the workplace.
3. Mobilizing support within the private sector, including the media, business groups, and community organizations.
4. Exchanging information and experiences among national law enforcement agencies and developing more effective mechanisms for these agencies to work together transnationally.
5. Regulating the flow of precursor and essential chemicals throughout the region.

In a sense, therefore, CICAD has done about as much as any multinational organization could to make it possible for the nations of the hemisphere to work together in this issue area. It is now entirely up to the members of the OAS themselves to take advantage of these avenues of cooperation and make them function effectively. In the absence of the political will and capability to take such action, CICAD's efforts will have no meaning.

The fundamental constraint on the evolution of an *effective* inter-American drug control regime, therefore, is national sovereignty. Even if the nations of the Americas express a potential willingness, for example, to adopt legislation to regulate the flow of precursor chemicals, they cannot be compelled to do so. Even more problematic is the effective implementation of such rules after they have become law. The latter concern is not so much a matter of political will as it is a matter of capability. Owing to the demonstrated capacity of the drug cartels to suborn officials charged with enforcing antidrug laws, the mere existence of such a statute could turn out to be rather watery gruel as far as curtailing drug production is concerned.

Another obvious constraint on CICAD's ability to carry out its statutory programs and to execute its priority lines of action is money. The penurious support afforded CICAD by OAS member states speaks far more persuasively about the actual priority attached to the objective than any of the resolutions and pronouncements they have promulgated. With an annual operating budget of less than $1 million, with *total* contributions to the Specific Fund less than $2 million and with a staff of thirteen, CICAD's ability to forge a workable drug-control regime is clearly limited. Support from outside the hemisphere may even come to dwarf contributions by OAS members themselves; Italy has been asked to donate $5 million for the Legal Development Project over the next five years, and the European Community has agreed to underwrite the activities of the Inter-American Information System. All of this raises doubts about whether OAS members want CICAD to be in the forefront of the war on drugs or merely a footnote.

It would seem evident, therefore, that a good deal more can be done. Clearly, if CICAD were adequately funded (and this would amount to a mere $5–6 million annually), it would be empowered to implement each of its statutory programs and its priority lines of action more vigorously. The real issue, however, is whether member states are prepared to subordinate certain national prerogatives in the interest of developing a viable drug-control regime in the Americas. Certain of CICAD's programs (such as sharing information via the data bank) involve virtually no sacrifice in this regard. Thus activities of this sort tend to be the stock in trade for entities such as CICAD. There is another set of measures, however, such as regulating the flow of precursor and essential chemicals, that does indeed begin to involve surrender of a nation's freedom of maneuver. This is also an issue for which it is imperative to secure unanimous support internationally if this cooperation is to bear fruit. It remains to be seen whether the global community is prepared to cleave together in the name of effective drug control.

If sensitivity about national sovereignty were not a limitation on the imagination of statesmen, still further steps could be taken that might deal a crushing blow to TDCs operating in the region. Among these might be the creation of a hemispheric court (and associated penal system) to try and to incarcerate perpetrators of this "crime against mankind." Another might be the formation of a multilateral force composed of highly trained, well-armed police units to assist national forces in controlling drug producing or processing regions. The particular utility of such an entity (which would comprise exogenenous units that serve for only a limited period in the affected country) would be the much reduced ability for drug kingpins to infiltrate and corrupt them. Such a force could also benefit from information and intelligence sharing among the countries involved. None of these measures are realistic possibilities at the moment because of the premium placed on preserving national sovereignty. It is conceivable, however, that successful implementation of CICAD's other cooperative ventures might gradually erode such concerns and allow more extensive (or intrusive) forms of cooperation to be contemplated.

While it may be satisfying to engage in such idealistic speculation, it is essential to maintain a sense of realism as well. Thus it is appropriate at this point to reflect on the second question raised above: Will these efforts be sufficient to bring drug trafficking under effective control? If we think exclusively in terms of CICAD's miniscule annual budget of $1 million and staff of thirteen, then the answer is clearly not affirmative. This is not to argue that an immense and costly bureaucracy is the answer, either. CICAD's role is vitally important because isolated efforts by individual countries will never deal adequately with this transnational phenomenon. Thus, the return on an investment in multilateral cooperation is likely to be great, *if* the willingness to exploit such a framework is also present.

If for a moment we assume that multilateral cooperation is to be forthcoming, will this be sufficient? While answering this question would involve more crystal-ball gazing than analysis, it is possible to engage in a degree of speculation. The illicit drug trade flourishes both because of the ease with which national boundaries can be penetrated by narcotraffickers and because of the impediment these same boundaries constitute for drug-control efforts regionally (owing to considerations of national sovereignty). A reasonable expectation would be for a future drug-control regime to neutralize (or perhaps even reverse) this disadvantage. Whether such a regime would be sufficient to reduce the scourge of drugs to tolerable limits is still impossible to predict. It is evident, however, that this inherently transnational phenomenon will never be dealt with adequately without a viable regime of multilateral cooperation among the states of the Americas.

## NOTES

1. Michael J. Dziedzic, "The Transnational Drug Trade and Regional Security," *Survival* 31, 6 (November-December 1989): 533–48.
2. AG. Res. 699 (XIV–0/84), Fourteenth Regular Session, Brasilia, Brazil, 12–17 November 1984.
3. Organization of American States, *Inter-American Program of Action of Rio de Janeiro against the Illicit Use and Production of Narcotic Drugs and Psychotropic Substances and Traffic Therein*, 24 April 1986 (Washington, D.C.: Organization of American States, 1986).
4. Ibid, 4.
5. AG. Res. 817 (XVI–0/86), Sixteenth Regular Session, Guatemala City, Guatemala, 10–15 November 1986.
6. The desire to collaborate with the PADF has not produced results, to date.
7. OEA/Ser/L/XVI.5.1, CICAD/CIECC/doc.33/90 rev. 1 (Washington, D.C.: 17 July 1990, 8).

## BIBLIOGRAPHY

Dziedzic, Michael J. "The Transnational Drug Trade and Regional Security." *Survival* 31, 6 (November-December 1989): 533–48.

"Inter-American Drug Abuse Control Commission (CICAD) Holds Ninth Session." *International Enforcement Law Reporter* (May 1991): 190–92.

Lee, Rensselaer W. III. *The White Labyrinth: Cocaine and Political Power*. New Brunswick, N.J.: Transaction Publishers, 1989.

Organization of American States. *Inter-American Program of Action of Rio de Janeiro against the Illicit Use and Production of Narcotic Drugs and Psychotropic Sub-*

*stances and Traffic Therein*. Washington, D.C.: Organization of American States, 24 April 1986.

U.S. Department of State, Bureau of International Narcotics Matters. *International Narcotics Control Strategy Report*. Washington, D.C.: U.S. Department of State, March 1991.

26

# United Nations' Activities in International Drug Control

ROBIN ROLLEY

## INTRODUCTION

In order to effectuate real solutions to the growing drug crisis, there must be an international narcotics-control system that will facilitate and promote meaningful international cooperation. The success of such an international scheme of control, however, rests ultimately on the cooperation and will of the members of the world community. As the harmful effects of drug abuse have been made known (harm not only to the individual abuser but to society as well), the will of the international community to combat drug trafficking has increased. This can be seen by the fact that 106 countries participated in the negotiations of the 1988 United Nations Convention against Illicit Traffic in Narcotic Drugs and Psychotropic Substances (the UN Drug Convention). International cooperation, however, is a constant struggle due to the cultural and legal diversities of the countries involved. Despite the complexities of developing an international control system, the United Nations (UN) is progressing in its attempt to solve the drug problem.

This chapter first presents the historical background of the UN's international narcotics-control system, setting forth the treaties that existed prior to the establishment of the UN; the UN's assumption of the powers previously held by the League of Nations in narcotics control; and the UN conventions, such as the Single Convention on Narcotic Drugs, which led up to the 1988 UN Drug Convention. Second, the 1988 UN Drug Convention is analyzed with respect to the ways in which the 1988 convention encompasses and strengthens the narcotic-control mechanisms of previous treaties. Third, the Comprehensive Multidisciplinary Outline of Future Activities in Drug Abuse Control, as an example of UN policy, is discussed, and it is shown how such policy has been incorporated into UN treaties. Finally, the chapter summarizes the Political Declaration and Global Program of Action, adopted by the General Assembly in February 1990, and illustrates how it reaffirms the provisions set forth in previous treaties and concludes by examining how each of the United Nations' treaties demonstrate the UN's progress in establishing an international system of control.

## HISTORICAL BACKGROUND OF THE UN's INTERNATIONAL NARCOTICS-CONTROL SYSTEM

Four basic categories of narcotic substances are covered by international agreements: (1) opium and morphine, which are both produced from the poppy seed; (2) cocaine, which is produced from the coca bush; (3) cannabis sativa, which is also referred to as Indian hemp, hashish, marijuana, and bhang, depending on its geographical location; and (4) psychotropic substances, which are chemically manufactured rather than agriculturally produced drugs. International control of some of these substances began as early as 1909.

In 1909, prior to the establishment of the United Nations and even before the League of Nations was created, thirteen powers concerned with the Far East formed an Opium Commission to discuss the Chinese opium problem. This meeting led to The Hague Convention of 1912, which is the first time that international cooperation in the control of narcotic drugs came into force.

Later, the League of Nations, the predecessor to the UN, created an Advisory Committee on Traffic in Opium and Other Dangerous Drugs. The purpose of this committee was to provide the League's council with assistance and advice on drug-trafficking issues as well as to develop international legislation on such matters. On February 19, 1925, the Geneva Convention was signed, which strengthened existing tactics for supervising the transfer of narcotics. According to the Geneva Convention:

> Governments were required to submit to the newly created Permanent Central Opium Board annual statistics concerning production of opium and coca leaves; the manufacture, consumption, and stocks of narcotic drugs, and quarterly reports on the import and export of such drugs (not including opium and coca leaves). [The Convention] also established the system of import certificates and export authorizations requiring governmental approval of each import and export.[1]

The next convention created under the League of Nations was the Convention for Limiting the Manufacture and Regulating the Distribution of Narcotic Drugs. This convention, signed in Geneva on July 13, 1931, limited the world manufacture of drugs to medical and scientific needs. Members to the 1931 convention bound themselves to a restricted quantity of drugs to be manufactured in and imported to their particular country. The last treaty concluded under the League of Nations is the Convention for the Suppression of the Illicit Traffic in Dangerous Drugs. This convention, signed in Geneva on June 26, 1936, attempted to tighten the loopholes used by offenders to escape prosecution by facilitating the extradition of such offenders.

After World War II, the United Nations was established and given the power (under the Geneva Protocol of 1946) to carry on the League's functions under the various narcotics treaties. During the UN's first session, the Economic and Social Council created the Commission on Narcotic Drugs to replace the League's Committee on Traffic in Opium and Other Dangerous Drugs. Next came the Paris Protocol of 1948, which granted the World Health Organization the authority to control all addictive drugs. Third was the Opium Protocol of 1953, which restricted the use of opium to scientific and medical needs.

The most important multilateral treaty through 1972 is the Single Convention on Narcotic Drugs of 1961, which came into effect on December 15, 1964, and has since been amended. This convention has had great support; more than half of the members of the United Nations have ratified it. The objective of the Single Convention was to unify preexisting multilateral treaties involving narcotics control and to simplify the international control machinery. Therefore, for all parties to the Single Convention the earlier treaties no longer existed, and they are bound only to the provisions of the Single Convention, with the exception of the 1936 Convention on Illicit Traffic, which continues independent of the Single Convention. The Single Convention was able to simplify the international control machinery by merging the Permanent Central Opium Board and the Drug Supervisory Body into one unit: the International Narcotics Control Board (INCB). The functions of the INCB include the following:

1. Enforcing the provisions of the convention.
2. Securing estimates of drug requirements, existing stocks, production and consumption statistics, and statistics on seizures of unlawfully held drugs and publishing the results.
3. Requesting information, explanations, and public declarations by governments.
4. Recommending embargoes on imports and exports.
5. Gathering and publishing texts of laws and regulations concerning narcotics from signatory states.[2]

The Single Convention focuses on controlling the cultivation of plants from which narcotic substances can be produced. The treaty places the duty to punish violations of the convention upon the signatory state, making such violations a crime under municipal law. One significant aspect of the Single Convention is that it makes conspiracy to commit and attempts to commit drug-related offenses punishable crimes. Another important part of the Single Convention is that it recommends treatment and rehabilitation for those addicted to drugs. This more humane course of action was rarely incorporated into other treaties.

Despite the advances in international narcotics control made by the Single Convention, it suffers from many weaknesses. M. Cherif Bassiouni summarizes these weaknesses as follows:

1. [The Convention] rests essentially upon faithful cooperation by all parties in the context of their national decisions rather than upon effective international measures;

2. The limited authority given the international control bodies—the Commission on Narcotic Drugs and the International Narcotics Control Board—is apparently inadequate to halt or even to slow down the increasing illicit traffic;
3. The Convention lacks a precise obligation, machinery, and incentives for preventing overproduction of drugs;
4. It fails to clearly prohibit production of certain medically and scientifically unnecessary substances and drugs;
5. It has no direct controls over the execution of any treaty provision, particularly with respect to production controls which are very indirect;
6. It has no assignment of production quotas or production ceilings;
7. It does not prevent countries from entering into the production market;
8. The denunciation of the Convention is rather facile and operation outside its ambit is possible;
9. There is no international enforcement machinery (Interpol has no jurisdictional authority); and
10. There are no international sanctions applicable to individual offenders.[3]

The Single Convention was also deficient in that it did not cover psychotropic substances; therefore, in 1971 the Convention on Psychotropic Substances was adopted by a UN conference in Vienna. This convention provides strict international control over thirty-two substances having hallucinogenic effects, including LSD, mescaline, "pep pills," and barbiturate-type sleeping pills.

In 1972, the Single Convention on Narcotic Drugs was amended by the Geneva Protocol. Although it still lacked any substantial enforcement capabilities, improvements were made in the areas of informational input and output, sanctions, extradition, technical assistance, treatment and rehabilitation, competence of the board, and preventative measures.

In spite of obvious weaknesses in the different treaties over the years, there has been progress in establishing an international narcotics-control system. The 1961 Single Convention, for example, begins to touch on the idea that not only is it important to restrict the supply of narcotics but also to look deeper into the reason there is such a demand for them, hinting at the need to educate, treat, and rehabilitate those addicted to drugs. As the drug problem penetrates more and more societies worldwide, countries are starting to realize the need to work together toward a better system of control. With previous UN treaties setting the foundation, this is precisely what more than 106 countries attempted to do in negotiating the 1988 United Nations Convention against Illicit Traffic in Narcotic Drugs and Psychotropic Substances (UN Drug Convention).

## UN DRUG CONVENTION

The UN Drug Convention was signed on December 19, 1988, and went into force on November 11, 1990. The new drug convention is a significant improvement over previous treaties. One reason for this is the amount of support the convention received throughout its drafting stage. Other reasons include the breadth of areas covered by the convention and the strengthening of enforcement measures. The purpose of the convention is to deal more effectively with illicit drug trafficking through cooperation among signatories. Signatories are obligated to enact legislative and administrative measures in their respective domestic systems which coincide with the fundamental elements of the convention. Thus, many provisions of the convention can be enforced under the domestic law of individual systems, and offenders are no longer assured of escaping prosecution simply because the convention conflicts with a country's domestic law. Parties are expressly prohibited, however, from intervening into those functions that are reserved for other parties under its domestic law.

### Offense and Sanctions

Under Article 3 of the convention, signatories are required to criminalize in their domestic law certain offenses should they be committed intentionally:

1. The production, manufacture, extraction, preparation, offering, offering for sale, distribution, sale, delivery on any terms whatsoever, brokerage, dispatch, dispatch in transit, transport, importation or exportation of any narcotic drug or any psychotropic substance contrary to the provisions of the 1961 Convention, the 1961 Convention as amended, or the 1971 Convention;
2. The cultivation of opium poppy, coca bush, or cannabis plant for the purposes of the production of narcotic drugs contrary to the provisions of the 1961 Convention and the 1961 Convention as amended;
3. The possession or purchase of any narcotic drug or psychotropic substance for the purpose of any of the activities enumerated in (1) above;
4. The manufacture, transport, or distribution of equipment [or] materials, . . . knowing they will be used in or for the illicit cultivation, production, or manufacture of narcotic drugs or psychotropic substances;
5. The organization, management, or financing of any of the offenses enumerated in (1), (2), (3), or (4) above.[4]

Other offenses included in Article 3 concern money laundering. Any transfer of property, knowing that property is derived from one of the offenses listed above, is also to be criminalized under domestic law. Also, the concealment or disguise of property known to be derived from the above offenses is likewise a crime.

Article 3 lists the other following offenses to be criminalized under domestic law, but states that these offenses are subject to the constitutional principles and basic concepts of a signatory's legal system:

1. The acquisition, possession, or use of property, knowing, at the time of receipt, that such property was derived from an offense or offenses established in accordance with

subparagraph (a) of this paragraph or from an act of participation in such offense or offenses;

2. The possession of equipment or materials or substances listed in Table I and Table II, knowing that they are being or are to be used in or for the illicit cultivation, production, or manufacture of narcotic drugs or psychotropic substances;
3. Publicly inciting or inducing others, by any means, to commit any of the offenses established in accordance with this article or to use narcotic drugs or psychotropic substances illicitly;
4. Participation in, association or conspiracy to commit, attempts to commit and aiding, abetting, facilitating, and counselling the commission of any of the offenses established in accordance with this article.[5]

Since the four offenses listed above are subject to the constitutional provisions of the individual party's legal system, enforcement of these offenses depends on the interaction with the constitutional provisions. With the existing diversity among various legal systems, it will be difficult to enforce consistently the criminalization of the above four offenses. Overall, however, Article 3 tends to go beyond previous treaties and to strengthen enforcement capacities by requiring signatories to incorporate most of the provisions of the convention into their domestic law. Article 3 also requires parties to make offenders liable to sanctions. Parties may, in addition to or in some cases as an alternative to such sanctions, provide treatment, education, rehabilitation, or social reintegration.

The 1988 UN Drug Convention also obligates signatories to ensure that factual circumstances establishing the commission of an offense be considered by courts and other competent authorities which have jurisdiction, particularly with respect to serious crimes. The convention stresses that parties maximize the effectiveness of law enforcement measures whenever using their discretionary powers in the prosecution of an offender under domestic law. In all, many of the provisions of Article 3 are aimed at the prosecution and sanctioning of offenders, attempting to create stronger enforcement capabilities despite the differing legal systems of the parties to the convention.

## Confiscation

In attempting to take the profit out of drug-related crimes, the 1988 UN Drug Convention includes a section on confiscation. Specifically, Article 5 states that:

Each Party shall adopt such measures as may be necessary to enable confiscation of:

(a) Proceeds derived from offenses established in accordance with article 3, paragraph 1, or property the value of which corresponds to that of such proceeds;

(b) Narcotic drugs and psychotropic substances, materials and equipment of other instrumentalities used in or intended for use in any manner in offenses established in accordance with article 3, paragraph 1.[6]

Along with the requirements listed above, the convention orders signatories to adopt measures that will enable its authorities to identify, trace, and freeze or seize proceeds, property, instrumentalities, or other items for later confiscation. In implementing the provisions of Article 5, parties are required to empower their courts or competent authorities to turn over bank, commercial, or financial records. Claims of bank secrecy are no grounds for declining access to such records. Hence, Article 5 not only tries to deter crime by confiscating the proceeds of criminal activity, but also tightens possible loopholes on acts of money laundering by making bank records available.

In order to further implement the confiscation measures of Article 5, the convention requires a country, which receives a request from another country with jurisdiction over a covered offense, to submit the request to its competent authorities for confiscation. The requested party then must take measures to identify, trace, and freeze or seize proceeds, property, instrumentalities, or other items. All actions and decisions of the requested party are to be made in accordance with the country's domestic law and procedural rules as well as with any bilateral or multilateral treaty to which it may be bound in relation to the requesting party. This provision, in recognizing bilateral and multilateral treaties and urging adherence to them, serves to enhance international cooperation in confiscation.

Article 5 of the UN Drug Convention also states that, when a party is working on a confiscation request, it may give special consideration to concluding agreements on:

1. Contributing the value of such proceeds and property, or funds derived from the sale of such proceeds or property, or a substantial part thereof, to intergovernmental bodies specializing in the fight against illicit traffic in and abuse of narcotic drugs and psychotropic substances;
2. Sharing with other Parties, on a regular or case-by-case basis, such proceeds or property, or funds derived from the sale of such proceeds or property, in accordance with its domestic law, administrative procedures, or bilateral or multilateral agreements entered into for this purpose.[7]

This provision creates a means for strengthening enforcement of the convention inasmuch as proceeds obtained from property or materials that have been confiscated may be used to improve already existing programs for fighting drug trafficking and abuse. More specifically, this provision strengthens such UN institutions as the United Nations Fund for Drug Control (UNFDAC), which has now been reorganized into the UN International Drug Programme, as discussed below, by allowing funds to be contributed to intergovernmental bodies combatting narcotics.

Property that has been intermingled with property acquired from legitimate sources is liable to confiscation up to the assessed value of the intermingled proceeds.[8] Also, each party may consider reversing the burden of proof regarding the lawful origin of alleged proceeds or other property liable to confiscation, so long as it is consistent with the party's domestic law and in the nature of its judicial proceedings.[9] Article 5, however, does not allow the rights of bona fide third parties to be prejudiced. This, then, offers potential protection to those who provide legal assistance to defendants in narcotics cases. Hence, the confiscation provisions not only offer an incentive for law enforcement agents to prosecute offenses, but also provide a means for such agents to fight for the control of narcotics.

## Extradition

The UN Drug Convention makes all offenses, which were previously established under Article 3, subject to extradition. Parties may require, however, that extradition is conditional on the existence of a treaty between it and other parties. If a party does not make extradition conditional on the existence of a treaty, then it is obligated to recognize the offenses under the convention as extraditable offenses.[10] These provisions attempt to compel prosecution of those allegedly involved in narcotics-related offenses and are, therefore, a great improvement over earlier treaties. The extradition provisions in this convention are weakened, however, by leaving extradition subject to compatibility with the law of the requested party. Nevertheless, strengths outweigh weaknesses in the extradition provisions. Parties, of whom extradition has been requested, may, when circumstances warrant it and at the request of the requesting party, take an alleged offender into custody to ensure that offender's presence at extradition proceedings.[11] Article 6 further states

> Without prejudice to the exercise of any criminal jurisdiction established in accordance with its domestic law, a Party in whose territory an alleged offender is found shall:
>
> a) If it does not extradite him in respect of an offense established in accordance with Article 3, paragraph 1 . . . submit the case to its competent authorities for the purpose of prosecution, unless otherwise agreed with the requesting party.[12]

Thus, if extradition is denied by a party, then that party is still obligated, if allowable under that party's domestic law, to prosecute the alleged offender within its own system. Another enhanced law enforcement mechanism under the convention is that, where extradition for the purpose of enforcing a sentence is denied by a requesting party, that party is required to consider enforcing the sentence under the laws of its own system, when the requesting party so demands. Parties to the convention are also urged to expedite extradition procedures and to conclude bilateral and multilateral agreements in order to enhance the effectiveness of extradition. Therefore, the extradition provisions of the 1988 UN Drug Convention are a substantial improvement over earlier treaties, greatly advancing countries' abilities to prosecute offenders and enforce antidrug laws. In August 1990, a model extradition convention, adopted by the Eighth UN

Crime Congress and subsequently by the UN General Assembly, provides a model for all countries to use.

## Mutual Legal Assistance

Article 7 of the 1988 UN Drug Convention involves mutual legal assistance, and it is designed to make investigations, prosecutions, and judicial proceedings related to narcotics cases easier. Mutual legal assistance includes the following:

1. Taking evidence or statements from persons;
2. Effecting service of judicial documents;
3. Executing searches and seizures;
4. Examining objects and sites;
5. Providing information and evidentiary items;
6. Providing originals or certified copies of relevant documents and records, including bank, financial, corporate, or business records; and
7. Identifying or tracing proceeds, property, instrumentalities, or other things for evidentiary purposes.[13]

The mutual legal assistance provisions are an important aid to law enforcement. Without such assistance, many prosecutions cannot be realized due to a lack of admissible evidence or support for the claim. Mutual legal assistance also enables prosecutors to ascertain probable cause and, therefore, to extradite and try offenders who are overseas. Another enhancement, which the mutual legal assistance provisions incorporate, is that parties are not allowed to decline assistance based on bank secrecy regulations. Bank secrecy laws have previously stifled litigation; therefore, not allowing bank secrecy laws as a reason for declining legal assistance greatly increases the chances that drug offenders will be prosecuted. Parties to the convention must delegate authorities who will have the power to and responsibility of executing requests for mutual legal assistance.[14] Thus, complaints about earlier treaties that sufficient powers were not delegated in order to implement treaty provisions are rectified in the 1988 UN Drug Convention with respect to mutual legal assistance.

Under the following circumstances, a request for mutual legal assistance may be refused:

1. If the request is not made in conformity with [the Convention];
2. If the requested Party considers that execution of the request is likely to prejudice its sovereignty, security, *ordre public*, or other essential interests;
3. If the authorities of the requested Party would be prohibited by its domestic law from carrying out the action requested with regard to any similar offense, had it been subject to investigation, prosecution, or proceedings under their own jurisdiction; and

4. If it would be contrary to the legal system of the requested Party relating to mutual legal assistance for the request to be granted.[15]

The requested party must give reasons for any refusal of mutual legal assistance. Mutual legal assistance may also be postponed by a requested party, if such assistance would interfere with any ongoing proceedings. A witness, expert, or other person who travels to another country to assist in a judicial proceeding is given safe conduct and will not be subject to punishment for fifteen days (or an agreed-upon time) after his presence is no longer required.

The provisions allowing a request for mutual legal assistance to be denied show that it is still difficult to get around the great diversities within different legal systems. Denial of assistance is allowed when such assistance would conflict with a party's own judicial system or prejudice its sovereignty. Despite the possibility of denial, the convention requires that signatories afford the widest measure of mutual legal assistance possible, and the binding language of the convention supports cooperation among parties to provide assistance in a way that was nonexistent in earlier treaties. To further assist in concluding mutual legal assistance agreements, in August 1990, a model mutual legal assistance treaty (MLAT) was adopted by the Eighth UN Crime Congress and subsequently by the UN General Assembly.

## Other Significant Parts of the 1988 UN Drug Convention

Article 9 of the convention stresses cooperation and communication among signatories in working toward effective law enforcement in drug offenses. It obligates parties to cooperate with one another when conducting inquiries and to establish and maintain channels of communication.[16] Parties are also required under Article 9(2) to develop or improve training programs for law enforcement and customs personnel. Similarly, parties must share their expertise in areas concerning illicit traffic in narcotic drugs and psychotropic substances.[17]

Signatories are required to take appropriate measures in order to monitor the manufacture and distribution of narcotic substances as defined by the convention.[18] Specifically, parties must "(1) establish and maintain a system to monitor international trade in narcotic substances and (2) require that imports and exports be properly labelled and documented."[19] The convention allows for parties to apply stricter or more severe measures than those listed in the 1988 UN Drug Convention. Furthermore,

[a] Any measures taken pursuant to this Convention by Parties shall not be less stringent than the provisions applicable to the eradication of illicit cultivation of plants containing narcotic and psychotropic substances and to the elimination of illicit demand for narcotic

drugs and psychotropic substances under the provisions of the 1961 Convention, the 1961 Convention as amended, and the 1971 Convention.[20]

Accordingly, parties may enter into any bilateral or multilateral agreements that are directed toward eliminating or reducing illicit demand for narcotic drugs and psychotropic substances.

The 1988 UN Drug Convention strengthens the capacity of UN institutions to combat narcotics in two distinct ways. One way is through the new functions the convention provides for the Commission on Narcotic Drugs (which is now part of the reorganized UN International Drug Control Programme) of the Economic and Social Council. The commission is authorized to review the operation of the convention and may make suggestions and general recommendations based on the examination of the information received from the parties. The commission may also call the attention of the INCB (now part of the reorganized UN International Drug Control Programme), which was established by the Single Convention on Narcotic Drugs, to any matters that are relevant to the functions of the board. It is obligated, on any matter referred to it by the board under Article 22, to take whatever action it deems appropriate. Finally, the commission may draw the attention of nonparties to the decisions and recommendations that it adopts, in order that they might consider taking similar action.[21]

The second way the 1988 UN Drug Convention strengthens the capacity of UN institutions to combat narcotics is through the additional responsibilities given to the board. The board is authorized, when it deems necessary, to call upon the party concerned to adopt such remedial measures as seem, under the circumstances, to be necessary for the execution of the provisions of Articles 12, 13, and 16 regarding substances frequently used in the illicit manufacture of narcotic drugs or psychotropic substances, materials and equipment, and commercial documents and labelling of exports. If the board finds that the party concerned has not taken the remedial measures it has been asked to take, then the board may call the attention of the parties, the council, and the commission to the matter.[22]

In all, the 1988 UN Drug Convention represents significant progress in establishing an international system of control over narcotic drugs and psychotropic substances. Despite weaknesses, such as provisions only obligating parties when the convention is not in conflict with a country's domestic laws, the convention promises wide application, since more than 106 countries participated in its drafting. The 1988 UN Drug Convention is also a great improvement over previous treaties because it strengthens the ability of law enforcement agencies to combat trafficking in illicit substances. Provisions for increased international cooperation, stiffer sanctions, extradition, and asset forfeiture all work toward achieving this goal. Although international control still relies on the cooperation and will of the members of the world community, the 1988 convention has increased control mechanisms and has strengthened the authority of international organizations.

## COMPREHENSIVE MULTIDISCIPLINARY OUTLINE OF FUTURE ACTIVITIES IN DRUG ABUSE CONTROL

The Comprehensive Multidisciplinary Outline of Future Activities in Drug Abuse Control (the outline) is a compilation of recommendations directed toward governments and organizations, setting forth practical measures by which they can improve their fight against drug abuse and illicit narcotics trafficking. It is not a legally binding document, but rather a document representative of UN policy, which governments are encouraged to adapt, according to each country's economic and social conditions, to their national law. The outline consists of four chapters which cover the main elements involved in fighting drug abuse and illicit trafficking: the prevention and reduction of illicit demand, the control of supply, action against illicit trafficking, and treatment and rehabilitation. Each chapter specifies targets, pointing out the goal to be achieved and the action to be taken at the national level (by governments, professional associations, academic institutions, nongovernmental organizations, communities, parents, and individuals); at the regional level (by regional intergovernmental and nongovermental organizations and bodies); and at the international level (by international organizations, particularly those of the United Nations system). In reading the outline, it is possible to see how the 1988 UN Drug Convention supports and follows UN policy as portrayed in the outline. Most regional organizations, such as the later Inter-American Drug Abuse Commission (CICAD), and national governments have also relied heavily on the outline in establishing and assessing antidrug policies.

### Prevention and Reduction of the Illicit Demand for Narcotic Drugs and Psychotropic Substances

One target of this chapter is the need to understand the patterns of drug abuse and the extent of existing misuse. It recommends studies to be done on all levels (governmental, regional, and international) in order to monitor trends of abuse and to evaluate the effectiveness of preventive policies, training, and other instruments. Another target is organizing comprehensive systems for the collection and evaluation of data. Here, the UN recommends that standardized instruments be applied. A third target is the prevention of drug abuse and illicit trafficking through education. It is suggested that preventive education is most effective when it is integrated into the overall framework of academic, social, and cultural learning. Thus, a healthy, drug-free life-style must be promoted as a primary goal in all of these areas. Other targets include prevention of drug abuse in the workplace and the development of prevention programs by civic, community, and special interest groups and by law enforcement agencies. Also included is the need to provide and promote facilities, materials, and funding for drug-free leisure-time activities. It is suggested that governments and organizations take advantage of the media in their campaigns to promote a drug-free life-style.

The 1988 UN Drug Convention attempts to enforce these recommendations by requiring that parties adopt appropriate measures aimed at eliminating or reducing the illicit demand for narcotic drugs and psychotropic substances, with a view to reducing human suffering and eliminating financial incentives for illicit traffic. The convention specifically states that these measures may be based on the recommendations of the United Nations, specialized agencies of the United Nations such as the World Health Organization, and other competent international organizations, and on the Comprehensive Multidisciplinary Outline adopted by the International Conference on Drug Abuse and Illicit Trafficking, held in 1987, as it pertains to governmental and nongovernmental agencies and private efforts in the fields of prevention, treatment, and rehabilitation.[23] Hence, the 1988 convention attempts to enforce UN policy on eliminating the demand side of drug abuse and illicit trafficking.

## Control of Supply

This chapter gives recommendations on how to improve control over the cultivation, production, manufacture, and use of and international trade in narcotic and psychotropic substances. One suggestion is that countries obtain annual estimates on the availability and utilization of narcotics and psychotropic substances for legitimate medical purposes. The UN also recommends that countries monitor exports of narcotic drugs and psychotropic substances. Joint training courses for customs and other law enforcement officers organized by the Division of Narcotic Drugs and other relevant organizations can be used to improve reporting of suspect movements of drugs. States are urged to report on their efforts to locate and eliminate the illicit cultivation of narcotic plants in their annual report to the secretary general of the UN. Another target in attempting to control the supply of illicit substances is to redevelop areas formerly under illicit drug crop cultivation. International assistance is strongly recommended so that such areas will no longer be economically dependent on illicit crops. It is then suggested that the results of successful integrated rural development and crop substitution programs be made available to the general public so that other countries will be encouraged to undertake similar programs.

UN policies on controlling the supply of illicit substances have been implemented in the 1988 UN Drug Convention. By requiring that parties document and label exports, the 1988 convention attempts to monitor illicit trafficking of narcotics. The Single Convention also works to control the supply if illicit substances by securing estimates of drug requirements, requesting information, and gathering statistics on the production and consumption of drugs.

### Suppression of Illicit Trafficking

The targets focused on in this chapter are disrupting major trafficking networks, promoting the use of controlled delivery, facilitation of extradition, providing mutual judicial and legal assistance, allowing samples of bulk seizures of drugs to be used as evidence, requiring forfeiture of the instruments and proceeds of illicit drug trafficking, strengthening external border control, controlling the use of the international mails for drug trafficking, and controlling ships on the high seas and aircrafts in international airspace. All of these targets are provided for in the 1988 UN Drug Convention, which, in turn, shows direct enforcement of UN policy.

### Treatment and Rehabilitation

Here, the Comprehensive Multidisciplinary Outline suggests that countries inventory available modalities and techniques of treatment and rehabilitation. Another concern mentioned in the outline is the need to reduce the incidence of diseases and the number of infections transmitted through drug-using habits. Care for drug-addicted offenders within the criminal justice system is also recommended along with the social reintegration of persons who have undergone programs for treatment and rehabilitation.

Most of these UN policies have been incorporated into the 1988 UN Drug Convention by urging parties to provide treatment, rehabilitation, and social reintegration in addition to or in place of conviction or punishment for drug crimes. Even the Single Convention requested that signatories develop treatment and rehabilitation programs for those addicted to drugs. In all, many of the recommendations within the Comprehensive Multidisciplinary Outline are being enforced by the 1988 UN Drug Convention. The outline, however, does list many suggestions for improving or furthering the systems of narcotics control already in place.

## POLITICAL DECLARATION AND GLOBAL PROGRAM OF ACTION

The Political Declaration and Global Program of Action (Program of Action) adopted by the General Assembly in February 1990, which is devoted to increasing international cooperation against illicit production, supply, demand, trafficking, and distribution of narcotic drugs and psychotropic substances, is the most recent attempt to improve the international control system. The Program of Action reaffirms the provisions set forth in the Single Convention on Narcotic Drugs of 1961, the 1972 Protocol Amending the Single Convention on Narcotic Drugs of 1961, the Convention on Psychotropic Substances of 1971, and the United Nations Convention against Illicit Traffic in Narcotic Drugs and Psychotropic Substances adopted in 1988. In particular, member states of the United

Nations pledge to intensify their efforts in the fields of health, education, and public information in order to reduce illicit demand. They also undertake to apply, as appropriate, the recommendations of the Comprehensive Multidisciplinary Outline of Future Activities in Drug Abuse Control.

Activities of the Program of Action include analyzing the causes generating illicit demand for narcotic drugs and psychotropic substances in order to fight drug abuse at the root of the problem and using information and assistance provided by the United Nations in establishing treatment and rehabilitation programs worldwide. States are required to take all necessary measures to establish monitoring and control systems to prevent diversion from legitimate purposes of specific chemical substances and equipment frequently used in the illicit manufacture of narcotic drugs and psychotropic substances, as already provided for in Articles 12 and 13 of the 1988 UN Drug Convention. In attempting to further earlier conventions, UN member states invite the International Narcotics Control Board to advise and extend technical assistance upon request by such states. The Program of Action declares that mechanisms will be developed to prevent the banking system and other financial institutions from being used for the processing and laundering of drug-related money. In accordance with the 1988 convention, states are required to enact legislation to prevent the use of the banking system for processing and laundering drug money. At the same time, states are to consider using forfeited property and proceeds for activities to combat drug abuse and illicit trafficking. The Program of Action also requires states to study and promote measures to protect the judiciary from any form of exposure or intimidation that might threaten its integrity and independence. These measures are significant in that many judicial systems, especially those less stable ones, are apt to be influenced or even controlled by the drug cartels in their own countries, often because of fear and intimidation. Finally, the Program of Action requires the strengthening of the United Nations drug-control organs and their secretariats. The Program of Action is to be continuously monitored on its progress and implementation. Its overall goal is to intensify and sustain international, regional, and national efforts in the fight against drug abuse.

## REORGANIZATION OF UN DRUG ACTIVITIES

With organized crime beginning to expand both the markets and the routes for drug traffic to take advantage of new travel and trade in Europe, the United Nations has begun to reorganize and redirect its antidrug efforts.

Organizationally, the United Nations is merging three agencies—the Division of Narcotic Drugs, the United Nations Fund for Drug Abuse Control, and the International Narcotics Control Board—into a single organization, which will be known as the United Nation International Drug Control Programme.

Giorgio Giacomelli, a former senior Italian diplomat who in March 1991 began his position as the new head of the UN International Drug Control Programme, is expected to emphasize a more vigorous attack against money laundering and especially to try to sever the ability of organized crime to channel money into legitimate businesses.

The annual meeting of the UN Commission of Narcotic Drugs was held for ten days starting on April 29, 1991. The three UN drug agencies employ approximately 150 people in Vienna and 50 in fifteen other offices worldwide. They implement and monitor treaties on legal drug production and operation intervention programs to attempt to alter the economic and cultural bases of the Third World countries that produce opium and coca leaves.

The biggest need will be for the UN and other law enforcement agencies to persuade member governments around the world that its strategy for combatting drug trafficking is worthy of investment. Currently the three UN agencies have a combined annual budget of $80 million, which does not begin to enable the agencies to compete against organized criminals. The UN hopes that, once the consolidation of the three agencies makes them more efficient and reduces duplication, the UN will be able to persuade member governments to contribute more money to battle organized drug traffickers.

## CONCLUSION

The United Nations is increasing its efforts in international drug control. The 1988 UN Drug Convention incorporates underlying UN policy as seen in the Comprehensive Multidisciplinary Outline, while at the same time it encompasses control mechanisms of previous treaties and attempts to strengthen those mechanisms. The United Nations encourages countries to support its efforts to control illicit use and trafficking of narcotic drugs and psychotropic substances in its Global Program of Action. Support for UN efforts can be seen by the bilateral agreements that have been created and modeled after the 1988 UN Drug Convention. An example of this is the Narcotics Cooperation Agreement between the United States and Mexico. This agreement focuses on attacking drug-dependency problems in four main ways: prevention and reduction of the illicit demand for narcotics and psychotropic substances, control of supply, suppression of illicit traffic, and treatment and rehabilitation. Despite increased international concern over the drug crisis, countries must continue to cooperate in their efforts to improve the international system in each of the four main areas of the UN outline: prevention and reduction of demand, control of supply, suppression of illicit trafficking, and treatment and rehabilitation. Furthermore, in order to effectuate real solutions to the drug problem, countries must put their will into fighting illicit drug trafficking and into action by signing existing treaties and adhering to them.

## NOTES

1. M. Cherif Bassiouni, "The International Narcotics Control System," in M. Bassiouni and V. Nanda, eds., *Treatise on International Criminal Law* (New York: Practicing Law Institute, 1973), 539.

2. Ibid, 542.
3. Ibid, 542–43.
4. United Nations Economic and Social Council, *United Nations Convention against Illicit Traffic in Narcotic Drugs and Psychotropic Substances*, adopted 19 December 1988 [E/Conf. 82/15 (Vienna, Austria), Art. 3(1)] (hereinafter cited as UN Drug Convention).
5. Ibid, Article 3(1) (c).
6. Ibid, Article 5(1).
7. Ibid, Article 5(5) (b).
8. Ibid, Article 5(6) (b).
9. Ibid, Article 5(7).
10. Ibid, Article 6(4).
11. Ibid, Article 6(8).
12. Ibid, Article 6(9) (a).
13. Ibid, Article 7(2).
14. Ibid, Article 7(8).
15. Ibid, Article 7(15).
16. Ibid, Article 9(1) (a) and (b).
17. Ibid, Article 9(3).
18. Ibid, Article 12(8).
19. Ibid, Article 12(9) (a) and (d).
20. Ibid, Article 14(1).
21. Ibid, Article 21(a), (b), (c), and (f).
22. Ibid, Article 22(1) (b) (i) and (iii).
23. Ibid, Article 14(4).

## BIBLIOGRAPHY

Bassiouni, M. Cherif. "The International Narcotics Control System." In *Treatise on International Criminal Law*, edited by M. Bassiouni and V. Nanda. New York: Practicing Law Institute, 1973.

Kochinke, Clemens and Bruce Zagaris. "U.N. Prepares for 8th Congress on Crime Prevention and Treatment." *International Enforcement Law Reporter* 6, 4 (April 1990): 149–50.

United Nations. *Declaration of the International Conference on Drug Abuse and Illicit Trafficking and Comprehensive Multidisciplinary Outline of Future Activities in Drug Abuse Control*. New York: Division of Narcotic Drugs, 1988.

———. *Final Act of the United Nations Conference for the Adoption of a Convention against Illicit Traffic in Narcotic Drugs and Psychotropic Substances*. E/Conf. 82/14. New York: Economic and Social Council, 19 December 1988.

———. *Political Declaration and Global Program of Action*. A/S–17/11. New York: United Nations, 23 February 1990.

———. *United Nations Convention against Illicit Traffic in Narcotic Drugs and Psychotropic Substances*. E/Conf. 82/15. New York: Economic and Social Council, 19 December 1988.

Zagaris, Bruce. "Developments in International Judicial Assistance and Related Matters." *Denver Journal of International Law and Policy* 18, 3 (4 April 1989): 339–386.

———. "Dollar Diplomacy: International Enforcement of Money Movement and Related Matters—a United States Perspective." 1989. *The George Washington Journal of International Law and Economics*, George Washington University.

# Appendix: Tables

**Table 1**
**Net Production of Opium, 1987–1991 (metric tons)**

| | 1991est. | 1990 | 1989 | 1988 | 1987 |
|---|---|---|---|---|---|
| Afghanistan | 400 | 415 | 585 | 750 | 600 |
| Iran | 300 | 300 | 300 | 300 | 300 |
| Pakistan | 125 | 165 | 130 | 205 | 205 |
| Total SW Asia | 825 | 880 | 1,015 | 1,255 | 1,105 |
| Burma | 2,250 | 2,250 | 2,430 | 1,285 | 835 |
| Laos | 250 | 275 | 375 | 255 | 225 |
| Thailand | 39 | 40 | 50 | 28 | 24 |
| Total SE Asia | 2,539 | 2,565 | 2,855 | 1,568 | 1,084 |
| Lebanon | 40 | 32 | 45 | na | na |
| Guatemala | 10 | 13 | 12 | 8 | 3 |
| Mexico | 55 | 62 | 66 | 50 | 50 |
| Total | 105 | 107 | 123 | 58 | 53 |
| Total Opium | 3,569 | 3,552 | 3,993 | 2,881 | 2,242 |

Source: Bureau of International Narcotics Matters, U.S. Department of State, International Narcotics Control Strategy Report, March 1991 (Washington, D.C.: U. S. Department of State, March 1991), p. 22.

**Table 2**
**Net Production of Coca Leaf, 1987–1991 (metric tons)**

| | 1991est | 1990 | 1989 | 1988 | 1987 |
|---|---|---|---|---|---|
| Bolivia | 56,500 | 64,400 | 68,300 | 58,500 | 46,500 |
| Colombia | 31,000 | 32,100 | 33,900 | 27,200 | 20,500 |
| Peru | 138,300 | 138,300 | 137,300 | 125,900 | 124,000 |
| Ecuador | 100 | 120 | 150 | 240 | 300 |
| Total Coca Leaf | 225,900 | 234,920 | 239,650 | 211,840 | 191,300 |

Source: Bureau of International Narcotics Matters, International Narcotics Control Strategy Report, March 1991 (Washington, D.C.: U.S. Department of State, March 1991), p. 22.

**Table 3**
**Net Production of Marijuana, 1987–1991 (metric tons)**

| | 1991est. | 1990 | 1989 | 1988 | 1987 |
|---|---|---|---|---|---|
| Mexico | 18,000 | 19,715 | 30,200 | 5,655 | 5,933 |
| Colombia | 1,500 | 1,500 | 2,800 | 7,775 | 5,600 |
| Jamaica | 600 | 825 | 190 | 405 | 460 |
| Belize | 50 | 60 | 65 | 120 | 200 |
| Others | 3,500 | 3,500 | 3,500 | 3,500 | 1,500 |
| Total Marijuana | 23,650 | 25,600 | 36,755 | 17,455 | 13,693 |

Source: Bureau of International Narcotics Matters, International Narcotics Control Strategy Report, March 1991 (Washington, D.C.: U.S. Department of State, March 1991), p. 22.

**Table 4**
**Net Production of Hashish, 1987–1991 (metric tons)**

| | 1991est | 1990 | 1989 | 1988 | 1987 |
|---|---|---|---|---|---|
| Lebanon | 100 | 100 | 905 | 700 | 700 |
| Pakistan | 200 | 200 | 200 | 200 | 200 |
| Afghanistan | 300 | 300 | 300 | 300 | 300 |
| Morocco | 85 | 85 | 85 | 85 | 60 |
| Total Hashish | 685 | 685 | 1,490 | 1,285 | 1,260 |

Source: Bureau of International Narcotics Matters, International Narcotics Control Strategy Report, March 1991 (Washington, D.C.: U.S. Department of State, March 1991), p. 22.

**Table 5**
**Selected Countries and Money Laundering Laws (as of September 1991)**

| Country | Money Laundering is A Criminal Act | Free Convertibility of Currency |
|---|---|---|
| Australia | Yes | Yes |
| Canada | Yes | Yes |
| Colombia | No | Yes |
| France | Yes | Yes |
| Germany | No (legislation pending) | Yes |
| Japan | No (legislation pending) | Yes |
| Luxembourg | Yes | Yes |
| Singapore | No (legislation pending) | Yes |
| Soviet Union | No | No |
| Spain | Yes | Yes |
| Switzerland | Yes | Yes |
| Turkey | No (legislation pending) | Yes |
| United Kingdom | Yes | Yes |
| United States | Yes | Yes |
| Uruguay | No | Yes |

Source: Scott B. MacDonald, "Anti-Money Laundering Regimes in Europe and Canada", Comptroller of the Currency Quarterly (Summer 1991), pp. 8-13.

# Bibliographic Essay

Literature on the international drug trade is extensive and growing rapidly in the early 1990s. Two of the earliest books on the international drug trade are Brian Freemantle, *The Fix: Inside the World Drug Trade* (New York: Tor Books, 1985, 1986) and James Mills, *The Underground Empire: Where Crime and Governments Embrace* (Garden City, New Jersey: Doubleday & Company, 1986). Freemantle's book is well worth reading as it provides a global approach to issues, discussing in detail the production, transportation and abuse of the major drugs in the global market—cocaine and heroin. Although the book is now overtaken by current events and the chapter pertaining to Bolivia is superficial, this is a classic. Mills's book is an exercise in reading stamina, considering its great length (1,185 pages). If the reader can master the sheer volume of what is thrown at them—the drug trade from the continental United States to Bangkok to Medellín—the benefit is attaining a feel of the trade. However, readers should be aware that Mills is not always accurate with his information. Another major overview piece, of considerable brevity compared to Mills, is Louis Kraar, "The Drug Trade," *Fortune*, June 20, 1988. Kraar covers the drug trade in all its international components.

On the official side, one of the best sources for information is the U.S. Department of State's annual *International Narcotics Control Strategy Report*. Published and released every March, this book is an excellent source of data. It is broken down into the following sections: policy and program developments for the year (with discussions on cocaine, opium, heroin and money laundering); plans for the future (encompassing Latin America and the Caribbean, Asia and Africa and global support); fiscal year summary; legislative basis for policy; international training; other U.S. government assistance; and area reports (South America, Mexico and Central America, the Caribbean, Southwest Asia, Southeast Asia and the Pacific, Europe and the Middle East, Africa, and financial mechanisms and money laundering). There are also detailed tables with estimates of production and exportation of drugs as well as amounts of drugs seized and destroyed. The quality and usefulness of the *International Narcotics Control Strategy Report* has improved considerably through the late 1980s and early 1990s.

The U.S. government has published other similar reports that are worth mention. Two studies by President Richard Nixon's National Commission on Marijuana and Drug Abuse are useful in providing insight into U.S. policy and attitudes about drug control policies in the 1970s: *Marijuana: A Signal of Misunderstanding* (Washington, D.C.: U.S. Government Printing Office, 1972) and *Drug Use in America: Problem in Perspective* (Washington, D.C.: U.S. Government Printing Office, 1973). Moving ahead a few years to the Reagan administration, two studies contain valuable information on the international drug trade and money laundering: The President's Commission on Organized Crime, *America's Habit: Drug Abuse, Drug Trafficking, and Organized Crime* (Washington, D.C.: U.S. Government Printing Office, March 1986) and *The Cash Connection: Organized Crime, Financial Institutions and Money Laundering* (Washington, D.C.: U.S. Government Printing Office, October 1984). Another noteworthy publication on the official side is from the Permanent Subcommittee on Investigations of the Committee on Governmental Affairs, United States Senate, *Crime and Secrecy: The Use of Offshore Banks and Companies* (Washington, D.C.: U.S. Government Printing Office, 1985).

Other books worth examining on the drug issue in the United States include: Rufus King, *The Drug Hang-up* (Springfield, Ill.: Charles C. Thomas, Publisher, 1972); David F. Musto, *The American Disease: Origins of Narcotic Control* (New Haven, Ct.: Yale University Library, 1973); Thomas Szasz, *Ceremonial Chemistry: The Ritual Persecution of Drugs, Addicts, and Pushers* (Holmes Beach, Fla.: Learning Publications, 1974, revised edition 1984); and Arnold S. Trebach, *The Great Drug War: And Radical Proposals that Could Make America Safe Again* (New York: Macmillan Publishing Company, 1987). For information on U.S. overseas drug policy see the excellent work of Raphael F. Perl, *International Narcotics Control and Foreign Assistance Certification: Requirements, Procedures, Timetables and Guidelines* (Washington, D.C.: U.S. Senate, Committee on Foreign Relations, March 1988); "The U.S. Congress, International Drug Policy, and the Anti-Drug Abuse Act of 1988," *Journal of Interamerican Studies and World Affairs* 30, Nos. 2 & 3 (Summer/Fall 1988); and his edited book, *Drugs and Foreign Policy: A Critical Review* (Boulder, Colorado: Westview Press, 1991). A critical view of U.S. drug policy and a pro-legalization of drugs piece worth noting and often cited is Ethan Nadelmann, "U.S. Drug Policy: A Bad Export," *Foreign Policy*, No. 70 (Spring 1988): 83–108; and a letter in response to Nadelmann from Congressmen Charles Rangel and Benjamin A. Gilman in *Foreign Policy* No. 71 (Summer 1988): 199–200. Another critical view of U.S. drug policy is provided by Bruce Bagley, "U.S. Foreign Policy and the War on Drugs: Analysis of a Policy Failure," *Journal of Interamerican Studies and World Affairs* (Summer/Fall 1988): 198–213.

On the subject of U.S. anti-money laundering efforts see Bruce Zagaris, "Dollar Diplomacy: International Enforcement of Money Movement and Related Matters—A United States Perspective," *The George Washington Journal of International Law and Economics* 22, No. 3 (1989): 465–552. For a comparative piece on U.S., European and Canadian anti-drug money laundering laws see Scott B. MacDonald, "Anti-Money Laundering Regimes in Europe and Canada," *Comptroller of the Currency Quarterly* (June 1991): 8–11.

The emergence of cocaine in the 1980s spawned a growing literature largely oriented to Latin America and in particular, Colombia, Bolivia, Peru and Mexico. One of the best works is Rensselaer W. Lee III, *The White Labyrinth: Cocaine and Political Power* (New Brunswick, New Jersey: Transaction Publishers, 1989). This book is well researched and provides an excellent overview of the cocaine trade in Latin America. Another groundbreaking book is Deborah Pacini and Christine Franquemont, editors, *Coca and Cocaine:*

*Effects on People and Policy in Latin America* (Petersborough, New Hampshire: Transcript Publishing Company, 1986). One major book from Colombia is essential reading: Fabio Castillo, *Los jinetes de la cocaína* (the jockeys of cocaine) (Bogotá, Colombia: Editorial Documentos Periodisticas, 1987). Castillo was a journalist for a major Colombian newspaper and after publishing this book he was forced to live outside the country because his book mentions people by name. Other worthwhile reading on the Latin American drug trade is Bruce Bagley, "Colombia and the War on Drugs," *Foreign Affairs* (Fall 1988): 70–92; Alain Delpirou and Alain Labrousse, *Coca Coke: Produtores, Consumdores, traficantes e governantes* (São Paulo: Editora Brasiliense, 1988); Paul Eddy with Hugo Sabogal and Sara Walden, *The Cocaine Wars* (New York: W. W. Norton and Company, 1988); Guy Gugliotta and Jeff Leen, *Kings of Cocaine: Inside the Medellín Cartel—An Astonishing True Story of Murder, Money, and International Corruption* (New York: Simon and Schuster, 1989); Scott B. MacDonald, *Mountain High, White Avalanche: Cocaine and Power in the Andean States and Panama* (New York: Praeger and the Center for Strategic and International Studies Washington Papers Series, 1989); by the same author, *Dancing on a Volcano: The Latin American Drug Trade* (New York: Praeger, 1988); Edmundo Morales, *Cocaine: White Gold Rush in Peru* (Tuscon: University of Arizona Press, 1989); and Elaine Shannon, *Desperados: Latin Drug Lords, U.S. Lawmen, and the War America Can't Win* (New York: Viking, 1988).

On the legal side of international drug control and money laundering see Secretariat for Legal Affairs, *Comparative Study of the Legal Regime on Drug Control in Ten South American Member States of the Organization of American States* (Washington, D.C.: Organization of American States, 1988). Though outdated, this study is comprehensive and provides some idea of the legal systems maintained by key Latin American countries for dealing with drug control. Another noteworthy article dealing with the legal system is Mark Andrew Sherman, "United States International Drug Control Policy, Extradition, and the Rule of Law in Colombia," *NOVA Law Review*, Vol. 15 (Spring 1991): 661–701. Two articles that deal with the narco-money laundering issue in Europe are Bruce Zagaris and Ange Fantauzzi, "Breaking the Connection," *Security Management* (June 1989): 47–52 and Bruce Zagaris and Markus Bornheim, "International Cooperation Against Money Laundering in the European Integration Context," *1992—The External Impact of European Unification* (November 3, 1989): 13–16.

Research on drug activities and criminal organizations involved in the Far East's heroin trade worth noting include the following: Alfred W. McCoy, *The Politics of Heroin in Southwest Asia* (New York: Harper and Row, 1972); W. P. Morgan, *Triad Societies in Hong Kong* (Hong Kong: The Government Printer, 1960); the scholarly work of Jean Chesneaux, *Secret Societies in China in the Nineteenth and Twentieth Centuries* (New York: Heinemann, 1971); an excellent piece from Jon A. Wiant, "Narcotics in the Golden Triangle," *Washington Quarterly* 8, No. 4 (Fall 1988): 130–37; and Martin Booth's journalistic, *The Triads: The Growing Global Threat from the Chinese Societies* (New York: St. Martin's Press, 1990).

Literature on the international drug trade in other countries worth noting includes for the United Kingdom: Horace Freeland Judson, *Heroin Addiction in Britain* (New York: Harcourt Brace Jovanovich, 1973); Philip Bean, *The Social Control of Drugs* (London: Martin Robertson & Company, 1974); and The Home Office, *United Kingdom Action on Drug Abuse—The Government's Strategy* (London: The Home Office, 1990); for Canada: Victor Malarek, *Merchants of Misery: Inside Canada's Illegal Drug Scene*

(Toronto: McClelland & Stewart, 1989, 1990); for Italy: Claire Sterling, *Octopus: The Long Reach of the International Sicilian Mafia* (New York: W. W. Norton & Company, 1990); and for Iran: Gerald T. McLaughlin, ''The Poppy Is Not an Ordinary Flower: A Survey of Drug Policy in Iran,'' *Fordham Law Review* 44 (1976): 701–72.

# Index

# About the Contributors

LUIZA THEREZA BAPTISTA DE MATTOS is a Prosecutor for the State of Rio de Janeiro and a Professor of Penal Law at the Law Faculty of Candido Mendes University. She is also a member of the Institute of Brazilian and Portuguese Law in Rio de Janeiro and a member of the Brazilian Bar Association. In 1990–1991, she received a Hubert Humphrey Grant to study law in the United States.

SARAH BARBER is a paralegal at the firm of Brownstein, Zeidman & Schomer in Washington, D.C. She was the assistant editor of the *International Enforcement Law Reporter* and holds a B.A. from Bates College.

LOREN CAIN is a National Bank Examiner at the Office of the Comptroller of the Currency. He has worked and travelled extensively through Asia and Europe and conducted research in the United Kingdom. In 1989, he was on a rotational assignment in the Office of the Comptroller of the Currency's Washington headquarters, where he conducted a major study of Central and Eastern European banking systems. He has a Bachelor of Foreign Service from Georgetown University, Washington, D.C.

DAVID L. CRUM is a Vice President at American Security Bank, N.A. in Washington, D.C. He received his M.A. in Canadian Studies and International Economics from the Johns Hopkins University's School of Advanced International Studies in Washington, D.C. and joined the bank as an international economist. He is the co-editor of *The Global Debt Crisis: Forecasting the Future*, and has published on Canadian issues in *Export Today, The International Trader of Northern Virginia*, and in the Americas Series with the Center for Strategic and International Studies (CSIS) in Washington, D.C.

MICHAEL J. DZIEDZIC is a Lt. Col. with the U.S. Air Force and a tenured professor in the Department of Political Science at the U.S. Air Force Academy. He received his M.A. from the Tufts University's Fletcher School of Law and Diplomacy and his Ph.D. from the University of Texas, Austin. While a Research Associate at the International Institute for Strategic Studies in London from 1987–1989, he wrote *Mexico: Converging Challenges*. He has written extensively on security issues concerning the United States and Mexico and conducted field research in Latin America, Europe, and at the Organization of American States in Washington, D.C.

EDUARDO GAMARRA is an assistant professor of Political Science at Florida International University. He is the co-author of *Revolution and Reaction: Bolivia 1964–1985* and author of numerous articles on L.A. politics. He has also been the co-editor of the *Latin American and Caribbean Contemporary Record*.

SUSAN S. HARDESTY is the managing editor of *Middle East Insight* (Washington, D.C.). She received her Bachelor of Foreign Service from Georgetown University and her M.A. from George Washington University. She has worked on Capitol Hill with members of Congress and at the Export-Import Bank of the United States.

BARBARA JAHANSOOZI is an Intelligence Research Specialist for the U.S. Drug Enforcement Administration since 1985. Prior to that position she worked for the Federal Bureau of Investigation. She received her B.A. from Ceder Crest College, Allentown, Pennsylvania and a M.B.A. in International Business from Southeastern University in Washington, D.C. She speaks Farsi and has travelled extensively through Latin America and parts of the Middle East.

ELIZABETH KINGMA received her B.A. from Emory College and her J.D. from the University of Georgia Law School. She is currently working at the Commodity Futures Trading Commission and chairs the American Bar Association's Sub-Committee on International Asset Forfeiture.

RENSSELAER W. LEE III is president of Global Advisory Services, Inc., a Virginia-based company that consults on international development issues, and an associate scholar at the Foreign Policy Research Institute in Philadelphia. He has testified on drug trafficking and drug abuse issues before the House Subcommittee on Western Hemispheric Affairs and other congressional forums. He has conducted research on the narcotics issue in Latin America and most recently in the Soviet Union and is the author of numerous articles as well as *The White Labyrinth: Cocaine and Political Power*.

DEBRA A. LIANG is the Production Editor of *Journal for Democracy* (Washington, D.C.). She received her B.A. in Political Science from Trinity College in Hartford, Connecticut in 1988 and has been accepted at the University of London's School of Oriental and African Studies for a M.A. program in Southeast Asian Studies.

SCOTT B. MACDONALD is an international economic advisor at the Office of the Comptroller of the Currency in Washington, D.C. Prior to that position, he was the Chief International Economist at Maryland National Bank and American Security Bank, N.A., in Baltimore and Washington, D.C. respectively, and was the Unit Manager for International and Specialized Industries Unit in the Loan Administration of Connecticut National Bank. He received his Ph.D. in Political Science from the University of Connecticut in 1985; his M.A. in Area Studies (the Far East) from the University of London's School of Oriental and African Studies in 1979; and B.A. in Political Science and History from Trinity College in Hartford, Connecticut, in 1978. He is the author of *Trinidad and Tobago: Democracy and Development in the Caribbean; Dancing on a Volcano: The Latin American Drug Trade*; and *Mountain High, White Avalanche: Cocaine and Power in the Andean States and Panama*. He has co-edited *The Caribbean After Grenada, The Global Debt Crisis: Forecasting the Future, The Politics of the Caribbean Basin Sugar Trade*, and *The Latin American Debt Crisis in the 1990s*. His articles have appeared in *Middle East Insight, Journal of Inter-American Studies and World Affairs, The Times of the Americas, LatinFinance, Leaders, Repères Bulletin économique et financier, Caribbean Review*, and *SAIS Review*. He is currently working on a book about the European Community in the 1990s.

RAPHAEL FRANCIS PERL is a Specialist in International Affairs with the Congressional Research Service of the U.S. Library of Congress in Washington, D.C. He received his Bachelor for Foreign Service from the Georgetown School of Foreign Service in 1968 and J.D. from Georgetown University Law School in 1971. He is author of *International Narcotics Control and Foreign Assistance Certification: Requirements, Procedures, Timetables and Guidelines* and editor of *Drugs and Foreign Policy: A Critical Review*. He has also published numerous articles on U.S. drug policy in publications such as *Journal of Interamerican Studies and World Affairs*.

ROBIN ROLLEY received her J.D. from the Washington College of Law in 1991. She is currently working on a M.A. in Justice. Her B.A. in Political Science and German was achieved in 1988. Rolley served as a legal intern for the International Human Rights Law Group in the Fall of 1989 and worked on the *International Enforcement Law Reporter* in the Spring of 1990 in concurrence with an independent study project on the U.S. lawyer's role in improving criminal justice in Central America. She also worked as a summer law clerk for the Department of Justice in 1990 and in the International Human Rights Law Clinic at the Washington College of Law during the 1990–1991 school year. She is a member of the Equal Justice Foundation, the Phi Delta Law Fraternity, and a student member of the American Bar Association.

LAURA VÁSQUEZ is a candidate for a J.D. at the law school at the State University of New York, in Buffalo, New York and holds a M.A. from the Johns Hopkins' University School of Advanced International Studies in Washington, D.C. She has done considerable work on Latin American affairs and published in *Times of the Americas*.

CAROLINE S. WEST received her B.A. from Lehigh University with a double major in journalism and international affairs. She is currently a candidate for a J.D. and a M.A. in international affairs at the University of Pittsburgh. In 1990, she was the assistant editor of the *European Journal of International Affairs*. She has travelled extensively throughout Eastern Europe and lived in Italy and Mexico.

GOVERT FRANK VAN DE WIJNGAART is a member of the Faculty of Social Sciences, Utrecht University. He has been affiliated with the Addiction Research Institute. For many years Dr. van de Wijngaart has been active in research and has contributed many scholarly articles on the Dutch approach to drug abuse. He has also been active in many international organizations as a speaker and writer on drug prevention and treatment.

BRUCE ZAGARIS is a partner with the firm of Cameron & Hornbostel in Washington, D.C. He received his B.A. in 1969, J.D. in 1972, and LLM in 1973 from George Washington University. In addition, he received graduate legal diplomas from the Stockholm University, Sweden in 1975 and the Free University, Brussels in 1976. He was a consultant for the United Nations on organized crime and has worked for 12 foreign governments and 3 international organizations. Zagaris is co-chair of the Committee on International Criminal Law for the American Bar Association and sits on the Executive Committee and Board of the American Society for International Law. He is also an adjunct professor of International Criminal Business Law at Fordham University School of Law. Additionally, he is the founder and editor-in-chief of the *International Enforcement Law Reporter*, co-editor of three books, and author of *Foreign Investment in the United States* (Praeger, 1980). He has published numerous articles on international legal issues and has travelled extensively in Europe, the Caribbean, and Latin America.